Published by
Lion Publishing plc
Sandy Lane West, Oxford, England
ISBN 0 7459 2042 X
ISBN 0 7459 2043 8 (gift edition)
Albatross Books Pty Ltd
PO Box 320, Sutherland, NSW 2232, Australia
ISBN 0 7324 0291 3
ISBN 0 7324 0472 X (gift edition)
Produced by Creative Publishing, Bath.
Bible text from the Holy Bible,
New International Version, (Anglicised edition),
published by Hodder and Stoughton Ltd.,
© International Bible Society 1973, 1978, 1984.
Used by permission

First edition 1991

Acknowledgments

© Pictures: Creative Slide Library.
Additional photographs: Lion Publishing/
David Townsend, Susanna Burton
British Library Cataloguing in Publication Data
(Applied for)

Printed and bound in Singapore by Star Standard Industries

Distributed in the U.S. by Zondervan Publishing House, Grand Rapids, Michigan.

Thru The Year
NEW TESTAMENT in *Color*

**New
International
Version**

ZondervanPublishingHouse

A Division of HarperCollins*Publishers*

Foreword

Most people know something about the Bible — particularly the NewTestament. The Lord's Prayer, the beatitudes, 'the greatest of these is love', the story of the cross, these and other beautiful passages have a way of sticking in our minds.

Yet the New Testament is far more than a collection of separate stories and sayings. It is a library of books: four Gospels, the narrative of Christianity's first years, twenty-one letters and a strange vision.

Taken together, these books tell a story. It begins a little over a year before Jesus was born in Bethlehem and it ends nearly a century later, with an old man dreaming on the island of Patmos. Galilee and Jerusalem are the scene of the first four books; the others range through the region from Jerusalem across the eastern Mediterranean and as far as Rome.

It is all too possible to know our few favourite verses but to miss out on the story. Like any story, we have to read it right through to get the point. We have to follow all the threads, the plots and the sub-plots. We need to become acquainted with the characters and enter their world.

What better way to read the amazing story of the New Testament than the five-minutes-a-day method provided by this book? The translation is fluent and readable, the selections helpfully arranged. Good reading.

Contents

Key New Testament Themes

The reader can follow each of these central themes and beliefs through the New Testament by using the carefully selected lists of references below.

ASCENSION, THE   At the end of his time on earth, Jesus took up again his eternal glory.

Matthew 28:16-20; Luke 24:50-52; John 1:51; 3:13; 6:62; Acts 1:9-11; Romans 10:6; Ephesians 4:8-12; Hebrews 9:24; Revelation 7:2

BAPTISM   New believers were washed in water as a sign of their new life in Christ.

Matthew 3:11, 13-17; 28:19; Mark 1:5; 10:38-39; John 3:5; Acts 1:5; 2:38,41; 8:12-16; 16:33; 19:3-5; Romans 6:1-6; 1 Corinthians 1:13-15; 12:13; Colossians 2:11-15; Titus 3:4-7; 1 Peter 3:21

BREAKING BREAD   Jesus taught his disciples to take bread and wine in memory of his death.

Matthew 26:17-30; Mark 14:12-26; Luke 22:7-20; 24:28-31; John 6:53-58; Acts 2:42; 20:11; 1 Corinthians 10:16-22; 11:17-34; Revelation 19:5-9

CHURCH, THE   All who follow Jesus are called into a new community.

Matthew 16:18; 18:17; Luke 12:32-34; Acts 2:47; 4:32-35; 5:11; 7:38; 20:28; Romans 16:3-5; 1 Corinthians 1:2; 11:18; 12:27; Ephesians 1:22-23; 5:23-32; Colossians 1:18,24; 1 Timothy 3:15; Hebrews 12:22-24; 1 Peter 2:4-10

COVENANT WITH GOD   Prophets had predicted a 'new covenant' - a new basis for relationship between God and his people.

Luke 1:72; 22:20; Acts 3:25; Romans 9:4; Galatians 3:15-17; Ephesians 2:12; Hebrews 8:6-13; 12:24

DEATH OF JESUS, THE   He died to bring us to God.

Matthew 1:21; 16:21; 26:26-29; 27:27-54; Mark 10:45; 15:21-47; Luke 12:49-50; 22:14-23; John 1:29; 12:24; 19:1-37; Acts 2:22-23; 3:15; 4:10; 8:32-35; 10:38-43; Romans 3:23-25; 5:6-10; 8:1-3; 1 Corinthians 1:22-25; 5:7; 15:3; 2 Corinthians 5:14-21; Galatians 2:20; 3:13; Ephesians 1:7; 2:13,16; Philippians 2:5-10; 3:10; Colossians 1:20; 2:13-15; 3:3;

1 Thessalonians 2:15; 1 Timothy 1:15; 2:5; 2 Timothy 1:10; Titus 3:4-7; Hebrews 2:14-18; 5:7-9; 7:26-27; 9:12-14; 10:11-14,19-22; 12:2; 1 Peter 1:11,18-19; 2:21-24; 3:18; 1 John 1:7; Revelation 1:5-7,9-10

DISCIPLES   To be a disciple is to follow Jesus and learn from him.

Matthew 28:18-20; Mark 1:16-20; 3:13-15; Luke 9:1-6,57-62; 14:25-33; John 1:35-51; Galatians 2:20-21; Ephesians 6:10-20; Philippians 3:12-16; 1 Timothy 6:11-16

FAITH   Faith means putting our whole trust in Jesus alone.

Mark 2:5; 6:5-6; 10:52; Luke 7:2-10; John 1:12; 3:15-16; 5:24; 6:68-69; 9:35-38; Acts 2:38-39; 16:31; Romans 1:17; 4:18-22; 5:1; 10:6-13; Galatians 2:20; 3:11-14,23-29; Ephesians 2:8-9; 1 Timothy 4:1; 6:12; 2 Timothy 1:12; Hebrews 11:1,6,8-10; 12:1-2; 1 John 5:1,4; Revelation 3:19-20

GOD THE CREATOR   God created the world and us in it; he keeps everything in being.

Matthew 6:28-34; Luke 13:1-5; John 1:1-4; 5:17; Acts 4:24-25; 14:17; 17:23-31; Romans 1:20-23; 8:18-23,38-39; 1 Corinthians 8:6; 10:26; Colossians 1:15-20; Hebrews 1:1-3; 4:11; 10:6; 11:3

GOD THE FATHER   Jesus taught his followers to call God 'our Father'.

Matthew 5:16,45,48; 6:4,9; 11:25-27; Mark 14:36; Luke 11:11-13; 15:11-32; John 1:14; 5:36-37; 10:15,30; 11:41; 14:2-7; 17:1; Romans 8:15; 1 Corinthians 8:6; 2 Corinthians 1:3; Galatians 4:6; Ephesians 3:14-15; Hebrews 12:7-9; 1 Peter 1:2-3; 1 John 1:2-3

GOD THE TRINITY   Father, Son and Holy Spirit: God the three-in-one.

Matthew 3:13-17; 28:19; John 14:15-23; 15:26; 16:13-15; Acts 2:33-34; 1 Corinthians 12:4-6; 2 Corinthians 13:13; Galatians 4:4-6; Ephesians 2:18; 4:4-6; Philippians 3:3; Hebrews 10:10-17; 1 John 5:1-12

Key New Testament Themes

GOD REVEALS HIMSELF He has made himself known to humanity in the whole story recorded in the Bible, and above all in his Son.

Luke 10:21-22; John 12:38; 16:12-15,25; Romans 1:17-18; 1 Corinthians 2:10; 14:6; Galatians 1:12,15-16; Hebrews 1:1-3; 1 Peter 1:10-12; Revelation 1:1

HOLY SPIRIT, THE Jesus' work did not end when he died and rose; the Holy Spirit of God continues what Jesus began.

Matthew 3:16; 4:1; Luke 1:41; 4:18; 11:13; John 3:6-8; 4:24; 14:17; 15:26; 16:7-15; Acts 2:1-18; 8:29; Romans 8:2-16; 1 Corinthians 2:11-14; 3:16; 6:19; 12:4-13; 2 Corinthians 3:6,17; Galatians 4:6; 5:22-25; Ephesians 1:13; 4:4; 5:18; 6:17; 1 Thessalonians 4:8; 5:19; 2 Timothy 1:7

HOPE Soon or late, God's purposes will come to fruition.

Matthew 24:13-14; Romans 5:2; 15:4-6,13; 1 Corinthians 15:51-58; 2 Corinthians 1:15-22; 4:16-18; Ephesians 1:13-14; 1 Thessalonians 4:13-18; 2 Timothy 1:12; Titus 2:11-13; Hebrews 6:17-20; 11:8-16; 1 Peter 1:3-5; 1 John 3:2-3; Revelation 21:1-22:21

IMAGE OF GOD, THE God created men and women to reflect his own nature.

Romans 8:28; 1 Corinthians 11:7; 15:49; 2 Corinthians 3:18; 4:4; Philippians 2:5-10; Colossians 1:15; 3:10; Hebrews 1:3; James 3:9

JESUS: GOD MADE MAN In him, God lived a fully human life.

Matthew 1:20-23; 4:1-11; Mark 13:32; 14:32-36; Luke 2:39-52; 10:21; John 1:10-14; 4:7; 6:38; 12:27-28; Acts 2:22; 10:38-40; 13:23-25; Romans 8:3; Galatians 4:4; Philippians 2:5-11; 1 Timothy 2:5; 3:16; Hebrews 2:17-18; 4:15; 5:7-10; 1 Peter 4:1; 1 John 4:1-3

JESUS THE MESSIAH Since Old Testament days, Jews had expected God's chosen leader - the 'Messiah' (or 'Christ').

Matthew 21:1-9; Mark 8:27-30; 14:60-64; Luke 1:32-33; 2:11; 3:16-21; 7:18-23; John 4:25-26; 14:1-15:27; Acts 2:36; 3:18-26;

1 Corinthians 1:23-24; 1 Peter 2:21-25

JESUS THE REDEEMER He paid the price to redeem (or 'ransom') humanity from slavery to sin.

Mark 10:45; Luke 1:68; John 8:34-36; Acts 8:32-36; Romans 3:24-26; 1 Corinthians 6:19-20; 2 Corinthians 5:14-21; Galatians 3:13; 5:1; Ephesians 1:7; Colossians 1:14; 1 Timothy 2:5-6; 1 Peter 1:18-19; Revelation 5:9-10

JESUS THE TEACHER His was the deepest and yet the most accessible of teaching.

Matthew 5:1-7:29; 13:1-52; 16:21-23; 18:1-15; 21:23-27; 22:15-46; 25:1-46; 28:16-20; Mark 1:14-15; 3:13-15; 4:1-20; 11:18; 13:1-37; Luke 2:46-47; 4:16-22; 6:39-40; 9:1-6; 10:25-37; 11:1-13; 15:1-32; 19:47-48; 24:25-27; John 3:1-13; 7:14-18; 13:1-17; 14:1-10; 16:12-14

JESUS THE WORD John used this term of Jesus, the one who gives meaning to everything.

John 1:1-18; Hebrews 1:1-3; Revelation 19:13

JUDGMENT We are all accountable to God for how we live.

Matthew 3:7-12; 11:20-23; 13:37-43; 25:31-46; Luke 16:19-31; John 3:18-21; 5:23-29; Acts 10:42; 17:30-31; Romans 1:18-32; 2:6-11; 14:10-12; 1 Corinthians 3:10-15; 4:3-5; 2 Corinthians 5:10; 2 Thessalonians 1:5-10; 2 Timothy 4:1; Hebrews 2:2-3; 9:27; 10:26-31; 1 Peter 4:5; 2 Peter 3:7-13; 1 John 4:17; Revelation 20:11-15; 22:10-13

JUSTICE Jesus placed a high value on 'justice, mercy and truth'.

Matthew 23:1-5,23-28; Mark 6:20; Luke 1:46-55; 10:29-37; Romans 1:32; 13:1-7; 2 Timothy 4:8; 1 Peter 3:13; Revelation 15:3; 16:5-7

KINGDOM OF GOD, THE The Jews longed for a new king, but Jesus established the kingdom (or 'rule') of God in human hearts.

Matthew 3:1-3; 4:23-25; 6:10; 13:1-52; 16:13-20,28; 25:1-46; Mark 4:11; 10:23; 14:25; Luke 9:1-2; 17:20-21; 19:11; John 18:36; Acts 1:6; Romans 14:17; 1 Corinthians 4:20; 6:9-10; 15:50; Revelation 1:9

Key New Testament Themes

LAW, GOD'S   Many looked to law-keeping to earn God's favour, but Jesus said he had 'fulfilled' the Law.

Matthew 5:17-20; 22:37-40; Mark 2:24-28; Romans 2:12-16; 3:20; 4:13-15; 5:12-15; 7:4-12,21-25; 13:10; 15:1-7; Galatians 2:16-20; 3:13,21-25; 4:3-5; James 2:8

LOVE   Love is the hub of the way of life Jesus taught.

Luke 6:35; 10:25-37; John 3:16; 13:1; 14:21-24; 21:15-17; Romans 5:5,8; 8:37-39; 1 Corinthians 13:1-13; Galatians 2:20; Ephesians 3:17-19; 5:2; Colossians 3:14; 1 Thessalonians 5:13; James 2:8-13; 1 Peter 1:22; 1 John 3:14-18; 4:7-12

MALE AND FEMALE   Jesus valued women highly; the practical implications of this are still being worked out.

Matthew 19:4; Luke 7:36-50; 8:1-3; John 4:4-42; 20:1-18; 1 Corinthians 11:3-16; Galatians 3:28; 1 Peter 3:4

MARRIAGE AND THE FAMILY   Marriage is at the centre of a web of relationships which affect everyone.

Matthew 1:18-25; 19:3-9; Luke 20:34; John 2:1-2; 19:26-27; 1 Corinthians 7:10-11,33-34,38; Ephesians 5:21-6:4; Colossians 3:18-21; Hebrews 13:4

MISSION   'As my Father sent me,' said Jesus, 'so I send you.'

Matthew 3:1; 3:23-24; 9:35; 28:18-20; Mark 1:32-34; 3:14-19; 6:34; 10:43-45; Luke 7:22; 10:1-11; 15:3-32; 19:1-10; John 1:9-18; 5:25-27; 6:35-40; 10:7-16; 17:6-26; Acts 1:6-9; 2:37-42; 9:26-30; 10:34-43; 11:18; 13:1-3; 20:18-28; Romans 1:16; 3:21-26; 5:6-11; 10:9-15; 15:15-21; 16:1-16; 1 Corinthians 1:32; 2:1-4; 9:19-23; 2 Corinthians 5:11-21; 8:8-9; Galatians 1:6-9; Ephesians 1:3-10; 2:13-17; 3:7-13; Philippians 2:5-11; Colossians 1:15-20,29; 1 Thessalonians 1:8-10; 1 Timothy 11:12-17; 2 Timothy 2:1-7; 4:2-5

MONEY   Money is important, but money itself is not real wealth.

Matthew 6:19-21,25-33; Luke 6:24; 9:3; 12:16-21; 16:19-31; 18:18-30; 19:1-10; Acts 5:1-11; 8:18-20; 2 Corinthians 8:9; 1 Timothy 6:6-10,17-19; James 1:9-11; 2:5-7; Revelation 3:17-18

NEIGHBOUR, THE

'Who is my neighbour?' Jesus was asked. He answered with a parable.

Matthew 5:43-48; Luke 10:25-37; Romans 13:9; 1 Corinthians 10:23-33; Galatians 5:14; 6:2,10; Philippians 2:1-4; 2 Thessalonians 3:11-15; Hebrews 13:1-2; James 1:27; 2:1-8,15-17; 1 Peter 3:8-12

NEW CREATION   When people are linked to Jesus Christ in faith, their lives are made new.

Matthew 18:1-4; Luke 4:16-21; John 3:3-5; Acts 3:19-21; Romans 6:4; 8:18-23; 2 Corinthians 5:17; Colossians 3:1-10; Titus 3:4-7; Revelation 21:1-7

POWERS OF EVIL   Jesus believed he was in conflict with a personal force of evil.

Matthew 4:1-11; 7:22; 12:22-29; 17:18; Mark 1:23-27; Luke 4:33-35; 8:2,27-33; 9:1; John 8:44-48; 13:2; 1 Corinthians 5:5; Ephesians 4:27; 6:11-12; Colossians 2:8-15; Hebrews 2:14-15; 1 Peter 5:8; 1 John 3:8-10; Revelation 2:10; 12:9-10; 20:10

PRAYER   Prayer is our lifeline to God.

Matthew 6:7-15; 7:7-11; 26:39,41; Mark 1:35; Luke 9:28-29; 11:9-13; John 14:13; 17:1-26; Acts 4:31; 9:11; 10:9; 12:5; Romans 8:16-17,26-27; Ephesians 1:15-17; 3:14-21; 6:18; Philippians 1:9-11; Colossians 1:9-10; 4:3; 1 Thessalonians 3:10; 5:17; 1 Timothy 2:1-8; James 5:16; 1 John 5:14-15; Jude 20; Revelation 22:20

RAISED FROM DEATH   Jesus' death was not in vain, but the prelude to a great victory.

Matthew 22:23-33; 28:1-15; Mark 16:1-8; Luke 24:1-43; John 5:28-29; 6:39-40; 11:25-26; 20:1-28; 21:1-14; Acts 2:29-32; Romans 1:4; 6:4; 8:11; 14:9; 1 Corinthians 15:3-23, 35-58; 2 Corinthians 4:14; Philippians 3:20-21; 1 Thessalonians 4:13-14; Revelation 1:17-18

Key New Testament Themes

REPENTANCE   Following Jesus involves changing our mind and our direction, to live his new way.

Matthew 3:2; Mark 1:14-15; Luke 3:8; 15:7; 24:47; Acts 3:19; 17:30; 2 Corinthians 7:8-10; 1 Thessalonians 1:9; Hebrews 6:1-6

SAVED   Everyone needs to be set free and made whole.

Matthew 25:31-46; Mark 2:5-11; Luke 4:16-21; 15:4-32; 18:9-14,35-43; 19:1-10; John 3:1-17; 4:10-14,42; 5:24; 6:69; 9:35-39; 10:10,27-29; 17:3; Acts 2:38; 3:13-19; 4:12; 9:3-19; 10:43; 16:22-34; Romans 1:16-17; 3:21-26; 5:1-10; 8:1-4; 10:4-9; 1 Corinthians 1:18-25,30; 2 Corinthians 6:2; Galatians 2:20; 3:13; 5:1; Ephesians 1:3-14; 2:8-10; Philippians 3:4-11; Colossians 1:3-5,13-23; 1 Thessalonians 1:10; 1 Timothy 1:15; 2:3-5; 4:10; 2 Timothy 1:9-10; Titus 3:4-7; Hebrews 2:3-4,9-10; 9:23-28; 1 Peter 1:3-9,18-23; 2:2-4,21-25; 3:18-22; 1 John 3:1-8,16; 4:9-10; Revelation 7:9-11; 12:10-11

SERVICE   To belong to Jesus involves 'ministry'-serving other people as he did.

Mark 3:13-19; 10:42-45; John 13:3-7; Acts 6:1-7; Romans 12:4-8; 13:4-6; 2 Corinthians 3:1-6; 4:1-7; 5:18-20; Ephesians 4:11-13; Colossians 1:7,23; 1 Timothy 1:12; 3:1-13; 5:17; 2 Timothy 1:3-7; 1 Peter 4:10-11; 5:1-5

SIN   All human beings, although made in God's image, have a tendency to spoil their great potential.

Matthew 1:21; 3:6; 26:28; Mark 1:4; 2:5-7; 7:14-23; John 1:29; 3:16-21; Acts 2:38; Romans 3:23-25; 5:12-13; 6:1-6; 8:2-3; Galatians 1:4; 2:17-21; Titus 3:11; Hebrews 1:3; 7:27; 10:2; 1 Peter 2:22-24; 3:18; 1 John 1:7-10; 3:8

SPIRITUAL GIFTS   God gives abilities beyond natural ones, for service and for worship.

Matthew 25:14-30; Luke 11:13; Acts 2:17; 8:17-21; Romans 12:3-8; 1 Corinthians 12:1-13, 27-30; 14:14-16; Ephesians 1:17; 4:11-12,30; 2 Timothy 1:7; 1 Peter 4:10-11

STATE, THE   God instituted human powers, but his own authority remains higher.

Mark 12:13-17; John 19:10-11; Acts 5:27-29; 17:26; 19:35-41; Romans 13:1-7; Philippians 3:20; Colossians 2:15; 1 Timothy 2:1-4; 1 Peter 2:13-17; Revelation 11:15; 18:1-24

SUFFERING   Pain and sadness are hard to understand, but Jesus experienced them deeply himself.

Mark 8:34-35; 13:5-13; 14:32-36; John 19:1-30; Romans 8:22-23; 2 Corinthians 1:3-9; 11:23-28; 12:7-10; Philippians 1:29; Colossians 1:24; 1 Timothy 2:3; 5:8; 12:4-11; 1 Peter 1:6-7; 2:18-25; Revelation 21:4

WAR AND PEACE   Jesus was the 'Prince of peace'. So must his followers be pacifists?

Matthew 24:6-8; Luke 1:79; 2:14; 19:42; Romans 3:17; 15:33; Ephesians 2:14-17; 6:15; Hebrews 7:2; Revelation 6:4

WORK AND REST   Work is part of being human, but life is more than work.

Ephesians 4:28; Colossians 3:23-24; 2 Thessalonians 3:6-13; Hebrews 3:11; 4:3-10

WORSHIP   Worship means giving God honour and acknowledging his supremacy.

Matthew 2:2,8,11; 4:9-10; 28:16-17; Mark 5:6; Luke 2:13-14; John 4:20-24; 9:38; 17:1-5; Acts 2:43-47; 16:25; 17:23; Philippians 3:3; Colossians 3:16; Revelation 4:8-11; 22:8-9

DAY 1
MARK 1. 1 — 20

1 John the Baptist Prepares the Way

The beginning of the gospel about Jesus Christ, the Son of God.

[2] It is written in Isaiah the prophet:

'I will send my messenger
  ahead of you,
  who will prepare your
    way' -
[3] 'a voice of one calling in the
    desert,
  "Prepare the way for the Lord,
    make straight paths for
      him." '

[4] And so John came, baptising in the desert region and preaching a baptism of repentance for the forgiveness of sins. [5] The whole Judean countryside and all the people of Jerusalem went out to him. Confessing their sins, they were baptised by him in the Jordan River. [6] John wore clothing made of camel's hair, with a leather belt round his waist, and he ate locusts and wild honey. [7] And this was his message: 'After me will come one more powerful than I, the thongs of whose sandals I am not worthy to stoop down and untie. [8] I baptise you with water, but he will baptise you with the Holy Spirit.'

The Baptism and Temptation of Jesus

[9] At that time Jesus came from Nazareth in Galilee and was baptised by John in the Jordan. [10] As Jesus was coming up out of the water, he saw heaven being torn open and the Spirit descending on him like a dove. [11] And a voice came from heaven: 'You are my Son, whom I love; with you I am well pleased.'

[12] At once the Spirit sent him out into the desert, [13] and he was in the desert for forty days, being tempted by Satan. He was with the wild animals, and angels attended him.

The Calling of the First Disciples

[14] After John was put in prison, Jesus went into Galilee, proclaiming the good news of God. [15] 'The time has come,' he said. 'The kingdom of God is near. Repent and believe the good news!'

[16] As Jesus walked beside the Sea of Galilee, he saw Simon and his brother Andrew casting a net into the lake, for they were fishermen. [17] 'Come, follow me,' Jesus said, 'and I will make you fishers of men.' [18] At once they left their nets and followed him.

[19] When he had gone a little farther, he saw James son of Zebedee and his brother John in a boat, preparing their nets. [20] Without delay he called them, and they left their father Zebedee in the boat with the hired men and followed him.

The Spirit descended on him like a dove.

DAY 2

MARK 1. 21 — 45

Jesus Drives Out an Evil Spirit

21 They went to Capernaum, and when the Sabbath came, Jesus went into the synagogue and began to teach. 22 The people were amazed at his teaching, because he taught them as one who had authority, not as the teachers of the law. 23 Just then a man in their synagogue who was possessed by an evil spirit cried out, 24 'What do you want with us, Jesus of Nazareth? Have you come to destroy us? I know who you are - the Holy One of God!' 25 'Be quiet!' said Jesus sternly. 'Come out of him!' 26 The evil spirit shook the man violently and came out of him with a shriek.

27 The people were all so amazed that they asked each other, 'What is this? A new teaching - and with authority! He even gives orders to evil spirits and they obey him.' 28 News about him spread quickly over the whole region of Galilee.

Jesus Heals Many

29 As soon as they left the synagogue, they went with James and John to the home of Simon and Andrew. 30 Simon's mother-in-law was in bed with a fever, and they told Jesus about her. 31 So he went to her, took her hand and helped her up. The fever left her and she began to wait on them.

32 That evening after sunset the people brought to Jesus all the sick and demon-possessed. 33 The whole town gathered at the door, 34 and Jesus healed many who had various diseases. He also drove out many demons, but he would not let the demons speak because they knew who he was.

Jesus Prays in a Solitary Place

35 Very early in the morning, while it was still dark, Jesus got up, left the house and went off to a solitary place, where he prayed. 36 Simon and his companions

'I know who you are - the Holy One of God!'

went to look for him, 37 and when they found him, they exclaimed: 'Everyone is looking for you!'

38 Jesus replied, 'Let us go somewhere else - to the nearby villages - so that I can preach there also. That is why I have come.' 39 So he travelled throughout Galilee, preaching in their synagogues and driving out demons.

A Man With Leprosy

40 A man with leprosy came to him and begged him on his knees, 'If you are willing, you can make me clean.' 41 Filled with compassion, Jesus reached out his hand and touched the man. 'I am willing,' he said. 'Be clean!' 42 Immediately the leprosy left him and he was cured.

43 Jesus sent him away at once with a strong warning: 44 'See that you don't tell this to anyone. But go, show yourself to the priest and offer the sacrifices that Moses commanded for your cleansing, as a testimony to them.' 45 Instead he went out and began to talk freely, spreading the news. As a result, Jesus could no longer enter a town openly but stayed outside in lonely places. Yet the people still came to him from everywhere.

DAY 3

MARK 2. 1 — 17

Jesus Heals a Paralytic

2 A few days later, when Jesus again entered Capernaum, the people heard that he had come home. ² So many gathered that there was no room left, not even outside the door, and he preached the word to them. ³ Some men came, bringing to him a paralytic, carried by four of them. ⁴ Since they could not get him to Jesus because of the crowd, they made an opening in the roof above Jesus and, after digging through it, lowered the mat the paralysed man was lying on. ⁵ When Jesus saw their faith, he said to the paralytic, 'Son, your sins are forgiven.'

⁶ Now some teachers of the law were sitting there, thinking to themselves, ⁷ 'Why does this fellow talk like that? He's blaspheming! Who can forgive sins but God alone?'

⁸ Immediately Jesus knew in his spirit that this was what they were thinking in their hearts, and he said to them, 'Why are you thinking these things? ⁹ Which is easier: to say to the paralytic, "Your sins are forgiven," or to say, "Get up, take your mat and walk"? ¹⁰ But that you may know that the Son of Man has authority on earth to forgive sins. . . .' He said to the paralytic, ¹¹ 'I tell you, get up, take your mat and go home.' ¹² He got up, took his mat and walked out in full view of them all. This amazed everyone and they praised God, saying, 'We have never seen anything like this!'

The Calling of Levi

¹³ Once again Jesus went out beside the lake. A large crowd came to him, and he began to teach them. ¹⁴ As he walked along, he saw Levi son of Alphaeus sitting at the tax collector's booth. 'Follow me,' Jesus told him, and Levi got up and followed him.

¹⁵ While Jesus was having dinner at Levi's house, many tax collectors and 'sinners' were eating with him and his disciples, for there were many who followed him. ¹⁶ When the teachers of the law who were Pharisees saw him eating with the 'sinners' and tax collectors, they asked his disciples: 'Why does he eat with tax collectors and "sinners"?'

¹⁷ On hearing this, Jesus said to them, 'It is not the healthy who need a doctor, but the sick. I have not come to call the righteous, but sinners.'

DAY 4

MARK 2. 18 — 3.6

Jesus Questioned About Fasting

¹⁸ Now John's disciples and the Pharisees were fasting. Some people came and asked Jesus, 'How is it that John's disciples and the disciples of the Pharisees are fasting, but yours are not?'

¹⁹ Jesus answered, 'How can the guests of the bridegroom fast while he is with them? They cannot, so long as they have him with them. ²⁰ But the time will come when the bridegroom will be taken from them, and on that day they will fast.

²¹ 'No-one sews a patch of unshrunk cloth on an old garment. If he does, the new piece will pull away from the old, making the tear worse. ²² And no-one

pours new wine into old wineskins. If he does, the wine will burst the skins, and both the wine and the wineskins will be ruined. No, he pours new wine into new wineskins.'

Lord of the Sabbath

[23] One Sabbath Jesus was going through the cornfields, and as his disciples walked along, they began to pick some ears of corn. [24] The Pharisees said to him, 'Look, why are they doing what is unlawful on the Sabbath?'

[25] He answered, 'Have you never read what David did when he and his companions were hungry and in need? [26] In the days of Abiathar the high priest, he entered the house of God and ate the consecrated bread, which is lawful only for priests to eat. And he also gave some to his companions.'

[27] Then he said to them, 'The Sabbath was made for man, not man for the Sabbath. [28] So the Son of Man is Lord even of the Sabbath.'

3 Another time he went into the synagogue, and a man with a shrivelled hand was there. [2] Some of them were looking for a reason to accuse Jesus, so they watched him closely to see if he would heal him on the Sabbath. [3] Jesus said to the man with the shrivelled hand, 'Stand up in front of everyone.'

[4] Then Jesus asked them, 'Which is lawful on the Sabbath: to do good or to do evil, to save life or to kill?' But they remained silent.

[5] He looked round at them in anger and, deeply distressed at their stubborn hearts, said to the man, 'Stretch out your hand.' He stretched it out, and his hand was completely restored. [6] Then the Pharisees went out and began to plot with the Herodians how they might kill Jesus.

...as his disciples walked along, they began to pick some ears of corn.

DAY 5

MARK 3. 7 — 35

Crowds Follow Jesus

[7] Jesus withdrew with his disciples to the lake, and a large crowd from Galilee followed. [8] When they heard all he was doing, many people came to him from Judea, Jerusalem, Idumea, and the regions across the Jordan and around Tyre and Sidon. [9] Because of the crowd he told his disciples to have a small boat ready for him, to keep the people from crowding him. [10] For he had healed many, so that those with diseases were pushing forward to touch him. [11] Whenever the evil spirits saw him, they fell down before him and cried out, 'You are the Son of God.' [12] But he gave them strict orders not to tell who he was.

The Appointing of the Twelve Apostles

[13] Jesus went up on a mountainside and called to him those he wanted, and they came to him. [14] He appointed twelve - designating them apostles - that they might be with him and that he might send them out to preach [15] and to have authority to drive out demons. [16] These are the twelve he appointed: Simon (to whom he gave the name Peter); [17] James son of Zebedee and his brother John (to them he gave the name Boanerges, which means Sons of Thunder); [18] Andrew, Philip, Bartholomew, Matthew, Thomas, James son of Alphaeus, Thaddaeus, Simon the Zealot [19] and Judas Iscariot, who betrayed him.

Jesus and Beelzebub

[20] Then Jesus entered a house, and again a crowd gathered, so that he and his disciples were not even able to eat. [21] When his family heard about this, they went to take charge of him, for they said, 'He is out of his mind.'

[22] And the teachers of the law who came down from Jerusalem said, 'He is possessed by Beelzebub! By the prince of demons he is driving out demons.'

[23] So Jesus called them and spoke to them in parables: 'How can Satan drive out Satan? [24] If a kingdom is divided against itself, that kingdom cannot stand. [25] If a house is divided against itself, that house cannot stand. [26] And if Satan opposes himself and is divided, he cannot stand; his end has come. [27] In fact, no-one can enter a strong man's house and carry off his possessions unless he first ties up the strong man. Then he can rob his house. [28] I tell you the truth, all the sins and blasphemies of men will be forgiven them. [29] But whoever blasphemes against the Holy Spirit will never be forgiven; he is guilty of an eternal sin.'

[30] He said this because they were saying, 'He has an evil spirit.'

Jesus' Mother and Brothers

[31] Then Jesus' mother and brothers arrived. Standing outside, they sent someone in to call him. [32] A crowd was sitting around him, and they told him, 'Your mother and brothers are outside looking for you.'

[33] 'Who are my mother and my brothers?' he asked.

[34] Then he looked at those seated in a circle around him and said, 'Here are my mother and my brothers! [35] Whoever does God's will is my brother and sister and mother.'

DAY 6

MARK 4. 1 — 20

4 **The Parable of the Sower**
Again Jesus began to teach by the lake. The crowd that gathered round him was so large that he got into a boat and sat in it out on the lake, while all the people were along the shore at the water's edge. ² He taught them many things by parables, and in his teaching said: ³ 'Listen! A farmer went out to sow his seed. ⁴ As he was scattering the seed, some fell along the

---

'The secret of the kingdom of God has been given to you.'

---

path, and the birds came and ate it up. ⁵ Some fell on rocky places, where it did not have much soil. It sprang up quickly, because the soil was shallow. ⁶ But when the sun came up, the plants were scorched, and they withered because they had no root. ⁷ Other seed fell among thorns, which grew up and choked the plants, so that they did not bear grain. ⁸ Still other seed fell on good soil. It came up, grew and produced a crop, multiplying thirty, sixty, or even a hundred times.'

⁹ Then Jesus said, 'He who has ears to hear, let him hear.'

¹⁰ When he was alone, the Twelve and the others around him asked him about the parables. ¹¹ He told them, 'The secret of the kingdom of God has been given to you. But to those on the outside everything is said in parables ¹² so that,

"they may be ever seeing but never perceiving, and ever hearing but never understanding; otherwise they might turn and be forgiven!" '

¹³ Then Jesus said to them, 'Don't you understand this parable? How then will you understand any parable? ¹⁴ The farmer sows the word. ¹⁵ Some people are like seed along the path, where the word is sown. As soon as they hear it, Satan comes and takes away the word that was sown in them. ¹⁶ Others, like seed sown on rocky places, hear the word and at once receive it with joy. ¹⁷ But since they have no root, they last only a short time. When trouble or persecution comes because of the word, they quickly fall away. ¹⁸ Still others, like seed sown among thorns, hear the word; ¹⁹ but the worries of this life, the deceitfulness of wealth and the desires for other things come in and choke the word, making it unfruitful. ²⁰ Others, like seed sown on good soil, hear the word, accept it, and produce a crop - thirty, sixty or even a hundred times what was sown.'

Other seed fell among thorns . . .

DAY 7

MARK 4. 21 — 41

A Lamp on a Stand

²¹ He said to them, 'Do you bring in a lamp to put it under a bowl or a bed? Instead, don't you put it on its stand? ²² For whatever is hidden is meant to be disclosed, and whatever is concealed is meant to be brought out into the open. ²³ If anyone has ears to hear, let him hear.'

²⁴ 'Consider carefully what you hear,' he continued. 'With the measure you use, it will be measured to you - and even more. ²⁵ Whoever has will be given more; whoever does not have, even what he has will be taken from him.'

The Parable of the Growing Seed

²⁶ He also said, 'This is what the kingdom of God is like. A man scatters seed on the ground. ²⁷ Night and day, whether he sleeps or gets up, the seed sprouts and grows, though he does not know how. ²⁸ All by itself the soil produces corn - first the stalk, then the ear, then the full grain in the ear. ²⁹ As soon as the grain is ripe, he puts the sickle to it, because the harvest has come.'

The Parable of the Mustard Seed

³⁰ Again he said, 'What shall we say the kingdom of God is like, or what parable shall we use to describe it? ³¹ It is like a mustard seed, which is the smallest seed you plant in the ground. ³² Yet when planted, it grows and becomes the largest of all garden plants, with such big branches that the birds of the air can perch in its shade.'

³³ With many similar parables Jesus spoke the word to them, as much as they could understand. ³⁴ He did not say anything to them without using a parable. But when he was alone with his own disciples, he explained everything.

Jesus Calms the Storm

³⁵ That day when evening came, he said to his disciples, 'Let us go over to the other side.' ³⁶ Leaving the crowd behind, they took him along, just as he was, in the boat. There were also other boats with him. ³⁷ A furious squall came up, and the waves broke over the boat, so that it was nearly swamped. ³⁸ Jesus was in the stern, sleeping on a cushion. The disciples woke him and said to him, 'Teacher, don't you care if we drown?'

³⁹ He got up, rebuked the wind and said to the waves, 'Quiet! Be still!' Then the wind died down and it was completely calm.

⁴⁰ He said to his disciples, 'Why are you so afraid? Do you still have no faith?'

⁴¹ They were terrified and asked each other, 'Who is this? Even the wind and the waves obey him!'

DAY 8

MARK 5. 1 — 20

The Healing of a Demon-possessed Man

5 They went across the lake to the region of the Gerasenes. ² When Jesus got out of the boat, a man with an evil spirit came from the tombs to meet him. ³ This man lived in the tombs, and no-one could bind him any more, not even with a chain. ⁴ For he had often been chained hand and foot, but he tore the chains apart and broke the irons on his feet. No-one was strong enough to subdue him. ⁵ Night and day among the tombs and in the hills he would

They (the disciples) were terrified and asked each other, 'Who is this? Even the wind and the waves obey him!'

cry out and cut himself with stones.

[6] When he saw Jesus from a distance, he ran and fell on his knees in front of him. [7] He shouted at the top of his voice, 'What do you want with me, Jesus, Son of the Most High God? Swear to God that you won't torture me!' [8] For Jesus had said to him, 'Come out of this man, you evil spirit!'

[9] Then Jesus asked him, 'What is your name?'

'My name is Legion,' he replied, 'for we are many.' [10] And he begged Jesus again and again not to send them out of the area.

[11] A large herd of pigs was feeding on the nearby hillside. [12] The demons begged Jesus, 'Send us among the pigs; allow us to go into them.' [13] He gave them permission, and the evil spirits came out and went into the pigs. The herd, about two thousand in number, rushed down the steep bank into the lake and were drowned.

[14] Those tending the pigs ran off and reported this in the town and countryside, and the people went out to see what had happened. [15] When they came to Jesus, they saw the man who had been possessed by the legion of demons, sitting there, dressed and in his right mind; and they were afraid. [16] Those who had seen it told the people what had happened to the demon-possessed man - and told about the pigs as well. [17] Then the people began to plead with Jesus to leave their region.

[18] As Jesus was getting into the boat, the man who had been demon-possessed begged to go with him. [19] Jesus did not let him, but said, 'Go home to your family and tell them how much the Lord has done for you, and how he has had mercy on you.' [20] So the man went away and began to tell in the Decapolis how much Jesus had done for him. And all the people were amazed.

DAY 9

MARK 5. 21 — 43

A Dead Girl and a Sick Woman

²¹ When Jesus had again crossed over by boat to the other side of the lake, a large crowd gathered round him while he was by the lake. ²² Then one of the synagogue rulers, named Jairus, came there. Seeing Jesus, he fell at his feet ²³ and pleaded earnestly with him, 'My little daughter is dying. Please come and put your hands on her so that she will be healed and live.' ²⁴ So Jesus went with him.

A large crowd followed and pressed around him. ²⁵ And a woman was there who had been subject to bleeding for twelve years. ²⁶ She had suffered a great deal under the care of many doctors and had spent all she had, yet instead of getting better she grew worse. ²⁷ When she heard about Jesus, she came up behind him in the crowd and touched his cloak, ²⁸ because she thought, 'If I just touch his clothes, I will be healed.' ²⁹ Immediately her bleeding stopped and she felt in her body that she was freed from her suffering.

³⁰ At once Jesus realised that power had gone out from him. He turned around in the crowd and asked, 'Who touched my clothes?'

³¹ 'You see the people crowding against you,' his disciples answered, 'and yet you can ask, "Who touched me?" '

³² But Jesus kept looking around to see who had done it. ³³ Then the woman, knowing what had happened to her, came and fell at his feet and, trembling with fear, told him the whole truth. ³⁴ He said to her, 'Daughter, your faith has healed you. Go in peace and be freed from your suffering.'

³⁵ While Jesus was still speaking, some men came from the house of Jairus, the synagogue ruler. 'Your daughter is dead,' they said. 'Why bother the teacher any more?'

³⁶ Ignoring what they said, Jesus told the synagogue ruler, 'Don't be afraid; just believe.'

³⁷ He did not let anyone follow him except Peter, James and John the brother of James. ³⁸ When they came to the home of the synagogue ruler, Jesus saw a commotion, with people crying

---

He took her by the hand and said to her 'Talitha koum!' (which means, 'Little girl, I say to you, get up!').

---

and wailing loudly. ³⁹ He went in and said to them, 'Why all this commotion and wailing? The child is not dead but asleep.' ⁴⁰ But they laughed at him.

After he put them all out, he took the child's father and mother and the disciples who were with him, and went in where the child was. ⁴¹ He took her by the hand and said to her, *'Talitha koum!'* (which means, 'Little girl, I say to you, get up!'). ⁴² Immediately the girl stood up and walked around (she was twelve years old). At this they were completely astonished. ⁴³ He gave strict orders not to let anyone know about this, and told them to give her something to eat.

DAY 10

MARK 6. 1 — 13

6 **A Prophet Without Honour**
Jesus left there and went to his home town, accompanied by his disciples. ² When the Sabbath came, he began to teach in the synagogue, and many who heard him were amazed.

'Where did this man get these things?' they asked. 'What's this wisdom that has been given him, that he even does miracles! ³ Isn't this the carpenter? Isn't this Mary's son and the brother of James, Joseph, Judas and Simon? Aren't his sisters here with us?' And they took offence at him.

⁴ Jesus said to them, 'Only in his home town, among his relatives and in his own house is a prophet without honour.' ⁵ He could not do any miracles there, except lay his hands on a few sick people and heal them. ⁶ And he was amazed at their lack of faith.

Jesus Sends Out the Twelve

Then Jesus went round teaching from village to village. ⁷ Calling the Twelve to him, he sent them out two by two and gave them authority over evil spirits.

⁸ These were his instructions: 'Take nothing for the journey except a staff - no bread, no bag, no money in your belts. ⁹ Wear sandals but not an extra tunic. ¹⁰ Whenever you enter a house, stay there until you leave that town. ¹¹ And if any place will not welcome you or listen to you, shake the dust off your feet when you leave, as a testimony against them.'

¹² They went out and preached that people should repent. ¹³ They drove out many demons and anointed many sick people with oil and healed them.

They went out and preached that people should repent.

DAY 11

MARK 6. 14 — 29

John the Baptist Beheaded

[14] King Herod heard about this, for Jesus' name had become well known. Some were saying, 'John the Baptist has been raised from the dead, and that is why miraculous powers are at work in him.'

[15] Others said, 'He is Elijah.'

And still others claimed, 'He is a prophet, like one of the prophets of long ago.'

[16] But when Herod heard this, he said, 'John, the man I beheaded, has been raised from the dead!'

[17] For Herod himself had given orders to have John arrested, and he had him bound and put in prison. He did this because of Herodias, his brother Philip's wife, whom he had married. [18] For John had been saying to Herod, 'It is not lawful for you to have your brother's wife.' [19] So Herodias nursed a grudge against John and wanted to kill him. But she was not able to, [20] because Herod feared John and protected him, knowing him to be a righteous and holy man. When Herod heard John, he was greatly puzzled; yet he liked to listen to him.

[21] Finally the opportune time came. On his birthday Herod gave a banquet for his high officials and military commanders and the leading men of Galilee. [22] When the daughter of Herodias came in and danced, she pleased Herod and his dinner guests.

The king said to the girl, 'Ask me for anything you want, and I'll give it to you.' [23] And he promised her with an oath, 'Whatever you ask I will give you, up to half my kingdom.'

[24] She went out and said to her mother, 'What shall I ask for?'

'The head of John the Baptist,' she answered.

[25] At once the girl hurried in to the king with the request: 'I want you to give me right now the head of John the Baptist on a platter.'

[26] The king was greatly distressed, but because of his oaths and his dinner guests he did not want to refuse her. [27] So he immediately sent an executioner with orders to bring John's head. The man went, beheaded John in the prison, [28] and brought back his head on a platter. He presented it to the girl, and she gave it to her mother. [29] On hearing of this, John's disciples came and took his body and laid it in a tomb.

DAY 12

MARK 6. 30 — 56

Jesus Feeds the Five Thousand

[30] The apostles gathered round Jesus and reported to him all they had done and taught. [31] Then, because so many people were coming and going that they did not even have a chance to eat, he said to them 'Come with me by yourselves to a quiet place and get some rest.'

[32] So they went away by themselves in boat to a solitary place. [33] But many who saw them leaving recognised them and ran on foot from all the towns and got there ahead of them. [34] When Jesus landed and saw a large crowd, he had compassion on them, because they were like sheep withou a shepherd. So he began teaching them

many things.

³⁵ By this time it was late in the day, so his disciples came to him. 'This is a remote place,' they said, 'and it's already very late. ³⁶ Send the people away so that they can go to the surrounding countryside and villages and buy themselves something to eat.'

³⁷ But he answered, 'You give them something to eat.'

They said to him, 'That would take eight months of a man's wages! Are we to go and spend that much on bread and give it to them to eat?'

³⁸ 'How many loaves do you have?' he asked. 'Go and see.'

When they found out, they said, 'Five - and two fish.'

³⁹ Then Jesus directed them to have all the people sit down in groups on the green grass. ⁴⁰ So they sat down in groups of hundreds and fifties. ⁴¹ Taking the five loaves and the two fish and looking up to heaven, he gave thanks and broke the loaves. Then he gave them to his disciples to set before the people. He also divided the two fish among them all. ⁴² They all ate and were satisfied, ⁴³ and the disciples picked up twelve basketfuls of broken pieces of bread and fish. ⁴⁴ The number of the men who had eaten was five thousand.

Jesus Walks on the Water

⁴⁵ Immediately Jesus made his disciples get into the boat and go on ahead of him to Bethsaida, while he dismissed the crowd. ⁴⁶ After leaving them, he went up on a mountainside to pray.

⁴⁷ When evening came, the boat was in the middle of the lake, and he was alone on land. ⁴⁸ He saw the disciples straining at the oars, because the wind was against them. About the fourth watch of the night he went out to them, walking on the lake. He was about to pass by them, ⁴⁹ but when they saw him walking on the lake, they thought he was a ghost. They cried out, ⁵⁰ because they all saw him and were terrified.

Immediately he spoke to them and said, 'Take courage! It is I. Don't be afraid.' ⁵¹ Then he climbed into the boat with them, and the wind died down. They were completely amazed, ⁵² for they

> ## 'Take courage! It is I. Don't be afraid.'

had not understood about the loaves; their hearts were hardened.

⁵³ When they had crossed over, they landed at Gennesaret and anchored there. ⁵⁴ As soon as they got out of the boat, people recognised Jesus. ⁵⁵ They ran throughout that whole region and carried the sick on mats to wherever they heard he was. ⁵⁶ And wherever he went - into villages, towns or countryside - they placed the sick in the market-places. They begged him to let them touch even the edge of his cloak, and all who touched him were healed.

He had compassion on them because they were like sheep without a shepherd.

DAY 13

MARK 7. 1 — 23

7 **Clean and Unclean**
The Pharisees and some of the teachers of the law who had come from Jerusalem gathered round Jesus and [2] saw some of his disciples eating food with hands that were 'unclean', that is, unwashed. [3] (The Pharisees and all the Jews do not eat unless they give their hands a ceremonial washing, holding to the tradition of the elders. [4] When they come from the market-place they do not eat unless they wash. And they observe many other traditions, such as the washing of cups, pitchers and kettles.)
[5] So the Pharisees and teachers of the law asked Jesus, 'Why don't your disciples live according to the tradition of the elders instead of eating their food with "unclean" hands?'
[6] He replied, 'Isaiah was right when he prophesied about you hypocrites; as it is written:

"These people honour me
with their lips,
but their hearts are far
from me.
[7] They worship me in vain;
their teachings are but
rules taught by men."

[8] You have let go of the commands of God and are holding on to the traditions of men.'
[9] And he said to them: 'You have a fine way of setting aside the commands of God in order to observe your own traditions! [10] For Moses said, "Honour your father and your mother," and, "Anyone who curses his father or mother must be put to death." [11] But you say that if a man says to his father or mother: "Whatever help you might otherwise have received from me is Corban" (that is, a gift devoted to God), [12] then you no longer let him do anything for his father or mother. [13] Thus you nullify the word of God by your tradition that you have handed down. And you do many things like that.'
[14] Again Jesus called the crowd to him and said, 'Listen to me, everyone, and understand this. [15] Nothing outside a man can make him "unclean" by going into him. Rather, it is what comes out of a man that makes him "unclean".'
[17] After he had left the crowd and entered the house, his disciples asked him about this parable. [18] 'Are you so dull?' he asked. 'Don't you see that nothing that enters a man from the outside can make him "unclean"? [19] For it doesn't go into his heart but into his stomach, and then

> "Honour your father and your mother," and, "Anyone who curses his father or mother must be put to death."

out of his body.' (In saying this, Jesus declared all foods 'clean'.)
[20] He went on: 'What comes out of a man is what makes him "unclean". [21] For from within, out of men's hearts, come evil thoughts, sexual immorality, theft, murder, adultery, [22] greed, malice, deceit, lewdness, envy, slander, arrogance and folly. [23] All these evils come from inside and make a man "unclean".'

DAY 14

MARK 7. 24 — 37

The Faith of a Syro-Phoenician Woman

[24] Jesus left that place and went to the vicinity of Tyre. He entered a house and did not want anyone to know it; yet he could not keep his presence secret. [25] In fact, as soon as she heard about him, a woman whose little daughter was possessed by an

[30] She went home and found her child lying on the bed, and the demon gone.

The Healing of a Deaf and Mute Man

[31] Then Jesus left the vicinity of Tyre and went through Sidon, down to the Sea of Galilee and into the region of the Decapolis. [32] There some people brought to him a man who was deaf and could hardly talk, and they begged him to place his hand on the man.

[33] After he took him aside, away from the crowd, Jesus put his fingers into the man's ears. Then he spat and touched the

He looked up to heaven...

evil spirit came and fell at his feet. [26] The woman was a Greek, born in Syrian Phoenicia. She begged Jesus to drive the demon out of her daughter.

[27] 'First let the children eat all they want,' he told her, 'for it is not right to take the children's bread and toss it to their dogs.'

[28] 'Yes, Lord,' she replied, 'but even the dogs under the table eat the children's crumbs.'

[29] Then he told her, 'For such a reply, you may go; the demon has left your daughter.'

man's tongue. [34] He looked up to heaven and with a deep sigh said to him, 'Ephphatha!' (which means, 'Be opened!'). [35] At this, the man's ears were opened, his tongue was loosened and he began to speak plainly.

[36] Jesus commanded them not to tell anyone. But the more he did so, the more they kept talking about it. [37] People were overwhelmed with amazement. 'He has done everything well,' they said. 'He even makes the deaf hear and the mute speak.'

DAY 15

MARK 8. 1 — 26

8 **Jesus Feeds the Four Thousand** During those days another large crowd gathered. Since they had nothing to eat, Jesus called his disciples to him and said, [2] 'I have compassion for these people; they have already been with me three days and have nothing to eat. [3] If I send them home hungry, they will collapse on the way, because some of them have come a long distance.'

[4] His disciples answered, 'But where in this remote place can anyone get enough bread to feed them?'

[5] 'How many loaves do you have?' Jesus asked.

'Seven,' they replied.

[6] He told the crowd to sit down on the ground. When he had taken the seven loaves and given thanks, he broke them and gave them to his disciples to set before the people, and they did so. [7] They had a few small fish as well; he gave thanks for them also and told the disciples to distribute them. [8] The people ate and were satisfied. Afterwards the disciples picked up seven basketfuls of broken pieces that were left over. [9] About four thousand men were present. And having sent them away, [10] he got into the boat with his disciples and went to the region of Dalmanutha.

[11] The Pharisees came and began to question Jesus. To test him, they asked him for a sign from heaven. [12] He sighed deeply and said, 'Why does this generation ask for a miraculous sign? I tell you the truth, no sign will be given to it.' [13] Then he left them, got back into the boat and crossed to the other side.

The Yeast of the Pharisees and Herod

[14] The disciples had forgotten to bring bread, except for one loaf they had with them in the boat. [15] 'Be careful,' Jesus warned them. 'Watch out for the yeast of the Pharisees and that of Herod.'

[16] They discussed this with one another and said, 'It is because we have no bread.'

[17] Aware of their discussion, Jesus asked them: 'Why are you talking about having no bread? Do you still not see or understand? Are your hearts hardened? [18] Do you have eyes but fail to see, and ears but fail to hear? And don't you remember? [19] When I broke the five loaves for the five thousand, how many basketfuls of pieces did you pick up?'

'Twelve,' they replied.

[20] 'And when I broke the seven loaves for the four thousand, how many basketfuls of pieces did you pick up?'

They answered, 'Seven.'

[21] He said to them, 'Do you still not understand?'

The Healing of a Blind Man at Bethsaida

[22] They came to Bethsaida, and some people brought a blind man and begged Jesus to touch him. [23] He took the blind man by the hand and led him outside the village. When he had spat on the man's eyes and put his hands on him, Jesus asked, 'Do you see anything?'

[24] He looked up and said, 'I see people; they look like trees walking around.'

[25] Once more Jesus put his hands on the man's eyes. Then his eyes were opened, his sight was restored, and he saw everything clearly. [26] Jesus sent him home saying, 'Don't go into the village.'

DAY 16

MARK 8. 27 — 9.1

Peter's Confession of Christ

²⁷ Jesus and his disciples went on to the villages around Caesarea Philippi. On the way he asked them, 'Who do people say I am?'

²⁸ They replied, 'Some say John the Baptist; others say Elijah; and still others, one of the prophets.'

²⁹ 'But what about you?' he asked. 'Who do you say I am?'

Peter answered, 'You are the Christ.'

³⁰ Jesus warned them not to tell anyone about him.

Jesus Predicts His Death

³¹ He then began to teach them that the Son of Man must suffer many things and be rejected by the elders, chief priests and teachers of the law, and that he must be killed and after three days rise again. ³² He spoke plainly about this, and Peter took him aside and began to rebuke him.

³³ But when Jesus turned and looked at his disciples, he rebuked Peter. 'Get behind me, Satan!' he said. 'You do not have in mind the things of God, but the things of men.'

³⁴ Then he called the crowd to him along with his disciples and said: 'If anyone would come after me, he must deny himself and take up his cross and follow me. ³⁵ For whoever wants to save his life will lose it, but whoever loses his

> ### 'What good is it for a man to gain the whole world, yet forfeit his soul?'

life for me and for the gospel will save it. ³⁶ What good is it for a man to gain the whole world, yet forfeit his soul? ³⁷ Or what can a man give in exchange for his soul? ³⁸ If anyone is ashamed of me and my words in this adulterous and sinful generation, the Son of Man will be ashamed of him when he comes in his Father's glory with the holy angels.'

9 And he said to them, 'I tell you the truth, some who are standing here will not taste death before they see the kingdom of God come with power.'

(Jesus said) 'You do not have in mind the things of God, but the things of men.'

DAY 17

MARK 9. 2 — 13

The Transfiguration

[2] After six days Jesus took Peter, James and John with him and led them up a high mountain, where they were all alone. There he was transfigured before them. [3] His clothes became dazzling white, whiter than anyone in the world could bleach them. [4] And there appeared before them Elijah and Moses, who were talking with Jesus.

[5] Peter said to Jesus, 'Rabbi, it is good for us to be here. Let us put up three shelters - one for you, one for Moses and one for Elijah.' [6] (He did not know what to say, they were so frightened.)

[7] Then a cloud appeared and enveloped them, and a voice came from the cloud: 'This is my Son, whom I love. Listen to him!'

[8] Suddenly, when they looked round, they no longer saw anyone with them except Jesus.

[9] As they were coming down the mountain, Jesus gave them orders not to tell anyone what they had seen until the Son of Man had risen from the dead. [10] They kept the matter to themselves, discussing what 'rising from the dead' meant.

[11] And they asked him, 'Why do the teachers of the law say that Elijah must come first?' [12] Jesus replied, 'To be sure, Elijah does come first, and restores all things. Why then is it written that the Son of Man must suffer much and be rejected? [13] But I tell you, Elijah has come and they have done to him everything they wished, just as it is written about him.'

...and a voice came from the cloud: 'This is my Son, whom I love. Listen to him!'

DAY 18

MARK 9. 14 — 29

The Healing of a Boy With an Evil Spirit

¹⁴ When they came to the other disciples, they saw a large crowd around them and

> **'Teacher, I brought you my son, who is possessed by a spirit that has robbed him of speech.'**

the teachers of the law arguing with them. ¹⁵ As soon as all the people saw Jesus, they were overwhelmed with wonder and ran to greet him.

¹⁶ 'What are you arguing with them about?' he asked.

¹⁷ A man in the crowd answered, 'Teacher, I brought you my son, who is possessed by a spirit that has robbed him of speech. ¹⁸ Whenever it seizes him, it throws him to the ground. He foams at the mouth, gnashes his teeth and becomes rigid. I asked your disciples to drive out the spirit, but they could not.'

¹⁹ 'O unbelieving generation,' Jesus replied, 'how long shall I stay with you? How long shall I put up with you? Bring the boy to me.'

²⁰ So they brought him. When the spirit saw Jesus, it immediately threw the boy into a convulsion. He fell to the ground and rolled around, foaming at the mouth.

²¹ Jesus asked the boy's father, 'How long has he been like this?'

'From childhood,' he answered. ²² 'It has often thrown him into fire or water to kill him. But if you can do anything, take pity on us and help us.'

²³ ' "If you can"?' said Jesus. 'Everything is possible for him who believes.'

²⁴ Immediately the boy's father exclaimed, 'I do believe; help me overcome my unbelief!'

²⁵ When Jesus saw that a crowd was running to the scene, he rebuked the evil spirit. 'You deaf and mute spirit,' he said, 'I command you, come out of him and never enter him again.'

²⁶ The spirit shrieked, convulsed him violently and came out. The boy looked so much like a corpse that many said, 'He's dead.' ²⁷ But Jesus took him by the hand and lifted him to his feet, and he stood up.

²⁸ After Jesus had gone indoors, his disciples asked him privately, 'Why couldn't we drive it out?'

²⁹ He replied, 'This kind can come out only by prayer.'

> **'The Son of Man is going to be betrayed into the hands of men. They will kill him, and after three days he will rise.'**

³⁰ They left that place and passed through Galilee. Jesus did not want anyone to know where they were, ³¹ because he was teaching his disciples. He said to them, 'The Son of Man is going to be betrayed into the hands of men. They will kill him, and after three days he will rise.' ³² But they did not understand what he meant and were afraid to ask him about it.

DAY 19

MARK 9. 30 — 50

Who Is the Greatest?

[33] They came to Capernaum. When he was in the house, he asked them, 'What were you arguing about on the road?' [34] But they kept quiet because on the way they had argued about who was the greatest.

[35] Sitting down, Jesus called the Twelve and said, 'If anyone wants to be first, he must be the very last, and the servant of all.'

[36] He took a little child and had him stand among them. Taking him in his arms, he said to them, [37] 'Whoever welcomes one of these little children in my name welcomes me; and whoever welcomes me does not welcome me but the one who sent me.'

Whoever Is Not Against Us Is for Us

[38] 'Teacher,' said John, 'we saw a man driving out demons in your name and we told him to stop, because he was not one of us.'

[39] 'Do not stop him,' Jesus said. 'No-one who does a miracle in my name can in the next moment say anything bad about me, [40] for whoever is not against us is for us. [41] I tell you the truth, anyone who gives you a cup of water in my name because you belong to Christ will certainly not lose his reward.'

Causing to Sin

[42] 'And if anyone causes one of these little ones who believe in me to sin, it would be better for him to be thrown into the sea with a large millstone tied around his neck. [43] If your hand causes you to sin, cut it off. It is better for you to enter life maimed than with two hands to go into hell, where the fire never goes out. [45] And if your foot causes you to sin, cut it off. It is better for you to enter life crippled than to have two feet and be thrown into hell. [47] And if your eye causes you to sin, pluck it out. It is better for you to enter the kingdom of God with one eye than to have two eyes and be thrown into hell, [48] where

> **'No-one who does a miracle in my name can in the next moment say anything bad about me, for whoever is not against us is for us. '**

"their worm does not die,
    and the fire is not quenched."

[49] Everyone will be salted with fire. [50] 'Salt is good, but if it loses its saltiness, how can you make it salty again? Have salt in yourselves, and be at peace with each other.'

DAY 20

MARK 10. 1 — 16

10

Divorce

Jesus then left that place and went into the region of Judea and across the Jordan. Again crowds of people came to him, and as was his custom he taught them.

[2] Some Pharisees came and tested him by asking, 'Is it lawful for a man to divorce his wife?'

[3] 'What did Moses command you?' he replied.

[4] They said, 'Moses permitted a man to write a certificate of divorce and send her away.'

[5] 'It was because your hearts were hard that Moses wrote you this law,' Jesus replied. [6] 'But at the beginning of creation God "made them male and female". [7] "For this reason a man will leave his father and mother and be united to his wife, [8] and the two will become one flesh" So they are no longer two, but one. [9] Therefore what God has joined together, let man not separate.'

[10] When they were in the house again, the disciples asked Jesus about this. He answered, 'Anyone who divorces his wife and marries another woman commits adultery against her. [12] And if she divorces her husband and marries another man, she commits adultery.'

The Little Children and Jesus

[3] People were bringing little children to Jesus to have him touch them, but the disciples rebuked them. [14] When Jesus saw this, he was indignant. He said to them, 'Let the little children come to me, and

> **'Let the little children come to me, and do not hinder them, for the kingdom of God belongs to such as these.'**

do not hinder them, for the kingdom of God belongs to such as these. [15] I tell you the truth, anyone who will not receive the kingdom of God like a little child will never enter it.' [16] And he took the children in his arms, put his hands on them and blessed them.

(Jesus) said to them, '. . .the kingdom of God belongs to such as these.'

DAY 21

MARK 10. 17 — 31

The Rich Young Man

[17] As Jesus started on his way, a man ran up to him and fell on his knees before him. 'Good teacher,' he asked, 'what must I do to inherit eternal life?'

[18] 'Why do you call me good?' Jesus answered. 'No-one is good - except God alone. [19] You know the commandments: "Do not murder, do not commit adultery, do not steal, do not give false testimony, do not defraud, honour your father and mother." '

[20] 'Teacher,' he declared, 'all these I have kept since I was a boy.'

[21] Jesus looked at him and loved him. 'One thing you lack,' he said. 'Go, sell

'Children, how hard it is to enter the kingdom of God!'

everything you have and give to the poor, and you will have treasure in heaven. Then come, follow me.'

[22] At this the man's face fell. He went away sad, because he had great wealth.

[23] Jesus looked around and said to his disciples, 'How hard it is for the rich to enter the kingdom of God!'

[24] The disciples were amazed at his words. But Jesus said again, 'Children, how hard it is to enter the kingdom of God! [25] It is easier for a camel to go through the eye of a needle than for a

rich man to enter the kingdom of God.'

[26] The disciples were even more amazed, and said to each other, 'Who then can be saved?'

[27] Jesus looked at them and said, 'With man this is impossible, but not with God; all things are possible with God.'

[28] Peter said to him, 'We have left everything to follow you!'

[29] 'I tell you the truth,' Jesus replied, 'no-one who has left home or brothers or sisters or mother or father or children or fields for me and the gospel [30] will fail to receive a hundred times as much in this present age (homes, brothers, sisters, mothers, children and fields - and with them, persecutions) and in the age to come, eternal life. [31] But many who are first will be last, and the last first.'

'It is easier for a camel to go through the eye of a needle than for a rich man to enter the kingdom of God.'

DAY 22

MARK 10. 32 — 52

Jesus Again Predicts His Death

[32] They were on their way up to Jerusalem, with Jesus leading the way, and the disciples were astonished, while those who followed were afraid. Again he took the Twelve aside and told them what was going to happen to him. [33] 'We are going up to Jerusalem,' he said, 'and the Son of Man will be betrayed to the chief priests and teachers of the law. They will condemn him to death and will hand him over to the Gentiles, [34] who will mock him and spit on him, flog him and kill him. Three days later he will rise.'

The Request of James and John

[35] Then James and John, the sons of Zebedee, came to him. 'Teacher,' they said, 'we want you to do for us whatever we ask.'

[36] 'What do you want me to do for you?' he asked.

[37] They replied, 'Let one of us sit at your right and the other at your left in your glory.'

[38] 'You don't know what you are asking,' Jesus said. 'Can you drink the cup I drink or be baptised with the baptism I am baptised with?'

[39] 'We can,' they answered. Jesus said to them, 'You will drink the cup I drink and be baptised with the baptism I am baptised with, [40] but to sit at my right or left is not for me to grant. These places belong to those for whom they have been prepared.'

[41] When the ten heard about this, they became indignant with James and John. [42] Jesus called them together and said, 'You know that those who are regarded as rulers of the Gentiles lord it over them, and their high officials exercise authority over them. [43] Not so with you. Instead, whoever wants to become great among you must be your servant, [44] and whoever wants to be first must be slave of all. [45] For even the Son of Man did not come to be served, but to serve, and to give his life as a ransom for many.'

Blind Bartimaeus Receives His Sight

[46] Then they came to Jericho. As Jesus and his disciples, together with a large crowd, were leaving the city, a blind man, Bartimaeus (that is, the Son of Timaeus), was sitting by the roadside begging. [47] When he heard that it was Jesus of Nazareth, he began to shout, 'Jesus, Son of David, have mercy on me!'

[48] Many rebuked him and told him to be quiet, but he shouted all the more, 'Son of David, have mercy on me!'

[49] Jesus stopped and said, 'Call him.'

So they called to the blind man, 'Cheer up! On your feet! He's calling you.' [50] Throwing his cloak aside, he jumped to his feet and came to Jesus. [51] 'What do you want me to do for

---

Many rebuked him and told him to be quiet, but he shouted all the more, 'Son of David, have mercy on me!'

---

you?' Jesus asked him.

The blind man said, 'Rabbi, I want to see.'

[52] 'Go,' said Jesus, 'your faith has healed you.' Immediately he received his sight and followed Jesus along the road.

DAY 23

MARK 11. 1 — 19

11 The Triumphal Entry

As they approached Jerusalem and came to Bethphage and Bethany at the Mount of Olives, Jesus sent two of his disciples, ² saying to them, 'Go to the village ahead of you, and just as you enter it, you will find a colt tied there, which no-one has ever ridden. Untie it and bring it here.³ If anyone asks you, "Why are you doing this?" tell him, "The Lord needs it and will send it back here shortly. " '

⁴ They went and found a colt outside in the street, tied at a doorway. As they untied it, ⁵ some people standing there asked, 'What are you doing, untying that colt?' ⁶ They answered as Jesus had told

---

'Hosanna in the highest!'

---

them to, and the people let them go. ⁷ When they brought the colt to Jesus and threw their cloaks over it, he sat on it. ⁸ Many people spread their cloaks on the road, while others spread branches they had cut in the fields. ⁹ Those who went ahead and those who followed shouted,

'Hosanna!'

'Blessed is he who comes in
the name of the Lord!'

¹⁰ 'Blessed is the coming
kingdom of our father David!'
'Hosanna in the highest!'

¹¹ Jesus entered Jerusalem and went to the temple. He looked around at everything, but since it was already late, he went out to Bethany with the Twelve.

Jesus Clears the Temple

¹² The next day as they were leaving Bethany, Jesus was hungry. ¹³ Seeing in the distance a fig-tree in leaf, he went to find out if it had any fruit. When he reached it, he found nothing but leaves, because it was not the season for figs.

"My house will be called a house of prayer for all nations."

---

¹⁴ Then he said to the tree, 'May no-one ever eat fruit from you again.' And his disciples heard him say it.

¹⁵ On reaching Jerusalem, Jesus entered the temple area and began driving out those who were buying and selling there. He overturned the tables of the money changers and the benches of those selling doves, ¹⁶ and would not allow anyone to carry merchandise through the temple courts. ¹⁷ And as he taught them, he said, 'Is it not written:

"My house will be called
a house of prayer for all
nations"?

But you have made it "a den of robbers".'
¹⁸ The chief priests and the teachers of the law heard this and began looking for a way to kill him, for they feared him, because the whole crowd was amazed at his teaching.
¹⁹ When evening came, they went out of the city.

DAY 24

MARK 11. 20 — 33

The Withered Fig-Tree

²⁰ In the morning, as they went along, they saw the fig-tree withered from the roots. ²¹ Peter remembered and said to Jesus, 'Rabbi, look! The fig-tree you cursed has withered!'

anything against anyone, forgive him, so that your Father in heaven may forgive you your sins.'

The Authority of Jesus Questioned

²⁷ They arrived again in Jerusalem, and while Jesus was walking in the temple courts, the chief priests, the teachers of the law and the elders came to him. ²⁸ 'By what authority are you doing these things?' they asked. 'And who gave you authority to do this?'

²⁹ Jesus replied, 'I will ask you one

'Whatever you ask for in prayer, believe that you have received it, and it will be yours.'

²² 'Have faith in God,' Jesus answered. ²³ 'I tell you the truth, if anyone says to this mountain, "Go, throw yourself into the sea," and does not doubt in his heart but believes that what he says will happen, it

'Have faith in God.'

will be done for him. ²⁴ Therefore I tell you, whatever you ask for in prayer, believe that you have received it, and it will be yours. ²⁵ And when you stand praying, if you hold

question. Answer me, and I will tell you by what authority I am doing these things. ³⁰ John's baptism - was it from heaven, or from men? Tell me!'

³¹ They discussed it among themselves and said, 'If we say, "From heaven", he will ask, "Then why didn't you believe him?" ³² But if we say, "From men". . . .' (They feared the people, for everyone held that John really was a prophet.)

³³ So they answered Jesus, 'We don't know.' Jesus said, 'Neither will I tell you by what authority I am doing these things.'

DAY 25

MARK 12. 1 — 17

12 **The Parable of the Tenants**
He then began to speak to them in parables: 'A man planted a vineyard. He put a wall around it, dug a pit for the winepress and built a watchtower. Then he rented the vineyard to some farmers and went away on a journey. ² At harvest time he sent a servant to the tenants to collect from them some of the fruit of the vineyard. ³ But they seized him, beat him and sent him away empty-handed. ⁴ Then he sent another servant to them; they struck this man on the head and treated him shamefully. ⁵ He sent still another, and that one they killed. He sent many others; some of them they beat, others they killed.
⁶ 'He had one left to send, a son, whom he loved. He sent him last of all, saying, "They will respect my son."
⁷ 'But the tenants said to one

> **'This is the heir. Come, let's kill him, and the inheritance will be ours.'**

another, "This is the heir. Come, let's kill him, and the inheritance will be ours." ⁸ So they took him and killed him, and threw him out of the vineyard.
⁹ 'What then will the owner of the vineyard do? He will come and kill those tenants and give the vineyard to others. ¹⁰ Haven't you read this scripture:

> "The stone the builders rejected
> has become the capstone;
> ¹¹ the Lord has done this,
> and it is marvellous in our eyes"?'

¹² Then they looked for a way to arrest him because they knew he had spoken the parable against them. But

> **'Give to Caesar what is Caesar's and to God what is God's.'**

they were afraid of the crowd; so they left him and went away.

Paying Taxes to Caesar

¹³ Later they sent some of the Pharisees and Herodians to Jesus to catch him in his words. ¹⁴ They came to him and said 'Teacher, we know you are a man of integrity. You aren't swayed by men, because you pay no attention to who they are; but you teach the way of God in accordance with the truth. Is it right to pay taxes to Caesar or not? ¹⁵ Should we pay or shouldn't we?'
But Jesus knew their hypocrisy. 'Why are you trying to trap me?' he asked. 'Bring me a denarius and let me look at it.' ¹⁶ They brought the coin, and he asked them, 'Whose portrait is this? And whose inscription?'
'Caesar's,' they replied.
¹⁷ Then Jesus said to them, 'Give to Caesar what is Caesar's and to God what is God's.'
And they were amazed at him.

DAY 26

MARK 12. 18 — 34

Marriage at the Resurrection

[18] Then the Sadducees, who say there is no resurrection, came to him with a question. [19] 'Teacher,' they said, 'Moses wrote for us that if a man's brother dies and leaves a wife but no children, the man must marry the widow and have children for his brother. [20] Now there were seven brothers. The first one married and died without leaving any children. [21] The second one married the widow, but he also died, leaving no child. It was the same with the third. [22] In fact, none of the seven left any children. Last of all, the woman died too. [23] At the resurrection whose wife will she be, since the seven were married to her?'

[24] Jesus replied, 'Are you not in error because you do not know the Scriptures or the power of God? [25] When the dead rise, they will neither marry nor be given in marriage; they will be like the angels in heaven. [26] Now about the dead rising - have you not read in the book of Moses, in the account of the bush, how God said to him, "I am the God of Abraham, the God of Isaac, and the God of Jacob"? [27] He is not the God of the dead, but of the living. You are badly mistaken!'

The Greatest Commandment

[28] One of the teachers of the law came and heard them debating. Noticing that Jesus had given them a good answer, he asked him, 'Of all the commandments, which is the most important?' [29] 'The most important one,' answered Jesus, 'is this: Hear, O Israel, the Lord our God, the Lord is one. [30] Love the Lord your God with all your heart and with all your soul and with all your mind and with all your strength." [31] The second is this: "Love your neighbour as yourself." There is no commandment greater than these.'

[32] 'Well said, teacher,' the man replied. 'You are right in saying that God is one and there is no other but him. [33] To love him with all your heart, with all your understanding and with all your strength, and to love your neighbour as yourself is more important than all burnt offerings and sacrifices.'

[34] When Jesus saw that he had answered wisely, he said to him, 'You are not far from the kingdom of God.' And from then on no-one dared ask him any more questions.

'Love your neighbour as yourself.'

DAY 27

MARK 12. 35 — 13.2

Whose Son is the Christ?

[35] While Jesus was teaching in the temple courts, he asked, 'How is it that the teachers of the law say that the Christ is the son of David? [36] David himself, speaking by the Holy Spirit, declared:

> "The Lord said to my Lord:
> 'Sit at my right hand
> until I put your enemies
> under your feet." '

[37] David himself calls him "Lord". How then can he be his son?'

The large crowd listened to him with delight.

[38] As he taught, Jesus said, 'Watch out for the teachers of the law. They like to walk around in flowing robes and be greeted in the market-places, [39] and have the most important seats in the synagogues and the places of honour at banquets. [40] They devour widows' houses and for a show make lengthy prayers. Such men will be punished most severely.'

The Widow's Offering

[41] Jesus sat down opposite the place where the offerings were put and watched the crowd putting their money into the temple treasury. Many rich people threw in large amounts. [42] But a poor widow came and put in two very small copper coins, worth only a fraction of a penny.

[43] Calling his disciples to him, Jesus said, 'I tell you the truth, this poor widow has put more into the treasury than all the others. [44] They all gave out of their wealth; but she, out of her poverty, put in everything - all she had to live on.'

13 Signs of the End of the Age

As he was leaving the temple, one of his disciples said to him, 'Look, Teacher! What massive stones! What magnificent buildings!' [2] 'Do you see all these great buildings?' replied Jesus. 'Not one stone here will be left on another; every one will be thrown down.'

DAY 28

MARK 13. 3 — 23

[3] As Jesus was sitting on the Mount of Olives opposite the temple, Peter, James, John and Andrew asked him privately, [4] 'Tell us, when will these things happen? And what will be the sign that they are all about to be fulfilled?'

[5] Jesus said to them: 'Watch out that no-one deceives you. [6] Many will come in my name, claiming, "I am he," and will deceive many. [7] When you hear of wars and rumours of wars, do not be alarmed. Such things must happen, but the end is still to come. [8] Nation will rise against nation, and kingdom against kingdom. There will be earthquakes in various places, and famines. These are the beginning of birth-pains.

[9] 'You must be on your guard. You will be handed over to the local councils and flogged in the synagogues. On account of me you will stand before governors and kings as witnesses to them. [10] And the gospel must first be preached

'Not one stone here will be left on another; every one will be thrown down.'

to all nations. [11] Whenever you are arrested and brought to trial, do not worry beforehand about what to say. Just say whatever is given you at the time, for it is not you speaking, but the Holy Spirit.

[12] 'Brother will betray brother to death, and a father his child. Children will rebel against their parents and have them put to death. [13] All men will hate you because of me, but he who stands firm to the end will be saved.

[14] 'When you see "the abomination that causes desolation" standing where it does not belong - let the reader understand - then let those who are in Judea flee to the mountains. [15] Let no-one on the roof of his house go down or enter the house to take anything out. [16] Let no-one in the field go back to get his cloak. [17] How dreadful it will be in those days for pregnant women and nursing mothers! [18] Pray that this will not take place in winter, [19] because those will be days of distress unequalled from the beginning, when God created the world, until now - and never to be equalled again. [20] If the Lord had not cut short those days, no-one would survive. But for the sake of the elect, whom he has chosen, he has shortened them. [21] At that time if anyone says to you, "Look, here is the Christ!" or, "Look, there he is!" do not believe it. [22] For false Christs and false prophets will appear and perform signs and miracles to deceive the elect - if that were possible. [23] So be on your guard; I have told you everything ahead of time.

DAY 29

MARK 13. 24 — 37

²⁴ 'But in those days, following that distress,

' "the sun will be darkened,
and the moon will not give
its light;
²⁵ the stars will fall from the sky,
and the heavenly bodies
will be shaken."

²⁶ 'At that time men will see the Son of Man coming in clouds with great power and glory. ²⁷ And he will send his angels and gather his elect from the four winds, from the ends of the earth to the ends of the heavens.

²⁸ 'Now learn this lesson from the fig-tree: As soon as its twigs get tender

---

> "The sun will be darkened,
> and the moon will not
> give its light;
> the stars will fall from
> the sky..."

---

and its leaves come out, you know that summer is near. ²⁹ Even so, when you see these things happening, you know that it is near, right at the door. ³⁰ I tell you the truth, this generation will certainly not pass away until all these things have happened. ³¹ Heaven and earth will pass away, but my words will never pass away.

The Day and Hour Unknown

³² 'No-one knows about that day or hour, not even the angels in heaven, nor the Son, but only the Father. ³³ Be on guard! Be alert! You do not know when that time will come. ³⁴ It's like a man going away: He leaves his house and puts his servants in charge, each with his assigned task, and tells the one at the door to keep watch.

³⁵ 'Therefore keep watch because you do not know when the owner of the house will come back - whether in the evening, or at midnight, or when the cock crows, or at dawn. ³⁶ If he comes suddenly, do not let him find you sleeping. ³⁷ What I say to you, I say to everyone: "Watch!" '

'Heaven and earth will pass away, but my words will never pass away.'

DAY 30

MARK 14. 1 — 11

14 Jesus Anointed at Bethany

Now the Passover and the Feast of Unleavened Bread were only two days away, and the chief priests and the teachers of the law were looking for some sly way to arrest Jesus and kill him. ² 'But not during the Feast,' they said, 'or the people may riot.'

³ While he was in Bethany, reclining at the table in the home of a man known as Simon the Leper, a woman came with an alabaster jar of very expensive perfume, made of pure nard. She broke

> **'But not during the Feast,' they said, 'or the people may riot.'**

the jar and poured the perfume on his head.

⁴ Some of those present were saying indignantly to one another, 'Why this waste of perfume? ⁵ It could have been sold for more than a year's wages and the money given to the poor.' And they rebuked her harshly.

⁶ 'Leave her alone,' said Jesus. 'Why are you bothering her? She has done a beautiful thing to me. ⁷ The poor you will always have with you, and you can help them any time you want. But you will not always have me. ⁸ She did what she could. She poured perfume on my body beforehand to prepare for my burial. ⁹ I

tell you the truth, wherever the gospel is preached throughout the world, what she has done will also be told, in memory of her.'

> **Then Judas Iscariot, one of the Twelve, went to the chief priests to betray Jesus to them.**

¹⁰ Then Judas Iscariot, one of the Twelve, went to the chief priests to betray Jesus to them. ¹¹ They were delighted to hear this and promised to give him money. So he watched for an opportunity to hand him over.

'The poor you will always have with you.'

DAY 31

MARK 14. 12 — 31

The Lord's Supper

[12] On the first day of the Feast of Unleavened Bread, when it was customary to sacrifice the Passover lamb, Jesus' disciples asked him, 'Where do you want us to go and make preparations for you to eat the Passover?'

[13] So he sent two of his disciples, telling them, 'Go into the city, and a man carrying a jar of water will meet you. Follow him. [14] Say to the owner of the house he enters, "The Teacher asks: Where is my guest room, where I may eat the Passover with my disciples?" [15] He will show you a large upper room, furnished and ready. Make preparations for us there.'

[16] The disciples left, went into the city and found things just as Jesus had told them. So they prepared the Passover.

[17] When evening came, Jesus arrived with the Twelve. [18] While they were reclining at the table eating, he said, 'I tell you the truth, one of you will betray me - one who is eating with me.'

[19] They were saddened, and one by one they said to him, 'Surely not I?'

> **'I tell you the truth, one of you will betray me - one who is eating with me.'**

[20] 'It is one of the Twelve,' he replied, 'one who dips bread into the bowl with me. [21] The Son of Man will go just as it is written about him. But woe to that man who betrays the Son of Man! It would be better for him if he had not been born.'

[22] While they were eating, Jesus took bread, gave thanks and broke it, and gave it to his disciples, saying, 'Take it; this is my body.'

[23] Then he took the cup, gave thanks and offered it to them, and they all drank from it.

> **'Take it; this is my body.'**

[24] 'This is my blood of the covenant, which is poured out for many,' he said to them. [25] 'I tell you the truth, I will not drink again of the fruit of the vine until that day when I drink it anew in the kingdom of God.'

[26] When they had sung a hymn, they went out to the Mount of Olives.

Jesus Predicts Peter's Denial

[27] 'You will all fall away,' Jesus told them, 'for it is written:

> "I will strike the shepherd,
> and the sheep will be
> scattered."

[28] But after I have risen, I will go ahead of you into Galilee.'

[29] Peter declared, 'Even if all fall away, I will not.'

[30] 'I tell you the truth,' Jesus answered, 'today - yes, tonight - before the cock crows twice you yourself will disown me three times.'

[31] But Peter insisted emphatically, 'Even if I have to die with you, I will never disown you.' And all the others said the same.

DAY 32

MARK 14. 32 — 52

Gethsemane

³² They went to a place called Gethsemane, and Jesus said to his disciples, 'Sit here while I pray.' ³³ He took Peter, James and John along with him, and he began to be deeply distressed and troubled. ³⁴ 'My soul is overwhelmed with sorrow to the point of death,' he said to them. 'Stay here and keep watch.'

³⁵ Going a little farther, he fell to the ground and prayed that if possible the hour might pass from him. ³⁶ 'Abba, Father,' he said, 'everything is possible for you. Take this cup from me. Yet not what I will, but what you will.'

³⁷ Then he returned to his disciples and found them sleeping. 'Simon,' he said to Peter, 'are you asleep? Could you not keep watch for one hour? ³⁸ Watch and pray so that you will not fall into temptation. The spirit is willing, but the body is weak.'

³⁹ Once more he went away and prayed the same thing. ⁴⁰ When he came back, he again found them sleeping, because their eyes were heavy. They did not know what to say to him.

⁴¹ Returning the third time, he said to them, 'Are you still sleeping and resting? Enough! The hour has come. Look, the Son of Man is betrayed into the hands of sinners. ⁴² Rise! Let us go! Here comes my betrayer!'

Jesus Arrested

⁴³ Just as he was speaking, Judas, one of the Twelve, appeared. With him was a crowd armed with swords and clubs, sent from the chief priests, the teachers of the law, and the elders.

⁴⁴ Now the betrayer had arranged a signal with them: 'The one I kiss is the man; arrest him and lead him away under guard.' ⁴⁵ Going at once to Jesus, Judas said, 'Rabbi!' and kissed him. ⁴⁶ The men seized Jesus and arrested him. ⁴⁷ Then one of those standing near drew his sword and struck the servant of the high priest, cutting off his ear.

⁴⁸ 'Am I leading a rebellion,' said Jesus, 'that you have come out with swords and clubs to capture me? ⁴⁹ Every day I was with you, teaching in the temple courts, and you did not arrest me. But the Scriptures must be fulfilled.' ⁵⁰ Then everyone deserted him and fled.

⁵¹ A young man, wearing nothing but a linen garment, was following Jesus. When they seized him, ⁵² he fled naked, leaving his garment behind.

'The hour has come.'

DAY 33

MARK 14. 53 — 72

Before the Sanhedrin

⁵³ They took Jesus to the high priest, and all the chief priests, elders and teachers of the law came together. ⁵⁴ Peter followed him at a distance, right into the courtyard of the high priest. There he sat with the guards and warmed himself at the fire.

⁵⁵ The chief priests and the whole Sanhedrin were looking for evidence against Jesus so that they could put him to death, but they did not find any. ⁵⁶ Many testified falsely against him, but their statements did not agree.

⁵⁷ Then some stood up and gave this false testimony against him: ⁵⁸ 'We heard him say, "I will destroy this man-made temple and in three days will build another, not made by man." ' ⁵⁹ Yet even then their testimony did not agree.

⁶⁰ Then the high priest stood up before them and asked Jesus, 'Are you not going to answer? What is this testimony that these men are bringing against you?' ⁶¹ But Jesus remained silent and gave no answer.

> **'And you will see
> the Son of Man sitting at the
> right hand of the Mighty One
> and coming on the clouds of
> heaven.'**

Again the high priest asked him, 'Are you the Christ, the Son of the Blessed One?'

⁶² 'I am,' said Jesus. 'And you will see the Son of Man sitting at the right hand of the Mighty One and coming on the clouds of heaven.'

⁶³ The high priest tore his clothes. 'Why do we need any more witnesses?' he asked. ⁶⁴ 'You have heard the blasphemy. What do you think?'

They all condemned him as worthy of death.⁶⁵ Then some began to spit at him; they blindfolded him, struck him with their fists, and said, 'Prophesy!' And the guards took him and beat him.

Peter Disowns Jesus

⁶⁶ While Peter was below in the courtyard, one of the servant girls of the high priest came by. ⁶⁷ When she saw Peter warming himself, she looked closely at him.

'You also were with that Nazarene, Jesus,' she said.

> **'Surely you are one of them,
> for you are a Galilean.'**

⁶⁸ But he denied it. 'I don't know or understand what you're talking about,' he said, and went out into the entrance.

⁶⁹ When the servant girl saw him there, she said again to those standing around, 'This fellow is one of them.' ⁷⁰ Again he denied it.

After a little while, those standing near said to Peter, 'Surely you are one of them, for you are a Galilean.'

⁷¹ He began to call down curses on himself, and he swore to them, 'I don't know this man you're talking about.'

⁷² Immediately the cock crowed the second time. Then Peter remembered the word Jesus had spoken to him: 'Before the cock crows twice you will disown me three times.' And he broke down and wept.

DAY 34

MARK 15. 1 — 20

15 Jesus Before Pilate

Very early in the morning, the chief priests, with the elders, the teachers of the law and the whole Sanhedrin, reached a decision. They bound Jesus, led him away and turned him over to Pilate.

[2] 'Are you the king of the Jews?' asked Pilate.

'Yes, it is as you say,' Jesus replied.

[3] The chief priests accused him of many things. [4] So again Pilate asked him, 'Aren't you going to answer? See how many things they are accusing you of.'

[5] But Jesus still made no reply, and Pilate was amazed.

[6] Now it was the custom at the Feast to release a prisoner whom the people requested. [7] A man called Barabbas was in prison with the insurrectionists who had committed murder in the uprising. [8] The crowd came up and asked Pilate to do for them what he usually did.

[9] 'Do you want me to release to you the king of the Jews?' asked Pilate,

[10] knowing it was out of envy that the chief priests had handed Jesus over to him. [11] But the chief priests stirred up the crowd to have Pilate release Barabbas instead.

[12] 'What shall I do, then, with the one you call the king of the Jews?' Pilate asked them.

[13] 'Crucify him!' they shouted.

[14] 'Why? What crime has he committed?' asked Pilate.

But they shouted all the louder, 'Crucify him!'

[15] Wanting to satisfy the crowd, Pilate released Barabbas to them. He had Jesus flogged, and handed him over to be crucified.

The Soldiers Mock Jesus

[16] The soldiers led Jesus away into the palace (that is, the Praetorium) and called together the whole company of soldiers. [17] They put a purple robe on him, then twisted together a crown of thorns and set it on him. [18] And they began to call out to him, 'Hail, king of the Jews!' [19] Again and again they struck him on the head with a staff and spat on him. Falling on their knees, they paid homage to him. [20] And when they had mocked him, they took off the purple robe and put his own clothes on him. Then they led him out to crucify him.

Then they led him out to crucify him.

DAY 35

MARK 15. 21 — 47

The Crucifixion

²¹ A certain man from Cyrene, Simon, the father of Alexander and Rufus, was passing by on his way in from the country, and they forced him to carry the cross. ²² They brought Jesus to the place called Golgotha (which means The Place of the Skull). ²³ Then they offered him wine mixed with myrrh, but he did not take it. ²⁴ And they crucified him. Dividing up his clothes, they cast lots to see what each would get.

²⁵ It was the third hour when they crucified him. ²⁶ The written notice of the charge against him read: THE KING OF THE JEWS. ²⁷ They crucified two robbers with him, one on his right and one on his left. ²⁹ Those who passed by hurled insults at him, shaking their heads and saying, 'So! You who are going to destroy the temple and build it in three days, ³⁰ come down from the cross and save yourself!'

³¹ In the same way the chief priests and the teachers of the law mocked him among themselves. 'He saved others,' they said, 'but he can't save himself! ³² Let this Christ, this King of Israel, come down now from the cross, that we may see and believe.' Those crucified with him also heaped insults on him.

The Death of Jesus

³³ At the sixth hour darkness came over the whole land until the ninth hour. ³⁴ And at the ninth hour Jesus cried out in a loud voice, *'Eloi, Eloi, lama sabachthani?'* - which means, 'My God, my God, why have you forsaken me?'

³⁵ When some of those standing near heard this, they said, 'Listen, he's calling Elijah.'

³⁶ One man ran, filled a sponge with wine vinegar, put it on a stick, and offered it to Jesus to drink. 'Now leave him alone. Let's see if Elijah comes to take him down,' he said.

³⁷ With a loud cry, Jesus breathed his last.

³⁸ The curtain of the temple was torn in two from top to bottom. ³⁹ And when the centurion, who stood there in front of Jesus, heard his cry and saw how he died, he said, 'Surely this man was the Son of God!'

⁴⁰ Some women were watching from a distance. Among them were Mary Magdalene, Mary the mother of James the younger and of Joses, and Salome. ⁴¹ In Galilee these women had followed him and cared for his needs. Many other women who had come up with him to Jerusalem were also there.

The Burial of Jesus

⁴² It was Preparation Day (that is, the day before the Sabbath). So as evening approached, ⁴³ Joseph of Arimathea, a prominent member of the Council, who was himself waiting for the kingdom of God, went boldly to Pilate and asked for Jesus' body. ⁴⁴ Pilate was surprised to hear that he was already dead. Summoning the centurion, he asked him if Jesus had already died. ⁴⁵ When he learned from the centurion that it was so, he gave the body to Joseph. ⁴⁶ So Joseph bought some linen cloth, took down the body, wrapped it in the linen, and placed it in a tomb cut out of rock. Then he rolled a stone against the entrance of the tomb. ⁴⁷ Mary Magdalene and Mary the mother of Joses saw where he was laid.

DAY 36

MARK 16. 1 — 20

16 **The Resurrection**
When the Sabbath was over, Mary Magdalene, Mary the mother of James, and Salome bought spices so that they might go to anoint Jesus' body. [2] Very early on the first day of the week, just after sunrise, they were on their way to the tomb [3] and they asked each other, 'Who will roll the stone away from the entrance of the tomb?'

[4] But when they looked up, they saw that the stone, which was very large, had been rolled away. [5] As they entered the tomb, they saw a young man dressed in a white robe sitting on the right side, and they were alarmed.

[6] 'Don't be alarmed,' he said. 'You are looking for Jesus the Nazarene, who was crucified. He has risen! He is not here. See the place where they laid him. [7] But go, tell his disciples and Peter, "He is going ahead of you into Galilee. There you will see him, just as he told you." '

[8] Trembling and bewildered, the women went out and fled from the tomb. They said nothing to anyone, because they were afraid.

―――――――――――――

[The most reliable early manuscripts and other ancient witnesses do not have Mark 16:9–20.]

[9] When Jesus rose early on the first day of the week, he appeared first to Mary Magdalene, out of whom he had driven seven demons. [10] She went and told those who had been with him and who were mourning and weeping. [11] When they heard that Jesus was alive and that she had seen him, they did not believe it.

[12] Afterwards Jesus appeared in a different form to two of them while they were walking in the country. [13] These returned and reported it to the rest; but they did not believe them either.

[14] Later Jesus appeared to the Eleven as they were eating; he rebuked them for their lack of faith and their stubborn refusal to believe those who had seen him after he had risen.

[15] He said to them, 'Go into all the world and preach the good news to all creation. [16] Whoever believes and is baptised will be saved, but whoever does not believe will be condemned. [17] And

―――――――――――――

'Go into all the world and preach the good news to all creation.'

―――――――――――――

these signs will accompany those who believe: In my name they will drive out demons; they will speak in new tongues; [18] they will pick up snakes with their hands; and when they drink deadly poison, it will not hurt them at all; they will place their hands on sick people, and they will get well.'

[19] After the Lord Jesus had spoken to them, he was taken up into heaven and he sat at the right hand of God. [20] Then the disciples went out and preached everywhere, and the Lord worked with them and confirmed his word by the signs that accompanied it.

DAY 37

1 PETER 1. 1 — 12

1 Peter, an apostle of Jesus Christ,

To God's elect, strangers in the world, scattered throughout Pontus, Galatia, Cappadocia, Asia and Bithynia, [2] who have been chosen according to the foreknowledge of God the Father, through the sanctifying work of the Spirit, for obedience to Jesus Christ and sprinkling by his blood:

Grace and peace be yours in abundance.

Praise to God for a Living Hope

[3] Praise be to the God and Father of our Lord Jesus Christ! In his great mercy he has given us new birth into a living hope through the resurrection of Jesus Christ from the dead, [4] and into an inheritance that can never perish, spoil or fade - kept in heaven for you, [5] who through faith are shielded by God's power until the coming of the salvation that is ready to be revealed in the last time. [6] In this you greatly rejoice, though now for a little while you may have had to suffer grief in all kinds of trials. [7] These have come so that your faith - of greater worth than gold, which perishes even though refined by fire - may be proved genuine and may result in praise, glory and honour when Jesus Christ is revealed. [8] Though you have not seen him, you love him; and even though you do not see him now, you believe in him and are filled with an inexpressible and glorious joy, [9] for you are receiving the goal of your faith, the salvation of your souls.

[10] Concerning this salvation, the prophets, who spoke of the grace that was to come to you, searched intently and with the greatest care, [11] trying to find out the time and circumstances to which the Spirit of Christ in them was pointing

Praise be to the God and Father of our Lord Jesus Christ!

when he predicted the sufferings of Christ and the glories that would follow. [12] It was revealed to them that they were not serving themselves but you, when they spoke of the things that have now been told you by those who have preached the gospel to you by the Holy Spirit sent from heaven. Even angels long to look into these things.

DAY 38

1 PETER 1. 13 — 25

Be Holy

[13] Therefore, prepare your minds for action; be self-controlled; set your hope fully on the grace to be given you when Jesus Christ is revealed. [14] As obedient children, do not conform to the evil desires you had when you lived in ignorance. [15] But just as he who called you is holy, so be holy in all you do; [16] for it is written: 'Be holy, because I am holy.'

[17] Since you call on a Father who judges each man's work impartially, live your lives as strangers here in reverent

The grass withers and the flowers fall, but the word of the Lord stands for ever.

ear. [18] For you know that it was not with perishable things such as silver or gold that you were redeemed from the empty way of life handed down to you from your forefathers, [19] but with the precious blood of Christ, a lamb without blemish or defect. [20] He was chosen before the creation of the world, but was revealed in these last times for your sake. Through him you believe in God, who raised him from the dead and glorified him, and so your faith and hope are in God.

[22] Now that you have purified yourselves by obeying the truth so that you have sincere love for your brothers,

love one another deeply, from the heart. [23] For you have been born again, not of perishable seed, but of imperishable, through the living and enduring word of God. [24] For,

'All men are like grass,
  and all their glory is like the flowers
of the field;
  the grass withers and the flowers fall,
[25]but the word of the Lord stands for
  ever.'

And this is the word that was preached to you.

DAY 39

1 PETER 2. 1 — 10

2 Therefore, rid yourselves of all malice and all deceit, hypocrisy, envy, and slander of every kind. [2] Like newborn babies, crave pure spiritual milk, so that by it you may grow up in your salvation, [3] now that you have tasted that the Lord is good.

The Living Stone and a Chosen People

[4] As you come to him, the living Stone - rejected by men but chosen by God and precious to him - [5] you also, like living stones, are being built into a spiritual house to be a holy priesthood, offering spiritual sacrifices acceptable to God through Jesus Christ. [6] For in Scripture

> 'The stone the builders rejected has become the capstone.'

it says:

> 'See, I lay a stone in Zion,
>   a chosen and precious cornerstone,
> and the one who trusts in him
>   will never be put to shame.'

[7] Now to you who believe, this stone is precious. But to those who do not believe,

> 'The stone the builders rejected has become the capstone,'

[8] and,

> 'A stone that causes men to stumble and a rock that makes them fall.'

They stumble because they disobey the message - which is also what they were destined for.

[9] But you are a chosen people, a royal priesthood, a holy nation, a people belonging to God, that you may declare the praises of him who called you out of darkness into his wonderful light. [10] Once you were not a people, but now you are the people of God; once you had not received mercy, but now you have received mercy.

... like living stones being built into a spiritual house...

DAY 40

1 PETER 2. 11 — 25

Dear friends, I urge you, as aliens
d strangers in the world, to abstain
m sinful desires, which war against
ur soul. ¹² Live such good lives among
e pagans that, though they accuse you
doing wrong, they may see your good
eds and glorify God on the day he visits
.

ubmission to Rulers and lasters

Submit yourselves for the Lord's sake to
ery authority instituted among men:
hether to the king, as the supreme
thority, ¹⁴ or to governors, who are sent
him to punish those who do wrong and
commend those who do right. ¹⁵ For it
God's will that by doing good you
ould silence the ignorant talk of foolish
en. ¹⁶ Live as free men, but do not use
ur freedom as a cover-up for evil; live as
rvants of God. ¹⁷ Show proper respect to
eryone: Love the brotherhood of
lievers, fear God, honour the king.

¹⁸ Slaves, submit yourselves to your
asters with all respect, not only to those
ho are good and considerate, but also to
ose who are harsh. ¹⁹ For it is
mmendable if a man bears up under the
in of unjust suffering because he is
nscious of God. ²⁰ But how is it to your
edit if you receive a beating for doing
rong and endure it? But if you suffer for
ing good and you endure it, this is
mmendable before God. ²¹ To this you
ere called, because Christ suffered for
u, leaving you an example, that you
ould follow in his steps.

²² 'He committed no sin,
and no deceit was found in his
mouth.'

²³ When they hurled their insults at
him, he did not retaliate; when he
suffered, he made no threats. Instead, he
entrusted himself to him who judges
justly. ²⁴ He himself bore our sins in his
body on the tree, so that we might die to
sins and live for righteousness; by his
wounds you have been healed. ²⁵ For you
were like sheep going astray, but now you
have returned to the Shepherd and
Overseer of your souls.

Christ suffered for you, leaving an example,
that you should follow in his footsteps.

DAY 41

1 PETER 3. 1 — 22

3 **Wives and Husbands**
Wives, in the same way be
submissive to your husbands so
that, if any of them do not believe the
word, they may be won over without
words by the behaviour of their wives,
[2] when they see the purity and reverence
of your lives. [3] Your beauty should not
come from outward adornment, such as
braided hair and the wearing of gold
jewellery and fine clothes. [4] Instead, it
should be that of your inner self, the
unfading beauty of a gentle and quiet
spirit, which is of great worth in God's
sight. [5] For this is the way the holy
women of the past who put their hope in
God used to make themselves beautiful.
They were submissive to their own
husbands, [6] like Sarah, who obeyed
Abraham and called him her master. You
are her daughters if you do what is right
and do not give way to fear.

[7] Husbands, in the same way be
considerate as you live with your wives,
and treat them with respect as the weaker
partner and as heirs with you of the
gracious gift of life, so that nothing will
hinder your prayers.

Suffering for Doing Good

[8] Finally, all of you, live in harmony with
one another; be sympathetic, love as
brothers, be compassionate and humble.
[9] Do not repay evil with evil or insult with
insult, but with blessing, because to this
you were called so that you may inherit a
blessing. [10] For,

'Whoever would love life
and see good days
must keep his tongue from evil
and his lips from deceitful speech.
[11] He must turn from evil and do good
he must seek peace and pursue it.
[12] For the eyes of the Lord are on the
righteous
and his ears are attentive to their
prayer,
but the face of the Lord is against
those who do evil.'

[13] Who is going to harm you if you
are eager to do good? [14] But even if you
should suffer for what is right, you are
blessed. 'Do not fear what they fear; do n
be frightened.' [15] But in your hearts set
apart Christ as Lord. Always be prepared
to give an answer to everyone who asks
you to give the reason for the hope that
you have. But do this with gentleness and
respect, [16] keeping a clear conscience, so
that those who speak maliciously against
your good behaviour in Christ may be
ashamed of their slander. [17] It is better, if
is God's will, to suffer for doing good than
for doing evil. [18] For Christ died for sins
once for all, the righteous for the
unrighteous, to bring you to God. He was
put to death in the body but made alive b
the Spirit, [19] through whom also he went
and preached to the spirits in prison [20] wh
disobeyed long ago when God waited
patiently in the days of Noah while the
ark was being built. In it only a few
people, eight in all, were saved through
water, [21] and this water symbolises baptism
that now saves you also - not the remova
of dirt from the body but the pledge of a
good conscience towards God. It saves yo
by the resurrection of Jesus Christ, [22] who
has gone into heaven and is at God's righ
hand - with angels, authorities and powe
in submission to him.

DAY 42

1 PETER 4. 1 — 19

Living for God

Therefore, since Christ suffered in his body, arm yourselves also with e same attitude, because he who has ffered in his body is done with sin. [2] As result, he does not live the rest of his rthly life for evil human desires, but

> **Above all, love each other deeply, because love covers over a multitude of sins.**

ther for the will of God. [3] For you have ent enough time in the past doing what gans choose to do - living in bauchery, lust, drunkenness, orgies, rousing and detestable idolatry. [4] They ink it strange that you do not plunge ith them into the same flood of ssipation, and they heap abuse on you. But they will have to give account to him ho is ready to judge the living and the ad. [6] For this is the reason the gospel was eached even to those who are now dead, that they might be judged according to en in regard to the body, but live cording to God in regard to the spirit. [7] The end of all things is near. herefore be clear minded and self-ntrolled so that you can pray. [8] Above l, love each other deeply, because love vers over a multitude of sins. [9] Offer spitality to one another without umbling. [10] Each one should use hatever gift he has received to serve hers, faithfully administering God's

grace in its various forms. [11] If anyone speaks, he should do it as one speaking the very words of God. If anyone serves, he should do it with the strength God provides, so that in all things God may be praised through Jesus Christ. To him be the glory and the power for ever and ever. Amen.

Suffering for Being a Christian

[12] Dear friends, do not be surprised at the painful trial you are suffering, as though something strange were happening to you. [13] But rejoice that you participate in the sufferings of Christ, so that you may be overjoyed when his glory is revealed. [14] If you are insulted because of the name of Christ, you are blessed, for the Spirit of glory and of God rests on you. [15] If you suffer, it should not be as a murderer or thief or any other kind of criminal, or even as a meddler. [16] However, if you suffer as a Christian, do not be ashamed, but praise God that you bear that name. [17] For it is time for judgment to begin with

> **'If it is hard for the righteous to be saved, what will become of the ungodly and the sinner?'**

the family of God; and if it begins with us, what will the outcome be for those who do not obey the gospel of God? [18] And,

> 'If it is hard for the righteous to be saved, what will become of the ungodly and the sinner?'

[19] So then, those who suffer according to God's will should commit themselves to their faithful Creator and continue to do good.

DAY 43

1 PETER 5. 1 — 14

5 **To Elders and Young Men**
To the elders among you, I appeal as a fellow-elder, a witness of Christ's sufferings and one who also will share in the glory to be revealed: ² Be shepherds of God's flock that is under your care, serving as overseers - not because you must, but because you are willing, as God wants you to be; not greedy for money, but eager to serve; ³ not lording it over those entrusted to

⁶ Humble yourselves, therefore, under God's mighty hand, that he may lift you up in due time. ⁷ Cast all your anxiety on him because he cares for you.

⁸ Be self-controlled and alert. Your enemy the devil prowls around like a roaring lion looking for someone to devour. ⁹ Resist him, standing firm in the faith, because you know that your brothers throughout the world are undergoing the same kind of sufferings.

¹⁰ And the God of all grace, who called you to his eternal glory in Christ, after you have suffered a little while, will himself restore you and make you strong, firm and steadfast. ¹¹ To him be the power for ever and ever. Amen.

Cast all your anxiety on him because he cares for you.

you, but being examples to the flock. ⁴ And when the Chief Shepherd appears, you will receive the crown of glory that will never fade away.

⁵ Young men, in the same way be submissive to those who are older. All of you, clothe yourselves with humility towards one another, because,

'God opposes the proud
  but gives grace to the humble.'

Final Greetings

¹² With the help of Silas, whom I regard as a faithful brother, I have written to you briefly, encouraging you and testifying that this is the true grace of God. Stand fast in it.

¹³ She who is in Babylon, chosen together with you, sends you her greetings, and so does my son Mark. ¹⁴ Greet one another with a kiss of love.

Peace to all of you who are in Christ

DAY 44

2 PETER 1. 1 — 21

1 Simon Peter, a servant and apostle of Jesus Christ

To those who through the righteousness of our God and Saviour Jesus Christ have received a faith as precious as ours:

2 Grace and peace be yours in abundance through the knowledge of God and of Jesus our Lord.

Making One's Calling and Election Sure

3 His divine power has given us everything we need for life and godliness through our knowledge of him who called us by his own glory and goodness. 4 Through these he has given us his very great and precious promises, so that through them you may participate in the divine nature and escape the corruption in the world caused by evil desires.

5 For this very reason, make every effort to add to your faith goodness; and to goodness, knowledge; 6 and to knowledge, self-control; and to self-control, perseverance; and to perseverance, godliness; 7 and to godliness, brotherly kindness; and to brotherly kindness, love. 8 For if you possess these qualities in increasing measure, they will keep you from being ineffective and unproductive in your knowledge of our Lord Jesus Christ. 9 But if anyone does not have them, he is short-sighted and blind, and has forgotten that he has been cleansed from

his past sins.

10 Therefore, my brothers, be all the more eager to make your calling and election sure. For if you do these things, you will never fall, 11 and you will receive a rich welcome into the eternal kingdom of our Lord and Saviour Jesus Christ.

Prophecy of Scripture

12 So I will always remind you of these things, even though you know them and are firmly established in the truth you now have. 13 I think it is right to refresh your memory as long as I live in the tent of this body, 14 because I know that I will soon put it aside, as our Lord Jesus Christ has made clear to me. 15 And I will make every effort to see that after my departure you will always be able to remember these things.

16 We did not follow cleverly invented stories when we told you about the power and coming of our Lord Jesus Christ, but we were eye-witnesses of his majesty. 17 For he received honour and glory from God the Father when the voice came to him from the Majestic Glory, saying, 'This is my Son, whom I love; with him I am well pleased.' 18 We ourselves heard this voice that came from heaven when we were with him on the sacred mountain.

19 And we have the word of the prophets made more certain, and you will do well to pay attention to it, as to a light shining in a dark place, until the day dawns and the morning star rises in your hearts. 20 Above all, you must understand that no prophecy of Scripture came about by the prophet's own interpretation. 21 For prophecy never had its origin in the will of man, but men spoke from God as they were carried along by the Holy Spirit.

DAY 45

2 PETER 2. 1 — 22

2 False Teachers and Their Destruction

But there were also false prophets among the people, just as there will be false teachers among you. They will secretly introduce destructive heresies, even denying the sovereign Lord who bought them - bringing swift destruction on themselves. [2] Many will follow their shameful ways and will bring the way of truth into disrepute. [3] In their greed these teachers will exploit you with stories they have made up. Their condemnation has long been hanging over them, and their destruction has not been sleeping.

[4] For if God did not spare angels when they sinned, but sent them to hell, putting them into gloomy dungeons to be held for judgment; [5] if he did not spare the ancient world when he brought the flood on its ungodly people, but protected Noah, a preacher of righteousness, and seven others; [6] if he condemned the cities of Sodom and Gomorrah by burning them to ashes, and made them an example of what is going to happen to the ungodly; [7] and if he rescued Lot, a righteous man, who was distressed by the filthy lives of lawless men [8] (for that righteous man, living among them day after day, was tormented in his righteous soul by the lawless deeds he saw and heard) - [9] if this is so, then the Lord knows how to rescue godly men from trials and to hold the unrighteous for the day of judgment, while continuing their punishment. [10] This is especially true of those who follow the corrupt desire of the sinful nature and despise authority.

Bold and arrogant, these men are not afraid to slander celestial beings; [11] yet even angels, although they are stronger and more powerful, do not bring slanderous accusations against such beings in the presence of the Lord. [12] But these men blaspheme in matters they do not understand. They are like brute beasts, creatures of instinct, born only to be caught and destroyed, and like beasts they too will perish.

[13] They will be paid back with harm for the harm they have done. Their idea of pleasure is to carouse in broad daylight. They are blots and blemishes, revelling in their pleasures while they feast with you. [14] With eyes full of adultery, they never stop sinning; they seduce the unstable; they are experts in greed - an accursed brood! [15] They have left the straight way and wandered off to follow the way of Balaam son of Beor, who loved the wages of wickedness. [16] But he was rebuked for his wrongdoing by a donkey - a beast without speech - who spoke with a man's voice and restrained the prophet's madness.

[17] These men are springs without water and mists driven by a storm. Blackest darkness is reserved for them. [18] For they mouth empty, boastful words and, by appealing to the lustful desires of sinful human nature, they entice people who are just escaping from those who live in error. [19] They promise them freedom, while they themselves are slaves of depravity - for a man is a slave to whatever has mastered him. [20] If they have escaped the corruption of the world by knowing our Lord and Saviour Jesus Christ and are again entangled in it and overcome, they are worse off at the end than they were at the beginning. [21] It would have been better for them not have known the way of righteousness, than to have known it and then to turn their backs on the sacred command that was passed on to them. [22] Of them the proverbs are true: 'A dog returns to its vomit,' and, 'A sow that is washed goes back to her wallowing in the mud.'

DAY 46

2 PETER 3. 1 — 18

The Day of the Lord

Dear friends, this is now my second letter to you. I have written both them as reminders to stimulate you to ꞉olesome thinking. ² I want you to ꞉all the words spoken in the past by the ꞉ly prophets and the command given by ꞉r Lord and Saviour through your ꞉ostles.

³ First of all, you must understand ꞉at in the last days scoffers will come, ꞉offing and following their own evil ꞉sires. ⁴ They will say, 'Where is this ꞉oming" he promised? Ever since our ꞉hers died, everything goes on as it has ꞉ce the beginning of creation.' ⁵ But ꞉ey deliberately forget that long ago by ꞉od's word the heavens existed and the ꞉rth was formed out of water and by ꞉ter. ⁶ By these waters also the world of ꞉at time was deluged and destroyed. ⁷ By ꞉e same word the present heavens and ꞉rth are reserved for fire, being kept for ꞉e day of judgment and destruction of ꞉godly men.

⁸ But do not forget this one thing, ꞉ar friends: With the Lord a day is like a ꞉ousand years, and a thousand years are ꞉e a day. ⁹ The Lord is not slow in ꞉eping his promise, as some understand ꞉wness. He is patient with you, not ꞉anting anyone to perish, but everyone ꞉ come to repentance.

¹⁰ But the day of the Lord will come ꞉e a thief. The heavens will disappear ꞉ith a roar; the elements will be ꞉stroyed by fire, and the earth and everything in it will be laid bare. ¹¹ Since everything will be destroyed in this way, what kind of people ought you to be? You ought to live holy and godly lives ¹² as you look forward to the day of God and speed its coming. That day will bring about the destruction of the heavens by fire, and the elements will melt in the heat. ¹³ But in keeping with his promise we are looking forward to a new heaven and a new earth, the home of righteousness.

¹⁴ So then, dear friends, since you are looking forward to this, make every

> **With the Lord a day is like a thousand years, and a thousand years are like a day.**

effort to be found spotless, blameless and at peace with him. ¹⁵ Bear in mind that our Lord's patience means salvation, just as our dear brother Paul also wrote to you with the wisdom that God gave him. ¹⁶ He writes the same way in all his letters, speaking in them of these matters. His letters contain some things that are hard to understand, which ignorant and unstable people distort, as they do the other Scriptures, to their own destruction.

¹⁷ Therefore, dear friends, since you already know this, be on your guard so that you may not be carried away by the error of lawless men and fall from your secure position. ¹⁸ But grow in the grace and knowledge of our Lord and Saviour Jesus Christ. To him be glory both now and for ever! Amen.

DAY 47

JOHN 1. 1 — 18

1 **The Word Became Flesh**
In the beginning was the Word, and the Word was with God, and the Word was God. [2] He was with God in the beginning.

[3] Through him all things were made; without him nothing was made that has been made. [4] In him was life, and that life was the light of men. [5] The light shines in the darkness, but the darkness has not understood it.

[6] There came a man who was sent from God; his name was John. [7] He came as a witness to testify concerning that light, so that through him all men might believe. [8] He himself was not the light; he came only as a witness to the light. [9] The true light that gives light to every man was coming into the world.

[10] He was in the world, and though the world was made through him, the world did not recognise him. [11] He came to that which was his own, but his own did not receive him. [12] Yet to all who received him, to those who believed in his name, he gave the right to become children of God - [13] children born not of natural descent, nor of human decision or a husband's will, but born of God.

[14] The Word became flesh and made his dwelling among us. We have seen his glory, the glory of the One and Only, who came from the Father, full of grace and truth.

[15] John testifies concerning him. He cries out, saying, 'This was he of whom I said, "He who comes after me has surpassed me because he was before me." [16] From the fulness of his grace we have all received one blessing after another. [17] For the law was given through Moses; grace and truth came through Jesus Christ. [18] No-one has ever seen God, but God the One and Only, who is at the Father's side, has made him known.

DAY 48

JOHN 1. 19 — 34

John the Baptist Denies Being the Christ

[19] Now this was John's testimony when the Jews of Jerusalem sent priests and Levites to ask him who he was. [20] He did not fail to confess, but confessed freely, 'I am not the Christ.'

[21] They asked him, 'Then who are you? Are you Elijah?'

He said, 'I am not.'

'Are you the Prophet?'

He answered, 'No.'

[22] Finally they said, 'Who are you? Give us an answer to take back to those who sent us. What do you say about yourself?'

' Make straight the way for the Lord.'

[23] John replied in the words of Isaiah the prophet, 'I am the voice of one calling in the desert, "Make straight the way for the Lord." '

[24] Now some Pharisees who had been

The light that shines in the darkness.

nt ²⁵ questioned him, 'Why then do you
ptise if you are not the Christ, nor
ijah, nor the Prophet?'

²⁶ 'I baptise with water,' John replied,
ut among you stands one you do not
ıow. ²⁷ He is the one who comes after
e, the thongs of whose sandals I am not
orthy to untie.'

²⁸ This all happened at Bethany on
e other side of the Jordan, where John
ıs baptising.

sus the Lamb of God

The next day John saw Jesus coming
wards him and said, 'Look, the Lamb of
od, who takes away the sin of the
world! ³⁰ This is the one I meant when I
said, "A man who comes after me has
surpassed me because he was before me."
³¹ I myself did not know him, but the
reason I came baptising with water was
that he might be revealed to Israel.'

³² Then John gave this testimony: 'I
saw the Spirit come down from heaven as
a dove and remain on him. ³³ I would not
have known him, except that the one
who sent me to baptise with water told
me, "The man on whom you see the
Spirit come down and remain is he who
will baptise with the Holy Spirit." ³⁴ I
have seen and I testify that this is the Son
of God.'

DAY 49

JOHN 1. 35 — 51

Jesus' First Disciples

[35] The next day John was there again with two of his disciples. [36] When he saw Jesus passing by, he said, 'Look, the Lamb of God!'

[37] When the two disciples heard him say this, they followed Jesus. [38] Turning round, Jesus saw them following and asked, 'What do you want?'

They said, 'Rabbi' (which means Teacher), 'where are you staying?'

[39] 'Come,' he replied, 'and you will see.'

So they went and saw where he was staying, and spent that day with him. It was about the tenth hour.

[40] Andrew, Simon Peter's brother, was one of the two who heard what John had said and who had followed Jesus. [41] The first thing Andrew did was to find his brother Simon and tell him, 'We have found the Messiah' (that is, the Christ). [42] And he brought him to Jesus.

Jesus looked at him and said, 'You are Simon son of John. You will be called Cephas' (which, when translated, is Peter).

Jesus Calls Philip and Nathanael

[43] The next day Jesus decided to leave for Galilee. Finding Philip, he said to him, 'Follow me.'

[44] Philip, like Andrew and Peter, was from the town of Bethsaida. [45] Philip found Nathanael and told him, 'We have found the one Moses wrote about in the Law, and about whom the prophets also wrote - Jesus of Nazareth, the son of Joseph.'

[46] 'Nazareth! Can anything good come from there?' Nathanael asked.

'Come and see,' said Philip.

[47] When Jesus saw Nathanael approaching, he said of him, 'Here is a true Israelite, in whom there is nothing false.'

[48] 'How do you know me?' Nathanael asked.

Jesus answered, 'I saw you while you were still under the fig-tree before Philip called you.'

[49] Then Nathanael declared, 'Rabbi, you are the Son of God; you are the King of Israel.'

[50] Jesus said, 'You believe because I told you I saw you under the fig-tree. You shall see greater things than that.' [51] He then added, 'I tell you the truth, you shall see heaven open, and the angels of God ascending and descending on the Son of Man.'

You shall see heaven ope

DAY 50

JOHN 2. 1 — 25

2 **Jesus Changes Water to Wine**
On the third day a wedding took place at Cana in Galilee. Jesus' mother was there, [2] and Jesus and his disciples had also been invited to the wedding. When the wine was gone, Jesus' mother said to him, 'They have no more wine.'

[4] 'Dear woman, why do you involve me?' Jesus replied, 'My time has not yet come.'

[5] His mother said to the servants, 'Do whatever he tells you.'

[6] Nearby stood six stone water jars, the kind used by the Jews for ceremonial washing, each holding from twenty to thirty gallons.

[7] Jesus said to the servants, 'Fill the jars with water'; so they filled them to the brim.

[8] Then he told them, 'Now draw some out and take it to the master of the banquet.'

They did so, [9] and the master of the banquet tasted the water that had been turned into wine. He did not realise where it had come from, though the servants who had drawn the water knew. Then he called the bridegroom aside [10] and said, 'Everyone brings out the choice wine first and then the cheaper wine after the guests have had too much to drink; but you have saved the best till now.'

[11] This, the first of his miraculous signs, Jesus performed at Cana in Galilee. He thus revealed his glory, and his disciples put their faith in him.

Jesus Clears the Temple

[12] After this he went down to Capernaum with his mother and brothers and his disciples. There they stayed for a few days.

[13] When it was almost time for the Jewish Passover, Jesus went up to Jerusalem. [14] In the temple courts he found men selling cattle, sheep and doves, and others sitting at tables exchanging money. [15] So he made a whip out of cords, and drove all from the temple area, both sheep and cattle; he scattered the coins of the money changers and overturned their tables. [16] To those who sold doves he said, 'Get these out of here! How dare you turn my Father's house into a market!'

[17] His disciples remembered that it is written, 'Zeal for your house will consume me.'

[18] Then the Jews demanded of him, 'What miraculous sign can you show us to prove your authority to do all this?'

[19] Jesus answered them, 'Destroy this temple, and I will raise it again in three days.'

[20] The Jews replied, 'It has taken forty-six years to build this temple, and you are going to raise it in three days?' [21] But the temple he had spoken of was his body. [22] After he was raised from the dead, his disciples recalled what he had said. Then they believed the Scripture and the words that Jesus had spoken.

[23] Now while he was in Jerusalem at the Passover Feast, many people saw the miraculous signs he was doing and believed in his name. [24] But Jesus would not entrust himself to them, for he knew all men. [25] He did not need man's testimony about man, for he knew what was in a man.

DAY 51

JOHN 3. 1 — 21

3 **Jesus Teaches Nicodemus** Now there was a man of the Pharisees named Nicodemus, a member of the Jewish ruling council. [2] He came to Jesus at night and said, 'Rabbi, we know you are a teacher who has come from God. For no-one could perform the miraculous signs you are doing if God were not with him.'

[3] In reply Jesus declared, 'I tell you the truth, no-one can see the kingdom of God unless he is born again.'

[4] 'How can a man be born when he is old?' Nicodemus asked. 'Surely he cannot enter a second time into his mother's womb to be born!'

[5] Jesus answered, 'I tell you the truth, no-one can enter the kingdom of God unless he is born of water and the Spirit. [6] Flesh gives birth to flesh, but the Spirit gives birth to spirit. [7] You should not be surprised at my saying, "You must be born again." [8] The wind blows wherever it pleases. You hear its sound, but you cannot tell where it comes from

---

'I tell you the truth, no-one can enter the kingdom of God unless he is born of water and the Spirit.'

---

or where it is going. So it is with everyone born of the Spirit.'

[9] 'How can this be?' Nicodemus asked.

[10] 'You are Israel's teacher,' said Jesus, 'and do you not understand these things [11] I tell you the truth, we speak of what we know, and we testify to what we have seen, but still you people do not accept our testimony. [12] I have spoken to you of earthly things and you do not believe; how then will you believe if I speak of heavenly things? [13] No-one has ever gone into heaven except the one who came

---

'For God so loved the world that he gave his one and only Son, that whoever believes in him shall not perish but have eternal life.'

---

from heaven - the Son of Man. [14] Just as Moses lifted up the snake in the desert, so the Son of Man must be lifted up, [15] that everyone who believes in him may have eternal life.

[16] 'For God so loved the world that he gave his one and only Son, that whoever believes in him shall not perish but have eternal life. [17] For God did not send his Son into the world to condemn the world, but to save the world through him. [18] Whoever believes in him is not condemned, but whoever does not believe stands condemned already because he has not believed in the name of God's one and only Son. [19] This is the verdict: Light has come into the world, but men loved darkness instead of light because their deeds were evil. [20] Everyone who does evil hates the light, and will not come into the light for fear that his deeds will be exposed. [21] But whoever lives by the truth comes into the light, so that it may be seen plainly that what he has done has been done through God.'

DAY 52

JOHN 3. 22 — 36

hn the Baptist's Testimony bout Jesus

After this, Jesus and his disciples went t into the Judean countryside, where he ent some time with them, and baptised. Now John also was baptising at Aenon ar Salim, because there was plenty of ter, and people were constantly coming be baptised. [24] (This was before John s put in prison.) [25] An argument veloped between some of John's ciples and a certain Jew over the tter of ceremonial washing. [26] They me to John and said to him, 'Rabbi, at man who was with you on the other le of the Jordan - the one you testified out - well, he is baptising, and everyone going to him.'

[27] To this John replied, 'A man can receive only what is given him from heaven. [28] You yourselves can testify that I said, "I am not the Christ but am sent ahead of him." [29] The bride belongs to the bridegroom. The friend who attends the bridegroom waits and listens for him, and is full of joy when he hears the bridegroom's voice. That joy is mine, and it is now complete. [30] He must become greater; I must become less.

[31] 'The one who comes from above is above all; the one who is from the earth belongs to the earth, and speaks as one from the earth. The one who comes from heaven is above all. [32] He testifies to what he has seen and heard, but no-one accepts his testimony. [33] The man who has accepted it has certified that God is truthful. [34] For the one whom God has sent speaks the words of God, for God gives the Spirit without limit. [35] The Father loves the Son and has placed everything in his hands. [36] Whoever believes in the Son has eternal life, but whoever rejects the Son will not see life, for God's wrath remains on him.'

Whoever believes in the Son has eternal life.

DAY 53

JOHN 4. 1 — 26

4 **Jesus Talks With a Samaritan Woman**

The Pharisees heard that Jesus was gaining and baptising more disciples than John, [2] although in fact it was not Jesus who baptised, but his disciples. [3] When the Lord learned of this, he left Judea and went back once more to Galilee.

[4] Now he had to go through Samaria. [5] So he came to a town in Samaria called Sychar, near the plot of ground Jacob had given to his son Joseph. [6] Jacob's well was there, and Jesus, tired as he was from the journey, sat down by the well. It was about the sixth hour.

[7] When a Samaritan woman came to draw water, Jesus said to her, 'Will you give me a drink?' [8] (His disciples had gone into the town to buy food.)

> **'...whoever drinks the water I give him will never thirst.'**

[9] The Samaritan woman said to him, 'You are a Jew and I am a Samaritan woman. How can you ask me for a drink?' (For Jews do not associate with Samaritans.)

[10] Jesus answered her, 'If you knew the gift of God and who it is that asks you for a drink, you would have asked him and he would have given you living water.'

[11] 'Sir,' the woman said, 'you have nothing to draw with and the well is deep. Where can you get this living water? [12] Are you greater than our father Jacob, who gave us the well and drank from it himself, as did also his sons and his flocks and herds?'

[13] Jesus answered, 'Everyone who drinks this water will be thirsty again, [14] but whoever drinks the water I give him will never thirst. Indeed, the water I give him will become in him a spring of water welling up to eternal life.'

[15] The woman said to him, 'Sir, give me this water so that I won't get thirsty and have to keep coming here to draw water.'

[16] He told her, 'Go, call your husband and come back.'

[17] 'I have no husband,' she replied.

Jesus said to her, 'You are right when you say you have no husband. [18] The fact is, you have had five husbands, and the man you now have is not your husband. What you have just said is quite true.'

[19] 'Sir,' the woman said, 'I can see that you are a prophet. [20] Our fathers worshipped on this mountain, but you Jews claim that the place where we must worship is in Jerusalem.'

[21] Jesus declared, 'Believe me, woman, a time is coming when you will worship the Father neither on this mountain nor in Jerusalem. [22] You Samaritans worship what you do not know; we worship what we do know, for salvation is from the Jews. [23] Yet a time is coming and has now come when the true worshippers will worship the Father in spirit and truth, for they are the kind of worshippers the Father seeks. [24] God is spirit, and his worshippers must worship in spirit and in truth.'

[25] The woman said, 'I know that Messiah' (called Christ) 'is coming. When he comes, he will explain everything to us.'

[26] Then Jesus declared, 'I who speak to you am he.'

DAY 54

JOHN 4. 27 — 54

The Disciples Rejoin Jesus

Just then his disciples returned and were surprised to find him talking with a woman. But no-one asked, 'What do you want?' or 'Why are you talking with her?' [28] Then, leaving her water jar, the woman went back to the town and said to the people, [29] 'Come, see a man who told me everything I ever did. Could this be the Christ?' [30] They came out of the town and made their way towards him.

[31] Meanwhile his disciples urged him, 'Rabbi, eat something.'

[32] But he said to them, 'I have food to eat that you know nothing about.'

[33] Then his disciples said to each other, 'Could someone have brought him food?'

[34] 'My food,' said Jesus, 'is to do the will of him who sent me and to finish his work. [35] Do you not say, "Four months more and then the harvest"? I tell you, open your eyes and look at the fields! They are ripe for harvest. [36] Even now the reaper draws his wages, even now he harvests the crop for eternal life, so that the sower and the reaper may be glad together. [37] Thus the saying "One sows and another reaps" is true. [38] I sent you to reap what you have not worked for. Others have done the hard work, and you have reaped the benefits of their labour.'

Many Samaritans Believe

[39] Many of the Samaritans from that town believed in him because of the woman's testimony, 'He told me everything I ever did.' [40] So when the Samaritans came to him, they urged him to stay with them, and he stayed two days. [41] And because of his words many more became believers.

[42] They said to the woman, 'We no longer believe just because of what you said; now we have heard for ourselves, and we know that this man really is the Saviour of the world.'

Jesus Heals the Official's Son

[43] After the two days he left for Galilee. [44] (Now Jesus himself had pointed out that a prophet has no honour in his own country.) [45] When he arrived in Galilee, the Galileans welcomed him. They had seen all that he had done in Jerusalem at the Passover Feast, for they also had been there.

[46] Once more he visited Cana in Galilee, where he had turned the water into wine. And there was a certain royal official whose son lay sick at Capernaum. [47] When this man heard that Jesus had arrived in Galilee from Judea, he went to him and begged him to come and heal his son, who was close to death.

[48] 'Unless you people see miraculous signs and wonders,' Jesus told him, 'you will never believe.'

[49] The royal official said, 'Sir, come down before my child dies.'

[50] Jesus replied, 'You may go. Your son will live.'

The man took Jesus at his word and departed. [51] While he was still on the way, his servants met him with the news that his boy was living. [52] When he enquired as to the time when his son got better, they said to him, 'The fever left him yesterday at the seventh hour.'

[53] Then the father realised that this was the exact time at which Jesus had said to him, 'Your son will live.' So he and all his household believed.

[54] This was the second miraculous sign that Jesus performed, having come from Judea to Galilee.

DAY 55

JOHN 5. 1 — 18

5 **The Healing at the Pool**
Some time later, Jesus went up to
Jerusalem for a feast of the Jews.
[2] Now there is in Jerusalem near the
Sheep Gate a pool, which in Aramaic is
called Bethesda and which is surrounded
by five covered colonnades. [3] Here a great
number of disabled people used to lie -
the blind, the lame, the paralysed. [5] One
who was there had been an invalid for
thirty-eight years. [6] When Jesus saw him
lying there and learned that he had been
in this condition for a long time, he asked
him, 'Do you want to get well?'

[7] 'Sir,' the invalid replied, 'I have
no-one to help me into the pool when
the water is stirred. While I am trying to
get in, someone else goes down ahead of
me.'

[8] Then Jesus said to him, 'Get up!
Pick up your mat and walk.' [9] At once the
man was cured; he picked up his mat and
walked.

The day on which this took place was
a Sabbath, [10] and so the Jews said to the
man who had been healed, 'It is the
Sabbath; the law forbids you to carry your
mat.'

[11] But he replied, 'The man who made
me well said to me, "Pick up your mat and
walk."'

[12] So they asked him, 'Who is this
fellow who told you to pick it up and
walk?'

[13] The man who was healed had no
idea who it was, for Jesus had slipped
away into the crowd that was there.

[14] Later Jesus found him at the temple
and said to him, 'See, you are well again.
Stop sinning or something worse may
happen to you.' [15] The man went away
and told the Jews that it was Jesus who
had made him well.

Life Through the Son

[16] So, because Jesus was doing these thing
on the Sabbath, the Jews persecuted him
[17] Jesus said to them, 'My Father is alway
at his work to this very day, and I, too, a
working.' [18] For this reason the Jews tried
all the harder to kill him; not only was h
breaking the Sabbath, but he was even
calling God his own Father, making
himself equal with God.

DAY 56

JOHN 5. 19 — 30

[19] Jesus gave them this answer: 'I tell
you the truth, the Son can do nothing b
himself; he can do only what he sees his
Father doing, because whatever the
Father does the Son also does. [20] For the
Father loves the Son and shows him all
he does. Yes, to your amazement he will
show him even greater things than these
[21] For just as the Father raises the dead
and gives them life, even so the Son give
life to whom he is pleased to give it.
[22] Moreover, the Father judges no-one,
but has entrusted all judgment to the
Son, [23] that all may honour the Son just
as they honour the Father. He who does
not honour the Son does not honour the
Father, who sent him.

[24] 'I tell you the truth, whoever
hears my word and believes him who ser
me has eternal life and will not be
condemned; he has crossed over from
death to life. [25] I tell you the truth, a tim

is coming and has now come when the dead will hear the voice of the Son of God and those who hear will live. ²⁶ For as the Father has life in himself, so he has granted the Son to have life in himself. ²⁷ And he has given him authority to judge because he is the Son of Man.

²⁸ 'Do not be amazed at this, for a time is coming when all who are in their graves will hear his voice ²⁹ and come out - those who have done good will rise to live, and those who have done evil will rise to be condemned. ³⁰ By myself I can do nothing; I judge only as I hear, and my judgment is just, for I seek not to please myself but him who sent me.

DAY 57

JOHN 5. 31 — 47

Testimonies About Jesus

³¹ 'If I testify about myself, my testimony is not valid. ³² There is another who testifies in my favour, and I know that his testimony about me is valid.

³³ 'You have sent to John and he has testified to the truth. ³⁴ Not that I accept human testimony; but I mention it that you may be saved. ³⁵ John was a lamp that burned and gave light, and you chose for a time to enjoy his light.

³⁶ 'I have testimony weightier than that of John. For the very work that the Father has given me to finish, and which I am doing, testifies that the Father has sent me. ³⁷ And the Father who sent me has himself testified concerning me. You have never heard his voice nor seen his form, ³⁸ nor does his word dwell in you, for you do not believe the one he sent. ³⁹ You diligently study the Scriptures

because you think that by them you possess eternal life. These are the Scriptures that testify about me, ⁴⁰ yet you refuse to come to me to have life.

⁴¹ 'I do not accept praise from men, ⁴² but I know you. I know that you do not have the love of God in your hearts. ⁴³ I have come in my Father's name, and you do not accept me; but if someone else comes in his own name, you will accept him. ⁴⁴ How can you believe if you accept praise from one another, yet make no effort to obtain the praise that comes from the only God?

⁴⁵ 'But do not think I will accuse you before the Father. Your accuser is Moses, on whom your hopes are set. ⁴⁶ If you believed Moses, you would believe me, for he wrote about me. ⁴⁷ But since you do not believe what he wrote, how are you going to believe what I say?'

'John was a lamp that burned and gave light.'

DAY 58
JOHN 6. 1 — 24

6 **Jesus Feeds the Five Thousand**
Some time after this, Jesus crossed to the far shore of the Sea of Galilee (that is, the Sea of Tiberias), [2] and a great crowd of people followed him because they saw the miraculous signs he had performed on the sick. [3] Then Jesus went up on a mountainside and sat down with his disciples. [4] The Jewish Passover Feast was near.

[5] When Jesus looked up and saw a great crowd coming towards him, he said to Philip, 'Where shall we buy bread for these people to eat?' [6] He asked this only to test him, for he already had in mind what he was going to do.

[7] Philip answered him, 'Eight months' wages would not buy enough bread for each one to have a bite!'

[8] Another of his disciples, Andrew, Simon Peter's brother, spoke up, [9] 'Here is a boy with five small barley loaves and two small fish, but how far will they go among so many?'

[10] Jesus said, 'Make the people sit down.' There was plenty of grass in that place, and the men sat down, about five thousand of them. [11] Jesus then took the loaves, gave thanks, and distributed to those who were seated as much as they wanted. He did the same with the fish.

[12] When they had all had enough to eat, he said to his disciples, 'Gather the pieces that are left over. Let nothing be wasted.' [13] So they gathered them and filled twelve baskets with the pieces of the five barley loaves left over by those who had eaten.

[14] After the people saw the miraculous sign that Jesus did, they began to say, 'Surely this is the Prophet who is to come into the world.' [15] Jesus, knowing that they intended to come and make him king by force, withdrew again to a mountain by himself.

Jesus Walks on the Water
[16] When evening came, his disciples went down to the lake, [17] where they got into a boat and set off across the lake for Capernaum. By now it was dark, and Jesus had not yet joined them. [18] A strong wind was blowing and the waters grew rough. [19] When they had rowed three or three and a half miles, they saw Jesus approaching the boat, walking on the water; and they were terrified. [20] But he said to them, 'It is I; don't be afraid.' [21] Then they were willing to take him into the boat, and immediately the boat reached the shore where they were heading.

[22] The next day the crowd that had stayed on the opposite shore of the lake realised that only one boat had been there, and that Jesus had not entered it with his disciples, but that they had gone away alone. [23] Then some boats from Tiberias landed near the place where the people had eaten the bread after the Lord had given thanks. [24] Once the crowd realised that neither Jesus nor his disciples were there, they got into the boats and went to Capernaum in search of Jesus.

DAY 59
JOHN 6. 25 — 59

Jesus the Bread of Life
[25] When they found him on the other side of the lake, they asked him, 'Rabbi, when did you get here?'

[26] Jesus answered, 'I tell you the truth, you are looking for me, not because you saw miraculous signs but because you ate the

oaves and had your fill. [27] Do not work for food that spoils, but for food that endures to eternal life, which the Son of Man will give you. On him God the Father has placed his seal of approval.'

[28] Then they asked him, 'What must we do to do the works God requires?'

[29] Jesus answered, 'The work of God is this: to believe in the one he has sent.'

[30] So they asked him, 'What miraculous sign then will you give that we may see it and believe you? What will you do? [31] Our forefathers ate the manna in the desert; as it is written: "He gave them bread from heaven to eat." '

[32] Jesus said to them, 'I tell you the truth, it is not Moses who has given you the bread from heaven, but it is my Father who gives you the true bread from heaven. [33] For the bread of God is he who comes down from heaven and gives life to the world.'

[34] 'Sir,' they said, 'from now on give us this bread.'

[35] Then Jesus declared, 'I am the bread of life. He who comes to me will never go hungry, and he who believes in me will never be thirsty. [36] But as I told you, you have seen me and still you do not believe. [37] All that the Father gives me will come to me, and whoever comes to me I will never drive away. [38] For I have come down from heaven not to do my will but to do the will of him who sent me. [39] And this is the will of him who sent me, that I shall lose none of all that he has given me, but raise them up at the last day. [40] For my Father's will is that everyone who looks to the Son and believes in him shall have eternal life, and I will raise him up at the last day.'

[41] At this the Jews began to grumble about him because he said, 'I am the bread that came down from heaven.' [42] They said, 'Is this not Jesus, the son of Joseph, whose father and mother we know? How can he now say, "I came down from heaven"?'

[43] 'Stop grumbling among yourselves,' Jesus answered. [44] 'No-one can come to me unless the Father who sent me draws him, and I will raise him up at the last day. [45] It is written in the Prophets: "They will all be taught by God." Everyone who listens to the Father and learns from him comes to me. [46] No-one has seen the Father except the one who is from God; only he has seen the Father. [47] I tell you the truth, he who believes has everlasting life. [48] I am the bread of life. [49] Your forefathers ate the manna in the desert, yet they died. [50] But here is the bread that comes down from heaven, which a man may eat and not die. [51] I am the living bread that came down from heaven. If anyone eats of this bread, he will live for ever. This bread is my flesh, which I will give for the life of the world.'

[52] Then the Jews began to argue sharply

'This bread is my flesh, which I will give for the life of the world.'

---

among themselves, 'How can this man give us his flesh to eat?'

[53] Jesus said to them, 'I tell you the truth, unless you can eat the flesh of the Son of Man and drink his blood, you have no life in you. [54] Whoever eats my flesh and drinks my blood has eternal life, and I will raise him up at the last day. [55] For my flesh is real food and my blood is real drink. [56] Whoever eats my flesh and drinks my blood remains in me, and I in him. [57] Just as the living Father sent me and I live because of the Father, so the one who feeds on me will live because of me. [58] This is the bread that came down from heaven. Your forefathers ate manna and died, but he who feeds on this bread will live for ever.' [59] He said this while teaching in the synagogue in Capernaum.

DAY 60
JOHN 6. 60 — 71

Many Disciples Desert Jesus

[60] On hearing it, many of his disciples said, 'This is a hard teaching. Who can accept it?'

[61] Aware that his disciples were grumbling about this, Jesus said to them, 'Does this offend you? [62] What if you see the Son of Man ascend to where he was before! [63] The Spirit gives life; the flesh counts for nothing. The words I have spoken to you are spirit and they are life.

> **'The Spirit gives life; the flesh counts for nothing.'**

[64] Yet there are some of you who do not believe.' For Jesus had known from the beginning which of them did not believe and who would betray him. [65] He went on to say, 'This is why I told you that no-one can come to me unless the Father has enabled him.'

[66] From this time many of his disciples turned back and no longer followed him.

[67] 'You do not want to leave too, do you?' Jesus asked the Twelve. [68] Simon Peter answered him, 'Lord, to whom shall we go? You have the words of eternal life. [69] We believe and know that you are the Holy One of God.'

[70] Then Jesus replied, 'Have I not chosen you, the Twelve? Yet one of you is a devil!' [71] (He meant Judas, the son of Simon Iscariot, who, though one of the Twelve, was later to betray him.)

'The words I have spoken to you are spirit and they are life.'

DAY 61

JOHN 7. 1 — 24

Jesus Goes to the Feast of Tabernacles

After this, Jesus went around in Galilee, purposely staying away from Judea because the Jews there were waiting to take his life. ² But when the Jewish

---

'The right time for me has not yet come.'

Feast of Tabernacles was near, ³ Jesus' brothers said to him, 'You ought to leave here and go to Judea, so that your disciples may see the miracles you do. ⁴No-one who wants to become a public figure acts in secret. Since you are doing these things, show yourself to the world.' ⁵ For even his own brothers did not believe in him.

⁶ Therefore Jesus told them, 'The right time for me has not yet come; for you any time is right. ⁷ The world cannot hate you, but it hates me because I testify that what it does is evil. ⁸ You go to the Feast. I am not yet going up to this Feast, because for me the right time has not yet come.' ⁹Having said this, he stayed in Galilee.

¹⁰ However, after his brothers had left for the Feast, he went also, not publicly, but in secret. ¹¹ Now at the Feast the Jews were watching for him and asking, 'Where is that man?'

¹² Among the crowds there was widespread whispering about him. Some said, 'He is a good man.'

Others replied, 'No, he deceives the people.' ¹³ But no-one would say anything publicly about him for fear of the Jews.

Jesus Teaches at the Feast

¹⁴ Not until halfway through the Feast did Jesus go up to the temple courts and begin to teach. ¹⁵ The Jews were amazed and asked, 'How did this man get such learning without having studied?'

¹⁶ Jesus answered, 'My teaching is not my own. It comes from him who sent me. ¹⁷ If anyone chooses to do God's will, he will find out whether my teaching comes from God or whether I speak on my own. ¹⁸ He who speaks on his own does so to gain honour for himself, but he who works for the honour of the one who sent him is a man of truth; there is nothing false about him. ¹⁹ Has not Moses given you the law? Yet not one of you keeps the law. Why are you trying to kill me?'

²⁰ 'You are demon-possessed,' the crowd answered. 'Who is trying to kill you?'

²¹ Jesus said to them, 'I did one miracle, and you are all astonished. ²² Yet,

---

Jesus said to them, 'I did one miracle, and you are all astonished.'

---

because Moses gave you circumcision (though actually it did not come from Moses, but from the patriarchs), you circumcise a child on the Sabbath. ²³ Now if a child can be circumcised on the Sabbath so that the law of Moses may not be broken, why are you angry with me for healing the whole man on the Sabbath? ²⁴ Stop judging by mere appearances, and make a right judgment.'

DAY 62

JOHN 7. 25 — 53

Is Jesus the Christ?

²⁵ At that point some of the people of Jerusalem began to ask, 'Isn't this the man they are trying to kill? ²⁶ Here he is, speaking publicly, and they are not saying a word to him. Have the authorities really concluded that he is the Christ? ²⁷ But we know where this man is from; when the Christ comes, no-one will know where he is from.'

²⁸ Then Jesus, still teaching in the temple courts, cried out, 'Yes, you know me, and you know where I am from. I am not here on my own, but he who sent me is true. You do not know him, ²⁹ but I know him because I am from him and he sent me.'

³⁰ At this they tried to seize him, but no-one laid a hand on him, because his time had not yet come. ³¹ Still, many in the crowd put their faith in him. They said, 'When the Christ comes, will he do more miraculous signs than this man?'

³² The Pharisees heard the crowd whispering such things about him. Then the chief priests and the Pharisees sent temple guards to arrest him.

³³ Jesus said, 'I am with you for only a short time, and then I go to the one who sent me. ³⁴ You will look for me, but you will not find me; and where I am, you cannot come.'

³⁵ The Jews said to one another, 'Where does this man intend to go that we cannot find him? Will he go where our people live scattered among the Greeks, and teach the Greeks? ³⁶ What did he mean when he said, "You will look for me, but you will not find me," and "Where I am, you cannot come"?'

³⁷ On the last and greatest day of the Feast, Jesus stood and said in a loud voice, 'If anyone is thirsty, let him come to me and drink. ³⁸ Whoever believes in me, as the Scripture has said, streams of living water will flow from within him.' ³⁹ By this he meant the Spirit, whom those who believed in him were later to receive. Up to that time the Spirit had not been given, since Jesus had not yet been glorified.

⁴⁰ On hearing his words, some of the people said, 'Surely this man is the Prophet.'

⁴¹ Others said, 'He is the Christ.'

Still others asked, 'How can the Christ come from Galilee? ⁴² Does not the Scripture say that the Christ will come from David's family and from Bethlehem, the town where David lived?' ⁴³ Thus the people were divided because of Jesus. ⁴⁴ Some wanted to seize him, but no-one laid a hand on him.

Unbelief of the Jewish Leaders

⁴⁵ Finally the temple guards went back to the chief priests and Pharisees, who asked them, 'Why didn't you bring him in?'

⁴⁶ 'No-one ever spoke the way this man does,' the guards declared.

⁴⁷ 'You mean he has deceived you also?' the Pharisees retorted. ⁴⁸ 'Has any of the rulers or of the Pharisees believed in him? ⁴⁹ No! But this mob that knows nothing of the law - there is a curse on them.'

⁵⁰ Nicodemus, who had gone to Jesus earlier and who was one of their own number, asked, ⁵¹ 'Does our law condemn a man without first hearing him to find out what he is doing?'

⁵² They replied, 'Are you from Galilee, too? Look into it, and you will find that a prophet does not come out of Galilee.'

⁵³ Then Jesus went to his home.

DAY 63

JOHN 8. 1 — 30

8 But Jesus went to the Mount of Olives. [2] At dawn he appeared again in the temple courts, where all the people gathered round him, and he sat down to teach them. [3] The teachers of the law and the Pharisees brought in a woman caught in adultery. They made her stand before the group [4] and said to Jesus, 'Teacher, this woman was caught in the act of adultery. [5] In the Law Moses commanded us to stone such women. Now what do you say?' [6] They were using this question as a trap, in order to have a basis for accusing him.

But Jesus bent down and started to write on the ground with his finger. [7] When they kept on questioning him, he straightened up and said to them, 'If any one of you is without sin, let him be the first to throw a stone at her.' [8] Again he stooped down and wrote on the ground.

[9] At this, those who heard began to go away one at a time, the older ones first, until only Jesus was left, with the woman still standing there. [10] Jesus straightened up and asked her, 'Woman, where are they? Has no-one condemned you?'

[11] 'No-one, sir,' she said.

'Then neither do I condemn you,' Jesus declared. 'Go now and leave your life of sin.'

The Validity of Jesus' Testimony

[12] When Jesus spoke again to the people, he said, 'I am the light of the world. Whoever follows me will never walk in darkness, but will have the light of life.'

[13] The Pharisees challenged him, 'Here you are, appearing as your own witness; your testimony is not valid.'

[14] Jesus answered, 'Even if I testify on my own behalf, my testimony is valid, for I know where I came from and where I am going. But you have no idea where I come from or where I am going. [15] You judge by human standards; I pass judgment on no-one. [16] But if I do judge, my decisions are right, because I am not alone. I stand with the Father, who sent me. [17] In your own Law it is written that the testimony of two men is valid. [18] I am one who testifies for myself; my other witness is the Father, who sent me.'

[19] Then they asked him, 'Where is your father?'

'You do not know me or my Father,' Jesus replied. 'If you knew me, you would know my Father also.' [20] He spoke these words while teaching in the temple area near the place where the offerings were put. Yet no-one seized him, because his time had not yet come.

[21] Once more Jesus said to them, 'I am going away, and you will look for me, and you will die in your sin. Where I go, you cannot come.'

[22] This made the Jews ask, 'Will he kill himself? Is that why he says, "Where I go, you cannot come"?'

[23] But he continued, 'You are from below; I am from above. You are of this world; I am not of this world. [24] I told you that you would die in your sins; if you do not believe that I am [the one I claim to be], you will indeed die in your sins.'

[25] 'Who are you?' they asked.

'Just what I have been claiming all along,' Jesus replied. [26] 'I have much to say in judgment of you. But he who sent me is reliable, and what I have heard from him I tell the world.'

[27] They did not understand that he was telling them about his Father. [28] So Jesus said, 'When you have lifted up the

Son of Man, then you will know that I am [the one I claim to be] and that I do nothing on my own but speak just what the Father has taught me. [29] The one who sent me is with me; he has not left me alone, for I always do what pleases him.' [30] Even as he spoke, many put their faith in him.

DAY 64

JOHN 8. 31 — 59

The Children of Abraham

[31] To the Jews who had believed him, Jesus said, 'If you hold to my teaching, you are really my disciples. [32] Then you will know the truth, and the truth will set you free.'

[33] They answered him, 'We are Abraham's descendants and have never been slaves of anyone. How can you say that we shall be set free?'

[34] Jesus replied, 'I tell you the truth, everyone who sins is a slave to sin. [35] Now a slave has no permanent place in the family, but a son belongs to it for ever. [36] So if the Son sets you free, you will be free indeed. [37] I know you are Abraham's descendants. Yet you are ready to kill me, because you have no room for my word. [38] I am telling you what I have seen in the Father's presence, and you do what you have heard from your father.'

[39] 'Abraham is our father,' they answered.

'If you were Abraham's children,' said Jesus, 'then you would do the things Abraham did. [40] As it is, you are determined to kill me, a man who has told you the truth that I heard from God. Abraham did not do such things. [41] You are doing the things your own father does.'

'We are not illegitimate children,' they protested. 'The only Father we have is God himself.'

The Children of the Devil

[42] Jesus said to them, 'If God were your Father, you would love me, for I came from God and now am here. I have not come on my own; but he sent me. [43] Why is my language not clear to you? Because you are unable to hear what I say. [44] You belong to your father, the devil, and you want to carry out your father's desire. He was a murderer from the beginning, not holding to the truth, for there is no truth in him. When he lies, he speaks his native language, for he is a liar and the father of lies. [45] Yet because I tell the truth, you do not believe me! [46] Can any of you prove me guilty of sin? If I am

'The truth will set you free.'

telling the truth, why don't you believe me? [47] He who belongs to God hears what God says. The reason you do not hear is that you do not belong to God.'

The Claims of Jesus About Himself

[48] The Jews answered him, 'Aren't we right in saying that you are a Samaritan and demon-possessed?'

[49] 'I am not possessed by a demon,' said Jesus, 'but I honour my Father and you dishonour me. [50] I am not seeking glory for myself; but there is one who seeks it, and he is the judge. [51] I tell you the truth, if anyone keeps my word, he will never see death.'

[52] At this the Jews exclaimed, 'Now we know that you are demon-possessed! Abraham died and so did the prophets, yet you say that if anyone keeps your word, he will never taste death. [53] Are you greater than our father Abraham? He died, and so did the prophets. Who do you think you are?'

[54] Jesus replied, 'If I glorify myself, my glory means nothing. My Father, whom you claim as your God, is the one who glorifies me. [55] Though you do not know him, I know him. If I said I did not, I would be a liar like you, but I do know him and keep his word. [56] Your father Abraham rejoiced at the thought of seeing my day; he saw it and was glad.'

[57] 'You are not yet fifty years old,' the Jews said to him, 'and you have seen Abraham!'

[58] 'I tell you the truth,' Jesus answered, 'before Abraham was born, I am!' [59] At this, they picked up stones to stone him, but Jesus hid himself, slipping away from the temple grounds.

DAY 65
JOHN 9. 1 — 41

9 Jesus Heals a Man Born Blind

As he went along, he saw a man blind from birth. [2] His disciples asked him, 'Rabbi, who sinned, this man or his parents, that he was born blind?'

[3] 'Neither this man nor his parents sinned,' said Jesus, 'but this happened so that the work of God might be displayed in his life. [4] As long as it is day, we must

> 'I am not seeking glory for myself; but there is one who seeks it, and he is the judge.'

do the work of him who sent me. Night is coming, when no-one can work. [5] While I am in the world, I am the light of the world.'

[6] Having said this, he spat on the ground, made some mud with the saliva, and put it on the man's eyes. [7] 'Go,' he told him, 'wash in the Pool of Siloam' (this word means Sent). So the man went and washed, and came home seeing.

[8] His neighbours and those who had formerly seen him begging asked, 'Isn't this the same man who used to sit and beg?' [9] Some claimed that he was.

Others said, ' No, he only looks like him.'

But he himself insisted, 'I am the man.'

[10] 'How then were your eyes opened?' they demanded.

[11] He replied, 'The man they call

Jesus made some mud and put it on my eyes. He told me to go to Siloam and wash. So I went and washed, and then I could see.'

¹² 'Where is this man?' they asked him.

'I don't know,' he said.

The Pharisees Investigate the Healing

¹³ They brought to the Pharisees the man who had been blind. ¹⁴ Now the day on which Jesus had made the mud and opened the man's eyes was a Sabbath. ¹⁵ Therefore the Pharisees also asked him how he had received his sight. 'He put mud on my eyes,' the man replied, 'and I washed, and now I see.'

¹⁶ Some of the Pharisees said, 'This man is not from God, for he does not keep the Sabbath.'

But others asked, 'How can a sinner do such miraculous signs?' So they were divided.

¹⁷ Finally they turned again to the blind man, 'What have you to say about him? It was your eyes he opened.'

The man replied, 'He is a prophet.'

¹⁸ The Jews still did not believe that he had been blind and had received his sight until they sent for the man's parents. ¹⁹ 'Is this your son?' they asked. 'Is this the one you say was born blind? How is it that now he can see?'

²⁰ 'We know he is our son,' the parents answered, 'and we know he was born blind. ²¹ But how he can see now, or who opened his eyes, we don't know. Ask him. He is of age; he will speak for himself.' ²² His parents said this because they were afraid of the Jews, for already the Jews had decided that anyone who acknowledged that Jesus was the Christ would be put out of the synagogue. ²³ That was why his parents said, 'He is of age; ask him.'

²⁴ A second time they summoned the man who had been blind. 'Give glory to God,' they said. 'We know this man is a sinner.'

²⁵ He replied, 'Whether he is a sinner or not, I don't know. One thing I do know. I was blind but now I see!'

²⁶ Then they asked him, 'What did he do to you? How did he open your eyes?'

²⁷ He answered, 'I have told you already and you did not listen. Why do you want to hear it again? Do you want to become his disciples, too?'

²⁸ Then they hurled insults at him and said, 'You are this fellow's disciple! We are disciples of Moses! ²⁹ We know that God spoke to Moses, but as for this fellow, we don't even know where he comes from.'

³⁰ The man answered, 'Now that is remarkable! You don't know where he comes from, yet he opened my eyes. ³¹ We know that God does not listen to sinners. He listens to the godly man who does his will. ³² Nobody has ever heard of opening the eyes of a man born blind. ³³ If this man were not from God, he could do nothing.'

³⁴ To this they replied, 'You were steeped in sin at birth; how dare you lecture us!' And they threw him out.

Spiritual Blindness

³⁵ Jesus heard that they had thrown him out, and when he found him, he said, 'Do you believe in the Son of Man?'

³⁶ 'Who is he, sir?' the man asked. 'Tell me so that I may believe in him.'

³⁷ Jesus said, 'You have now seen him; in fact, he is the one speaking with you.'

³⁸ Then the man said, 'Lord, I believe,' and he worshipped him.

³⁹ Jesus said, 'For judgment I have come into this world, so that the blind will see and those who see will become blind.'

⁴⁰ Some Pharisees who were with him heard him say this and asked, 'What? Are we blind too?'

⁴¹ Jesus said, 'If you were blind, you would not be guilty of sin; but now that you claim you can see, your guilt remains.

DAY 66

JOHN 10. 1 — 21

10 The Shepherd and His Flock

'I tell you the truth, the man who does not enter the sheep pen by the gate, but climbs in by some other way, is a thief and a robber. ² The man who enters by the gate is the shepherd of his sheep. ³ The watchman opens the gate for him, and the sheep listen to his voice. He calls his own sheep by name and leads them out. ⁴ When he has brought out all his own, he goes on ahead of them, and his sheep follow him because they know his voice. ⁵ But they will never follow a stranger; in fact, they will run away from him because they do not recognise a stranger's voice.' ⁶ Jesus used this figure of speech, but they did not understand what he was telling them.

⁷ Therefore Jesus said again, 'I tell you the truth, I am the gate for the sheep. ⁸ All who ever came before me were thieves and robbers, but the sheep did not listen to them. ⁹ I am the gate; whoever enters through me will be saved. He will come in and go out, and find pasture. ¹⁰ The thief comes only to steal and kill and destroy; I have come that they may have life, and have it to the full.

¹¹ 'I am the good shepherd. The good shepherd lays down his life for the sheep.

¹² The hired hand is not the shepherd who owns the sheep. So when he sees the wolf coming, he abandons the sheep and runs away. Then the wolf attacks the flock and scatters it. ¹³ The man runs away because he is a hired hand and cares nothing for the sheep.

¹⁴ 'I am the good shepherd; I know my sheep and my sheep know me - ¹⁵ just as the Father knows me and I know the Father - and I lay down my life for the sheep. ¹⁶ I have other sheep that are not of this sheep pen. I must bring them also. They too will listen to my voice, and there shall be one flock and one shepherd. ¹⁷ The reason my Father loves me is that I lay down my life - only to take it up again. ¹⁸ No-one takes it from me, but I lay it down of my own accord. I have authority to lay it down and authority to take it up again. This command I received from my Father.'

¹⁹ At these words the Jews were again divided. ²⁰ Many of them said, 'He is demon-possessed and raving mad. Why listen to him?'

²¹ But others said, 'These are not the sayings of a man possessed by a demon. Can a demon open the eyes of the blind?'

'Whoever enters through me will be saved.'

DAY 67

JOHN 10. 22 — 42

The Unbelief of the Jews

²² Then came the Feast of Dedication at Jerusalem. It was winter, ²³ and Jesus was in the temple area walking in Solomon's Colonnade. ²⁴ The Jews gathered round him, saying, 'How long will you keep us in suspense? If you are the Christ, tell us plainly.'

²⁵ Jesus answered, 'I did tell you, but you do not believe. The miracles I do in the Father. For which of these do you stone me?'

³³ 'We are not stoning you for any of these,' replied the Jews, ' but for blasphemy, because you, a mere man, claim to be God.'

³⁴ Jesus answered them, 'Is it not written in your Law, "I have said you are gods"? ³⁵ If he called them "gods", to whom the word of God came - and the Scripture cannot be broken - ³⁶ what about the one whom the Father set apart as his very own and sent into the world? Why then do you accuse me of blasphemy because I said, "I am God's Son"? ³⁷ Do not believe me unless I do what my Father does. ³⁸ But if I do it, even though

'I give them eternal life, and they shall never perish.'

my Father's name speak for me, ²⁶ but you do not believe because you are not my sheep. ²⁷ My sheep listen to my voice; I know them, and they follow me. ²⁸ I give them eternal life, and they shall never perish; no-one can snatch them out of my hand. ²⁹ My Father, who has given them to me, is greater than all; no-one can snatch them out of my Father's hand. ³⁰ I and the Father are one.'

³¹ Again the Jews picked up stones to stone him, ³² but Jesus said to them, 'I have shown you many great miracles from

you do not believe me, believe the miracles, that you may know and understand that the Father is in me, and I in the Father.' ³⁹ Again they tried to seize him, but he escaped their grasp.

⁴⁰ Then Jesus went back across the Jordan to the place where John had been baptising in the early days. Here he stayed ⁴¹ and many people came to him. They said, 'Though John never performed a miraculous sign, all that John said about this man was true.' ⁴² And in that place many believed in Jesus.

DAY 68

JOHN 11. 1 — 27

11
The Death of Lazarus

Now a man named Lazarus was sick. He was from Bethany, the village of Mary and her sister Martha. ² This Mary, whose brother Lazarus now lay sick, was the same one who poured perfume on the Lord and wiped his feet with her hair. ³ So the sisters sent word to Jesus, 'Lord, the one you love is sick.'

⁴ When he heard this, Jesus said, 'This sickness will not end in death. No, it is for God's glory so that God's Son may be glorified through it.' ⁵ Jesus loved Martha and her sister and Lazarus. ⁶ Yet when he heard that Lazarus was sick, he stayed where he was two more days.

⁷ Then he said to his disciples, 'Let us go back to Judea.'

⁸ 'But Rabbi,' they said, 'a short while ago the Jews tried to stone you, and yet you are going back there?'

⁹ Jesus answered, 'Are there not twelve hours of daylight? A man who walks by day will not stumble, for he sees by this world's light. ¹⁰ It is when he walks by night that he stumbles, for he has no light.'

¹¹ After he had said this, he went on to tell them, 'Our friend Lazarus has fallen asleep; but I am going there to wake him up.'

¹² His disciples replied, 'Lord, if he sleeps, he will get better.' ¹³ Jesus had been speaking of his death, but his disciples thought he meant natural sleep.

¹⁴ So then he told them plainly, 'Lazarus is dead, ¹⁵ and for your sake I am glad I was not there, so that you may believe. But let us go to him.'

¹⁶ Then Thomas (called Didymus) said to the rest of the disciples, 'Let us also go, that we may die with him.'

Jesus Comforts the Sisters

¹⁷ On his arrival, Jesus found that Lazarus had already been in the tomb for four days. ¹⁸ Bethany was less than two miles from Jerusalem, ¹⁹ and many Jews had

> 'I am the resurrection and the life. He who believes in me will live, even though he dies; and whoever lives and believes in me will never die. Do you believe this?'

come to Martha and Mary to comfort them in the loss of their brother. ²⁰ When Martha heard that Jesus was coming, she went out to meet him, but Mary stayed at home.

²¹ 'Lord,' Martha said to Jesus, 'if you had been here, my brother would not have died. ²² But I know that even now God will give you whatever you ask.'

²³ Jesus said to her, 'Your brother will rise again.'

²⁴ Martha answered, 'I know he will rise again in the resurrection at the last day.'

²⁵ Jesus said to her, 'I am the resurrection and the life. He who believes in me will live, even though he dies; ²⁶ and whoever lives and believes in me will never die. Do you believe this?'

²⁷ 'Yes, Lord,' she told him, 'I believe that you are the Christ, the Son of God, who was to come into the world.'

DAY 69

JOHN 11. 28 — 57

²⁸ And after she had said this, she went back and called her sister Mary aside. 'The Teacher is here,' she said, 'and is asking for you.' ²⁹ When Mary heard this, she got up quickly and went to him. ³⁰ Now Jesus had not yet entered the village, but was still at the place where Martha had met him. ³¹ When the Jews who had been with Mary in the house, comforting her, noticed how quickly she got up and went out, they followed her, supposing she was going to the tomb to mourn there.

³² When Mary reached the place where Jesus was and saw him, she fell at his feet and said, 'Lord, if you had been here, my brother would not have died.'

³³ When Jesus saw her weeping, and the Jews who had come along with her also weeping, he was deeply moved in spirit and troubled. ³⁴ 'Where have you laid him?' he asked.

'Come and see, Lord,' they replied.

³⁵ Jesus wept.

³⁶ Then the Jews said, 'See how he loved him!'

³⁷ But some of them said, 'Could not he who opened the eyes of the blind man have kept this man from dying?'

Jesus Raises Lazarus From the Dead

³⁸ Jesus, once more deeply moved, came to the tomb. It was a cave with a stone laid across the entrance. ³⁹ 'Take away the stone,' he said.

'But, Lord,' said Martha, the sister of the dead man, 'by this time there is a bad odour, for he has been there four days.'

⁴⁰ Then Jesus said, 'Did I not tell you that if you believed, you would see the glory of God?'

⁴¹ So they took away the stone. Then Jesus looked up and said, 'Father, I thank you that you have heard me. ⁴² I knew that you always hear me, but I said this for the benefit of the people standing here, that they may believe that you sent me.'

⁴³ When he had said this, Jesus called in a loud voice, 'Lazarus, come out!' ⁴⁴ The dead man came out, his hands and feet wrapped with strips of linen, and a cloth around his face.

Jesus said to them, 'Take off the grave clothes and let him go.'

The Plot to Kill Jesus

⁴⁵ Therefore many of the Jews who had come to visit Mary, and had seen what Jesus did, put their faith in him. ⁴⁶ But some of them went to the Pharisees and told them what Jesus had done. ⁴⁷ Then the chief priests and the Pharisees called a meeting of the Sanhedrin.

'What are we accomplishing?' they asked. 'Here is this man performing many miraculous signs. ⁴⁸ If we let him go on like this, everyone will believe in him, and then the Romans will come and take away both our place and our nation.'

⁴⁹ Then one of them, named Caiaphas, who was high priest that year, spoke up, 'You know nothing at all! ⁵⁰ You do not realise that it is better for you that one man die for the people than that the whole nation perish.'

⁵¹ He did not say this on his own, but as high priest that year he prophesied that Jesus would die for the Jewish nation, ⁵² and not only for that nation but also for the scattered children of God, to bring them together and make them one. ⁵³ So

om that day on they plotted to take his
e.

⁵⁴ Therefore Jesus no longer moved
out publicly among the Jews. Instead
e withdrew to a region near the desert,
a village called Ephraim, where he
ayed with his disciples.

⁵⁵ When it was almost time for the
wish Passover, many went up from the
ountry to Jerusalem for their ceremonial
eansing before the Passover. ⁵⁶ They
ept looking for Jesus, and as they stood
the temple area they asked one
nother, 'What do you think? Isn't he
oming to the Feast at all?' ⁵⁷ But the
ief priests and Pharisees had given
rders that if anyone found out where
sus was, he should report it so that they
ight arrest him.

DAY 70

JOHN 12. 1 — 15

12 Jesus Anointed at Bethany

Six days before the Passover,
sus arrived at Bethany, where Lazarus
ved, whom Jesus had raised from the
ead. ² Here a dinner was given in Jesus'
onour. Martha served, while Lazarus was
mong those reclining at the table with
im. ³ Then Mary took about a pint of
ure nard, an expensive perfume; she
oured it on Jesus' feet and wiped his feet
ith her hair. And the house was filled
ith the fragrance of the perfume.

⁴ But one of his disciples, Judas
scariot, who was later to betray him,
bjected, ⁵ 'Why wasn't this perfume sold
nd the money given to the poor? It was
orth a year's wages.' ⁶ He did not say this
because he cared about the poor but
because he was a thief; as keeper of the
money bag, he used to help himself to
what was put into it.

⁷ 'Leave her alone,' Jesus replied.' [It
was intended] that she should save this
perfume for the day of my burial. ⁸ You
will always have the poor among you, but
you will not always have me.'

'Blessed is he who comes in the name of the Lord!'

⁹ Meanwhile a large crowd of Jews
found out that Jesus was there and came,
not only because of him but also to see
Lazarus, whom he had raised from the
dead. ¹⁰ So the chief priests made plans to
kill Lazarus as well, ¹¹ for on account of
him many of the Jews were going over to
Jesus and putting their faith in him.

The Triumphal Entry

¹² The next day the great crowd that had
come for the Feast heard that Jesus was
on his way to Jerusalem. ¹³ They took
palm branches and went out to meet him,
shouting,

'Hosanna!'

'Blessed is he who comes in the name
of the Lord!'

'Blessed is the King of Israel!'

¹⁴ Jesus found a young donkey and sat
upon it, as it is written,

¹⁵ 'Do not be afraid, O Daughter of
Zion;
see, your king is coming,
seated on a donkey's colt.'

DAY 71

JOHN 12. 16 — 50

[16] At first his disciples did not understand all this. Only after Jesus was glorified did they realise that these things had been written about him and that they had done these things to him.
[17] Now the crowd that was with him when he called Lazarus from the tomb and raised him from the dead continued to spread the word. [18] Many people, because they had heard that he had given this miraculous sign, went out to meet him.
[19] So the Pharisees said to one another, 'See, this is getting us nowhere. Look how the whole world has gone after him!'

Jesus Predicts His Death

[20] Now there were some Greeks among those who went up to worship at the Feast. [21] They came to Philip, who was from Bethsaida in Galilee, with a request. 'Sir,' they said, 'we would like to see Jesus.' [22] Philip went to tell Andrew; Andrew and Philip in turn told Jesus.
[23] Jesus replied, 'The hour has come for the Son of Man to be glorified. [24] I tell you the truth, unless a grain of wheat falls to the ground and dies, it remains only a single seed. But if it dies, it produces many seeds. [25] The man who loves his life will lose it, while the man who hates his life in this world will keep it for eternal life. [26] Whoever serves me must follow me; and where I am, my servant also will be. My Father will honour the one who serves me.
[27] 'Now my heart is troubled, and what shall I say? "Father, save me from this hour"? No, it was for this very reason I came to this hour. [28] Father, glorify your name!'

Then a voice came from heaven, 'I have glorified it, and will glorify it again.
[29] The crowd that was there and heard it said it had thundered; others said an angel had spoken to him.
[30] Jesus said, 'This voice was for your benefit, not mine. [31] Now is the time for judgment on this world; now the prince of this world will be driven out. [32] But I, when I am lifted up from the earth, will draw all men to myself.' [33] He said this to show the kind of death he was going to die.
[34] The crowd spoke up, 'We have heard from the Law that the Christ will remain for ever, so how can you say, "The Son of Man must be lifted up"? Who is this "Son of Man"?'
[35] Then Jesus told them, 'You are going to have the light just a little while longer. Walk while you have the light, before darkness overtakes you. The man who walks in the dark does not know where he is going. [36] Put your trust in the light while you have it, so that you may become sons of light.' When he had finished speaking, Jesus left and hid himself from them.

The Jews Continue in Their Unbelief

[37] Even after Jesus had done all these miraculous signs in their presence, they still would not believe in him. [38] This was to fulfil the word of Isaiah the prophet:

'Lord, who has believed our message and to whom has the arm of the Lord been revealed?'

[39] For this reason they could not believe, because, as Isaiah says elsewhere

[40] 'He has blinded their eyes and deadened their hearts,

so they can neither see with their eyes, nor understand with their hearts, nor turn - and I would heal them.'

⁴¹ Isaiah said this because he saw Jesus' ory and spoke about him.

⁴² Yet at the same time many even nong the leaders believed in him. But ∶cause of the Pharisees they would not ɔnfess their faith for fear they would be ʊt out of the synagogue; ⁴³ for they loved ̵aise from men more than praise from ̵od.

⁴⁴ Then Jesus cried out, 'When a man ∊lieves in me, he does not believe in me nly, but in the one who sent me. When he looks at me, he sees the one ‛ho sent me. ⁴⁶ I have come into the ̵orld as a light, so that no-one who ∊lieves in me should stay in darkness.

⁴⁷ 'As for the person who hears my ̵ords but does not keep them, I do not ɪdge him. For I did not come to judge ɪe world, but to save it. ⁴⁸ There is a ɪdge for the one who rejects me and does ɔt accept my words; that very word ̵hich I spoke will condemn him at the ɪst day. ⁴⁹ For I did not speak of my own ɪccord, but the Father who sent me ɔmmanded me what to say and how to ɪy it. ⁵⁰ I know that his command leads ɔ eternal life. So whatever I say is just ̵hat the Father has told me to say.'

DAY 72

JOHN 13. 1 — 17

13 Jesus Washes His Disciples' Feet

It was just before the Passover ̵east. Jesus knew that the time had come ̵or him to leave this world and go to the Father. Having loved his own who were in the world, he now showed them the full extent of his love.

² The evening meal was being served, and the devil had already prompted Judas Iscariot, son of Simon, to betray Jesus. ³ Jesus knew that the Father had put all things under his power, and that he had come from God and was returning to God; ⁴ so he got up from the meal, took off his outer clothing, and wrapped a towel round his waist. ⁵ After that, he poured water into a basin and began to wash his disciples' feet, drying them with the towel that was wrapped round him.

⁶ He came to Simon Peter, who said to him, 'Lord, are you going to wash my feet?'

⁷ Jesus replied, 'You do not realise now what I am doing, but later you will understand.'

⁸ 'No,' said Peter, 'you shall never wash my feet.'

Jesus answered, 'Unless I wash you, you have no part with me.'

⁹ 'Then, Lord,' Simon Peter replied, 'not just my feet but my hands and my head as well!'

¹⁰ Jesus answered, 'A person who has had a bath needs only to wash his feet; his whole body is clean. And you are clean, though not every one of you.' ¹¹ For he knew who was going to betray him, and that was why he said not every one was clean.

¹² When he had finished washing their feet, he put on his clothes and returned to his place. 'Do you understand what I have done for you?' he asked them. ¹³ 'You call me "Teacher" and "Lord", and rightly so, for that is what I am. ¹⁴ Now that I, your Lord and Teacher, have washed your feet, you also should wash one another's feet. ¹⁵ I have set you an example that you should do as I have done for you. ¹⁶ I tell you the truth, no

servant is greater than his master, nor is a messenger greater than the one who sent him. [17] Now that you know these things, you will be blessed if you do them.

DAY 73

JOHN 13. 18 — 38

Jesus Predicts His Betrayal

[18] 'I am not referring to all of you; I know those I have chosen. But this is to fulfil

---

'He who shares my bread has lifted up his heel against me.'

---

the scripture: "He who shares my bread has lifted up his heel against me."

[19] 'I am telling you now before it happens, so that when it does happen you will believe that I am He. [20] I tell you the truth, whoever accepts anyone I send accepts me; and whoever accepts me accepts the one who sent me.'

[21] After he had said this, Jesus was troubled in spirit and testified, 'I tell you the truth, one of you is going to betray me.'

[22] His disciples stared at one another, at a loss to know which of them he meant. [23] One of them, the disciple whom Jesus loved, was reclining next to him. [24] Simon Peter motioned to this disciple and said, 'Ask him which one he means.'

[25] Leaning back against Jesus, he asked him, 'Lord, who is it?'

[26] Jesus answered, 'It is the one to whom I will give this piece of bread when I have dipped it in the dish.' Then, dipping the piece of bread, he gave it to Judas Iscariot, son of Simon. [27] As soon as

Judas took the bread, Satan entered into him.

'What you are about to do, do quickly,' Jesus told him, [28] but no-one at the meal understood why Jesus said this to him. [29] Since Judas had charge of the money, some thought Jesus was telling him to buy what was needed for the Fea or to give something to the poor. [30] As soon as Judas had taken the bread, he went out. And it was night.

Jesus Predicts Peter's Denial

[31] When he was gone, Jesus said, 'Now is the Son of Man glorified and God is glorified in him. [32] If God is glorified in him, God will glorify the Son in himself and will glorify him at once.

[33] 'My children, I will be with you only a little longer. You will look for me, and just as I told the Jews, so I tell you now: Where I am going, you cannot come.

[34] 'A new command I give you: Love one another. As I have loved you, you must love one another. [35] By this all men will know that you are my disciples, if you love one another.'

[36] Simon Peter asked him, 'Lord, where are you going?'

Jesus replied, 'Where I am going, you cannot follow now, but you will follow later.'

[37] Peter asked, 'Lord, why can't I

'Lord, where are you going?'

---

follow you now? I will lay down my life for you.'

[38] Then Jesus answered, 'Will you really lay down your life for me? I tell you the truth, before the cock crows, you will disown me three times!'

'...I have come that they may have life, and have it to the full.'

DAY 74

JOHN 14. 1 — 31

14 Jesus Comforts His Disciples

'Do not let your hearts be troubled. Trust in God; trust also in me. [2] In my Father's house are many rooms; if it were not so, I would have told you. I am going there to prepare a place for you. [3] And if I go and prepare a place for you, I will come back and take you to be with me that you also may be where I am. [4] You know the way to the place where I am going.'

Jesus the Way to the Father

[5] Thomas said to him, 'Lord, we don't know where you are going, so how can we know the way?'

[6] Jesus answered, 'I am the way and the truth and the life. No-one comes to the Father except through me. [7] If you really knew me, you would know my Father as well. From now on, you do know him and have seen him.'

[8] Philip said, 'Lord, show us the Father and that will be enough for us.'

[9] Jesus answered: 'Don't you know me, Philip, even after I have been among you such a long time? Anyone who has seen me has seen the Father. How can you say, "Show us the Father"? [10] Don't you believe that I am in the Father, and that the Father is in me? The words I say to you are not just my own. Rather, it is the Father, living in me, who is doing his work. [11] Believe me when I say that I am in the Father and the Father is in me; or at least believe on the evidence of the miracles themselves. [12] I tell you the truth, anyone who has faith in me will ● what I have been doing. He will do eve greater things than these, because I am going to the Father. [13] And I will do whatever you ask in my name, so that t Son may bring glory to the Father. [14] Yo may ask me for anything in my name, a I will do it.

Jesus Promises the Holy Spirit

[15] 'If you love me, you will obey what I command. [16] And I will ask the Father, and he will give you another Counsello to be with you for ever - [17] the Spirit of truth. The world cannot accept him, because it neither sees him nor knows him. But you know him, for he lives wit you and will be in you. [18] I will not leav you as orphans; I will come to you. [19] Before long, the world will not see m any more, but you will see me. Because

> ## 'If you love me, you will obe what I command.'

live, you also will live. [20] On that day yo will realise that I am in my Father, and you are in me, and I am in you. [21] Whoever has my commands and obe them, he is the one who loves me. He who loves me will be loved by my Fath and I too will love him and show myse to him.'

[22] Then Judas (not Judas Iscariot) said, 'But, Lord, why do you intend to show yourself to us and not to the worl [23] Jesus replied, 'If anyone loves me he will obey my teaching. My Father w love him, and we will come to him and make our home with him. [24] He who do not love me will not obey my teaching. These words you hear are not my own;

ey belong to the Father who sent me. [25] 'All this I have spoken while still th you. [26] But the Counsellor, the Holy irit, whom the Father will send in my me, will teach you all things and will nind you of everything I have said to u. [27] Peace I leave with you; my peace I ve you. I do not give to you as the world es. Do not let your hearts be troubled d do not be afraid.

[28] 'You heard me say, "I am going ay and I am coming back to you." If u loved me, you would be glad that I going to the Father, for the Father is eater than I. [29] I have told you now fore it happens, so that when it does ppen you will believe. [30] I will not eak with you much longer, for the ince of this world is coming. He has no ld on me, [31] but the world must learn at I love the Father and that I do actly what my Father has commanded e.

'Come now; let us leave.

DAY 75
JOHN 15. 1 — 18

15 The Vine and the Branches

'I am the true vine, and my ther is the gardener. [2] He cuts off every anch in me that bears no fruit, while ery branch that does bear fruit he anes so that it will be even more itful. [3] You are already clean because of e word I have spoken to you. [4] Remain me, and I will remain in you. No anch can bear fruit by itself; it must nain in the vine. Neither can you bear it unless you remain in me.

[5] 'I am the vine; you are the branches.

If a man remains in me and I in him, he will bear much fruit; apart from me you can do nothing. [6] If anyone does not remain in me, he is like a branch that is thrown away and withers; such branches

---

'But the Counsellor, the Holy Spirit, whom the Father will send in my name, will teach you all things and will remind you of everything I have said to you.'

---

are picked up, thrown into the fire and burned. [7] If you remain in me and my words remain in you, ask whatever you wish, and it will be given you. [8] This is to my Father's glory, that you bear much fruit, showing yourselves to be my disciples.

[9] 'As the Father has loved me, so have I loved you. Now remain in my love. [10] If you obey my commands, you will remain in my love, just as I have obeyed my Father's commands and remain in his love. [11] I have told you this so that my joy may be in you and that your joy may be complete. [12] My command is this: Love each other as I have loved you. [13] Greater love has no-one than this, that he lay down his life for his friends. [14] You are my friends if you do what I command. [15] I no longer call you servants, because a servant does not know his master's business. Instead, I have called you friends, for everything that I learned from my Father I have made known to you. [16] You did not choose me, but I chose you and appointed you to go and bear fruit - fruit that will last. Then the Father will give you whatever you ask in my name. [17] This is my command: Love each other.

DAY 76
JOHN 15. 18 — 27

The World Hates the Disciples

[18] 'If the world hates you, keep in mind that it hated me first. [19] If you belonged to the world, it would love you as its own. As it is, you do not belong to the world, but I have chosen you out of the world. That is why the world hates you. [20] Remember the words I spoke to you: "No servant is greater than his master." If they persecuted me, they will persecute

you also. If they obeyed my teaching, t| will obey yours also. [21] They will treat y| this way because of my name, for they | not know the One who sent me. [22] If I | had not come and spoken to them, the| would not be guilty of sin. Now, howev| they have no excuse for their sin. [23] He | who hates me hates my Father as well. | I had not done among them what no-c| else did, they would not be guilty of sir| But now they have seen these miracles| and yet they have hated both me and r| Father. [25] But this is to fulfil what is written in their Law: "They hated me without reason."

[26] 'When the Counsellor comes, whom I will send to you from the Fath| the Spirit of truth who goes out from t| Father, he will testify about me. [27] And | you also must testify, for you have been| with me from the beginning.

'If the world hates you, keep in mind that it hated me first.'

DAY 77
JOHN 16. 1 — 33

16 'All this I have told you so that you will not go astray. [2] They will put you out of t| synagogue; in fact, a time is coming wh| anyone who kills you will think he is offering a service to God. [3] They will d| such things because they have not kno| the Father or me. [4] I have told you this that when the time comes you will remember that I warned you. I did not t| you this at first because I was with you.

The Work of the Holy Spirit

[5] 'Now I am going to him who sent me,| yet none of you asks me, "Where are y| going?" [6] Because I have said these thin| you are filled with grief. [7] But I tell you

truth: It is for your good that I am
ng away. Unless I go away, the
unsellor will not come to you; but if I
I will send him to you. [8] When he
mes, he will convict the world of guilt
regard to sin and righteousness and
lgment: [9] in regard to sin, because men
not believe in me; [10] in regard to
hteousness, because I am going to the
ther, where you can see me no longer;
nd in regard to judgment, because the
nce of this world now stands
ndemned.

[12] 'I have much more to say to you,
re than you can now bear. [13] But when
, the Spirit of truth, comes, he will
ide you into all truth. He will not speak
his own; he will speak only what he
ars, and he will tell you what is yet to
me. [14] He will bring glory to me by
king from what is mine and making it
own to you. [15] All that belongs to the
ther is mine. That is why I said the
irit will take from what is mine and
ke it known to you.

[16] 'In a little while you will see me
more, and then after a little while you
ll see me.'

he Disciples' Grief Will Turn to
y

Some of his disciples said to one
other, 'What does he mean by saying,
a little while you will see me no more,
d then after a little while you will see
,' and "Because I am going to the
ther"?' [18] They kept asking, 'What does
mean by "a little while"? We don't
derstand what he is saying.'

[19] Jesus saw that they wanted to ask
m about this, so he said to them, 'Are
u asking one another what I meant
en I said, "In a little while you will see
no more, and then after a little while
u will see me"? [20] I tell you the truth,
you will weep and mourn while the world
rejoices. You will grieve, but your grief
will turn to joy. [21] A woman giving birth
to a child has pain because her time has
come; but when her baby is born she
forgets the anguish because of her joy that
a child is born into the world. [22] So with
you: Now is your time of grief, but I will
see you again and you will rejoice, and
no-one will take away your joy. [23] In that
day you will no longer ask me anything. I
tell you the truth, my Father will give you
whatever you ask in my name. [24] Until
now you have not asked for anything in
my name. Ask and you will receive, and
your joy will be complete.

[25] 'Though I have been speaking
figuratively, a time is coming when I will
no longer use this kind of language but
will tell you plainly about my Father. [26] In
that day you will ask in my name. I am
not saying that I will ask the Father on
your behalf. [27] No, the Father himself
loves you because you have loved me and
have believed that I came from God. [28] I
came from the Father and entered the
world; now I am leaving the world and
going back to the Father.'

[29] Then Jesus' disciples said, 'Now
you are speaking clearly and without
figures of speech. [30] Now we can see that
you know all things and that you do not
even need to have anyone ask you
questions. This makes us believe that you
came from God.'

[31] 'You believe at last!' Jesus
answered. [32] 'But a time is coming, and
has come, when you will be scattered,
each to his own home. You will leave me
all alone. Yet I am not alone, for my
Father is with me.

[33] 'I have told you these things, so
that in me you may have peace. In this
world you will have trouble. But take
heart! I have overcome the world.'

DAY 78

JOHN 17. 1 — 26

17 ### Jesus Prays for Himself
After Jesus said this, he looked towards heaven and prayed:

'Father, the time has come. Glorify your Son, that your Son may glorify you. [2] For you granted him authority over all people that he might give eternal life to all those you have given him. [3] Now this is eternal life: that they may know you, the only true God, and Jesus Christ, whom you have sent. [4] I have brought you glory on earth by completing the work you gave me to do. [5] And now, Father, glorify me in your presence with the glory I had with you before the world began.

Jesus Prays for His Disciples

[6] 'I have revealed you to those whom you gave me out of the world. They were yours; you gave them to me and they have obeyed your word. [7] Now they know that everything you have given me comes from you. [8] For I gave them the words you gave me and they accepted them. They knew with certainty that I came from you, and they believed that you sent me. [9] I pray for them. I am not praying for the world, but for those you have given me, for they are yours. [10] All I have is yours, and all you have is mine. And glory has come to me through them. [11] I will remain in the world no longer, but they are still in the world, and I am coming to you. Holy Father, protect them by the power of your name - the name you gave me - so that they ma[y] be one as we are one. [12] While I was with them, I protected them and ke[pt] them safe by that name you gave me. None has been lost except the one doomed to destruction so that Scripture would be fulfilled.

[13] 'I am coming to you now, but [I] say these things while I am still in th[e] world, so that they may have the ful[l] measure of my joy within them. [14] I have given them your word and the world has hated them, for they are n[ot] of the world any more than I am of [the] world. [15] My prayer is not that you t[ake] them out of the world but that you protect them from the evil one. [16] Th[ey] are not of the world, even as I am n[ot] of it. [17] Sanctify them by the truth; your word is truth. [18] As you sent me into the world, I have sent them int[o] the world. [19] For them I sanctify mys[elf] that they too may be truly sanctified[.]

Jesus Prays for All Believers

[20] 'My prayer is not for them alone. [I] pray also for those who will believe [in] me through their message, [21] that all [of] them may be one, Father, just as you are in me and I am in you. May the[y] also be in us so that the world may believe that you have sent me. [22] I h[ave] given them the glory that you gave [me] that they may be one as we are one: in them and you in me. May they b[e] brought to complete unity to let the world know that you sent me and ha[ve] loved them even as you have loved m[e.]

[24] 'Father, I want those you have given me to be with me where I am, and to see my glory, the glory you ha[ve] given me because you loved me befo[re] the creation of the world.

[25] 'Righteous Father, though the world does not know you, I know yo[u]

and they know that you have sent me. [26] I have made you known to them, and will continue to make you known in order that the love you have for me may be in them and that I myself may be in them.'

DAY 79

JOHN 18. 1 — 14

18 ### Jesus Arrested

When he had finished praying, Jesus left with his disciples and crossed the Kidron Valley. On the other side there was an olive grove, and he and his disciples went into it.

[2] Now Judas, who betrayed him, knew the place, because Jesus had often met

'Who is it you want?'

there with his disciples. [3] So Judas came to the grove, guiding a detachment of soldiers and some officials from the chief priests and Pharisees. They were carrying torches, lanterns and weapons.

[4] Jesus, knowing all that was going to happen to him, went out and asked them, 'Who is it you want?'

[5] 'Jesus of Nazareth,' they replied.

'I am he,' Jesus said. (And Judas the traitor was standing there with them.) When Jesus said, 'I am he,' they drew back and fell to the ground.

[7] Again he asked them, 'Who is it you want?'

And they said, 'Jesus of Nazareth.'

[8] 'I told you that I am he,' Jesus answered. 'If you are looking for me, then

let these men go.' [9] This happened so that the words he had spoken would be fulfilled: 'I have not lost one of those you gave me.'

[10] Then Simon Peter, who had a sword, drew it and struck the high priest's servant, cutting off his right ear. (The servant's name was Malchus.)

[11] Jesus commanded Peter, 'Put your sword away! Shall I not drink the cup the Father has given me?'

Jesus Taken to Annas

[12] Then the detachment of soldiers with its commander and the Jewish officials arrested Jesus. They bound him [13] and brought him first to Annas, who was the father-in-law of Caiaphas, the high priest that year. [14] Caiaphas was the one who had advised the Jews that it would be good if one man died for the people.

DAY 80

JOHN 18. 15 — 27

Peter's First Denial

[15] Simon Peter and another disciple were following Jesus. Because this disciple was known to the high priest, he went with Jesus into the high priest's courtyard, [16] but Peter had to wait outside at the door. The other disciple, who was known to the high priest, came back, spoke to the girl on duty there and brought Peter in.

[17] 'You are not one of his disciples, are you?' the girl at the door asked Peter.

He replied, 'I am not.'

[18] It was cold, and the servants and officials stood round a fire they had made to keep warm. Peter also was standing with them, warming himself.

The High Priest Questions Jesus

[19] Meanwhile, the high priest questioned Jesus about his disciples and his teaching.

[20] 'I have spoken openly to the world,' Jesus replied. 'I always taught in synagogues or at the temple, where all the Jews come together. I said nothing in secret. [21] Why question me? Ask those who heard me. Surely they know what I said.'

[22] When Jesus said this, one of the officials near by struck him in the face. 'Is this the way you answer the high priest?' he demanded.

[23] 'If I said something wrong,' Jesus replied, 'testify as to what is wrong. But if I spoke the truth, why did you strike me?' [24] Then Annas sent him, still bound, to Caiaphas the high priest.

Peter's Second and Third Denials

[25] As Simon Peter stood warming himself, he was asked, 'You are not one of his disciples, are you?'

He denied it, saying, 'I am not.'

[26] One of the high priest's servants, a relative of the man whose ear Peter had cut off, challenged him, 'Didn't I see you with him in the olive grove?' [27] Again Peter denied it, and at that moment a cock began to crow.

DAY 81

JOHN 18.28 — 19.16

Jesus Before Pilate

[28] Then the Jews led Jesus from Caiaphas to the palace of the Roman governor. By now it was early morning, and to avoid ceremonial uncleanness the Jews did not enter the palace; they wanted to be able to eat the Passover. [29] So Pilate came out to them and asked, 'What charges are y bringing against this man?'

[30] 'If he were not a criminal,' they replied, 'we would not have handed him over to you.'

[31] Pilate said, 'Take him yourselves and judge him by your own law.'

'But we have no right to execute anyone,' the Jews objected. [32] This happened so that the words Jesus had spoken indicating the kind of death he was going to die would be fulfilled.

[33] Pilate then went back inside the palace, summoned Jesus and asked him, 'Are you the king of the Jews?'

[34] 'Is that your own idea,' Jesus asked 'or did others talk to you about me?'

[35] 'Am I a Jew?' Pilate replied. 'It was your people and your chief priests who handed you over to me. What is it you have done?'

[36] Jesus said, 'My kingdom is not of this world. If it were, my servants would

'My kingdom is not of this world.'

fight to prevent my arrest by the Jews. B now my kingdom is from another place.'

[37] 'You are a king, then!' said Pilate.

Jesus answered, 'You are right in saying I am a king. In fact, for this reaso I was born, and for this I came into the world, to testify to the truth. Everyone c the side of truth listens to me.'

[38] 'What is truth?' Pilate asked. With this he went out again to the Jews and said, 'I find no basis for a charge against him. [39] But it is your custom for me to release to you one prisoner at the time c the Passover. Do you want me to release "the king of the Jews"?'

[40] They shouted back, 'No, not

m! Give us Barabbas!' Now Barabbas
d taken part in a rebellion.

19 Jesus Sentenced to be Crucified

Then Pilate took Jesus and
d him flogged. ² The soldiers twisted
gether a crown of thorns and put it on
s head. They clothed him in a purple
be ³ and went up to him again and
ain, saying, 'Hail, king of the Jews!'
ad they struck him in the face.

⁴ Once more Pilate came out and
d to the Jews, 'Look, I am bringing him
t to you to let you know that I find no
sis for a charge against him.' ⁵ When
us came out wearing the crown of
orns and the purple robe, Pilate said to
em, 'Here is the man!'

⁶ As soon as the chief priests and
eir officials saw him, they shouted,
rucify! Crucify!'

But Pilate answered, 'You take him
d crucify him. As for me, I find no basis
a charge against him.'

⁷ The Jews insisted, 'We have a law,
d according to that law he must die,
cause he claimed to be the Son of
od.'

⁸ When Pilate heard this, he was
en more afraid, ⁹ and he went back
side the palace. 'Where do you come
om?' he asked Jesus, but Jesus gave him
answer. ¹⁰ 'Do you refuse to speak to
?' Pilate said. 'Don't you realise I have
wer either to free you or to crucify you?'

¹¹ Jesus answered, 'You would have
power over me if it were not given to
u from above. Therefore the one who
nded me over to you is guilty of a
ater sin.'

¹² From then on, Pilate tried to set
us free, but the Jews kept shouting, 'If
u let this man go, you are no friend of
esar. Anyone who claims to be a king

The soldiers...twisted together a crown of thorns.

opposes Caesar.'

¹³ When Pilate heard this, he brought
Jesus out and sat down on the judge's seat
at a place known as the Stone Pavement
(which in Aramaic is Gabbatha). ¹⁴ It was
the day of Preparation of Passover Week,
about the sixth hour.

'Here is your king,' Pilate said to the
Jews.

¹⁵ But they shouted, 'Take him
away! Take him away! Crucify him!'

'Shall I crucify your king?' Pilate
asked.

'We have no king but Caesar,' the
chief priests answered.

¹⁶ Finally Pilate handed him over to
them to be crucified.

DAY 82

JOHN 19. 17 — 42

The Crucifixion

So the soldiers took charge of Jesus.
[17] Carrying his own cross, he went out to the place of the Skull (which in Aramaic is called Golgotha). [18] Here they crucified him, and with him two others - one on each side and Jesus in the middle.

[19] Pilate had a notice prepared and fastened to the cross. It read: JESUS OF NAZARETH, THE KING OF THE JEWS. [20] Many of the Jews read this sign, for the place where Jesus was crucified was near the city, and the sign was written in Aramaic, Latin and Greek. [21] The chief priests of the Jews protested to Pilate, 'Do not write "The King of the Jews", but that this man claimed to be king of the Jews.'

[22] Pilate answered, 'What I have written, I have written.'

[23] When the soldiers crucified Jesus, they took his clothes, dividing them into four shares, one for each of them, with the undergarment remaining. This garment was seamless, woven in one piece from top to bottom.

[24] 'Let's not tear it,' they said to one another. 'Let's decide by lot who will get it.'

This happened that the scripture might be fulfilled which said,

'They divided my garments among
  them
and cast lots for my clothing.'

So this is what the soldiers did.

[25] Near the cross of Jesus stood his mother, his mother's sister, Mary the wife of Clopas, and Mary Magdalene. [26] When Jesus saw his mother there, and the disciple whom he loved standing near h he said to his mother, 'Dear woman, he is your son,' [27] and to the disciple, 'Here your mother.' From that time on, this disciple took her into his home.

The Death of Jesus

[28] Later, knowing that all was now completed, and so that the Scripture would be fulfilled, Jesus said, 'I am thirsty.' [29] A jar of wine vinegar was the so they soaked a sponge in it, put the sponge on a stalk of the hyssop plant, a lifted it to Jesus' lips. [30] When he had received the drink, Jesus said, 'It is finished.' With that, he bowed his head and gave up his spirit.

[31] Now it was the day of Preparation and the next day was to be a special Sabbath. Because the Jews did not wan the bodies left on the crosses during the Sabbath, they asked Pilate to have the legs broken and the bodies taken down [32] The soldiers therefore came and brok the legs of the first man who had been crucified with Jesus, and then those of other. [33] But when they came to Jesus ar found that he was already dead, they di not break his legs. [34] Instead, one of the soldiers pierced Jesus' side with a spear, bringing a sudden flow of blood and water. [35] The man who saw it has given testimony, and his testimony is true. He knows that he tells the truth, and he testifies so that you also may believe. [36] These things happened so that the scripture would be fulfilled: 'Not one of his bones will be broken,' [37] and, as another scripture says, 'They will look at the one they have pierced.'

The Burial of Jesus

[38] Later, Joseph of Arimathea asked Pila for the body of Jesus. Now Joseph was a

isciple of Jesus, but secretly because he
ared the Jews. With Pilate's permission,
e came and took the body away. [39] He
as accompanied by Nicodemus, the man
ho earlier had visited Jesus at night.
Iicodemus brought a mixture of myrrh
nd aloes, about seventy-five pounds.
Taking Jesus' body, the two of them
rapped it, with the spices, in strips of
nen. This was in accordance with
wish burial customs. [41] At the place
here Jesus was crucified, there was a
arden, and in the garden a new tomb, in
hich no-one had ever been laid.
Because it was the Jewish day of
reparation and since the tomb was near
y, they laid Jesus there.

DAY 83
JOHN 20. 1 — 18

2 0 ### The Empty Tomb
Early on the first day of the
week, while it was still dark,
lary Magdalene went to the tomb and
w that the stone had been removed
om the entrance. [2] So she came
nning to Simon Peter and the other
sciple, the one Jesus loved, and said,
'hey have taken the Lord out of the
mb, and we don't know where they
ve put him!'
[3] So Peter and the other disciple
arted for the tomb. [4] Both were running,
t the other disciple outran Peter and
ached the tomb first. [5] He bent over and
oked in at the strips of linen lying there
t did not go in. [6] Then Simon Peter,
ho was behind him, arrived and went

into the tomb. He saw the strips of linen
lying there, [7] as well as the burial cloth
that had been around Jesus' head. The
cloth was folded up by itself, separate
from the linen. [8] Finally the other
disciple, who had reached the tomb first,
also went inside. He saw and believed.
[9] (They still did not understand from
Scripture that Jesus had to rise from the
dead.)

Jesus Appears to Mary Magdalene
[10] Then the disciples went back to their
homes, [11] but Mary stood outside the
tomb crying. As she wept, she bent over
to look into the tomb [12] and saw two
angels in white, seated where Jesus' body
had been, one at the head and the other
at the foot.
[13] They asked her, 'Woman, why are
you crying?'
'They have taken my Lord away,'
she said, 'and I don't know where they
have put him.' [14] At this, she turned
round and saw Jesus standing there, but
she did not realise that it was Jesus.
[15] 'Woman,' he said, 'why are you
crying? Who is it you are looking for?'
Thinking he was the gardener, she
said, 'Sir, if you have carried him away,
tell me where you have put him, and I
will get him.'
[16] Jesus said to her, 'Mary.'
She turned towards him and cried out
in Aramaic, 'Rabboni!' (which means
Teacher).
[17] Jesus said, 'Do not hold on to me,
for I have not yet returned to the Father.
Go instead to my brothers and tell them,
"I am returning to my Father and your
Father, to my God and your God." '
[18] Mary Magdalene went to the
disciples with the news: 'I have seen the
Lord!' And she told them that he had
said these things to her.

DAY 84

JOHN 20. 19 — 31

Jesus Appears to His Disciples

[19] On the evening of that first day of the week, when the disciples were together, with the doors locked for fear of the Jews, Jesus came and stood among them and said, 'Peace be with you!' [20] After he said this, he showed them his hands and side.

when Jesus came. [25] So the other discipl told him, 'We have seen the Lord!'

But he said to them, 'Unless I see the nail marks in his hands and put my finger where the nails were, and put my hand into his side, I will not believe it.'

[26] A week later his disciples were in the house again, and Thomas was with them. Though the doors were locked, Jesus came and stood among them and said, 'Peace be with you!' [27] Then he sai to Thomas, 'Put your finger here; see m hands. Reach out your hand and put it into my side. Stop doubting and believe

'Peace be with you!'

The disciples were overjoyed when they saw the Lord.

[21] Again Jesus said, 'Peace be with you! As the Father has sent me, I am sending you.' [22] And with that he breathed on them and said, 'Receive the Holy Spirit. [23] If you forgive anyone his sins, they are forgiven; if you do not forgive them, they are not forgiven.'

Jesus Appears to Thomas

[24] Now Thomas (called Didymus), one of the Twelve, was not with the disciples

[28] Thomas said to him, 'My Lord and my God!'

[29] Then Jesus told him, 'Because you have seen me, you have believed; blesse are those who have not seen and yet ha believed.'

[30] Jesus did many other miraculous signs in the presence of his disciples, which are not recorded in this book.
[31] But these are written that you may believe that Jesus is the Christ, the Son God, and that by believing you may hav life in his name.

DAY 85

JOHN 21. 1 — 25

21 **Jesus and the Miraculous Catch of Fish**
Afterwards Jesus appeared
ain to his disciples, by the Sea of
berias. It happened this way: [2] Simon
·ter, Thomas (called Didymus),
athanael from Cana in Galilee, the sons
Zebedee, and two other disciples were
gether. [3] 'I'm going out to fish,' Simon
·ter told them, and they said, 'We'll go
th you.' So they went out and got into
·e boat, but that night they caught
thing.

[4] Early in the morning, Jesus stood
· the shore, but the disciples did not
alise that it was Jesus.

[5] He called out to them, 'Friends,
·ven't you any fish?'

'No,' they answered.

[6] He said, 'Throw your net on the
·ht side of the boat and you will find
·me.' When they did, they were unable
· haul the net in because of the large
·mber of fish.

[7] Then the disciple whom Jesus loved
·id to Peter, 'It is the Lord!' As soon as
·mon Peter heard him say, 'It is the
·rd,' he wrapped his outer garment
·und him (for he had taken it off) and
·mped into the water. [8] The other
·sciples followed in the boat, towing the
·t full of fish, for they were not far from
·ore, about a hundred yards. [9] When
·ey landed, they saw a fire of burning
·als there with fish on it, and some
·ead.

[10] Jesus said to them, 'Bring some of
·e fish you have just caught.'

[11] Simon Peter climbed aboard and dragged the net ashore. It was full of large fish, 153, but even with so many the net was not torn. [12] Jesus said to them, 'Come and have breakfast.' None of the disciples dared ask him, 'Who are you?' They knew it was the Lord. [13] Jesus came, took the bread and gave it to them, and did the same with the fish. [14] This was now the third time Jesus appeared to his disciples after he was raised from the dead.

Jesus Reinstates Peter

[15] When they had finished eating, Jesus said to Simon Peter, 'Simon son of John, do you truly love me more than these?'

'Yes, Lord,' he said, 'you know that I love you.'

Jesus said, 'Feed my lambs.'

[16] Again Jesus said, 'Simon son of

> **'Simon son of John, do you truly love me more than these?'**

do you truly love me?'

He answered, 'Yes, Lord, you know that I love you.'

Jesus said, 'Take care of my sheep.'

[17] The third time he said to him, 'Simon son of John, do you love me?'

Peter was hurt because Jesus asked him the third time, 'Do you love me?' He said, 'Lord, you know all things; you know that I love you.'

Jesus said, 'Feed my sheep. [18] I tell you the truth, when you were younger you dressed yourself and went where you wanted; but when you are old you will stretch out your hands, and someone else will dress you and lead you where you do not want to go.' ¹⁹ Jesus said this to indicate the kind of death by which Peter would glorify God. Then he said to him, 'Follow me!'

²⁰ Peter turned and saw that the disciple whom Jesus loved was following them. (This was the one who had leaned back against Jesus at the supper and had said, 'Lord, who is going to betray you?') ²¹ When Peter saw him, he asked, 'Lord, what about him?'

²² Jesus answered, 'If I want him to remain alive until I return, what is that to you? You must follow me.' ²³ Because of this, the rumour spread among the brothers that this disciple would not die. But Jesus did not say that he would not die; he only said, 'If I want him to remain alive until I return, what is that to you?'

²⁴ This is the disciple who testifies these things and who wrote them down. We know that his testimony is true.

²⁵ Jesus did many other things as well. If every one of them were written down, I suppose that even the whole world would not have room for the books that would be written.

Jesus said, 'Follow

DAY 86

JUDE 1 — 25

de, a servant of Jesus Christ and a
other of James,

To those who have been called, who
e loved by God the Father and kept by
sus Christ:

² Mercy, peace and love be yours in
undance.

he Sin and Doom of Godless
en

Dear friends, although I was very eager to
rite to you about the salvation we share,
elt I had to write and urge you to
ntend for the faith that was once for all
trusted to the saints. ⁴ For certain men
ose condemnation was written about
ng ago have secretly slipped in among
u. They are godless men, who change
e grace of our God into a licence for
morality and deny Jesus Christ our only
vereign and Lord.

⁵ Though you already know all this, I
nt to remind you that the Lord
livered his people out of Egypt, but later
stroyed those who did not believe.
And the angels who did not keep their
sitions of authority but abandoned their
n home - these he has kept in darkness,
und with everlasting chains for
dgment on the great Day. ⁷ In a similar
y, Sodom and Gomorrah and the
rrounding towns gave themselves up to
xual immorality and perversion. They
rve as an example of those who suffer
e punishment of eternal fire.

⁸ In the very same way, these
dreamers pollute their own bodies, reject
authority and slander celestial beings.
⁹ But even the archangel Michael, when
he was disputing with the devil about the
body of Moses, did not dare to bring a
slanderous accusation against him, but
said, 'The Lord rebuke you!' ¹⁰ Yet these
men speak abusively against whatever they
do not understand; and what things they
do understand by instinct, like
unreasoning animals - these are the very
things that destroy them.

¹¹ Woe to them! They have taken
the way of Cain; they have rushed for
profit into Balaam's error; they have been
destroyed in Korah's rebellion.

¹² These men are blemishes at your
love feasts, eating with you without the
slightest qualm - shepherds who feed only
themselves. They are clouds without rain,
blown along by the wind; autumn trees,
without fruit and uprooted - twice dead.
¹³ They are wild waves of the sea, foaming
up their shame; wandering stars, for whom
blackest darkness has been reserved for
ever.

¹⁴ Enoch, the seventh from Adam,
prophesied about these men: 'See, the
Lord is coming with thousands upon
thousands of his holy ones ¹⁵ to judge
everyone, and to convict all the ungodly
of all the ungodly acts they have done in
the ungodly way, and of all the harsh
words ungodly sinners have spoken against
him.' ¹⁶ These men are grumblers and
fault-finders; they follow their own evil
desires; they boast about themselves and
flatter others for their own advantage.

A Call to Persevere

¹⁷ But, dear friends, remember what the
apostles of our Lord Jesus Christ foretold.
¹⁸ They said to you, 'In the last times there
will be scoffers who will follow their own
ungodly desires.' ¹⁹ These are the men who

divide you, who follow mere natural instincts and do not have the Spirit.

[20] But you, dear friends, build yourselves up in your most holy faith and pray in the Holy Spirit. [21] Keep yourselves in God's love as you wait for the mercy of our Lord Jesus Christ to bring you to eternal life.

[22] Be merciful to those who doubt; [23] snatch others from the fire and save them; to others show mercy, mixed with fear - hating even the clothing stained by corrupted flesh.

Doxology

[24] To him who is able to keep you from falling and to present you before his glorious presence without fault and with great joy - [25] to the only God our Saviour be glory, majesty, power and authority, through Jesus Christ our Lord, before all ages, now and for evermore! Amen.

Mercy, peace and love be yours in abundan

DAY 87

1 JOHN 1. 1 — 2.6

1 **The Word of Life**
That which was from the beginning, which we have heard, which we have seen with our eyes, which we have looked at and our hands have touched - this we proclaim concerning the Word of life. [2] The life appeared; we have seen it and testify to it, and we proclaim to you the eternal life, which was with the Father and has appeared to us. [3] We proclaim to you what we have seen and heard, so that you also may have

---

And our fellowship is with the Father and with his Son, Jesus Christ.

---

fellowship with us. And our fellowship is with the Father and with his Son, Jesus Christ. [4] We write this to make our joy complete.

Walking in the Light
This is the message we have heard from him and declare to you: God is light; in him there is no darkness at all. [6] If we claim to have fellowship with him yet walk in the darkness, we lie and do not live by the truth. [7] But if we walk in the light, as he is in the light, we have fellowship with one another, and the blood of Jesus, his Son, purifies us from all sin. [8] If we claim to be without sin, we deceive ourselves and the truth is not in us. [9] If we confess our sins, he is faithful and just and will forgive us our sins and purify us from all

unrighteousness. [10] If we claim we have not sinned, we make him out to be a liar and his word has no place in our lives.

2 My dear children, I write this to you so that you will not sin. But if anybody does sin, we have one who speaks to the Father in our defence - Jesus Christ, the Righteous One. [2] He is the atoning sacrifice for our sins, and not only for ours but also for the sins of the whole world.

[3] We know that we have come to know him if we obey his commands. [4] The man who says, 'I know him,' but does not do what he commands is a liar, and the truth is not in him. [5] But if anyone obeys his word, God's love is truly made complete in him. This is how we know we are in him: [6] Whoever claims to live in him must walk as Jesus did.

God is light; in him there is no darkness at all.

DAY 88

1 JOHN 2. 7 — 27

[7] Dear friends, I am not writing you a new command but an old one, which you have had since the beginning. This old command is the message you have heard. [8] Yet I am writing you a new command; its truth is seen in him and you, because the darkness is passing and the true light is already shining.
[9] Anyone who claims to be in the light but hates his brother is still in the darkness. [10] Whoever loves his brother lives in the light, and there is nothing in him to make him stumble. [11] But whoever hates his brother is in the darkness and walks around in the darkness; he does not know where he is going, because the darkness has blinded him.

[12] I write to you, dear children,
because your sins have been forgiven
on account of his name.
[13] I write to you, fathers,
because you have known him who is
from the beginning.
I write to you, young men,
because you have overcome the evil
one.
I write to you, dear children,
because you have known the Father.
[14] I write to you, fathers,
because you have known him who is
from the beginning.
I write to you, young men,
because you are strong,
and the word of God lives in you,
and you have overcome the evil one.

Do Not Love the World

[15] Do not love the world or anything in the world. If anyone loves the world, the love of the Father is not in him. [16] For everything in the world - the cravings of sinful man, the lust of his eyes and the boasting of what he has and does - comes not from the Father but from the world. [17] The world and its desires pass away, but the man who does the will of God lives for ever.

Warning Against Antichrists

[18] Dear children, this is the last hour; and as you have heard that the antichrist is coming, even now many antichrists have come. This is how we know it is the last hour. [19] They went out from us, but they did not really belong to us. For if they had belonged to us, they would have remained with us; but their going showed that none of them belonged to us.
[20] But you have an anointing from the Holy One, and all of you know the truth. [21] I do not write to you because you do not know the truth, but because you do know it and because no lie comes from the truth. [22] Who is the liar? It is the man who denies that Jesus is the Christ. Such a man is the antichrist - he denies the Father and the Son. [23] No-one who denies the Son has the Father; whoever acknowledges the Son has the Father also.
[24] See that what you have heard from the beginning remains in you. If it does, you also will remain in the Son and in the Father. [25] And this is what he promised us - even eternal life.[26] I am writing these things to you about those who are trying to lead you astray.
[27] As for you, the anointing you received from him remains in you, and you do not need anyone to teach you. But as his anointing teaches you about all things and as that anointing is real, not counterfeit - just as it has taught you, remain in him.

DAY 89

1 JOHN 2. 28 — 3. 24

Children of God

28 And now, dear children, continue in him, so that when he appears we may be confident and unashamed before him at his coming. 29 If you know that he is righteous, you know that everyone who does what is right has been born of him.

3 How great is the love the Father has lavished on us, that we should be called children of God! And that is what we are! The reason the world does not know us is that it did not know him. 2 Dear friends, now we are children of God, and what we will be has not yet been made known. But we know that when he appears, we shall be like him, for we shall see him as he is. 3 Everyone who has this hope in him purifies himself, just as he is pure.

4 Everyone who sins breaks the law; in fact, sin is lawlessness. 5 But you know that he appeared so that he might take away our sins. And in him is no sin. 6 No-one who lives in him keeps on sinning. No-one who continues to sin has either seen him or known him.

7 Dear children, do not let anyone lead you astray. He who does what is right is righteous, just as he is righteous. 8 He who does what is sinful is of the devil, because the devil has been sinning from the beginning. The reason the Son of God appeared was to destroy the devil's work. 9 No-one who is born of God will continue to sin, because God's seed remains in him; he cannot go on sinning, because he has been born of God. 10 This

is how we know who the children of God are and who the children of the devil are: Anyone who does not do what is right is not a child of God; nor is anyone who does not love his brother.

Love One Another

11 This is the message you heard from the beginning: We should love one another. 12 Do not be like Cain, who belonged to the evil one and murdered his brother. And why did he murder him? Because his own actions were evil and his brother's were righteous. 13 Do not be surprised, my brothers, if the world hates you. 14 We know that we have passed from death to life, because we love our brothers. Anyone who does not love remains in death. 15 Anyone who hates his brother is a murderer, and you know that no murderer has eternal life in him.

16 This is how we know what love is: Jesus Christ laid down his life for us. And we ought to lay down our lives for our brothers. 17 If anyone has material possessions and sees his brother in need but has no pity on him, how can the love of God be in him? 18 Dear children, let us not love with words or tongue but with actions and in truth. 19 This then is how we know that we belong to the truth, and how we set our hearts at rest in his presence 20 whenever our hearts condemn us. For God is greater than our hearts, and he knows everything.

21 Dear friends, if our hearts do not condemn us, we have confidence before God 22 and receive from him anything we ask, because we obey his commands and do what pleases him. 23 And this is his command: to believe in the name of his Son, Jesus Christ, and to love one another as he commanded us. 24 Those who obey his commands live in him, and he in them. And this is how we know that he lives in us: We know it by the Spirit he gave us.

DAY 90
1 JOHN 4. 1 — 21

4 Test the Spirits

Dear friends, do not believe every spirit, but test the spirits to see whether they are from God, because many false prophets have gone out into the world. [2] This is how you can recognise the Spirit of God: Every spirit that acknowledges that Jesus Christ has come in the flesh is from God, [3] but every spirit that does not acknowledge Jesus is not from God. This is the spirit of the antichrist, which you have heard is coming and even now is already in the world.

[4] You, dear children, are from God and have overcome them, because the one who is in you is greater than the one who is in the world. [5] They are from the world and therefore speak from the viewpoint of the world, and the world

We are from God, and whoever knows God listens to us.

listens to them. [6] We are from God, and whoever knows God listens to us; but whoever is not from God does not listen to us. This is how we recognise the Spirit of truth and the spirit of falsehood.

God's Love and Ours

[7] Dear friends, let us love one another, for love comes from God. Everyone who loves has been born of God and knows God. [8] Whoever does not love does not know God, because God is love. [9] This is how God showed his love among us: He sent his one and only Son into the world that we might live through him. [10] This is love: not that we loved God, but that he loved us and sent his Son as an atoning sacrifice for our sins. [11] Dear friends, since God so loved us, we also ought to love one another. [12] No-one has ever seen God; but if we love one another, God lives in us and his love is made complete in us.

[13] We know that we live in him and he in us, because he has given us of his

Whoever loves God must also love his brother.

Spirit. [14] And we have seen and testify that the Father has sent his Son to be the Saviour of the world. [15] If anyone acknowledges that Jesus is the Son of God, God lives in him and he in God. [16] And so we know and rely on the love God has for us.

God is love. Whoever lives in love lives in God, and God in him. [17] In this way, love is made complete among us so that we will have confidence on the day of judgment, because in this world we are like him. [18] There is no fear in love. But perfect love drives out fear, because fear has to do with punishment. The one who fears is not made perfect in love.

[19] We love because he first loved us. [20] If anyone says, 'I love God,' yet hates his brother, he is a liar. For anyone who does not love his brother, whom he has seen, cannot love God, whom he has not seen. [21] And he has given us this command: Whoever loves God must also love his brother.

Whoever loves God must also love his brother.

DAY 91

1 JOHN 5. 1 — 21

5 Faith in the Son of God

Everyone who believes that Jesus is the Christ is born of God, and everyone who loves the father loves his child as well. [2] This is how we know that we love the children of God: by loving God and carrying out his commands. [3] This is love for God: to obey his commands. And his commands are not

> **This is how we know that we love the children of God: by loving God and carrying out his commands.**

burdensome, [4] for everyone born of God overcomes the world. This is the victory that has overcome the world, even our faith. [5] Who is it that overcomes the world? Only he who believes that Jesus is the Son of God.

[6] This is the one who came by water and blood - Jesus Christ. He did not come by water only, but by water and blood. And it is the Spirit who testifies, because the Spirit is the truth. [7] For there are three that testify: [8] the Spirit, the water and the blood; and the three are in agreement. [9] We accept man's testimony, but God's testimony is greater because it is the testimony of God, which he has given about his Son. [10] Anyone who believes in the Son of God has this testimony in his heart. Anyone who does

not believe God has made him out to be a liar, because he has not believed the testimony God has given about his Son. [11] And this is the testimony: God has given us eternal life, and this life is in his Son. [12] He who has the Son has life; he who does not have the Son of God does not have life.

Concluding Remarks

[13] I write these things to you who believe in the name of the Son of God so that you may know that you have eternal life. [14] This is the confidence we have in approaching God: that if we ask anything according to his will, he hears us. [15] And if we know that he hears us - whatever we ask - we know that we have what we asked of him.

[16] If anyone sees his brother commit a sin that does not lead to death, he should pray and God will give him life. I refer to those whose sin does not lead to death. There is a sin that leads to death. I am not saying that he should pray about that. [17] All wrongdoing is sin, and there is sin that does not lead to death.

[18] We know that anyone born of God does not continue to sin; the one who was born of God keeps him safe, and the evil one cannot harm him. [19] We know that we are children of God, and that the whole world is under the control of the evil one. [20] We know also that the Son of God has come and has given us understanding, so that we may know him who is true. And we are in him who is true - even in his Son Jesus Christ. He is the true God and eternal life.

[21] Dear children, keep yourselves from idols.

DAY 92

2 JOHN 1 — 13

The elder,

To the chosen lady and her children, whom I love in the truth - and not I only, but also all who know the truth - ² because of the truth, which lives in us and will be with us for ever:

walk in obedience to his commands. As you have heard from the beginning, his command is that you walk in love.

⁷ Many deceivers, who do not acknowledge Jesus Christ as coming in the flesh, have gone out into the world. Any such person is the deceiver and the antichrist. ⁸ Watch out that you do not lose what you have worked for, but that you may be rewarded fully. ⁹ Anyone who runs ahead and does not continue in the teaching of Christ does not have God; whoever continues in the teaching has

Walk in obedience to his commands.

³ Grace, mercy and peace from God the Father and from Jesus Christ, the Father's Son, will be with us in truth and love.

⁴ It has given me great joy to find some of your children walking in the truth, just as the Father commanded us. ⁵ And now, dear lady, I am not writing you a new command but one we have had from the beginning. I ask that we love one another. ⁶ And this is love: that we

both the Father and the Son. ¹⁰ If anyone comes to you and does not bring this teaching, do not take him into your house or welcome him. ¹¹ Anyone who welcomes him shares in his wicked work. ¹² I have much to write to you, but I do not want to use paper and ink. Instead, I hope to visit you and talk with you face to face, so that our joy may be complete.

¹³ The children of your chosen sister send their greetings.

DAY 93

3 JOHN 1 — 15

The elder,

To my dear friend Gaius, whom I love in the truth.

² Dear friend, I pray that you may enjoy good health and that all may go well with you, even as your soul is getting along well. ³ It gave me great joy to have some brothers come and tell about your faithfulness to the truth and how you continue to walk in the truth. ⁴ I have no greater joy than to hear that my children are walking in the truth.

⁵ Dear friend, you are faithful in what you are doing for the brothers, even though they are strangers to you. ⁶ They have told the church about your love. You will do well to send them on their way in a manner worthy of God. ⁷ It was for the sake of the Name that they went

They have told the church about your love.

out, receiving no help from the pagans. ⁹ We ought therefore to show hospitality to such men so that we may work together for the truth.

⁹ I wrote to the church, but Diotrephes, who loves to be first, will have nothing to do with us. ¹⁰ So if I come, I will call attention to what he is doing, gossiping maliciously about us. Not satisfied with that, he refuses to welcome the brothers. He also stops those who

want to do so and puts them out of the church.

¹¹ Dear friend, do not imitate what is evil but what is good. Anyone who does what is good is from God. Anyone who does what is evil has not seen God.
¹² Demetrius is well spoken of by everyone - and even by the truth itself. We also speak well of him, and you know that our testimony is true.

¹³ I have much to write to you, but I do not want to do so with pen and ink.
¹⁴ I hope to see you soon, and we will talk face to face.

¹⁵ Peace to you. The friends here send their greetings. Greet the friends there by name.

My children are walking in the truth

DAY 94

HEB. 1. 1 — 14

1 The Son Superior to Angels

In the past God spoke to our forefathers through the prophets at many times and in various ways, ² but in these last days he has spoken to us by his son, whom he appointed heir of all things, and through whom he made the universe. ³ The Son is the radiance of God's glory and the exact representation of his being, sustaining all things by his powerful word. After he had provided purification for sins, he sat down at the right hand of the Majesty in heaven. ⁴ So

> **'In the beginning, O Lord, you laid the foundations of the earth, and the heavens are the work of your hands.'**

he became as much superior to the angels as the name he has inherited is superior to theirs.
⁵ For to which of the angels did God ever say,

'You are my Son;
today I have become your Father'?

Or again,

'I will be his Father,
and he will be my Son'?

And again, when God brings his firstborn into the world, he says,

'Let all God's angels worship him.'

⁷ In speaking of the angels he says,

'He makes his angels winds,
his servants flames of fire.'

⁸ But about the Son he says,

'Your throne, O God, will last for
ever and ever,
and righteousness will be the
sceptre of your kingdom.
⁹ You have loved righteousness and
hated wickedness;
therefore God, your God, has set
you above your companions
by anointing you with the oil of joy.'

¹⁰ He also says,

'In the beginning, O Lord, you laid
the foundations of the earth,
and the heavens are the work of
your hands.
¹¹ They will perish, but you remain;
they will all wear out like a
garment.
¹² You will roll them up like a robe;
like a garment they will be changed.
But you remain the same,
and your years will never end.'

¹³ To which of the angels did God ever
say,

'Sit at my right hand
until I make your enemies
a footstool for your feet'?

¹⁴ Are not all angels ministering spirits
sent to serve those who will inherit
salvation?

DAY 95

HEB. 2. 1 — 18

2 **Warning to Pay Attention**
We must pay more careful attention, therefore, to what we have heard, so that we do not drift away. ² For if the message spoken by angels was binding, and every violation and disobedience received its just punishment, ³ how shall we escape if we ignore such a great salvation? This salvation, which was first announced by the Lord, was confirmed to us by those who heard him. ⁴ God also testified to it by signs, wonders and various miracles, and gifts of the Holy Spirit distributed according to his will.

Jesus Made Like His Brothers

⁵ It is not to angels that he has subjected the world to come, about which we are speaking. ⁶ But there is a place where someone has testified:

> 'What is man that you are mindful of him,
>> the son of man that you care for him?
> ⁷ You made him a little lower than the angels;
>> you crowned him with glory and honour
> ⁸ and put everything under his feet.'

In putting everything under him, God left nothing that is not subject to him. Yet at present we do not see everything subject to him. ⁹ But we see Jesus, who was made à little lower than the angels, now crowned with glory and honour because he suffered death, so that by the grace of God he might taste death for everyone. ¹⁰ In bringing many sons to glory, it was fitting that God, for whom and through whom everything exists, should make the author of their salvation perfect through suffering. ¹¹ Both the one who makes men holy and those who are made holy are of the same family. So Jesus is not ashamed to call them brothers. ¹² He says,

> 'I will declare your name to my brothers;
>> in the presence of the congregation I will sing your praises.'

¹³ And again,

> 'I will put my trust in him.'

And again he says,

> 'Here am I, and the children God has given me.'

¹⁴ Since the children have flesh and blood, he too shared in their humanity so that by his death he might destroy him who holds the power of death - that is, the devil - ¹⁵ and free those who all their lives were held in slavery by their fear of death. ¹⁶ For surely it is not angels he helps, but Abraham's descendants. ¹⁷ For this reason he had to be made like his brothers in every way, in order that he might become a merciful and faithful high priest in service to God, and that he might make atonement for the sins of the people. ¹⁸ Because he himself suffered when he was tempted, he is able to help those who are being tempted.

DAY 96

HEB. 3. 1 — 19

3 **Jesus Greater Than Moses**
Therefore, holy brothers, who
share in the heavenly calling, fix
our thoughts on Jesus, the apostle and
high priest whom we confess. ² He was
faithful to the one who appointed him,
just as Moses was faithful in all God's
house. ³ Jesus has been found worthy of
greater honour than Moses, just as the
builder of a house has greater honour
than the house itself. ⁴ For every house is
built by someone, but God is the builder
of everything. ⁵ Moses was faithful as a
servant in all God's house, testifying to
what would be said in the future. ⁶ But
Christ is faithful as a son over God's
house. And we are his house, if we hold
on to our courage and the hope of which
we boast.

Warning Against Unbelief

So, as the Holy Spirit says:

'Today, if you hear his voice,
⁸ do not harden your hearts as you
did in the rebellion, during the
time of testing in the desert,
⁹ where your fathers tested and tried
me and for forty years saw
what I did.
¹⁰ That is why I was angry with that
generation,
and I said, "Their hearts are always
going astray,
and they have not known my ways."
¹¹ So I declared on oath in my anger,
"They shall never enter my rest." '

¹² See to it, brothers, that none of you
has a sinful, unbelieving heart that turns
away from the living God. ¹³ But
encourage one another daily, as long as it
is called Today, so that none of you may
be hardened by sin's deceitfulness. ¹⁴ We
have come to share in Christ if we hold
firmly till the end the confidence we had
at first. ¹⁵ As has just been said:

'Today, if you hear his voice,
do not harden your hearts
as you did in the rebellion.'

¹⁶ Who were they who heard and
rebelled? Were they not all those Moses
led out of Egypt? ¹⁷ And with whom was
he angry for forty years? Was it not with
those who sinned, whose bodies fell in
the desert? ¹⁸ And to whom did God
swear that they would never enter his rest
if not to those who disobeyed? ¹⁹ So we
see that they were not able to enter,
because of their unbelief.

God is the builder of everything.

DAY 97
HEB. 4. 1 — 16

4 **A Sabbath-rest for the People of God**
Therefore, since the promise of entering his rest still stands, let us be careful that none of you be found to have fallen short of it. [2] For we also have had the gospel preached to us, just as they did; but the message they heard was of no value to them, because those who heard did not combine it with faith. [3] Now we who have believed enter that rest, just as God has said,

'So I declared on oath in my anger,
"They shall never enter my rest."'

And yet his work has been finished since the creation of the world. [4] For somewhere he has spoken about the seventh day in these words: 'And on the seventh day God rested from all his work.' [5] And again in the passage above he says, 'They shall never enter my rest.'

[6] It still remains that some will enter that rest, and those who formerly had the gospel preached to them did not go in, because of their disobedience. [7] Therefore God again set a certain day, calling it Today, when a long time later he spoke through David, as was said before:

'Today, if you hear his voice,
do not harden your hearts.'

[8] For if Joshua had given them rest, God would not have spoken later about another day. [9] There remains, then, a Sabbath-rest for the people of God; [10] for anyone who enters God's rest also rests from his own work, just as God did from his. [11] Let us, therefore, make every effort to enter that rest, so that no-one will fall by following their example of disobedience.

[12] For the word of God is living and active. Sharper than any double-edged sword, it penetrates even to dividing soul and spirit, joints and marrow; it judges the thoughts and attitudes of the heart. [13] Nothing in all creation is hidden from God's sight. Everything is uncovered and laid bare before the eyes of him to whom we must give account.

Jesus the Great High Priest
[14] Therefore, since we have a great high priest who has gone through the heavens, Jesus the Son of God, let us hold firmly to the faith we profess. [15] For we do not have a high priest who is unable to sympathise with our weaknesses, but we have one who has been tempted in every way, just as we are - yet was without sin. [16] Let us then approach the throne of grace with confidence, so that we may receive mercy and find grace to help us in our time of need.

DAY 98
HEB. 5. 1 — 6.20

5 Every high priest is selected from among men and is appointed to represent them in matters related to God, to offer gifts and sacrifices for sins. [2] He is able to deal gently with those who are ignorant and are going astray, since he himself is subject to weakness. [3] This is why he has to offer sacrifices for

We have this hope as an anchor.

is own sins, as well as for the sins of the eople.

⁴No-one takes this honour upon imself; he must be called by God, just as Aaron was. ⁵ So Christ also did not take pon himself the glory of becoming a igh priest. But God said to him,

'You are my Son;
today I have become your Father.'

And he says in another place,

'You are a priest for ever,
in the order of Melchizedek.'

⁷ During the days of Jesus' life on earth, he offered up prayers and petitions with loud cries and tears to the one who could save him from death, and he was heard because of his reverent submission. ⁸ Although he was a son, he learned obedience from what he suffered ⁹ and, once made perfect, he became the source of eternal salvation for all who obey him ¹⁰ and was designated by God to be high priest in the order of Melchizedek.

Warning Against Falling Away

[11] We have much to say about this, but it is hard to explain because you are slow to learn. [12] In fact, though by this time you ought to be teachers, you need someone to teach you the elementary truths of God's word all over again. You need milk, not solid food! [13] Anyone who lives on milk, being still an infant, is not acquainted with the teaching about righteousness. [14] But solid food is for the mature, who by constant use have trained themselves to distinguish good from evil.

6 Therefore let us leave the elementary teachings about Christ and go on to maturity, not laying again the foundation of repentance from acts that lead to death, and of faith in God, [2] instruction about baptisms, the laying on of hands, the resurrection of the dead, and eternal judgment. [3] And God permitting, we will do so.

[4] It is impossible for those who have once been enlightened, who have tasted the heavenly gift, who have shared in the Holy Spirit, [5] who have tasted the goodness of the word of God and the powers of the coming age, [6] if they fall away, to be brought back to repentance, because to their loss they are crucifying the Son of God all over again and subjecting him to public disgrace.

[7] Land that drinks in the rain often falling on it and that produces a crop useful to those for whom it is farmed receives the blessing of God. [8] But land that produces thorns and thistles is worthless and is in danger of being cursed. In the end it will be burned.

[9] Even though we speak like this, dear friends, we are confident of better things in your case - things that accompany salvation. [10] God is not unjust; he will not forget your work and the love you have shown him as you have helped his people and continue to help them. [11] We want each of you to show this same diligence the very end, in order to make your hope sure. [12] We do not want you to become lazy, but to imitate those who through faith and patience inherit what has been promised.

The Certainty of God's Promise

[13] When God made his promise to Abraham, since there was no-one greater for him to swear by, he swore by himself [14] saying, 'I will surely bless you and give you many descendants.' [15] And so after waiting patiently, Abraham received what was promised.

[16] Men swear by someone greater than themselves, and the oath confirms what said and puts an end to all argument. [17] Because God wanted to make the unchanging nature of his purpose very clear to the heirs of what was promised, he confirmed it with an oath. [18] God did this so that, by two unchangeable things in which it is impossible for God to lie, we who have fled to take hold of the hope offered to us may be greatly

'You are my Son; today I have become your Father.'

encouraged. [19] We have this hope as an anchor for the soul, firm and secure. It enters the inner sanctuary behind the curtain, [20] where Jesus, who went before us, has entered on our behalf. He has become a high priest for ever, in the order of Melchizedek.

DAY 99

HEB. 7. 1 — 28

7 **Melchizedek the Priest**
This Melchizedek was king of
Salem and priest of God Most
High. He met Abraham returning from
the defeat of the kings and blessed him,
and Abraham gave him a tenth of
everything. First, his name means 'king of
righteousness' ; then also, 'king of Salem'
means ' king of peace.' ³ Without father
or mother, without genealogy, without
beginning of days or end of life, like the
Son of God he remains a priest for ever.

⁴ Just think how great he was: Even
the patriarch Abraham gave him a tenth
of the plunder! ⁵ Now the law requires
the descendants of Levi who become
priests to collect a tenth from the people
that is, their brothers - even though
their brothers are descended from
Abraham. ⁶ This man, however, did not
trace his descent from Levi, yet he
collected a tenth from Abraham and
blessed him who had the promises.
And without doubt the lesser person is
blessed by the greater. ⁸ In the one case,
the tenth is collected by men who die;
but in the other case, by him who is
declared to be living. ⁹ One might even
say that Levi, who collects the tenth,
paid the tenth through Abraham,
¹⁰ because when Melchizedek met
Abraham, Levi was still in the body of
his ancestor.

Jesus Like Melchizedek
¹¹ If perfection could have been attained
through the Levitical priesthood (for on

the basis of it the law was given to the
people), why was there still need for
another priest to come - one in the order
of Melchizedek, not in the order of
Aaron? ¹² For when there is a change of
the priesthood, there must also be a
change of the law. ¹³ He of whom these
things are said belonged to a different
tribe, and no-one from that tribe has
ever served at the altar. ¹⁴ For it is clear
that our Lord descended from Judah, and
in regard to that tribe Moses said
nothing about priests. ¹⁵ And what we
have said is even more clear if another
priest like Melchizedek appears, ¹⁶ one
who has become a priest not on the basis
of a regulation as to his ancestry but on
the basis of the power of an
indestructible life. ¹⁷ For it is declared:

'You are a priest for ever,
in the order of Melchizedek.'

¹⁸ The former regulation is set aside
because it was weak and useless ¹⁹ (for the
law made nothing perfect), and a better
hope is introduced, by which we draw
near to God.
²⁰ And it was not without an oath!
Others became priests without any oath,
²¹ but he became a priest with an oath
when God said to him:

'The Lord has sworn
and will not change his mind:
"You are a priest for ever." '

²² Because of this oath, Jesus has become
the guarantee of a better covenant.
²³ Now there have been many of
those priests, since death prevented them
from continuing in office; ²⁴ but because
Jesus lives for ever, he has a permanent
priesthood. ²⁵ Therefore he is able to save
completely those who come to God

through him, because he always lives to intercede for them.

²⁶ Such a high priest meets our need - one who is holy, blameless, pure, set apart from sinners, exalted above the heavens. ²⁷ Unlike the other high priests, he does not need to offer sacrifices day after day, first for his own sins, and then for the sins of the people. He sacrificed for their sins once for all when he offered himself. ²⁸ For the law appoints as high priests men who are weak; but the oath, which came after the law, appointed the Son, who has been made perfect for ever.

DAY 100

HEB. 8. 1 — 13

8 **The High Priest of a New Covenant**
The point of what we are saying is this: We do have such a high priest, who sat down at the right hand of the throne of the Majesty in heaven, ² and who serves in the sanctuary, the true tabernacle set up by the Lord, not by man.

³ Every high priest is appointed to offer both gifts and sacrifices, and so it was necessary for this one also to have something to offer. ⁴ If he were on earth, he would not be a priest, for there are already men who offer the gifts prescribed by the law. ⁵ They serve at a sanctuary that is a copy and shadow of what is in heaven. This is why Moses was warned when he was about to build the tabernacle: 'See to it that you make everything according to the pattern shown you on the mountain.' ⁶ But the ministry Jesus has received is as superior

to theirs as the covenant of which he is mediator is superior to the old one, and is founded on better promises.

⁷ For if there had been nothing wrong with that first covenant, no place would have been sought for another. ⁸ But God found fault with the people and said:

'The time is coming, declares the Lord,
  when I will make a new covenant
with the house of Israel
  and with the house of Judah.
⁹ It will not be like the covenant
  I made with their forefathers
when I took them by the hand
  to lead them out of Egypt,
because they did not remain faithful
  to my covenant,
and I turned away from them,
          declares the Lord.
¹⁰ This is the covenant I will make
  with the house of Israel
after that time, declares the Lord.
I will put my laws in their minds
  and write them on their hearts.
I will be their God,
  and they will be my people.
¹¹ No longer will a man teach his
  neighbour,
  or a man his brother, saying,
  "Know the Lord,"
because they will all know me,
  from the least of them to the
  greatest.
¹² For I will forgive their wickedness
  and will remember their sins no
  more.'

¹³ By calling this covenant 'new', he has made the first one obsolete; and what is obsolete and ageing will soon disappear.

DAY 101

HEB. 9. 1 — 28

Worship in the Earthly Tabernacle

Now the first covenant had ulations for worship and also an thly sanctuary. [2] A tabernacle was set In its first room were the lampstand, table and the consecrated bread; this s called the Holy Place. [3] Behind the ond curtain was a room called the st Holy Place, [4] which had the golden ar of incense and the gold-covered ark the covenant. This ark contained the d jar of manna, Aaron's staff that had dded, and the stone tablets of the venant. [5] Above the ark were the erubim of the Glory, overshadowing atonement cover. But we cannot cuss these things in detail now.

[6] When everything had been anged like this, the priests entered ularly into the outer room to carry on eir ministry. [7] But only the high priest ered the inner room, and that only ce a year, and never without blood, ich he offered for himself and for the s the people had committed in orance. [8] The Holy Spirit was showing this that the way into the Most Holy ce had not yet been disclosed as long the first tabernacle was still standing. his is an illustration for the present e, indicating that the gifts and rifices being offered were not able to ar the conscience of the worshipper. They are only a matter of food and nk and various ceremonial washings - ernal regulations applying until the e of the new order.

The Blood of Christ

[11] When Christ came as high priest of the good things that are already here, he went through the greater and more perfect tabernacle that is not man-made, that is to say, not a part of this creation. [12] He did not enter by means of the blood of goats and calves; but he entered the Most Holy Place once for all by his own blood, having obtained eternal redemption. [13] The blood of goats and bulls and the ashes of a heifer sprinkled on those who are ceremonially unclean sanctify them so that they are outwardly clean. [14] How much more, then, will the blood of Christ, who through the eternal Spirit offered himself unblemished to God, cleanse our consciences from acts that lead to death, so that we may serve the living God!

[15] For this reason Christ is the mediator of a new covenant, that those who are called may receive the promised eternal inheritance - now that he has died as a ransom to set them free from the sins committed under the first covenant.

[16] In the case of a will, it is necessary to prove the death of the one who made it, [17] because a will is in force only when somebody has died; it never takes effect while the one who made it is living. [18] This is why even the first covenant was not put into effect without blood. [19] When Moses had proclaimed every commandment of the law to all the people, he took the blood of calves, together with water, scarlet wool and branches of hyssop, and sprinkled the scroll and all the people. [20] He said, 'This is the blood of the covenant, which God has commanded you to keep.' [21] In the same way, he sprinkled with the blood both the tabernacle and everything used in its ceremonies. [22] In fact, the law

requires that nearly everything be cleansed with blood, and without the shedding of blood there is no forgiveness. [23] It was necessary, then, for the copies of the heavenly things to be purified with these sacrifices, but the heavenly things themselves with better sacrifices than these. [24] For Christ did not enter a man-made sanctuary that was only a copy of the true one; he entered heaven itself, now to appear for us in God's presence. [25]Nor did he enter heaven to offer himself again and again, the way the high priest enters the Most Holy Place every year with blood that is not his own. [26] Then Christ would have had to suffer many times since the creation of the world. But now he has appeared once for all at the end of the ages to do away with sin by the sacrifice of himself. [27] Just as man is destined to die once, and after that to face judgment, [28] so Christ was sacrificed once to take away the sins of many people; and he will appear a second time, not to bear sin, but to bring salvation to those who are waiting for him.

DAY 102

HEB. 10. 1 — 18

10

Christ's Sacrifice Once for All

The law is only a shadow of the good things that are coming - not the realities themselves. For this reason it can never, by the same sacrifices repeated endlessly year after year, make perfect those who draw near to worship. [2] If it could, would they not have stopped being offered? For the worshippers would have been cleansed once for all, and would no longer

have felt guilty for their sins. [3] But those sacrifices are an annual reminder of sins, [4] because it is impossible for the blood of bulls and goats to take away sins.

[5] Therefore, when Christ came into the world, he said:

'Sacrifice and offering you did not desire,
  but a body you prepared for me;
[6] with burnt offerings and sin offerings you were not pleased.'
[7] Then I said, "Here I am - it is written about me in the scroll -
  I have come to do your will, O God.'

[8] First he said, 'Sacrifices and offerings, burnt offerings and sin offerings you did r desire, nor were you pleased with them' (although the law required them to be made). [9] Then he said, 'Here I am, I have come to do your will.' He sets aside the fi to establish the second. [10] And by that wi we have been made holy through the sacrifice of the body of Jesus Christ once all.

[11] Day after day every priest stands and performs his religious duties; again ar again he offers the same sacrifices, which can never take away sins. [12] But when thi priest had offered for all time one sacrific for sins, he sat down at the right hand of God. [13] Since that time he waits for his enemies to be made his footstool, [14]becau by one sacrifice he has made perfect for e those who are being made holy.

[15] The Holy Spirit also testifies to us about this. First he says:

[16] 'This is the covenant I will make wi them after that time, says the Lord.
I will put my laws in their hearts,
  and I will write them on their minc

[17] Then he adds:

'Their sins and lawless acts
I will remember no more.'

And where these have been forgiven,
re is no longer any sacrifice for sin.

DAY 103
HEB. 10. 19 — 39

Call to Persevere

erefore, brothers, since we have
nfidence to enter the Most Holy Place
the blood of Jesus, 20 by a new and
ing way opened for us through the
rtain, that is, his body, 21 and since we
ve a great priest over the house of God,
et us draw near to God with a sincere
art in full assurance of faith, having our
arts sprinkled to cleanse us from a
lty conscience and having our bodies
shed with pure water. 23 Let us hold
swervingly to the hope we profess, for
who promised is faithful. 24 And let us
nsider how we may spur one another
towards love and good deeds. 25 Let us
t give up meeting together, as some are
the habit of doing, but let us encourage
e another - and all the more as you see
e Day approaching.

26 If we deliberately keep on sinning
er we have received the knowledge of
e truth, no sacrifice for sins is left, 27 but
ly a fearful expectation of judgment
d of raging fire that will consume the
emies of God. 28 Anyone who rejected
e law of Moses died without mercy on
e testimony of two or three witnesses.
How much more severely do you think
man deserves to be punished who has
mpled the Son of God under foot, who

has treated as an unholy thing the blood
of the covenant that sanctified him, and
who has insulted the Spirit of grace? 30 For
we know him who said, 'It is mine to
avenge; I will repay,' and again, 'The Lord
will judge his people.' 31 It is a dreadful
thing to fall into the hands of the living
God.

32 Remember those earlier days after
you had received the light, when you
stood your ground in a great contest in
the face of suffering. 33 Sometimes you
were publicly exposed to insult and persecution; at other times you stood side by
side with those who were so treated.
34 You sympathised with those in prison
and joyfully accepted the confiscation of
your property, because you knew that you
yourselves had better and lasting
possessions.

'He who is coming will come and will not delay.'

35 So do not throw away your
confidence; it will be richly rewarded.
36 You need to persevere so that when you
have done the will of God, you will
receive what he has promised. 37 For in
just a very little while,

'He who is coming will come and will
not delay.
38 But my righteous one will live by
faith.
And if he shrinks back,
I will not be pleased with him.'

39 But we are not of those who shrink
back and are destroyed, but of those who
believe and are saved.

DAY 104

HEB. 11. 1 — 22

11 **By Faith**
Now faith is being sure of what we hope for and certain of what we do not see. [2] This is what the ancients were commended for.

[3] By faith we understand that the universe was formed at God's command, so that what is seen was not made out of what was visible.

[4] By faith Abel offered God a better sacrifice than Cain did. By faith he was commended as a righteous man, when God spoke well of his offerings. And by faith he still speaks, even though he is dead.

[5] By faith Enoch was taken from this life, so that he did not experience death; he could not be found, because God had taken him away. For before he was taken, he was commended as one who pleased God. [6] And without faith it is impossible to please God, because anyone who comes to him must believe that he exists and that he rewards those who earnestly seek him.

[7] By faith Noah, when warned about things not yet seen, in holy fear built an ark to save his family. By his faith he condemned the world and became heir of the righteousness that comes by faith.

[8] By faith Abraham, when called to go to a place he would later receive as his inheritance, obeyed and went, even though he did not know where he was going. [9] By faith he made his home in the promised land like a stranger in a foreign country; he lived in tents, as did Isaac and Jacob, who were heirs with him of the same promise. [10] For he was looking forward to the city with foundations, whose architect and builder is God.

[11] By faith Abraham, even though he was past age - and Sarah herself was barren - was enabled to become a fathe because he considered him faithful wh had made the promise. [12] And so from one man, and he as good as dead, came descendants as numerous as the stars in the sky and as countless as the sand on the seashore.

[13] All these people were still living by faith when they died. They did not receive the things promised; they only saw them and welcomed them from a distance. And they admitted that they were aliens and strangers on earth. [14] People who say such things show tha they are looking for a country of their own. [15] If they had been thinking of the country they had left, they would have had opportunity to return. [16] Instead, th were longing for a better country - a heavenly one. Therefore God is not ashamed to be called their God, for he has prepared a city for them.

[17] By faith Abraham, when God test him, offered Isaac as a sacrifice. He who had received the promises was about to sacrifice his one and only son, [18] even though God had said to him, 'It is throu Isaac that your offspring will be reckone [19] Abraham reasoned that God could ra the dead, and figuratively speaking, he did receive Isaac back from death.

[20] By faith Isaac blessed Jacob and Esau in regard to their future.

[21] By faith Jacob, when he was dyin blessed each of Joseph's sons, and worshipped as he leaned on the top of l staff.

[22] By faith Joseph, when his end wa near, spoke about the exodus of the Israelites from Egypt and gave instructic about his bones.

DAY 105

HEB. 11. 23 — 40

By faith Moses' parents hid him for ree months after he was born, because ey saw he was no ordinary child, and ey were not afraid of the king's edict. [24] By faith Moses, when he had grown , refused to be known as the son of araoh's daughter. [25] He chose to be ill-ated along with the people of God her than to enjoy the pleasures of sin a short time. [26] He regarded disgrace

because she welcomed the spies, was not killed with those who were disobedient. [32] And what more shall I say? I do not have time to tell about Gideon, Barak, Samson, Jephthah, David, Samuel and the prophets, [33] who through faith conquered kingdoms, administered justice, and gained what was promised; who shut the mouths of lions, [34] quenched the fury of the flames, and escaped the edge of the sword; whose weakness was turned to strength; and who became powerful in battle and routed foreign armies. [35] Women received back their dead, raised to life again. Others were tortured and refused to be released, so that they might gain a better resurrection.

The universe was formed at God's command.

r the sake of Christ as of greater value an the treasures of Egypt, because he is looking ahead to his reward. [27] By th he left Egypt, not fearing the king's ger; he persevered because he saw him no is invisible. [28] By faith he kept the ssover and the sprinkling of blood, so at the destroyer of the firstborn would t touch the firstborn of Israel.

[29] By faith the people passed through e Red Sea as on dry land; but when the yptians tried to do so, they were drowned.

[30] By faith the walls of Jericho fell, er the people had marched around em for seven days.

[31] By faith the prostitute Rahab,

[36] Some faced jeers and flogging, while still others were chained and put in prison. [37] They were stoned; they were sawn in two; they were put to death by the sword. They went about in sheepskins and goatskins, destitute, persecuted and ill-treated - [38] the world was not worthy of them. They wandered in deserts and mountains, and in caves and holes in the ground.

[39] These were all commended for their faith, yet none of them received what had been promised. [40] God had planned something better for us so that only together with us would they be made perfect.

DAY 106

HEB. 12. 1 — 29

12

God Disciplines His Sons

Therefore, since we are surrounded by such a great cloud of witnesses, let us throw off everything that hinders and the sin that so easily entangles, and let us run with perseverance the race marked out for us. [2] Let us fix our eyes on Jesus, the author and perfecter of our faith, who for the joy set before him endured the cross, scorning its shame, and sat down at the right hand of the throne of God. [3] Consider him who endured such opposition from sinful men, so that you will not grow weary and lose heart.

[4] In your struggle against sin, you have not yet resisted to the point of shedding your blood. [5] And you have forgotten that word of encouragement that addresses you as sons:

'My son, do not make light of the
  Lord's discipline,
 and do not lose heart when he
  rebukes you,
[6] because the Lord disciplines those
  he loves, and he punishes
  everyone he accepts as a son.'

[7] Endure hardship as discipline; God is treating you as sons. For what son is not disciplined by his father? [8] If you are not disciplined (and everyone undergoes discipline), then you are illegitimate children and not true sons. [9] Moreover, we have all had human fathers who disciplined us and we respected them for it. How much more should we submit to the Father of our spirits and live! [10] Our fathers disciplined us for a little while as they thought best; but God disciplines us for our good, that we may share in his holiness. [11] No discipline seems pleasant at the time, but painful. Later on, however, it produces a harvest of righteousness and peace for those who have been trained by it.

[12] Therefore, strengthen your feeble arms and weak knees! [13] 'Make level paths for your feet,' so that the lame may not be disabled, but rather healed.

Warning Against Refusing God

[14] Make every effort to live in peace with all men and to be holy; without holiness no-one will see the Lord. [15] See to it that no-one misses the grace of God and that no bitter root grows up to cause trouble and defile many. [16] See that no-one is sexually immoral, or is godless like Esau

---

Therefore, strengthen your feeble arms and weak knees!

---

who for a single meal sold his inheritance rights as the oldest son. [17] Afterwards, as you know, when he wanted to inherit this blessing, he was rejected. He could bring about no change of mind, though he sought the blessing with tears.

[18] You have not come to a mountain that can be touched and that is burning with fire; to darkness, gloom and storm; [19] to a trumpet blast or to such a voice speaking words that those who heard it begged that no further word be spoken to them, [20] because they could not bear what was commanded: 'If even an animal touches the mountain, it must be stoned.' [21] The sight was so terrifying that Moses

, 'I am trembling with fear.'
²² But you have come to Mount Zion,
he heavenly Jerusalem, the city of the
ng God. You have come to thousands
n thousands of angels in joyful
mbly, ²³ to the church of the firstborn,
se names are written in heaven. You
e come to God, the judge of all men,
he spirits of righteous men made
ect, ²⁴ to Jesus the mediator of a new
enant, and to the sprinkled blood that
aks a better word than the blood of Abel.
²⁵ See to it that you do not refuse
who speaks. If they did not escape
en they refused him who warned them

on earth, how much less will we, if we
turn away from him who warns us from
heaven? ²⁶ At that time his voice shook
the earth, but now he has promised,
'Once more I will shake not only the
earth but also the heavens.' ²⁷ The words
'once more' indicate the removing of
what can be shaken - that is, created
things - so that what cannot be shaken
may remain.
²⁸ Therefore, since we are receiving a
kingdom that cannot be shaken, let us be
thankful, and so worship God acceptably
with reverence and awe, ²⁹ for our God is
a consuming fire.

Let us run with perseverance the race marked out for us.

DAY 107

HEB. 13. 1 — 25

13 **Concluding Exhortations** Keep on loving each other as brothers. [2] Do not forget to entertain strangers, for by so doing some people have entertained angels without knowing it. [3] Remember those in prison as if you were their fellow-prisoners, and those who are ill-treated as if you yourselves were suffering.

[4] Marriage should be honoured by all, and the marriage bed kept pure, for God will judge the adulterer and all the sexually immoral. [5] Keep your lives free from the love of money and be content with what you have, because God has said,

'Never will I leave you;
    never will I forsake you.'

[6] So we say with confidence,

'The Lord is my helper;
    I will not be afraid.
    What can man do to me?'

[7] Remember your leaders, who spoke the word of God to you. Consider the outcome of their way of life and imitate their faith. [8] Jesus Christ is the same yesterday and today and for ever. [9] Do not be carried away by all kinds of strange teachings. It is good for our hearts to be strengthened by grace, not by ceremonial foods, which are of no value to those who eat them. [10] We have an altar from which those who minister at the tabernacle have no right to eat. [11] The high priest carries the blood of animals into the Most Holy Place as a s offering, but the bodies are burned outside the camp. [12] And so Jesus also suffered outside the city gate to make th people holy through his own blood. [13] L us, then, go to him outside the camp, bearing the disgrace he bore. [14] For here we do not have an enduring city, but we are looking for the city that is to come.

[15] Through Jesus, therefore, let us continually offer to God a sacrifice of praise - the fruit of lips that confess his name. [16] And do not forget to do good and to share with others, for with such sacrifices God is pleased.

[17] Obey your leaders and submit to their authority. They keep watch over you as men who must give an account. Obey them so that their work will be a joy, not a burden, for that would be of n advantage to you.

[18] Pray for us. We are sure that we have a clear conscience and desire to liv honourably in every way. [19] I particularly urge you to pray so that I may be restore to you soon.

[20] May the God of peace, who throug the blood of the eternal covenant brougl back from the dead our Lord Jesus, that great Shepherd of the sheep, [21] equip yo with everything good for doing his will, and may he work in us what is pleasing him, through Jesus Christ, to whom be glory for ever and ever. Amen.

[22] Brothers, I urge you to bear with my word of exhortation, for I have written you only a short letter.

[23] I want you to know that our broth Timothy has been released. If he arrives soon, I will come with him to see you.

[24] Greet all your leaders and all God people. Those from Italy send you their greetings.

[25] Grace be with you all.

DAY 108

ACTS 1. 1 — 26

1 Jesus Taken Up Into Heaven

In my former book, Theophilus, I rote about all that Jesus began to do and teach [2] until the day he was taken up heaven, after giving instructions rough the Holy Spirit to the apostles he ad chosen. [3] After his suffering, he nowed himself to these men and gave nany convincing proofs that he was live. He appeared to them over a period

> **'Lord, are you at this time going to restore the kingdom to Israel?'**

f forty days and spoke about the ingdom of God. [4] On one occasion, hile he was eating with them, he gave nem this command: 'Do not leave erusalem, but wait for the gift my Father romised, which you have heard me peak about. [5] For John baptised with ater, but in a few days you will be aptised with the Holy Spirit.'

[6] So when they met together, they sked him, 'Lord, are you at this time oing to restore the kingdom to Israel?'

[7] He said to them: 'It is not for you to now the times or dates the Father has set y his own authority. [8] But you will eceive power when the Holy Spirit omes on you; and you will be my itnesses in Jerusalem, and in all Judea nd Samaria, and to the ends of the arth.'

[9] After he said this, he was taken up before their very eyes, and a cloud hid him from their sight.

[10] They were looking intently up into the sky as he was going, when suddenly two men dressed in white stood beside them. [11] 'Men of Galilee,' they said, 'why do you stand here looking into the sky? This same Jesus, who has been taken from you into heaven, will come back in the same way you have seen him go into heaven.'

He was taken up before their very eyes, and a cloud hid him from their sight.

Matthias Chosen to Replace Judas

[12] Then they returned to Jerusalem from the hill called the Mount of Olives, a Sabbath day's walk from the city. [13] When they arrived, they went upstairs to the room where they were staying. Those present were Peter, John, James and Andrew; Philip and Thomas, Bartholomew and Matthew; James son of Alphaeus and Simon the Zealot, and Judas son of James. [14] They all joined together constantly in prayer, along with the women and Mary the mother of Jesus, and with his brothers.

[15] In those days Peter stood up among the believers (a group numbering about a hundred and twenty) [16] and said, 'Brothers, the Scripture had to be fulfilled which the Holy Spirit spoke long ago through the mouth of David concerning Judas, who served as guide for those who arrested Jesus - [17] he was one of our number and shared in this ministry.'

'May his place be deserted; let there be no-one to dwell in it.'

[18] (With the reward he got for his wickedness, Judas bought a field; there he fell headlong, his body burst open and all his intestines spilled out. [19] Everyone in Jerusalem heard about this, so they called that field in their language Akeldama, that is, Field of Blood.)

[20] 'For,' said Peter, 'it is written in the Book of Psalms,

"May his place be deserted;
let there be no-one to dwell in it,"

and,

"May another take his place of leadership."

[21] Therefore it is necessary to choose one of the men who have been with us the whole time the Lord Jesus went in and out among us, [22] beginning from John's baptism to the time when Jesus was taken

'May another take his place of leadership.'

up from us. For one of these must become a witness with us of his resurrection.'

[23] So they proposed two men: Joseph called Barsabbas (also known as Justus) and Matthias. [24] Then they prayed, 'Lord, you know everyone's heart. Show us which of these two you have chosen [25] to take over this apostolic ministry, which Judas left to go where he belongs.' [26] Then they cast lots, and the lot fell to Matthias, so he was added to the eleven apostles.

DAY 109

ACTS 2. 1 — 28

2 ### The Holy Spirit Comes at Pentecost

When the day of Pentecost came, they were all together in one place. [2] Suddenly a sound like the blowing of a violent wind came from heaven and filled the whole house where they were sitting. [3] They saw what seemed to be tongues of fire that separated and came to rest on each of them. [4] All of them were filled th the Holy Spirit and began to speak other tongues as the Spirit enabled them. [5] Now there were staying in Jerusalem od-fearing Jews from every nation under aven. [6] When they heard this sound, a owd came together in bewilderment, cause each one heard them speaking in s own language. [7] Utterly amazed, they ked: 'Are not all these men who are eaking Galileans? [8] Then how is it that ch of us hears them in his own native nguage? [9] Parthians, Medes and Elames; residents of Mesopotamia, Judea and appadocia, Pontus and Asia, [10] Phrygia d Pamphylia, Egypt and the parts of bya near Cyrene; visitors from Rome (both Jews and converts to Judaism); retans and Arabs - we hear them claring the wonders of God in our own ngues!' [12] Amazed and perplexed, they ked one another, 'What does this mean?' [13] Some, however, made fun of them d said, 'They have had too much wine.'

eter Addresses the Crowd

Then Peter stood up with the Eleven, ised his voice and addressed the crowd: ellow Jews and all of you who live in rusalem, let me explain this to you; sten carefully to what I say. [15] These men re not drunk, as you suppose. It's only ine in the morning! [16] No, this is what as spoken by the prophet Joel:

[17] "In the last days, God says,
    I will pour out my Spirit on all
        people.
    Your sons and daughters will
        prophesy,
    your young men will see visions,
    your old men will dream dreams.
[18] Even on my servants, both men and
        women,
    I will pour out my Spirit in those days,
    and they will prophesy.

[19] I will show wonders in the heaven
        above
    and signs on the earth below,
    blood and fire and billows of smoke.
[20] The sun will be turned to darkness
    and the moon to blood
    before the coming of the great and
        glorious day of the Lord.
[21] And everyone who calls on the name
    of the Lord will be saved."

[22] 'Men of Israel, listen to this: Jesus of Nazareth was a man accredited by God to you by miracles, wonders and signs, which God did among you through him, as you yourselves know. [23] This man was handed over to you by God's set purpose and foreknowledge; and you, with the help of wicked men, put him to death by

'I will pour out my Spirit on all people.'

nailing him to the cross. [24] But God raised him from the dead, freeing him from the agony of death, because it was impossible for death to keep its hold on him. [25] David said about him:

"I saw the Lord always before me.
    Because he is at my right hand,
    I will not be shaken.
[26] Therefore my heart is glad and my
        tongue rejoices;
    my body also will live in hope,
[27] because you will not abandon me
        to the grave,
    nor will you let your Holy One see
        decay.
[28] You have made known to me the
        paths of life;
    you will fill me with joy in your
        presence."

DAY 110
ACTS 2. 29 — 47

'The promise is for you and your children'

²⁹ 'Brothers, I can tell you confidently that the patriarch David died and was buried, and his tomb is here to this day. ³⁰ But he was a prophet and knew that God had promised him on oath that he would place one of his descendants on his throne. ³¹ Seeing what was ahead, he spoke of the resurrection of the Christ, that he was not abandoned to the grave, nor did his body see decay. ³² God has raised this Jesus to life, and we are all witnesses of the fact. ³³ Exalted to the right hand of God, he has received from the Father the promised Holy Spirit and has poured out what you now see and hear. ³⁴ For David did not ascend to heaven, and yet he said,

"The Lord said to my Lord:
Sit at my right hand
³⁵ until I make your enemies
a footstool for your feet."

³⁶ 'Therefore let all Israel be assured of this: God has made this Jesus, whom you crucified, both Lord and Christ.'
³⁷ When the people heard this, they were cut to the heart and said to Peter and the other apostles, 'Brothers, what shall we do?'
³⁸ Peter replied, 'Repent and be baptised, every one of you, in the name of Jesus Christ for the forgiveness of your sins. And you will receive the gift of the Holy Spirit. ³⁹ The promise is for you and your children and for all who are far off - for all whom the Lord our God will call.'

⁴⁰ With many other words he warned them; and he pleaded with them, 'Save yourselves from this corrupt generation.' ⁴¹ Those who accepted his message were baptised, and about three thousand were added to their number that day.

The Fellowship of the Believers
⁴² They devoted themselves to the apostles' teaching and to the fellowship, to the breaking of bread and to prayer. ⁴³ Everyone was filled with awe, and many wonders and miraculous signs were done by the apostles. ⁴⁴ All the believers were together and had everything in common ⁴⁵ Selling their possessions and goods, they gave to anyone as he had need. ⁴⁶ Every day they continued to meet together in the temple courts. They broke bread in their homes and ate together with glad and sincere hearts, ⁴⁷ praising God and enjoying the favour of all the people. And the Lord added to their number daily those who were being saved

DAY 111

ACTS 3. 1 — 26

3 ### Peter Heals the Crippled Beggar

One day Peter and John were going up to the temple at the time of prayer - at three in the afternoon. [2] Now a man crippled from birth was being carried to the temple gate called Beautiful, where he was put every day to beg from those going into the temple courts. [3] When he saw Peter and John about to enter, he asked them for money. [4] Peter looked straight at him, as did John. Then Peter said, 'Look at us!' So the man gave them his attention, expecting to get something from them.

[6] Then Peter said, 'Silver or gold I do not have, but what I have I give you. In the name of Jesus Christ of Nazareth, walk.' [7] Taking him by the right hand, he helped him up, and instantly the man's feet and ankles became strong. [8] He jumped to his feet and began to walk. Then he went with them into the temple courts, walking and jumping, and praising God. [9] When all the people saw him walking and praising God, [10] they recognised him as the same man who used to sit begging at the temple gate called Beautiful, and they were filled with wonder and amazement at what had happened to him.

Peter Speaks to the Onlookers

While the beggar held on to Peter and John, all the people were astonished and came running to them in the place called Solomon's Colonnade. [12] When Peter saw this, he said to them: 'Men of Israel, why does this surprise you? Why do you stare at us as if by our own power or godliness we had made this man walk? [13] The God of Abraham, Isaac and Jacob, the God of our fathers, has glorified his servant Jesus. You handed him over to be killed, and you disowned him before Pilate, though he had decided to let him go. [14] You disowned the Holy and Righteous One and asked that a murderer be released to you. [15] You killed the author of life, but God raised him from the dead. We are witnesses of this. [16] By faith in the name of Jesus, this man whom you see and know was made strong. It is Jesus' name and the faith that comes through him that has given this complete healing to him, as you can all see.

[17] 'Now, brothers, I know that you acted in ignorance, as did your leaders. [18] But this is how God fulfilled what he had foretold through all the prophets, saying that his Christ would suffer. [19] Repent, then, and turn to God, so that your sins may be wiped out, that times of refreshing may come from the Lord, [20] and that he may send the Christ, who has been appointed for you - even Jesus. [21] He must remain in heaven until the time comes for God to restore everything, as he promised long ago through his holy prophets. [22] For Moses said, 'The Lord your God will raise up for you a prophet like me from among your own people; you must listen to everything he tells you. [23] Anyone who does not listen to him will be completely cut off from among his people.'

[24] 'Indeed, all the prophets from Samuel on, as many as have spoken, have foretold these days. [25] And you are heirs of the prophets and of the covenant God made with your fathers. He said to Abraham, "Through your offspring all peoples on earth will be blessed." [26] When God raised up his servant, he sent him first to you to bless you by turning each of you from your wicked ways.'

DAY 112

ACTS 4. 1 — 22

4 ## Peter and John Before the Sanhedrin

The priests and the captain of the temple guard and the Sadducees came up to Peter and John while they were speaking to the people. [2] They were greatly disturbed because the apostles were teaching the people and proclaiming in Jesus the resurrection of the dead. [3] They seized Peter and John, and because it was evening, they put them in jail until the next day. [4] But many who heard the message believed, and the number of men grew to about five thousand.

'The stone you builders rejected ...has become the capstone.'

[5] The next day the rulers, elders and teachers of the law met in Jerusalem. [6] Annas the high priest was there, and so were Caiaphas, John, Alexander and the other men of the high priest's family. [7] They had Peter and John brought before them and began to question them: 'By what power or what name did you do this?' [8] Then Peter, filled with the Holy Spirit, said to them: 'Rulers and elders of the people! [9] If we are being called to account today for an act of kindness shown to a cripple and are asked how he was healed, [10] then know this, you and all the people of Israel: It is by the name of Jesus Christ of Nazareth, whom you crucified but whom God raised from the dead, that this man stands before you

healed. [11] He is

"the stone you builders rejected,
which has become the capstone."

[12] Salvation is found in no-one else, for there is no other name under heaven given to men by which we must be saved. [13] When they saw the courage of Peter and John and realised that they

'Judge for yourselves...'

were unschooled, ordinary men, they were astonished and they took note that these men had been with Jesus. [14] But since they could see the man who had been healed standing there with them, there was nothing they could say. [15] So they ordered them to withdraw from the Sanhedrin and then conferred together. [16] 'What are we going to do with these men?' they asked. 'Everybody living in Jerusalem knows they have done an outstanding miracle, and we cannot deny it. [17] But to stop this thing from spreading any further among the people, we must warn these men to speak no longer to anyone in this name.' [18] Then they called them in again and commanded them not to speak or teach at all in the name of Jesus. [19] But Peter and John replied, 'Judge for yourselves whether it is right in God's sight to obey you rather than God. [20] For we cannot help speaking about what we have seen and heard.' [21] After further threats they let them go. They could not decide how to punish them, because all the people were praising God for what had happened. [22] For the man who was miraculously healed was over forty years old.

DAY 113

ACTS 4. 23 — 37

The Believers' Prayer

On their release, Peter and John went back to their own people and reported all that the chief priests and elders had said to them. ²⁴ When they heard this, they raised their voices together in prayer to God. 'Sovereign Lord,' they said, 'you made the heaven and the earth and the sea, and everything in them. ²⁵ You spoke by the Holy Spirit through the mouth of your servant, our father David:

"Why do the nations rage
    and the peoples plot in vain?
²⁶ The kings of the earth take their stand
    and the rulers gather together
against the Lord
    and against his Anointed One."

Indeed Herod and Pontius Pilate met together with the Gentiles and the people of Israel in this city to conspire against your holy servant Jesus, whom you anointed. ²⁸ They did what your power and will had decided beforehand should happen. ²⁹ Now, Lord, consider their threats and enable your servants to speak

'Stretch out your hand...'

your word with great boldness. ³⁰ Stretch out your hand to heal and perform miraculous signs and wonders through the name of your holy servant Jesus.'
³¹ After they prayed, the place where they were meeting was shaken. And they were all filled with the Holy Spirit and spoke the word of God boldly.

The Believers Share Their Possessions

³² All the believers were one in heart and mind. No-one claimed that any of his possessions was his own, but they shared everything they had. ³³ With great power the apostles continued to testify to the resurrection of the Lord Jesus, and much grace was upon them all. ³⁴ There were no needy persons among them. For from time to time those who owned lands or houses sold them, brought the money from the sales ³⁵ and put it at the apostles' feet, and it was distributed to anyone as he had need.

³⁶ Joseph, a Levite from Cyprus, whom the apostles called Barnabas (which means Son of Encouragement), ³⁷ sold a field he owned and brought the money and put it at the apostles' feet.

They shared everything they had.

DAY 114
ACTS 5. 1 — 16

5 ### Ananias and Sapphira
Now a man named Ananias, together with his wife Sapphira, also sold a piece of property. [2] With his wife's full knowledge he kept back part of the money for himself, but brought the rest and put it at the apostles' feet.

[3] Then Peter said, 'Ananias, how is it that Satan has so filled your heart that you have lied to the Holy Spirit and have kept for yourself some of the money you received for the land? [4] Didn't it belong to you before it was sold? And after it was sold, wasn't the money at your disposal?

'How could you agree to test the Spirit of the Lord?'

What made you think of doing such a thing? You have not lied to men but to God.'

[5] When Ananias heard this, he fell down and died. And great fear seized all who heard what had happened. [6] Then the young men came forward, wrapped up his body, and carried him out and buried him.

[7] About three hours later his wife came in, not knowing what had happened. [8] Peter asked her, 'Tell me, is this the price you and Ananias got for the land?'

'Yes,' she said, 'that is the price.'

[9] Peter said to her, 'How could you agree to test the Spirit of the Lord? Look! The feet of the men who buried your husband are at the door, and they will carry you out also.'

[10] At that moment she fell down at his feet and died. Then the young men came in and, finding her dead, carried her out and buried her beside her husband. [11] Great fear seized the whole church and all who heard about these events.

The Apostles Heal Many
[12] The apostles performed many miraculous signs and wonders among the people. And all the believers used to meet together in Solomon's Colonnade. [13] No-one else dared join them, even though they were highly regarded by the people. [14] Nevertheless, more and more men and women believed in the Lord and were added to their number. [15] As a result, people brought the sick into the streets and laid them on beds and mats so that at least Peter's shadow might fall on some of them as he passed by. [16] Crowds gathered also from the towns around Jerusalem, bringing their sick and those tormented by evil spirits, and all of them were healed.

DAY 115
ACTS 5. 17 — 42

The Apostles Persecuted
[17] Then the high priest and all his associates, who were members of the party of the Sadducees, were filled with jealousy. [18] They arrested the apostles and put them in the public jail. [19] But during the night an angel of the Lord opened the doors of the jail and brought them out. [20] 'Go, stand in the temple courts,' he said

nd tell the people the full message of
his new life.'

²¹ At daybreak they entered the
temple courts, as they had been told, and
began to teach the people.

When the high priest and his
associates arrived, they called together
the Sanhedrin - the full assembly of the
elders of Israel - and sent to the jail for
the apostles. ²² But on arriving at the jail,
the officers did not find them there. So
they went back and reported, ²³ 'We found
the jail securely locked, with the guards
standing at the doors; but when we
opened them, we found no-one inside.'
On hearing this report, the captain of
the temple guard and the chief priests
were puzzled, wondering what would
come of this.

²⁵ Then someone came and said,
'Look! The men you put in jail are
standing in the temple courts teaching
the people.' ²⁶ At that, the captain went
with his officers and brought the apostles.
They did not use force, because they
feared that the people would stone them.

²⁷ Having brought the apostles, they
made them appear before the Sanhedrin
to be questioned by the high priest.
'We gave you strict orders not to teach
in this name,' he said. 'Yet you have filled
Jerusalem with your teaching and are
determined to make us guilty of this
man's blood.'

²⁹ Peter and the other apostles replied:
'We must obey God rather than men!
³⁰ The God of our fathers raised Jesus from
the dead - whom you had killed by
hanging him on a tree. ³¹ God exalted
him to his own right hand as Prince and
Saviour that he might give repentance
and forgiveness of sins to Israel. ³² We are
witnesses of these things, and so is the
Holy Spirit, whom God has given to
those who obey him.'

³³ When they heard this, they were
furious and wanted to put them to death.
³⁴ But a Pharisee named Gamaliel, a
teacher of the law, who was honoured by
all the people, stood up in the Sanhedrin
and ordered that the men be put outside
for a little while. ³⁵ Then he addressed
them: 'Men of Israel, consider carefully
what you intend to do to these men.
³⁶ Some time ago Theudas appeared,
claiming to be somebody, and about four
hundred men rallied to him. He was
killed, all his followers were dispersed,
and it all came to nothing. ³⁷ After him,
Judas the Galilean appeared in the days of
the census and led a band of people in

'We must obey God rather
than men!'

revolt. He too was killed, and all his
followers were scattered. ³⁸ Therefore, in
the present case I advise you: Leave these
men alone! Let them go! For if their
purpose or activity is of human origin, it
will fail. ³⁹ But if it is from God, you will
not be able to stop these men; you will
only find yourselves fighting against
God.'

⁴⁰ His speech persuaded them. They
called the apostles in and had them
flogged. Then they ordered them not to
speak in the name of Jesus, and let them
go.

⁴¹ The apostles left the Sanhedrin,
rejoicing because they had been counted
worthy of suffering disgrace for the Name.
⁴² Day after day, in the temple courts and
from house to house, they never stopped
teaching and proclaiming the good news
that Jesus is the Christ.

DAY 116

ACTS 6. 1 — 15

6 **The Choosing of the Seven**
In those days when the number of disciples was increasing, the Grecian Jews among them complained against the Hebraic Jews because their widows were being overlooked in the daily distribution of food. ² So the Twelve gathered all the disciples together and said, 'It would not be right for us to neglect the ministry of the word of God in order to wait on tables. ³ Brothers, choose seven men from among you who are known to be full of the Spirit and wisdom. We will turn this responsibility over to them ⁴ and will give our attention to prayer and the ministry of the word.'

⁵ This proposal pleased the whole group. They chose Stephen, a man full of faith and of the Holy Spirit; also Philip, Procorus, Nicanor, Timon, Parmenas, and Nicolas from Antioch, a convert to Judaism. ⁶ They presented these men to the apostles, who prayed and laid their hands on them.

⁷ So the word of God spread. The number of disciples in Jerusalem increased rapidly, and a large number of priests became obedient to the faith.

Stephen Seized

⁸ Now Stephen, a man full of God's grace and power, did great wonders and miraculous signs among the people. ⁹ Opposition arose, however, from members of the Synagogue of the Freedmen (as it was called) - Jews of Cyrene and Alexandria as well as the provinces of Cilicia and Asia. These men began to argue with Stephen, ¹⁰ but they could not stand up against his wisdom or the Spirit by whom he spoke.

¹¹ Then they secretly persuaded some men to say, 'We have heard Stephen speak words of blasphemy against Moses and against God.'

¹² So they stirred up the people and the elders and the teachers of the law. They seized Stephen and brought him before the Sanhedrin. ¹³ They produced false witnesses, who testified, 'This fellow never stops speaking against this holy place and against the law. ¹⁴ For we have heard him say that this Jesus of Nazareth will destroy this place and change the customs Moses handed down to us.'

¹⁵ All who were sitting in the Sanhedrin looked intently at Stephen, and they saw that his face was like the face of an angel.

The word of God spread.

DAY 117

ACTS 7. 1 — 36

7 Stephen's Speech to the Sanhedrin

Then the high priest asked him, 'Are these charges true?'

[2] To this he replied: 'Brothers and fathers, listen to me! The God of glory appeared to our father Abraham while he was still in Mesopotamia, before he lived

'Brothers and fathers, listen to me!'

in Haran. [3] "Leave your country and your people," God said, "and go to the land I will show you."

[4] 'So he left the land of the Chaldeans and settled in Haran. After the death of his father, God sent him to this land where you are now living. [5] He gave him no inheritance here, not even a foot of ground. But God promised him that he and his descendants after him would possess the land, even though at that time Abraham had no child. [6] God spoke to him in this way: "Your descendants will be strangers in a country not their own, and they will be enslaved and ill-treated for four hundred years. [7] But I will punish the nation they serve as slaves," God said, "and afterwards they will come out of that country and worship me in this place." [8] Then he gave Abraham the covenant of circumcision. And Abraham became the father of Isaac and circumcised him eight days after his

birth. Later Isaac became the father of Jacob, and Jacob became the father of the twelve patriarchs.

[9] 'Because the patriarchs were jealous of Joseph, they sold him as a slave into Egypt. But God was with him [10] and rescued him from all his troubles. He gave Joseph wisdom and enabled him to gain the goodwill of Pharaoh king of Egypt; so he made him ruler over Egypt and all his palace.

[11] 'Then a famine struck all Egypt and Canaan, bringing great suffering, and our fathers could not find food. [12] When Jacob heard that there was grain in Egypt, he sent our fathers on their first visit. [13] On their second visit, Joseph told his brothers who he was, and Pharaoh learned about Joseph's family. [14] After this, Joseph sent for his father Jacob and his whole family, seventy-five in all. [15] Then Jacob went down to Egypt, where he and our fathers died. [16] Their bodies were brought back to Shechem and placed in the tomb that Abraham had bought from the sons of Hamor at Shechem for a certain sum of money.

[17] 'As the time drew near for God to fulfil his promise to Abraham, the number of our people in Egypt greatly increased. [18] Then another king, who knew nothing about Joseph, became ruler of Egypt. [19] He dealt treacherously with our people and oppressed our forefathers by forcing them to throw out their newborn babies so that they would die.

[20] 'At that time Moses was born, and he was no ordinary child. For three months he was cared for in his father's house. [21] When he was placed outside, Pharaoh's daughter took him and brought him up as her own son. [22] Moses was educated in all the wisdom of the Egyptians and was powerful in speech and action.

²³ 'When Moses was forty years old, he decided to visit his fellow Israelites. ²⁴ He saw one of them being ill-treated by an Egyptian, so he went to his defence and avenged him by killing the Egyptian. ²⁵ Moses thought that his own people would realise that God was using him to rescue them, but they did not. ²⁶ The next day Moses came upon two Israelites who were fighting. He tried to reconcile them by saying, "Men, you are brothers; why do you want to hurt each other?"

²⁷ 'But the man who was ill-treating the other pushed Moses aside and said, "Who made you ruler and judge over us? ²⁸ Do you want to kill me as you killed the Egyptian yesterday?" ²⁹ When Moses heard this, he fled to Midian, where he settled as a foreigner and had two sons.

³⁰ 'After forty years had passed, an angel appeared to Moses in the flames of a burning bush in the desert near Mount Sinai. ³¹ When he saw this, he was amazed at the sight. As he went over to look more closely, he heard the Lord's voice: ³² "I am the God of your fathers, the God of Abraham, Isaac and Jacob." Moses trembled with fear and did not dare to look.

³³ 'Then the Lord said to him, "Take off your sandals; the place where you are standing is holy ground. ³⁴ I have indeed seen the oppression of my people in Egypt. I have heard their groaning and have come down to set them free. Now come, I will send you back to Egypt."

³⁵ 'This is the same Moses whom they had rejected with the words, "Who made you ruler and judge?" He was sent to be their ruler and deliverer by God himself, through the angel who appeared to him in the bush. ³⁶ He led them out of Egypt and did wonders and miraculous signs in Egypt, at the Red Sea and for forty years in the desert.

'I have heard their groaning and have come down to set them free.'

DAY 118

ACTS 7. 37 — 60

⁷ 'This is that Moses who told the Israelites, "God will send you a prophet like me from your own people." ³⁸ He was in the assembly in the desert, with the angel who spoke to him on Mount Sinai, and with our fathers; and he received living words to pass on to us.

³⁹ 'But our fathers refused to obey him. Instead, they rejected him and in their hearts turned back to Egypt. ⁴⁰ They told Aaron, "Make us gods who will go before us. As for this fellow Moses who led us out of Egypt - we don't know what has happened to him!" ⁴¹ That was the time they made an idol in the form of a calf. They brought sacrifices to it and held a celebration in honour of what their hands had made. ⁴² But God turned away and gave them over to the worship of the heavenly bodies. This agrees with what is written in the book of the prophets:

"Did you bring me sacrifices and
    offerings for forty years in the desert,
    O house of Israel?
⁴³ You have lifted up the shrine of Molech
    and the star of your god Rephan,
    the idols you made to worship.
    Therefore I will send you into exile
    beyond Babylon."

⁴⁴ 'Our forefathers had the tabernacle of the Testimony with them in the desert. It had been made as God directed Moses, according to the pattern he had seen. ⁴⁵ Having received the tabernacle, our fathers under Joshua brought it with them when they took the land from the nations God drove out before them. It remained in the land until the time of David, ⁴⁶ who enjoyed God's favour and asked that he might provide a dwelling-place for the God of Jacob. ⁴⁷ But it was Solomon who built the house for him.

⁴⁸ 'However, the Most High does not live in houses made by men. As the prophet says:

⁴⁹ "Heaven is my throne,
    and the earth is my footstool.
    What kind of house will you build
        for me?
                    says the Lord.
    Or where will my resting place be?
⁵⁰ Has not my hand made all these things?"

⁵¹ 'You stiff-necked people,with uncircumcised hearts and ears! You are just like your fathers: You always resist the Holy Spirit! ⁵² Was there ever a prophet your fathers did not persecute? They even killed those who predicted the coming of the Righteous One. And now you have betrayed and murdered him - ⁵³ you who have received the law that was put into effect through angels but have not obeyed it.'

The Stoning of Stephen

⁵⁴ When they heard this, they were furious and gnashed their teeth at him. ⁵⁵ But Stephen, full of the Holy Spirit, looked up to heaven and saw the glory of God, and Jesus standing at the right hand of God. ⁵⁶ 'Look,' he said, 'I see heaven open and the Son of Man standing at the right hand of God.'

⁵⁷ At this they covered their ears and, yelling at the top of their voices, they all rushed at him, ⁵⁸ dragged him out of the city and began to stone him. Meanwhile, the witnesses laid their clothes at the feet of a young man named Saul.

⁵⁹ While they were stoning him, Stephen prayed, 'Lord Jesus, receive my spirit.' ⁶⁰ Then he fell on his knees and cried out, 'Lord, do not hold this sin against them.' When he had said this, he fell asleep.

DAY 119
ACTS 8. 1 — 25

8 And Saul was there, giving approval to his death.

The Church Persecuted and Scattered

On that day a great persecution broke out against the church at Jerusalem, and all except the apostles were scattered throughout Judea and Samaria. ² Godly men buried Stephen and mourned deeply for him. ³ But Saul began to destroy the church. Going from house to house, he dragged off men and women and put them in prison.

Philip in Samaria

⁴ Those who had been scattered preached the word wherever they went. ⁵ Philip went down to a city in Samaria and proclaimed the Christ there. ⁶ When the crowds heard Philip and saw the miraculous signs he did, they all paid close attention to what he said. ⁷ With shrieks, evil spirits came out of many, and many paralytics and cripples were healed. ⁸ So there was great joy in that city.

Simon the Sorcerer

⁹ Now for some time a man named Simon had practised sorcery in the city and amazed all the people of Samaria.

He boasted that he was someone great, ¹⁰ and all the people, both high and low, gave him their attention and exclaimed 'This man is the divine power known as the Great Power.' ¹¹ They followed him because he had amazed them for a long time with his magic. ¹² But when they believed Philip as he preached the good news of the kingdom of God and the name of Jesus Christ, they were baptised, both men and women. ¹³ Simon himself believed and was baptised. And he followed Philip everywhere, astonished by the great signs and miracles he saw.

¹⁴ When the apostles in Jerusalem heard that Samaria had accepted the word of God, they sent Peter and John to them. ¹⁵ When they arrived, they prayed for them that they might receive the Holy Spirit, ¹⁶ because the Holy Spirit had not yet come upon any of them; they had simply been baptised into the name of the Lord Jesus. ¹⁷ Then Peter and John placed their hands on them, and they received the Holy Spirit.

¹⁸ When Simon saw that the Spirit was given at the laying on of the apostles' hands, he offered them money ¹⁹ and said, 'Give me also this ability so that everyone on whom I lay my hands may receive the Holy Spirit.'

²⁰ Peter answered: 'May your money perish with you, because you thought you could buy the gift of God with money! ²¹ You have no part or share in this ministry, because your heart is not right before God. ²² Repent of this wickedness and pray to the Lord. Perhaps he will forgive you for having such a thought in your heart. ²³ For I see that you are full of bitterness and captive to sin.'

²⁴ Then Simon answered, 'Pray to the Lord for me so that nothing you have said may happen to me.'

²⁵ When they had testified and proclaimed the word of the Lord, Peter and John returned to Jerusalem, preaching the gospel in many Samaritan villages.

DAY 120

ACTS 8. 26 — 40

Philip and the Ethiopian

²⁶ Now an angel of the Lord said to Philip, 'Go south to the road - the desert road - that goes down from Jerusalem to Gaza.' ²⁷ So he started out, and on his way he met an Ethiopian eunuch, an important official in charge of all the treasury of Candace, queen of the Ethiopians. This man had gone to Jerusalem to worship, ²⁸ and on his way home was sitting in his chariot reading the book of Isaiah the prophet. ²⁹ The Spirit told Philip, 'Go to that chariot and stay near it.'

³⁰ Then Philip ran up to the chariot and heard the man reading Isaiah the prophet. 'Do you understand what you are reading?' Philip asked.

³¹ 'How can I,' he said, 'unless someone explains it to me?' So he invited Philip to come up and sit with him.

³² The eunuch was reading this passage of Scripture:

'He was led like a sheep to the
   slaughter,
   and as a lamb before the shearer is
   silent,
   so he did not open his mouth.
³³ In his humiliation he was deprived of
   justice.
   Who can speak of his descendants?
   For his life was taken from the earth.'

They came to some water and Philip baptised him.

³⁴ The eunuch asked Philip, 'Tell me, please, who is the prophet talking about, himself or someone else?' ³⁵ Then Philip began with that very passage of Scripture and told him the good news about Jesus.

³⁶ As they travelled along the road, they came to some water and the eunuch said, 'Look, here is water. Why shouldn't I be baptised?' ³⁸ And he gave orders to stop the chariot. Then both Philip and the eunuch went down into the water and Philip baptised him. ³⁹ When they came up out of the water, the Spirit of the Lord suddenly took Philip away, and the eunuch did not see him again, but went on his way rejoicing. ⁴⁰ Philip, however, appeared at Azotus and travelled about, preaching the gospel in all the towns until he reached Caesarea.

DAY 121

ACTS 9. 1 — 31

9 **Saul's Conversion**
Meanwhile, Saul was still
breathing out murderous threats
against the Lord's disciples. He went to
the high priest [2] and asked him for letters
to the synagogues in Damascus, so that if
he found any there who belonged to the
Way, whether men or women, he might
take them as prisoners to Jerusalem. [3] As
he neared Damascus on his journey,
suddenly a light from heaven flashed
around him. [4] He fell to the ground and
heard a voice say to him, 'Saul, Saul, why
do you persecute me?'
[5] 'Who are you, Lord?' Saul asked.
'I am Jesus, whom you are persecuting,'
he replied. [6] 'Now get up and go into the
city, and you will be told what you must
do.'
[7] The men travelling with Saul stood

'Saul, Saul, why do you persecute me?'

there speechless; they heard the sound
but did not see anyone. [8] Saul got up from
the ground, but when he opened his eyes
he could see nothing. So they led him by
the hand into Damascus. [9] For three days
he was blind, and did not eat or drink
anything.
[10] In Damascus there was a disciple
named Ananias. The Lord called to him
in a vision, 'Ananias!'
'Yes, Lord,' he answered.

[11] The Lord told him, 'Go to the
house of Judas on Straight Street and ask
for a man from Tarsus named Saul, for he
is praying. [12] In a vision he has seen a man
named Ananias come and place his hands
on him to restore his sight.'
[13] 'Lord,' Ananias answered, 'I
have heard many reports about this man

'I will show him how much he must suffer for my name.'

and all the harm he has done to your
saints in Jerusalem. [14] And he has come
here with authority from the chief priests
to arrest all who call on your name.'
[15] But the Lord said to Ananias, 'Go!
This man is my chosen instrument to
carry my name before the Gentiles and
their kings and before the people of Israel.
[16] I will show him how much he must
suffer for my name.'
[17] Then Ananias went to the house
and entered it. Placing his hands on Saul,
he said, 'Brother Saul, the Lord - Jesus,
who appeared to you on the road as you
were coming here - has sent me so that
you may see again and be filled with the
Holy Spirit.' [18] Immediately, something
like scales fell from Saul's eyes, and he
could see again. He got up and was
baptised, [19] and after taking some food, he
regained his strength.

Saul in Damascus and Jerusalem
Saul spent several days with the disciples
in Damascus. [20] At once he began to
preach in the synagogues that Jesus is the
Son of God. [21] All those who heard him
were astonished and asked, 'Isn't he the
man who caused havoc in Jerusalem
among those who call on this name? And
hasn't he come here to take them as

risoners to the chief priests?' ²² Yet Saul grew more and more powerful and baffled he Jews living in Damascus by proving hat Jesus is the Christ.

²³ After many days had gone by, the ews conspired to kill him, ²⁴ but Saul earned of their plan. Day and night they ept close watch on the city gates in order to kill him. ²⁵ But his followers took him by night and lowered him in a basket hrough an opening in the wall.

²⁶ When he came to Jerusalem, he ried to join the disciples, but they were ll afraid of him, not believing that he eally was a disciple. ²⁷ But Barnabas took him and brought him to the apostles. He old them how Saul on his journey had een the Lord and that the Lord had poken to him, and how in Damascus he had preached fearlessly in the name of esus. ²⁸ So Saul stayed with them and moved about freely in Jerusalem, speaking oldly in the name of the Lord. ²⁹ He alked and debated with the Grecian ews, but they tried to kill him. ³⁰ When he brothers learned of this, they took him down to Caesarea and sent him off to Tarsus.

³¹ Then the church throughout Judea, Galilee and Samaria enjoyed a ime of peace. It was strengthened; and encouraged by the Holy Spirit, it grew in numbers, living in the fear of the Lord.

DAY 122

ACTS 9. 32 — 43

Aeneas and Dorcas

³² As Peter travelled about the country, he went to visit the saints in Lydda. ³³ There he found a man named Aeneas, a paralytic who had been bedridden for eight years. ³⁴ 'Aeneas,' Peter said to him, 'Jesus Christ heals you. Get up and tidy up your mat.' Immediately Aeneas got up. ³⁵ All those who lived in Lydda and

---

'Jesus Christ heals you. Get up and tidy up your mat.' Immediately Aeneas got up.

Sharon saw him and turned to the Lord.

³⁶ In Joppa there was a disciple named Tabitha (which, when translated, is Dorcas), who was always doing good and helping the poor. ³⁷ About that time she became sick and died, and her body was washed and placed in an upstairs room. ³⁸ Lydda was near Joppa; so when the disciples heard that Peter was in Lydda, they sent two men to him and urged him, 'Please come at once!'

³⁹ Peter went with them, and when he arrived he was taken upstairs to the room. All the widows stood around him, crying and showing him the robes and other clothing that Dorcas had made while she was still with them.

⁴⁰ Peter sent them all out of the room; then he got down on his knees and prayed. Turning towards the dead woman, he said, 'Tabitha, get up.' She opened her eyes, and seeing Peter she sat up. ⁴¹ He took her by the hand and helped her to her feet. Then he called the believers and the widows and presented her to them alive. ⁴² This became known all over Joppa, and many people believed in the Lord. ⁴³ Peter stayed in Joppa for some time with a tanner named Simon.

DAY 123

ACTS 10. 1 — 38

10 Cornelius Calls for Peter

At Caesarea there was a man named Cornelius, a centurion in what was known as the Italian Regiment. [2] He and all his family were devout and God-fearing; he gave generously to those in need and prayed to God regularly. [3] One day at about three in the afternoon he had a vision. He distinctly saw an angel of God, who came to him and said, 'Cornelius!'

[4] Cornelius stared at him in fear. 'What is it, Lord?' he asked.

The angel answered, 'Your prayers and gifts to the poor have come up as a memorial offering before God. [5] Now send men to Joppa to bring back a man named Simon who is called Peter. [6] He is staying with Simon the tanner, whose house is by the sea.'

[7] When the angel who spoke to him had gone, Cornelius called two of his servants and a devout soldier who was one of his attendants. [8] He told them everything that had happened and sent them to Joppa.

Peter's Vision

[9] About noon the following day as they were on their journey and approaching the city, Peter went up on the roof to pray. [10] He became hungry and wanted something to eat, and while the meal was being prepared, he fell into a trance. [11] He saw heaven opened and something like a large sheet being let down to earth by its four corners. [12] It contained all kinds of four-footed animals, as well as reptiles of the earth and birds of the air. [13] Then a voice told him, 'Get up, Peter. Kill and eat.'

[14] ' Surely not, Lord!' Peter replied. 'I have never eaten anything impure or unclean.'

[15] The voice spoke to him a second time, 'Do not call anything impure that God has made clean.'

[16] This happened three times, and immediately the sheet was taken back to heaven.

[17] While Peter was wondering about the meaning of the vision, the men sent by Cornelius found out where Simon's house was and stopped at the gate. [18] They called out, asking if Simon who was known as Peter was staying there.

[19] While Peter was still thinking about the vision, the Spirit said to him, 'Simon, three men are looking for you. [20] So get up and go downstairs. Do not hesitate to go with them, for I have sent them.'

[21] Peter went down and said to the men, 'I'm the one you're looking for. Why have you come?'

[22] The men replied, 'We have come from Cornelius the centurion. He is a righteous and God-fearing man, who is respected by all the Jewish people. A holy angel told him to have you come to his house so that he could hear what you have to say.' [23] Then Peter invited the men into the house to be his guests.

Peter at Cornelius' House

The next day Peter started out with them and some of the brothers from Joppa went along. [24] The following day he arrived in Caesarea. Cornelius was expecting them and had called together his relatives and close friends. [25] As Peter entered the house, Cornelius met him and fell at his feet in reverence. [26] But Peter made him et up. 'Stand up,' he said, 'I am only a man myself.'

²⁷ Talking with him, Peter went inside and found a large gathering of people. ²⁸ He said to them: 'You are well aware that it is against our law for a Jew to associate with a Gentile or visit him. But God has shown me that I should not call any man impure or unclean. ²⁹ So when I was sent for, I came without raising any objection. May I ask why you sent for me?'

³⁰ Cornelius answered: 'Four days ago I was in my house praying at this hour, at three in the afternoon. Suddenly a man in shining clothes stood before me ³¹ and said, "Cornelius, God has heard your prayer and remembered your gifts to the poor. ³² Send to Joppa for Simon who is called Peter. He is a guest in the home of Simon the tanner, who lives by the sea."

³³ So I sent for you immediately, and it was good of you to come. Now we are all here in the presence of God to listen to everything the Lord has commanded you to tell us.'

³⁴ Then Peter began to speak: 'I now realise how true it is that God does not show favouritism ³⁵ but accepts men from every nation who fear him and do what is right. ³⁶ You know the message God sent to the people of Israel, telling the good news of peace through Jesus Christ, who is Lord of all. ³⁷ You know what has happened throughout Judea, beginning in Galilee after the baptism that John preached - ³⁸ how God anointed Jesus of Nazareth with the Holy Spirit and power, and how he went around doing good and healing all who were under the power of the devil, because God was with him.

'Do not call anything impure that God has made clean.'

DAY 124

ACTS 10. 39 — 11.18

[39] 'We are witnesses of everything he did in the country of the Jews and in Jerusalem. They killed him by hanging him on a tree, [40] but God raised him from the dead on the third day and caused him to be seen. [41] He was not seen by all the people, but by witnesses whom God had already chosen - by us who ate and drank with him after he rose from the dead. [42] He commanded us to preach to the people and to testify that he is the one whom God appointed as judge of the living and the dead. [43] All the prophets testify about him that everyone who believes in him receives forgiveness of sins through his name.'

[44] While Peter was still speaking these words, the Holy Spirit came on all who heard the message. [45] The circumcised believers who had come with Peter were astonished that the gift of the Holy Spirit had been poured out even on the Gentiles. [46] For they heard them speaking in tongues and praising God.

Then Peter said, [47] 'Can anyone keep these people from being baptised with water? They have received the Holy Spirit just as we have.' [48] So he ordered that they be baptised in the name of Jesus Christ. Then they asked Peter to stay with them for a few days.

11 **Peter Explains His Actions** The apostles and the brothers throughout Judea heard that the Gentiles also had received the word of God. [2] So when Peter went up to Jerusalem, the circumcised believers criticised him [3] and said, 'You went into the house of uncircumcised men and ate with them.'

[4] Peter began and explained everything to them precisely as it had happened: [5] 'I was in the city of Joppa praying, and in a trance I saw a vision. I saw something like a large sheet being let down from heaven by its four corners, and it came down to where I was. [6] I looked into it and saw four-footed animals of the earth, wild beasts, reptiles, and birds of the air. [7] Then I heard a voice telling me, "Get up, Peter. Kill and eat."

[8] 'I replied, "Surely not, Lord! Nothing impure or unclean has ever entered my mouth."

[9] 'The voice spoke from heaven a second time, "Do not call anything impure that God has made clean." [10] This happened three times, and then it was pulled up to heaven again.

[11] 'Right then three men who had been sent to me from Caesarea stopped at the house where I was staying. [12] The Spirit told me to have no hesitation about going with them. These six brothers also went with me, and we entered the man's house. [13] He told us how he had seen an angel appear in his house and say, "Send to Joppa for Simon who is called Peter. [14] He will bring you a message through which you and all your household will be saved."

[15] 'As I began to speak, the Holy Spirit came on them as he had come on us at the beginning. [16] Then I remembered what the Lord had said: "John baptised with water, but you will be baptised with the Holy Spirit." [17] So if God gave them the same gift as he gave us, who believed in the Lord Jesus Christ, who was I to think that I could oppose God?'

[18] When they heard this, they had no further objections and praised God, saying, 'So then, God has granted even the Gentiles repentance unto life.'

DAY 125

ACTS 11. 19 — 30

he Church in Antioch

Now those who had been scattered by
e persecution in connection with
ephen travelled as far as Phoenicia,
prus and Antioch, telling the message
ly to Jews. [20] Some of them, however,
en from Cyprus and Cyrene, went to
ntioch and began to speak to Greeks
o, telling them the good news about
e Lord Jesus. [21] The Lord's hand was
th them, and a great number of people
lieved and turned to the Lord.

[22] News of this reached the ears of the
urch at Jerusalem, and they sent
rnabas to Antioch. [23] When he arrived
d saw the evidence of the grace of God,
was glad and encouraged them all to
main true to the Lord with all their
arts. [24] He was a good man, full of the
ly Spirit and faith, and a great number
people were brought to the Lord.

[25] Then Barnabas went to Tarsus to

> ## He was a good man, full of the
> ## Holy Spirit and faith.

ok for Saul, [26] and when he found him,
brought him to Antioch. So for a
hole year Barnabas and Saul met with
e church and taught great numbers of
ople. The disciples were called
hristians first at Antioch.

[27] During this time some prophets
me down from Jerusalem to Antioch.
One of them, named Agabus, stood up

and through the Spirit predicted that a
severe famine would spread over the
entire Roman world. (This happened
during the reign of Claudius.) [29] The
disciples, each according to his ability,
decided to provide help for the brothers
living in Judea. [30] This they did, sending
their gift to the elders by Barnabas and
Saul.

They helped their brothers.

DAY 126

ACTS 12. 1 — 25

12 Peter's Miraculous Escape From Prison

It was about this time that King Herod arrested some who belonged to the church, intending to persecute them. [2] He had James, the brother of John, put to death with the sword. [3] When he saw that this pleased the Jews, he proceeded to seize Peter also. This happened during the Feast of Unleavened Bread. [4] After arresting him, he put him in prison, handing him over to be guarded by four squads of four soldiers each. Herod intended to bring him out for public trial after the Passover.

[5] So Peter was kept in prison, but the

'Quick, get up!' he said, and the chains fell of Peter's wrists.

church was earnestly praying to God for him.

[6] The night before Herod was to bring him to trial, Peter was sleeping between two soldiers, bound with two chains, and sentries stood guard at the entrance. [7] Suddenly an angel of the Lord appeared and a light shone in the cell. He struck Peter on the side and woke him up. 'Quick, get up!' he said, and the chains fell off Peter's wrists.

[8] Then the angel said to him, 'Put on your clothes and sandals.' And Peter did so. 'Wrap your cloak around you and follow me,' the angel told him. [9] Peter followed him out of the prison, but he had no idea that what the angel was doing was really happening; he thought he was seeing a vision. [10] They passed the first and second guards and came to the iron gate leading to the city. It opened for them by itself, and they went through it. When they had walked the length of one

'Now I know without a doubt that the Lord sent his angel and rescued me...'

street, suddenly the angel left him.

[11] Then Peter came to himself and said, 'Now I know without a doubt that the Lord sent his angel and rescued me from Herod's clutches and from everything the Jewish people were anticipating.'

[12] When this had dawned on him, he went to the house of Mary the mother of John, also called Mark, where many people had gathered and were praying. [13] Peter knocked at the outer entrance, and a servant girl named Rhoda came to answer the door. [14] When she recognised Peter's voice, she was so overjoyed she ran back without opening it and exclaimed, 'Peter is at the door!'

[15] 'You're out of your mind,' they told her. When she kept insisting that it was so, they said, ' It must be his angel.'

[16] But Peter kept on knocking, and when they opened the door and saw him, they were astonished. [17] Peter motioned with his hand for them to be quiet and described how the Lord had brought him out of prison. 'Tell James and the brothers about this,' he said, and then he left for another place.

[18] In the morning, there was no small commotion among the soldiers as to what had become of Peter. [19] After Herod had a thorough search made for him and did

find him, he cross-examined the
ards and ordered that they be executed.

erod's Death

en Herod went from Judea to Caesarea
d stayed there a while. [20] He had been
arrelling with the people of Tyre and
lon; they now joined together and
ight an audience with him. Having
ured the support of Blastus, a trusted
sonal servant of the king, they asked
peace, because they depended on the
1g's country for their food supply.
[21] On the appointed day Herod,
aring his royal robes, sat on his throne
d delivered a public address to the
ople. [22] They shouted, 'This is the voice
a god, not of a man.' [23] Immediately,
cause Herod did not give praise to God,
angel of the Lord struck him down,
d he was eaten by worms and died.
[24] But the word of God continued to
crease and spread.
[25] When Barnabas and Saul had
ished their mission, they returned from
rusalem, taking with them John, also
lled Mark.

DAY 127

ACTS 13. 1 — 12

13 Barnabas and Saul Sent Off

In the church at Antioch
ere were prophets and teachers:
rnabas, Simeon called Niger, Lucius of
yrene, Manaen (who had been brought
 with Herod the tetrarch) and Saul.
Vhile they were worshipping the Lord
d fasting, the Holy Spirit said, 'Set

apart for me Barnabas and Saul for the
work to which I have called them.' [3] So
after they had fasted and prayed, they
placed their hands on them and sent
them off.

On Cyprus

[4] The two of them, sent on their way by
the Holy Spirit, went down to Seleucia
and sailed from there to Cyprus. [5] When
they arrived at Salamis, they proclaimed
the word of God in the Jewish synagogues.
John was with them as their helper.

'This is the voice of a god.'

[6] They travelled through the whole
island until they came to Paphos. There
they met a Jewish sorcerer and false
prophet named Bar-Jesus, [7] who was an
attendant of the proconsul, Sergius
Paulus. The proconsul, an intelligent
man, sent for Barnabas and Saul because
he wanted to hear the word of God. [8] But
Elymas the sorcerer (for that is what his
name means) opposed them and tried to
turn the proconsul from the faith. [9] Then
Saul, who was also called Paul, filled with
the Holy Spirit, looked straight at Elymas
and said, [10] 'You are a child of the devil
and an enemy of everything that is right!
You are full of all kinds of deceit and
trickery. Will you never stop perverting
the right ways of the Lord? [11] Now the
hand of the Lord is against you. You are
going to be blind, and for a time you will
be unable to see the light of the sun.'
Immediately mist and darkness came
over him, and he groped about, seeking
someone to lead him by the hand.
[12] When the proconsul saw what had
happened, he believed, for he was amazed
at the teaching about the Lord.

DAY 128
ACTS 13. 13 — 52

In Pisidian Antioch

[13] From Paphos, Paul and his companions sailed to Perga in Pamphylia, where John left them to return to Jerusalem. [14] From Perga they went on to Pisidian Antioch. On the Sabbath they entered the synagogue and sat down. [15] After the reading from the Law and the Prophets, the synagogue rulers sent word to them, saying, 'Brothers, if you have a message of encouragement for the people, please speak.'

[16] Standing up, Paul motioned with his hand and said: 'Men of Israel and you Gentiles who worship God, listen to me! [17] The God of the people of Israel chose our fathers; he made the people prosper during their stay in Egypt, with mighty power he led them out of that country, [18] he endured their conduct for about forty years in the desert, [19] he overthrew seven nations in Canaan and gave their land to his people as their inheritance. [20] All this took about 450 years.

'After this, God gave them judges until the time of Samuel the prophet. [21] Then the people asked for a king, and he gave them Saul son of Kish, of the tribe of Benjamin, who ruled for forty years. [22] After removing Saul, he made David their king. He testified concerning him: "I have found David son of Jesse a man after my own heart; he will do everything I want him to do."

[23] 'From this man's descendants God has brought to Israel the Saviour Jesus, as he promised. [24] Before the coming of Jesus, John preached repentance and

God raised him from the dead.

baptism to all the people of Israel. [25] As John was completing his work, he said: "Who do you think I am? I am not that one. No, but he is coming after me, whose sandals I am not worthy to untie.

[26] 'Brothers, children of Abraham, and you God-fearing Gentiles, it is to us that this message of salvation has been sent. [27] The people of Jerusalem and their rulers did not recognise Jesus, yet in condemning him they fulfilled the words of the prophets that are read every Sabbath. [28] Though they found no proper ground for a death sentence, they asked Pilate to have him executed. [29] When they had carried out all that was written about him, they took him down from the tree and laid him in a tomb. [30] But God raised him from the dead, [31] and for many days was seen by those who had travelled with him from Galilee to Jerusalem. They are now his witnesses to our people.

³² 'We tell you the good news: What
d promised our fathers ³³ he has
illed for us, their children, by raising
esus. As it is written in the second
lm:

'You are my Son;
today I have become your Father.'

he fact that God raised him from the
d, never to decay, is stated in these
rds:

'I will give you the holy and sure
blessings promised to David.'

³⁵ So it is stated elsewhere:

'You will not let your Holy One
see decay.'

³⁶ 'For when David had served God's
pose in his own generation, he fell
eep; he was buried with his fathers and
body decayed. ³⁷ But the one whom
d raised from the dead did not see
ay.

³⁸ 'Therefore, my brothers, I want
to know that through Jesus the
giveness of sins is proclaimed to you.
hrough him everyone who believes is
tified from everything you could not be
tified from by the law of Moses. ⁴⁰ Take
e that what the prophets have said
s not happen to you:

'Look, you scoffers,
wonder and perish,
for I am going to do something in
your days that you would never
believe, even if someone told you." '

⁴² As Paul and Barnabas were leaving
synagogue, the people invited them
speak further about these things on the

next Sabbath. ⁴³ When the congregation
was dismissed, many of the Jews and
devout converts to Judaism followed Paul
and Barnabas, who talked with them and
urged them to continue in the grace of
God.

⁴⁴ On the next Sabbath almost the
whole city gathered to hear the word of the
Lord. ⁴⁵ When the Jews saw the crowds,
they were filled with jealousy and talked
abusively against what Paul was saying.

⁴⁶ Then Paul and Barnabas answered

'You are my Son; today I have become your Father.'

them boldly: 'We had to speak the word
of God to you first. Since you reject it
and do not consider yourselves worthy of
eternal life, we now turn to the Gentiles.
⁴⁷ For this is what the Lord has
commanded us:

"I have made you a light for the
Gentiles,
that you may bring salvation
to the ends of the earth." '

⁴⁸ When the Gentiles heard this,
they were glad and honoured the word of
the Lord; and all who were appointed for
eternal life believed.

⁴⁹ The word of the Lord spread
through the whole region. ⁵⁰ But the Jews
incited the God-fearing women of high
standing and the leading men of the city.
They stirred up persecution against Paul
and Barnabas, and expelled them from
their region. ⁵¹ So they shook the dust
from their feet in protest against them and
went to Iconium. ⁵² And the disciples were
filled with joy and with the Holy Spirit.

DAY 129

ACTS 14. 1 — 28

14 In Iconium

At Iconium Paul and Barnabas went as usual into the Jewish synagogue. There they spoke so effectively that a great number of Jews and Gentiles believed. [2] But the Jews who refused to believe stirred up the Gentiles and poisoned their minds against the brothers. [3] So Paul and Barnabas spent considerable time there, speaking boldly for the Lord, who confirmed the message of his grace by enabling them to do miraculous signs and wonders. [4] The people of the city were divided; some sided with the Jews, others with the apostles. [5] There was a plot afoot among the Gentiles and Jews, together with their leaders, to ill-treat them and stone them. [6] But they found out about it and fled to the Lycaonian cities of Lystra and Derbe and to the surrounding country, [7] where they continued to preach the good news.

In Lystra and Derbe

[8] In Lystra there sat a man crippled in his feet, who was lame from birth and had never walked. [9] He listened to Paul as he was speaking. Paul looked directly at him, saw that he had faith to be healed [10] and called out, 'Stand up on your feet!' At that, the man jumped up and began to walk.

[11] When the crowd saw what Paul had done, they shouted in the Lycaonian language, 'The gods have come down to us in human form!' [12] Barnabas they called Zeus, and Paul they called Hermes because he was the chief speaker. [13] The priest of Zeus, whose temple was just outside the city, brought bulls and wreaths to the city gates because he and the crowd wanted to offer sacrifices to them.

[14] But when the apostles Barnabas and Paul heard of this, they tore their clothes and rushed out into the crowd shouting: [15] 'Men, why are you doing t? We too are only men, human like you. We are bringing you good news, telling you to turn from these worthless thing the living God, who made heaven and

'Men, why are you doing this?'

earth and sea and everything in them. [16] In the past, he let all nations go the own way. [17] Yet he has not left himself without testimony: He has shown kindness by giving you rain from heav and crops in their seasons; he provides you with plenty of food and fills your hearts with joy.' [18] Even with these wo they had difficulty keeping the crowd from sacrificing to them.

[19] Then some Jews came from Anti and Iconium and won the crowd over. They stoned Paul and dragged him outside the city, thinking he was dead [20] But after the disciples had gathered round him, he got up and went back i the city. The next day he and Barnaba left for Derbe.

The Return to Antioch in Syr

[21] They preached the good news in tha city and won a large number of discip Then they returned to Lystra, Iconiun and Antioch, [22] strengthening the disciples and encouraging them to rem

e to the faith. 'We must go through
ny hardships to enter the kingdom of
d,' they said. [23] Paul and Barnabas
pointed elders for them in each church
d, with prayer and fasting, committed
em to the Lord, in whom they had put
eir trust. [24] After going through Pisidia,
ey came into Pamphylia, [25] and when
ey had preached the word in Perga,
ey went down to Attalia.

[26] From Attalia they sailed back to
ntioch, where they had been committed
the grace of God for the work they had
w completed. [27] On arriving there, they
hered the church together and
ported all that God had done through
em and how he had opened the door of
th to the Gentiles. [28] And they stayed
ere a long time with the disciples.

DAY 130

ACTS 15. 1 — 35

5 The Council at Jerusalem

Some men came down from
dea to Antioch and were teaching the
thers: 'Unless you are circumcised,
cording to the custom taught by Moses,
u cannot be saved.' [2] This brought Paul
d Barnabas into sharp dispute and
bate with them. So Paul and Barnabas
re appointed, along with some other
ievers, to go up to Jerusalem to see the
ostles and elders about this question.
he church sent them on their way, and
they travelled through Phoenicia and
maria, they told how the Gentiles had
en converted. This news made all the
thers very glad. [4] When they came to
rusalem, they were welcomed by the

church and the apostles and elders, to
whom they reported everything God had
done through them.

[5] Then some of the believers who
belonged to the party of the Pharisees
stood up and said, 'The Gentiles must be
circumcised and required to obey the law
of Moses.'

[6] The apostles and elders met to
consider this question. [7] After much
discussion, Peter got up and addressed
them: 'Brothers, you know that some time
ago God made a choice among you that
the Gentiles might hear from my lips the
message of the gospel and believe. [8] God,
who knows the heart, showed that he
accepted them by giving the Holy Spirit
to them, just as he did to us. [9] He made
no distinction between us and them, for
he purified their hearts by faith. [10] Now
then, why do you try to test God by
putting on the necks of the disciples a
yoke that neither we nor our fathers have
been able to bear? [11] No! We believe it is
through the grace of our Lord Jesus that
we are saved, just as they are.'

[12] The whole assembly became silent
as they listened to Barnabas and Paul
telling about the miraculous signs and
wonders God had done among the
Gentiles through them. [13] When they
finished, James spoke up: 'Brothers, listen
to me. [14] Simon has described to us how
God at first showed his concern by taking
from the Gentiles a people for himself.
[15] The words of the prophets are in
agreement with this, as it is written:

[16] "After this I will return
    and rebuild David's fallen tent.
  Its ruins I will rebuild,
    and I will restore it,
[17] that the remnant of men may seek
    the Lord,
  and all the Gentiles who bear

my name,
says the Lord, who does these things
[18] that have been known for ages."

[19] 'It is my judgment, therefore, that we should not make it difficult for the Gentiles who are turning to God. [20] Instead we should write to them, telling them to abstain from food polluted by idols, from sexual immorality, from the meat of strangled animals and from blood. [21] For Moses has been preached in every city from the earliest times and is read in the synagogues on every Sabbath.'

The Council's Letter to Gentile Believers

[22] Then the apostles and elders, with the whole church, decided to choose some of their own men and send them to Antioch with Paul and Barnabas. They chose Judas (called Barsabbas) and Silas, two men who were leaders among the brothers. [23] With them they sent the following letter:

The apostles and elders, your brothers,

To the Gentile believers in Antioch, Syria and Cilicia:

Greetings.

[24] We have heard that some went out from us without our authorisation and disturbed you, troubling your minds by what they said. [25] So we all agreed to choose some men and send them to you with our dear friends Barnabas and Paul - [26] men who have risked their lives for the name of our Lord Jesus Christ. [27] Therefore we are sending Judas and Silas to confirm by word of mouth what we are writing. [28] It seemed good to the Holy Spirit and to us not to burden you with anything beyond

The blessing of pe

the following requirements: [29] You are abstain from food sacrificed to idols, fr blood, from the meat of strangled anim and from sexual immorality. You will d well to avoid these things.

Farewell.

[30] The men were sent off and went down to Antioch, where they gathered the church together and delivered the letter. [31] The people read it and were gl for its encouraging message. [32] Judas an Silas, who themselves were prophets, s much to encourage and strengthen the brothers. [33] After spending some time there, they were sent off by the brother with the blessing of peace to return to those who had sent them. [35] But Paul a Barnabas remained in Antioch, where they and many others taught and preached the word of the Lord.

DAY 131

GAL. 1. 1 — 24

Paul, an apostle - sent not from men nor by man, but by Jesus Christ and God the Father, who ʒed him from the dead - ² and all the ʙthers with me,

To the churches in Galatia:

³ Grace and peace to you from God ʀ Father and the Lord Jesus Christ, ho gave himself for our sins to rescue ɾrom the present evil age, according to

Grace and peace to you from God our Father

ɘ will of our God and Father, ⁵ to whom glory for ever and ever. Amen.

ʘ Other Gospel

am astonished that you are so quickly ʒerting the one who called you by the ɪce of Christ and are turning to a ɾerent gospel - ⁷ which is really no ʒpel at all. Evidently some people are ɾowing you into confusion and are ʴing to pervert the gospel of Christ. ʙut even if we or an angel from heaven ɔuld preach a gospel other than the one ɘ preached to you, let him be eternally ndemned! ⁹ As we have already said, so ʍw I say again: If anybody is preaching you a gospel other than what you cepted, let him be eternally ndemned!

¹⁰ Am I now trying to win the proval of men, or of God? Or am I trying to please men? If I were still trying to please men, I would not be a servant of Christ.

Paul Called by God

¹¹ I want you to know, brothers, that the gospel I preached is not something that man made up. ¹² I did not receive it from any man, nor was I taught it; rather, I received it by revelation from Jesus Christ.

¹³ For you have heard of my previous way of life in Judaism, how intensely I persecuted the church of God and tried to destroy it. ¹⁴ I was advancing in Judaism beyond many Jews of my own age and was extremely zealous for the traditions of my fathers. ¹⁵ But when God, who set me apart from birth and called me by his grace, was pleased ¹⁶ to reveal his Son in me so that I might preach him among the Gentiles, I did not consult any man, ¹⁷ nor did I go up to Jerusalem to see those who were apostles before I was, but I went immediately into Arabia and later returned to Damascus.

¹⁸ Then after three years, I went up to Jerusalem to get acquainted with Peter and stayed with him fifteen days. ¹⁹ I saw none of the other apostles - only James, the Lord's brother. ²⁰ I assure you before God that what I am writing to you is no lie. ²¹ Later I went to Syria and Cilicia. ²² I

And they praised God because of me.

was personally unknown to the churches of Judea that are in Christ. ²³ They only heard the report: 'The man who formerly persecuted us is now preaching the faith he once tried to destroy.' ²⁴ And they praised God because of me.

DAY 132

GAL. 2. 1 — 21

2 Paul Accepted by the Apostles

Fourteen years later I went up again to Jerusalem, this time with Barnabas. I took Titus along also. [2] I went in response to a revelation and set before them the gospel that I preach among the Gentiles. But I did this privately to those who seemed to be leaders, for fear that I was running or had run my race in vain. [3] Yet not even Titus, who was with me, was compelled to be circumcised, even though he was a Greek. [4] [This matter arose] because some false brothers had infiltrated our ranks to spy on the freedom we have in Christ Jesus and to make us slaves. [5] We did not give in to them for a moment, so that the truth of the gospel might remain with you.

[6] As for those who seemed to be important - whatever they were makes no difference to me; God does not judge by external appearance - those men added nothing to my message. [7] On the contrary, they saw that I had been entrusted with the task of preaching the gospel to the Gentiles, just as Peter had been to the Jews. [8] For God, who was at work in the ministry of Peter as an apostle to the Jews, was also at work in my ministry as an apostle to the Gentiles. [9] James, Peter and John, those reputed to be pillars, gave me and Barnabas the right hand of fellowship when they recognised the grace given to me. They agreed that we should go to the Gentiles, and they to the Jews. [10] All they asked was that we should continue to remember the poor, the very thing I was eager to do.

Paul Opposes Peter

[11] When Peter came to Antioch, I opposed him to his face, because he was clearly in the wrong. [12] Before certain men came from James, he used to eat with the Gentiles. But when they arrived he began to draw back and separate himself from the Gentiles because he was afraid of those who belonged to the circumcision group. [13] The other Jews joined him in his hypocrisy, so that by their hypocrisy even Barnabas was led astray.

[14] When I saw that they were not acting in line with the truth of the gospel I said to Peter in front of them all, 'You are a Jew, yet you live like a Gentile and not like a Jew. How is it, then, that you force Gentiles to follow Jewish customs?

[15] 'We who are Jews by birth and not "Gentile sinners" [16] know that a man is not justified by observing the law, but by faith in Jesus Christ. So we, too, have put our faith in Christ Jesus that we may be justified by faith in Christ and not by observing the law, because by observing the law no-one will be justified.

[17] 'If, while we seek to be justified in Christ, it becomes evident that we ourselves are sinners, does that mean that Christ promotes sin? Absolutely not! [18] I rebuild what I destroyed, I prove that I am a law-breaker. [19] For through the law I died to the law so that I might live for God. [20] I have been crucified with Christ and I no longer live, but Christ lives in me. The life I live in the body, I live by faith in the Son of God, who loved me and gave himself for me. [21] I do not set aside the grace of God, for if righteousness could be gained through the law, Christ died for nothing!'

DAY 133

GAL. 3. 1 — 20

Faith or Observance of the Law

You foolish Galatians! Who has ҍitched you? Before your very eyes ᴜs Christ was clearly portrayed as ᴄified. [2] I would like to learn just one ng from you: Did you receive the Spirit observing the law, or by believing what ᴜ heard? [3] Are you so foolish? After ɡinning with the Spirit, are you now ing to attain your goal by human ᴏrt? [4] Have you suffered so much for ᴄhing - if it really was for nothing? ᴊoes God give you his Spirit and work racles among you because you observe ᴇ law, or because you believe what you ard?

[6] Consider Abraham: 'He believed ᴏd, and it was credited to him as ᴄhteousness.' [7] Understand, then, that ᴏse who believe are children of ᴏraham. [8] The Scripture foresaw that ᴏd would justify the Gentiles by faith, d announced the gospel in advance to ᴏraham: 'All nations will be blessed ᴛough you.' [9] So those who have faith ᴇ blessed along with Abraham, the man faith.

[10] All who rely on observing the law ᴇ under a curse, for it is written: ᴜursed is everyone who does not ᴏntinue to do everything written in the ᴏok of the Law.' [11] Clearly no-one is ᴛstified before God by the law, because, he righteous will live by faith.' [12] The ᴠ is not based on faith; on the ᴏntrary, 'The man who does these ᴉngs will live by them.'

[13] Christ redeemed us from the curse of the law by becoming a curse for us, for it is written: 'Cursed is everyone who is hung on a tree.' [14] He redeemed us in order that the blessing given to Abraham might come to the Gentiles through Christ Jesus, so that by faith we might receive the promise of the Spirit.

The Law and the Promise

[15] Brothers, let me take an example from everyday life. Just as no-one can set aside or add to a human covenant that has been duly established, so it is in this case. [16] The promises were spoken to Abraham and to his seed. The Scripture does not say 'and to seeds', meaning many people, but 'and to your seed', meaning one person, who is Christ. [17] What I mean is this: The law, introduced 430 years later, does not set aside the covenant previously established by God and thus do away with the promise. [18] For if the inheritance depends on the law, then it no longer depends on a promise; but God in his grace gave it to Abraham through a promise.

> **Does God give you his Spirit and work miracles among you because you observe the law, or because you believe what you heard?**

[19] What, then, was the purpose of the law? It was added because of transgressions until the Seed to whom the promise referred had come. The law was put into effect through angels by a mediator. [20] A mediator, however, does not represent just one party; but God is one.

DAY 134

GAL. 3. 21 — 4.7

²¹ Is the law, therefore, opposed to the promises of God? Absolutely not! For if a law had been given that could impart life, then righteousness would certainly have come by the law. ²² But the Scripture declares that the whole world is a prisoner of sin, so that what was promised, being given through faith in Jesus Christ, might be given to those who believe.

²³ Before this faith came, we were held prisoners by the law, locked up until faith should be revealed. ²⁴ So the law was put in charge to lead us to Christ that we might be justified by faith. ²⁵ Now that faith has come, we are no longer under the supervision of the law.

Sons of God

²⁶ You are all sons of God through faith in Christ Jesus, ²⁷ for all of you who were baptised into Christ have clothed yourselves with Christ. ²⁸ There is neither Jew nor Greek, slave nor free, male nor female, for you are all one in Christ Jesus. ²⁹ If you belong to Christ, then you are Abraham's seed, and heirs according to the promise.

4 What I am saying is that as long as the heir is a child, he is no different from a slave, although he owns the whole estate. ² He is subject to guardians and trustees until the time set by his father. ³ So also, when we were children, we were in slavery under the basic principles of the world. ⁴ But when the time had fully come, God sent his Son, born of a woman, born under law,

⁵ to redeem those under law, that we might receive the full rights of sons. ⁶ Because you are sons, God sent the Spirit of his Son into our hearts, the Spirit who calls out, 'Abba, Father.' ⁷ So you are no longer a slave, but a son; and since you are a son, God has made you also an heir.

No longer a slave.

DAY 135

GAL. 4. 8 — 31

...ul's Concern for the Galatians

...ormerly, when you did not know God,
...u were slaves to those who by nature
...e not gods. ⁹ But now that you know
...od - or rather are known by God - how
...t that you are turning back to those
...ak and miserable principles? Do you
...sh to be enslaved by them all over
...in? ¹⁰ You are observing special days
...d months and seasons and years! ¹¹ I
...r for you, that somehow I have wasted
...y efforts on you.

¹² I plead with you, brothers, become
...e me, for I became like you. You have

> **I plead with you, brothers,
> :come like me, for I became like
> you.**

...ne me no wrong. ¹³ As you know, it was
...cause of an illness that I first preached
...e gospel to you. ¹⁴ Even though my
...ness was a trial to you, you did not treat
...e with contempt or scorn. Instead, you
...lcomed me as if I were an angel of
...od, as if I were Christ Jesus himself.
...What has happened to all your joy? I
...n testify that, if you could have done
..., you would have torn out your eyes and
...ven them to me. ¹⁶ Have I now become
...ur enemy by telling you the truth?

¹⁷ Those people are zealous to win
...u over, but for no good. What they
...nt is to alienate you [from us], so that
...u may be zealous for them. ¹⁸ It is fine
...be zealous, provided the purpose is
...od, and to be so always and not just
...en I am with you. ¹⁹ My dear children,

for whom I am again in the pains of
childbirth until Christ is formed in you,
²⁰ how I wish I could be with you now and
change my tone, because I am perplexed
about you!

Hagar and Sarah

²¹ Tell me, you who want to be under the
law, are you not aware of what the law
says? ²² For it is written that Abraham had
two sons, one by the slave woman and
the other by the free woman. ²³ His son by
the slave woman was born in the ordinary
way; but his son by the free woman was
born as the result of a promise.

²⁴ These things may be taken
figuratively, for the women represent two
covenants. One covenant is from Mount
Sinai and bears children who are to be
slaves: This is Hagar. ²⁵ Now Hagar stands
for Mount Sinai in Arabia and corresponds
to the present city of Jerusalem, because
she is in slavery with her children. ²⁶ But
the Jerusalem that is above is free, and she
is our mother. ²⁷ For it is written:

'Be glad, O barren woman,
  who bears no children;
break forth and cry aloud,
  you who have no labour pains;
because more are the children of the
  desolate woman
than of her who has a husband.'

²⁸ Now you, brothers, like Isaac, are
children of promise. ²⁹ At that time the
son born in the ordinary way persecuted
the son born by the power of the Spirit. It
is the same now. ³⁰ But what does the
Scripture say? 'Get rid of the slave woman
and her son, for the slave woman's son
will never share in the inheritance with
the free woman's son.' ³¹ Therefore,
brothers, we are not children of the slave
woman, but of the free woman.

DAY 136

GAL. 5. 1 — 26

5 Freedom in Christ

It is for freedom that Christ has set us free. Stand firm, then, and do not let yourselves be burdened again by a yoke of slavery.

[2] Mark my words! I, Paul, tell you that if you let yourselves be circumcised, Christ will be of no value to you at all. [3] Again I declare to every man who lets himself be circumcised that he is required to obey the whole law. [4] You who are trying to be justified by law have been alienated from Christ; you have fallen away from grace. [5] But by faith we eagerly await through the Spirit the righteousness for which we hope. [6] For in Christ Jesus neither circumcision nor uncircumcision has any value. The only thing that counts is faith expressing itself through love.

[7] You were running a good race. Who cut in on you and kept you from obeying the truth? [8] That kind of persuasion does not come from the one who calls you. [9] 'A little yeast works through the whole batch of dough.' [10] I am confident in the Lord that you will take no other view.

You were running a good race.

The one who is throwing you into confusion will pay the penalty, whoever he may be. [11] Brothers, if I am still preaching circumcision, why am I still being persecuted? In that case the offence of the cross has been abolished. [12] As for those agitators, I wish they would go the whole way and emasculate themselves!

[13] You, my brothers, were called to b free. But do not use your freedom to indulge the sinful nature; rather, serve one another in love. [14] The entire law is summed up in a single command: 'Love your neighbour as yourself.' [15] If you keep on biting and devouring each other, watch out or you will be destroyed by each other.

Life by the Spirit

[16] So I say, live by the Spirit, and you wil not gratify the desires of the sinful natur [17] For the sinful nature desires what is contrary to the Spirit, and the Spirit wh is contrary to the sinful nature. They are in conflict with each other, so that you c not do what you want. [18] But if you are l by the Spirit, you are not under law.

'Love your neighbour as yourself.'

---

[19] The acts of the sinful nature are obvious: sexual immorality, impurity and debauchery; [20] idolatry and witchcraft; hatred, discord, jealousy, fits of rage, selfish ambition, dissensions, factions [21] and envy; drunkenness, orgies, and the like. I warn you, as I did before, that tho who live like this will not inherit the kingdom of God.

[22] But the fruit of the Spirit is love, joy, peace, patience, kindness, goodness, faithfulness, [23] gentleness and self-contro Against such things there is no law. [24] Those who belong to Christ Jesus hav crucified the sinful nature with its passions and desires. [25] Since we live by the Spirit, let us keep in step with the Spirit. [26] Let us not become conceited, provoking and envying each other.

DAY 137

GAL. 6. 1 — 18

Doing Good to All

Brothers, if someone is caught in a sin, you who are spiritual should restore him gently. But watch yourself, or you also may be tempted. ² Carry each other's burdens, and in this way you will fulfil the law of Christ. ³ If anyone thinks he is something when he is nothing, he

good, for at the proper time we will reap a harvest if we do not give up. ¹⁰ Therefore, as we have opportunity, let us do good to all people, especially to those who belong to the family of believers.

Not Circumcision but a New Creation

¹¹ See what large letters I use as I write to you with my own hand!

¹² Those who want to make a good impression outwardly are trying to compel you to be circumcised. The only reason they do this is to avoid being persecuted for the cross of Christ. ¹³ Not even those

Carry each other's burdens.

deceives himself. ⁴ Each one should test his own actions. Then he can take pride in himself, without comparing himself to somebody else, ⁵ for each one should carry his own load.

⁶ Anyone who receives instruction in the word must share all good things with his instructor.

⁷ Do not be deceived: God cannot be mocked. A man reaps what he sows. ⁸ The one who sows to please his sinful nature, from that nature will reap destruction; the one who sows to please the Spirit, from the Spirit will reap eternal life. ⁹ Let us not become weary in doing

who are circumcised obey the law, yet they want you to be circumcised that they may boast about your flesh. ¹⁴ May I never boast except in the cross of our Lord Jesus Christ, through which the world has been crucified to me, and I to the world.

¹⁵ Neither circumcision nor uncircumcision means anything; what counts is a new creation. ¹⁶ Peace and mercy to all who follow this rule, even to the Israel of God.

¹⁷ Finally, let no-one cause me trouble, for I bear on my body the marks of Jesus.

¹⁸ The grace of our Lord Jesus Christ be with your spirit, brothers. Amen.

DAY 138
ACTS 15.36 — 16.15

Disagreement Between Paul and Barnabas

[36] Some time later Paul said to Barnabas, 'Let us go back and visit the brothers in all the towns where we preached the word of the Lord and see how they are doing.' [37] Barnabas wanted to take John, also called Mark, with them, [38] but Paul did not think it wise to take him, because he had deserted them in Pamphylia and had not continued with them in the work. [39] They had such a sharp disagreement that they parted company. Barnabas took Mark and sailed for Cyprus, [40] but Paul chose Silas and left, commended by the brothers to the grace of the Lord. [41] He went through Syria and Cilicia, strengthening the churches.

16 Timothy Joins Paul and Silas

He came to Derbe and then to Lystra, where a disciple named Timothy lived, whose mother was a Jewess and a believer, but whose father was a Greek. [2] The brothers at Lystra and Iconium spoke well of him. [3] Paul wanted to take him along on the journey, so he circumcised him because of the Jews who lived in that area, for they all knew that his father was a Greek. [4] As they travelled from town to town, they delivered the decisions reached by the apostles and elders in Jerusalem for the people to obey. [5] So the churches were strengthened in the faith and grew daily in numbers.

Paul's Vision of the Man of Macedonia

[6] Paul and his companions travelled throughout the region of Phrygia and Galatia, having been kept by the Holy Spirit from preaching the word in the province of Asia. [7] When they came to the border of Mysia, they tried to enter Bithynia, but the Spirit of Jesus would not allow them to. [8] So they passed by Mysia and went down to Troas. [9] During the night Paul had a vision of a man of Macedonia standing and begging him, 'Come over to Macedonia and help us.' [10] After Paul had seen the vision, we got ready at once to leave for Macedonia, concluding that God had called us to preach the gospel to them.

Lydia's Conversion in Philippi

[11] From Troas we put out to sea and sailed straight for Samothrace, and the next day on to Neapolis. [12] From there we travelled to Philippi, a Roman colony and the leading city of that district of Macedonia. And we stayed there several days.

[13] On the Sabbath we went outside the city gate to the river, where we expected to find a place of prayer. We sat down and began to speak to the women who had gathered there. [14] One of those listening was a woman named Lydia, a dealer in purple cloth from the city of Thyatira, who was a worshipper of God. The Lord opened her heart to respond to Paul's message. [15] When she and the members of her household were baptised, she invited us to her home. 'If you consider me a believer in the Lord,' she said, 'come and stay at my house.' And she persuaded us.

DAY 139

ACTS 16. 16 — 40

aul and Silas in Prison

Once when we were going to the place of ayer, we were met by a slave girl who had a irit by which she predicted the future. She rned a great deal of money for her owners fortune-telling. [17] This girl followed Paul d the rest of us, shouting, 'These men are rvants of the Most High God, who are lling you the way to be saved.' [18] She kept is up for many days. Finally Paul became so oubled that he turned round and said to e spirit, 'In the name of Jesus Christ I mmand you to come out of her!' At that oment the spirit left her.

[19] When the owners of the slave girl alised that their hope of making money as gone, they seized Paul and Silas and agged them into the market-place to face e authorities. [20] They brought them before e magistrates and said, 'These men are ws, and are throwing our city into an roar [21] by advocating customs unlawful for Romans to accept or practise.'

[22] The crowd joined in the attack gainst Paul and Silas, and the agistrates ordered them to be stripped d beaten. [23] After they had been verely flogged, they were thrown into ison, and the jailer was commanded to ard them carefully. [24] Upon receiving ch orders, he put them in the inner cell d fastened their feet in the stocks.

[25] About midnight Paul and Silas ere praying and singing hymns to God, d the other prisoners were listening to em. [26] Suddenly there was such a olent earthquake that the foundations the prison were shaken. At once all the prison doors flew open, and everybody's chains came loose. [27] The jailer woke up, and when he saw the prison doors open, he drew his sword and was about to kill himself because he thought the prisoners had escaped. [28] But Paul shouted, 'Don't harm yourself! We are all here!'

[29] The jailer called for lights, rushed in and fell trembling before Paul and Silas. [30] He then brought them out and asked, 'Sirs, what must I do to be saved?' [31] They replied, 'Believe in the Lord Jesus, and you will be saved - you and your household.' [32] Then they spoke the word of the Lord to him and to all the others in his house. [33] At that hour of the night the jailer took them and washed their wounds; then immediately he and all his family were baptised. [34] The jailer brought them into his house and set a meal before them; he was filled with joy because he had come to believe in God - he and his whole family.

[35] When it was daylight, the magistrates sent their officers to the jailer with the order: 'Release those men.' [36] The jailer told Paul, 'The magistrates have ordered that you and Silas be released. Now you can leave. Go in peace.' [37] But Paul said to the officers: 'They beat us publicly without a trial, even though we are Roman citizens, and threw us into prison. And now do they want to get rid of us quietly? No! Let them come themselves and escort us out.' [38] The officers reported this to the magistrates, and when they heard that Paul and Silas were Roman citizens, they were alarmed. [39] They came to appease them and escorted them from the prison, requesting them to leave the city. [40] After Paul and Silas came out of the prison, they went to Lydia's house, where they met with the brothers and encouraged them. Then they left.

DAY 140

ACTS 17. 1 — 15

17

In Thessalonica

When they had passed through Amphipolis and Apollonia, they came to Thessalonica, where there was a Jewish synagogue. [2] As his custom was, Paul went into the synagogue, and on three Sabbath days he reasoned with them from the Scriptures, [3] explaining and proving that the Christ had to suffer and rise from the dead. 'This Jesus I am proclaiming to you is the Christ,' he said. [4] Some of the Jews were persuaded and joined Paul and Silas, as did a large number of God-fearing Greeks and not a few prominent women.

[5] But the Jews were jealous; so they rounded up some bad characters from the market-place, formed a mob and started a riot in the city. They rushed to Jason's house in search of Paul and Silas in order to bring them out to the crowd. [6] But when they did not find them, they dragged Jason and some other brothers before the city officials, shouting: 'These men who have caused trouble all over the world have now come here, [7] and Jason has welcomed them into his house. They are all defying Caesar's decrees, saying that there is another king, one called Jesus.' [8] When they heard this, the crowd and the city officials were thrown into turmoil. [9] Then they put Jason and the others on bail and let them go.

In Berea

[10] As soon as it was night, the brothers sent Paul and Silas away to Berea. On arriving there, they went to the Jewish synagogue. [11] Now the Bereans were of more noble character than the Thessalonians, for they received the message with great eagerness and examined the Scriptures every day to see if what Paul said was true. [12] Many of the Jews believed, as did also a number of prominent Greek women and many Greek men.

[13] When the Jews in Thessalonica learned that Paul was preaching the wor of God at Berea, they went there too, agitating the crowds and stirring them u [14] The brothers immediately sent Paul tc the coast, but Silas and Timothy stayed Berea. [15] The men who escorted Paul brought him to Athens and then left wi instructions for Silas and Timothy to joi him as soon as possible.

DAY 141

ACTS 17. 16 — 34

In Athens

[16] While Paul was waiting for them in Athens, he was greatly distressed to see that the city was full of idols. [17] So he reasoned in the synagogue with the Jew and the God-fearing Greeks, as well as i the market-place day by day with those who happened to be there. [18] A group of Epicurean and Stoic philosophers begar to dispute with him. Some of them aske 'What is this babbler trying to say?' Others remarked, 'He seems to be advocating foreign gods.' They said this because Paul was preaching the good news about Jesus and the resurrection. [19] Then they took him and brought him to a meeting of the Areopagus, where they said to him, 'May we know what th

God who has made the world and everything in it is the Lord of heaven.

·w teaching is that you are presenting? You are bringing some strange ideas to ·r ears, and we want to know what they ·an.' [21] (All the Athenians and the ·eigners who lived there spent their ·ne doing nothing but talking about and ·tening to the latest ideas.)

[22] Paul then stood up in the meeting the Areopagus and said: 'Men of ·thens! I see that in every way you are ·ry religious. [23] For as I walked around ·d looked carefully at your objects of ·rship, I even found an altar with this ·scription: TO AN UNKNOWN GOD. ·ow what you worship as something ·known I am going to proclaim to you.

[24] 'The God who made the world and ·erything in it is the Lord of heaven and ·rth and does not live in temples built ·' hands. [25] And he is not served by ·man hands, as if he needed anything, ·cause he himself gives all men life and ·eath and everything else. [26] From one ·an he made every nation of men, that ·ey should inhabit the whole earth; and · determined the times set for them and ·e exact places where they should live.

[27] God did this so that men would seek him and perhaps reach out for him and find him, though he is not far from each one of us. [28] "For in him we live and move and have our being." As some of your own poets have said, "We are his offspring."

[29] 'Therefore since we are God's offspring, we should not think that the divine being is like gold or silver or stone - an image made by man's design and skill. [30] In the past God overlooked such ignorance, but now he commands all people everywhere to repent. [31] For he has set a day when he will judge the world with justice by the man he has appointed. He has given proof of this to all men by raising him from the dead.'

[32] When they heard about the resurrection of the dead, some of them sneered, but others said, 'We want to hear you again on this subject.' [33] At that, Paul left the Council. [34] A few men became followers of Paul and believed. Among them was Dionysius, a member of the Areopagus, also a woman named Damaris, and a number of others.

DAY 142

1 THESS. 1. 1 — 2.16

1 Paul, Silas and Timothy,

To the church of the Thessalonians in God the Father and the Lord Jesus Christ:

Grace and peace to you.

Thanksgiving for the Thessalonians' Faith

[2] We always thank God for all of you, mentioning you in our prayers. [3] We continually remember before our God and Father your work produced by faith, your labour prompted by love, and your endurance inspired by hope in our Lord Jesus Christ.

[4] For we know, brothers loved by

We are not trying to please men but God, who tests our hearts.

God, that he has chosen you, [5] because our gospel came to you not simply with words, but also with power, with the Holy Spirit and with deep conviction. You know how we lived among you for your sake. [6] You became imitators of us and of the Lord; in spite of severe suffering, you welcomed the message with the joy given by the Holy Spirit. [7] And so you became a model to all the believers in Macedonia and Achaia. [8] The Lord's message rang out from you not only in Macedonia and Achaia - your faith in God has become known everywhere. Therefore we do not need to say anything about it, for they themselves report what kind of reception you gave us. They tell how you turned to God from idols to serve the living and true God, [10] and to wait for his Son from heaven, whom he raised from the dead Jesus, who rescues us from the coming wrath.

2 ### Paul's Ministry in Thessalonica

You know, brothers, that our visit to you was not a failure. [2] We had previously suffered and been insulted in Philippi, as you know, but with the help of our God we dared to tell you his gospel in spite of strong opposition. [3] For the appeal we make does not spring from error or impure motives, nor are we trying to trick you. [4] On the contrary, we speak as men approved by God to be entrusted with the gospel. We are not trying to please men but God, who tests our hearts. [5] You know we never used flattery, nor did we put on a mask to cover up greed - God is our witness. [6] We were not looking for praise from men, not from you or anyone else.

As apostles of Christ we could have been a burden to you, [7] but we were gentle among you, like a mother caring for her little children. [8] We loved you so much that we were delighted to share with you not only the gospel of God but our lives as well, because you had become so dear to us. [9] Surely you remember, brothers, our toil and hardship; we worked night and day in order not to be a burden to anyone while we preached the gospel of God to you.

[10] You are witnesses, and so is God, of how holy, righteous and blameless we were among you who believed. [11] For you know that we dealt with each of you as a

ther deals with his own children,
encouraging, comforting and urging you
live lives worthy of God, who calls you
to his kingdom and glory.

[13] And we also thank God
continually because, when you received
the word of God, which you heard from
, you accepted it not as the word of
men, but as it actually is, the word of
God, which is at work in you who
believe. [14] For you, brothers, became
imitators of God's churches in Judea,
which are in Christ Jesus: You suffered
from your own countrymen the same
things those churches suffered from the
Jews, [15] who killed the Lord Jesus and
the prophets and also drove us out.
They displease God and are hostile to
all men [16] in their effort to keep us from
speaking to the Gentiles so that they
may be saved. In this way they always
heap up their sins to the limit. The
wrath of God has come upon them at
last.

e continually remember before our God and Father your work produced by faith, your labour
ompted by love, and your endurance inspired by hope in our Lord Jesus Christ.

DAY 143

1 THESS. 2.17 — 4.12

Paul's Longing to See the Thessalonians

[17] But, brothers, when we were torn away from you for a short time (in person, not in thought), out of our intense longing we made every effort to see you. [18] For we wanted to come to you - certainly I, Paul, did, again and again - but Satan stopped us. [19] For what is our hope, our joy, or the crown in which we will glory in the presence of our Lord Jesus Christ when he comes? Is it not you? [20] Indeed, you are our glory and joy.

3 So when we could stand it no longer, we thought it best to be left by ourselves in Athens. [2] We sent Timothy, who is our brother and God's fellow-worker in spreading the gospel of Christ, to strengthen and encourage you in your faith, [3] so that no-one would be unsettled by these trials. You know quite well that we were destined for them. [4] In fact, when we were with you, we kept telling you that we would be persecuted. And it turned out that way, as you well know. [5] For this reason, when I could stand it no longer, I sent to find out about your faith. I was afraid that in some way the tempter might have tempted you and our efforts might have been useless.

Timothy's Encouraging Report

[6] But Timothy has just now come to us from you and has brought good news about your faith and love. He has told us that you always have pleasant memories of us and that you long to see us, just as we also long to see you. [7] Therefore,

brothers, in all our distress and persecution we were encouraged about you because of your faith. [8] For now we really live, since you are standing firm in the Lord. [9] How can we thank God enough for you in return for all the joy we have in the presence of our God because of you? [10] Night and day we pray most earnestly that we may see you again and supply what is lacking in your faith.

[11] Now may our God and Father himself and our Lord Jesus clear the way for us to come to you. [12] May the Lord make your love increase and overflow for each other and for everyone else, just as ours does for you. [13] May he strengthen your hearts so that you will be blameless and holy in the presence of our God and Father when our Lord Jesus comes with all his holy ones.

4 **Living to Please God**
Finally, brothers, we instructed you how to live in order to please God, as in fact you are living. Now we ask you and urge you in the Lord Jesus to do this more and more. [2] For you know what instructions we gave you by the authority of the Lord Jesus.

[3] It is God's will that you should be sanctified: that you should avoid sexual immorality; [4] that each of you should learn to control his own body in a way

---

May the Lord make your love increase and overflow for each other...

---

that is holy and honourable, [5] not in passionate lust like the heathen, who do not know God; [6] and that in this matter no-one should wrong his brother or take advantage of him. The Lord will punish en for all such sins, as we have already ›ld you and warned you. ⁷ For God did ›t call us to be impure, but to live a holy ›e. ⁸ Therefore, he who rejects this ›struction does not reject man but God, ho gives you his Holy Spirit.

⁹ Now about brotherly love we do not eed to write to you, for you yourselves ave been taught by God to love each ›her. ¹⁰ And in fact, you do love all the ›others throughout Macedonia. Yet we ›ge you, brothers, to do so more and ›ore.

¹¹ Make it your ambition to lead a ›iet life, to mind your own business and › work with your hands, just as we told ›u, ¹² so that your daily life may win the ›spect of outsiders and so that you will ›t be dependent on anybody.

DAY 144

1 THESS. 4.13 — 5.28

he Coming of the Lord

Brothers, we do not want you to be ›norant about those who fall asleep, or to ieve like the rest of men, who have no ›pe. ¹⁴ We believe that Jesus died and ›se again and so we believe that God ill bring with Jesus those who have ›llen asleep in him. ¹⁵ According to the ›rd's own word, we tell you that we who ›e still alive, who are left till the coming ⸴ the Lord, will certainly not precede ›ose who have fallen asleep. ¹⁶ For the ›rd himself will come down from ›aven, with a loud command, with the ›ice of the archangel and with the ›umpet call of God, and the dead in ›hrist will rise first. ¹⁷ After that, we who ›e still alive and are left will be caught

up together with them in the clouds to meet the Lord in the air. And so we will be with the Lord for ever. ¹⁸ Therefore encourage each other with these words.

5 Now, brothers, about times and dates we do not need to write to you, ² for you know very well that the day of the Lord will come like a thief in the night. ³ While people are saying, 'Peace and safety', destruction will come on them suddenly, as labour pains on a pregnant woman, and they will not escape.

⁴ But you, brothers, are not in darkness so that this day should surprise you like a thief. ⁵ You are all sons of the light and sons of the day. We do not belong to the night or to the darkness. ⁶ So then, let us not be like others, who are asleep, but let us be alert and self-controlled. ⁷ For those who sleep, sleep at night, and those who get drunk, get drunk at night. ⁸ But since we belong to the day, let us be self-controlled, putting on faith and love as a breastplate, and the hope of salvation as a helmet. ⁹ For God did not appoint us to suffer wrath but to receive salvation through our Lord Jesus Christ. ¹⁰ He died for us so that, whether we are awake or asleep, we may live together with him. ¹¹ Therefore encourage one another and build each other up, just as in fact you are doing.

Final Instructions

¹² Now we ask you, brothers, to respect those who work hard among you, who are over you in the Lord and who admonish you. ¹³ Hold them in the highest regard in love because of their work. Live in peace with each other. ¹⁴ And we urge you, brothers, warn those who are idle, encourage the timid, help the weak, be patient with everyone. ¹⁵ Make sure that

nobody pays back wrong for wrong, but always try to be kind to each other and to everyone else.

> **He died for us so that, whether we are awake or asleep, we may live together with him.**

[16] Be joyful always; [17] pray continually; [18] give thanks in all circumstances, for this is God's will for you in Christ Jesus.

[19] Do not put out the Spirit's fire; [20] do not treat prophecies with contempt.

[21] Test everything. Hold on to the good. [22] Avoid every kind of evil.

[23] May God himself, the God of peace, sanctify you through and through. May your whole spirit, soul and body be kept blameless at the coming of our Lord Jesus Christ. [24] The one who calls you is faithful and he will do it.

[25] Brothers, pray for us. [26] Greet all the brothers with a holy kiss. [27] I charge you before the Lord to have this letter read to all the brothers.

[28] The grace of our Lord Jesus Christ be with you.

Be joyful always.

DAY 145

2 THESS. 1.1 — 2.12

1 Paul, Silas and Timothy,

To the church of the Thessalonians in God our Father and the Lord Jesus Christ:

2 Grace and peace to you from God the Father and the Lord Jesus Christ.

Thanksgiving and Prayer

We ought always to thank God for you, brothers, and rightly so, because your faith is growing more and more, and the love every one of you has for each other is increasing. 4 Therefore, among God's churches we boast about your perseverance and faith in all the persecutions and trials you are enduring.

5 All this is evidence that God's judgment is right, and as a result you will be counted worthy of the kingdom of God, for which you are suffering. 6 God is just: He will pay back trouble to those who trouble you 7 and give relief to you who are troubled, and to us as well. This will happen when the Lord Jesus is revealed from heaven in blazing fire with his powerful angels. 8 He will punish those who do not know God and do not obey the gospel of our Lord Jesus. 9 They will be punished with everlasting destruction and shut out from the presence of the Lord and from the majesty of his power 10 on the day he comes to be glorified in his holy people and to be marvelled at among all those who have believed. This includes you, because you believed our testimony to you.

11 With this in mind, we constantly pray for you, that our God may count you worthy of his calling, and that by his power he may fulfil every good purpose of yours and every act prompted by your faith. 12 We pray this so that the name of our Lord Jesus may be glorified in you, and you in him, according to the grace of our God and the Lord Jesus Christ.

2 ## The Man of Lawlessness

Concerning the coming of our Lord Jesus Christ and our being gathered to him, we ask you, brothers, 2 not to become easily unsettled or alarmed by some prophecy, report or letter supposed to have come from us, saying that the day of the Lord has already come. 3 Don't let anyone deceive you in any way, for [that day will not come] until the rebellion occurs and the man of lawlessness is revealed, the man doomed to destruction. 4 He will oppose and will exalt himself over everything that is called God or is worshipped, so that he sets himself up in God's temple, proclaiming himself to be God.

5 Don't you remember that when I was with you I used to tell you these things? 6 And now you know what is holding him back, so that he may be revealed at the proper time. 7 For the secret power of lawlessness is already at work; but the one who now holds it back will continue to do so till he is taken out of the way. 8 And then the lawless one will be revealed, whom the Lord Jesus will overthrow with the breath of his mouth and destroy by the splendour of his coming. 9 The coming of the lawless one will be in accordance with the work of Satan displayed in all kinds of counterfeit miracles, signs and wonders, 10 and in every sort of evil that deceives those who are perishing. They perish because they

refused to love the truth and so be saved.
[11] For this reason God sends them a powerful delusion so that they will believe the lie [12] and so that all will be condemned who have not believed the truth but have delighted in wickedness.

DAY 146
2 THESS. 2.13 — 3.18

Stand Firm

[13] But we ought always to thank God for you, brothers loved by the Lord, because from the beginning God chose you to be saved through the sanctifying work of the Spirit and through belief in the truth. [14] He called you to this through our gospel, that you might share in the glory of our Lord Jesus Christ. [15] So then, brothers, stand firm and hold to the teachings we passed on to you, whether by word of mouth or by letter.

[16] May our Lord Jesus Christ himself and God our Father, who loved us and by his grace gave us eternal encouragement and good hope, [17] encourage your hearts and strengthen you in every good deed and word.

3 Request for Prayer

Finally, brothers, pray for us that the message of the Lord may spread rapidly and be honoured, just as it was with you. [2] And pray that we may be delivered from wicked and evil men, for not everyone has faith. [3] But the Lord is faithful, and he will strengthen and protect you from the evil one. [4] We have confidence in the Lord that you are doing and will continue to do the things we command. [5] May the Lord direct your hearts into God's love and Christ's perseverance.

Warning Against Idleness

[6] In the name of the Lord Jesus Christ, we command you, brothers, to keep away from every brother who is idle and does not live according to the teaching you received from us. [7] For you yourselves know how you ought to follow our example. We were not idle when we were with you, [8] nor did we eat anyone's food without paying for it. On the contrary, we worked night and day, labouring and toiling so that we would not be a burden to any of you. [9] We did this, not because we do not have the right to such help, but in order to make ourselves a model for you to follow. [10] For even when we were with you, we gave you this rule: 'If a man will not work, he shall not eat.'

[11] We hear that some among you are idle. They are not busy; they are busybodies. [12] Such people we command and urge in the Lord Jesus Christ to settle down and earn the bread they eat. [13] And as for you, brothers, never tire of doing what is right.

[14] If anyone does not obey our instruction in this letter, take special note of him. Do not associate with him, in order that he may feel ashamed. [15] Yet do not regard him as an enemy, but warn him as a brother.

Final Greetings

[16] Now may the Lord of peace himself give you peace at all times and in every way. The Lord be with all of you.

[17] I, Paul, write this greeting in my own hand, which is the distinguishing mark in all my letters. This is how I write.

[18] The grace of our Lord Jesus Christ be with you all.

DAY 147

ACTS 18. 1 — 23

18 **In Corinth**
After this, Paul left Athens and went to Corinth. ² There e met a Jew named Aquila, a native of ontus, who had recently come from Italy ith his wife Priscilla, because Claudius ad ordered all the Jews to leave Rome. aul went to see them, ³ and because he as a tentmaker as they were, he stayed nd worked with them. ⁴ Every Sabbath e reasoned in the synagogue, trying to ersuade Jews and Greeks.

⁵ When Silas and Timothy came from Macedonia, Paul devoted himself xclusively to preaching, testifying to the ews that Jesus was the Christ. ⁶ But when he Jews opposed Paul and became busive, he shook out his clothes in rotest and said to them, 'Your blood be n your own heads! I am clear of my esponsibility. From now on I will go to he Gentiles.'

⁷ Then Paul left the synagogue and vent next door to the house of Titius ustus, a worshipper of God. ⁸ Crispus, the ynagogue ruler, and his entire household elieved in the Lord; and many of the Corinthians who heard him believed and vere baptised.

⁹ One night the Lord spoke to Paul in a vision: 'Do not be afraid; keep on speaking, do not be silent. ¹⁰ For I am vith you, and no-one is going to attack nd harm you, because I have many eople in this city.' ¹¹ So Paul stayed for a year and a half, teaching them the word of God.

¹² While Gallio was proconsul of Achaia, the Jews made a united attack on Paul and brought him into court. ¹³ 'This man,' they charged, 'is persuading the people to worship God in ways contrary to the law.'

¹⁴ Just as Paul was about to speak, Gallio said to the Jews, 'If you Jews were making a complaint about some misdemeanour or serious crime, it would be reasonable for me to listen to you. ¹⁵ But since it involves questions about words and names and your own law - settle the matter yourselves. I will not be a judge of such things.' ¹⁶ So he had them ejected from the court. ¹⁷ Then they all turned on Sosthenes the synagogue ruler and beat him in front of the court. But Gallio showed no concern whatever.

Priscilla, Aquila and Apollos

¹⁸ Paul stayed on in Corinth for some time. Then he left the brothers and sailed for Syria, accompanied by Priscilla and Aquila. Before he sailed, he had his hair cut off at Cenchrea because of a vow he had taken. ¹⁹ They arrived at Ephesus, where Paul left Priscilla and Aquila. He himself went into the synagogue and reasoned with the Jews. ²⁰ When they asked him to spend more time with them, he declined. ²¹ But as he left, he promised, 'I will come back if it is God's will.' Then he set sail from Ephesus. ²² When he landed at Caesarea, he went up and greeted the church and then went down to Antioch.

²³ After spending some time in Antioch, Paul set out from there and travelled from place to place throughout the region of Galatia and Phrygia, strengthening all the disciples.

DAY 148

ACTS 18. 24 — 19.22

²⁴ Meanwhile a Jew named Apollos, a native of Alexandria, came to Ephesus. He was a learned man, with a thorough knowledge of the Scriptures. ²⁵ He had been instructed in the way of the Lord, and he spoke with great fervour and taught about Jesus accurately, though he knew only the baptism of John. ²⁶ He began to speak boldly in the synagogue. When Priscilla and Aquila heard him, they invited him to their home and explained to him the way of God more adequately.

²⁷ When Apollos wanted to go to Achaia, the brothers encouraged him and wrote to the disciples there to welcome him. On arriving, he was a great help to those who by grace had believed. ²⁸ For he vigorously refuted the Jews in public debate, proving from the Scriptures that Jesus was the Christ.

19 Paul in Ephesus

¹⁹ While Apollos was at Corinth, Paul took the road through the interior and arrived at Ephesus. There he found some disciples ² and asked them, 'Did you receive the Holy Spirit when you believed?'

They answered, 'No, we have not even heard that there is a Holy Spirit.'

³ So Paul asked, 'Then what baptism did you receive?'

'John's baptism,' they replied.

⁴ Paul said, 'John's baptism was a baptism of repentance. He told the people to believe in the one coming after him, that is, in Jesus.' ⁵ On hearing this, they were baptised into the name of the Lord Jesus. ⁶ When Paul placed his hands on them, the Holy Spirit came on them, an they spoke in tongues and prophesied. ⁷ There were about twelve men in all.

⁸ Paul entered the synagogue and spoke boldly there for three months, arguing persuasively about the kingdom of God. ⁹ But some of them became obstinate; they refused to believe and publicly maligned the Way. So Paul left them. He took the disciples with him an had discussions daily in the lecture hall o Tyrannus. ¹⁰ This went on for two years, so that all the Jews and Greeks who live in the province of Asia heard the word o the Lord.

¹¹ God did extraordinary miracles through Paul, ¹² so that even handkerchiefs and aprons that had touched him were taken to the sick, and

'Did you receive the Holy Spirit when you believed?'

their illnesses were cured and the evil spirits left them.

¹³ Some Jews who went around driving out evil spirits tried to invoke the name of the Lord Jesus over those who were demon-possessed. They would say, 'In the name of Jesus, whom Paul preaches, I command you to come out.' ¹⁴ Seven sons of Sceva, a Jewish chief priest, were doing this. ¹⁵ [One day] the evil spirit answered them, 'Jesus I know, and I know about Paul, but who are you?' ¹⁶ Then the man who had the evil spirit jumped on them and overpowered them all. He gave them such a beating that they ran out of the house naked and bleeding.

...the word of the Lord spread widely and grew in power.

¹⁷ When this became known to the Jews and Greeks living in Ephesus, they were all seized with fear, and the name of the Lord Jesus was held in high honour. ¹⁸ Many of those who believed now came and openly confessed their evil deeds. ¹⁹ A number who had practised sorcery brought their scrolls together and burned them publicly. When they calculated the value of the scrolls, the total came to fifty thousand drachmas. ²⁰ In this way the word of the Lord spread widely and grew in power.

²¹ After all this had happened, Paul decided to go to Jerusalem, passing through Macedonia and Achaia. 'After I have been there,' he said, 'I must visit Rome also.' ²² He sent two of his helpers, Timothy and Erastus, to Macedonia, while he stayed in the province of Asia a little longer.

DAY 149
ACTS 19. 23 — 41

The Riot in Ephesus

²³ About that time there arose a great disturbance about the Way. ²⁴ A silversmith named Demetrius, who made silver shrines of Artemis, brought in no little business for the craftsmen. ²⁵ He called them together, along with the workmen in related trades, and said: 'Men, you know we receive a good income from this business. ²⁶ And you see and hear how this fellow Paul has convinced and led astray large numbers of people here in Ephesus and in practically the whole province of Asia. He says that

man-made gods are no gods at all.
²⁷ There is danger not only that our trade will lose its good name, but also that the temple of the great goddess Artemis will be discredited, and the goddess herself, who is worshipped throughout the province of Asia and the world, will be robbed of her divine majesty.'

²⁸ When they heard this, they were furious and began shouting: 'Great is

'Great is Artemis of the Ephesians!'

Artemis of the Ephesians!' ²⁹ Soon the whole city was in an uproar. The people seized Gaius and Aristarchus, Paul's travelling companions from Macedonia, and rushed as one man into the theatre. ³⁰ Paul wanted to appear before the crowd, but the disciples would not let him. ³¹ Even some of the officials of the province, friends of Paul, sent him a message begging him not to venture into the theatre.

³² The assembly was in confusion: Some were shouting one thing, some another. Most of the people did not even know why they were there. ³³ The Jews pushed Alexander to the front, and some of the crowd shouted instructions to him. He motioned for silence in order to make a defence before the people. ³⁴ But when they realised he was a Jew, they all shouted in unison for about two hours: 'Great is Artemis of the Ephesians!'

³⁵ The city clerk quietened the crowd and said: 'Men of Ephesus, doesn't all the world know that the city of Ephesus is the guardian of the temple of the great Artemis and of her image, which fell from heaven? ³⁶ Therefore, since these facts are undeniable, you ought to be quiet and n[ot] do anything rash. ³⁷ You have brought these men here, though they have neith[er] robbed temples nor blasphemed our goddess. ³⁸ If, then, Demetrius and his fellow craftsmen have a grievance agains[t] anybody, the courts are open and there are proconsuls. They can press charges. ³⁹ If there is anything further you want t[o] bring up, it must be settled in a legal assembly. ⁴⁰ As it is, we are in danger of being charged with rioting because of today's events. In that case we would no[t] be able to account for this commotion, since there is no reason for it.' ⁴¹ After h[e] had said this, he dismissed the assembly.

Man-made gods are no gods at al[l]

DAY 150

1 COR. 1. 1 — 19

1 Paul, called to be an apostle of Christ Jesus by the will of God, and our brother Sosthenes,

² To the church of God in Corinth, ɔ those sanctified in Christ Jesus and ɪlled to be holy, together with all ɪose everywhere who call on the name f our Lord Jesus Christ - their Lord and ɪrs:

³ Grace and peace to you from God ɪur Father and the Lord Jesus Christ.

ʰanksgiving

ɪ always thank God for you because of ɪs grace given you in Christ Jesus. ⁵ For ɪ him you have been enriched in every ɪay - in all your speaking and in all your ɪnowledge - ⁶ because our testimony ɔout Christ was confirmed in you. Therefore you do not lack any spiritual

God, who has called you into fellowship with his Son Jesus Christ our Lord, is faithful.

ɪft as you eagerly wait for our Lord Jesus ʰrist to be revealed. ⁸ He will keep you ɪrong to the end, so that you will be ɪameless on the day of our Lord Jesus ʰrist. ⁹ God, who has called you into ɪllowship with his Son Jesus Christ our ɪrd, is faithful.

Divisions in the Church

¹⁰ I appeal to you, brothers, in the name of our Lord Jesus Christ, that all of you agree with one another so that there may be no

For Christ did not send me to baptise, but to preach the gospel.

divisions among you and that you may be perfectly united in mind and thought. ¹¹ My brothers, some from Chloe's household have informed me that there are quarrels among you. ¹² What I mean is this: One of you says, 'I follow Paul'; another, 'I follow Apollos'; another, 'I follow Cephas'; still another, 'I follow Christ.'

¹³ Is Christ divided? Was Paul crucified for you? Were you baptised into the name of Paul? ¹⁴ I am thankful that I did not baptise any of you except Crispus and Gaius, ¹⁵ so no-one can say that you were baptised into my name. (¹⁶ Yes, I also baptised the household of Stephanas; beyond that, I don't remember if I baptised anyone else.) ¹⁷ For Christ did not send me to baptise, but to preach the gospel - not with words of human wisdom, lest the cross of Christ be emptied of its power.

Christ the Wisdom and Power of God

¹⁸ For the message of the cross is foolishness to those who are perishing, but to us who are being saved it is the power of God. ¹⁹ For it is written:

'I will destroy the wisdom of the wise; the intelligence of the intelligent I will frustrate.'

DAY 151
1 COR. 1. 20 — 2. 16

[20] Where is the wise man? Where is the scholar? Where is the philosopher of this age? Has not God made foolish the wisdom of the world? [21] For since in the wisdom of God the world through its wisdom did not know him, God was pleased through the foolishness of what was preached to save those who believe. [22] Jews demand miraculous signs and Greeks look for wisdom, [23] but we preach Christ crucified: a stumbling-block to Jews and foolishness to Gentiles, [24] but to those whom God has called, both Jews and Greeks, Christ the power of God and the wisdom of God. [25] For the foolishness of God is wiser than man's wisdom, and the weakness of God is stronger than man's strength.

[26] Brothers, think of what you were when you were called. Not many of you were wise by human standards; not many were influential; not many were of noble birth. [27] But God chose the foolish things of the world to shame the wise; God chose the weak things of the world to shame the strong. [28] He chose the lowly things of this world and the despised things - and the things that are not - to nullify the things that are, [29] so that no-one may boast before him. [30] It is because of him that you are in Christ Jesus, who has become for us wisdom from God - that is, our righteousness, holiness and redemption. [31] Therefore, as it is written: 'Let him who boasts boast in the Lord.'

2 When I came to you, brothers, I did not come with eloquence or superior wisdom as I proclaimed to you the testimony about God. [2] For I resolved to know nothing while I was with you except Jesus Christ and him crucified. [3] I came to you in weakness and fear, and with much trembling. [4] My message and my preaching were not with wise and persuasive words, but with a demonstration of the Spirit's power, [5] so that your faith might not rest on men's wisdom, but on God's power.

Wisdom From the Spirit

[6] We do, however, speak a message of wisdom among the mature, but not the wisdom of this age or of the rulers of this age, who are coming to nothing. [7] No, we speak of God's secret wisdom, a wisdom that has been hidden and that God destined for our glory before time began. [8] None of the rulers of this age understood it, for if they had, they would not have crucified the Lord of glory. [9] However, as it is written:

'No eye has seen,
    no ear has heard,
no mind has conceived
    what God has prepared for those
        who love him'

[10] but God has revealed it to us by his Spirit.

The Spirit searches all things, even the deep things of God. [11] For who among men knows the thoughts of a man except the man's spirit within him? In the same way no-one knows the thoughts of God except the Spirit of God. [12] We have not received the spirit of the world but the Spirit who is from God, that we may understand what God has freely given us. [13] This is what we speak, not in words taught us by human wisdom but in words taught by the Spirit, expressing spiritual truths in spiritual words. [14] The man ithout the Spirit does not accept the ings that come from the Spirit of God, r they are foolishness to him, and he nnot understand them, because they e spiritually discerned. [15] The spiritual an makes judgments about all things, it he himself is not subject to any man's dgment:

[16] 'For who has known the mind of
   the Lord
   that he may instruct him?'

it we have the mind of Christ.

DAY 152
1 COR. 3. 1 — 23

3 **On Divisions in the Church**
Brothers, I could not address you as spiritual but as worldly - mere fants in Christ. [2] I gave you milk, not lid food, for you were not yet ready for Indeed, you are still not ready. [3] You e still worldly. For since there is jealousy id quarrelling among you, are you not orldly? Are you not acting like mere en? [4] For when one says, 'I follow Paul,' id another, 'I follow Apollos,' are you it mere men?

[5] What, after all, is Apollos? And hat is Paul? Only servants, through hom you came to believe - as the Lord is assigned to each his task. [6] I planted e seed, Apollos watered it, but God ade it grow. [7] So neither he who plants or he who waters is anything, but only od, who makes things grow. [8] The man ho plants and the man who waters have e purpose, and each will be rewarded cording to his own labour. [9] For we are od's fellow-workers; you are God's field,

God's building.
[10] By the grace God has given me, I laid a foundation as an expert builder, and someone else is building on it. But each one should be careful how he builds. [11] For no-one can lay any foundation other than the one already laid, which is Jesus Christ. [12] If any man builds on this foundation using gold, silver, costly stones, wood, hay or straw, [13] his work will be shown for what it is, because the Day will bring it to light. It will be revealed with fire, and the fire will test the quality of each man's work. [14] If what he has built survives, he will receive his reward. [15] If it is burned up, he will suffer loss; he himself will be saved, but only as one escaping through the flames.

[16] Don't you know that you yourselves are God's temple and that God's Spirit lives in you? [17] If anyone destroys God's temple, God will destroy

**I planted the seed,
Apollos watered it, but God
made it grow.**

him; for God's temple is sacred, and you are that temple.

[18] Do not deceive yourselves. If any one of you thinks he is wise by the standards of this age, he should become a 'fool' so that he may become wise. [19] For the wisdom of this world is foolishness in God's sight. As it is written: 'He catches the wise in their craftiness'; [20] and again, 'The Lord knows that the thoughts of the wise are futile.' [21] So then, no more boasting about men! All things are yours, [22] whether Paul or Apollos or Cephas or the world or life or death or the present or the future - all are yours, [23] and you are of Christ, and Christ is of God.

DAY 153

1 COR. 4. 1 — 21

4 **Apostles of Christ**
So then, men ought to regard us as servants of Christ and as those entrusted with the secret things of God. ² Now it is required that those who have been given a trust must prove faithful. ³ I care very little if I am judged by you or by any human court; indeed, I do not even

---

My conscience is clear, but that does not make me innocent.

---

judge myself. ⁴ My conscience is clear, but that does not make me innocent. It is the Lord who judges me. ⁵ Therefore judge nothing before the appointed time; wait till the Lord comes. He will bring to light what is hidden in darkness and will expose the motives of men's hearts. At that time each will receive his praise from God.
⁶ Now, brothers, I have applied these things to myself and Apollos for your benefit, so that you may learn from us the meaning of the saying, 'Do not go beyond what is written.' Then you will not take pride in one man over against another. ⁷ For who makes you different from anyone else? What do you have that you did not receive? And if you did receive it, why do you boast as though you did not? ⁸ Already you have all you want! Already you have become rich! You have become kings - and that without us! How I wish that you really had become kings so that we might be kings with you! ⁹ For it

seems to me that God has put us apostles on display at the end of the procession, like men condemned to die in the arena. We have been made a spectacle to the whole universe, to angels as well as to men. ¹⁰ We are fools for Christ, but you are so wise in Christ! We are weak, but you are strong! You are honoured, we are dishonoured! ¹¹ To this very hour we go hungry and thirsty, we are in rags, we are brutally treated, we are homeless. ¹² We work hard with our own hands. When we are cursed, we bless; when we are persecuted, we endure it; ¹³ when we are slandered, we answer kindly. Up to this moment we have become the scum of the earth, the refuse of the world.
¹⁴ I am not writing this to shame you but to warn you, as my dear children. ¹⁵ Even though you have ten thousand guardians in Christ, you do not have many fathers, for in Christ Jesus I became your father through the gospel. ¹⁶ Therefore I urge you to imitate me. ¹⁷ For this reason

---

Therefore I urge you to imitate me.

I am sending to you Timothy, my son whom I love, who is faithful in the Lord. He will remind you of my way of life in Christ Jesus, which agrees with what I teach everywhere in every church.
¹⁸ Some of you have become arrogant, as if I were not coming to you. ¹⁹ But I will come to you very soon, if the Lord is willing, and then I will find out not only how these arrogant people are talking, but what power they have. ²⁰ For the kingdom of God is not a matter of talk but of power. ²¹ What do you prefer? Shall I come to you with a whip, or in love and with a gentle spirit?

DAY 154

1 COR. 5. 1 — 13

5 **Expel the Immoral Brother!** It is actually reported that there is sexual immorality among you, and a kind that does not occur even among pagans: A man has his father's wife. ² And you are proud! Shouldn't you rather have been filled with grief and have put out of your fellowship the man who did this?

know that a little yeast works through the whole batch of dough? ⁷ Get rid of the old yeast that you may be a new batch without yeast - as you really are. For Christ, our Passover lamb, has been sacrificed. ⁸ Therefore let us keep the Festival, not with the old yeast, the yeast of malice and wickedness, but with bread without yeast, the bread of sincerity and truth.

⁹ I have written to you in my letter not to associate with sexually immoral people - ¹⁰ not at all meaning the people of this world who are immoral, or the greedy and swindlers, or idolaters. In that

Even though I am not physically present, I am with you in spirit.

Even though I am not physically present, I am with you in spirit. And I have already passed judgment on the one who did this, just as if I were present. When you are assembled in the name of our Lord Jesus and I am with you in spirit, and the power of our Lord Jesus is present, ⁵ hand this man over to Satan, so that the sinful nature may be destroyed and his spirit saved on the day of the Lord.

⁶ Your boasting is not good. Don't you

case you would have to leave this world. ¹¹ But now I am writing to you that you must not associate with anyone who calls himself a brother but is sexually immoral or greedy, an idolater or a slanderer, a drunkard or a swindler. With such a man do not even eat.

¹² What business is it of mine to judge those outside the church? Are you not to judge those inside? ¹³ God will judge those outside. 'Expel the wicked man from among you.'

DAY 155

1 COR. 6. 1 — 20

6 **Lawsuits Among Believers**
If any of you has a dispute with another, dare he take it before the ungodly for judgment instead of before the saints? [2] Do you not know that the saints will judge the world? And if you are to judge the world, are you not competent to judge trivial cases? [3] Do you not know that we will judge angels? How much more the things of this life! [4] Therefore, if you have disputes about such matters, appoint as judges even men of little account in the church! [5] I say this to shame you. Is it possible that there is nobody among you wise enough to judge a dispute between believers? [6] But instead, one brother goes to law against another - and this in front of unbelievers!

[7] The very fact that you have lawsuits among you means you have been completely defeated already. Why not rather be wronged? Why not rather be cheated? [8] Instead, you yourselves cheat and do wrong, and you do this to your brothers.

[9] Do you not know that the wicked will not inherit the kingdom of God? Do not be deceived: Neither the sexually immoral nor idolaters nor adulterers nor male prostitutes nor homosexual offenders [10] nor thieves nor the greedy nor drunkards nor slanderers nor swindlers will inherit the kingdom of God. [11] And that is what some of you were. But you were washed, you were sanctified, you were justified in the name of the Lord Jesus Christ and by the Spirit of our God.

Sexual Immorality

[12] 'Everything is permissible for me' - but not everything is beneficial. 'Everything is permissible for me' - but I will not be mastered by anything. [13] 'Food for the stomach and the stomach for food' - but God will destroy them both. The body is not meant for sexual immorality, but for the Lord, and the Lord for the body. [14] By his power God raised the Lord from the dead, and he will raise us also. [15] Do you not know that your bodies are members of Christ himself? Shall I then take the members of Christ and unite them with a prostitute? Never! [16] Do you not know that he who unites himself with a prostitute is one with her in body? For it is said, 'The two will become one flesh.' [17] But he who unites himself with the Lord is one with him in spirit.

[18] Flee from sexual immorality. All other sins a man commits are outside his body, but he who sins sexually sins against his own body. [19] Do you not know that your body is a temple of the Holy Spirit, who is in you, whom you have received from God? You are not your own; [20] you were bought at a price. Therefore honour God with your body.

DAY 156

1 COR. 7. 1 — 24

7 **Marriage**
Now for the matters you wrote about: It is good for a man not to marry. [2] But since there is so much immorality, each man should have his own wife, and each woman her own husband. [3] The husband should fulfil his

arital duty to his wife, and likewise the
ife to her husband. ⁴ The wife's body
oes not belong to her alone but also to
er husband. In the same way, the
usband's body does not belong to him
lone but also to his wife. ⁵ Do not
eprive each other except by mutual

But each man has his own gift from God; one has this gift, another has that.

onsent and for a time, so that you may
evote yourselves to prayer. Then come
gether again so that Satan will not
mpt you because of your lack of self-
ontrol. ⁶ I say this as a concession, not as
command. ⁷ I wish that all men were as
am. But each man has his own gift from
od; one has this gift, another has that.

⁸ Now to the unmarried and the
idows I say: It is good for them to stay
nmarried, as I am. ⁹ But if they cannot
ontrol themselves, they should marry, for
is better to marry than to burn with
ssion.

¹⁰ To the married I give this
ommand (not I, but the Lord): A wife
ust not separate from her husband.
But if she does, she must remain
nmarried or else be reconciled to her
usband. And a husband must not
vorce his wife.

¹² To the rest I say this (I, not the
rd): If any brother has a wife who is not
believer and she is willing to live with
m, he must not divorce her. ¹³ And if a
oman has a husband who is not a
liever and he is willing to live with her,
e must not divorce him. ¹⁴ For the
believing husband has been sanctified
rough his wife, and the unbelieving

wife has been sanctified through her
believing husband. Otherwise your
children would be unclean, but as it is,
they are holy.

¹⁵ But if the unbeliever leaves, let
him do so. A believing man or woman is
not bound in such circumstances; God
has called us to live in peace. ¹⁶ How do
you know, wife, whether you will save
your husband? Or, how do you know,
husband, whether you will save your wife?

¹⁷ Nevertheless, each one should
retain the place in life that the Lord
assigned to him and to which God has
called him. This is the rule I lay down in
all the churches. ¹⁸ Was a man already
circumcised when he was called? He
should not become uncircumcised. Was a
man uncircumcised when he was called?
He should not be circumcised.

¹⁹ Circumcision is nothing and
uncircumcision is nothing. Keeping God's
commands is what counts. ²⁰ Each one
should remain in the situation which he
was in when God called him. ²¹ Were you
a slave when you were called? Don't let it
trouble you - although if you can gain
your freedom, do so. ²² For he who was a
slave when he was called by the Lord is

For he who was a slave when he was called by the Lord is the Lord's freedman; similarly, he who was a free man when he was called is Christ's slave.

the Lord's freedman; similarly, he who
was a free man when he was called is
Christ's slave. ²³ You were bought at a
price; do not become slaves of men.
²⁴ Brothers, each man, as responsible to
God, should remain in the situation God
called him to.

DAY 157

1 COR. 7. 25 — 40

[25] Now about virgins: I have no command from the Lord, but I give a judgment as one who by the Lord's mercy is trustworthy. [26] Because of the present crisis, I think that it is good for you to remain as you are. [27] Are you married? Do not seek a divorce. Are you unmarried? Do not look for a wife. [28] But if you do marry, you have not sinned; and if a virgin marries, she has not sinned. But those who marry will face many troubles in this life, and I want to spare you this.

[29] What I mean, brothers, is that the time is short. From now on those who have wives should live as if they had none; [30] those who mourn, as if they did not; those who are happy, as if they were not; those who buy something, as if it were not theirs to keep; [31] those who use the things of the world, as if not engrossed in them. For this world in its present form is passing away.

[32] I would like you to be free from

I would like you to be free from concern.

concern. An unmarried man is concerned about the Lord's affairs - how he can please the Lord. [33] But a married man is concerned about the affairs of this world - how he can please his wife - [34] and his interests are divided. An unmarried

For this world in its present form is passing away.

oman or virgin is concerned about the
ord's affairs: Her aim is to be devoted to
e Lord in both body and spirit. But a
arried woman is concerned about the
airs of this world - how she can please
r husband. ³⁵ I am saying this for your
vn good, not to restrict you, but that
u may live in a right way in undivided
votion to the Lord.

³⁶ If anyone thinks he is acting
properly towards the virgin he is
gaged to, and if she is getting on in
ars and he feels he ought to marry, he
ould do as he wants. He is not sinning.
ey should get married. ³⁷ But the man
o has settled the matter in his own
nd, who is under no compulsion but
s control over his own will, and who
s made up his mind not to marry the
gin - this man also does the right
ing. ³⁸ So then, he who marries the
gin does right, but he who does not
rry her does even better.

³⁹ A woman is bound to her husband
long as he lives. But if her husband
s, she is free to marry anyone she
shes, but he must belong to the Lord.
n my judgment, she is happier if she
ys as she is - and I think that I too
ve the Spirit of God.

DAY 158
1 COR. 8. 1 — 13

Food Sacrificed to Idols

Now about food sacrificed to idols:
We know that we all possess
owledge. Knowledge puffs up, but love
lds up. ² The man who thinks he
ows something does not yet know as he
ght to know. ³ But the man who loves

God is known by God.

⁴ So then, about eating food sacrificed
to idols: We know that an idol is nothing
at all in the world and that there is no
God but one. ⁵ For even if there are so-
called gods, whether in heaven or on
earth (as indeed there are many 'gods'

> ...there is but one Lord,
> Jesus Christ, through whom
> all things came and
> through whom we live.

and many 'lords'), ⁶ yet for us there is but
one God, the Father, from whom all
things came and for whom we live; and
there is but one Lord, Jesus Christ,
through whom all things came and
through whom we live.

⁷ But not everyone knows this. Some
people are still so accustomed to idols
that when they eat such food they think
of it as having been sacrificed to an idol,
and since their conscience is weak, it is
defiled. ⁸ But food does not bring us near
to God; we are no worse if we do not eat,
and no better if we do.

⁹ Be careful, however, that the
exercise of your freedom does not become
a stumbling-block to the weak. ¹⁰ For if
anyone with a weak conscience sees you
who have this knowledge eating in an
idol's temple, won't he be emboldened to
eat what has been sacrificed to idols? ¹¹ So
this weak brother, for whom Christ died,
is destroyed by your knowledge. ¹² When
you sin against your brothers in this way
and wound their weak conscience, you
sin against Christ. ¹³ Therefore, if what I
eat causes my brother to fall into sin, I
will never eat meat again, so that I will
not cause him to fall.

DAY 159
1 COR. 9. 1 — 27

9 **The Rights of an Apostle**
Am I not free? Am I not an apostle? Have I not seen Jesus our Lord? Are you not the result of my work in the Lord? [2] Even though I may not be an apostle to others, surely I am to you! For you are the seal of my apostleship in the Lord.

[3] This is my defence to those who sit in judgment on me. [4] Don't we have the right to food and drink? [5] Don't we have the right to take a believing wife along with us, as do the other apostles and the Lord's brothers and Cephas? [6] Or is it only I and Barnabas who must work for a living?

[7] Who serves as a soldier at his own expense? Who plants a vineyard and does not eat of its grapes? Who tends a flock and does not drink of the milk? [8] Do I say this merely from a human point of view? Doesn't the Law say the same thing? [9] For it is written in the Law of Moses: 'Do not muzzle an ox while it is treading out the grain.' Is it about oxen that God is concerned? [10] Surely he says this for us, doesn't he? Yes, this was written for us, because when the ploughman ploughs and the thresher threshes, they ought to do so in the hope of sharing in the harvest. [11] If we have sown spiritual seed among you, is it too much if we reap a material harvest from you? [12] If others have this right of support from you, shouldn't we have it all the more?

But we did not use this right. On the contrary, we put up with anything rather than hinder the gospel of Christ. [13] Don't you know that those who work in the temple get their food from the temple, and those who serve at the altar share in what is offered on the altar? [14] In the sam

Woe to me if I do not preach the gospel!

way, the Lord has commanded that thos who preach the gospel should receive their living from the gospel.

[15] But I have not used any of these rights. And I am not writing this in the hope that you will do such things for me I would rather die than have anyone deprive me of this boast. [16] Yet when I preach the gospel, I cannot boast, for I a compelled to preach. Woe to me if I do not preach the gospel! [17] If I preach voluntarily, I have a reward; if not voluntarily, I am simply discharging the trust committed to me. [18] What then is my reward? Just this: that in preaching the gospel I may offer it free of charge, and so not make use of my rights in preaching it.

[19] Though I am free and belong to n man, I make myself a slave to everyone, to win as many as possible. [20] To the Jew I became like a Jew, to win the Jews. To those under the law I became like one under the law (though I myself am not under the law), so as to win those under the law. [21] To those not having the law I became like one not having the law (though I am not free from God's law bu am under Christ's law), so as to win tho not having the law. [22] To the weak I became weak, to win the weak. I have become all things to all men so that by a possible means I might save some. [23] I do

this for the sake of the gospel, that I
ay share in its blessings.

²⁴ Do you not know that in a race all
e runners run, but only one gets the
ize? Run in such a way as to get the
ize. ²⁵ Everyone who competes in the
mes goes into strict training. They do it
get a crown that will not last; but we
it to get a crown that will last for ever.
Therefore I do not run like a man
nning aimlessly; I do not fight like a
an beating the air. ²⁷ No, I beat my body
d make it my slave so that after I have
eached to others, I myself will not be
squalified for the prize.

DAY 160

1 COR. 10. 1 — 11.1

10 ### Warnings From Israel's History
For I do not want you to be
norant of the fact, brothers, that our
refathers were all under the cloud and
at they all passed through the sea.
They were all baptised into Moses in the
oud and in the sea. ³ They all ate the
me spiritual food ⁴ and drank the same
iritual drink; for they drank from the
iritual rock that accompanied them,
d that rock was Christ. ⁵ Nevertheless,
od was not pleased with most of them;
eir bodies were scattered over the
sert.

⁶ Now these things occurred as
amples to keep us from setting our
earts on evil things as they did. ⁷ Do not
idolaters, as some of them were; as it is
ritten: 'The people sat down to eat and
ink and got up to indulge in pagan
velry.' ⁸ We should not commit sexual

immorality, as some of them did - and in
one day twenty-three thousand of them
died. ⁹ We should not test the Lord, as
some of them did - and were killed by
snakes. ¹⁰ And do not grumble, as some of
them did - and were killed by the
destroying angel.

¹¹ These things happened to them as
examples and were written down as
warnings for us, on whom the fulfilment
of the ages has come. ¹² So, if you think
you are standing firm, be careful that you
don't fall! ¹³ No temptation has seized you
except what is common to man. And
God is faithful; he will not let you be
tempted beyond what you can bear. But
when you are tempted, he will also
provide a way out so that you can stand
up under it.

Idol Feasts and the Lord's Supper

¹⁴ Therefore, my dear friends, flee from
idolatry. ¹⁵ I speak to sensible people;
judge for yourselves what I say. ¹⁶ Is not
the cup of thanksgiving for which we give
thanks a participation in the blood of
Christ? And is not the bread that we
break a participation in the body of
Christ? ¹⁷ Because there is one loaf, we,
who are many, are one body, for we all
partake of the one loaf.

> **Do you not know that in a race
> all the runners run, but only one
> gets the prize?**

¹⁸ Consider the people of Israel: Do
not those who eat the sacrifices
participate in the altar? ¹⁹ Do I mean then
that a sacrifice offered to an idol is
anything, or that an idol is anything?
²⁰ No, but the sacrifices of pagans are
offered to demons, not to God, and I do

not want you to be participants with demons. [21] You cannot drink the cup of the Lord and the cup of demons too; you cannot have a part in both the Lord's table and the table of demons. [22] Are we trying to arouse the Lord's jealousy? Are we stronger than he?

The Believer's Freedom

[23] 'Everything is permissible' - but not everything is beneficial. 'Everything is permissible' - but not everything is constructive. [24] Nobody should seek his

[29] the other man's conscience, I mean, no yours. For why should my freedom be

For why should my freedom be judged by another's conscience?

judged by another's conscience? [30] If I tal part in the meal with thankfulness, why am I denounced because of something I thank God for?

The earth is the Lord's, and everything in it.

own good, but the good of others.

[25] Eat anything sold in the meat market without raising questions of conscience, [26] for, 'The earth is the Lord's, and everything in it.'

[27] If some unbeliever invites you to a meal and you want to go, eat whatever is put before you without raising questions of conscience. [28] But if anyone says to you, 'This has been offered in sacrifice,' then do not eat it, both for the sake of the man who told you and for conscience' sake -

[31] So whether you eat or drink or whatever you do, do it all for the glory of God. [32] Do not cause anyone to stumble, whether Jews, Greeks or the church of God - [33] even as I try to please everybody in every way. For I am not seeking my own good but the good of many, so that they may be saved.

11 Follow my example, as I follow the example of Christ.

DAY 161

1 COR. 11. 2 — 34

ropriety in Worship

praise you for remembering me in
erything and for holding to the
achings, just as I passed them on to you.
³ Now I want you to realise that the
ead of every man is Christ, and the head
the woman is man, and the head of
hrist is God. ⁴ Every man who prays or
ophesies with his head covered
shonours his head. ⁵ And every woman
ho prays or prophesies with her head
ncovered dishonours her head - it is just
though her head were shaved. ⁶ If a
oman does not cover her head, she
ould have her hair cut off; and if it is a
sgrace for a woman to have her hair cut
shaved off, she should cover her head.
A man ought not to cover his head,
nce he is the image and glory of God;
ut the woman is the glory of man. ⁸ For
an did not come from woman, but
oman from man; ⁹ neither was man
eated for woman, but woman for man.
For this reason, and because of the
ngels, the woman ought to have a sign of
uthority on her head.
¹¹ In the Lord, however, woman is
ot independent of man, nor is man
ndependent of woman. ¹² For as woman
ame from man, so also man is born of
oman. But everything comes from God.
Judge for yourselves: Is it proper for a
oman to pray to God with her head
ncovered? ¹⁴ Does not the very nature of
ings teach you that if a man has long
air, it is a disgrace to him, ¹⁵ but that if a
oman has long hair, it is her glory? For
ng hair is given to her as a covering. ¹⁶ If

anyone wants to be contentious about
this, we have no other practice - nor do
the churches of God.

The Lord's Supper

¹⁷ In the following directives I have no
praise for you, for your meetings do more
harm than good. ¹⁸ In the first place, I
hear that when you come together as a
church, there are divisions among you,
and to some extent I believe it. ¹⁹ No
doubt there have to be differences among
you to show which of you have God's
approval. ²⁰ When you come together, it is
not the Lord's Supper you eat, ²¹ for as you
eat, each of you goes ahead without
waiting for anybody else. One remains
hungry, another gets drunk. ²² Don't you
have homes to eat and drink in? Or do
you despise the church of God and
humiliate those who have nothing? What

> **'This is my body, which is for
> you; do this in remembrance
> of me.'**

shall I say to you? Shall I praise you for
this? Certainly not!
²³ For I received from the Lord what I
also passed on to you: The Lord Jesus, on
the night he was betrayed, took bread,
²⁴ and when he had given thanks, he
broke it and said, 'This is my body, which
is for you; do this in remembrance of me.'
²⁵ In the same way, after supper he took
the cup, saying, 'This cup is the new
covenant in my blood; do this, whenever
you drink it, in remembrance of me.'
²⁶ For whenever you eat this bread and
drink this cup, you proclaim the Lord's
death until he comes.
²⁷ Therefore, whoever eats the bread

or drinks the cup of the Lord in an unworthy manner will be guilty of sinning against the body and blood of the Lord. [28] A man ought to examine himself before he eats of the bread and drinks of the cup. [29] For anyone who eats and drinks without recognising the body of the Lord eats and drinks judgment on himself. [30] That is why many among you are weak and sick, and a number of you have fallen asleep. [31] But if we judged ourselves, we would not come under judgment. [32] When we are judged by the Lord, we are being disciplined so that we will not be condemned with the world.

[33] So then, my brothers, when you come together to eat, wait for each other. [34] If anyone is hungry, he should eat at home, so that when you meet together it may not result in judgment.

And when I come I will give further directions.

DAY 162

1 COR. 12. 1 — 31

12 **Spiritual Gifts**
Now about spiritual gifts, brothers, I do not want you to be ignorant. [2] You know that when you were pagans, somehow or other you were influenced and led astray to mute idols. [3] Therefore I tell you that no-one who is speaking by the Spirit of God says, 'Jesus be cursed,' and no-one can say, 'Jesus is Lord,' except by the Holy Spirit.

[4] There are different kinds of gifts, but the same Spirit. [5] There are different kinds of service, but the same Lord. [6] There are different kinds of working, but the same God works all of them in all men.

[7] Now to each one the manifestation of the Spirit is given for the common good. [8] To one there is given through the Spirit the message of wisdom, to another the message of knowledge by means of the same Spirit, [9] to another faith by the same Spirit, to another gifts of healing by that one Spirit, [10] to another miraculous powers, to another prophecy, to another distinguishing between spirits, to another speaking in different kinds of tongues, and to still another the interpretation of tongues. [11] All these are

---

For we were all baptised by one Spirit into one body.

---

the work of one and the same Spirit, and he gives them to each one, just as he determines.

One Body, Many Parts

[12] The body is a unit, though it is made up of many parts; and though all its parts are many, they form one body. So it is with Christ. [13] For we were all baptised by one Spirit into one body - whether Jews or Greeks, slave or free - and we were all given the one Spirit to drink.

[14] Now the body is not made up of one part but of many. [15] If the foot should say, 'Because I am not a hand, I do not belong to the body,' it would not for that reason cease to be part of the body. [16] And if the ear should say, 'Because I am not an eye, I do not belong to the body,' it would not for that reason cease to be part of the body. [17] If the whole body were an eye, where would the sense of hearing be? If the whole body were an ear, where would the sense of smell be? [18] But in fact God

arranged the parts in the body, every
e of them, just as he wanted them to
¹⁹ If they were all one part, where
uld the body be? ²⁰ As it is, there are
ny parts, but one body.
²¹ The eye cannot say to the hand,
on't need you!' And the head cannot
to the feet, 'I don't need you!' ²² On

the body, but that its parts should have
equal concern for each other. ²⁶ If one
part suffers, every part suffers with it; if
one part is honoured, every part rejoices
with it.
²⁷ Now you are the body of Christ,
and each one of you is a part of it. ²⁸ And
in the church God has appointed first of

We are the body of Christ.

e contrary, those parts of the body that
em to be weaker are indispensable,
and the parts that we think are less
nourable we treat with special honour.
d the parts that are unpresentable are
ated with special modesty, ²⁴ while our
esentable parts need no special
atment. But God has combined the
embers of the body and has given
eater honour to the parts that lacked it,
o that there should be no division in

all apostles, second prophets, third
teachers, then workers of miracles, also
those having gifts of healing, those able
to help others, those with gifts of
administration, and those speaking in
different kinds of tongues. ²⁹ Are all
apostles? Are all prophets? Are all
teachers? Do all work miracles? ³⁰ Do all
have gifts of healing? Do all speak in
tongues? Do all interpret? ³¹ But eagerly
desire the greater gifts.

DAY 163

1 COR. 13. 1 — 13

13 **Love**
And now I will show you the most excellent way.
If I speak in the tongues of men and of angels, but have not love, I am only a resounding gong or a clanging cymbal. [2] If I have the gift of prophecy and can fathom all mysteries and all knowledge, and if I have a faith that can move mountains, but have not love, I am nothing. [3] If I give all I possess to the poor and surrender my body to the flames, but have not love, I gain nothing.

Love is patient, love is kind. It does not envy, it does not boast, it is not proud.

---

[4] Love is patient, love is kind. It does not envy, it does not boast, it is not proud. [5] It is not rude, it is not self-seeking, it is not easily angered, it keeps no record of wrongs. [6] Love does not delight in evil but rejoices with the truth. [7] It always protects, always trusts, always hopes, always perseveres.

[8] Love never fails. But where there are prophecies, they will cease; where there are tongues, they will be stilled; where there is knowledge, it will pass away. [9] For we know in part and we prophesy in part, [10] but when perfection comes, the imperfect disappears. [11] When I was a child, I talked like a child, I thought like a child, I reasoned like a child. When I became a man, I put childish ways behind me. [12] Now we see but a poor reflection as in a mirror; then we shall see face to face. Now I know in part; then I shall know fully, even as I am fully known.

[13] And now these three remain: faith, hope and love. But the greatest of these love.

DAY 164

1 COR. 14. 1 — 25

14 **Gifts of Prophecy and Tongues**
Follow the way of love and eagerly desire spiritual gifts, especially the gift of prophecy. [2] For anyone who speaks in a tongue does not speak to men but to God. Indeed, no-one understands him; he utters mysteries with his spirit. [3] But everyone who prophesies speaks to men for their strengthening, encouragement and comfort. [4] He who speaks in a tongue edifies himself, but he who prophesies edifies the church. [5] I would like every one of you to speak in tongues, but I would rather have you prophesy. He who prophesies is greater than one who speaks in tongues, unless he interprets, so that the church may be edified.

[6] Now, brothers, if I come to you and speak in tongues, what good will I be to you, unless I bring you some revelation or knowledge or prophecy or word of instruction? [7] Even in the case of lifeless things that make sounds, such as the flute or harp, how will anyone know what tune is being played unless there is a distinction in the notes? [8] Again, if the trumpet does not sound a clear call, who

I get ready for battle? [9] So it is with ... . Unless you speak intelligible words ...h your tongue, how will anyone know ...at you are saying? You will just be ...aking into the air. [10] Undoubtedly ...re are all sorts of languages in the ...rld, yet none of them is without ...aning. [11] If then I do not grasp the ...aning of what someone is saying, I am ...oreigner to the speaker, and he is a ...eigner to me. [12] So it is with you. Since ...u are eager to have spiritual gifts, try to ...cel in gifts that build up the church.

[13] For this reason anyone who speaks ...a tongue should pray that he may ...erpret what he says. [14] For if I pray in a ...ngue, my spirit prays, but my mind is

church I would rather speak five intelligible words to instruct others than ten thousand words in a tongue.

[20] Brothers, stop thinking like children. In regard to evil be infants, but in your thinking be adults. [21] In the Law it is written:

'Through men of strange tongues
and through the lips of foreigners
I will speak to this people, but even
then they will not listen to me,'
says the Lord.

[22] Tongues, then, are a sign, not for believers but for unbelievers; prophecy, however, is for believers, not for

God is really among you.

...fruitful. [15] So what shall I do? I will pray ...th my spirit, but I will also pray with ...y mind; I will sing with my spirit, but I ...ll also sing with my mind. [16] If you are ...aising God with your spirit, how can ...e who finds himself among those who ...not understand say 'Amen' to your ...anksgiving, since he does not know ...hat you are saying? [17] You may be giving ...anks well enough, but the other man is ...ot edified.

[18] I thank God that I speak in ...ngues more than all of you. [19] But in the

unbelievers. [23] So if the whole church comes together and everyone speaks in tongues, and some who do not understand or some unbelievers come in, will they not say that you are out of your mind? [24] But if an unbeliever or someone who does not understand comes in while everybody is prophesying, he will be convinced by all that he is a sinner and will be judged by all, [25] and the secrets of his heart will be laid bare. So he will fall down and worship God, exclaiming, 'God is really among you!'

DAY 165

1 COR. 14. 26 — 40

Orderly Worship

[26] What then shall we say, brothers? When you come together, everyone has a hymn, or a word of instruction, a revelation, a tongue or an interpretation. All of these must be done for the strengthening of the church. [27] If anyone speaks in a tongue, two - or at the most three - should speak, one at a time, and someone must interpret. [28] If there is no interpreter, the speaker should keep quiet in the church and speak to himself and God.

[29] Two or three prophets should speak, and the others should weigh carefully what is said. [30] And if a revelation comes to someone who is sitting down, the first speaker should stop. [31] For you can all prophesy in turn so that everyone may be instructed and encouraged. [32] The spirits of prophets are subject to the control of prophets. [33] For God is not a God of disorder but of peace.

As in all the congregations of the saints, [34] women should remain silent in the churches. They are not allowed to speak, but must be in submission, as the Law says. [35] If they want to enquire about something, they should ask their own husbands at home; for it is disgraceful for a woman to speak in the church.

[36] Did the word of God originate with you? Or are you the only people it has reached? [37] If anybody thinks he is a prophet or spiritually gifted, let him acknowledge that what I am writing to you is the Lord's command. [38] If he ignores this, he himself will be ignored.

For God is not a God of disorder but of peace.

[39] Therefore, my brothers, be eager t prophesy, and do not forbid speaking in tongues. [40] But everything should be don in a fitting and orderly way.

DAY 166

1 COR. 15. 1 — 34

15 The Resurrection of Christ

Now, brothers, I want to remind you of the gospel I preached to you, which you received and on which you have taken your stand. [2] By this gospel you are saved, if you hold firmly t the word I preached to you. Otherwise, you have believed in vain.

[3] For what I received I passed on to

ou as of first importance: that Christ ied for our sins according to the criptures, ⁴ that he was buried, that he as raised on the third day according to ie Scriptures, ⁵ and that he appeared to eter, and then to the Twelve. ⁶ After iat, he appeared to more than five undred of the brothers at the same time, iost of whom are still living, though ome have fallen asleep. ⁷ Then he ppeared to James, then to all the postles, ⁸ and last of all he appeared to ie also, as to one abnormally born.

⁹ For I am the least of the apostles nd do not even deserve to be called an postle, because I persecuted the church f God. ¹⁰ But by the grace of God I am hat I am, and his grace to me was not ithout effect. No, I worked harder than ll of them - yet not I, but the grace of iod that was with me. ¹¹ Whether, then, was I or they, this is what we preach, nd this is what you believed.

he Resurrection of the Dead

But if it is preached that Christ has een raised from the dead, how can some f you say that there is no resurrection of he dead? ¹³ If there is no resurrection of he dead, then not even Christ has been aised. ¹⁴ And if Christ has not been aised, our preaching is useless and so is our faith. ¹⁵ More than that, we are then ound to be false witnesses about God, for ve have testified about God that he aised Christ from the dead. But he did iot raise him if in fact the dead are not aised. ¹⁶ For if the dead are not raised, hen Christ has not been raised either. ' And if Christ has not been raised, your aith is futile; you are still in your sins. ' Then those also who have fallen asleep n Christ are lost. ¹⁹ If only for this life we iave hope in Christ, we are to be pitied iore than all men.

²⁰ But Christ has indeed been raised from the dead, the firstfruits of those who have fallen asleep. ²¹ For since death came through a man, the resurrection of the dead comes also through a man. ²² For as in Adam all die, so in Christ all will be made alive. ²³ But each in his own turn: Christ, the firstfruits; then, when he comes, those who belong to him. ²⁴ Then the end will come, when he hands over the kingdom to God the Father after he has destroyed all dominion, authority and power. ²⁵ For he must reign until he has put all his enemies under his feet. ²⁶ The last enemy to be destroyed is death. ²⁷ For he 'has put everything under his feet'. Now when it says that 'everything' has been put under him, it is clear that this does not include God himself, who put everything under Christ. ²⁸ When he has done this, then the Son himself will be made subject to him who put everything under him, so that God may be all in all.

²⁹ Now if there is no resurrection, what will those do who are baptised for the dead? If the dead are not raised at all, why are people baptised for them? ³⁰ And as for us, why do we endanger ourselves every hour? ³¹ I die every day - I mean that, brothers - just as surely as I glory over you in Christ Jesus our Lord. ³² If I fought wild beasts in Ephesus for merely human reasons, what have I gained? If the dead are not raised,

'Let us eat and drink,
    for tomorrow we die.'

³³ Do not be misled: 'Bad company corrupts good character.' ³⁴ Come back to your senses as you ought, and stop sinning; for there are some who are ignorant of God - I say this to your shame.

DAY 167

1 COR. 15. 35 — 58

The Resurrection Body

[35] But someone may ask, 'How are the dead raised? With what kind of body will they come?' [36] How foolish! What you sow does not come to life unless it dies. [37] When you sow, you do not plant the

---

'How are the dead raised?'

---

body that will be, but just a seed, perhaps of wheat or of something else. [38] But God gives it a body as he has determined, and to each kind of seed he gives its own body. [39] All flesh is not the same: Men have one kind of flesh, animals have another, birds another and fish another. [40] There are also heavenly bodies and there are earthly bodies; but the splendour of the heavenly bodies is one kind, and the splendour of the earthly bodies is another. [41] The sun has one kind of splendour, the moon another and the stars another; and star differs from star in splendour.

[42] So will it be with the resurrection of the dead. The body that is sown is perishable, it is raised imperishable; [43] it is sown in dishonour, it is raised in glory; it is sown in weakness, it is raised in power; [44] it is sown a natural body, it is raised a spiritual body.

If there is a natural body, there is also a spiritual body. [45] So it is written: 'The first man Adam became a living being'; the last Adam, a life-giving spirit. [46] The spiritual did not come first, but the natural, and after that the spiritual. [47] The first man was of the dust of the earth, the second man from heaven. [48] As was the earthly man, so are those who are of the earth; and as is the man from heaven, so also are those who are of heaven. [49] And just as we have borne the likeness of the earthly man, so shall we bear the likeness of the man from heaven.

[50] I declare to you, brothers, that flesh and blood cannot inherit the kingdom of God, nor does the perishable inherit the imperishable. [51] Listen, I tell you a mystery: We will not all sleep, but we will all be changed - [52] in a flash, in the twinkling of an eye, at the last trumpet. For the trumpet will sound, the dead will be raised imperishable, and we will be changed. [53] For the perishable must clothe itself with the imperishable, and the mortal with immortality. [54] When the perishable has been clothed with the imperishable, and the mortal with immortality, then the saying that is written will come true: 'Death has been swallowed up in victory.'

[55] 'Where, O death, is your victory?
Where, O death, is your sting?'

[56] The sting of death is sin, and the power of sin is the law. [57] But thanks be to God! He gives us the victory through our Lord Jesus Christ.

[58] Therefore, my dear brothers, stand

He gives us the victory through our Lord Jesus Christ.

---

firm. Let nothing move you. Always give yourselves fully to the work of the Lord, because you know that your labour in the Lord is not in vain.

DAY 168

1 COR. 16. 1 — 24

16 The Collection for God's People

Now about the collection for od's people: Do what I told the alatian churches to do. ² On the first ay of every week, each one of you should t aside a sum of money in keeping with s income, saving it up, so that when I ome no collections will have to be made. Then, when I arrive, I will give letters of troduction to the men you approve and nd them with your gift to Jerusalem. ⁴ If seems advisable for me to go also, they ll accompany me.

ersonal Requests

After I go through Macedonia, I will ome to you - for I will be going through acedonia. ⁶ Perhaps I will stay with you vhile, or even spend the winter, so that u can help me on my journey, wherever ʒo. ⁷ I do not want to see you now and ake only a passing visit; I hope to spend me time with you, if the Lord permits. ut I will stay on at Ephesus until ntecost, ⁹ because a great door for fective work has opened to me, and ere are many who oppose me.

¹⁰ If Timothy comes, see to it that he s nothing to fear while he is with you, r he is carrying on the work of the Lord, st as I am. ¹¹ No-one, then, should refuse accept him. Send him on his way in ace so that he may return to me. I am pecting him along with the brothers.

¹² Now about our brother Apollos: trongly urged him to go to you with the others. He was quite unwilling to go

now, but he will go when he has the opportunity.

¹³ Be on your guard; stand firm in the faith; be men of courage; be strong. ¹⁴ Do everything in love.

¹⁵ You know that the household of Stephanas were the first converts in Achaia, and they have devoted themselves to the service of the saints. I urge you, brothers, ¹⁶ to submit to such as these and to everyone who joins in the work, and labours at it. ¹⁷ I was glad when

> **Be on your guard; stand firm in the faith; be men of courage; be strong.**

Stephanas, Fortunatus and Achaicus arrived, because they have supplied what was lacking from you. ¹⁸ For they refreshed my spirit and yours also. Such men deserve recognition.

Final Greetings

¹⁹ The churches in the province of Asia send you greetings. Aquila and Priscilla greet you warmly in the Lord, and so does the church that meets at their house. ²⁰ All the brothers here send you greetings. Greet one another with a holy kiss.

²¹ I, Paul, write this greeting in my own hand.

²² If anyone does not love the Lord - a curse be on him. Come, O Lord!

²³ The grace of the Lord Jesus be with you.

²⁴ My love to all of you in Christ Jesus. Amen.

DAY 169
ACTS 20. 1 — 16

20 Through Macedonia and Greece

When the uproar had ended, Paul sent for the disciples and, after encouraging them, said good-bye and set out for Macedonia. ² He travelled through that area, speaking many words of encouragement to the people, and finally arrived in Greece, ³ where he stayed three months. Because the Jews made a plot against him just as he was about to sail for Syria, he decided to go back through

---

He travelled through that area, speaking many words of encouragement to the people...

Macedonia. ⁴ He was accompanied by Sopater son of Pyrrhus from Berea, Aristarchus and Secundus from Thessalonica, Gaius from Derbe, Timothy also, and Tychicus and Trophimus from the province of Asia. ⁵ These men went on ahead and waited for us at Troas. ⁶ But we sailed from Philippi after the Feast of Unleavened Bread, and five days later joined the others at Troas, where we stayed seven days.

Eutychus Raised From the Dead at Troas

⁷ On the first day of the week we came together to break bread. Paul spoke to the people and, because he intended to leave the next day, kept on talking until midnight. ⁸ There were many lamps in the upstairs room where we were meeting. ⁹ Seated in a window was a young man named Eutychus, who was sinking into a deep sleep as Paul talked on and on. When he was sound asleep, he fell to the ground from the third storey and was picked up dead. ¹⁰ Paul went down, threw himself on the young man and put his arms around him. 'Don't be alarmed,' he said. 'He's alive!' ¹¹ Then he went upstairs again and broke bread and ate. After

---

'Don't be alarmed,' he said. 'He's alive!'

---

talking until daylight, he left. ¹² The people took the young man home alive and were greatly comforted.

Paul's Farewell to the Ephesian Elders

¹³ We went on ahead to the ship and sailed for Assos, where we were going to take Paul aboard. He had made this arrangement because he was going there on foot. ¹⁴ When he met us at Assos, we took him aboard and went on to Mitylene. ¹⁵ The next day we set sail from there and arrived off Kios. The day after that we crossed over to Samos, and on the following day arrived at Miletus. ¹⁶ Paul had decided to sail past Ephesus to avoid spending time in the province of Asia, for he was in a hurry to reach Jerusalem, if possible, by the day of Pentecost.

DAY 170

2 COR. 1. 1 — 2.4

1 Paul, an apostle of Christ Jesus by the will of God, and Timothy our brother,

To the church of God in Corinth, together with all the saints throughout Achaia:

² Grace and peace to you from God our Father and the Lord Jesus Christ.

The God of All Comfort

³ Praise be to the God and Father of our Lord Jesus Christ, the Father of compassion and the God of all comfort, ⁴ who comforts us in all our troubles, so that we can comfort those in any trouble with the comfort we ourselves have received from God. ⁵ For just as the sufferings of Christ flow over into our lives, so also through Christ our comfort overflows. ⁶ If we are distressed, it is for your comfort and salvation; if we are comforted, it is for your comfort, which produces in you patient endurance of the same sufferings we suffer. ⁷ And our hope for you is firm, because we know that just as you share in our sufferings, so also you share in our comfort.

⁸ We do not want you to be uninformed, brothers, about the hardships we suffered in the province of Asia. We were under great pressure, far beyond our ability to endure, so that we despaired even of life. ⁹ Indeed, in our hearts we felt the sentence of death. But this happened that we might not rely on ourselves but on God, who raises the dead. ¹⁰ He has

delivered us from such a deadly peril, and he will deliver us. On him we have set our hope that he will continue to deliver us, ¹¹ as you help us by your prayers. Then many will give thanks on our behalf for the gracious favour granted us in answer to the prayers of many.

Paul's Change of Plans

¹² Now this is our boast: Our conscience testifies that we have conducted ourselves in the world, and especially in our relations with you, in the holiness and sincerity that are from God. We have done so not according to worldly wisdom but according to God's grace. ¹³ For we do not write to you anything you cannot read or understand. And I hope that, ¹⁴ as you have understood us in part, you will come to understand fully that you can boast of us just as we will boast of you in the day of the Lord Jesus.

¹⁵ Because I was confident of this, I

> **Grace and peace to you from God our Father and the Lord Jesus Christ.**

planned to visit you first so that you might benefit twice. ¹⁶ I planned to visit you on my way to Macedonia and to come back to you from Macedonia, and then to have you send me on my way to Judea. ¹⁷ When I planned this, did I do it lightly? Or do I make my plans in a worldly manner so that in the same breath I say, 'Yes, yes' and 'No, no'?

¹⁸ But as surely as God is faithful, our message to you is not 'Yes' and 'No'. ¹⁹ For the Son of God, Jesus Christ, who was preached among you by me and Silas and Timothy, was not 'Yes' and 'No', but in

him it has always been 'Yes'. ²⁰For no matter how many promises God has made, they are 'Yes' in Christ. And so through him the 'Amen' is spoken by us to the glory of God. ²¹Now it is God who makes both us and you stand firm in Christ. He anointed us, ²²set his seal of ownership on us, and put his Spirit in our hearts as a deposit, guaranteeing what is to come.

²³I call God as my witness that it was in order to spare you that I did not return to Corinth. ²⁴Not that we lord it over your faith, but we work with you for your joy, because it is by faith you stand firm.

2 So I made up my mind that I would not make another painful visit to you. ²For if I grieve you, who is left to make me glad but you whom I have grieved? ³I wrote as I did so that when I came I should not be distressed by those who ought to make me rejoice. I had confidence in all of you, that you would all share my joy. ⁴For I wrote to you out of great distress and anguish of heart and with many tears, not to grieve you but to let you know the depth of my love for you.

DAY 171
2 COR. 2. 5—17

Forgiveness for the Sinner
⁵If anyone has caused grief, he has not so much grieved me as he has grieved all of you, to some extent - not to put it too severely. ⁶The punishment inflicted on him by the majority is sufficient for him. ⁷Now instead, you ought to forgive and comfort him, so that he will not be overwhelmed by excessive sorrow. ⁸I urge you, therefore, to reaffirm your love for him. ⁹The reason I wrote to you was to see if you would stand the test and be obedient in everything. ¹⁰If you forgive anyone, I also forgive him. And what I have forgiven - if there was anything to forgive - I have forgiven in the sight of Christ for your sake, ¹¹in order that Satan might not outwit us. For we are not unaware of his schemes.

Ministers of the New Covenant
¹²Now when I went to Troas to preach the gospel of Christ and found that the Lord had opened a door for me, ¹³I still had no peace of mind, because I did not

---

If you forgive anyone, I also forgive him.

---

find my brother Titus there. So I said good-bye to them and went on to Macedonia.

¹⁴But thanks be to God, who always leads us in triumphal procession in Christ and through us spreads everywhere the fragrance of the knowledge of him. ¹⁵For we are to God the aroma of Christ among those who are being saved and those who are perishing. ¹⁶To the one we are the smell of death; to the other, the fragrance of life. And who is equal to such a task? ¹⁷Unlike so many, we do not peddle the word of God for profit. On the contrary, in Christ we speak before God with sincerity, like men sent from God.

DAY 172

2 COR. 3. 1 — 18

3 Are we beginning to commend ourselves again? Or do we need, like some people, letters of recommendation to you or from you? You yourselves are our letter, written on our hearts, known and read by everybody. You show that you are a letter from Christ, the result of our ministry, written not with ink but with the Spirit of the living God, not on tablets of stone but on tablets of human hearts.

4 Such confidence as this is ours through Christ before God. 5 Not that we are competent in ourselves to claim anything for ourselves, but our competence comes from God. 6 He has made us competent as ministers of a new covenant - not of the letter but of the Spirit; for the letter kills, but the Spirit gives life.

The Glory of the New Covenant

7 Now if the ministry that brought death, which was engraved in letters on stone, came with glory, so that the Israelites could not look steadily at the face of Moses because of its glory, fading though it was, 8 will not the ministry of the Spirit be even more glorious? 9 If the ministry that condemns men is glorious, how much more glorious is the ministry that brings righteousness! 10 For what was glorious has no glory now in comparison with the surpassing glory. 11 And if what was fading away came with glory, how much greater is the glory of that which lasts!

12 Therefore, since we have such a hope, we are very bold. 13 We are not like Moses, who would put a veil over his face to keep the Israelites from gazing at it while the radiance was fading away. 14 But their minds were made dull, for to this day the same veil remains when the old covenant is read. It has not been removed, because only in Christ is it taken away. 15 Even to this day when Moses is read, a veil covers their hearts. 16 But whenever anyone turns to the Lord, the veil is taken away. 17 Now the Lord is the Spirit, and where the Spirit of the Lord is, there is freedom. 18 And we, who with unveiled faces all reflect the Lord's glory, are being transformed into his likeness with ever-increasing glory, which comes from the Lord, who is the Spirit.

...where the Spirit of the Lord is, there is freedom.

DAY 173

2 COR. 4.1 — 5.10

4 **Treasures in Jars of Clay**
Therefore, since through God's mercy we have this ministry, we do not lose heart. [2] Rather, we have renounced secret and shameful ways; we do not use deception, nor do we distort the word of God. On the contrary, by setting forth the truth plainly we commend ourselves to every man's conscience in the sight of God. [3] And even if our gospel is veiled, it is veiled to those who are perishing. [4] The god of this age has blinded the minds of unbelievers, so that they cannot see the light of the gospel of the glory of Christ, who is the image of God. [5] For we do not preach ourselves, but Jesus Christ as Lord, and ourselves as your servants for Jesus' sake. [6] For God, who said, 'Let light shine out of darkness,' made his light shine in our hearts to give us the light of the knowledge of the glory of God in the face of Christ.

[7] But we have this treasure in jars of clay to show that this all-surpassing power is from God and not from us. [8] We are hard pressed on every side, but not crushed; perplexed, but not in despair; [9] persecuted, but not abandoned; struck down, but not destroyed. [10] We always carry around in our body the death of Jesus, so that the life of Jesus may also be revealed in our body. [11] For we who are alive are always being given over to death for Jesus' sake, so that his life may be revealed in our mortal body. [12] So then, death is at work in us, but life is at work in you.

[13] It is written: 'I believed; therefore I have spoken.' With that same spirit of faith we also believe and therefore speak [14] because we know that the one who raised the Lord Jesus from the dead will also raise us with Jesus and present us with you in his presence. [15] All this is for your benefit, so that the grace that is reaching more and more people may cause thanksgiving to overflow to the glory of God.

[16] Therefore we do not lose heart. Though outwardly we are wasting away, yet inwardly we are being renewed day by day. [17] For our light and momentary troubles are achieving for us an eternal glory that far outweighs them all. [18] So we fix our eyes not on what is seen, but on what is unseen. For what is seen is temporary, but what is unseen is eternal.

5 **Our Heavenly Dwelling**
Now we know that if the earthly tent we live in is destroyed, we have a building from God, an eternal house in heaven, not built by human hands. [2] Meanwhile we groan, longing to be clothed with our heavenly dwelling, [3] because when we are clothed, we will not be found naked. [4] For while we are in this tent, we groan and are burdened, because we do not wish to be unclothed but to be clothed with our heavenly dwelling, so that what is mortal may be swallowed up by life. [5] Now it is God who has made us for this very purpose and has given us the Spirit as a deposit, guaranteeing what is to come.

[6] Therefore we are always confident and know that as long as we are at home in the body we are away from the Lord. [7] We live by faith, not by sight. [8] We are confident, I say, and would prefer to be away from the body and at home with the Lord. [9] So we make it our goal to please

im, whether we are at home in the body or away from it. [10] For we must all appear before the judgment seat of Christ, that each one may receive what is due to him for the things done while in the body, whether good or bad.

DAY 174

2 COR. 5. 11 — 6.13

The Ministry of Reconciliation

[11] Since, then, we know what it is to fear the Lord, we try to persuade men. What we are is plain to God, and I hope it is also plain to your conscience. [12] We are not trying to commend ourselves to you again, but are giving you an opportunity to take pride in us, so that you can answer those who take pride in what is seen rather than in what is in the heart. [13] If we are out of our mind, it is for the sake of God; if we are in our right mind, it is for you. [14] For Christ's love compels us, because we are convinced that one died for all, and therefore all died. [15] And he died for all, that those who live should no longer live for themselves but for him who died for them and was raised again.

[16] So from now on we regard no-one from a worldly point of view. Though we once regarded Christ in this way, we do so no longer. [17] Therefore, if anyone is in Christ, he is a new creation; the old has gone, the new has come! [18] All this is from God, who reconciled us to himself through Christ and gave us the ministry of reconciliation: [19] that God was reconciling the world to himself in Christ, not counting men's sins against them. And he has committed to us the message of reconciliation. [20] We are therefore Christ's ambassadors, as though God were making his appeal through us. We implore you on Christ's behalf: Be reconciled to God. [21] God made him who had no sin to be sin for us, so that in him we might become the righteousness of God.

6 As God's fellow-workers we urge you not to receive God's grace in vain. [2] For he says,

'In the time of my favour I heard you, and in the day of salvation I helped you.'

I tell you, now is the time of God's favour, now is the day of salvation.

Paul's Hardships

[3] We put no stumbling-block in anyone's path, so that our ministry will not be discredited. [4] Rather, as servants of God we commend ourselves in every way: in great endurance; in troubles, hardships and distresses; [5] in beatings, imprisonments and riots; in hard work, sleepless nights and hunger; [6] in purity, understanding, patience and kindness; in the Holy Spirit and in sincere love; [7] in truthful speech and in the power of God; with weapons of righteousness in the right hand and in the left; [8] through glory and dishonour, bad report and good report; genuine, yet regarded as impostors; [9] known, yet regarded as unknown; dying, and yet we live on; beaten, and yet not killed; [10] sorrowful, yet always rejoicing; poor, yet making many rich; having nothing, and yet possessing everything.

[11] We have spoken freely to you, Corinthians, and opened wide our hearts to you. [12] We are not withholding our affection from you, but you are withholding yours from us. [13] As a fair exchange - I speak as to my children - open wide your hearts also.

DAY 175

2 COR. 6.14 — 7.16

Do Not Be Yoked With Unbelievers

[14] Do not be yoked together with unbelievers. For what do righteousness and wickedness have in common? Or what fellowship can light have with darkness? [15] What harmony is there between Christ and Belial? What does a believer have in common with an unbeliever? [16] What agreement is there between the temple of God and idols? For we are the temple of the living God. As God has said:

'I will live with them and walk among them, and I will be their God, and they will be my people.'
[17] 'Therefore come out from them and be separate,
says the Lord
Touch no unclean thing, and I will receive you.'
[18] 'I will be a Father to you, and you will be my sons and daughters says the Lord Almighty

What fellowship can light have with darkness?

7 Since we have these promises, dear friends, let us purify ourselves from everything that contaminates body and spirit, perfecting holiness out of reverence for God.

Paul's Joy

Make room for us in your hearts. We have wronged no-one, we have corrupted no-one, we have exploited no-one. ³ I do not say this to condemn you; I have said before that you have such a place in our hearts that we would live or die with you. I have great confidence in you; I take great pride in you. I am greatly encouraged; in all our troubles my joy knows no bounds.

⁵ For when we came into Macedonia, this body of ours had no rest, but we were harassed at every turn - conflicts on the outside, fears within. ⁶ But God, who comforts the downcast, comforted us by the coming of Titus, ⁷ and not only by his coming but also by the comfort you had given him. He told us about your longing for me, your deep sorrow, your ardent concern for me, so that my joy was greater than ever.

⁸ Even if I caused you sorrow by my letter, I do not regret it. Though I did regret it - I see that my letter hurt you, but only for a little while - ⁹ yet now I am happy, not because you were made sorry, but because your sorrow led you to repentance. For you became sorrowful as God intended and so were not harmed in any way by us. ¹⁰ Godly sorrow brings repentance that leads to salvation and leaves no regret, but worldly sorrow brings death. ¹¹ See what this godly sorrow has produced in you: what earnestness, what eagerness to clear yourselves, what indignation, what alarm, what longing, what concern, what readiness to see justice done. At every point you have proved yourselves to be innocent in this matter. ¹² So even though I wrote to you, it was not on account of the one who did the wrong or of the injured party, but rather that before God you could see for yourselves how devoted to us you are. ¹³ By all this we are encouraged.

In addition to our own encouragement, we were especially delighted to see how happy Titus was, because his spirit has been refreshed by all of you. ¹⁴ I had boasted to him about you, and you have not embarrassed me. But just as everything we said to you was true, so our boasting about you to Titus has proved to be true as well. ¹⁵ And his affection for you is all the greater when he remembers that you were all obedient, receiving him with fear and trembling. ¹⁶ I am glad I can have complete confidence in you.

DAY 176

2 COR. 8. 1 — 24

8 Generosity Encouraged
And now, brothers, we want you to know about the grace that God has given the Macedonian churches. ² Out of the most severe trial, their overflowing joy and their extreme poverty welled up in rich generosity. ³ For

I have great confidence in you.

I testify that they gave as much as they were able, and even beyond their ability. Entirely on their own, ⁴ they urgently pleaded with us for the privilege of

At the present time your plenty will supply what they need...

sharing in this service to the saints. ⁵ And they did not do as we expected, but they gave themselves first to the Lord and then to us in keeping with God's will. ⁶ So we urged Titus, since he had earlier made a beginning, to bring also to completion this act of grace on your part. ⁷ But just as you excel in everything - in faith, in speech, in knowledge, in complete earnestness and in your love for us - see that you also excel in this grace of giving.

⁸ I am not commanding you, but I want to test the sincerity of your love by comparing it with the earnestness of others. ⁹ For you know the grace of our Lord Jesus Christ, that though he was rich, yet for your sakes he became poor, so that you through his poverty might become rich.

¹⁰ And here is my advice about what is best for you in this matter: Last year you were the first not only to give but also to have the desire to do so. ¹¹ Now finish the work, so that your eager willingness to do it may be matched by your completion of it, according to your means. ¹² For if the willingness is there, the gift is acceptable according to what one has, not according to what he does not have.

¹³ Our desire is not that others might be relieved while you are hard pressed, but that there might be equality. ¹⁴ At the present time your plenty will supply what they need, so that in turn their plenty will supply what you need. Then there will be equality, ¹⁵ as it is written: 'He who gathered much did not have too much, and he who gathered little did not have too little.'

Titus Sent to Corinth

¹⁶ I thank God, who put into the heart of Titus the same concern I have for you. ¹⁷ For Titus not only welcomed our appeal but he is coming to you with much enthusiasm and on his own initiative. ¹⁸ And we are sending along with him the brother who is praised by all the churches for his service to the gospel. ¹⁹ What is more, he was chosen by the churches to accompany us as we carry the offering, which we administer in order to honour the Lord himself and to show our eagerness to help. ²⁰ We want to avoid any criticism of the way we administer this liberal gift. ²¹ For we are taking pains to do what is right, not only in the eyes of the Lord but also in the eyes of men.

²² In addition, we are sending with them our brother who has often proved to us in many ways that he is zealous, and now even more so because of his great confidence in you. ²³ As for Titus, he is my partner and fellow-worker among you; as for our brothers, they are representatives of the churches and an honour to Christ. ²⁴ Therefore show these men the proof of your love and the reason for our pride in you, so that the churches can see it.

DAY 177

2 COR. 9. 1 — 15

9 There is no need for me to write to you about this service to the saints. [2] For I know your eagerness to help, and I have been boasting about it to the Macedonians, telling them that since last year you in Achaia were ready to give; and your enthusiasm has stirred most of them to action. [3] But I am sending the brothers in order that our boasting about you in this matter should not prove hollow, but that you may be ready, as I said you would be. [4] For if any Macedonians come with me and find you unprepared, we - not to say anything about you - would be ashamed of having been so confident. [5] So I thought it necessary to urge the brothers to visit you in advance and finish the arrangements for the generous gift you had promised. Then it will be ready as a generous gift, not as one grudgingly given.

Sowing Generously

Remember this: Whoever sows sparingly will also reap sparingly, and whoever sows generously will also reap generously. Each man should give what he has decided in his heart to give, not reluctantly or under compulsion, for God loves a cheerful giver. [8] And God is able to make all grace abound to you, so that in all things at all times, having all that you need, you will abound in every good work. [9] As it is written:

'He has scattered abroad his gifts
　　to the poor;
　　his righteousness endures for ever.'

Whoever sows sparingly will also reap sparingly, and whoever sows generously will reap generously.

[10] Now he who supplies seed to the sower and bread for food will also supply and increase your store of seed and will enlarge the harvest of your righteousness. [11] You will be made rich in every way so that you can be generous on every occasion, and through us your generosity will result in thanksgiving to God. [12] This service that you perform is not only supplying the needs of God's people but is also overflowing in many expressions of thanks to God. [13] Because of the service by which you have proved yourselves, men will praise God for the obedience that accompanies your confession of the gospel of Christ, and for your generosity in sharing with them and with everyone else. [14] And in their prayers for you their hearts will go out to you, because of the surpassing grace God has given you. [15] Thanks be to God for his indescribable gift!

DAY 178

2 COR. 10. 1 —18

10 **Paul's Defence of His Ministry**
By the meekness and gentleness of Christ, I appeal to you - I, Paul, who am 'timid' when face to face with you, but 'bold' when away! [2] I beg you that when I come I may not have to be as bold as I expect to be towards some people who think that we live by the standards of this world. [3] For though we live in the world, we do not wage war as the world does. [4] The weapons we fight with are not the weapons of the world. On the contrary, they have divine power to demolish strongholds. [5] We demolish arguments and every pretension that sets itself up against the knowledge of God, and we take captive every thought to make it obedient to Christ. [6] And we will be ready to punish every act of disobedience, once your obedience is complete.

[7] You are looking only on the surface of things. If anyone is confident that he belongs to Christ, he should consider again that we belong to Christ just as much as he. [8] For even if I boast somewhat freely about the authority the Lord gave us for building you up rather than pulling you down, I will not be ashamed of it. [9] I do not want to seem to be trying to frighten you with my letters. [10] For some say, 'His letters are weighty and forceful, but in person he is unimpressive and his speaking amounts to nothing.' [11] Such people should realise that what we are in our letters when we are absent, we will be in our actions when we are present.

[12] We do not dare to classify or compare ourselves with some who commend themselves. When they measure themselves by themselves and compare themselves with themselves, they are not wise. [13] We, however, will not boast beyond proper limits, but will confine our boasting to the field God has assigned to us, a field that reaches even to you. [14] We are not going too far in our boasting, as would be the case if we had not come to you, for we did get as far as you with the gospel of Christ. [15] Neither do we go beyond our limits by boasting of work done by others. Our hope is that, as your faith continues to grow, our area of activity among you will greatly expand, [16] so that we can preach the gospel in the regions beyond you. For we do not want to boast about work already done in another man's territory. [17] But, 'Let him who boasts boast in the Lord.' [18] For it is not the one who commends himself who is approved, but the one whom the Lord commends.

DAY 179

2 COR. 11. 1 — 33

11 **Paul and the False Apostles**
I hope you will put up with a little of my foolishness; but you are already doing that. [2] I am jealous for you with a godly jealousy. I promised you to one husband, to Christ, so that I might present you as a pure virgin to him. [3] But I am afraid that just as Eve was deceived by the serpent's cunning, your minds may somehow be led astray from your sincere

and pure devotion to Christ. ⁴For if someone comes to you and preaches a Jesus other than the Jesus we preached, or if you receive a different spirit from the one you received, or a different gospel from the one you accepted, you put up with it easily enough. ⁵But I do not think I am in the least inferior to those 'super-apostles'. ⁶I may not be a trained speaker, but I do have knowledge. We have made this perfectly clear to you in every way.

⁷Was it a sin for me to lower myself in order to elevate you by preaching the gospel of God to you free of charge? ⁸I robbed other churches by receiving support from them so as to serve you. ⁹And when I was with you and needed something, I was not a burden to anyone, for the brothers who came from Macedonia supplied what I needed. I have kept myself from being a burden to you in any way, and will continue to do so. ¹⁰As surely as the truth of Christ is in me, nobody in the regions of Achaia will stop this boasting of mine. ¹¹Why? Because I do not love you? God knows I do! ¹²And I will keep on doing what I am doing in order to cut the ground from under those who want an opportunity to be considered equal with us in the things they boast about.

¹³For such men are false apostles, deceitful workmen, masquerading as apostles of Christ. ¹⁴And no wonder, for Satan himself masquerades as an angel of light. ¹⁵It is not surprising, then, if his servants masquerade as servants of righteousness. Their end will be what their actions deserve.

Paul Boasts About His Sufferings

¹⁶I repeat: Let no-one take me for a fool. But if you do, then receive me just as you would a fool, so that I may do a little boasting. ¹⁷In this self-confident boasting I am not talking as the Lord would, but as a fool. ¹⁸Since many are boasting in the way the world does, I too will boast. ¹⁹You gladly put up with fools since you are so wise! ²⁰In fact, you even put up with anyone who enslaves you or exploits you or takes advantage of you or pushes himself forward or slaps you in the face. ²¹To my shame I admit that we were too weak for that!

What anyone else dares to boast about - I am speaking as a fool - I also dare to boast about. ²²Are they Hebrews? So am I. Are they Israelites? So am I. Are they Abraham's descendants? So am I. ²³Are they servants of Christ? (I am out of my mind to talk like this.) I am more. I have worked much harder, been in prison more frequently, been flogged more severely, and been exposed to death again and again. ²⁴Five times I received from the Jews the forty lashes minus one. ²⁵Three times I was beaten with rods, once I was stoned, three times I was shipwrecked, I spent a night and a day in the open sea, ²⁶I have been constantly on the move. I have been in danger from rivers, in danger from bandits, in danger from my own countrymen, in danger from Gentiles; in danger in the city, in danger in the country, in danger at sea; and in danger from false brothers. ²⁷I have laboured and toiled and have often gone without sleep; I have known hunger and thirst and have often gone without food; I have been cold and naked. ²⁸Besides everything else, I face daily the pressure of my concern for all the churches. ²⁹Who is weak, and I do not feel weak? Who is led into sin, and I do not inwardly burn?

³⁰If I must boast, I will boast of the things that show my weakness. ³¹The God and Father of the Lord Jesus, who is to be praised for ever, knows that I am not lying. ³²In Damascus the governor under King Aretas had the city of the Damascenes guarded in order to arrest me. ³³But I was lowered in a basket from a window in the wall and slipped through his hands.

DAY 180

2 COR. 12. 1 — 21

12 Paul's Vision and His Thorn

I must go on boasting. Although there is nothing to be gained, I will go on to visions and revelations from the Lord. ²I know a man in Christ who fourteen years ago was caught up to the third heaven. Whether it was in the body or out of the body I do not know - God knows. ³And I know that this man - whether in the body or apart from the body I do not know, but God knows - ⁴was caught up to paradise. He heard inexpressible things, things that man is not permitted to tell. ⁵I will boast about a man like that, but I will not boast about myself, except about my weaknesses. ⁶Even if I should choose to boast, I would not be a fool, because I would be speaking the truth. But I refrain, so no-one will think more of me than is warranted by what I do or say.

⁷To keep me from becoming conceited because of these surpassingly great revelations, there was given me a thorn in my flesh, a messenger of Satan, to torment me. ⁸Three times I pleaded with the Lord to take it away from me. ⁹But he said to me, 'My grace is sufficient for you, for my power is made perfect in weakness.' Therefore I will boast all the more gladly about my weaknesses, so that Christ's power may rest on me. ¹⁰That is why, for Christ's sake, I delight in weaknesses, in insults, in hardships, in persecutions, in difficulties. For when I am weak, then I am strong.

Paul's Concern for the Corinthians

¹¹I have made a fool of myself, but you drove me to it. I ought to have been commended by you, for I am not in the least inferior to the 'super-apostles', even though I am nothing. ¹²The things that mark an apostle - signs, wonders and miracles - were done among you with great perseverance. ¹³How were you inferior to the other churches, except that I was never a burden to you? Forgive me this wrong!

¹⁴Now I am ready to visit you for the third time, and I will not be a burden to you, because what I want is not your

If I love you more, will you love me less?

possessions but you. After all, children should not have to save up for their parents, but parents for their children. ¹⁵So I will very gladly spend for you everything I have and expend myself as well. If I love you more, will you love me less? ¹⁶Be that as it may, I have not been a burden to you. Yet, crafty fellow that I am, I caught you by trickery! ¹⁷Did I exploit you through any of the men I sent you? ¹⁸I urged Titus to go to you and I sent our brother with him. Titus did not exploit you, did he? Did we not act in the same spirit and follow the same course?

¹⁹Have you been thinking all along that we have been defending ourselves to you? We have been speaking in the sight of God as those in Christ; and everything we do, dear friends, is for your strengthening. ²⁰For I am afraid that when I come I may not find you as I want you to be, and you may not find me as you want me to be. I fear that there may

e quarrelling, jealousy, outbursts of nger, factions, slander, gossip, arrogance nd disorder. ²¹I am afraid that when I ome again my God will humble me efore you, and I will be grieved over nany who have sinned earlier and have ot repented of the impurity, sexual sin nd debauchery in which they have ndulged.

DAY 181

2 COR. 13. 1 — 14

13 Final Warnings
This will be my third visit to you. 'Every matter must be stablished by the testimony of two or hree witnesses.' ²I already gave you a varning when I was with you the second ime. I now repeat it while absent: On my eturn I will not spare those who sinned arlier or any of the others, ³since you are

Ve are weak but you are strong.

demanding proof that Christ is speaking through me. He is not weak in dealing with you, but is powerful among you. ⁴For to be sure, he was crucified in weakness, yet he lives by God's power. Likewise, we

For we cannot do anything against the truth, but only for the truth.

are weak in him, yet by God's power we will live with him to serve you.

⁵Examine yourselves to see whether you are in the faith; test yourselves. Do you not realise that Christ Jesus is in you - unless, of course, you fail the test? ⁶And I trust that you will discover that we have not failed the test. ⁷Now we pray to God that you will not do anything wrong. Not that people will see that we have stood the test but that you will do what is right even though we may seem to have failed. ⁸For we cannot do anything against the truth, but only for the truth. ⁹We are glad whenever we are weak but you are strong; and our prayer is for your perfection. ¹⁰This is why I write these things when I am absent, that when I come I may not have to be harsh in my use of authority - the authority the Lord gave me for building you up, not for tearing you down.

Final Greetings

¹¹Finally, brothers, good-bye. Aim for perfection, listen to my appeal, be of one mind, live in peace. And the God of love and peace will be with you.

¹²Greet one another with a holy kiss. ¹³All the saints send their greetings.

¹⁴May the grace of the Lord Jesus Christ, and the love of God, and the fellowship of the Holy Spirit be with you all.

DAY 182

ROM. 1. 1 — 17

1 Paul, a servant of Christ Jesus,
called to be an apostle and set
apart for the gospel of God - [2] the
gospel he promised beforehand through
his prophets in the Holy Scriptures
[3] regarding his Son, who as to his human
nature was a descendant of David, [4] and
who through the Spirit of holiness was
declared with power to be the Son of
God, by his resurrection from the dead:
Jesus Christ our Lord. [5] Through him and
for his name's sake, we received grace and
apostleship to call people from among all
the Gentiles to the obedience that comes
from faith. [6] And you also are among
those who are called to belong to Jesus
Christ.

[7] To all in Rome who are loved by
God and called to be saints:

Grace and peace to you from God
our Father and from the Lord Jesus
Christ.

Paul's Longing to Visit Rome

[8] First, I thank my God through Jesus
Christ for all of you, because your faith is
being reported all over the world. [9] God,
whom I serve with my whole heart in
preaching the gospel of his Son, is my
witness how constantly I remember you
[10] in my prayers at all times; and I pray
that now at last by God's will the way
may be opened for me to come to you.
[11] I long to see you so that I may
impart to you some spiritual gift to make
you strong - [12] that is, that you and I may

be mutually encouraged by each other's
faith. [13] I do not want you to be unaware,
brothers, that I planned many times to
come to you (but have been prevented
from doing so until now) in order that I
might have a harvest among you, just as
have had among the other Gentiles.
[14] I am bound both to Greeks and
non-Greeks, both to the wise and the
foolish. [15] That is why I am so eager to
preach the gospel also to you who are at
Rome.

**For in the gospel a
righteousness from God is
revealed...**

---

[16] I am not ashamed of the gospel,
because it is the power of God for the
salvation of everyone who believes: first
for the Jew, then for the Gentile. [17] For in
the gospel a righteousness from God is
revealed, a righteousness that is by faith
from first to last, just as it is written: 'The
righteous will live by faith.'

DAY 183

ROM. 1. 18 — 32

God's Wrath Against Mankind
[18] The wrath of God is being revealed
from heaven against all the godlessness
and wickedness of men who suppress the
truth by their wickedness, [19] since what
may be known about God is plain to
them, because God has made it plain to
them. [20] For since the creation of the

orld God's invisible qualities - his
ernal power and divine nature - have
en clearly seen, being understood from
hat has been made, so that men are
thout excuse.

²¹ For although they knew God, they
either glorified him as God nor gave
anks to him, but their thinking became
tile and their foolish hearts were

ones. ²⁷ In the same way the men also
abandoned natural relations with women
and were inflamed with lust for one
another. Men committed indecent acts
with other men, and received in
themselves the due penalty for their
perversion.

²⁸ Furthermore, since they did not
think it worth while to retain the

They served created things rather than the Creator.

rkened. ²² Although they claimed to be
ise, they became fools ²³ and exchanged
e glory of the immortal God for images
ade to look like mortal man and birds
d animals and reptiles.

²⁴ Therefore God gave them over in
e sinful desires of their hearts to sexual
ipurity for the degrading of their bodies
ith one another. ²⁵ They exchanged the
uth of God for a lie, and worshipped
d served created things rather than the
reator - who is for ever praised. Amen.

²⁶ Because of this, God gave them
er to shameful lusts. Even their women
changed natural relations for unnatural

knowledge of God, he gave them over to
a depraved mind, to do what ought not to
be done. ²⁹ They have become filled with
every kind of wickedness, evil, greed and
depravity. They are full of envy, murder,
strife, deceit and malice. They are gossips,
³⁰ slanderers, God-haters, insolent,
arrogant and boastful; they invent ways of
doing evil; they disobey their parents;
³¹ they are senseless, faithless, heartless,
ruthless. ³² Although they know God's
righteous decree that those who do such
things deserve death, they not only
continue to do these very things but also
approve of those who practise them.

DAY 184

ROM. 2. 1 — 16

2 ### God's Righteous Judgment

You, therefore, have no excuse, you who pass judgment on someone else, for at whatever point you judge the other, you are condemning yourself, because you who pass judgment do the same things. ² Now we know that God's judgment against those who do such things is based on truth. ³ So when you, a mere man, pass judgment on them and yet do the same things, do you think you will escape God's judgment? ⁴ Or do you show contempt for the riches of his kindness, tolerance and patience, not realising that God's kindness leads you towards repentance?

⁵ But because of your stubbornness and your unrepentant heart, you are storing up wrath against yourself for the day of God's wrath, when his righteous judgment will be revealed. ⁶ God 'will give to each person according to what he has done'. ⁷ To those who by persistence in doing good seek glory, honour and immortality, he will give eternal life. ⁸ But for those who are self-seeking and who reject the truth and follow evil, there will be wrath and anger. ⁹ There will be trouble and distress for every human being who does evil: first for the Jew, then for the Gentile; ¹⁰ but glory, honour and peace for everyone who does good: first for the Jew, then for the Gentile. ¹¹ For God does not show favouritism.

¹² All who sin apart from the law will also perish apart from the law, and all who sin under the law will be judged by the law. ¹³ For it is not those who hear the law who are righteous in God's sight, but it is those who obey the law who will be declared righteous. ¹⁴ (Indeed, when Gentiles, who do not have the law, do by nature things required by the law, they are a law for themselves, even though they do not have the law, ¹⁵ since they show that the requirements of the law are written on their hearts, their conscience also bearing witness, and their thoughts now accusing, now even defending them.) ¹⁶ This will take place on the day

---

God 'will give to each person according to what he has done'.

---

when God will judge men's secrets through Jesus Christ, as my gospel declares.

A light for those who are in the dark

DAY 185

ROM. 2. 17 — 3.8

The Jews and the Law

Now you, if you call yourself a Jew; if you rely on the law and brag about your relationship to God; [18] if you know his will and approve of what is superior because are instructed by the law; if you are convinced that you are a guide for the blind, a light for those who are in the dark, [20] an instructor of the foolish, a teacher of infants, because you have in the law the embodiment of knowledge and truth - [21] you, then, who teach others, do you not teach yourself? You who preach against stealing, do you steal? [22] You who say that people should not commit adultery, do you commit adultery? You who abhor idols, do you rob temples? [23] You who brag about the law, do you dishonour God by breaking

You who preach against stealing, do you steal?

the law? [24] As it is written: 'God's name is blasphemed among the Gentiles because of you.'

[25] Circumcision has value if you observe the law, but if you break the law, you have become as though you had not been circumcised. [26] If those who are not circumcised keep the law's requirements, will they not be regarded as though they were circumcised? [27] The one who is not circumcised physically and yet obeys the law will condemn you who, even though you have the written code and circumcision, are a law-breaker. [28] A man is not a Jew if he is only

...entrusted with the very words of God.

one outwardly, nor is circumcision merely outward and physical. [29] No, a man is a Jew if he is one inwardly; and circumcision is circumcision of the heart, by the Spirit, not by the written code. Such a man's praise is not from men, but from God.

3 God's Faithfulness

What advantage, then, is there in being a Jew, or what value is there in circumcision? [2] Much in every way! First of all, they have been entrusted with the very words of God.

[3] What if some did not have faith? Will their lack of faith nullify God's faithfulness? [4] Not at all! Let God be true, and every man a liar. As it is written:

'So that you may be proved right
when you speak
and prevail when you judge.'

[5] But if our unrighteousness brings out God's righteousness more clearly, what shall we say? That God is unjust in bringing his wrath on us? (I am using a human argument.) [6] Certainly not! If that were so, how could God judge the world? [7] Someone might argue, 'If my falsehood enhances God's truthfulness and so increases his glory, why am I still condemned as a sinner?' [8] Why not say - as we are being slanderously reported as saying and as some claim that we say 'Let us do evil that good may result'? Their condemnation is deserved.

DAY 186
ROM. 3.9 — 31

No-one is Righteous

[9] What shall we conclude then? Are we any better? Not at all! We have already made the charge that Jews and Gentiles alike are all under sin. [10] As it is written:

'There is no-one righteous, not even one;
[11]   there is no-one who understands,
    no-one who seeks God.
[12] All have turned away,
    they have together become worthless;
    there is no-one who does good,
    not even one.'
[13] 'Their throats are open graves;
    their tongues practise deceit.'
'The poison of vipers is on their lips.'
[14]   'Their mouths are full of cursing and bitterness.'
[15] 'Their feet are swift to shed blood;
[16]   ruin and misery mark their ways,
[17] and the way of peace they do not know.'
[18]   'There is no fear of God
    before their eyes.'

[19] Now we know that whatever the law says, it says to those who are under the law, so that every mouth may be silenced and the whole world held accountable to God. [20] Therefore no-one will be declared righteous in his sight by observing the law; rather, through the law we become conscious of sin.

Righteousness Through Faith

[21] But now a righteousness from God, apart from law, has been made known, to which the Law and the Prophets testify.

[22] This righteousness from God comes through faith in Jesus Christ to all who believe. There is no difference, [23] for all have sinned and fall short of the glory of God, [24] and are justified freely by his grace through the redemption that came by Christ Jesus. [25] God presented him as a sacrifice of atonement, through faith in his blood. He did this to demonstrate his justice, because in his forbearance he had left the sins committed beforehand unpunished [26] - he did it to demonstrate his justice at the present time, so as to be just and the one who justifies those who have faith in Jesus.

[27] Where, then, is boasting? It is excluded. On what principle? On that of observing the law? No, but on that of faith. [28] For we maintain that a man is justified by faith apart from observing the law. [29] Is God the God of Jews only? Is he not the God of Gentiles too? Yes, of Gentiles too, [30] since there is only one God, who will justify the circumcised by faith and the uncircumcised through that same faith. [31] Do we, then, nullify the law by this faith? Not at all! Rather, we uphold the law.

DAY 187
ROM. 4. 1 — 25

Abraham Justified by Faith

4 What then shall we say that Abraham, our forefather, discovered in this matter? [2] If, in fact, Abraham was justified by works, he had something to boast about - but not before God. [3] What does the Scripture say? 'Abraham believed God, and it was credited to him as righteousness.'

⁴Now when a man works, his wages are not credited to him as a gift, but as an obligation. ⁵However, to the man who does not work but trusts God who justifies the wicked, his faith is credited as righteousness. ⁶David says the same thing when he speaks of the blessedness of the man to whom God credits righteousness apart from works:

⁷ 'Blessed are they whose transgressions
    are forgiven, whose sins are covered.
⁸ Blessed is the man whose sin the Lord
    will never count against him.'

⁹Is this blessedness only for the circumcised, or also for the uncircumcised? We have been saying that Abraham's faith was credited to him as righteousness.

'Blessed are they whose transgressions are forgiven, whose sins are covered.'

Under what circumstances was it credited? Was it after he was circumcised, or before? It was not after, but before! And he received the sign of circumcision, a seal of the righteousness that he had by faith while he was still uncircumcised. So then, he is the father of all who believe but have not been circumcised, in order that righteousness might be credited to them. ¹²And he is also the father of the circumcised who not only are circumcised but who also walk in the footsteps of the faith that our father Abraham had before he was circumcised.

¹³It was not through law that Abraham and his offspring received the promise that he would be heir of the world, but through the righteousness that comes by faith. ¹⁴For if those who live by law are heirs, faith has no value and the promise is worthless, ¹⁵because law brings wrath. And where there is no law there is no transgression.

'I have made you a father of many nations.'

¹⁶Therefore, the promise comes by faith, so that it may be by grace and may be guaranteed to all Abraham's offspring - not only to those who are of the law but also to those who are of the faith of Abraham. He is the father of us all. ¹⁷As it is written: 'I have made you a father of many nations.' He is our father in the sight of God, in whom he believed - the God who gives life to the dead and calls things that are not as though they were.

¹⁸Against all hope, Abraham in hope believed and so became the father of many nations, just as it had been said to him, 'So shall your offspring be.' ¹⁹Without weakening in his faith, he faced the fact that his body was as good as dead - since he was about a hundred years old - and that Sarah's womb was also dead. ²⁰Yet he did not waver through unbelief regarding the promise of God, but was strengthened in his faith and gave glory to God, ²¹being fully persuaded that God had power to do what he had promised. ²²This is why 'it was credited to him as righteousness.' ²³The words 'it was credited to him' were written not for him alone, ²⁴but also for us, to whom God will credit righteousness - for us who believe in him who raised Jesus our Lord from the dead. ²⁵He was delivered over to death for our sins and was raised to life for our justification.

DAY 188
ROM. 5. 1 — 21

5 **Peace and Joy**
Therefore, since we have been justified through faith, we have peace with God through our Lord Jesus Christ, ²through whom we have gained access by faith into this grace in which we now stand. And we rejoice in the hope of the glory of God. ³Not only so, but we also rejoice in our sufferings, because we know that suffering produces perseverance; ⁴perseverance, character; and character, hope. ⁵And hope does not disappoint us, because God has poured out his love into our hearts by the Holy Spirit, whom he has given us.

And hope does not disappoint us.

⁶You see, at just the right time, when we were still powerless, Christ died for the ungodly. ⁷Very rarely will anyone die for a righteous man, though for a good man someone might possibly dare to die. ⁸But God demonstrates his own love for us in this: While we were still sinners, Christ died for us.

⁹Since we have now been justified by his blood, how much more shall we be saved from God's wrath through him! ¹⁰For if, when we were God's enemies, we were reconciled to him through the death of his Son, how much more, having been reconciled, shall we be saved through his life! ¹¹Not only is this so, but we also rejoice in God through our Lord Jesus Christ, through whom we have now received reconciliation.

Death Through Adam, Life Through Christ

¹²Therefore, just as sin entered the world through one man, and death through sin, and in this way death came to all men, because all sinned - ¹³for before the law was given, sin was in the world. But sin is not taken into account when there is no law. ¹⁴Nevertheless, death reigned from the time of Adam to the time of Moses, even over those who did not sin by breaking a command, as did Adam, who was a pattern of the one to come.

¹⁵But the gift is not like the trespass. For if the many died by the trespass of the one man, how much more did God's grace and the gift that came by the grace of the one man, Jesus Christ, overflow to the many! ¹⁶Again, the gift of God is not like the result of the one man's sin: The judgment followed one sin and brought condemnation, but the gift followed many trespasses and brought justification. ¹⁷For if, by the trespass of the one man, death reigned through that one man, how much more will those who receive God's abundant provision of grace and of the gift of righteousness reign in life through the one man, Jesus Christ.

¹⁸Consequently, just as the result of one trespass was condemnation for all men, so also the result of one act of righteousness was justification that brings life for all men. ¹⁹For just as through the disobedience of the one man the many were made sinners, so also through the obedience of the one man the many will be made righteous.

²⁰The law was added so that the trespass might increase. But where sin increased, grace increased all the more, ²¹so that, just as sin reigned in death, so also grace might reign through righteousness to bring eternal life through Jesus Christ our Lord.

DAY 189

ROM. 6. 1 — 23

Dead to Sin, Alive in Christ

What shall we say, then? Shall we go on sinning, so that grace may increase? ² By no means! We died to sin; how can we live in it any longer? ³ Or don't you know that all of us who were baptised into Christ Jesus were baptised into his death? ⁴ We were therefore buried with him through baptism into death in order that, just as Christ was raised from the dead through the glory of the Father, we too may live a new life.

⁵ If we have been united with him like this in his death, we will certainly also be united with him in his resurrection. ⁶ For we know that our old self was crucified with him so that the body of sin might be done away with, that we should no longer be slaves to sin - because anyone who has died has been freed from sin.

⁸ Now if we died with Christ, we believe that we will also live with him. ⁹ For we know that since Christ was raised from the dead, he cannot die again; death no longer has mastery over him. ¹⁰ The death he died, he died to sin once for all; but the life he lives, he lives to God.

¹¹ In the same way, count yourselves dead to sin but alive to God in Christ Jesus. ¹² Therefore do not let sin reign in your mortal body so that you obey its evil desires. ¹³ Do not offer the parts of your body to sin, as instruments of wickedness, but rather offer yourselves to God, as those who have been brought from death to life; and offer the parts of your body to him as instruments of righteousness. ¹⁴ For sin shall not be your master, because you are not under law, but under grace.

Slaves to Righteousness

¹⁵ What then? Shall we sin because we are not under law but under grace? By no means! ¹⁶ Don't you know that when you offer yourselves to someone to obey him as slaves, you are slaves to the one whom you obey - whether you are slaves to sin, which leads to death, or to obedience, which leads to righteousness? ¹⁷ But thanks be to God that, though you used to be slaves to sin, you wholeheartedly obeyed the form of teaching to which you were entrusted. ¹⁸ You have been set free from sin and have become slaves to righteousness.

¹⁹ I put this in human terms because you are weak in your natural selves. Just as you used to offer the parts of your body in slavery to impurity and to ever-increasing wickedness, so now offer them in slavery to righteousness leading to holiness. ²⁰ When you were slaves to sin, you were free from the control of righteousness. ²¹ What benefit did you

> **You have been set free from sin and have become slaves to righteousness.**

reap at that time from the things you are now ashamed of? Those things result in death! ²² But now that you have been set free from sin and have become slaves to God, the benefit you reap leads to holiness, and the result is eternal life. ²³ For the wages of sin is death, but the gift of God is eternal life in Christ Jesus our Lord.

DAY 190

ROM. 7. 1 — 25

7 ### An Illustration From Marriage

Do you not know, brothers - for I am speaking to men who know the law - that the law has authority over a man only as long as he lives? [2] For example, by law a married woman is bound to her husband as long as he is alive, but if her husband dies, she is released from the law of marriage. [3] So then, if she marries another man while her husband is still alive, she is called an adulteress. But if her husband dies, she is released from that law and is not an adulteress, even though she marries another man.

[4] So, my brothers, you also died to the law through the body of Christ, that you might belong to another, to him who was raised from the dead, in order that we might bear fruit to God. [5] For when we were controlled by the sinful nature, the sinful passions aroused by the law were at work in our bodies, so that we bore fruit for death. [6] But now, by dying to what once bound us, we have been released from the law so that we serve in the new way of the Spirit, and not in the old way of the written code.

Struggling With Sin

[7] What shall we say, then? Is the law sin? Certainly not! Indeed I would not have known what sin was except through the law. For I would not have known what coveting really was if the law had not said, 'Do not covet.' [8] But sin, seizing the opportunity afforded by the commandment, produced in me every kind of covetous desire. For apart from law, sin is dead. [9] Once I was alive apart from law; but when the commandment came, sin sprang to life and I died. [10] I found that the very commandment that was intended to bring life actually brought death. [11] For sin, seizing the opportunity afforded by the commandment, deceived me, and through the commandment put me to death. [12] So then, the law is holy, and the commandment is holy, righteous and good.

[13] Did that which is good, then, become death to me? By no means! But in order that sin might be recognised as sin, it produced death in me through what was good, so that through the commandment sin might become utterly sinful.

[14] We know that the law is spiritual; but I am unspiritual, sold as a slave to sin. [15] I do not understand what I do. For what I want to do I do not do, but what I hate I do. [16] And if I do what I do not want to do, I agree that the law is good. [17] As it is, it is no longer I myself who do it, but it is sin living in me. [18] I know that nothing good lives in me, that is, in my sinful nature. For I have the desire to do what is good, but I cannot carry it out. [19] For what I do is not the good I want to do; no, the evil I do not want to do - this I keep on doing. [20] Now if I do what I do not want to do, it is no longer I who do it, but it is sin living in me that does it.

[21] So I find this law at work: When I want to do good, evil is right there with me. [22] For in my inner being I delight in God's law; [23] but I see another law at work in the members of my body, waging war against the law of my mind and making me a prisoner of the law of sin at work within my members. [24] What a wretched man I am! Who will rescue me from this

)dy of death? [25] Thanks be to God -
rough Jesus Christ our Lord!

So then, I myself in my mind am a
ave to God's law, but in the sinful
ature a slave to the law of sin.

DAY 191
ROM. 8. 1 — 17

Life Through the Spirit
Therefore, there is now no
condemnation for those who are in
hrist Jesus, [2] because through Christ
sus the law of the Spirit of life set me
ee from the law of sin and death. [3] For
hat the law was powerless to do in that
was weakened by the sinful nature, God
d by sending his own Son in the
keness of sinful man to be a sin offering.
nd so he condemned sin in sinful man,
n order that the righteous requirements
the law might be fully met in us, who
) not live according to the sinful nature
it according to the Spirit.

hose who live according to the
nful nature have their minds set on
nat that nature desires; but those who
ve in accordance with the Spirit have
eir minds set on what the Spirit desires.
he mind of sinful man is death, but the
ind controlled by the Spirit is life and
ace; [7] the sinful mind is hostile to God.
does not submit to God's law, nor can it
» so. [8] Those controlled by the sinful
ature cannot please God.

[9] You, however, are controlled not by
e sinful nature but by the Spirit, if the
irit of God lives in you. And if anyone
es not have the Spirit of Christ, he
es not belong to Christ. [10] But if Christ
in you, your body is dead because of sin,

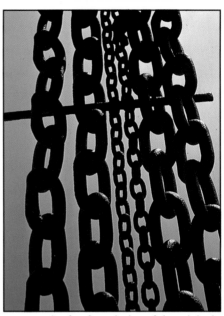

Set free from the law of sin and death.

yet your spirit is alive because of
righteousness. [11] And if the Spirit of him
who raised Jesus from the dead is living in
you, he who raised Christ from the dead
will also give life to your mortal bodies
through his Spirit, who lives in you.

[12] Therefore, brothers, we have an
obligation - but it is not to the sinful
nature, to live according to it. [13] For if you
live according to the sinful nature, you
will die; but if by the Spirit you put to
death the misdeeds of the body, you will
live, [14] because those who are led by the
Spirit of God are sons of God. [15] For you
did not receive a spirit that makes you a
slave again to fear, but you received the
Spirit of sonship. And by him we cry,
'Abba, Father.' [16] The Spirit himself
testifies with our spirit that we are God's
children. [17] Now if we are children, then
we are heirs - heirs of God and co-heirs
with Christ, if indeed we share in his
sufferings in order that we may also share
in his glory.

DAY 192

ROM. 8. 18 — 39

Future Glory

[18] I consider that our present sufferings are not worth comparing with the glory that will be revealed in us. [19] The creation waits in eager expectation for the sons of God to be revealed. [20] For the creation was subjected to frustration, not by its own choice, but by the will of the one who subjected it, in hope [21] that the creation itself will be liberated from its bondage to decay and brought into the glorious freedom of the children of God. [22] We know that the whole creation has been groaning as in the pains of childbirth right up to the present time. [23] Not only so, but we ourselves, who have the firstfruits of the Spirit, groan inwardly as we wait eagerly for our adoption as sons, the redemption of our bodies. [24] For in this hope we were saved. But hope that is seen is no hope at all. Who hopes for what he already has? [25] But if we hope for what we do not yet have, we wait for it patiently.

[26] In the same way, the Spirit helps us in our weakness. We do not know what we ought to pray for, but the Spirit himself intercedes for us with groans that words cannot express. [27] And he who searches our hearts knows the mind of the Spirit, because the Spirit intercedes for the saints in accordance with God's will.

More Than Conquerors

[28] And we know that in all things God works for the good of those who love him, who have been called according to his purpose. [29] For those God foreknew he also predestined to be conformed to the likeness of his Son, that he might be the firstborn among many brothers. [30] And those he predestined, he also called; those he called, he also justified; those he justified, he also glorified.

[31] What, then, shall we say in response to this? If God is for us, who can be against us? [32] He who did not spare his own Son, but gave him up for us all - how will he not also, along with him, graciously give us all things? [33] Who will bring any charge against those whom God has chosen? It is God who justifies. [34] Who is he that condemns? Christ Jesus

---

Who shall separate us from the love of Christ? Shall trouble or persecution or famine or nakedness or danger or sword?

---

who died - more than that, who was raised to life - is at the right hand of God and is also interceding for us. [35] Who shall separate us from the love of Christ? Shall trouble or hardship or persecution or famine or nakedness or danger or sword? [36] As it is written:

'For your sake we face death all day long
  we are considered as sheep to be
  slaughtered.'

[37] No, in all these things we are more than conquerors through him who loved us. [38] For I am convinced that neither death nor life, neither angels nor demons, neither the present nor the future, nor any powers, [39] neither height nor depth, nor anything else in all creation, will be able to separate us from the love of God that is in Christ Jesus our Lord.

DAY 193

ROM. 9. 1 — 29

God's Sovereign Choice

I speak the truth in Christ - I am not lying, my conscience confirms it in the Holy Spirit - ²I have great sorrow and ceasing anguish in my heart. ³For I could wish that I myself were cursed and cut off from Christ for the sake of my brothers, those of my own race, ⁴the people of Israel. Theirs is the adoption as sons; theirs the divine glory, the covenants, the receiving the law, the temple worship and the promises. ⁵Theirs are the patriarchs, and from them is traced the human ancestry of Christ, who is God over all, for ever praised! Amen.

⁶It is not as though God's word had failed. For not all who are descended from Israel are Israel. ⁷Nor because they are his descendants are they all Abraham's children. On the contrary, 'It is through Isaac that your offspring will be reckoned.' ⁸In other words, it is not the natural children who are God's children, but it is the children of the promise who are regarded as Abraham's offspring. ⁹For this was how the promise was stated: 'At the appointed time I will return, and Sarah will have a son.'

¹⁰Not only that, but Rebekah's children had one and the same father, our father Isaac. ¹¹Yet, before the twins were born or had done anything good or bad - in order that God's purpose in election might stand: ¹²not by works but by him who calls - she was told, 'The older will serve the younger.' ¹³Just as it is written: 'Jacob I loved, but Esau I hated.'

¹⁴What then shall we say? Is God unjust? Not at all! ¹⁵For he says to Moses,

'I will have mercy on whom I have mercy,
and I will have compassion on whom I have compassion.'

¹⁶It does not, therefore, depend on man's desire or effort, but on God's mercy. ¹⁷For the Scripture says to Pharaoh: 'I raised you up for this very purpose, that I might display my power in you and that my name might be proclaimed in all the earth.' ¹⁸Therefore God has mercy on whom he wants to have mercy, and he hardens whom he wants to harden.

¹⁹One of you will say to me: 'Then why does God still blame us? For who resists his will?' ²⁰But who are you, O man, to talk back to God? 'Shall what is formed say to him who formed it, "Why did you make me like this?" ' ²¹Does not the potter have the right to make out of the same lump of clay some pottery for noble purposes and some for common use?

²²What if God, choosing to show his wrath and make his power known, bore with great patience the objects of his wrath - prepared for destruction? ²³What if he did this to make the riches of his glory known to the objects of his mercy, whom he prepared in advance for glory - ²⁴even us, whom he also called, not only from the Jews but also from the Gentiles? ²⁵As he says in Hosea:

'I will call them "my people" who are not my people;
and I will call her "my loved one" who is not my loved one,'

²⁶and,

'It will happen that in the very place where it was said to them,
"You are not my people," they will be called "sons of the living God". '

[27] Isaiah cries out concerning Israel:

'Though the number of the Israelites
    be like the sand by the sea,
  only the remnant will be saved.
[28] For the Lord will carry out his
    sentence on earth with speed
    and finality.'

[29] It is just as Isaiah said previously:

'Unless the Lord Almighty
  had left us descendants,
we would have become like Sodom,
  we would have been like Gomorrah.'

DAY 194
ROM. 9. 30 — 10.21

Israel's Unbelief

[30] What then shall we say? That the
Gentiles, who did not pursue
righteousness, have obtained it, a
righteousness that is by faith; [31] but Israel,
who pursued a law of righteousness, has
not attained it. [32] Why not? Because they
pursued it not by faith but as if it were by
works. They stumbled over the
'stumbling-stone'. [33] As it is written:

'See, I lay in Zion a stone that causes
    men to stumble
  and a rock that makes them fall,
and the one who trusts in him will
    never be put to shame.'

10 Brothers, my heart's desire and
prayer to God for the Israelites
is that they may be saved. [2] For
I can testify about them that they are
zealous for God, but their zeal is not based

on knowledge. [3] Since they did not know
the righteousness that comes from God
and sought to establish their own, they
did not submit to God's righteousness.

> **'I was found by those who did
> not seek me; I revealed
> myself to those who did
> not ask for me.'**

[4] Christ is the end of the law so that there
may be righteousness for everyone who
believes.

[5] Moses describes in this way the
righteousness that is by the law: 'The
man who does these things will live by
them.' [6] But the righteousness that is by
faith says: 'Do not say in your heart,
"Who will ascend into heaven?"' (that is
to bring Christ down) [7] 'or "Who will
descend into the deep?"' (that is, to
bring Christ up from the dead). [8] But
what does it say? 'The word is near you;
is in your mouth and in your heart,' that
is, the word of faith we are proclaiming:
[9] That if you confess with your mouth,
'Jesus is Lord,' and believe in your heart
that God raised him from the dead, you
will be saved. [10] For it is with your heart
that you believe and are justified, and it
is with your mouth that you confess and
are saved. [11] As the Scripture says,
'Anyone who trusts in him will never be
put to shame.' [12] For there is no difference
between Jew and Gentile - the same Lord
is Lord of all and richly blesses all who
call on him, [13] for, 'Everyone who calls on
the name of the Lord will be saved.'

[14] How, then, can they call on the
one they have not believed in? And how
can they believe in the one of whom they
have not heard? And how can they hear

hout someone preaching to them?
nd how can they preach unless they
sent? As it is written, 'How beautiful
the feet of those who bring good
s!' [16]But not all the Israelites accepted
good news. For Isaiah says, 'Lord, who
believed our message?' [17]Consequently,
h comes from hearing the message,
the message is heard through the
d of Christ. [18]But I ask: Did they not
r? Of course they did:

'Their voice has gone out into
    all the earth,
their words to the ends of the world.'

gain I ask: Did Israel not understand?

First, Moses says,

'I will make you envious by those
    who are not a nation;
I will make you angry by a nation that
    has no understanding.'

[20]And Isaiah boldly says,

'I was found by those
    who did not seek me;
I revealed myself to those who
    did not ask for me.'

[21]But concerning Israel he says,

'All day long I have held out my
    hands to a disobedient and
    obstinate people.'

'Everyone who calls on the
name of the Lord will be
saved.'

DAY 195
ROM. 11. 1 — 12

11
The Remnant of Israel

I ask then: Did God reject his people? By no means! I am an Israelite myself, a descendant of Abraham, from the tribe of Benjamin. [2] God did not reject his people, whom he foreknew. Don't you know what the Scripture says in the passage about Elijah - how he appealed to God against Israel: [3] ' Lord, they have killed your prophets and torn down your altars; I am the only one left, and they are trying to kill me'? [4] And what was God's answer to him? 'I have reserved for myself seven thousand who have not bowed the knee to Baal.' [5] So too, at the present time there is a remnant chosen by grace. [6] And if by grace, then it is no longer by works; if it were, grace would no longer be grace. [7] What then? What Israel sought so earnestly it did not obtain, but the elect did. The others were hardened, [8] as it is written:

'God gave them a spirit of stupor,
    eyes so that they could not see
    and ears so that they could not hear,
to this very day.'

[9] And David says:

'May their table become a snare and
    a trap,
    a stumbling-block and a retribution
    for them.
[10] May their eyes be darkened so they
    cannot see,
    and their backs be bent for ever.'

Ingrafted Branches

[11] Again I ask: Did they stumble so as to fall beyond recovery? Not at all! Rather, because of their transgression, salvation has come to the Gentiles to make Israel

> **God did not reject his people, whom he foreknew.**

envious. [12] But if their transgression mea[n] riches for the world, and their loss mean[s] riches for the Gentiles, how much great[er] riches will their fulness bring!

DAY 196
ROM. 11. 13 — 36

[13] I am talking to you Gentiles. Inasmuch as I am the apostle to the Gentiles, I make much of my ministry [14] in the hope that I may somehow arouse my own people to envy and save some o[f] them. [15] For if their rejection is the reconciliation of the world, what will their acceptance be but life from the dead? [16] If the part of the dough offered a[s] firstfruits is holy, then the whole batch i[s] holy; if the root is holy, so are the branches.

[17] If some of the branches have been broken off, and you, though a wild olive shoot, have been grafted in among the others and now share in the nourishing sap from the olive root, [18] do not boast over those branches. If you do, consider this: You do not support the root, but th[e] root supports you. [19] You will say then, 'Branches were broken off so that I coul[d] be grafted in.' [20] Granted. But they were

ken off because of unbelief, and you
nd by faith. Do not be arrogant, but be
aid. ²¹ For if God did not spare the
tural branches, he will not spare you
her.
²² Consider therefore the kindness
d sternness of God: sternness to those
o fell, but kindness to you, provided
at you continue in his kindness.
herwise, you also will be cut off. ²³ And
hey do not persist in unbelief, they will
grafted in, for God is able to graft
em in again. ²⁴ After all, if you were cut
t of an olive tree that is wild by nature,
d contrary to nature were grafted into a
tivated olive tree, how much more
dily will these, the natural branches,
grafted into their own olive tree!

l Israel Will Be Saved

do not want you to be ignorant of this
stery, brothers, so that you may not be
nceited: Israel has experienced a
rdening in part until the full number of
e Gentiles has come in. ²⁶ And so all
ael will be saved, as it is written:

'The deliverer will come from Zion;
  he will turn godlessness away from
    Jacob.
²⁷ And this is my covenant with them
  when I take away their sins.'

²⁸ As far as the gospel is concerned,
ey are enemies on your account; but as
as election is concerned, they are

**'And this is my covenant
with them when I take away
their sins.'**

ed on account of the patriarchs, ²⁹ for
d's gifts and his call are irrevocable.

³⁰ Just as you who were at one time
disobedient to God have now received
mercy as a result of their disobedience,
³¹ so they too have now become

**'Who has ever given to God,
that God should repay him?'**

disobedient in order that they too may
now receive mercy as a result of God's
mercy to you. ³² For God has bound all
men over to disobedience so that he may
have mercy on them all.

Doxology
³³ Oh, the depth of the riches of the
  wisdom and knowledge of God!
How unsearchable his judgments,
  and his paths beyond tracing out!
³⁴ 'Who has known the mind of the Lord?
  Or who has been his counsellor?'
³⁵ 'Who has ever given to God,
  that God should repay him?'
³⁶ For from him and through him and
  to him are all things.
To him be the glory for ever! Amen.

DAY 197
ROM. 12. 1 — 21

12 **Living Sacrifices**
Therefore, I urge you, brothers, in view of God's mercy, to offer your bodies as living sacrifices, holy and pleasing to God - this is your spiritual act of worship. [2] Do not conform any longer to the pattern of this world, but be transformed by the renewing of your mind. Then you will be able to test and approve what God's will is - his good, pleasing and perfect will.

[3] For by the grace given me I say to every one of you: Do not think of yourself more highly than you ought, but rather think of yourself with sober judgment, in accordance with the measure of faith God has given you. [4] Just as each of us has one body with many members, and these members do not all have the same function, [5] so in Christ we who are many form one body, and each member belongs to all the others. [6] We have different gifts, according to the grace given us. If a man's gift is prophesying, let him use it in proportion to his faith. [7] If it is serving, let him serve; if it is teaching, let him teach; [8] if it is encouraging, let him encourage; if it is contributing to the needs of others, let him give generously; if it is leadership, let him govern diligently; if it is showing mercy, let him do it cheerfully.

Love
[9] Love must be sincere. Hate what is evil; cling to what is good. [10] Be devoted to one another in brotherly love. Honour one another above yourselves. [11] Never be lacking in zeal, but keep your spiritual fervour, serving the Lord. [12] Be joyful in hope, patient in affliction, faithful in prayer. [13] Share with God's people who are in need. Practise hospitality.

[14] Bless those who persecute you; bless and do not curse. [15] Rejoice with those who rejoice; mourn with those who mourn. [16] Live in harmony with one another. Do not be proud, but be willing to associate with people of low position. Do not be conceited.

Live in harmony with one another

¹⁷ Do not repay anyone evil for evil. Be careful to do what is right in the eyes of everybody. ¹⁸ If it is possible, as far as it depends on you, live at peace with everyone. ¹⁹ Do not take revenge, my friends, but leave room for God's wrath, for it is written: 'It is mine to avenge; I will repay,' says the Lord. ²⁰ On the contrary:

'If your enemy is hungry, feed him;
    if he is thirsty, give him something
    to drink.
In doing this, you will heap burning
    coals on his head.'

Do not be overcome by evil, but overcome evil with good.

DAY 198

ROM. 13. 1 — 14

13 Submission to the Authorities

Everyone must submit himself to the governing authorities, for there is no authority except that which God has established. The authorities that exist have been established by God. ² Consequently, he who rebels against the authority is rebelling against what God has instituted, and those who do so will bring judgment on themselves. ³ For rulers hold no terror for those who do right, but for those who do wrong. Do you want to be free from fear of the one in authority? Then do what is right and he will commend you. ⁴ For he is God's servant to do you good. But if you do wrong, be afraid, for he does not bear the sword for nothing. He is God's servant, an agent of wrath to bring punishment on the wrongdoer. ⁵ Therefore, it is necessary to submit to the authorities, not only because of possible punishment but also because of conscience.

⁶ This is also why you pay taxes, for the authorities are God's servants, who give their full time to governing. ⁷ Give everyone what you owe him: If you owe taxes, pay taxes; if revenue, then revenue; if respect, then respect; if honour, then honour.

Love, for the Day Is Near

⁸ Let no debt remain outstanding, except the continuing debt to love one another, for he who loves his fellow-man has fulfilled the law. ⁹ The commandments, 'Do not commit adultery,' 'Do not murder,' 'Do not steal,' 'Do not covet,' and whatever other commandment there may be, are summed up in this one rule: 'Love your neighbour as yourself.' ¹⁰ Love does no harm to its neighbour. Therefore love is the fulfilment of the law.

¹¹ And do this, understanding the present time. The hour has come for you to wake up from your slumber, because our salvation is nearer now than when we

'Love your neighbour as yourself.'

first believed. ¹² The night is nearly over; the day is almost here. So let us put aside the deeds of darkness and put on the armour of light. ¹³ Let us behave decently, as in the daytime, not in orgies and drunkenness, not in sexual immorality and debauchery, not in dissension and jealousy. ¹⁴ Rather, clothe yourselves with the Lord Jesus Christ, and do not think about how to gratify the desires of the sinful nature.

DAY 199

ROM. 14. 1 — 23

14 The Weak and the Strong

Accept him whose faith is weak, without passing judgment on disputable matters. ² One man's faith allows him to eat everything, but another man, whose faith is weak, eats only vegetables. ³ The man who eats everything must not look down on him who does not, and the man who does not eat everything must not condemn the man who does, for God has accepted him. ⁴ Who are you to judge someone else's servant? To his own master he stands or

---

'Every knee will bow before me.'

---

falls. And he will stand, for the Lord is able to make him stand.

⁵ One man considers one day more sacred than another; another man considers every day alike. Each one should be fully convinced in his own mind. ⁶ He who regards one day as special, does so to the Lord. He who eats meat, eats to the Lord, for he gives thanks to God; and he who abstains, does so to the Lord and gives thanks to God. ⁷ For none of us lives to himself alone and none of us dies to himself alone. ⁸ If we live, we live to the Lord; and if we die, we die to the Lord. So, whether we live or die, we belong to the Lord.

⁹ For this very reason, Christ died and returned to life so that he might be the Lord of both the dead and the living. ¹⁰ You, then, why do you judge your brother? Or why do you look down on your brother? For we will all stand before God's judgment seat. ¹¹ It is written:

' "As surely as I live," says the Lord,
"Every knee will bow before me;
every tongue will confess to God."

¹² So then, each of us will give an account of himself to God.

¹³ Therefore let us stop passing judgment on one another. Instead, make up your mind not to put any stumbling-block or obstacle in your brother's way. ¹⁴ As one who is in the Lord Jesus, I am fully convinced that no food is unclean in itself. But if anyone regards something as unclean, then for him it is unclean. ¹⁵ If your brother is distressed because of what you eat, you are no longer acting in love. Do not by your eating destroy your brother for whom Christ died. ¹⁶ Do not allow what you consider good to be spoken of as evil. ¹⁷ For the kingdom of God is not a matter of eating and drinking, but of righteousness, peace and joy in the Holy Spirit, ¹⁸ because anyone who serves Christ in this way is pleasing to God and approved by men.

¹⁹ Let us therefore make every effort to do what leads to peace and to mutual edification. ²⁰ Do not destroy the work of God for the sake of food. All food is clean, but it is wrong for a man to eat anything that causes someone else to stumble. ²¹ It is better not to eat meat or drink wine or to do anything else that will cause your brother to fall.

²² So whatever you believe about these things keep between yourself and God. Blessed is the man who does not condemn himself by what he approves. ²³ But the man who has doubts is condemned if he eats, because his eating is not from faith; and everything that does not come from faith is sin.

DAY 200

ROM. 15. 1 — 33

15 We who are strong ought to bear with the failings of the weak and not to please ourselves. ²Each of us should please his neighbour for his good, to build him up. ³For even Christ did not please himself but, as it is written: 'The insults of those who insult you have fallen on me.' ⁴For everything that was written in the past was written to teach us, so that through endurance and the encouragement of the Scriptures we might have hope.

'Praise the Lord, all you Gentiles...'

⁵May the God who gives endurance and encouragement give you a spirit of unity among yourselves as you follow Christ Jesus, ⁶so that with one heart and mouth you may glorify the God and Father of our Lord Jesus Christ.

⁷Accept one another, then, just as Christ accepted you, in order to bring praise to God. ⁸For I tell you that Christ has become a servant of the Jews on behalf of God's truth, to confirm the promises made to the patriarchs ⁹so that the Gentiles may glorify God for his mercy, as it is written:

'Therefore I will praise you among the
Gentiles;
I will sing hymns to your name.'

¹⁰Again, it says,

'Rejoice, O Gentiles, with his people.'

¹¹And again,

'Praise the Lord, all you Gentiles,
and sing praises to him, all you
peoples.'

¹²And again, Isaiah says,

'The Root of Jesse will spring up,
one who will arise to rule over the
nations;
the Gentiles will hope in him.'

¹³May the God of hope fill you with all joy and peace as you trust in him, so that you may overflow with hope by the power of the Holy Spirit.

Paul the Minister to the Gentiles

¹⁴I myself am convinced, my brothers, that you yourselves are full of goodness, complete in knowledge and competent to instruct one another. ¹⁵I have written to you quite boldly on some points, as if to remind you of them again, because of the grace God gave me ¹⁶to be a minister of Christ Jesus to the Gentiles with the priestly duty of proclaiming the gospel of God, so that the Gentiles might become an offering acceptable to God, sanctified by the Holy Spirit.

¹⁷Therefore I glory in Christ Jesus in my service to God. ¹⁸I will not venture to speak of anything except what Christ has accomplished through me in leading the Gentiles to obey God by what I have said and done - ¹⁹by the power of signs and miracles, through the power of the Spirit. So from Jerusalem all the way around to Illyricum, I have fully proclaimed the gospel of Christ. ²⁰It has always been my

ambition to preach the gospel where Christ was not known, so that I would not be building on someone else's foundation. [21] Rather, as it is written:

'Those who were not told about
   him will see,
   and those who have not heard will
   understand.'

[22] This is why I have often been hindered from coming to you.

Paul's Plan to Visit Rome

[23] But now that there is no more place for me to work in these regions, and since I have been longing for many years to see you, [24] I plan to do so when I go to Spain. I hope to visit you while passing through and to have you assist me on my journey there, after I have enjoyed your company for a while. [25] Now, however, I am on my way to Jerusalem in the service of the saints there. [26] For Macedonia and Achaia were pleased to make a contribution for the poor among the saints in Jerusalem. [27] They were pleased to do it, and indeed they owe it to them. For if the Gentiles have shared in the Jews' spiritual blessings, they owe it to the Jews to share with them their material blessings. [28] So after I have completed this task and have made sure that they have received this fruit, I will go to Spain and visit you on the way. [29] I know that when I come to you, I will come in the full measure of the blessing of Christ.

[30] I urge you, brothers, by our Lord Jesus Christ and by the love of the Spirit, to join me in my struggle by praying to God for me. [31] Pray that I may be rescued from the unbelievers in Judea and that my service in Jerusalem may be acceptable to the saints there, [32] so that by God's will I may come to you with joy

and together with you be refreshed. [33] The God of peace be with you all. Amen.

DAY 201
ROM. 16. 1 — 27

16 **Personal Greetings**
I commend to you our sister Phoebe, a servant of the church in Cenchrea. [2] I ask you to receive her in the Lord in a way worthy of the saints and to give her any help she may need from you, for she has been a great help to many people, including me.

[3] Greet Priscilla and Aquila, my fellow-
   workers in Christ Jesus. [4] They
   risked their lives for me. Not only
   but all the churches of the Gentile
   are grateful to them.
[5] Greet also the church that meets at
   their house.
Greet my dear friend Epenetus, who was
   the first convert to Christ in the
   province of Asia.
[6] Greet Mary, who worked very hard for
   you.
[7] Greet Andronicus and Junias, my
   relatives who have been in prison
   with me. They are outstanding
   among the apostles, and they were
   in Christ before I was.
[8] Greet Ampliatus, whom I love in the
   Lord.
[9] Greet Urbanus, our fellow-worker in
   Christ, and my dear friend Stachy
[10] Greet Apelles, tested and approved in
   Christ.
Greet those who belong to the househol
   of Aristobulus.
[11] Greet Herodion, my relative.

Greet those in the household of Narcissus who are in the Lord.

² Greet Tryphena and Tryphosa, those women who work hard in the Lord. Greet my dear friend Persis, another woman who has worked very hard in the Lord.

³ Greet Rufus, chosen in the Lord, and his mother, who has been a mother to me, too.

⁴ Greet Asyncritus, Phlegon, Hermes, Patrobas, Hermas and the brothers with them.

⁵ Greet Philologus, Julia, Nereus and his obedience, so I am full of joy over you; but I want you to be wise about what is good, and innocent about what is evil.

²⁰ The God of peace will soon crush Satan under your feet.

The grace of our Lord Jesus be with you.

²¹ Timothy, my fellow-worker, sends his greetings to you, as do Lucius, Jason and Sosipater, my relatives.

²² I, Tertius, who wrote down this letter, greet you in the Lord.

²³ Gaius, whose hospitality I and the whole church here enjoy, sends you

Be wise about what is good, and innocent about what is evil.

sister, and Olympas and all the saints with them.

⁶ Greet one another with a holy kiss. All the churches of Christ send greetings.

¹⁷ I urge you, brothers, to watch out for those who cause divisions and put obstacles in your way that are contrary to the teaching you have learned. Keep away from them. ¹⁸ For such people are not serving our Lord Christ, but their own appetites. By smooth talk and flattery they deceive the minds of naïve people. ¹⁹ Everyone has heard about your his greetings.

Erastus, who is the city's director of public works, and our brother Quartus send you their greetings.

²⁵ Now to him who is able to establish you by my gospel and the proclamation of Jesus Christ, according to the revelation of the mystery hidden for long ages past, ²⁶ but now revealed and made known through the prophetic writings by the command of the eternal God, so that all nations might believe and obey him - ²⁷ to the only wise God be glory for ever through Jesus Christ! Amen.

DAY 202

ACTS 20. 17 — 38

[17] From Miletus, Paul sent to Ephesus for the elders of the church. [18] When they arrived, he said to them: 'You know how I lived the whole time I was with you, from the first day I came into the province of Asia. [19] I served the Lord with great humility and with tears, although I was severely tested by the plots of the Jews. [20] You know that I have not hesitated to preach anything that would be helpful to you but have taught you publicly and from house to house. [21] I have declared to both Jews and Greeks that they must turn to God in repentance and have faith in our Lord Jesus.

[22] 'And now, compelled by the Spirit, I am going to Jerusalem, not knowing what will happen to me there. [23] I only know that in every city the Holy Spirit warns me that prison and hardships are facing me. [24] However, I consider my life worth nothing to me, if only I may finish the race and complete the task the Lord Jesus has given me - the task of testifying to the gospel of God's grace.

[25] 'Now I know that none of you among whom I have gone about preaching the kingdom will ever see me again. [26] Therefore, I declare to you today that I am innocent of the blood of all men. [27] For I have not hesitated to proclaim to you the whole will of God. [28] Keep watch over yourselves and all the flock of which the Holy Spirit has made you overseers. Be shepherds of the church of God, which he bought with his own blood. [29] I know that after I leave, savage wolves will come in among you and will not spare the flock. [30] Even from your own number men will arise and distort the truth in order to draw away disciples after them. [31] So be on your guard! Remember that for three years I never stopped warning each of you night and day with tears.

[32] 'Now I commit you to God and to the word of his grace, which can build you up and give you an inheritance among all those who are sanctified. [33] I have not coveted anyone's silver or gold or clothing. [34] You yourselves know that these hands of mine have supplied my own needs and the needs of my companions. [35] In everything I did, I showed you that by this kind of hard work we must help the weak, remembering the words the Lord Jesus himself said: "It is more blessed to give than to receive." '

[36] When he had said this, he knelt down with all of them and prayed. [37] They all wept as they embraced him and kissed him. [38] What grieved them most was his statement that they would never see his face again. Then they accompanied him to the ship.

DAY 203

ACTS 21. 1 — 26

21 On to Jerusalem
After we had torn ourselves away from them, we put out to sea and sailed straight to Cos. The next day we went to Rhodes and from there to Patara. [2] We found a ship crossing over to Phoenicia, went on board and set sail. [3] After sighting Cyprus and passing to the south of it, we sailed on to Syria. We

nded at Tyre, where our ship was to nload its cargo. ⁴Finding the disciples here, we stayed with them seven days. Through the Spirit they urged Paul not to o on to Jerusalem. ⁵But when our time was up, we left and continued on our way. All the disciples and their wives and

'Why are you weeping and breaking my heart?'

children accompanied us out of the city, and there on the beach we knelt to pray. After saying good-bye to each other, we went aboard the ship, and they returned home.

⁷We continued our voyage from Tyre and landed at Ptolemais, where we greeted the brothers and stayed with them for a day. ⁸Leaving the next day, we reached Caesarea and stayed at the house of Philip the evangelist, one of the Seven. ⁹He had four unmarried daughters who prophesied.

¹⁰After we had been there a number of days, a prophet named Agabus came down from Judea. ¹¹Coming over to us, he took Paul's belt, tied his own hands and feet with it and said, 'The Holy Spirit says, "In this way the Jews of Jerusalem will bind the owner of this belt and will hand him over to the Gentiles." '

¹²When we heard this, we and the people there pleaded with Paul not to go up to Jerusalem. ¹³Then Paul answered, 'Why are you weeping and breaking my heart? I am ready not only to be bound, but also to die in Jerusalem for the name of the Lord Jesus.' ¹⁴When he would not be dissuaded, we gave up and said, 'The Lord's will be done.'

¹⁵After this, we got ready and went up to Jerusalem. ¹⁶Some of the disciples from Caesarea accompanied us and brought us to the home of Mnason, where we were to stay. He was a man from Cyprus and one of the early disciples.

Paul's Arrival at Jerusalem

¹⁷When we arrived at Jerusalem, the brothers received us warmly. ¹⁸The next day Paul and the rest of us went to see James, and all the elders were present. ¹⁹Paul greeted them and reported in detail what God had done among the Gentiles through his ministry.

²⁰When they heard this, they praised God. Then they said to Paul: 'You see, brother, how many thousands of Jews have believed, and all of them are zealous for the law. ²¹They have been informed that you teach all the Jews who live among the Gentiles to turn away from Moses, telling them not to circumcise their children or live according to our customs. ²²What shall we do? They will certainly hear that you have come, ²³so do what we tell you. There are four men with us who have made a vow. ²⁴Take these men, join in their purification rites and pay their expenses, so that they can have their heads shaved. Then everybody will know there is no truth in these reports about you, but that you yourself are living in obedience to the law. ²⁵As for the Gentile believers, we have written to them our decision that they should abstain from food sacrificed to idols, from blood, from the meat of strangled animals and from sexual immorality.'

²⁶The next day Paul took the men and purified himself along with them. Then he went to the temple to give notice of the date when the days of purification would end and the offering would be made for each of them.

DAY 204

ACTS 21. 27 — 22.5

Paul Arrested

[27] When the seven days were nearly over, some Jews from the province of Asia saw Paul at the temple. They stirred up the whole crowd and seized him, [28] shouting,

---

The crowd that followed kept shouting, 'Away with him!'

'Men of Israel, help us! This is the man who teaches all men everywhere against our people and our law and this place. And besides, he has brought Greeks into the temple area and defiled this holy place.' [29] (They had previously seen Trophimus the Ephesian in the city with Paul and assumed that Paul had brought him into the temple area.)

[30] The whole city was aroused, and the people came running from all directions. Seizing Paul, they dragged him from the temple, and immediately the gates were shut. [31] While they were trying to kill him, news reached the commander of the Roman troops that the whole city of Jerusalem was in an uproar. [32] He at once took some officers and soldiers and ran down to the crowd. When the rioters saw the commander and his soldiers, they stopped beating Paul.

[33] The commander came up and arrested him and ordered him to be bound with two chains. Then he asked who he was and what he had done. [34] Some in the crowd shouted one thing

and some another, and since the commander could not get at the truth because of the uproar, he ordered that Paul be taken into the barracks. [35] When Paul reached the steps, the violence of the mob was so great he had to be carried by the soldiers. [36] The crowd that followed kept shouting, 'Away with him!'

Paul Speaks to the Crowd

[37] As the soldiers were about to take Paul into the barracks, he asked the commander, 'May I say something to you?'

'Do you speak Greek?' he replied. [38] 'Aren't you the Egyptian who started a revolt and led four thousand terrorists out into the desert some time ago?'

[39] Paul answered, 'I am a Jew, from Tarsus in Cilicia, a citizen of no ordinary city. Please let me speak to the people.'

[40] Having received the commander's permission, Paul stood on the steps and motioned to the crowd. When they were all silent, he said to them in Aramaic:

22 'Brothers and fathers, listen now to my defence.' [2] When they heard him speak to them in Aramaic, they became very quiet.

Then Paul said: [3] 'I am a Jew, born in Tarsus of Cilicia, but brought up in this city. Under Gamaliel I was thoroughly trained in the law of our fathers and was just as zealous for God as any of you are today. [4] I persecuted the followers of this Way to their death, arresting both men and women and throwing them into prison, [5] as also the high priest and all the Council can testify. I even obtained letters from them to their brothers in Damascus, and went there to bring these people as prisoners to Jerusalem to be punished.

DAY 205

ACTS 22.6 — 29

⁶ 'About noon as I came near Damascus, suddenly a bright light from heaven flashed around me. ⁷ I fell to the ground and heard a voice say to me, Saul! Saul! Why do you persecute me?" ⁸ ' "Who are you, Lord?" I asked.

' "I am Jesus of Nazareth, whom you are persecuting," he replied. ⁹ My companions saw the light, but they did not understand the voice of him who was speaking to me.

¹⁰ ' "What shall I do, Lord?" I asked.

' "Get up," the Lord said, "and go into Damascus. There you will be told all that you have been assigned to do." ¹¹ My companions led me by the hand into Damascus, because the brilliance of the light had blinded me.

¹² 'A man named Ananias came to see me. He was a devout observer of the law and highly respected by all the Jews living there. ¹³ He stood beside me and said, "Brother Saul, receive your sight!" And at that very moment I was able to see him.

¹⁴ 'Then he said: "The God of our fathers has chosen you to know his will and to see the Righteous One and to hear words from his mouth. ¹⁵ You will be his witness to all men of what you have seen and heard. ¹⁶ And now what are you waiting for? Get up, be baptised and wash your sins away, calling on his name."

¹⁷ 'When I returned to Jerusalem and was praying at the temple, I fell into a trance ¹⁸ and saw the Lord speaking. "Quick!" he said to me. "Leave Jerusalem immediately, because they will not accept your testimony about me."

¹⁹ ' "Lord," I replied, "these men know that I went from one synagogue to another to imprison and beat those who believe in you. ²⁰ And when the blood of your martyr Stephen was shed, I stood there giving my approval and guarding the clothes of those who were killing him."

²¹ 'Then the Lord said to me, "Go; I will send you far away to the Gentiles." '

Paul the Roman Citizen

²² The crowd listened to Paul until he said this. Then they raised their voices and shouted, 'Rid the earth of him! He's not fit to live!'

²³ As they were shouting and throwing off their cloaks and flinging dust into the air, ²⁴ the commander ordered Paul to be taken into the barracks. He directed that he be flogged and questioned in order to find out why the people were shouting at him like this.

²⁵ As they stretched him out to flog him, Paul said to the centurion standing there, 'Is it legal for you to flog a Roman citizen who hasn't even been found guilty?'

²⁶ When the centurion heard this, he went to the commander and reported it. 'What are you going to do?' he asked. 'This man is a Roman citizen.'

²⁷ The commander went to Paul and asked, 'Tell me, are you a Roman citizen?'

'Yes, I am,' he answered.

²⁸ Then the commander said, 'I had to pay a big price for my citizenship.'

'But I was born a citizen,' Paul replied.

²⁹ Those who were about to question him withdrew immediately. The commander himself was alarmed when he realised that he had put Paul, a Roman citizen, in chains.

DAY 206

ACTS 22. 30 — 23.22

Before the Sanhedrin

³⁰ The next day, since the commander wanted to find out exactly why Paul was being accused by the Jews, he released him and ordered the chief priests and all the Sanhedrin to assemble. Then he brought Paul and had him stand before them.

Paul looked straight at the Sanhedrin and said, 'My brothers, I have fulfilled my duty to God in all good conscience to this day.' ² At this the high priest Ananias ordered those standing near Paul to strike him on the mouth.

³ Then Paul said to him, 'God will strike you, you whitewashed wall! You sit there to judge me according to the law, yet you yourself violate the law by commanding that I be struck!'

⁴ Those who were standing near Paul said, 'You dare to insult God's high priest?'

⁵ Paul replied, 'Brothers, I did not realise that he was the high priest; for it is written: "Do not speak evil about the ruler of your people." '

⁶ Then Paul, knowing that some of them were Sadducees and the others

'My hope is in the resurrection of the dead.'

arisees, called out in the Sanhedrin, ly brothers, I am a Pharisee, the son of a arisee. I stand on trial because of my pe in the resurrection of the dead.' When he said this, a dispute broke out tween the Pharisees and the Sadducees, d the assembly was divided. [8] (The dducees say that there is no surrection, and that there are neither gels nor spirits, but the Pharisees knowledge them all.)

[9] There was a great uproar, and some the teachers of the law who were arisees stood up and argued vigorously. e find nothing wrong with this man,' ey said. 'What if a spirit or an angel has oken to him?' [10] The dispute became so olent that the commander was afraid aul would be torn to pieces by them. He rdered the troops to go down and take im away from them by force and bring im into the barracks.

[11] The following night the Lord stood ear Paul and said, 'Take courage! As you ave testified about me in Jerusalem, so ou must also testify in Rome.'

he Plot to Kill Paul

The next morning the Jews formed a onspiracy and bound themselves with an ath not to eat or drink until they had illed Paul. [13] More than forty men were nvolved in this plot. [14] They went to the hief priests and elders and said, 'We have aken a solemn oath not to eat anything ntil we have killed Paul. [15] Now then, ou and the Sanhedrin petition the ommander to bring him before you on he pretext of wanting more accurate nformation about his case. We are ready o kill him before he gets here.'

[16] But when the son of Paul's sister eard of this plot, he went into the arracks and told Paul.

[17] Then Paul called one of the cen-turions and said, 'Take this young man to the commander; he has something to tell him.' [18] So he took him to the commander.

The centurion said, 'Paul, the prisoner, sent for me and asked me to bring this young man to you because he has something to tell you.'

[19] The commander took the young man by the hand, drew him aside and asked, 'What is it you want to tell me?'

[20] He said: 'The Jews have agreed to ask you to bring Paul before the Sanhedrin tomorrow on the pretext of wanting more accurate information about him. [21] Don't give in to them, because more than forty of them are waiting in ambush for him. They have taken an oath not to eat or drink until they have killed him. They are ready now, waiting for your consent to their request.'

[22] The commander dismissed the young man and cautioned him, 'Don't tell anyone that you have reported this to me.'

DAY 207
ACTS 23. 23 — 24.9

Paul Transferred to Caesarea

[23] Then he called two of his centurions and ordered them, 'Get ready a detachment of two hundred soldiers, seventy horsemen and two hundred spearmen to go to Caesarea at nine tonight. [24] Provide mounts for Paul so that he may be taken safely to Governor Felix.'

[25] He wrote a letter as follows:

[26] Claudius Lysias,
To His Excellency,
Governor Felix:

Greetings.

²⁷ This man was seized by the Jews and they were about to kill him, but I came with my troops and rescued him, for I had learned that he is a Roman citizen. ²⁸ I wanted to know why they were accusing him, so I brought him to their Sanhedrin. ²⁹ I found that the accusation had to do with questions about their law, but there was no charge against him that deserved death or imprisonment. ³⁰ When I was informed of a plot to be carried out against the man, I sent him to you at once. I also ordered his accusers to present to you their case against him.

³¹ So the soldiers, carrying out their orders, took Paul with them during the night and brought him as far as Antipatris. ³² The next day they let the

---

'I will hear your case when your accusers get here.'

---

cavalry go on with him, while they returned to the barracks. ³³ When the cavalry arrived in Caesarea, they delivered the letter to the governor and handed Paul over to him. ³⁴ The governor read the letter and asked what province he was from. Learning that he was from Cilicia, ³⁵ he said, 'I will hear your case when your accusers get here.' Then he ordered that Paul be kept under guard in Herod's palace.

24 The Trial Before Felix

Five days later the high priest Ananias went down to Caesarea with some of the elders and a lawyer named Tertullus, and they brought their charges against Paul before the governor. ² When Paul was called in, Tertullus presented his case before Felix: 'We have enjoyed a long period of peace

---

'We have enjoyed a long period of peace under you, and your foresight has brought about reforms in this nation. '

---

under you, and your foresight has brought about reforms in this nation. ³ Everywhere and in every way, most excellent Felix, we acknowledge this with profound gratitude. ⁴ But in order not to weary you further, I would request that you be kind enough to hear us briefly.

⁵ 'We have found this man to be a troublemaker, stirring up riots among the Jews all over the world. He is a ringleader of the Nazarene sect ⁶ and even tried to desecrate the temple; so we seized him. ⁸ By examining him yourself you will be able to learn the truth about all these charges we are bringing against him.'

⁹ The Jews joined in the accusation, asserting that these things were true.

DAY 208
ACTS 24. 10 — 27

¹⁰ When the governor motioned for him to speak, Paul replied: 'I know that for a number of years you have been a judge over this nation; so I gladly make my

fence. [11] You can easily verify that no more than twelve days ago I went up to Jerusalem to worship. [12] My accusers did not find me arguing with anyone at the temple, or stirring up a crowd in the synagogues or anywhere else in the city. And they cannot prove to you the charges they are now making against me. However, I admit that I worship the God of our fathers as a follower of the Way, which they call a sect. I believe everything that agrees with the Law and that is written in the Prophets, [15] and I have the same hope in God as these men, that there will be a resurrection of both the righteous and the wicked. [16] So I strive always to keep my conscience clear before God and man.

[17] 'After an absence of several years, I came to Jerusalem to bring my people gifts for the poor and to present offerings.

'It is concerning the resurrection of the dead that I am on trial before you today.'

I was ceremonially clean when they found me in the temple courts doing this. There was no crowd with me, nor was I involved in any disturbance. [19] But there were some Jews from the province of Asia, who ought to be here before you and bring charges if they have anything against me. [20] Or these who are here should state what crime they found in me when I stood before the Sanhedrin - unless it was this one thing I shouted as I stood in their presence: "It is concerning the resurrection of the dead that I am on trial before you today." '

[22] Then Felix, who was well acquainted with the Way, adjourned the proceedings. 'When Lysias the commander comes,' he said, 'I will decide

'That's enough for now! You may leave. When I find it convenient, I will send for you.'

your case.' [23] He ordered the centurion to keep Paul under guard but to give him some freedom and permit his friends to take care of his needs.

[24] Several days later Felix came with his wife Drusilla, who was a Jewess. He sent for Paul and listened to him as he spoke about faith in Christ Jesus. [25] As Paul discoursed on righteousness, self-control and the judgment to come, Felix was afraid and said, 'That's enough for now! You may leave. When I find it convenient, I will send for you.' [26] At the same time he was hoping that Paul would offer him a bribe, so he sent for him frequently and talked with him.

[27] When two years had passed, Felix was succeeded by Porcius Festus, but because Felix wanted to grant a favour to the Jews, he left Paul in prison.

DAY 209

ACTS 25. 1 — 27

25 **The Trial Before Festus**
Three days after arriving in the province, Festus went up from Caesarea to Jerusalem, ²where the chief priests and Jewish leaders appeared before him and presented the charges against Paul. ³They urgently requested Festus, as a favour to them, to have Paul transferred to Jerusalem, for they were

> **'Let some of your leaders come with me and press charges against the man there, if he has done anything wrong.'**

preparing an ambush to kill him along the way. ⁴Festus answered, 'Paul is being held at Caesarea, and I myself am going there soon. ⁵Let some of your leaders come with me and press charges against the man there, if he has done anything wrong.'

⁶After spending eight or ten days with them, he went down to Caesarea, and the next day he convened the court and ordered that Paul be brought before him. ⁷When Paul appeared, the Jews who had come down from Jerusalem stood around him, bringing many serious charges against him, which they could not prove.

⁸Then Paul made his defence: 'I have done nothing wrong against the law of the Jews or against the temple or against Caesar.'

⁹Festus, wishing to do the Jews a favour, said to Paul, 'Are you willing to go up to Jerusalem and stand trial before me there on these charges?'

¹⁰Paul answered: 'I am now standing before Caesar's court, where I ought to be tried. I have not done any wrong to the Jews, as you yourself know very well. ¹¹If, however, I am guilty of doing anything deserving death, I do not refuse to die. But if the charges brought against me by these Jews are not true, no-one has the right to hand me over to them. I appeal to Caesar!'

¹²After Festus had conferred with his council, he declared: 'You have appealed to Caesar. To Caesar you will go!'

Festus Consults King Agrippa

¹³A few days later King Agrippa and Bernice arrived at Caesarea to pay their respects to Festus. ¹⁴Since they were spending many days there, Festus discussed Paul's case with the king. He said: 'There is a man here whom Felix left as a prisoner. ¹⁵When I went to Jerusalem the chief priests and elders of the Jews brought charges against him and asked that he be condemned.

¹⁶'I told them that it is not the Roman custom to hand over any man before he has faced his accusers and has had an opportunity to defend himself against their charges. ¹⁷When they came here with me, I did not delay the case, but convened the court the next day and ordered the man to be brought in. ¹⁸When his accusers got up to speak, they did not charge him with any of the crimes I had expected. ¹⁹Instead, they had some points of dispute with him about their own religion and about a dead man named Jesus whom Paul claimed was alive. ²⁰I was at a loss how to investigate such matters; so I asked if he would be

willing to go to Jerusalem and stand trial there on these charges. [21] When Paul made his appeal to be held over for the Emperor's decision, I ordered him to be held until I could send him to Caesar.'

[22] Then Agrippa said to Festus, 'I would like to hear this man myself.'

He replied, 'Tomorrow you will hear him.'

Paul Before Agrippa

[23] The next day Agrippa and Bernice came with great pomp and entered the audience room with the high ranking officers and the leading men of the city. At the command of Festus, Paul was

> **'I found he had done nothing deserving of death, but because he made his appeal to the Emperor I decided to send him to Rome.'**

brought in. [24] Festus said: 'King Agrippa, and all who are present with us, you see this man! The whole Jewish community has petitioned me about him in Jerusalem and here in Caesarea, shouting that he ought not to live any longer. [25] I found he had done nothing deserving of death, but because he made his appeal to the Emperor I decided to send him to Rome. [26] But I have nothing definite to write to His Majesty about him. Therefore I have brought him before all of you, and especially before you, King Agrippa, so that as a result of this investigation I may have something to write. [27] For I think it is unreasonable to send on a prisoner without specifying the charges against him.'

DAY 210
ACTS 26. 1 — 32

26 Then Agrippa said to Paul, 'You have permission to speak for yourself.'

So Paul motioned with his hand and began his defence: [2] 'King Agrippa, I consider myself fortunate to stand before you today as I make my defence against all the accusations of the Jews, [3] and especially so because you are well acquainted with all the Jewish customs and controversies. Therefore, I beg you to listen to me patiently.

[4] 'The Jews all know the way I have lived ever since I was a child, from the beginning of my life in my own country, and also in Jerusalem. [5] They have known me for a long time and can testify, if they are willing, that according to the strictest sect of our religion, I lived as a Pharisee. [6] 'And now it is because of my hope in what God has promised our fathers that I am on trial today. [7] This is the promise our twelve tribes are hoping to see fulfilled as they earnestly serve God day and night. O King, it is because of this hope that the Jews are accusing me. [8] Why should any of you consider it incredible that God raises the dead?

[9] 'I too was convinced that I ought to do all that was possible to oppose the name of Jesus of Nazareth. [10] And that is just what I did in Jerusalem. On the authority of the chief priests I put many of the saints in prison, and when they were put to death, I cast my vote against them. [11] Many a time I went from one synagogue to another to have them punished, and I tried to force them to

blaspheme. In my obsession against them, I even went to foreign cities to persecute them.

¹² 'On one of these journeys I was going to Damascus with the authority and commission of the chief priests. ¹³ About noon, O King, as I was on the road, I saw a light from heaven, brighter than the sun, blazing around me and my companions. ¹⁴ We all fell to the ground, and I heard a voice saying to me in Aramaic, "Saul, Saul, why do you persecute me? It is hard for you to kick against the goads."

¹⁵ 'Then I asked, "Who are you, Lord?"

' "I am Jesus, whom you are persecuting," the Lord replied. ¹⁶ "Now get up and stand on your feet. I have appeared to you to appoint you as a servant and as a witness of what you have seen of me and what I will show you. ¹⁷ I will rescue you from your own people and

'I will rescue you from your own people and from the Gentiles.'

from the Gentiles. I am sending you to them ¹⁸ to open their eyes and turn them from darkness to light, and from the power of Satan to God, so that they may receive forgiveness of sins and a place among those who are sanctified by faith in me."

¹⁹ 'So then, King Agrippa, I was not disobedient to the vision from heaven. ²⁰ First to those in Damascus, then to those in Jerusalem and in all Judea, and to the Gentiles also, I preached that they should repent and turn to God and prove their repentance by their deeds. ²¹ That is

why the Jews seized me in the temple courts and tried to kill me. ²² But I have had God's help to this very day, and so I stand here and testify to small and great alike. I am saying nothing beyond what the prophets and Moses said would happen - ²³ that the Christ would suffer and, as the first to rise from the dead,

...I have had God's help to this very day...

would proclaim light to his own people and to the Gentiles.'

²⁴ At this point Festus interrupted Paul's defence. 'You are out of your mind, Paul!' he shouted. 'Your great learning is driving you insane.'

²⁵ 'I am not insane, most excellent Festus,' Paul replied. 'What I am saying is true and reasonable. ²⁶ The king is familiar with these things, and I can speak freely to him. I am convinced that none of this has escaped his notice, because it was not done in a corner. ²⁷ King Agrippa, do you believe the prophets? I know you do.'

²⁸ Then Agrippa said to Paul, 'Do you think that in such a short time you can persuade me to be a Christian?'

²⁹ Paul replied, 'Short time or long - pray God that not only you but all who are listening to me today may become what I am, except for these chains.'

³⁰ The king rose, and with him the governor and Bernice and those sitting with them. ³¹ They left the room, and while talking with one another, they said 'This man is not doing anything that deserves death or imprisonment.'

³² Agrippa said to Festus, 'This man could have been set free if he had not appealed to Caesar.'

DAY 211

ACTS 27. 1 — 44

27 **Paul Sails for Rome**
When it was decided that we would sail for Italy, Paul and me other prisoners were handed over to centurion named Julius, who belonged the Imperial Regiment. ² We boarded a ip from Adramyttium about to sail for rts along the coast of the province of sia, and we put out to sea. Aristarchus, Macedonian from Thessalonica, was th us.

³ The next day we landed at Sidon; d Julius, in kindness to Paul, allowed m to go to his friends so they might ovide for his needs. ⁴ From there we put ut to sea again and passed to the lee of yprus because the winds were against us. When we had sailed across the open sea f the coast of Cilicia and Pamphylia, we nded at Myra in Lycia. ⁶ There the nturion found an Alexandrian ship iling for Italy and put us on board. ⁷ We ade slow headway for many days and d difficulty arriving off Cnidus. When e wind did not allow us to hold our urse, we sailed to the lee of Crete, pposite Salmone. ⁸ We moved along the ast with difficulty and came to a place lled Fair Havens, near the town of asea.

⁹ Much time had been lost, and iling had already become dangerous cause by now it was after the Fast. So aul warned them, ¹⁰ 'Men, I can see that ur voyage is going to be disastrous and ring great loss to ship and cargo, and to ur own lives also.' ¹¹ But the centurion, nstead of listening to what Paul said,

followed the advice of the pilot and of the owner of the ship. ¹² Since the harbour was unsuitable to winter in, the majority decided that we should sail on, hoping to reach Phoenix and winter there. This was a harbour in Crete, facing both south-west and north-west.

The Storm

¹³ When a gentle south wind began to blow, they thought they had obtained what they wanted; so they weighed anchor and sailed along the shore of Crete. ¹⁴ Before very long, a wind of hurricane force, called the 'north-easter', swept down from the island. ¹⁵ The ship was caught by the storm and could not head into the wind; so we gave way to it and were driven along. ¹⁶ As we passed to the lee of a small island called Cauda, we were hardly able to make the lifeboat secure. ¹⁷ When the men had hoisted it aboard, they passed ropes under the ship itself to hold it together. Fearing that they would run aground on the sand-bars of

> **'Men, you should have taken my advice not to sail from Crete.'**

Syrtis, they lowered the sea anchor and let the ship be driven along. ¹⁸ We took such a violent battering from the storm that the next day they began to throw the cargo overboard. ¹⁹ On the third day, they threw the ship's tackle overboard with their own hands. ²⁰ When neither sun nor stars appeared for many days and the storm continued raging, we finally gave up all hope of being saved.

²¹ After the men had gone a long time without food, Paul stood up before them and said: 'Men, you should have taken my

advice not to sail from Crete; then you would have spared yourselves this damage and loss. ²² But now I urge you to keep up your courage, because not one of you will be lost; only the ship will be destroyed. ²³ Last night an angel of the God whose I am and whom I serve stood beside me ²⁴ and said, "Do not be afraid, Paul. You must stand trial before Caesar; and God has graciously given you the lives of all who sail with you." ²⁵ So keep up your courage, men, for I have faith in God that it will happen just as he told me. ²⁶ Nevertheless, we must run aground on some island.'

Dashed against the rocks

The Shipwreck

²⁷ On the fourteenth night we were still being driven across the Adriatic Sea, when about midnight the sailors sensed they were approaching land. ²⁸ They took soundings and found that the water was one hundred and twenty feet deep. A short time later they took soundings again and found it was ninety feet deep. ²⁹ Fearing that we would be dashed against the rocks, they dropped four anchors from the stern and prayed for daylight. ³⁰ In an attempt to escape from the ship, the sailors let the lifeboat down into the sea, pretending they were going to lower some anchors from the bow. ³¹ Then Paul said to the centurion and the soldiers, 'Unless these men stay with the ship, you cannot be saved.' ³² So the soldiers cut the ropes that held the lifeboat and let it fall away.

³³ Just before dawn Paul urged them all to eat. 'For the last fourteen days,' he said, 'you have been in constant suspense and have gone without food - you haven't eaten anything. ³⁴ Now I urge you to take some food. You need it to survive. Not one of you will lose a single hair from his head.' ³⁵ After he said this, he took some bread and gave thanks to God in front of them all. Then he broke it and began to eat. ³⁶ They were all encouraged and ate some food themselves. ³⁷ Altogether there were 276 of us on board. ³⁸ When they had eaten as much as they wanted, they lightened the ship by throwing the grain into the sea.

³⁹ When daylight came, they did not recognise the land, but they saw a bay with a sandy beach, where they decided to run the ship aground if they could. ⁴⁰ Cutting loose the anchors, they left them in the sea and at the same time untied the ropes that held the rudders. Then they hoisted the foresail to the wind and made for the beach. ⁴¹ But the ship struck a sand-bar and ran aground. The bow stuck fast and would not move, and the stern was broken to pieces by the pounding of the surf.

⁴² The soldiers planned to kill the prisoners to prevent any of them from swimming away and escaping. ⁴³ But the centurion wanted to spare Paul's life and kept them from carrying out their plan. He ordered those who could swim to jump overboard first and get to land. ⁴⁴ The rest were to get there on planks or on pieces of the ship. In this way everyone reached land in safety.

DAY 212

ACTS 28. 1 — 16

28 **Ashore on Malta**
Once safely on shore, we found out that the island was called Malta. ² The islanders showed us unusual kindness. They built a fire and welcomed us all because it was raining and cold. ³ Paul gathered a pile of brushwood and, as he put it on the fire, a viper, driven out by the heat, fastened itself on his hand. ⁴ When the islanders saw the snake hanging from his hand, they said to each other, 'This man must be a murderer; for though he escaped from the sea, Justice has not allowed him to live.' ⁵ But Paul shook the snake off into the fire and suffered no ill effects. ⁶ The people expected him to swell up or suddenly fall dead, but after waiting a long time and seeing nothing unusual happen to him, they changed their minds and said he was a god.

⁷ There was an estate near by that belonged to Publius, the chief official of the island. He welcomed us to his home and for three days entertained us hospitably. ⁸ His father was sick in bed, suffering from fever and dysentery. Paul went in to see him and, after prayer, placed his hands on him and healed him. ⁹ When this had happened, the rest of the sick on the island came and were cured. ¹⁰ They honoured us in many ways and when we were ready to sail, they furnished us with the supplies we needed.

Arrival at Rome

¹¹ After three months we put out to sea in a ship that had wintered in the island. It was an Alexandrian ship with the figurehead of the twin gods Castor and Pollux. ¹² We put in at Syracuse and stayed there three days. ¹³ From there we set sail and arrived at Rhegium. The next day the south wind came up, and on the following day we reached Puteoli. ¹⁴ There we found some brothers who invited us to spend a week with them. And so we came to Rome. ¹⁵ The brothers there had heard that we were coming, and they travelled as far as the Forum of Appius and the Three Taverns to meet us. At the sight of these men Paul thanked God and was encouraged. ¹⁶ When we got to Rome, Paul was allowed to live by himself, with a soldier to guard him.

Brought safely to the shore.

DAY 213

ACTS 28. 17 — 31

Paul Preaches at Rome Under Guard

[17] Three days later he called together the leaders of the Jews. When they had assembled, Paul said to them: 'My brothers, although I have done nothing against our people or against the customs of our ancestors, I was arrested in Jerusalem and handed over to the Romans. [18] They examined me and wanted to release me, because I was not guilty of any crime deserving death. [19] But when the Jews objected, I was compelled to appeal to Caesar - not that I had any charge to bring against my own people. [20] For this reason I have asked to see you and talk with you. It is because of the hope of Israel that I am bound with this chain.'

[21] They replied, 'We have not received any letters from Judea concerning you, and none of the brothers who have come from there has reported or said anything bad about you. [22] But we want to hear what your views are, for we know that people everywhere are talking against this sect.'

[23] They arranged to meet Paul on a certain day, and came in even larger numbers to the place where he was staying. From morning till evening he explained and declared to them the kingdom of God and tried to convince them about Jesus from the Law of Moses and from the Prophets. [24] Some were convinced by what he said, but others would not believe. [25] They disagreed among themselves and began to leave after Paul had made this final statement: 'The Holy Spirit spoke the truth to your forefathers when he said through Isaiah the prophet:

[26] "Go to this people and say,
    'You will be ever hearing but never
        understanding;
    you will be ever seeing but never
        perceiving.'
[27] For this people's heart has become
        calloused;
    they hardly hear with their ears,
    and they have closed their eyes.
Otherwise they might see with their
    eyes, hear with their ears,
    understand with their hearts
and turn, and I would heal them."

[28] 'Therefore I want you to know that God's salvation has been sent to the Gentiles, and they will listen!'

[30] For two whole years Paul stayed there in his own rented house and welcomed all who came to see him. [31] Boldly and without hindrance he preached the kingdom of God and taught about the Lord Jesus Christ.

Otherwise they might see with their eye

DAY 214

PHIL. 1. 1 — 30

 Paul and Timothy, servants of Christ Jesus,

To all the saints in Christ Jesus at ilippi, together with the overseers and acons:

[2] Grace and peace to you from God r Father and the Lord Jesus Christ.

hanksgiving and Prayer

thank my God every time I remember u. [4] In all my prayers for all of you, I vays pray with joy [5] because of your rtnership in the gospel from the first y until now, [6] being confident of this, at he who began a good work in you ll carry it on to completion until the y of Christ Jesus.

[7] It is right for me to feel this way out all of you, since I have you in my art; for whether I am in chains or fending and confirming the gospel, all you share in God's grace with me. 'od can testify how I long for all of you th the affection of Christ Jesus.

[9] And this is my prayer: that your love y abound more and more in knowledge d depth of insight, [10] so that you may be le to discern what is best and may be re and blameless until the day of rist, [11] filled with the fruit of hteousness that comes through Jesus rist - to the glory and praise of God.

ul's Chains Advance the spel

Jow I want you to know, brothers, that

what has happened to me has really served to advance the gospel. [13] As a result, it has become clear throughout the whole palace guard and to everyone else that I am in chains for Christ. [14] Because of my chains, most of the brothers in the Lord have been encouraged to speak the word of God more courageously and fearlessly.

[15] It is true that some preach Christ out of envy and rivalry, but others out of goodwill. [16] The latter do so in love, knowing that I am put here for the defence of the gospel. [17] The former preach Christ out of selfish ambition, not sincerely, supposing that they can stir up trouble for me while I am in chains. [18] But what does it matter? The important thing is that in every way, whether from false motives or true, Christ is preached. And because of this I rejoice.

Yes, and I will continue to rejoice, [19] for I know that through your prayers and the help given by the Spirit of Jesus Christ, what has happened to me will turn out for my deliverance. [20] I eagerly expect and hope that I will in no way be ashamed, but will have sufficient courage so that now as always Christ will be exalted in my body, whether by life or by death. [21] For to me, to live is Christ and to die is gain. [22] If I am to go on living in the body, this will mean fruitful labour for me. Yet what shall I choose? I do not know! [23] I am torn between the two: I desire to depart and be with Christ, which is better by far; [24] but it is more necessary for you that I remain in the body. [25] Convinced of this, I know that I will remain, and I will continue with all of you for your progress and joy in the faith, [26] so that through my being with you again your joy in Christ Jesus will overflow on account of me.

[27] Whatever happens, conduct

yourselves in a manner worthy of the gospel of Christ. Then, whether I come and see you or only hear about you in my absence, I will know that you stand firm in one spirit, contending as one man for the faith of the gospel [28] without being frightened in any way by those who oppose you. This is a sign to them that they will be destroyed, but that you will be saved - and that by God. [29] For it has been granted to you on behalf of Christ not only to believe on him, but also to suffer for him, [30] since you are going through the same struggle you saw I had, and now hear that I still have.

DAY 215
PHIL. 2. 1 — 30

2 **Imitating Christ's Humility**
If you have any encouragement from being united with Christ, if any comfort from his love, if any fellowship with the Spirit, if any tenderness and compassion, [2] then make my joy complete by being like-minded, having the same love, being one in spirit and purpose. [3] Do nothing out of selfish ambition or vain conceit, but in humility consider others better than yourselves. [4] Each of you should look not only to your own interests, but also to the interests of others.
[5] Your attitude should be the same as that of Christ Jesus:

[6] Who, being in very nature God,
  did not consider equality with God
   something to be grasped,
[7] but made himself nothing,
  taking the very nature of a servant,

being made in human likeness.
[8] And being found in appearance as a man, he humbled himself
and became obedient to death - even death on a cross!
[9] Therefore God exalted him to the highest place and gave him the name that is above every name,
[10] that at the name of Jesus every knee should bow, in heaven and on earth and under the earth,
[11] and every tongue confess that Jesus Christ is Lord, to the glory of God the Father.

Shining as Stars
[12] Therefore, my dear friends, as you have always obeyed - not only in my presence but now much more in my absence - continue to work out your salvation with fear and trembling, [13] for it is God who works in you to will and to act according to his good purpose.
[14] Do everything without complaining or arguing, [15] so that you may become blameless and pure, children of God

---

'...at the name of Jesus every knee should bow, in heaven and on earth and under the earth...'

---

without fault in a crooked and depraved generation, in which you shine like stars in the universe [16] as you hold out the word of life - in order that I may boast on the day of Christ that I did not run or labour for nothing. [17] But even if I am being poured out like a drink offering on the sacrifice and service coming from your faith, I am glad and rejoice with all of you. [18] So you too should be glad and rejoice with me.

imothy and Epaphroditus

hope in the Lord Jesus to send
mothy to you soon, that I also may be
eered when I receive news about you.
have no-one else like him, who takes a
nuine interest in your welfare. [21] For
eryone looks out for his own interests,
t those of Jesus Christ. [22] But you know
at Timothy has proved himself, because
a son with his father he has served with
e in the work of the gospel. [23] I hope,
erefore, to send him as soon as I see
w things go with me. [24] And I am
nfident in the Lord that I myself will
me soon.

[25] But I think it is necessary to send
ck to you Epaphroditus, my brother,
fellow-worker and fellow-soldier, who is
also your messenger, whom you sent to
take care of my needs. [26] For he longs
for all of you and is distressed because
you heard he was ill. [27] Indeed he was
ill, and almost died. But God had
mercy on him, and not on him only but
also on me, to spare me sorrow upon
sorrow. [28] Therefore I am all the more
eager to send him, so that when you see
him again you may be glad and I may
have less anxiety. [29] Welcome him in
the Lord with great joy, and honour
men like him, [30] because he almost died
for the work of Christ, risking his life to
make up for the help you could not
give me.

You shine like stars.

DAY 216
PHIL. 3. 1 — 21

3 **No Confidence in the Flesh**
Finally, my brothers, rejoice in the Lord! It is no trouble for me to write the same things to you again, and it is a safeguard for you.
[2] Watch out for those dogs, those men who do evil, those mutilators of the flesh. [3] For it is we who are the circumcision, we who worship by the Spirit of God, who glory in Christ Jesus, and who put no confidence in the flesh - [4] though I myself have reasons for such confidence.

If anyone else thinks he has reasons to put confidence in the flesh, I have more: [5] circumcised on the eighth day, of the people of Israel, of the tribe of Benjamin, a Hebrew of Hebrews; in regard to the law, a Pharisee; [6] as for zeal, persecuting the church; as for legalistic righteousness, faultless.
[7] But whatever was to my profit I now consider loss for the sake of Christ.

...the surpassing greatness of knowing Christ Jesus my Lord.

[8] What is more, I consider everything a loss compared to the surpassing greatness of knowing Christ Jesus my Lord, for whose sake I have lost all things. I consider them rubbish, that I may gain Christ [9] and be found in him, not having a righteousness of my own that comes from the law, but that which is through faith in Christ - the righteousness that comes from God and is by faith. [10] I want to know Christ and the power of his resurrection and the fellowship of sharing in his sufferings, becoming like him in his death, [11] and so, somehow, to attain to the resurrection from the dead.

Pressing on Towards the Goal
[12] Not that I have already obtained all this, or have already been made perfect, but I press on to take hold of that for which Christ Jesus took hold of me. [13] Brothers, I do not consider myself yet to have taken hold of it. But one thing I do: Forgetting what is behind and straining

I press on towards the goal to win the prize.

towards what is ahead, [14] I press on towards the goal to win the prize for which God has called me heavenwards in Christ Jesus.
[15] All of us who are mature should take such a view of things. And if on some point you think differently, that too God will make clear to you. [16] Only let us live up to what we have already attained.
[17] Join with others in following my example, brothers, and take note of those who live according to the pattern we gave you. [18] For, as I have often told you before and now say again even with tears, many live as enemies of the cross of Christ. [19] Their destiny is destruction, their god is their stomach, and their glory is in their shame. Their mind is on earthly things. [20] But our citizenship is in heaven. And we eagerly await a Saviour from there, the Lord Jesus Christ, [21] who, by the power that enables him to bring everything under his control, will transform our lowly bodies so that they will be like his glorious body.

DAY 217

PHIL. 4. 1 — 23

4 Therefore, my brothers, you whom I love and long for, my joy and crown, that is how you should and firm in the Lord, dear friends!

xhortations

plead with Euodia and I plead with yntyche to agree with each other in the ord. ³Yes, and I ask you, loyal yoke-ellow, help these women who have ontended at my side in the cause of the ospel, along with Clement and the rest f my fellow-workers, whose names are in ne book of life.

⁴Rejoice in the Lord always. I will say again: Rejoice! ⁵Let your gentleness be vident to all. The Lord is near. ⁶Do not e anxious about anything, but in verything, by prayer and petition, with hanksgiving, present your requests to od. ⁷And the peace of God, which ranscends all understanding, will guard our hearts and your minds in Christ esus.

⁸Finally, brothers, whatever is true, vhatever is noble, whatever is right, vhatever is pure, whatever is lovely, vhatever is admirable - if anything is xcellent or praiseworthy - think about uch things. ⁹Whatever you have learned r received or heard from me, or seen in ne - put it into practice. And the God of eace will be with you.

Thanks for Their Gifts

¹I rejoice greatly in the Lord that at last ou have renewed your concern for me.

Indeed, you have been concerned, but you had no opportunity to show it. ¹¹I am not saying this because I am in need, for I have learned to be content whatever the circumstances. ¹²I know what it is to be in need, and I know what it is to have plenty. I have learned the secret of being content in any and every situation, whether well fed or hungry, whether living in plenty or in want. ¹³I can do everything through him who gives me strength.

¹⁴Yet it was good of you to share in my troubles. ¹⁵Moreover, as you Philippians know, in the early days of your acquaintance with the gospel, when I set out from Macedonia, not one church shared with me in the matter of giving and receiving, except you only; ¹⁶for even when I was in Thessalonica, you sent me aid again and again when I was in need. ¹⁷Not that I am looking for a gift, but I am looking for what may be credited to your account. ¹⁸I have received full payment and even more; I am amply supplied, now that I have received from Epaphroditus the gifts you sent. They are a fragrant offering, an acceptable sacrifice, pleasing to God. ¹⁹And my God will meet all your needs according to his glorious riches in Christ Jesus.

²⁰To our God and Father be glory for ever and ever. Amen.

Final Greetings

²¹Greet all the saints in Christ Jesus. The brothers who are with me send greetings. ²²All the saints send you greetings, especially those who belong to Caesar's household.

²³The grace of the Lord Jesus Christ be with your spirit. Amen.

DAY 218

EPH. 1. 1 — 23

1 Paul, an apostle of Christ Jesus by the will of God.

To the saints in Ephesus, the faithful in Christ Jesus:

[2] Grace and peace to you from God our Father and the Lord Jesus Christ.

Spiritual Blessings in Christ

[3] Praise be to the God and Father of our Lord Jesus Christ, who has blessed us in the heavenly realms with every spiritual blessing in Christ. [4] For he chose us in him before the creation of the world to be holy and blameless in his sight. In love [5] he predestined us to be adopted as his sons through Jesus Christ, in accordance with his pleasure and will - [6] to the praise of his glorious grace, which he has freely given us in the One he loves. [7] In him we have redemption through his blood, the forgiveness of sins, in accordance with the riches of God's grace [8] that he lavished on us with all wisdom and understanding. [9] And he made known to us the mystery of his will according to his good pleasure, which he purposed in Christ, [10] to be put into effect when the times will have reached their fulfilment - to bring all things in heaven and on earth together under one head, even Christ. [11] In him we were also chosen, having been predestined according to the plan of him who works out everything in conformity with the purpose of his will, [12] in order that we, who were the first to

hope in Christ, might be for the praise of his glory. [13] And you also were included in Christ when you heard the word of truth, the gospel of your salvation. Having believed, you were marked in him with a seal, the promised Holy Spirit, [14] who is a deposit guaranteeing our inheritance until the redemption of those who are God's possession - to the praise of his glory.

Thanksgiving and Prayer

[15] For this reason, ever since I heard about your faith in the Lord Jesus and your love for all the saints, [16] I have not stopped giving thanks for you, remembering you in my prayers. [17] I keep asking that the God of our Lord Jesus Christ, the glorious Father, may give you the Spirit of wisdom and revelation, so that you may know him better. [18] I pray also that the eyes of

---

That power is like the working of his mighty strength.

---

your heart may be enlightened in order that you may know the hope to which he has called you, the riches of his glorious inheritance in the saints, [19] and his incomparably great power for us who believe. That power is like the working of his mighty strength, [20] which he exerted in Christ when he raised him from the dead and seated him at his right hand in the heavenly realms, [21] far above all rule and authority, power and dominion, and every title that can be given, not only in the present age but also in the one to come. [22] And God placed all things under his feet and appointed him to be head over everything for the church, [23] which is his body, the fulness of him who fills everything in every way.

DAY 219

EPH. 2. 1 — 22

Made Alive in Christ

2 As for you, you were dead in your transgressions and sins, [2] in which you used to live when you followed the ways of this world and of the ruler of the kingdom of the air, the spirit who is now at work in those who are disobedient. All of us also lived among them at one time, gratifying the cravings of our sinful nature and following its desires and thoughts. Like the rest, we were by nature objects of wrath. [4] But because of his great love for us, God, who is rich in mercy, made us alive with Christ even when we were dead in transgressions - it is by grace you have been saved. [6] And God raised us up with Christ and seated us with him in the heavenly realms in Christ Jesus, [7] in order that in the coming ages he might show the incomparable riches of his grace, expressed in his kindness to us in Christ Jesus. [8] For it is by grace you have been saved, through faith - and this not from yourselves, it is the gift of God - not by works, so that no-one can boast. For we are God's workmanship, created in Christ Jesus to do good works, which God prepared in advance for us to do.

One in Christ

Therefore, remember that formerly you who are Gentiles by birth and called 'uncircumcised' by those who call themselves 'the circumcision' (that done in the body by the hands of men) - remember that at that time you were separate from Christ, excluded from citizenship in Israel and foreigners to the

For he himself is our peace.

covenants of the promise, without hope and without God in the world. [13] But now in Christ Jesus you who once were far away have been brought near through the blood of Christ.

[14] For he himself is our peace, who has made the two one and has destroyed the barrier, the dividing wall of hostility, [15] by abolishing in his flesh the law with its commandments and regulations. His purpose was to create in himself one new man out of the two, thus making peace, [16] and in this one body to reconcile both of them to God through the cross, by which he put to death their hostility. [17] He came and preached peace to you who were far away and peace to those who were near. [18] For through him we both have access to the Father by one Spirit.

[19] Consequently, you are no longer foreigners and aliens, but fellow-citizens with God's people and members of God's household, [20] built on the foundation of the apostles and prophets, with Christ Jesus himself as the chief cornerstone. [21] In him the whole building is joined together and rises to become a holy temple in the Lord. [22] And in him you too are being built together to become a dwelling in which God lives by his Spirit.

DAY 220
EPH. 3. 1 — 21

3 Paul the Preacher to the Gentiles

For this reason I, Paul, the prisoner of Christ Jesus for the sake of you Gentiles -

[2] Surely you have heard about the administration of God's grace that was given to me for you, [3] that is, the mystery made known to me by revelation, as I have already written briefly. [4] In reading this, then, you will be able to understand my insight into the mystery of Christ, [5] which was not made known to men in other generations as it has now been revealed by the Spirit to God's holy apostles and prophets. [6] This mystery is that through the gospel the Gentiles are heirs together with Israel, members together of one body, and sharers together in the promise in Christ Jesus.

[7] I became a servant of this gospel by the gift of God's grace given me through the working of his power. [8] Although I am less than the least of all God's people, this grace was given me: to preach to the Gentiles the unsearchable riches of Christ, [9] and to make plain to everyone the administration of this mystery, which for ages past was kept hidden in God, who created all things. [10] His intent was that now, through the church, the manifold wisdom of God should be made known to the rulers and authorities in the heavenly realms, [11] according to his eternal purpose which he accomplished in Christ Jesus our Lord. [12] In him and through faith in him we may approach God with freedom and confidence. [13] I ask you, therefore, not to be discouraged because of my sufferings for you, which are your glory.

A Prayer for the Ephesians

[14] For this reason I kneel before the Father, [15] from whom his whole family in heaven and on earth derives its name. [16] I pray that out of his glorious riches he m[ay] strengthen you with power through his Spirit in your inner being, [17] so that Chr[ist] may dwell in your hearts through faith. And I pray that you, being rooted and established in love, [18] may have power, together with all the saints, to grasp how wide and long and high and deep is the love of Christ, [19] and to know this love that surpasses knowledge - that you may be filled to the measure of all the fulnes[s] of God.

[20] Now to him who is able to do immeasurably more than all we ask or imagine, according to his power that is [at] work within us, [21] to him be glory in the church and in Christ Jesus throughout [all] generations, for ever and ever! Amen.

DAY 221
EPH. 4. 1 — 32

4 Unity in the Body of Chri[st]

As a prisoner for the Lord, then, [I] urge you to live a life worthy of t[he] calling you have received. [2] Be complete[ly] humble and gentle; be patient, bearing with one another in love. [3] Make every effort to keep the unity of the Spirit through the bond of peace. [4] There is on[e] body and one Spirit - just as you were called to one hope when you were calle[d] [5] one Lord, one faith, one baptism; [6] one

od and Father of all, who is over all and
through all and in all.
[7] But to each one of us grace has been
given as Christ apportioned it. [8] This is
why it says:

'When he ascended on high,
he led captives in his train
and gave gifts to men.'

What does 'he ascended' mean except
that he also descended to the lower,
earthly regions? [10] He who descended is
the very one who ascended higher than
all the heavens, in order to fill the whole
universe.) [11] It was he who gave some to
be apostles, some to be prophets, some to
be evangelists, and some to be pastors and
teachers, [12] to prepare God's people for
works of service, so that the body of
Christ may be built up [13] until we all reach
unity in the faith and in the knowledge of
the Son of God and become mature,
attaining to the whole measure of the
fullness of Christ.

[14] Then we will no longer be infants,
tossed back and forth by the waves, and
blown here and there by every wind of
teaching and by the cunning and
craftiness of men in their deceitful
scheming. [15] Instead, speaking the truth in
love, we will in all things grow up into
him who is the Head, that is, Christ.
From him the whole body, joined and
held together by every supporting
ligament, grows and builds itself up in
love, as each part does its work.

Living as Children of Light

So I tell you this, and insist on it in the
Lord, that you must no longer live as the
Gentiles do, in the futility of their
thinking. [18] They are darkened in their
understanding and separated from the life
of God because of the ignorance that is in

them due to the hardening of their hearts.
[19] Having lost all sensitivity, they have
given themselves over to sensuality so as
to indulge in every kind of impurity, with
a continual lust for more.

[20] You, however, did not come to
know Christ that way. [21] Surely you heard
of him and were taught in him in
accordance with the truth that is in Jesus.
[22] You were taught, with regard to your
former way of life, to put off your old self,
which is being corrupted by its deceitful
desires; [23] to be made new in the attitude
of your minds; [24] and to put on the new

'When he ascended on high,
he led captives in his train
and gave gifts to men.'

self, created to be like God in true
righteousness and holiness.

[25] Therefore each of you must put off
falsehood and speak truthfully to his
neighbour, for we are all members of one
body. [26] 'In your anger do not sin': Do not
let the sun go down while you are still
angry, [27] and do not give the devil a
foothold. [28] He who has been stealing
must steal no longer, but must work,
doing something useful with his own
hands, that he may have something to
share with those in need.

[29] Do not let any unwholesome talk
come out of your mouths, but only what
is helpful for building others up according
to their needs, that it may benefit those
who listen. [30] And do not grieve the Holy
Spirit of God, with whom you were sealed
for the day of redemption. [31] Get rid of all
bitterness, rage and anger, brawling and
slander, along with every form of malice.
[32] Be kind and compassionate to one
another, forgiving each other, just as in
Christ God forgave you.

DAY 222

EPH. 5. 1 — 33

5 Be imitators of God, therefore, as dearly loved children ² and live a life of love, just as Christ loved us and gave himself up for us as a fragrant offering and sacrifice to God.

³ But among you there must not be even a hint of sexual immorality, or of any kind of impurity, or of greed, because these are improper for God's holy people. ⁴ Nor should there be obscenity, foolish talk or coarse joking, which are out of place, but rather thanksgiving. ⁵ For of this you can be sure: No immoral, impure or greedy person - such a man is an idolater - has any inheritance in the kingdom of Christ and of God. ⁶ Let no-one deceive you with empty words, for because of such things God's wrath comes on those who are disobedient. ⁷ Therefore do not be partners with them.

⁸ For you were once darkness, but now you are light in the Lord. Live as children of light ⁹ (for the fruit of the light consists in all goodness, righteousness and truth) ¹⁰ and find out what pleases the Lord. ¹¹ Have nothing to do with the fruitless deeds of darkness, but rather expose them. ¹² For it is shameful even to mention what the disobedient do in secret. ¹³ But everything exposed by the light becomes visible, ¹⁴ for it is light that makes everything visible. This is why it is said:

'Wake up, O sleeper,
 rise from the dead,
 and Christ will shine on you.'

¹⁵ Be very careful, then, how you live not as unwise but as wise, ¹⁶ making the most of every opportunity, because the days are evil. ¹⁷ Therefore do not be foolish, but understand what the Lord's will is. ¹⁸ Do not get drunk on wine, whic leads to debauchery. Instead, be filled with the Spirit. ¹⁹ Speak to one another with psalms, hymns and spiritual songs. Sing and make music in your heart to th Lord, ²⁰ always giving thanks to God the Father for everything, in the name of ou Lord Jesus Christ.

²¹ Submit to one another out of reverence for Christ.

Wives and Husbands

²² Wives, submit to your husbands as to the Lord. ²³ For the husband is the head o the wife as Christ is the head of the church, his body, of which he is the Saviour. ²⁴ Now as the church submits to Christ, so also wives should submit to their husbands in everything.

²⁵ Husbands, love your wives, just as Christ loved the church and gave himsel up for her ²⁶ to make her holy, cleansing her by the washing with water through th word, ²⁷ and to present her to himself as a radiant church, without stain or wrinkle any other blemish, but holy and blameles ²⁸ In this same way, husbands ought to lov their wives as their own bodies. He who loves his wife loves himself. ²⁹ After all, n one ever hated his own body, but he feed and cares for it, just as Christ does the church - ³⁰ for we are members of his body ³¹ 'For this reason a man will leave his father and mother and be united to his wife, and the two will become one flesh.' ³² This is a profound mystery - but I am talking about Christ and the church. ³³ However, each one of you also must lov his wife as he loves himself, and the wife must respect her husband.

DAY 223

EPH. 6. 1 — 24

Children and Parents

6 Children, obey your parents in the Lord, for this is right. ²'Honour your father and mother' - which is the first commandment with a promise - that it may go well with you and that you may enjoy long life on the earth.'
⁴Fathers, do not exasperate your children; instead, bring them up in the training and instruction of the Lord.

Slaves and Masters

Slaves, obey your earthly masters with respect and fear, and with sincerity of heart, just as you would obey Christ. Obey them not only to win their favour when their eye is on you, but like slaves of Christ, doing the will of God from your heart. ⁷Serve wholeheartedly, as if you were serving the Lord, not men, ⁸because you know that the Lord will reward everyone for whatever good he does, whether he is slave or free.
⁹And masters, treat your slaves in the same way. Do not threaten them, since you know that he who is both their Master and yours is in heaven, and there is no favouritism with him.

The Armour of God

Finally, be strong in the Lord and in his mighty power. ¹¹Put on the full armour of God so that you can take your stand against the devil's schemes. ¹²For our struggle is not against flesh and blood, but against the rulers, against the authorities, against the powers of this dark world and against the spiritual forces of evil in

the heavenly realms. ¹³Therefore put on the full armour of God, so that when the day of evil comes, you may be able to stand your ground, and after you have done everything, to stand. ¹⁴Stand firm then, with the belt of truth buckled round your waist, with the breastplate of righteousness in place, ¹⁵and with your feet fitted with the readiness that comes from the gospel of peace. ¹⁶In addition to

'Honour your father and mother.'

all this, take up the shield of faith, with which you can extinguish all the flaming arrows of the evil one. ¹⁷Take the helmet of salvation and the sword of the Spirit, which is the word of God. ¹⁸And pray in the Spirit on all occasions with all kinds of prayers and requests. With this in mind, be alert and always keep on praying for all the saints.
¹⁹Pray also for me, that whenever I open my mouth, words may be given me so that I will fearlessly make known the mystery of the gospel, ²⁰for which I am an ambassador in chains. Pray that I may declare it fearlessly, as I should.

Final Greetings

²¹Tychicus, the dear brother and faithful servant in the Lord, will tell you everything, so that you also may know how I am and what I am doing. ²²I am sending him to you for this very purpose, that you may know how we are, and that he may encourage you.
²³Peace to the brothers, and love with faith from God the Father and the Lord Jesus Christ. ²⁴Grace to all who love our Lord Jesus Christ with an undying love.

DAY 224

COL. 1. 1—23

1 Paul, an apostle of Christ Jesus by the will of God, and Timothy our brother.

[2] To the holy and faithful brothers in Christ at Colosse:

Grace and peace to you from God our Father.

Thanksgiving and Prayer

[3] We always thank God, the Father of our Lord Jesus Christ, when we pray for you, [4] because we have heard of your faith in Christ Jesus and of the love you have for all the saints - [5] the faith and love that spring from the hope that is stored up for you in heaven and that you have already heard about in the word of truth, the gospel [6] that has come to you. All over the world this gospel is bearing fruit and growing, just as it has been doing among you since the day you heard it and understood God's grace in all its truth. [7] You learned it from Epaphras, our dear fellow-servant, who is a faithful minister of Christ on our behalf, [8] and who also told us of your love in the Spirit.

[9] For this reason, since the day we heard about you, we have not stopped praying for you and asking God to fill you with the knowledge of his will through all spiritual wisdom and understanding. [10] And we pray this in order that you may live a life worthy of the Lord and may please him in every way: bearing fruit in every good work, growing in the knowledge of God, [11] being strengthened with all power according to his glorious might so that you may have great endurance and patience, and joyfully [12] giving thanks to the Father, who has qualified you to share in the inheritance of the saints in the kingdom of light. [13] For he has rescued us from the dominion of darkness and brought us into the kingdom of the Son he loves, [14] in whom we have redemption, the forgiveness of sins.

The Supremacy of Christ

[15] He is the image of the invisible God, the firstborn over all creation. [16] For by him all things were created: things in heaven and on earth, visible and invisible, whether thrones or powers or rulers or authorities; all things were created by him and for him. [17] He is befor all things, and in him all things hold together. [18] And he is the head of the body, the church; he is the beginning and the firstborn from among the dead, so that in everything he might have the supremacy. [19] For God was pleased to have all his fulness dwell in him, [20] and through him to reconcile to himself all things, whether things on earth or things in heaven, by making peace through his blood, shed on the cross.

[21] Once you were alienated from God and were enemies in your minds because of your evil behaviour. [22] But now he has reconciled you by Christ's physical body through death to present you holy in his sight, without blemish and free from accusation - [23] if you continue in your faith, established and firm, not moved from the hope held out in the gospel. This is the gospel that you heard and tha has been proclaimed to every creature under heaven, and of which I, Paul, have become a servant.

DAY 225

COL. 1. 24 — 2.19

Paul's Labour for the Church

Now I rejoice in what was suffered for you, and I fill up in my flesh what is still lacking in regard to Christ's afflictions, for the sake of his body, which is the church. [25] I have become its servant by the commission God gave me to present to you the word of God in its fulness - [26] the mystery that has been kept hidden for ages and generations, but is now disclosed to the saints. [27] To them God has chosen to make known among the Gentiles the glorious riches of this mystery, which is Christ in you, the hope of glory.

[28] We proclaim him, admonishing and teaching everyone with all wisdom, so that we may present everyone perfect in Christ. [29] To this end I labour, struggling with all his energy, which so powerfully works in me.

[2] I want you to know how much I am struggling for you and for those at Laodicea, and for all who have not met me personally. [2] My purpose is that they may be encouraged in heart and united in love, so that they may have the full riches of complete understanding, in order that they may know the mystery of God, namely, Christ, [3] in whom are hidden all the treasures of wisdom and knowledge. [4] I tell you this so that no-one may deceive you by fine-sounding arguments. [5] For though I am absent from you in body, I am present with you in spirit and delight to see how orderly you are and how firm your faith in Christ is.

Freedom from Human Regulations Through Life with Christ

[6] So then, just as you received Christ Jesus as Lord, continue to live in him, [7] rooted and built up in him, strengthened in the faith as you were taught, and overflowing with thankfulness.

[8] See to it that no-one takes you captive through hollow and deceptive philosophy, which depends on human tradition and the basic principles of this world rather than on Christ.

[9] For in Christ all the fulness of the Deity lives in bodily form, [10] and you have been given fulness in Christ, who is the Head over every power and authority. [11] In him you were also circumcised, in the putting off of the sinful nature, not with a circumcision done by the hands of men but with the circumcision done by Christ, [12] having been buried with him in baptism and raised with him through your faith in the power of God, who raised him from the dead.

[13] When you were dead in your sins and in the uncircumcision of your sinful nature, God made you alive with Christ. He forgave us all our sins, [14] having cancelled the written code, with its regulations, that was against us and that stood opposed to us; he took it away, nailing it to the cross. [15] And having disarmed the powers and authorities, he made a public spectacle of them, triumphing over them by the cross.

[16] Therefore do not let anyone judge you by what you eat or drink, or with regard to a religious festival, a New Moon celebration or a Sabbath day. [17] These are a shadow of the things that were to come; the reality, however, is found in Christ. [18] Do not let anyone who delights in false humility and the worship of angels disqualify you for the prize. Such a person

goes into great detail about what he has seen, and his unspiritual mind puffs him up with idle notions. [19] He has lost connection with the Head, from whom the whole body, supported and held together by its ligaments and sinews, grows as God causes it to grow.

DAY 226
COL. 2.20 — 3.17

[20] Since you died with Christ to the basic principles of this world, why, as though you still belonged to it, do you submit to its rules: [21] 'Do not handle! Do not taste! Do not touch!'? [22] These are all destined to perish with use, because they are based on human commands and teachings. [23] Such regulations indeed have an appearance of wisdom, with their self-imposed worship, their false humility and

'Do not handle! Do not taste!'

their harsh treatment of the body, but they lack any value in restraining sensual indulgence.

3 **Rules for Holy Living** Since, then, you have been raised with Christ, set your hearts on things above, where Christ is seated at the right hand of God. [2] Set your minds on things above, not on earthly things. [3] For you died, and your life is now hidden with Christ in God. [4] When Christ, who is your life, appears, then you also will appear with him in glory.

[5] Put to death, therefore, whatever belongs to your earthly nature: sexual immorality, impurity, lust, evil desires and greed, which is idolatry. [6] Because of

You used to walk in these ways, in the life you once lived.

these, the wrath of God is coming. [7] You used to walk in these ways, in the life you once lived. [8] But now you must rid yourselves of all such things as these: anger, rage, malice, slander and filthy language from your lips. [9] Do not lie to each other, since you have taken off your old self with its practices [10] and have put on the new self, which is being renewed in knowledge in the image of its Creator. [11] Here there is no Greek or Jew, circumcised or uncircumcised, barbarian, Scythian, slave or free, but Christ is all, and is in all.

[12] Therefore, as God's chosen people, holy and dearly loved, clothe yourselves with compassion, kindness, humility, gentleness and patience. [13] Bear with each other and forgive whatever grievances you may have against one another. Forgive as the Lord forgave you. [14] And over all these virtues put on love, which binds them all together in perfect unity.

[15] Let the peace of Christ rule in your hearts, since as members of one body you were called to peace. And be thankful. [16] Let the word of Christ dwell in you richly as you teach and admonish one another with all wisdom, and as you sing psalms, hymns and spiritual songs with gratitude in your hearts to God. [17] And whatever you do, whether in word or deed, do it all in the name of the Lord Jesus, giving thanks to God the Father through him.

DAY 227

COL. 3.18 — 4.18

Rules for Christian Households

Wives, submit to your husbands, as is
fitting in the Lord. [19] Husbands, love your wives and do
not be harsh with them. [20] Children, obey your parents in
everything, for this pleases the Lord. [21] Fathers, do not embitter your
children, or they will become
discouraged.

[22] Slaves, obey your earthly masters in
everything; and do it, not only when
their eye is on you and to win their
favour, but with sincerity of heart and
reverence for the Lord. [23] Whatever you
do, work at it with all your heart, as
working for the Lord, not for men, [24] since
you know that you will receive an
inheritance from the Lord as a reward. It
the Lord Christ you are serving.
Anyone who does wrong will be repaid
for his wrong, and there is no favouritism.

Masters, provide your slaves with
what is right and fair, because you
know that you also have a Master
in heaven.

Further Instructions

Devote yourselves to prayer, being
watchful and thankful. [3] And pray for us,
too, that God may open a door for our
message, so that we may proclaim the
mystery of Christ, for which I am in
chains. [4] Pray that I may proclaim it
clearly, as I should. [5] Be wise in the way
you act towards outsiders; make the most
of every opportunity. [6] Let your
conversation be always full of grace,
seasoned with salt, so that you may know
how to answer everyone.

Final Greetings

[7] Tychicus will tell you all the news about
me. He is a dear brother, a faithful
minister and fellow-servant in the Lord.
[8] I am sending him to you for the express
purpose that you may know about our
circumstances and that he may encourage
your hearts. [9] He is coming with
Onesimus, our faithful and dear brother,
who is one of you. They will tell you
everything that is happening here.
[10] My fellow-prisoner Aristarchus
sends you his greetings, as does Mark,
the cousin of Barnabas. (You have
received instructions about him; if he
comes to you, welcome him.) [11] Jesus,
who is called Justus, also sends greetings.
These are the only Jews among my
fellow-workers for the kingdom of God,
and they have proved a comfort to me.
[12] Epaphras, who is one of you and a
servant of Christ Jesus, sends greetings.
He is always wrestling in prayer for you,
that you may stand firm in all the will of
God, mature and fully assured. [13] I vouch
for him that he is working hard for you
and for those at Laodicea and Hierapolis.
[14] Our dear friend Luke, the doctor, and
Demas send greetings. [15] Give my
greetings to the brothers at Laodicea,
and to Nympha and the church in her
house.
[16] After this letter has been read to
you, see that it is also read in the church
of the Laodiceans and that you in turn
read the letter from Laodicea.
[17] Tell Archippus: 'See to it that you
complete the work you have received in
the Lord.'
[18] I, Paul, write this greeting in my
own hand. Remember my chains. Grace
be with you.

DAY 228
PHILEMON 1 — 25

Paul, a prisoner of Christ Jesus, and Timothy our brother,

To Philemon our dear friend and fellow-worker, [2] to Apphia our sister, to Archippus our fellow-soldier and to the church that meets in your home:

[3] Grace to you and peace from God our Father and the Lord Jesus Christ.

Thanksgiving and Prayer
[4] I always thank my God as I remember you in my prayers, [5] because I hear about your faith in the Lord Jesus and your love for all the saints. [6] I pray that you may be active in sharing your faith, so that you will have a full understanding of every good thing we have in Christ. [7] Your love has given me great joy and encouragement, because you, brother, have refreshed the hearts of the saints.

Paul's Plea for Onesimus
[8] Therefore, although in Christ I could be bold and order you to do what you ought to do, [9] yet I appeal to you on the basis of love. I then, as Paul - an old man and now also a prisoner of Christ Jesus - [10] I appeal to you for my son Onesimus, who became my son while I was in chains. [11] Formerly he was useless to you, but now he has become useful both to you and to me. [12] I am sending him - who is my very heart - back to you. [13] I would have liked to keep him with me so that he could take your place in helping me while I am in chains for the gospel. [14] But I did not want to do anything without your consent, so that any favour you do will be spontaneous and not forced. [15] Perhaps the reason he was separated from you for a little while was that you might have him back for good - [16] no longer as a slave but better than a slave, as a dear brother. He is very dear to me but even dearer to you, both as a man and as a brother in the Lord.

[17] So if you consider me a partner, welcome him as you would welcome me. [18] If he has done you any wrong or owes you anything, charge it to me. [19] I, Paul, am writing this with my own hand. I will pay it back - not to mention that you owe me your very self. [20] I do wish, brother, that I may have some benefit from you in the Lord; refresh my heart in Christ. [21] Confident of your obedience, I write to you, knowing that you will do even more than I ask.

[22] And one thing more: Prepare a guest room for me, because I hope to be restored to you in answer to your prayers.

[23] Epaphras, my fellow-prisoner in Christ Jesus, sends you greetings. [24] And so do Mark, Aristarchus, Demas and Luke, my fellow-workers.

[25] The grace of the Lord Jesus Christ be with your spirit.

DAY 229
1 TIM. 1. 1 — 20

1 Paul, an apostle of Christ Jesus by the command of God our Saviour and of Christ Jesus our hope.

[2] To Timothy my true son in the faith

Grace, mercy and peace from God the Father and Christ Jesus our Lord.

Warning Against False Teachers of the Law

As I urged you when I went into Macedonia, stay there in Ephesus so that you may command certain men not to teach false doctrines any longer ⁴ nor to devote themselves to myths and endless genealogies. These promote controversies rather than God's work - which is by faith. ⁵ The goal of this command is love, which comes from a pure heart and a good conscience and a sincere faith. Some have wandered away from these and turned to meaningless talk. ⁷ They want to be teachers of the law, but they do not know what they are talking about or what they so confidently affirm.

We know that the law is good if one uses it properly. ⁹ We also know that law is made not for the righteous but for lawbreakers and rebels, the ungodly and sinful, the unholy and irreligious; for those who kill their fathers or mothers, for murderers, ¹⁰ for adulterers and perverts, for slave traders and liars and perjurers - and for whatever else is contrary to the sound doctrine ¹¹ that conforms to the glorious gospel of the blessed God, which he entrusted to me.

The Lord's Grace to Paul

¹² I thank Christ Jesus our Lord, who has given me strength, that he considered me faithful, appointing me to his service. ¹³ Even though I was once a blasphemer and a persecutor and a violent man, I was shown mercy because I acted in ignorance and unbelief. ¹⁴ The grace of our Lord was poured out on me abundantly, along with the faith and love that are in Christ Jesus. ¹⁵ Here is a trustworthy saying that deserves full acceptance: Christ Jesus came into the world to save sinners - of whom I am the worst. ¹⁶ But for that very reason I was shown mercy so that in me, the worst of sinners, Christ Jesus might display his unlimited patience as an example for those who would believe on him and receive eternal life. ¹⁷ Now to the King eternal, immortal, invisible, the only God, be honour and glory for ever and ever. Amen.

¹⁸ Timothy, my son, I give you this instruction in keeping with the prophecies once made about you, so that by following them you may fight the good fight, ¹⁹ holding on to faith and a good conscience. Some have rejected these and so have shipwrecked their faith. ²⁰ Among them are Hymenaeus and Alexander, whom I have handed over to Satan to be taught not to blaspheme.

Love comes from a pure heart, a good conscience and a sincere faith.

DAY 230

1 TIM. 2. 1 — 3. 16

2 Instructions on Worship

I urge, then, first of all, that requests, prayers, intercession and thanksgiving be made for everyone - ²for kings and all those in authority, that we may live peaceful and quiet lives in all godliness and holiness. ³This is good, and pleases God our Saviour, ⁴who wants all men to be saved and to come to a knowledge of the truth. ⁵For there is one God and one mediator between God and men, the man Christ Jesus, ⁶who gave himself as a ransom for all men - the testimony given in its proper time. ⁷And for this purpose I was appointed a herald and an apostle - I am telling the truth, I am not lying - and a teacher of the true faith to the Gentiles.

⁸I want men everywhere to lift up holy hands in prayer, without anger or disputing.

⁹I also want women to dress modestly, with decency and propriety, not with braided hair or gold or pearls or expensive clothes, ¹⁰but with good deeds, appropriate for women who profess to worship God.

¹¹A woman should learn in quietness and full submission. ¹²I do not permit a woman to teach or to have authority over a man; she must be silent. ¹³For Adam was formed first, then Eve. ¹⁴And Adam was not the one deceived; it was the woman who was deceived and became a sinner. ¹⁵But women will be saved through childbearing - if they continue in faith, love and holiness with propriety.

3 Overseers and Deacons

Here is a trustworthy saying: If anyone sets his heart on being an overseer, he desires a noble task. ²Now the overseer must be above reproach, the husband of but one wife, temperate, self-controlled, respectable, hospitable, able to teach, ³not given to drunkenness, not violent but gentle, not quarrelsome, not a lover of money. ⁴He must manage his own family well and see that his children obey him with proper respect. ⁵(If anyone does not know how to manage his own family, how can he take care of God's church?) ⁶He must not be a recent convert, or he may become conceited and fall under the same judgment as the devil. ⁷He must also have a good reputation with outsiders, so that he will not fall into disgrace and into the devil's trap.

⁸Deacons, likewise, are to be men worthy of respect, sincere, not indulging in much wine, and not pursuing dishonest gain. ⁹They must keep hold of the deep truths of the faith with a clear conscience. ¹⁰They must first be tested; and then if there is nothing against them, let them serve as deacons.

¹¹In the same way, their wives are to be women worthy of respect, not malicious talkers but temperate and trustworthy in everything.

¹²A deacon must be the husband of but one wife and must manage his children and his household well. ¹³Those who have served well gain an excellent standing and great assurance in their faith in Christ Jesus.

¹⁴Although I hope to come to you soon, I am writing you these instructions so that, ¹⁵if I am delayed, you will know how people ought to conduct themselves in God's household, which is the church of the living God, the pillar and

foundation of the truth. ¹⁶Beyond all question, the mystery of godliness is great:

He appeared in a body,
　was vindicated by the Spirit,
was seen by angels,
　was preached among the nations,
was believed on in the world,
　was taken up in glory.

DAY 231

1 TIM. 4. 1 — 16

4 Instructions to Timothy

The Spirit clearly says that in later times some will abandon the faith and follow deceiving spirits and things taught by demons. ²Such teachings come through hypocritical liars, whose consciences have been seared as with a hot iron. ³They forbid people to marry and order them to abstain from certain foods, which God created to be received with thanksgiving by those who believe and who know the truth. ⁴For everything God created is good, and nothing is to be rejected if it is received with thanksgiving, ⁵because it is consecrated by the word of God and prayer.

⁶If you point these things out to the brothers, you will be a good minister of Christ Jesus, brought up in the truths of the faith and of the good teaching that you have followed. ⁷Have nothing to do with godless myths and old wives' tales; rather, train yourself to be godly. ⁸For physical training is of some value, but godliness has value for all things, holding promise for both the present life and the life to come.

⁹This is a trustworthy saying that deserves full acceptance ¹⁰(and for this we labour and strive), that we have put our hope in the living God, who is the Saviour of all men, and especially of those who believe.

¹¹Command and teach these things. ¹²Don't let anyone look down on you because you are young, but set an example for the believers in speech, in life, in love, in faith and in purity. ¹³Until I come, devote yourself to the public reading of Scripture, to preaching and to teaching. ¹⁴Do not neglect your gift, which was given you through a prophetic message when the body of elders laid their hands on you.

¹⁵Be diligent in these matters; give yourself wholly to them, so that everyone may see your progress. ¹⁶Watch your life and doctrine closely. Persevere in them, because if you do, you will save both yourself and your hearers.

Godliness has value for all things.

DAY 232
1 TIM. 5. 1 — 6.2

5 ### Advice About Widows, Elders and Slaves
Do not rebuke an older man harshly, but exhort him as if he were your father. Treat younger men as brothers, [2] older women as mothers, and younger women as sisters, with absolute purity.

[3] Give proper recognition to those widows who are really in need. [4] But if a widow has children or grandchildren, these should learn first of all to put their religion into practice by caring for their own family and so repaying their parents and grandparents, for this is pleasing to God. [5] The widow who is really in need and left all alone puts her hope in God and continues night and day to pray and to ask God for help. [6] But the widow who lives for pleasure is dead even while she lives. [7] Give the people these instructions, too, so that no-one may be open to blame. [8] If anyone does not provide for his relatives, and especially for his immediate family, he has denied the faith and is worse than an unbeliever.

[9] No widow may be put on the list of widows unless she is over sixty, has been faithful to her husband, [10] and is well known for her good deeds, such as bringing up children, showing hospitality, washing the feet of the saints, helping those in trouble and devoting herself to all kinds of good deeds.

[11] As for younger widows, do not put them on such a list. For when their sensual desires overcome their dedication to Christ, they want to marry. [12] Thus they bring judgment on themselves, because they have broken their first pledge. [13] Besides, they get into the habit of being idle and going about from house to house. And not only do they become idlers, but also gossips and busybodies, saying things they ought not to. [14] So I counsel younger widows to marry, to have children, to manage their homes and to give the enemy no opportunity for slander. [15] Some have in fact already turned away to follow Satan.

[16] If any woman who is a believer has widows in her family, she should help them and not let the church be burdened with them, so that the church can help those widows who are really in need.

[17] The elders who direct the affairs of the church well are worthy of double honour, especially those whose work is preaching and teaching. [18] For the Scripture says, 'Do not muzzle the ox while it is treading out the grain,' and 'The worker deserves his wages.' [19] Do not entertain an accusation against an elder unless it is brought by two or three witnesses. [20] Those who sin are to be rebuked publicly, so that the others may take warning.

[21] I charge you, in the sight of God and Christ Jesus and the elect angels, to keep these instructions without partiality, and to do nothing out of favouritism.

[22] Do not be hasty in the laying on of hands, and do not share in the sins of others. Keep yourself pure.

[23] Stop drinking only water, and use a little wine because of your stomach and your frequent illnesses.

[24] The sins of some men are obvious, reaching the place of judgment ahead of them; the sins of others trail behind them. [25] In the same way, good deeds are obvious, and even those that are not cannot be hidden.

All who are under the yoke of slavery should consider their masters worthy of full respect, so that God's name and our teaching may not be slandered. ² Those who have believing masters are not to show less respect for them because they are brothers. Instead, they are to serve them even better, because those who benefit from their service are believers, and dear to them. These are the things you are to teach and urge on them.

DAY 233

1 TIM. 6. 3 — 21

Love of Money

If anyone teaches false doctrines and does not agree to the sound instruction of our Lord Jesus Christ and to godly teaching, ⁴ he is conceited and understands nothing. He has an unhealthy interest in controversies and quarrels about words that result in envy, strife, malicious talk, evil suspicions ⁵ and constant friction between men of corrupt mind, who have been robbed of the truth and who think that godliness is a means to financial gain.

⁶ But godliness with contentment is great gain. ⁷ For we brought nothing into the world, and we can take nothing out of it. ⁸ But if we have food and clothing, we will be content with that. ⁹ People who want to get rich fall into temptation and a trap and into many foolish and harmful desires that plunge men into ruin and destruction. ¹⁰ For the love of money is a root of all kinds of evil. Some people, eager for money, have wandered from the faith and pierced themselves with many griefs.

Paul's Charge to Timothy

¹¹ But you, man of God, flee from all this, and pursue righteousness, godliness, faith, love, endurance and gentleness. ¹² Fight the good fight of the faith. Take hold of the eternal life to which you were called when you made your good confession in the presence of many witnesses. ¹³ In the sight of God, who gives life to everything, and of Christ Jesus, who while testifying before Pontius Pilate made the good confession, I charge you ¹⁴ to keep this command without spot or blame until the appearing of our Lord Jesus Christ, ¹⁵ which God will bring about in his own time - God, the blessed and only Ruler, the King of kings and Lord of lords, ¹⁶ who alone is immortal and who lives in unapproachable light, whom no-one has seen or can see. To him be honour and might for ever. Amen.

¹⁷ Command those who are rich in this present world not to be arrogant nor to put their hope in wealth, which is so

Grace be with you.

uncertain, but to put their hope in God, who richly provides us with everything for our enjoyment. ¹⁸ Command them to do good, to be rich in good deeds, and to be generous and willing to share. ¹⁹ In this way they will lay up treasure for themselves as a firm foundation for the coming age, so that they may take hold of the life that is truly life.

²⁰ Timothy, guard what has been entrusted to your care. Turn away from godless chatter and the opposing ideas of what is falsely called knowledge, ²¹ which some have professed and in so doing have wandered from the faith.

Grace be with you.

DAY 234
TITUS 1. 1 — 16

1 Paul, a servant of God and an apostle of Jesus Christ for the faith of God's elect and the knowledge of the truth that leads to godliness - ² a faith and knowledge resting on the hope of eternal life, which God, who does not lie, promised before the beginning of time, ³ and at his appointed season he brought his word to light through the preaching entrusted to me by the command of God our Saviour,

⁴ To Titus, my true son in our common faith:

Grace and peace from God the Father and Christ Jesus our Saviour.

Titus' Task on Crete
⁵ The reason I left you in Crete was that you might straighten out what was left unfinished and appoint elders in every town, as I directed you. ⁶ An elder must be blameless, the husband of but one wife, a man whose children believe and are not open to the charge of being wild and disobedient. ⁷ Since an overseer is entrusted with God's work, he must be blameless - not overbearing, not quick-tempered, not given to drunkenness, not violent, not pursuing dishonest gain. ⁸ Rather he must be hospitable, one who loves what is good, who is self-controlled, upright, holy and disciplined. ⁹ He must hold firmly to the trustworthy message as it has been taught, so that he can encourage others by sound doctrine and

refute those who oppose it.

¹⁰ For there are many rebellious people, mere talkers and deceivers, especially those of the circumcision group. ¹¹ They must be silenced, because they are ruining whole households by teaching things they ought not to teach - and that for the sake of dishonest gain. ¹² Even one of their own prophets has said, 'Cretans are always liars, evil brutes, lazy gluttons.' ¹³ This testimony is true. Therefore, rebuke them sharply, so that they will be sound in the faith ¹⁴ and will pay no attention to Jewish myths or to the commands of those who reject the truth. ¹⁵ To the pure, all things are pure, but to those who are corrupted and do not believe, nothing is pure. In fact, both their minds and consciences are corrupted. ¹⁶ They claim to know God, but by their actions they deny him. They are detestable, disobedient and unfit for doing anything good.

DAY 235
TITUS 2. 1 — 3.15

2 **What Must Be Taught to Various Groups**
You must teach what is in accord with sound doctrine. ² Teach the older men to be temperate, worthy of respect, self-controlled, and sound in faith, in love and in endurance.

³ Likewise, teach the older women to be reverent in the way they live, not to be slanderers or addicted to much wine, but to teach what is good. ⁴ Then they can train the younger women to love their husbands and children, ⁵ to be self-controlled and pure, to be busy at home,

be kind, and to be subject to their usbands, so that no-one will malign the ord of God.

⁶Similarly, encourage the young men) be self-controlled. ⁷In everything set em an example by doing what is good. i your teaching show integrity, eriousness ⁸and soundness of speech that annot be condemned, so that those who ppose you may be ashamed because they ave nothing bad to say about us.

⁹Teach slaves to be subject to their asters in everything, to try to please em, not to talk back to them, ¹⁰and not) steal from them, but to show that they an be fully trusted, so that in every way ey will make the teaching about God ur Saviour attractive.

¹¹For the grace of God that brings lvation has appeared to all men. ¹²It aches us to say 'No' to ungodliness and orldly passions, and to live self- ontrolled, upright and godly lives in this resent age, ¹³while we wait for the essed hope - the glorious appearing of ur great God and Saviour, Jesus Christ, who gave himself for us to redeem us om all wickedness and to purify for imself a people that are his very own, ager to do what is good.

¹⁵These, then, are the things you hould teach. Encourage and rebuke with ll authority. Do not let anyone despise ou.

3 Doing What is Good

Remind the people to be subject to rulers and authorities, to be bedient, to be ready to do whatever is ood, ²to slander no-one, to be peaceable nd considerate, and to show true umility towards all men.

³At one time we too were foolish, isobedient, deceived and enslaved by ll kinds of passions and pleasures. We lived in malice and envy, being hated and hating one another. ⁴But when the kindness and love of God our Saviour appeared, ⁵he saved us, not because of righteous things we had done, but because of his mercy. He saved us through the washing of rebirth and renewal by the Holy Spirit, ⁶whom he poured out on us generously through Jesus Christ our Saviour, ⁷so that, having been justified by his grace, we might become heirs having the hope of eternal life. ⁸This is a trustworthy saying. And I want you to stress these things, so that those who have trusted in God may be careful to devote themselves to doing what is good. These things are excellent and profitable for everyone.

⁹But avoid foolish controversies and genealogies and arguments and quarrels about the law, because these are unprofitable and useless. ¹⁰Warn a divisive person once, and then warn him a second time. After that, have nothing to do with him. ¹¹You may be sure that such a man is warped and sinful; he is self-condemned.

Final Remarks

¹²As soon as I send Artemas or Tychicus to you, do your best to come to me at Nicopolis, because I have decided to winter there. ¹³Do everything you can to help Zenas the lawyer and Apollos on their way and see that they have everything they need. ¹⁴Our people must learn to devote themselves to doing what is good, in order that they may provide for daily necessities and not live unproductive lives.

¹⁵Everyone with me sends you greetings. Greet those who love us in the faith.

Grace be with you all.

DAY 236
2 TIM. 1. 1 — 18

1 Paul, an apostle of Christ Jesus by the will of God, according to the promise of life that is in Christ Jesus.

² To Timothy, my dear son:

Grace, mercy and peace from God the Father and Christ Jesus our Lord.

Encouragement to Be Faithful
³ I thank God, whom I serve, as my forefathers did, with a clear conscience, as night and day I constantly remember you in my prayers. ⁴ Recalling your tears, I long to see you, so that I may be filled with joy. ⁵ I have been reminded of your sincere faith, which first lived in your grandmother Lois and in your mother Eunice and, I am persuaded, now lives in you also. ⁶ For this reason I remind you to fan into flame the gift of God, which is in you through the laying on of my hands. ⁷ For God did not give us a spirit of timidity, but a spirit of power, of love and of self-discipline.

⁸ So do not be ashamed to testify about our Lord, or ashamed of me his prisoner. But join with me in suffering for the gospel, by the power of God, ⁹ who has saved us and called us to a holy life - not because of anything we have done but because of his own purpose and grace. This grace was given us in Christ Jesus before the beginning of time, ¹⁰ but it has now been revealed through the appearing of our Saviour, Christ Jesus, who has destroyed death and has brought life and immortality to light through the gospel. ¹¹ And of this gospel I was appointed a herald and an apostle and a teacher. ¹² That is why I am suffering as I am. Yet I am not ashamed, because I know whom I have believed, and am convinced that he is able to guard what I have entrusted to him for that day.

¹³ What you heard from me, keep as the pattern of sound teaching, with faith and love in Christ Jesus. ¹⁴ Guard the good deposit that was entrusted to you - guard it with the help of the Holy Spirit who lives in us.

¹⁵ You know that everyone in the province of Asia has deserted me, including Phygelus and Hermogenes. ¹⁶ May the Lord show mercy to the household of Onesiphorus, because he often refreshed me and was not ashamed of my chains. ¹⁷ On the contrary, when he was in Rome, he searched hard for me until he found me. ¹⁸ May the Lord grant that he will find mercy from the Lord on that day! You know very well in how many ways he helped me in Ephesus.

Fan into flame the gift of God.

DAY 237

2 TIM. 2. 1 — 26

2 You then, my son, be strong in the grace that is in Christ Jesus. [2] And the things you have heard me say in the presence of many witnesses entrust to reliable men who will also be qualified to teach others. [3] Endure hardship with us like a good soldier of Christ Jesus. [4] None serving as a soldier gets involved in civilian affairs - he wants to please his commanding officer. [5] Similarly, if anyone competes as an athlete, he does not receive the victor's crown unless he competes according to the rules. [6] The hardworking farmer should be the first to receive a share of the crops. [7] Reflect on what I am saying, for the Lord will give you insight into all this.

[8] Remember Jesus Christ, raised from the dead, descended from David. This is my gospel, [9] for which I am suffering even to the point of being chained like a criminal. But God's word is not chained. [10] Therefore I endure everything for the sake of the elect, that they too may obtain the salvation that is in Christ Jesus, with eternal glory.

[11] Here is a trustworthy saying:

If we died with him,
we will also live with him;
[12] if we endure,
we will also reign with him.
If we disown him,
he will also disown us;
[13] if we are faithless,
he will remain faithful,
for he cannot disown himself.

A Workman Approved by God

[14] Keep reminding them of these things. Warn them before God against quarrelling about words; it is of no value, and only ruins those who listen. [15] Do your best to present yourself to God as one approved, a workman who does not need to be ashamed and who correctly handles the word of truth. [16] Avoid godless chatter, because those who indulge in it will become more and more ungodly. [17] Their teaching will spread like gangrene. Among them are Hymenaeus and Philetus, [18] who have wandered away from the truth. They say that the resurrection has already taken place, and they destroy the faith of some. [19] Nevertheless, God's solid foundation stands firm, sealed with this inscription: 'The Lord knows those who are his,' and, 'Everyone who confesses the name of the Lord must turn away from wickedness.'

[20] In a large house there are articles not only of gold and silver, but also of wood and clay; some are for noble purposes and some for ignoble. [21] If a man cleanses himself from the latter, he will be an instrument for noble purposes, made holy, useful to the Master and prepared to do any good work.

[22] Flee the evil desires of youth, and pursue righteousness, faith, love and peace, along with those who call on the Lord out of a pure heart. [23] Don't have anything to do with foolish and stupid arguments, because you know they produce quarrels. [24] And the Lord's servant must not quarrel; instead, he must be kind to everyone, able to teach, not resentful. [25] Those who oppose him he must gently instruct, in the hope that God will grant them repentance leading them to a knowledge of the truth, [26] and that they will come to their senses and escape from the trap of the devil, who has taken them captive to do his will.

DAY 238

2 TIM. 3. 1 — 17

3 Godlessness in the Last Days

But mark this: There will be terrible times in the last days. ²People will be lovers of themselves, lovers of money, boastful, proud, abusive, disobedient to their parents, ungrateful, unholy, ³without love, unforgiving, slanderous, without self-control, brutal, not lovers of the good, ⁴treacherous, rash, conceited, lovers of pleasure rather than lovers of God - ⁵having a form of godliness but denying its power. Have nothing to do with them.

⁶They are the kind who worm their way into homes and gain control over weak-willed women, who are loaded down with sins and are swayed by all kinds of evil desires, ⁷always learning but never able to acknowledge the truth. ⁸Just as Jannes and Jambres opposed Moses, so also these men oppose the truth - men of depraved minds, who, as far as the faith is concerned, are rejected. ⁹But they will not get very far because, as in the case of those men, their folly will be clear to everyone.

Paul's Charge to Timothy

¹⁰You, however, know all about my teaching, my way of life, my purpose, faith, patience, love, endurance, ¹¹persecutions, sufferings - what kinds of things happened to me in Antioch, Iconium and Lystra, the persecutions I endured. Yet the Lord rescued me from all of them. ¹²In fact, everyone who wants to live a godly life in Christ Jesus will be persecuted, ¹³while evil men and impostors will go from bad to worse, deceiving and being deceived. ¹⁴But as for you, continue in what you have learned and have become convinced of, because you know those from whom you learned it, ¹⁵and how from infancy you have known the holy Scriptures, which are able to make you wise for salvation through faith in Christ Jesus. ¹⁶All Scripture is God-breathed and is useful for teaching, rebuking, correcting and training in righteousness, ¹⁷so that the man of God may be thoroughly equipped for every good work.

DAY 239

2 TIM. 4. 1 — 22

4 In the presence of God and of Christ Jesus, who will judge the living and the dead, and in view of his appearing and his kingdom, I give you this charge: ²Preach the Word; be prepared in season and out of season; correct, rebuke and encourage - with great patience and careful instruction.

Preach the Word; be prepared in season and out of season.

³For the time will come when men will not put up with sound doctrine. Instead, to suit their own desires, they will gather around them a great number of teachers to say what their itching ears want to hear. ⁴They will turn their ears away from

e truth and turn aside to myths. ⁵But
ᴜ, keep your head in all situations,
dure hardship, do the work of an
angelist, discharge all the duties of your
nistry.

⁶For I am already being poured out
e a drink offering, and the time has
me for my departure. ⁷I have fought the
od fight, I have finished the race, I
ve kept the faith. ⁸Now there is in

¹⁴Alexander the metalworker did me
a great deal of harm. The Lord will repay
him for what he has done. ¹⁵You too
should be on your guard against him,
because he strongly opposed our message.
¹⁶At my first defence, no-one came to
my support, but everyone deserted me.
May it not be held against them. ¹⁷But
the Lord stood at my side and gave me
strength, so that through me the message

The Lord will rescue me.

re for me the crown of righteousness,
ich the Lord, the righteous Judge, will
ard to me on that day - and not only to
, but also to all who have longed for
 appearing.

ersonal Remarks

o your best to come to me quickly, ¹⁰for
mas, because he loved this world, has
serted me and has gone to
essalonica. Crescens has gone to
latia, and Titus to Dalmatia. ¹¹Only
ke is with me. Get Mark and bring him
th you, because he is helpful to me in
 ministry. ¹²I sent Tychicus to Ephesus.
Vhen you come, bring the cloak that I
t with Carpus at Troas, and my scrolls,
ecially the parchments.

might be fully proclaimed and all the
Gentiles might hear it. And I was
delivered from the lion's mouth. ¹⁸The
Lord will rescue me from every evil attack
and will bring me safely to his heavenly
kingdom. To him be glory for ever and
ever. Amen.

Final Greetings

¹⁹Greet Priscilla and Aquila and the
household of Onesiphorus. ²⁰Erastus
stayed in Corinth, and I left Trophimus
sick in Miletus. ²¹Do your best to get here
before winter. Eubulus greets you, and so
do Pudens, Linus, Claudia and all the
brothers.

²²The Lord be with your spirit. Grace
be with you.

DAY 240

MATT. 1. 1 — 25

1 The Genealogy of Jesus

A record of the genealogy of Jesus Christ the son of David, the son of Abraham:

² Abraham was the father of Isaac,
Isaac the father of Jacob,
Jacob the father of Judah and his
brothers,
³ Judah the father of Perez and Zerah,
whose mother was Tamar,
Perez the father of Hezron,
Hezron the father of Ram,
⁴ Ram the father of Amminadab,
Amminadab the father of Nahshon,
Nahshon the father of Salmon,
⁵ Salmon the father of Boaz, whose
mother was Rahab,
Boaz the father of Obed, whose mother
was Ruth,
Obed the father of Jesse,
⁶ and Jesse the father of King David.

David was the father of Solomon, whose
mother had been Uriah's wife,
⁷ Solomon the father of Rehoboam,
Rehoboam the father of Abijah,
Abijah the father of Asa,
⁸ Asa the father of Jehoshaphat,
Jehoshaphat the father of Jehoram,
Jehoram the father of Uzziah,
⁹ Uzziah the father of Jotham,
Jotham the father of Ahaz,
Ahaz the father of Hezekiah,
¹⁰ Hezekiah the father of Manasseh,
Manasseh the father of Amon,
Amon the father of Josiah,
¹¹ and Josiah the father of Jeconiah

and his brothers at the time of the exile to Babylon.

¹² After the exile to Babylon:
Jeconiah was the father of Shealtiel,
Shealtiel the father of Zerubbabel,
¹³ Zerubbabel the father of Abiud,
Abiud the father of Eliakim,
Eliakim the father of Azor,
¹⁴ Azor the father of Zadok,
Zadok the father of Akim,
Akim the father of Eliud,
¹⁵ Eliud the father of Eleazar,
Eleazar the father of Matthan,
Matthan the father of Jacob,
¹⁶ and Jacob the father of Joseph, the
husband of Mary, of whom was born
Jesus, who is called Christ.

¹⁷ Thus there were fourteen generations in all from Abraham to David, fourteen from David to the exile to Babylon, and fourteen from the exile to the Christ.

The Birth of Jesus Christ

¹⁸ This is how the birth of Jesus Christ came about: His mother Mary was pledged to be married to Joseph, but before they came together, she was found to be with child through the Holy Spirit.

> **'She will give birth to a son, and you are to give him the name Jesus.'**

¹⁹ Because Joseph her husband was a righteous man and did not want to expose her to public disgrace, he had in mind to divorce her quietly.
²⁰ But after he had considered this, an angel of the Lord appeared to him in a dream and said, 'Joseph son of David, do

t be afraid to take Mary home as your
fe, because what is conceived in her is
om the Holy Spirit. ²¹ She will give birth

a son, and you are to give him the
me Jesus, because he will save his
ople from their sins.'

²² All this took place to fulfil what the
rd had said through the prophet:
The virgin will be with child and will
ve birth to a son, and they will call him
manuel' - which means, 'God with us.'

²⁴ When Joseph woke up, he did what
e angel of the Lord had commanded
m and took Mary home as his wife.
But he had no union with her until she
ve birth to a son. And he gave him the
me Jesus.

DAY 241

MATT. 2. 1 — 23

The Visit of the Magi

After Jesus was born in Bethlehem
in Judea, during the time of King
erod, Magi from the east came to
rusalem ² and asked, 'Where is the one
ho has been born king of the Jews? We
w his star in the east and have come to
orship him.'

³ When King Herod heard this he was
sturbed, and all Jerusalem with him.
When he had called together all the
ople's chief priests and teachers of the
w, he asked them where the Christ was
be born. ⁵ 'In Bethlehem in Judea,'
ey replied, 'for this is what the prophet
s written:

⁶ "But you, Bethlehem, in the land of
      Judah,
   are by no means least among the

rulers of Judah;
for out of you will come a ruler
   who will be the shepherd
   of my people Israel." '

⁷ Then Herod called the Magi secretly
and found out from them the exact time
the star had appeared. ⁸ He sent them to
Bethlehem and said, 'Go and make a
careful search for the child. As soon as
you find him, report to me, so that I too
may go and worship him.'

⁹ After they had heard the king, they
went on their way, and the star they had
seen in the east went ahead of them until
it stopped over the place where the child
was. ¹⁰ When they saw the star, they were
overjoyed. ¹¹ On coming to the house,
they saw the child with his mother Mary,
and they bowed down and worshipped
him. Then they opened their treasures
and presented him with gifts of gold and
of incense and of myrrh. ¹² And having
been warned in a dream not to go back to
Herod, they returned to their country by
another route.

The Escape to Egypt

¹³ When they had gone, an angel of the
Lord appeared to Joseph in a dream. 'Get
up,' he said, 'take the child and his
mother and escape to Egypt. Stay there
until I tell you, for Herod is going to
search for the child to kill him.'

¹⁴ So he got up, took the child and his
mother during the night and left for
Egypt, ¹⁵ where he stayed until the death
of Herod. And so was fulfilled what the
Lord had said through the prophet: 'Out
of Egypt I called my son.'

¹⁶ When Herod realised that he had
been outwitted by the Magi, he was
furious, and he gave orders to kill all the
boys in Bethlehem and its vicinity who
were two years old and under, in

accordance with the time he had learned from the Magi. ⁱ⁷ Then what was said through the prophet Jeremiah was fulfilled:

ⁱ⁸ 'A voice is heard in Ramah,
  weeping and great mourning,
Rachel weeping for her children
  and refusing to be comforted,
because they are no more.'

The Return to Nazareth

ⁱ⁹ After Herod died, an angel of the Lord appeared in a dream to Joseph in Egypt ²⁰ and said, 'Get up, take the child and his mother and go to the land of Israel, for those who were trying to take the child's life are dead.'

²¹ So he got up, took the child and his mother and went to the land of Israel. ²² But when he heard that Archelaus was reigning in Judea in place of his father

'Get up, take the child and his mother and go to the land of Israel'

Herod, he was afraid to go there. Having been warned in a dream, he withdrew to the district of Galilee, ²³ and he went and lived in a town called Nazareth. So was fulfilled what was said through the prophets: 'He will be called a Nazarene.'

They followed the star.

DAY 242
MATT. 3. 1 — 17

3 **John the Baptist Prepares the Way**
In those days John the Baptist ame, preaching in the Desert of Judea nd saying, 'Repent, for the kingdom of eaven is near.' ³ This is he who was oken of through the prophet Isaiah:

'A voice of one calling in the desert,
"Prepare the way for the Lord,
make straight paths for him." '

⁴ John's clothes were made of camel's air, and he had a leather belt round his

'Prepare the way for the Lord, make straight paths for him!'

'He will baptise you with the Holy Spirit and with fire.'

aist. His food was locusts and wild oney. ⁵ People went out to him from rusalem and all Judea and the whole gion of the Jordan. ⁶ Confessing their ns, they were baptised by him in the rdan River.

⁷ But when he saw many of the narisees and Sadducees coming to where e was baptising, he said to them: 'You ood of vipers! Who warned you to flee om the coming wrath? ⁸ Produce fruit in eeping with repentance. ⁹ And do not ink you can say to yourselves, "We have oraham as our father." I tell you that t of these stones God can raise up ildren for Abraham. ¹⁰ The axe is eady at the root of the trees, and every e that does not produce good fruit will

be cut down and thrown into the fire.

¹¹ 'I baptise you with water for repentance. But after me will come one who is more powerful than I, whose sandals I am not fit to carry. He will baptise you with the Holy Spirit and with fire. ¹² His winnowing fork is in his hand, and he will clear his threshing-floor, gathering his wheat into the barn and burning up the chaff with unquenchable fire.'

The Baptism of Jesus
¹³ Then Jesus came from Galilee to the Jordan to be baptised by John. ¹⁴ But John tried to deter him, saying, 'I need to be baptised by you, and do you come to me?'

¹⁵ Jesus replied, 'Let it be so now; it is proper for us to do this to fulfil all righteousness.' Then John consented.

¹⁶ As soon as Jesus was baptised, he went up out of the water. At that moment heaven was opened, and he saw the Spirit of God descending like a dove and lighting on him. ¹⁷ And a voice from heaven said, 'This is my Son, whom I love; with him I am well pleased.'

DAY 243

MATT. 4. 1 — 25

4 The Temptation of Jesus
Then Jesus was led by the Spirit into the desert to be tempted by the devil. [2] After fasting for forty days and forty nights, he was hungry. [3] The tempter came to him and said, 'If you are the Son of God, tell these stones to become bread.'

[4] Jesus answered, 'It is written: "Man does not live on bread alone, but on every word that comes from the mouth of God." '

[5] Then the devil took him to the holy city and had him stand on the highest point of the temple. [6] 'If you are the Son of God,' he said, 'throw yourself down. For it is written:

"He will command his angels
concerning you,
and they will lift you up in their hands,
so that you will not strike your foot
against a stone." '

[7] Jesus answered him, 'It is also written: "Do not put the Lord your God to the test." '

[8] Again, the devil took him to a very high mountain and showed him all the kingdoms of the world and their splendour. [9] 'All this I will give you,' he said, 'if you will bow down and worship me.'

[10] Jesus said to him, 'Away from me, Satan! For it is written: "Worship the Lord your God, and serve him only." '

[11] Then the devil left him, and angels came and attended him.

Jesus Begins to Preach

[12] When Jesus heard that John had been put in prison, he returned to Galilee. [13] Leaving Nazareth, he went and lived in Capernaum, which was by the lake in the area of Zebulun and Naphtali - [14] to fulfil what was said through the prophet Isaiah

[15] 'Land of Zebulun and land of
Naphtali,
the way to the sea, along the Jordan
Galilee of the Gentiles -
[16] the people living in darkness
have seen a great light;
on those living in the land of the
shadow of death
a light has dawned.'

[17] From that time on Jesus began to preach, 'Repent, for the kingdom of heaven is near.'

The Calling of the First Disciple

[18] As Jesus was walking beside the Sea of Galilee, he saw two brothers, Simon called Peter and his brother Andrew. They were casting a net into the lake, for they were fishermen. [19] 'Come, follow me Jesus said, 'and I will make you fishers of men.' [20] At once they left their nets

---

'Man does not live on bread alone...'

---

and followed him.

[21] Going on from there, he saw two other brothers, James son of Zebedee an his brother John. They were in a boat with their father Zebedee, preparing the nets. Jesus called them, [22] and immediate they left the boat and their father and followed him.

esus Heals the Sick

Jesus went throughout Galilee, teaching their synagogues, preaching the good ews of the kingdom, and healing every sease and sickness among the people. News about him spread all over Syria, nd people brought to him all who were with various diseases, those suffering vere pain, the demon-possessed, those ving seizures, and the paralysed, and he ealed them. ²⁵ Large crowds from Galilee, e Decapolis, Jerusalem, Judea and the gion across the Jordan followed him.

DAY 244

MATT. 5. 1 — 20

The Beatitudes

Now when he saw the crowds, he went up on a mountainside and t down. His disciples came to him, ² and began to teach them, saying:

³ 'Blessed are the poor in spirit,
  for theirs is the kingdom of heaven.
⁴ Blessed are those who mourn,
  for they will be comforted.
⁵ Blessed are the meek,
  for they will inherit the earth.
⁶ Blessed are those who hunger and
  thirst for righteousness,
  for they will be filled.
⁷ Blessed are the merciful,
  for they will be shown mercy.
⁸ Blessed are the pure in heart,
  for they will see God.
⁹ Blessed are the peacemakers,
  for they will be called sons of God.
¹⁰ Blessed are those who are
  persecuted because of

righteousness,
  for theirs is the kingdom of heaven.

¹¹ 'Blessed are you when people insult you, persecute you and falsely say all kinds of evil against you because of me. ¹² Rejoice and be glad, because great is your reward in heaven, for in the same way they persecuted the prophets who were before you.

Salt and Light

¹³ 'You are the salt of the earth. But if the salt loses its saltiness, how can it be made salty again? It is no longer good for anything, except to be thrown out and trampled by men. ¹⁴ 'You are the light of the world. A city on a hill cannot be hidden. ¹⁵ Neither do people light a lamp and put it under a bowl. Instead they put it on its stand, and it gives light to everyone in the house. ¹⁶ In the same way, let your light shine before men, that they may see your good deeds and praise your Father in heaven.

The Fulfilment of the Law

¹⁷ 'Do not think that I have come to abolish the Law or the Prophets; I have not come to abolish them but to fulfil them. ¹⁸ I tell you the truth, until heaven and earth disappear, not the smallest letter, not the least stroke of a pen, will by any means disappear from the Law until everything is accomplished. ¹⁹ Anyone who breaks one of the least of these commandments and teaches others to do the same will be called least in the kingdom of heaven, but whoever practises and teaches these commands will be called great in the kingdom of heaven. ²⁰ For I tell you that unless your righteousness surpasses that of the Pharisees and the teachers of the law, you will certainly not enter the kingdom of heaven.

DAY 245

MATT. 5. 21 — 48

Murder

[21] 'You have heard that it was said to the people long ago, "Do not murder, and anyone who murders will be subject to judgment." [22] But I tell you that anyone who is angry with his brother will be subject to judgment. Again, anyone who says to his brother, "Raca," is answerable to the Sanhedrin. But anyone who says, "You fool!" will be in danger of the fire of hell.

[23] 'Therefore, if you are offering your gift at the altar and there remember that your brother has something against you, [24] leave your gift there in front of the altar. First go and be reconciled to your brother; then come and offer your gift.

[25] 'Settle matters quickly with your adversary who is taking you to court. Do it while you are still with him on the way, or he may hand you over to the judge, and the judge may hand you over to the officer, and you may be thrown into prison. [26] I tell you the truth, you will not get out until you have paid the last penny.

Adultery

[27] 'You have heard that it was said, "Do not commit adultery." [28] But I tell you that anyone who looks at a woman lustfully has already committed adultery with her in his heart. [29] If your right eye causes you to sin, gouge it out and throw it away. It is better for you to lose one part of your body than for your whole body to be thrown into hell. [30] And if your right hand causes you to sin, cut it off and throw it

away. It is better for you to lose one part of your body than for your whole body to go into hell.

Divorce

[31] 'It has been said, "Anyone who divorce his wife must give her a certificate of divorce." [32] But I tell you that anyone wh divorces his wife, except for marital unfaithfulness, causes her to become an adulteress, and anyone who marries the divorced woman commits adultery.

Oaths

[33] 'Again, you have heard that it was said to the people long ago, "Do not break your oath, but keep the oaths you have made to the Lord." [34] But I tell you, Do not swear at all: either by heaven, for it God's throne; [35] or by the earth, for it is his footstool; or by Jerusalem, for it is th city of the Great King. [36] And do not swear by your head, for you cannot mak even one hair white or black. [37] Simply your "Yes" be "Yes", and your "No", "No anything beyond this comes from the ev one.

An Eye for an Eye

[38] 'You have heard that it was said, "Eye for eye, and tooth for tooth." [39] But I tell you, Do not resist an evil person. If someone strikes you on the right cheek, turn to him the other also. [40] And if someone wants to sue you and take your tunic, let him have your cloak as well. [4] someone forces you to go one mile, go with him two miles. [42] Give to the one who asks you, and do not turn away fro the one who wants to borrow from you.

Love for Enemies

[43] 'You have heard that it was said, "Lov your neighbour and hate your enemy." [44] But I tell you: Love your enemies and

ay for those who persecute you, [45] that
u may be sons of your Father in heaven.
e causes his sun to rise on the evil and
e good, and sends rain on the righteous
d the unrighteous. [46] If you love those
ho love you, what reward will you get?
re not even the tax collectors doing
at? [47] And if you greet only your
others, what are you doing more than
hers? Do not even pagans do that? [48] Be
rfect, therefore, as your heavenly
ther is perfect.

DAY 246

MATT. 6. 1 — 18

Giving to the Needy

'Be careful not to do your "acts of
righteousness" before men, to be
en by them. If you do, you will have no
ward from your Father in heaven.

[2] 'So when you give to the needy, do
ot announce it with trumpets, as the
ypocrites do in the synagogues and on
e streets, to be honoured by men. I tell
u the truth, they have received their
ward in full. [3] But when you give to the
eedy, do not let your left hand know
hat your right hand is doing, [4] so that
ur giving may be in secret. Then your
ther, who sees what is done in secret,
ill reward you.

rayer

And when you pray, do not be like the
ypocrites, for they love to pray standing
the synagogues and on the street
rners to be seen by men. I tell you the
uth, they have received their reward in
ll. [6] But when you pray, go into your
om, close the door and pray to your
ther, who is unseen. Then your Father,

who sees what is done in secret, will
reward you. [7] And when you pray, do not

> **'Love your enemies and pray
> for those who persecute you,
> that you may be sons of your
> Father in heaven.'**

keep on babbling like pagans, for they
think they will be heard because of their
many words. [8] Do not be like them, for
your Father knows what you need before
you ask him.

[9] 'This, then, is how you should pray:

"Our Father in heaven,
hallowed be your name,
[10] your kingdom come,
your will be done
on earth as it is in heaven.
[11] Give us today our daily bread.
[12] Forgive us our debts,
as we also have forgiven our debtors.
[13] And lead us not into temptation,
but deliver us from the evil one."

[14] 'For if you forgive men when they
sin against you, your heavenly Father will
also forgive you. [15] But if you do not
forgive men their sins, your Father will
not forgive your sins.

Fasting

[16] 'When you fast, do not look sombre as
the hypocrites do, for they disfigure their
faces to show men they are fasting. I tell
you the truth, they have received their
reward in full. [17] But when you fast, put oil
on your head and wash your face, [18] so
that it will not be obvious to men that
you are fasting, but only to your Father,
who is unseen; and your Father, who sees
what is done in secret, will reward you.

DAY 247

MATT. 6. 19 — 34

Treasures in Heaven

¹⁹ 'Do not store up for yourselves treasures on earth, where moth and rust destroy, and where thieves break in and steal. ²⁰ But store up for yourselves treasures in heaven, where moth and rust do not destroy, and where thieves do not break in and steal. ²¹ For where your treasure is, there your heart will be also.

²² 'The eye is the lamp of the body. If your eyes are good, your whole body will be full of light. ²³ But if your eyes are bad, your whole body will be full of darkness. If then the light within you is darkness, how great is that darkness!

²⁴ 'No-one can serve two masters. Either he will hate the one and love the other, or he will be devoted to the one and despise the other. You cannot serve both God and Money.

Do Not Worry

²⁵ 'Therefore I tell you, do not worry about your life, what you will eat or drink; or about your body, what you will wear. Is not life more important than food, and the body more important than clothes? ²⁶ Look at the birds of the air; they do not sow or reap or store away in barns, and yet your heavenly Father feeds them. Are you not much more valuable than they? ²⁷ Who of you by worrying can add a single hour to his life?

²⁸ 'And why do you worry about clothes? See how the lilies of the field grow. They do not labour or spin. ²⁹ Yet I tell you that not even Solomon in all his splendour was dressed like one of these.

³⁰ If that is how God clothes the grass of the field, which is here today and tomorrow is thrown into the fire, will he not much more clothe you, O you of little faith? ³¹ So do not worry, saying, "What shall we eat?" or "What shall we drink?" or "What shall we wear?" ³² For the pagans run after all these things, and your heavenly Father knows that you need them. ³³ But seek first his kingdom and his righteousness, and all these things will be given to you as well. ³⁴ Therefore do not worry about tomorrow, for tomorrow will worry about itself. Each day has enough trouble of its own.

DAY 248

MATT. 7. 1 — 29

Judging Others

7 'Do not judge, or you too will be judged. ² For in the same way as you judge others, you will be judged, and with the measure you use, it will be measured to you.

³ 'Why do you look at the speck of sawdust in your brother's eye and pay no attention to the plank in your own eye? ⁴ How can you say to your brother, "Let me take the speck out of your eye," when all the time there is a plank in your own eye? ⁵ You hypocrite, first take the plank out of your own eye, and then you will see clearly to remove the speck from your brother's eye.

⁶ 'Do not give dogs what is sacred; do not throw your pearls to pigs. If you do, they may trample them under their feet, and then turn and tear you to pieces.

Ask, Seek, Knock

⁷ 'Ask and it will be given to you; seek and you will find; knock and the door will be

ened to you. [8] For everyone who asks
ceives; he who seeks finds; and to him
ho knocks, the door will be opened.

[9] 'Which of you, if his son asks for
read, will give him a stone? [10] Or if he
ks for a fish, will give him a snake? [11] If
ou, then, though you are evil, know how
o give good gifts to your children, how
uch more will your Father in heaven
ve good gifts to those who ask him! [12] So
n everything, do to others what you
ould have them do to you, for this sums
p the Law and the Prophets.

he Narrow and Wide Gates

'Enter through the narrow gate. For
ide is the gate and broad is the road that
ads to destruction, and many enter
rough it. [14] But small is the gate and
arrow the road that leads to life, and
nly a few find it.

'Ask and it will be given to you; seek and you will
find; knock and the door will be opened to you.'

Tree and Its Fruit

'Watch out for false prophets. They come
o you in sheep's clothing, but inwardly
ney are ferocious wolves. [16] By their fruit
ou will recognise them. Do people pick
rapes from thornbushes, or figs from
histles? [17] Likewise every good tree bears
ood fruit, but a bad tree bears bad fruit.
A good tree cannot bear bad fruit, and a
ad tree cannot bear good fruit. [19] Every
ree that does not bear good fruit is cut
own and thrown into the fire. [20] Thus, by
heir fruit you will recognise them.

[21] 'Not everyone who says to me,
Lord, Lord," will enter the kingdom of
eaven, but only he who does the will of
y Father who is in heaven. [22] Many will
ay to me on that day, "Lord, Lord, did we
ot prophesy in your name, and in your
ame drive out demons and perform
nany miracles?" [23] Then I will tell them
lainly, "I never knew you. Away from
e, you evildoers!"

The Wise and Foolish Builders

[24] 'Therefore everyone who hears these
words of mine and puts them into
practice is like a wise man who built his
house on the rock. [25] The rain came down,
the streams rose, and the winds blew and
beat against that house; yet it did not fall,
because it had its foundation on the rock.
[26] But everyone who hears these words of
mine and does not put them into practice
is like a foolish man who built his house
on sand. [27] The rain came down, the
streams rose, and the winds blew and beat
against that house, and it fell with a great
crash.'

[28] When Jesus had finished saying
these things, the crowds were amazed at
his teaching, [29] because he taught as one
who had authority, and not as their
teachers of the law.

DAY 249

MATT. 8. 1 — 27

The Man With Leprosy

8 When he came down from the mountainside, large crowds followed him. [2] A man with leprosy came and knelt before him and said, 'Lord, if you are willing, you can make me clean.'

[3] Jesus reached out his hand and touched the man. 'I am willing,' he said. 'Be clean!' Immediately he was cured of his leprosy. [4] Then Jesus said to him, 'See that you don't tell anyone. But go, show yourself to the priest and offer the gift Moses commanded, as a testimony to them.'

The Faith of the Centurion

[5] When Jesus had entered Capernaum, a centurion came to him, asking for help. [6] 'Lord,' he said, 'my servant lies at home paralysed and in terrible suffering.'

[7] Jesus said to him, 'I will go and heal him.'

[8] The centurion replied, 'Lord, I do not deserve to have you come under my roof. But just say the word, and my servant will be healed. [9] For I myself am a man under authority, with soldiers under

---

'I will go and heal him.'

---

me. I tell this one, "Go," and he goes; and that one, "Come," and he comes. I say to my servant, "Do this," and he does it.'

[10] When Jesus heard this, he was astonished and said to those following

him, 'I tell you the truth, I have not found anyone in Israel with such great faith. [11] I say to you that many will come from the east and the west, and will take their places at the feast with Abraham, Isaac and Jacob in the kingdom of heaven. [12] But the subjects of the kingdom will be thrown outside, into the darkness where there will be weeping and gnashing of teeth.'

[13] Then Jesus said to the centurion, 'Go! It will be done just as you believed would.' And his servant was healed at that very hour.

Jesus Heals Many

[14] When Jesus came into Peter's house, he saw Peter's mother-in-law lying in bed with a fever. [15] He touched her hand and the fever left her, and she got up and began to wait on him.

[16] When evening came, many who were demon-possessed were brought to him, and he drove out the spirits with a word and healed all the sick. [17] This was to fulfil what was spoken through the prophet Isaiah:

'He took up our infirmities
and carried our diseases.'

The Cost of Following Jesus

[18] When Jesus saw the crowd around him, he gave orders to cross to the other side of the lake. [19] Then a teacher of the law came to him and said, 'Teacher, I will follow you wherever you go.'

[20] Jesus replied, 'Foxes have holes and birds of the air have nests, but the Son of Man has nowhere to lay his head.'

[21] Another disciple said to him, 'Lord, first let me go and bury my father.'

[22] But Jesus told him, 'Follow me, and let the dead bury their own dead.'

'What kind of man is this? Even the winds and the waves obey him!'

sus Calms the Storm

hen he got into the boat and his ciples followed him. ²⁴ Without rning, a furious storm came up on the e, so that the waves swept over the at. But Jesus was sleeping. ²⁵ The ciples went and woke him, saying, rd, save us! We're going to drown!'

²⁶ He replied, 'You of little faith, why are you so afraid?' Then he got up and rebuked the winds and the waves, and it was completely calm.

²⁷ The men were amazed and asked, 'What kind of man is this? Even the winds and the waves obey him!'

DAY 250

MATT. 8. 28 — 9.17

The Healing of Two Demon-possessed Men

²⁸ When he arrived at the other side in the region of the Gadarenes, two demon-possessed men coming from the tombs met him. They were so violent that no-one could pass that way. ²⁹ 'What do you want with us, Son of God?' they shouted. 'Have you come here to torture us before the appointed time?'

³⁰ Some distance from them a large herd of pigs was feeding. ³¹ The demons begged Jesus, 'If you drive us out, send us into the herd of pigs.'

³² He said to them, 'Go!' So they came out and went into the pigs, and the whole herd rushed down the steep bank into the lake and died in the water. ³³ Those tending the pigs ran off, went into the town and reported all this, including what had happened to the demon-possessed men. ³⁴ Then the whole town went out to meet Jesus. And when they saw him, they pleaded with him to leave their region.

9 **Jesus Heals a Paralytic**
Jesus stepped into a boat, crossed over and came to his own town. ² Some men brought to him a paralytic, lying on a mat. When Jesus saw their faith, he said to the paralytic, 'Take heart, son; your sins are forgiven.'

³ At this, some of the teachers of the law said to themselves, 'This fellow is blaspheming!'

⁴ Knowing their thoughts, Jesus said, 'Why do you entertain evil thoughts in your hearts? ⁵ Which is easier: to say, "Your sins are forgiven," or to say, "Get up and walk"? ⁶ But so that you may know that th Son of Man has authority on earth to forgive sins...' Then he said to the

'What do you want with us, Son of God?'

paralytic, 'Get up, take your mat and go home.' ⁷ And the man got up and went home. ⁸ When the crowd saw this, they were filled with awe; and they praised Go who had given such authority to men.

The Calling of Matthew

⁹ As Jesus went on from there, he saw a man named Matthew sitting at the tax collector's booth. 'Follow me,' he told him, and Matthew got up and followed him.

¹⁰ While Jesus was having dinner at Matthew's house, many tax collectors ar 'sinners' came and ate with him and his disciples. ¹¹ When the Pharisees saw this they asked his disciples, 'Why does your teacher eat with tax collectors and "sinners"?'

¹² On hearing this, Jesus said, 'It is no the healthy who need a doctor, but the sick. ¹³ But go and learn what this means "I desire mercy, not sacrifice." For I have not come to call the righteous, but sinners.'

Jesus Questioned About Fasting

¹⁴ Then John's disciples came and asked him, 'How is it that we and the Pharisee fast, but your disciples do not fast?'

¹⁵ Jesus answered, 'How can the gues of the bridegroom mourn while he is wi them? The time will come when the

degroom will be taken from them; then
~y will fast.
¹⁶'No-one sews a patch of unshrunk
~th on an old garment, for the patch
l pull away from the garment, making
~ tear worse. ¹⁷Neither do men pour
w wine into old wineskins. If they do,
~ skins will burst, the wine will run out
~d the wineskins will be ruined. No,
~y pour new wine into new wineskins,
~d both are preserved.'

DAY 251
MATT. 9. 18 — 38

Dead Girl and a Sick Woman

While he was saying this, a ruler came
~d knelt before him and said, 'My
~ghter has just died. But come and put
~r hand on her, and she will live.'
~sus got up and went with him, and so
~ his disciples.
²⁰Just then a woman who had been
~ject to bleeding for twelve years came
behind him and touched the edge of

'If I only touch his cloak, I will be healed.'

cloak. ²¹She said to herself, 'If I only
~ch his cloak, I will be healed.'
²²Jesus turned and saw her. 'Take
~rt, daughter,' he said, 'your faith has
~led you.' And the woman was healed
~m that moment.
²³When Jesus entered the ruler's
~use and saw the flute players and the
~sy crowd, ²⁴he said, 'Go away. The girl
~ot dead but asleep.' But they laughed

at him. ²⁵After the crowd had been put
outside, he went in and took the girl by
the hand, and she got up. ²⁶News of this
spread through all that region.

Jesus Heals the Blind and Mute

²⁷As Jesus went on from there, two blind
men followed him, calling out, 'Have
mercy on us, Son of David!'
²⁸When he had gone indoors, the
blind men came to him, and he asked
them, 'Do you believe that I am able to
do this?'
'Yes, Lord,' they replied.
²⁹Then he touched their eyes and
said, 'According to your faith will it be
done to you;' ³⁰and their sight was
restored. Jesus warned them sternly, 'See
that no-one knows about this.' ³¹But they
went out and spread the news about him
all over that region.
³²While they were going out, a man
who was demon-possessed and could not
talk was brought to Jesus. ³³And when the
demon was driven out, the man who had
been mute spoke. The crowd was amazed
and said, 'Nothing like this has ever been
seen in Israel.'
³⁴But the Pharisees said, 'It is by the
prince of demons that he drives out
demons.'

The Workers Are Few

³⁵Jesus went through all the towns and
villages, teaching in their synagogues,
preaching the good news of the kingdom
and healing every disease and sickness.
³⁶When he saw the crowds, he had
compassion on them, because they were
harassed and helpless, like sheep without
a shepherd. ³⁷Then he said to his
disciples, 'The harvest is plentiful but the
workers are few. ³⁸Ask the Lord of the
harvest, therefore, to send out workers
into his harvest field.'

DAY 252

MATT. 10. 1 — 25

10 Jesus Sends Out the Twelve

He called his twelve disciples to him and gave them authority to drive out evil spirits and to heal every disease and sickness.

² These are the names of the twelve apostles: first, Simon (who is called Peter) and his brother Andrew; James son of Zebedee, and his brother John; ³ Philip and Bartholomew; Thomas and Matthew the tax collector; James son of Alphaeus, and Thaddaeus; ⁴ Simon the Zealot and Judas Iscariot, who betrayed him.

⁵ These twelve Jesus sent out with the following instructions: 'Do not go among the Gentiles or enter any town of the Samaritans. ⁶ Go rather to the lost sheep of Israel. ⁷ As you go, preach this message: "The kingdom of heaven is near." ⁸ Heal the sick, raise the dead, cleanse those who have leprosy, drive out demons.

'A student is not above his teacher, nor a servant above his master.'

Freely you have received, freely give. ⁹ Do not take along any gold or silver or copper in your belts; ¹⁰ take no bag for the journey, or extra tunic, or sandals or a staff; for the worker is worth his keep. ¹¹ 'Whatever town or village you enter, search for some worthy person there and stay at his house until you leave. ¹² As you enter the home, give it your greeting. ¹³ If the home is deserving let your peace rest on it; if it is not, let your peace return to you. ¹⁴ If anyone will not welcome you or listen to your words shake the dust off your feet when you leave that home or town. ¹⁵ I tell you the

'The kingdom of heaven is near'

truth, it will be more bearable for Sodom and Gomorrah on the day of judgment than for that town. ¹⁶ I am sending you out like sheep among wolves. Therefore be as shrewd as snakes and as innocent as doves.

¹⁷ 'Be on your guard against men; the will hand you over to the local councils and flog you in their synagogues. ¹⁸ On m account you will be brought before governors and kings as witnesses to them and to the Gentiles. ¹⁹ But when they arrest you, do not worry about what to s or how to say it. At that time you will be given what to say, ²⁰ for it will not be you speaking, but the Spirit of your Father speaking through you.

²¹ 'Brother will betray brother to death, and a father his child; children w rebel against their parents and have the put to death. ²² All men will hate you because of me, but he who stands firm to the end will be saved. ²³ When you are persecuted in one place, flee to another. tell you the truth, you will not finish going through the cities of Israel before the Son of Man comes.

²⁴ 'A student is not above his teache nor a servant above his master. ²⁵ It is enough for the student to be like his teacher, and the servant like his master. the head of the house has been called Beelzebub, how much more the member of his household!

DAY 253

MATT. 10. 26 — 42

[25] 'So do not be afraid of them. There is nothing concealed that will not be disclosed, or hidden that will not be made known. [27] What I tell you in the dark, speak in the daylight; what is whispered in your ear, proclaim from the roofs. [28] Do not be afraid of those who kill the body but cannot kill the soul. Rather, be afraid to bring peace, but a sword. [35] For I have come to turn

"a man against his father,
    a daughter against her mother,
a daughter-in-law against her
    mother-in-law -
[36]   a man's enemies will be the
    members of his own household."

[37] 'Anyone who loves his father or mother more than me is not worthy of me; anyone who loves his son or daughter more than me is not worthy of me; [38] and anyone who does not take his cross and

'So don't be afraid; you are worth more than many sparrows.'

of the One who can destroy both soul and body in hell. [29] Are not two sparrows sold for a penny? Yet not one of them will fall to the ground apart from the will of your Father. [30] And even the very hairs of your head are all numbered. [31] So don't be afraid; you are worth more than many sparrows.

[32] 'Whoever acknowledges me before men, I will also acknowledge him before my Father in heaven. [33] But whoever disowns me before men, I will disown him before my Father in heaven.

[34] 'Do not suppose that I have come to bring peace to the earth. I did not come follow me is not worthy of me. [39] Whoever finds his life will lose it, and whoever loses his life for my sake will find it.

[40] 'He who receives you receives me, and he who receives me receives the one who sent me. [41] Anyone who receives a prophet because he is a prophet will receive a prophet's reward, and anyone who receives a righteous man because he is a righteous man will receive a righteous man's reward. [42] And if anyone gives even a cup of cold water to one of these little ones because he is my disciple, I tell you the truth, he will certainly not lose his reward.'

DAY 254
MATT. 11. 1 — 30

11 **Jesus and John the Baptist**
After Jesus had finished instructing his twelve disciples, he went on from there to teach and preach in the towns of Galilee.

[2] When John heard in prison what Christ was doing, he sent his disciples [3] to ask him, 'Are you the one who was to come, or should we expect someone else?'

[4] Jesus replied, 'Go back and report to John what you hear and see: [5] The blind receive sight, the lame walk, those who have leprosy are cured, the deaf hear, the dead are raised, and the good news is preached to the poor. [6] Blessed is the man who does not fall away on account of me.'

[7] As John's disciples were leaving, Jesus began to speak to the crowd about John: 'What did you go out into the desert to see? A reed swayed by the wind? [8] If not, what did you go out to see? A man dressed in fine clothes? No, those who wear fine clothes are in kings' palaces. [9] Then what did you go out to see? A prophet? Yes, I tell you, and more than a prophet. [10] This is the one about whom it is written:

"I will send my messenger ahead of
you,
who will prepare your way before
you."

[11] I tell you the truth: Among those born of women there has not risen anyone greater than John the Baptist; yet he who is least in the kingdom of heaven is greater than he. [12] From the days of John the Baptist until now, the kingdom of heaven has been forcefully advancing, and forceful men lay hold of it. [13] For all the Prophets and the Law prophesied until John. [14] And if you are willing to accept it, he is the Elijah who was to come. [15] He who has ears, let him hear.

[16] 'To what can I compare this generation? They are like children sitting in the market-places and calling out to others:

[17] "'We played the flute for you,
and you did not dance;
we sang a dirge,
and you did not mourn."

[18] For John came neither eating nor drinking, and they say, "He has a demon. [19] The Son of Man came eating and drinking, and they say, "Here is a glutton and a drunkard, a friend of tax collectors and 'sinners'." But wisdom is proved right by her actions.'

Woe on Unrepentant Cities

[20] Then Jesus began to denounce the cities in which most of his miracles had been performed, because they did not repent. [21] 'Woe to you, Korazin! Woe to you, Bethsaida! If the miracles that were performed in you had been performed in Tyre and Sidon, they would have repented long ago in sackcloth and ashes. [22] But I tell you, it will be more bearable for Tyre and Sidon on the day of judgment than for you. [23] And you, Capernaum, will you be lifted up to the skies? No, you will go down to the depths. If the miracles that were performed in you had been performed in Sodom, it would have remained to this day. [24] But I tell you that it will be more bearable for Sodom on the day of judgment than for you.'

Rest for the Weary

[5] At that time Jesus said, 'I praise you, Father, Lord of heaven and earth, because you have hidden these things from the wise and learned, and revealed them to little children. [26] Yes, Father, for this was your good pleasure.

[27] 'All things have been committed to me by my Father. No-one knows the Son except the Father, and no-one knows the Father except the Son and those to whom the Son chooses to reveal him.

[28] 'Come to me, all you who are weary and burdened, and I will give you rest. [9] Take my yoke upon you and learn from me, for I am gentle and humble in heart, and you will find rest for your souls. [30] For my yoke is easy and my burden is light.'

DAY 255

MATT. 12. 1 — 21

12

Lord of the Sabbath

At that time Jesus went through the cornfields on the Sabbath. His disciples were hungry and began to pick some ears of corn and eat them. [2] When the Pharisees saw this, they said to him, 'Look! Your disciples are doing what is unlawful on the Sabbath.'

[3] He answered, 'Haven't you read what David did when he and his companions were hungry? [4] He entered the house of God, and he and his companions ate the consecrated bread which was not lawful for them to do, but only for the priests. [5] Or haven't you read in the Law that on the Sabbath the priests in the temple desecrate the day and yet are innocent? [6] I tell you that one greater than the temple is here. [7] If you had known what these words mean, "I desire mercy, not sacrifice," you would not have condemned the innocent. [8] For the Son of Man is Lord of the Sabbath.'

[9] Going on from that place, he went into their synagogue, and [10] a man with a shrivelled hand was there. Looking for a reason to accuse Jesus, they asked him, 'Is it lawful to heal on the Sabbath?'

[11] He said to them, 'If any of you has a sheep and it falls into a pit on the Sabbath, will you not take hold of it and lift it out? [12] How much more valuable is a man than a sheep! Therefore it is lawful to do good on the Sabbath.'

[13] Then he said to the man, 'Stretch out your hand.' So he stretched it out and it was completely restored, just as sound as the other. [14] But the Pharisees went out and plotted how they might kill Jesus.

God's Chosen Servant

[15] Aware of this, Jesus withdrew from that place. Many followed him, and he healed all their sick, [16] warning them not to tell who he was. [17] This was to fulfil what was spoken through the prophet Isaiah:

[18] 'Here is my servant whom I have chosen,
the one I love, in whom I delight;
I will put my Spirit on him,
and he will proclaim justice to the nations.
[19] He will not quarrel or cry out;
no-one will hear his voice in the streets.
[20] A bruised reed he will not break,
and a smouldering wick he will not snuff out,
till he leads justice to victory.
[21] In his name the nations will put their hope.'

DAY 256

MATT. 12. 22 — 37

Jesus and Beelzebub

²² Then they brought him a demon-possessed man who was blind and mute, and Jesus healed him, so that he could both talk and see. ²³ All the people were astonished and said, 'Could this be the Son of David?'

²⁴ But when the Pharisees heard this, they said, 'It is only by Beelzebub, the prince of demons, that this fellow drives out demons.'

²⁵ Jesus knew their thoughts and said to them, 'Every kingdom divided against itself will be ruined, and every city or household divided against itself will not stand. ²⁶ If Satan drives out Satan, he is divided against himself. How then can his kingdom stand? ²⁷ And if I drive out demons by Beelzebub, by whom do your people drive them out? So then, they will be your judges. ²⁸ But if I drive out demons by the Spirit of God, then the kingdom of God has come upon you.

²⁹ 'Or again, how can anyone enter a strong man's house and carry off his possessions unless he first ties up the strong man? Then he can rob his house.

³⁰ 'He who is not with me is against me, and⋅he who does not gather with me scatters. ³¹ And so I tell you, every sin and blasphemy will be forgiven men, but the blasphemy against the Spirit will not be forgiven. ³² Anyone who speaks a word against the Son of Man will be forgiven, but anyone who speaks against the Holy Spirit will not be forgiven, either in this age or in the age to come.

³³ 'Make a tree good and its fruit will be good, or make a tree bad and its fruit will be bad, for a tree is recognised by its fruit. ³⁴ You brood of vipers, how can you who are evil say anything good? For out of the overflow of the heart the mouth speaks. ³⁵ The good man brings good things out of the good stored up in him,

---

> **'He who is not with me is against me, and he who does not gather with me scatters.'**

---

and the evil man brings evil things out of the evil stored up in him. ³⁶ But I tell you that men will have to give account on the day of judgment for every careless word they have spoken. ³⁷ For by your words you will be acquitted, and by your words you will be condemned.'

DAY 257

MATT. 12. 38 — 50

The Sign of Jonah

³⁸ Then some of the Pharisees and teachers of the law said to him, 'Teacher, we want to see a miraculous sign from you.'

³⁹ He answered, 'A wicked and adulterous generation asks for a miraculous sign! But none will be given except the sign of the prophet Jonah. ⁴⁰ For as Jonah was three days and three nights in the belly of a huge fish, so the Son of Man will be three days and three nights in the heart of the earth. ⁴¹ The men of Nineveh will stand up at the judgment with this generation and condemn it; for they repented at the

reaching of Jonah, and now one greater
~~~~an Jonah is here. [42] The Queen of the
~~~~outh will rise at the judgment with this
~~~~eneration and condemn it; for she came
~~~~om the ends of the earth to listen to
~~~~olomon's wisdom, and now one greater
~~~~an Solomon is here.

how it will be with this wicked
generation.'

Jesus' Mother and Brothers

[46] While Jesus was still talking to the
crowd, his mother and brothers stood
outside, wanting to speak to him.

'Whoever does the will of my Father in heaven is my brother and sister and mother.'

[43] 'When an evil spirit comes out of a
~~~~an, it goes through arid places seeking
~~~~st and does not find it. [44] Then it says, "I
~~~~ill return to the house I left." When it
~~~~rives, it finds the house unoccupied,
~~~~vept clean and put in order. [45] Then it
~~~~oes and takes with it seven other spirits
~~~~ore wicked than itself, and they go in
~~~~d live there. And the final condition of
~~~~at man is worse than the first. That is

Someone told him, 'Your mother and
brothers are standing outside, wanting to
speak to you.'
[48] He replied to him, 'Who is my
mother, and who are my brothers?'
[49] Pointing to his disciples, he said, 'Here
are my mother and my brothers. [50] For
whoever does the will of my Father in
heaven is my brother and sister and
mother.'

DAY 258

MATT. 13. 1 — 23

13

The Parable of the Sower

That same day Jesus went out of the house and sat by the lake. ²Such large crowds gathered round him that he got into a boat and sat in it, while all the people stood on the shore. ³Then he told them many things in parables, saying: 'A farmer went out to sow his seed. ⁴As he was scattering the seed, some fell along the path, and the birds came and ate it up. ⁵Some fell on rocky places, where it did not have much soil. It sprang up quickly, because the soil was shallow. ⁶But when the sun came up, the plants were scorched, and they withered because they had no root. ⁷Other seed fell among thorns, which grew up and choked the plants. ⁸Still other seed fell on good soil, where it produced a crop - a hundred, sixty or thirty times what was sown. ⁹He who has ears, let him hear.'

¹⁰The disciples came to him and asked, 'Why do you speak to the people in parables?'

¹¹He replied, 'The knowledge of the secrets of the kingdom of heaven has been given to you, but not to them. ¹²Whoever has will be given more, and he will have an abundance. Whoever does not have, even what he has will be taken from him. ¹³This is why I speak to them in parables:

Though seeing, they do not see;
though hearing, they do not hear or understand.

¹⁴In them is fulfilled the prophecy of Isaiah:

"You will be ever hearing but never understanding;
you will be ever seeing but never perceiving.
¹⁵For this people's heart has become calloused;
they hardly hear with their ears,
and they have closed their eyes.
Otherwise they might see with their eyes, hear with their ears,
understand with their hearts
and turn, and I would heal them.'

¹⁶'But blessed are your eyes because they see, and your ears because they he ¹⁷For I tell you the truth, many prophet and righteous men longed to see what see but did not see it, and to hear what you hear but did not hear it.

¹⁸'Listen then to what the parable the sower means: ¹⁹When anyone hear the message about the kingdom and do

---

'The knowledge of the secret of the kingdom of heaven has been given to you.'

---

not understand it, the evil one comes a snatches away what was sown in his heart. This is the seed sown along the path. ²⁰The one who received the seed that fell on rocky places is the man wh hears the word and at once receives it with joy. ²¹But since he has no root, he lasts only a short time. When trouble c persecution comes because of the word he quickly falls away. ²²The one who received the seed that fell among the thorns is the man who hears the word,

it the worries of this life and the
ceitfulness of wealth choke it, making
unfruitful. ²³ But the one who received
e seed that fell on good soil is the man
ho hears the word and understands it.
e produces a crop, yielding a hundred,
xty or thirty times what was sown.'

DAY 259
MATT. 13. 24 — 52

he Parable of the Weeds

Jesus told them another parable: 'The
ngdom of heaven is like a man who
wed good seed in his field. ²⁵ But while
eryone was sleeping, his enemy came
d sowed weeds among the wheat, and
ent away. ²⁶ When the wheat sprouted
d formed ears, then the weeds also
peared.

²⁷ 'The owner's servants came to him
d said, "Sir, didn't you sow good seed in
ur field? Where then did the weeds
me from?"

²⁸ ' "An enemy did this," he replied.
'The servants asked him, "Do you
ant us to go and pull them up?"

²⁹ ' "No," he answered, "because while
u are pulling the weeds, you may root
the wheat with them. ³⁰ Let both grow
gether until the harvest. At that time I
ill tell the harvesters: First collect the
eeds and tie them in bundles to be
rned; then gather the wheat and bring
into my barn." '

he Parables of the Mustard
eed and the Yeast

He told them another parable: 'The
ngdom of heaven is like a mustard seed,
hich a man took and planted in his

field. ³² Though it is the smallest of all
your seeds, yet when it grows, it is the
largest of garden plants and becomes a
tree, so that the birds of the air come and
perch in its branches.'

³³ He told them still another parable:
'The kingdom of heaven is like yeast that

'The kingdom of heaven is like a man who sowed good seed in his field.'

a woman took and mixed into a large
amount of flour until it worked all
through the dough.'

³⁴ Jesus spoke all these things to the
crowd in parables; he did not say
anything to them without using a parable.
³⁵ So was fulfilled what was spoken
through the prophet:

'I will open my mouth in parables,
I will utter things hidden since the
creation of the world.'

The Parable of the Weeds Explained

³⁶ Then he left the crowd and went into
the house. His disciples came to him and
said, 'Explain to us the parable of the
weeds in the field.'

³⁷ He answered, 'The one who sowed
the good seed is the Son of Man. ³⁸ The
field is the world, and the good seed
stands for the sons of the kingdom. The
weeds are the sons of the evil one, ³⁹ and
the enemy who sows them is the devil.
The harvest is the end of the age, and the
harvesters are angels.

⁴⁰ 'As the weeds are pulled up and
burned in the fire, so it will be at the end
of the age. ⁴¹ The Son of Man will send
out his angels, and they will weed out of

'The kingdom of heaven is like a
that was let down into the lake a
caught all kinds of fish. When it w
full, the fisherman pulled it up on
shore. Then they sat down a
collected the good fish in baskets, t
threw the bad awa

his kingdom everything that causes sin
and all who do evil. ⁴²They will throw
them into the fiery furnace, where there
will be weeping and gnashing of teeth.
⁴³Then the righteous will shine like the
sun in the kingdom of their Father. He
who has ears, let him hear.

The Parables of the Hidden Treasure and the Pearl

⁴⁴'The kingdom of heaven is like treasure
hidden in a field. When a man found it,
he hid it again, and then in his joy went
and sold all he had and bought that field.

⁴⁵'Again, the kingdom of heaven is
like a merchant looking for fine pearls.
⁴⁶When he found one of great value, he
went away and sold everything he had
and bought it.

The Parable of the Net

⁴⁷'Once again, the kingdom of heaven is
like a net that was let down into the lake

and caught all kinds of fish. ⁴⁸When it
was full, the fishermen pulled it up on th
shore. Then they sat down and collected
the good fish in baskets, but threw the
bad away. ⁴⁹This is how it will be at the

'Have you understood all these things?'

end of the age. The angels will come an
separate the wicked from the righteous
⁵⁰and throw them into the fiery furnace,
where there will be weeping and gnashi
of teeth.

⁵¹'Have you understood all these
things?' Jesus asked.

'Yes,' they replied.

⁵²He said to them, 'Therefore every
teacher of the law who has been instruct
about the kingdom of heaven is like the
owner of a house who brings out of his
storeroom new treasures as well as old.'

DAY 260

MATT. 13. 53 — 14.21

Prophet Without Honour

When Jesus had finished these parables, he moved on from there. [54] Coming to his home town, he began teaching the people in their synagogue, and they were amazed. 'Where did this man get this wisdom and these miraculous powers?' they asked. 'Isn't this the carpenter's son? Isn't his mother's name Mary, and aren't his brothers James, Joseph, Simon and Judas? Aren't all his sisters with us? Where then did this man get all these things?' And they took offence at him.

But Jesus said to them, 'Only in his home town and in his own house is a prophet without honour.'

[58] And he did not do many miracles there because of their lack of faith.

14

John the Baptist Beheaded

At that time Herod the tetrarch heard the reports about Jesus, and he said to his attendants, 'This is John the Baptist; he has risen from the dead! That is why miraculous powers are at work in him.'

[3] Now Herod had arrested John and bound him and put him in prison because of Herodias, his brother Philip's wife, [4] for John had been saying to him: 'It is not lawful for you to have her.' [5] Herod wanted to kill John, but he was afraid of the people, because they considered him a prophet.

[6] On Herod's birthday the daughter of Herodias danced for them and pleased Herod so much [7] that he promised with an oath to give her whatever she asked. [8] Prompted by her mother, she said, 'Give me here on a platter the head of John the Baptist.' [9] The king was distressed, but because of his oaths and his dinner guests, he ordered that her request be granted [10] and had John beheaded in the prison. [11] His head was brought in on a platter and given to the girl, who carried it to her mother. [12] John's disciples came and took his body and buried it. Then they went and told Jesus.

Jesus Feeds the Five Thousand

[13] When Jesus heard what had happened, he withdrew by boat privately to a solitary place. Hearing of this, the crowds followed him on foot from the towns. [14] When Jesus landed and saw a large crowd, he had compassion on them and healed their sick.

[15] As evening approached, the disciples came to him and said, 'This is a remote place, and it's already getting late. Send the crowds away, so that they can go to the villages and buy themselves some food.'

[16] Jesus replied, 'They do not need to go away. You give them something to eat.'

[17] 'We have here only five loaves of bread and two fish,' they answered.

[18] 'Bring them here to me,' he said. [19] And he directed the people to sit down on the grass. Taking the five loaves and the two fish and looking up to heaven, he gave thanks and broke the loaves. Then he gave them to the disciples, and the disciples gave them to the people. [20] They all ate and were satisfied, and the disciples picked up twelve basketfuls of broken pieces that were left over. [21] The number of those who ate was about five thousand men, besides women and children.

DAY 261

MATT. 14. 22 — 36

Jesus Walks on the Water

²² Immediately Jesus made the disciples get into the boat and go on ahead of him to the other side, while he dismissed the crowd. ²³ After he had dismissed them, he went up on a mountainside by himself to pray. When evening came, he was there alone, ²⁴ but the boat was already a considerable distance from land, buffeted by the waves because the wind was against it.

²⁵ During the fourth watch of the night Jesus went out to them, walking on the lake. ²⁶ When the disciples saw him walking on the lake, they were terrified.

> **'You of little faith,' he said, 'why did you doubt?'**

'It's a ghost,' they said, and cried out in fear.

²⁷ But Jesus immediately said to them: 'Take courage! It is I. Don't be afraid.'

²⁸ 'Lord, if it's you,' Peter replied, 'tell me to come to you on the water.'

²⁹ 'Come,' he said.

Then Peter got down out of the boat, walked on the water and came towards Jesus. ³⁰ But when he saw the wind, he was afraid and, beginning to sink, cried out, 'Lord, save me!'

³¹ Immediately Jesus reached out his hand and caught him. 'You of little faith,' he said, 'why did you doubt?'

³² And when they climbed into the boat, the wind died down. ³³ Then those

who were in the boat worshipped him, saying, 'Truly you are the Son of God.'

³⁴ When they had crossed over, they landed at Gennesaret. ³⁵ And when the men of that place recognised Jesus, they sent word to all the surrounding country. People brought all their sick to him ³⁶ and begged him to let the sick just touch the edge of his cloak, and all who touched him were healed.

The boat was already a considerable distance from land.

DAY 262

MATT. 15. 1 — 28

15 **Clean and Unclean**
Then some Pharisees and
teachers of the law came to
sus from Jerusalem and asked, ² 'Why do
ur disciples break the tradition of the
ders? They don't wash their hands
fore they eat!'

³ Jesus replied, 'And why do you
eak the command of God for the sake
your tradition? ⁴ For God said,
Honour your father and mother" and
Anyone who curses his father or mother
ust be put to death." ⁵ But you say that
a man says to his father or mother,
Whatever help you might otherwise
ave received from me is a gift devoted
God," ⁶ he is not to "honour his
ther" with it. Thus you nullify the word
f God for the sake of your tradition.
You hypocrites! Isaiah was right when
e prophesied about you:

⁸ "These people honour me with their
lips, but their hearts are far from me.
⁹ They worship me in vain;
their teachings are but rules taught
by men." '

¹⁰ Jesus called the crowd to him and
aid, 'Listen and understand. ¹¹ What goes
ato a man's mouth does not make him
unclean", but what comes out of his
nouth, that is what makes him
unclean".'

¹² Then the disciples came to him and
sked, 'Do you know that the Pharisees
vere offended when they heard this?'

¹³ He replied, 'Every plant that my
heavenly Father has not planted will be
pulled up by the roots. ¹⁴ Leave them; they
are blind guides. If a blind man leads a
blind man, both will fall into a pit.'

¹⁵ Peter said, 'Explain the parable to
us.'

¹⁶ 'Are you still so dull?' Jesus asked
them. ¹⁷ 'Don't you see that whatever
enters the mouth goes into the stomach
and then out of the body? ¹⁸ But the
things that come out of the mouth come
from the heart, and these make a man
"unclean". ¹⁹ For out of the heart come
evil thoughts, murder, adultery, sexual
immorality, theft, false testimony, slander.
²⁰ These are what make a man "unclean";
but eating with unwashed hands does not
make him "unclean".'

The Faith of the Canaanite Woman

²¹ Leaving that place, Jesus withdrew to
the region of Tyre and Sidon. ²² A
Canaanite woman from that vicinity
came to him, crying out, 'Lord, Son of
David, have mercy on me! My daughter is
suffering terribly from demon-possession.'

²³ Jesus did not answer a word. So his
disciples came to him and urged him,
'Send her away, for she keeps crying out
after us.'

²⁴ He answered, 'I was sent only to the
lost sheep of Israel.'

²⁵ The woman came and knelt before
him. 'Lord, help me!' she said.

²⁶ He replied, 'It is not right to take
the children's bread and toss it to their
dogs.'

²⁷ 'Yes, Lord,' she said, 'but even the
dogs eat the crumbs that fall from their
masters' table.'

²⁸ Then Jesus answered, 'Woman, you
have great faith! Your request is granted.'
And her daughter was healed from that
very hour.

DAY 263

MATT. 15. 29 — 16.12

Jesus Feeds the Four Thousand

[29] Jesus left there and went along the Sea of Galilee. Then he went up on a mountainside and sat down. [30] Great crowds came to him, bringing the lame, the blind, the crippled, the mute and many others, and laid them at his feet; and he healed them. [31] The people were amazed when they saw the mute speaking, the crippled made well, the lame walking and the blind seeing. And they praised the God of Israel.

[32] Jesus called his disciples to him and said, 'I have compassion for these people; they have already been with me three days and have nothing to eat. I do not want to send them away hungry, or they may collapse on the way.'

[33] His disciples answered, 'Where could we get enough bread in this remote place to feed such a crowd?'

[34] 'How many loaves do you have?' Jesus asked.

'Seven,' they replied, 'and a few small fish.'

[35] He told the crowd to sit down on the ground. [36] Then he took the seven loaves and the fish, and when he had given thanks, he broke them and gave them to the disciples, and they in turn to the people. [37] They all ate and were satisfied. Afterwards the disciples picked up seven basketfuls of broken pieces that were left over. [38] The number of those who ate was four thousand, besides women and children. [39] After Jesus had sent the crowd away, he got into the boat and went to the vicinity of Magadan.

The Demand for a Sign

16 The Pharisees and Sadducees came to Jesus and tested him by asking him to show them a sign from heaven.

[2] He replied, 'When evening comes, you say, "It will be fair weather, for the sky is red," [3] and in the morning, "Today it will be stormy, for the sky is red and overcast." You know how to interpret the appearance of the sky, but you cannot interpret the signs of the times. [4] A wicked and adulterous generation looks for a miraculous sign, but none will be given it except the sign of Jonah.' Jesus then left them and went away.

The Yeast of the Pharisees and Sadducees

[5] When they went across the lake, the disciples forgot to take bread. [6] 'Be careful,' Jesus said to them. 'Be on your guard against the yeast of the Pharisees and Sadducees.'

[7] They discussed this among themselves and said, 'It is because we didn't bring any bread.'

[8] Aware of their discussion, Jesus asked, 'You of little faith, why are you talking among yourselves about having no bread? [9] Do you still not understand? Don't you remember the five loaves for the five thousand, and how many basketfuls you gathered? [10] Or the seven loaves for the four thousand, and how many basketfuls you gathered? [11] How is it you don't understand that I was not talking to you about bread? But be on your guard against the yeast of the Pharisees and Sadducees.' [12] Then they understood that he was not telling them to guard against the yeast used in bread, but against the teaching of the Pharisees and Sadducees.

DAY 264

MATT. 16. 13 — 28

Peter's Confession of Christ

¹³ When Jesus came to the region of Caesarea Philippi, he asked his disciples, 'Who do people say the Son of Man is?'

¹⁴ They replied, 'Some say John the Baptist; others say Elijah; and still others, Jeremiah or one of the prophets.'

¹⁵ 'But what about you?' he asked. 'Who do you say I am?'

¹⁶ Simon Peter answered, 'You are the Christ, the Son of the living God.'

¹⁷ Jesus replied, 'Blessed are you, Simon son of Jonah, for this was not revealed to you by man, but by my Father in heaven. ¹⁸ And I tell you that you are Peter, and on this rock I will build my church, and the gates of Hades will not overcome it. ¹⁹ I will give you the keys of the kingdom of heaven; whatever you bind on earth will be bound in heaven, and whatever you loose on earth will be loosed in heaven.' ²⁰ Then he warned his disciples not to tell anyone that he was the Christ.

Jesus Predicts His Death

²¹ From that time on Jesus began to explain to his disciples that he must go to Jerusalem and suffer many things at the hands of the elders, chief priests and teachers of the law, and that he must be killed and on the third day be raised to life.

²² Peter took him aside and began to rebuke him. 'Never, Lord!' he said. 'This shall never happen to you!'

²³ Jesus turned and said to Peter, 'Get behind me, Satan! You are a stumbling-block to me; you do not have in mind the things of God, but the things of men.'

²⁴ Then Jesus said to his disciples, 'If anyone would come after me, he must deny himself and take up his cross and follow me. ²⁵ For whoever wants to save his life will lose it, but whoever loses his life for me will find it. ²⁶ What good will it be for a man if he gains the whole world, yet forfeits his soul? Or what can a man give in exchange for his soul? ²⁷ For the Son of Man is going to come in his Father's glory with his angels, and then he

> **'If anyone would come after me, he must deny himself and take up his cross and follow me.'**

will reward each person according to what he has done. ²⁸ I tell you the truth, some who are standing here will not taste death before they see the Son of Man coming in his kingdom.'

'What good will it be for a man if he gains the whole world, yet forfeits his soul?'

DAY 265

MATT. 17. 1 — 23

The Transfiguration

17 After six days Jesus took with him Peter, James and John the brother of James, and led them up a high mountain by themselves. ² There he was transfigured before them. His face shone like the sun, and his clothes became as white as the light. ³ Just then there appeared before them Moses and Elijah, talking with Jesus.

⁴ Peter said to Jesus, 'Lord, it is good for us to be here. If you wish, I will put up three shelters - one for you, one for Moses and one for Elijah.'

⁵ While he was still speaking, a bright cloud enveloped them, and a voice from the cloud said, 'This is my Son, whom I love; with him I am well pleased. Listen to him!'

⁶ When the disciples heard this, they fell face down to the ground, terrified. ⁷ But Jesus came and touched them. 'Get up,' he said. 'Don't be afraid.' ⁸ When they looked up, they saw no-one except Jesus.

⁹ As they were coming down the mountain, Jesus instructed them, 'Don't tell anyone what you have seen, until the Son of Man has been raised from the dead.'

¹⁰ The disciples asked him, 'Why then do the teachers of the law say that Elijah must come first?'

¹¹ Jesus replied, 'To be sure, Elijah comes and will restore all things. ¹² But I tell you, Elijah has already come, and they did not recognise him, but have done to him everything they wished. In the same way the Son of Man is going to suffer at their hands.' ¹³ Then the disciples understood that he was talking to them about John the Baptist.

The Healing of a Boy With a Demon

¹⁴ When they came to the crowd, a man approached Jesus and knelt before him. ¹⁵ 'Lord, have mercy on my son,' he said. 'He has seizures and is suffering greatly. He often falls into the fire or into the water. ¹⁶ I brought him to your disciples, but they could not heal him.'

¹⁷ 'O unbelieving and perverse generation,' Jesus replied, 'how long shall I stay with you? How long shall I put up with you? Bring the boy here to me.' ¹⁸ Jesus rebuked the demon, and it came

> 'This is my Son, whom I love; with him I am well pleased. Listen to him!'

out of the boy, and he was healed from that moment.

¹⁹ Then the disciples came to Jesus in private and asked, 'Why couldn't we drive it out?'

²⁰ He replied, 'Because you have so little faith. I tell you the truth, if you have faith as small as a mustard seed, you can say to this mountain, "Move from here to there" and it will move. Nothing will be impossible for you.'

²² When they came together in Galilee, he said to them, 'The Son of Man is going to be betrayed into the hands of men. ²³ They will kill him, and on the third day he will be raised to life.' And the disciples were filled with grief.

DAY 266
MATT. 17. 24 — 18.14

The Temple Tax

²⁴ After Jesus and his disciples arrived in Capernaum, the collectors of the two-drachma tax came to Peter and asked, 'Doesn't your teacher pay the temple tax?'

²⁵ 'Yes, he does,' he replied.

When Peter came into the house, Jesus was the first to speak. 'What do you think, Simon?' he asked. 'From whom do the kings of the earth collect duty and taxes - from their own sons or from others?'

²⁶ 'From others,' Peter answered.

'Then the sons are exempt,' Jesus said to him. ²⁷ 'But so that we may not offend them, go to the lake and throw out your line. Take the first fish you catch; open its mouth and you will find a four-drachma coin. Take it and give it to them for my tax and yours.'

18
The Greatest in the Kingdom of Heaven
At that time the disciples came to Jesus and asked, 'Who is the greatest in the kingdom of heaven?'

² He called a little child and had him stand among them. ³ And he said: 'I tell you the truth, unless you change and

'Who is the greatest in the kingdom of heaven?'

become like little children, you will never enter the kingdom of heaven. ⁴ Therefore, whoever humbles himself like this child is the greatest in the kingdom of heaven.

⁵ 'And whoever welcomes a little child like this in my name welcomes me. ⁶ But if anyone causes one of these little ones who believe in me to sin, it would be better for him to have a large millstone hung around his neck and to be drowned in the depths of the sea.

⁷ 'Woe to the world because of the things that cause people to sin! Such

'See that you do not look down on one of these little ones.'

things must come, but woe to the man through whom they come! ⁸ If your hand or your foot causes you to sin, cut it off and throw it away. It is better for you to enter life maimed or crippled than to have two hands or two feet and be thrown into eternal fire. ⁹ And if your eye causes you to sin, gouge it out and throw it away. It is better for you to enter life with one eye than to have two eyes and be thrown into the fire of hell.

The Parable of the Lost Sheep

¹⁰ 'See that you do not look down on one of these little ones. For I tell you that their angels in heaven always see the face of my Father in heaven.

¹² 'What do you think? If a man owns a hundred sheep, and one of them wanders away, will he not leave the ninety-nine on the hills and go to look for the one that wandered off? ¹³ And if he finds it, I tell you the truth, he is happier about that one sheep than about the ninety-nine that did not wander off. ¹⁴ In the same way your Father in heaven is not willing that any of these little ones should be lost.

DAY 267

MATT. 18. 15 — 35

A Brother Who Sins Against You

[15] 'If your brother sins against you, go and show him his fault, just between the two of you. If he listens to you, you have won your brother over. [16] But if he will not listen, take one or two others along, so that "every matter may be established by

> 'I tell you the truth, whatever you bind on earth will be bound in heaven, and whatever you loose on earth will be loosed in heaven.'

the testimony of two or three witnesses." [17] If he refuses to listen to them, tell it to the church; and if he refuses to listen even to the church, treat him as you would a pagan or a tax collector. [18] 'I tell you the truth, whatever you bind on earth will be bound in heaven, and whatever you loose on earth will be loosed in heaven. [19] 'Again, I tell you that if two of you on earth agree about anything you ask for, it will be done for you by my Father in heaven. [20] For where two or three come together in my name, there am I with them.'

The Parable of the Unmerciful Servant

[21] Then Peter came to Jesus and asked, 'Lord, how many times shall I forgive my brother when he sins against me? Up to seven times?'

[22] Jesus answered, 'I tell you, not seven times, but seventy-seven times.

[23] 'Therefore, the kingdom of heaven is like a king who wanted to settle accounts with his servants. [24] As he began the settlement, a man who owed him ten thousand talents was brought to him. [25] Since he was not able to pay, the master ordered that he and his wife and his children and all that he had be sold to repay the debt.

[26] 'The servant fell on his knees before him. "Be patient with me," he begged, "and I will pay back everything." [27] The servant's master took pity on him, cancelled the debt and let him go.

[28] 'But when that servant went out, he found one of his fellow-servants who owed him a hundred denarii. He grabbed him and began to choke him. "Pay back what you owe me!" he demanded.

[29] 'His fellow-servant fell to his knees and begged him, "Be patient with me, and I will pay you back."

[30] 'But he refused. Instead, he went off and had the man thrown into prison until he could pay the debt. [31] When the other servants saw what had happened, they were greatly distressed and went and told their master everything that had happened.

[32] 'Then the master called the servant in. "You wicked servant," he said, "I cancelled all that debt of yours because you begged me to. [33] Shouldn't you have had mercy on your fellow-servant just as I had on you?" [34] In anger his master turned him over to the jailers to be tortured, until he should pay back all he owed.

[35] 'This is how my heavenly Father will treat each of you unless you forgive your brother from your heart.'

DAY 268

MATT. 19. 1 — 15

19 Divorce

When Jesus had finished saying these things, he left Galilee and went into the region of Judea to the other side of the Jordan. ² Large crowds followed him, and he healed them there.

³ Some Pharisees came to him to test him. They asked, 'Is it lawful for a man to divorce his wife for any and every reason?'

⁴ 'Haven't you read,' he replied, 'that at the beginning the Creator "made them male and female", ⁵ and said, "For this reason a man will leave his father and mother and be united to his wife, and the two will become one flesh"? ⁶ So they are no longer two, but one. Therefore what God has joined together, let man not separate.'

⁷ 'Why then,' they asked, 'did Moses command that a man give his wife a certificate of divorce and send her away?'

⁸ Jesus replied, 'Moses permitted you to divorce your wives because your hearts were hard. But it was not this way from the beginning. ⁹ I tell you that anyone who divorces his wife, except for marital unfaithfulness, and marries another woman commits adultery.'

¹⁰ The disciples said to him, 'If this is the situation between a husband and wife, it is better not to marry.'

¹¹ Jesus replied, 'Not everyone can accept this word, but only those to whom it has been given. ¹² For some are eunuchs because they were born that way; others were made that way by men; and others have renounced marriage because of the kingdom of heaven. The one who can accept this should accept it.'

The Little Children and Jesus

¹³ Then little children were brought to Jesus for him to place his hands on them and pray for them. But the disciples rebuked those who brought them.

¹⁴ Jesus said, 'Let the little children come to me, and do not hinder them, for the kingdom of heaven belongs to such as these.' ¹⁵ When he had placed his hands on them, he went on from there.

'Let the little children come to me.'

DAY 269

MATT. 19. 16 — 30

The Rich Young Man

¹⁶ Now a man came up to Jesus and asked, 'Teacher, what good thing must I do to get eternal life?'

¹⁷ 'Why do you ask me about what is good?' Jesus replied. 'There is only One who is good. If you want to enter life, obey the commandments.'

¹⁸ 'Which ones?' the man enquired.

Jesus replied, ' "Do not murder, do not commit adultery, do not steal, do not give false testimony, ¹⁹ honour your father and mother," and "love your neighbour as yourself." '

²⁰ 'All these I have kept,' the young man said. 'What do I still lack?'

²¹ Jesus answered, 'If you want to be perfect, go, sell your possessions and give to the poor, and you will have treasure in heaven. Then come, follow me.'

²² When the young man heard this, he went away sad, because he had great wealth.

²³ Then Jesus said to his disciples, 'I

> **'It is easier for a camel to go through the eye of a needle than for a rich man to enter the kingdom of God.'**

tell you the truth, it is hard for a rich man to enter the kingdom of heaven. ²⁴ Again I tell you, it is easier for a camel to go through the eye of a needle than for a rich man to enter the kingdom of God.'

²⁵ When the disciples heard this, they

'You will have treasure in heaven.'

re greatly astonished and asked, 'Who
en can be saved?'

²⁶ Jesus looked at them and said,
'ith man this is impossible, but with
od all things are possible.'

²⁷ Peter answered him, 'We have left
erything to follow you! What then will
ere be for us?'

²⁸ Jesus said to them, 'I tell you the
ith, at the renewal of all things, when
e Son of Man sits on his glorious
rone, you who have followed me will
o sit on twelve thrones, judging the
elve tribes of Israel. ²⁹ And everyone
o has left houses or brothers or sisters
father or mother or children or fields
r my sake will receive a hundred times
much and will inherit eternal life.
But many who are first will be last, and
any who are last will be first.

DAY 270

MATT. 20. 1 — 16

20 The Parable of the Workers in the Vineyard

'For the kingdom of heaven is
e a landowner who went out early in
e morning to hire men to work in his
neyard. ² He agreed to pay them a
narius for the day and sent them into
s vineyard.

³ 'About the third hour he went out
d saw others standing in the market-
ace doing nothing. ⁴ He told them, "You
o go and work in my vineyard, and I
ll pay you whatever is right." ⁵ So they
nt.

'He went out again about the sixth

hour and the ninth hour and did the same
thing. ⁶ About the eleventh hour he went
out and found still others standing
around. He asked them, "Why have you
been standing here all day long doing
nothing?"

⁷ ' "Because no-one has hired us,"
they answered.

'He said to them, "You also go and
work in my vineyard."

'So the last will be first, and the first will be last.'

⁸ 'When evening came, the owner of
the vineyard said to his foreman, "Call
the workers and pay them their wages,
beginning with the last ones hired and
going on to the first."

⁹ 'The workers who were hired about
the eleventh hour came and each
received a denarius. ¹⁰ So when those
came who were hired first, they expected
to receive more. But each one of them
also received a denarius. ¹¹ When they
received it, they began to grumble against
the landowner. ¹² "These men who were
hired last worked only one hour," they
said, "and you have made them equal to
us who have borne the burden of the
work and the heat of the day."

¹³ 'But he answered one of them,
"Friend, I am not being unfair to you.
Didn't you agree to work for a denarius?
¹⁴ Take your pay and go. I want to give the
man who was hired last the same as I gave
you. ¹⁵ Don't I have the right to do what I
want with my own money? Or are you
envious because I am generous?"

¹⁶ 'So the last will be first, and the first
will be last.'

DAY 271

MATT. 20. 17 — 34

Jesus Again Predicts His Death

[17] Now as Jesus was going up to Jerusalem, he took the twelve disciples aside and said to them, [18] 'We are going up to Jerusalem, and the Son of Man will be betrayed to the chief priests and the teachers of the law. They will condemn him to death [19] and will turn him over to the Gentiles to be mocked and flogged and crucified. On the third day he will be raised to life!'

A Mother's Request

[20] Then the mother of Zebedee's sons came to Jesus with her sons and, kneeling down, asked a favour of him.

> 'You will indeed drink from my cup, but to sit at my right or left is not for me to grant.'

[21] 'What is it you want?' he asked.

She said, 'Grant that one of these two sons of mine may sit at your right and the other at your left in your kingdom.'

[22] 'You don't know what you are asking,' Jesus said to them. 'Can you drink the cup I am going to drink?'

'We can,' they answered.

[23] Jesus said to them, 'You will indeed drink from my cup, but to sit at my right or left is not for me to grant. These places belong to those for whom they have been prepared by my Father.'

[24] When the ten heard about this, they were indignant with the two brothers. [25] Jesus called them together an said, 'You know that the rulers of the Gentiles lord it over them, and their hig officials exercise authority over them. [26] Not so with you. Instead, whoever wants to become great among you must be your servant, [27] and whoever wants to be first must be your slave - [28] just as the Son of Man did not come to be served, but to serve, and to give his life as a ransom for many.'

Two Blind Men Receive Sight

[29] As Jesus and his disciples were leaving Jericho, a large crowd followed him. [30] Two blind men were sitting by the roadside, and when they heard that Jesu was going by, they shouted, 'Lord, Son o David, have mercy on us!'

[31] The crowd rebuked them and told them to be quiet, but they shouted all th louder, 'Lord, Son of David, have mercy on us!'

[32] Jesus stopped and called them. 'What do you want me to do for you?' he asked.

[33] 'Lord,' they answered, 'we want ou sight.'

[34] Jesus had compassion on them and touched their eyes. Immediately they received their sight and followed him.

DAY 272

MATT. 21. 1 — 22

21 The Triumphal Entry

As they approached Jerusale and came to Bethphage on the Mount of Olives, Jesus sent two

isciples, ² saying to them, 'Go to the
village ahead of you, and at once you will
find a donkey tied there, with her colt by
her. Untie them and bring them to me.
If anyone says anything to you, tell him
that the Lord needs them, and he will
send them right away.'
⁴ This took place to fulfil what was
spoken through the prophet:

⁵ 'Say to the Daughter of Zion,
    "See, your king comes to you,
gentle and riding on a donkey,
    on a colt, the foal of a donkey."'

⁶ The disciples went and did as Jesus
had instructed them. ⁷ They brought the
donkey and the colt, placed their cloaks
on them, and Jesus sat on them. ⁸ A very
large crowd spread their cloaks on the
road, while others cut branches from the
trees and spread them on the road. ⁹ The
crowds that went ahead of him and those
that followed shouted,

'Hosanna to the Son of David!'

'Blessed is he who comes in the name
    of the Lord!'

'Hosanna in the highest!'

¹⁰ When Jesus entered Jerusalem, the
whole city was stirred and asked, 'Who is
this?'
¹¹ The crowds answered, 'This is Jesus,
the prophet from Nazareth in Galilee.'

Jesus at the Temple

Jesus entered the temple area and drove
out all who were buying and selling there.
He overturned the tables of the money
changers and the benches of those selling
doves. ¹³ 'It is written,' he said to them,
'"My house will be called a house of

prayer," but you are making it a "den of
robbers".'
¹⁴ The blind and the lame came to
him at the temple, and he healed them.
¹⁵ But when the chief priests and the
teachers of the law saw the wonderful

'Hosanna to the Son of David.'

things he did and the children shouting
in the temple area, 'Hosanna to the Son
of David,' they were indignant.
¹⁶ 'Do you hear what these children
are saying?' they asked him.
'Yes,' replied Jesus, 'have you never
read,

"From the lips of children and infants
    you have ordained praise"?'

¹⁷ And he left them and went out of
the city to Bethany, where he spent the
night.

The Fig-Tree Withers

¹⁸ Early in the morning, as he was on his
way back to the city, he was hungry.
¹⁹ Seeing a fig-tree by the road, he went up
to it but found nothing on it except
leaves. Then he said to it, 'May you never
bear fruit again!' Immediately the tree
withered.
²⁰ When the disciples saw this, they
were amazed. 'How did the fig-tree wither
so quickly?' they asked.
²¹ Jesus replied, 'I tell you the truth, if
you have faith and do not doubt, not only
can you do what was done to the fig-tree,
but also you can say to this mountain,
"Go, throw yourself into the sea," and it
will be done. ²² If you believe, you will
receive whatever you ask for in prayer.'

DAY 273

MATT. 21. 23 — 46

The Authority of Jesus Questioned

²³ Jesus entered the temple courts, and, while he was teaching, the chief priests and the elders of the people came to him. 'By what authority are you doing these things?' they asked. 'And who gave you this authority?'

²⁴ Jesus replied, 'I will also ask you one question. If you answer me, I will tell you

---

'By what authority are you doing these things?'

---

by what authority I am doing these things. ²⁵ John's baptism - where did it come from? Was it from heaven, or from men?'

They discussed it among themselves and said, 'If we say, "From heaven", he will ask, "Then why didn't you believe him?" ²⁶ But if we say, "From men" - we are afraid of the people, for they all hold that John was a prophet.'

²⁷ So they answered Jesus, 'We don't know.'

Then he said, 'Neither will I tell you by what authority I am doing these things.

The Parable of the Two Sons

²⁸ 'What do you think? There was a man who had two sons. He went to the first and said, "Son, go and work today in the vineyard."

²⁹ ' "I will not," he answered, but later he changed his mind and went.

³⁰ 'Then the father went to the other son and said the same thing. He answered, "I will, sir," but he did not go.

³¹ 'Which of the two did what his father wanted?'

'The first,' they answered.

Jesus said to them, 'I tell you the truth, the tax collectors and the prostitutes are entering the kingdom of God ahead of you. ³² For John came to you to show you the way of righteousness, and you did not believe him, but the tax collectors and the prostitutes did. And even after you saw this, you did not repent and believe him.

The Parable of the Tenants

³³ 'Listen to another parable: There was a landowner who planted a vineyard. He put a wall around it, dug a winepress in it and built a watchtower. Then he rented the vineyard to some farmers and went away on a journey. ³⁴ When the harvest time approached, he sent his servants to the tenants to collect his fruit.

³⁵ 'The tenants seized his servants; they beat one, killed another, and stoned a third. ³⁶ Then he sent other servants to them, more than the first time, and the tenants treated them in the same way. ³⁷ Last of all, he sent his son to them. "They will respect my son," he said.

³⁸ 'But when the tenants saw the son, they said to each other, "This is the heir. Come, let's kill him and take his inheritance." ³⁹ So they took him and threw him out of the vineyard and killed him.

⁴⁰ 'Therefore, when the owner of the vineyard comes, what will he do to those tenants?'

⁴¹ 'He will bring those wretches to a wretched end,' they replied, 'and he will

ent the vineyard to other tenants, who will give him his share of the crop at harvest time.'

⁴²Jesus said to them, 'Have you never read in the Scriptures:

"The stone the builders rejected
    has become the capstone;
the Lord has done this,
    and it is marvellous in our eyes"?

⁴³'Therefore I tell you that the kingdom of God will be taken away from you and given to a people who will produce its fruit. ⁴⁴He who falls on this stone will be broken to pieces, but he on whom it falls will be crushed.'

⁴⁵When the chief priests and the Pharisees heard Jesus' parables, they knew he was talking about them. ⁴⁶They looked for a way to arrest him, but they were afraid of the crowd because the people held that he was a prophet.

DAY 274

MATT. 22. 1 — 22

22 ### The Parable of the Wedding Banquet

Jesus spoke to them again in parables, saying: ²'The kingdom of heaven is like a king who prepared a wedding banquet for his son. ³He sent his servants to those who had been invited to the banquet to tell them to come, but they refused to come.

⁴'Then he sent some more servants and said, "Tell those who have been invited that I have prepared my dinner: My oxen and fattened cattle have been slaughtered, and everything is ready.

Come to the wedding banquet."

⁵'But they paid no attention and went off - one to his field, another to his business. ⁶The rest seized his servants, ill-treated them and killed them. ⁷The king was enraged. He sent his army and destroyed those murderers and

---

'Go to the street corners and invite to the banquet anyone you find.'

---

burned their city.

⁸'Then he said to his servants, "The wedding banquet is ready, but those I invited did not deserve to come. ⁹Go to the street corners and invite to the banquet anyone you find." ¹⁰So the servants went out into the streets and gathered all the people they could find, both good and bad, and the wedding hall was filled with guests.

¹¹'But when the king came in to see the guests, he noticed a man there who was not wearing wedding clothes. ¹²"Friend," he asked, "how did you get in here without wedding clothes?" The man was speechless.

¹³'Then the king told the attendants, "Tie him hand and foot, and throw him outside, into the darkness, where there will be weeping and gnashing of teeth."

¹⁴'For many are invited, but few are chosen.'

Paying Taxes to Caesar

¹⁵Then the Pharisees went out and laid plans to trap him in his words. ¹⁶They sent their disciples to him along with the Herodians. 'Teacher,' they said, 'we know you are a man of integrity and that you teach the way of God in accordance with

'Many are invited but few are chosen.'

the truth. You aren't swayed by men, because you pay no attention to who they

'Give to Caesar what is Caesar's, and to God what is God's.'

are. [17] Tell us then, what is your opinion? Is it right to pay taxes to Caesar or not?'

[18] But Jesus, knowing their evil intent, said, 'You hypocrites, why are you trying to trap me? [19] Show me the coin used for paying the tax.' They brought him a denarius, [20] and he asked them, 'Whose portrait is this? And whose inscription?'

[21] 'Caesar's,' they replied.

Then he said to them, 'Give to Caesar what is Caesar's, and to God what is God's.'

[22] When they heard this, they were amazed. So they left him and went away.

DAY 275

MATT. 22. 23 — 46

Marriage at the Resurrection

That same day the Sadducees, who say here is no resurrection, came to him with question. ²⁴ 'Teacher,' they said, 'Moses old us that if a man dies without having

---

'Love the Lord your God with all your heart and with all your soul and with all your mind.'

---

children, his brother must marry the widow and have children for him. ²⁵ Now here were seven brothers among us. The first one married and died, and since he had no children, he left his wife to his brother. ²⁶ The same thing happened to he second and third brother, right on own to the seventh. ²⁷ Finally, the woman died. ²⁸ Now then, at the resurrection, whose wife will she be of the even, since all of them were married to her?'

²⁹ Jesus replied, 'You are in error because you do not know the Scriptures or the power of God. ³⁰ At the resurrection people will neither marry nor be given in marriage; they will be like the angels in heaven. ³¹ But about the resurrection of the dead - have you not read what God said to you, ³² "I am the God of Abraham, the God of Isaac, and the God of Jacob"? He is not the God of the dead but of the living.'

³³ When the crowds heard this, they were astonished at his teaching.

The Greatest Commandment

³⁴ Hearing that Jesus had silenced the Sadducees, the Pharisees got together. ³⁵ One of them, an expert in the law, tested him with this question: ³⁶ 'Teacher, which is the greatest commandment in the Law?'

³⁷ Jesus replied: ' "Love the Lord your God with all your heart and with all your soul and with all your mind." ³⁸ This is the first and greatest commandment. ³⁹ And the second is like it: "Love your neighbour as yourself." ⁴⁰ All the Law and the Prophets hang on these two commandments.'

Whose Son Is the Christ?

⁴¹ While the Pharisees were gathered together, Jesus asked them, ⁴² 'What do you think about the Christ? Whose son is he?'

'The son of David,' they replied.

⁴³ He said to them, 'How is it then that David, speaking by the Spirit, calls

---

'What do you think about the Christ? Whose son is he?'

---

him "Lord"? For he says,

⁴⁴ "The Lord said to my Lord:
'Sit at my right hand
until I put your enemies
under your feet.' "

⁴⁵ 'If then David calls him "Lord", how can he be his son?' ⁴⁶ No-one could say a word in reply, and from that day on no-one dared to ask him any more questions.

DAY 276

MATT. 23. 1 — 28

23 Seven Woes

Then Jesus said to the crowds and to his disciples: [2] 'The teachers of the law and the Pharisees sit in Moses' seat. [3] So you must obey them and do everything they tell you. But do not do what they do, for they do not practise what they preach. [4] They tie up heavy loads and put them on men's shoulders, but they themselves are not willing to lift a finger to move them.

[5] 'Everything they do is done for men

'And do not call anyone on earth "father", for you have one Father, and he is in heaven.'

---

to see: They make their phylacteries wide and the tassels on their garments long; [6] they love the place of honour at banquets and the most important seats in the synagogues; [7] they love to be greeted in the market-places and to have men call them "Rabbi".

[8] 'But you are not to be called "Rabbi", for you have only one Master and you are all brothers. [9] And do not call anyone on earth "father", for you have one Father, and he is in heaven. [10] Nor are you to be called "teacher", for you have one Teacher, the Christ. [11] The greatest among you will be your servant. [12] For whoever exalts himself will be humbled, and whoever humbles himself will be exalted.

[13] 'Woe to you, teachers of the law and Pharisees, you hypocrites! You shut the kingdom of heaven in men's faces. You yourselves do not enter, nor will you let those enter who are trying to.

[15] 'Woe to you, teachers of the law and Pharisees, you hypocrites! You travel over land and sea to win a single convert, and when he becomes one, you make him twice as much a son of hell as you are.

[16] 'Woe to you, blind guides! You say, "If anyone swears by the temple, it means nothing; but if anyone swears by the gold of the temple, he is bound by his oath." [17] You blind fools! Which is greater: the gold, or the temple that makes the gold sacred? [18] You also say, "If anyone swears by the altar, it means nothing; but if anyone swears by the gift on it, he is bound by his oath." [19] You blind men! Which is greater: the gift, or the altar that makes the gift sacred? [20] Therefore, he who swears by the altar swears by it and by everything on it. [21] And he who swears by the temple swears by it and by the one who dwells in it. [22] And he who swears by heaven swears by God's throne and by the one who sits on it.

[23] 'Woe to you, teachers of the law and Pharisees, you hypocrites! You give a tenth of your spices - mint, dill and cummin. But you have neglected the more important matters of the law - justice, mercy and faithfulness. You should have practised the latter, without neglecting the former. [24] You blind guides! You strain out a gnat but swallow a camel.

[25] 'Woe to you, teachers of the law and Pharisees, you hypocrites! You clean the outside of the cup and dish, but inside they are full of greed and self-indulgence. [26] Blind Pharisee! First clean the inside of the cup and dish, and then the outside also will be clean.

[27] 'Woe to you, teachers of the law

nd Pharisees, you hypocrites! You are ike whitewashed tombs, which look beautiful on the outside but on the inside are full of dead men's bones and everything unclean. ²⁸ In the same way, on the outside you appear to people as righteous but on the inside you are full of hypocrisy and wickedness.

DAY 277

MATT. 23. 29 — 24.2

⁹ 'Woe to you, teachers of the law and Pharisees, you hypocrites! You build tombs for the prophets and decorate the graves of the righteous. ³⁰ And you say, "If we had lived in the days of our forefathers, we would not have taken part with them in shedding the blood of the prophets." ³¹ So you testify against yourselves that you are the descendants of those who murdered the prophets. ³² Fill up, then, the measure of the sin of your forefathers!

³³ 'You snakes! You brood of vipers! How will you escape being condemned to hell? ³⁴ Therefore I am sending you prophets and wise men and teachers. Some of them you will kill and crucify; others you will flog in your synagogues and pursue from town to town. ³⁵ And so upon you will come all the righteous blood that has been shed on earth, from the blood of righteous Abel to the blood of Zechariah son of Berakiah, whom you murdered between the temple and the altar. ³⁶ I tell you the truth, all this will come upon this generation.

³⁷ 'O Jerusalem, Jerusalem, you who kill the prophets and stone those sent to you, how often I have longed to gather your children together, as a hen gathers her chicks under her wings, but you were not willing. ³⁸ Look, your house is left to you desolate. ³⁹ For I tell you, you will not see me again until you say, "Blessed is he who comes in the name of the Lord." '

24 Signs of the End of the Age

Jesus left the temple and was walking away when his disciples came up to him to call his attention to its buildings. ² 'Do you see all these things?' he asked. 'I tell you the truth, not one stone here will be left on another; every one will be thrown down.'

'Whoever humbles himself will be exalted.'

DAY 278

MATT. 24. 3 — 31

[3] As Jesus was sitting on the Mount of Olives, the disciples came to him privately. 'Tell us,' they said, 'when will this happen, and what will be the sign of your coming and of the end of the age?' [4] Jesus answered: 'Watch out that no-one deceives you. [5] For many will come in my name, claiming, "I am the Christ," and will deceive many. [6] You will hear of wars and rumours of wars, but see to it that you are not alarmed. Such things must happen, but the end is still to come.

'And this gospel of the kingdom will be preached in the whole world as a testimony to all nations.'

---

[7] Nation will rise against nation, and kingdom against kingdom. There will be famines and earthquakes in various places. [8] All these are the beginning of birth-pains.

[9] 'Then you will be handed over to be persecuted and put to death, and you will be hated by all nations because of me. [10] At that time many will turn away from the faith and will betray and hate each other, [11] and many false prophets will appear and deceive many people. [12] Because of the increase of wickedness, the love of most will grow cold, [13] but he who stands firm to the end will be saved. [14] And this gospel of the kingdom will be preached in the whole world as a testimony to all nations, and then the end will come.

[15] 'So when you see standing in the holy place "the abomination that causes desolation", spoken of through the prophet Daniel - let the reader understand - [16] then let those who are in Judea flee to the mountains. [17] Let no-one on the roof of his house go down to take anything out of the house. [18] Let no-one in the field go back to get his cloak. [19] How dreadful it will be in those days for pregnant women and nursing mothers! [20] Pray that your flight will not take place in winter or on the Sabbath. [21] For then there will be great distress, unequalled from the beginning of the world until now - and never to be equalled again. [22] If those days had not been cut short, no-one would survive, but for the sake of the elect those days will be shortened. [23] At that time if anyone says to you, "Look, here is the Christ!" or, "There he is!" do not believe it. [24] For false Christs and false prophets will appear and perform great signs and miracles to deceive even the elect - if that were possible. [25] See, I have told you ahead of time.

[26] 'So if anyone tells you, "There he is, out in the desert," do not go out; or, "Here he is, in the inner rooms," do not believe it. [27] For as lightning that comes from the east is visible even in the west, so will be the coming of the Son of Man. [28] Wherever there is a carcass, there the vultures will gather.

[29] 'Immediately after the distress of those days

"the sun will be darkened,
    and the moon will not give its light;
the stars will fall from the sky,
    and the heavenly bodies will be shaken."

³⁰'At that time the sign of the Son of Man will appear in the sky, and all the nations of the earth will mourn. They will see the Son of Man coming on the clouds of the sky, with power and great glory. ³¹And he will send his angels with a loud trumpet call, and they will gather his elect from the four winds, from one end of the heavens to the other.

DAY 279
MATT. 24. 32 — 25.13

³²Now learn this lesson from the fig-tree: As soon as its twigs get tender and its leaves come out, you know that summer is near. ³³Even so, when you see all these things, you know that it is near, right at the door. ³⁴I tell you the truth, this generation will certainly not pass away until all these things have happened. ³⁵Heaven and earth will pass away, but my words will never pass away.

The Day and Hour Unknown

³⁶'No-one knows about that day or hour, not even the angels in heaven, nor the Son, but only the Father. ³⁷As it was in the days of Noah, so it will be at the coming of the Son of Man. ³⁸For in the days before the flood, people were eating and drinking, marrying and giving in marriage, up to the day Noah entered the ark; ³⁹and they knew nothing about what would happen until the flood came and took them all away. That is how it will be at the coming of the Son of Man. ⁴⁰Two men will be in the field; one will be taken and the other left. ⁴¹Two women will be grinding with a hand mill; one will be taken and the other left.

⁴²'Therefore keep watch, because you do not know on what day your Lord will come. ⁴³But understand this: If the owner of the house had known at what time of night the thief was coming, he would have kept watch and would not have let his house be broken into. ⁴⁴So you also must be ready, because the Son of Man will come at an hour when you do not expect him.

⁴⁵'Who then is the faithful and wise servant, whom the master has put in charge of the servants in his household to give them their food at the proper time? ⁴⁶It will be good for that servant whose master finds him doing so when he returns. ⁴⁷I tell you the truth, he will put him in charge of all his possessions. ⁴⁸But

'Heaven and earth will pass away, but my words will never pass away.'

suppose that servant is wicked and says to himself, "My master is staying away a long time," ⁴⁹and he then begins to beat his fellow-servants and to eat and drink with drunkards. ⁵⁰The master of that servant will come on a day when he does not expect him and at an hour he is not aware of. ⁵¹He will cut him to pieces and assign him a place with the hypocrites, where there will be weeping and gnashing of teeth.'

25 The Parable of the Ten Virgins

'At that time the kingdom of heaven will be like ten virgins who took their lamps and went out to meet the bridegroom. ²Five of them were foolish

'Therefore keep watch, because you do not know the day or the hou

and five were wise. ³ The foolish ones took their lamps but did not take any oil with them. ⁴ The wise, however, took oil in jars along with their lamps. ⁵ The

> **'Therefore keep watch, because you do not know the day or the hour.'**

bridegroom was a long time in coming, and they all became drowsy and fell asleep.

⁶ 'At midnight the cry rang out: "Here's the bridegroom! Come out to meet him!"

⁷ 'Then all the virgins woke up and trimmed their lamps. ⁸ The foolish ones said to the wise, "Give us some of your oil; our lamps are going out."

⁹ ' "No," they replied, "there may not be enough for both us and you. Instead, go to those who sell oil and buy some for yourselves."

¹⁰ 'But while they were on their way to buy the oil, the bridegroom arrived. The virgins who were ready went in with him to the wedding banquet. And the door was shut.

¹¹ 'Later the others also came. "Sir! Sir!" they said. "Open the door for us!"

¹² 'But he replied, "I tell you the truth, I don't know you."

¹³ 'Therefore keep watch, because you do not know the day or the hour.

DAY 280

MATT. 25. 14 — 30

...he Parable of the Talents

...Again, it will be like a man going on a ...urney, who called his servants and ...trusted his property to them. ¹⁵ To one ... gave five talents of money, to another

---

'I will put you in charge of many things. Come and share your master's happiness!'

...o talents, and to another one talent, ...ch according to his ability. Then he ...nt on his journey. ¹⁶ The man who had ...ceived the five talents went at once and ...t his money to work and gained five ...ore. ¹⁷ So also, the one with the two ...lents gained two more. ¹⁸ But the man ...ho had received the one talent went off, ...g a hole in the ground and hid his ...aster's money.

¹⁹ 'After a long time the master of ...ose servants returned and settled ...counts with them. ²⁰ The man who had ...ceived the five talents brought the ...her five. "Master," he said, "you ...trusted me with five talents. See, I ...ve gained five more."

²¹ 'His master replied, "Well done, ...od and faithful servant! You have been ...ithful with a few things; I will put you ... charge of many things. Come and ...are your master's happiness!"

²² 'The man with the two talents also came. "Master," he said, "you entrusted me with two talents; see, I have gained two more."

²³ 'His master replied, "Well done, good and faithful servant! You have been faithful with a few things; I will put you in charge of many things. Come and share your master's happiness!"

²⁴ 'Then the man who had received the one talent came. "Master," he said, "I knew that you are a hard man, harvesting where you have not sown and gathering where you have not scattered seed. ²⁵ So I was afraid and went out and hid your talent in the ground. See, here is what belongs to you."

²⁶ 'His master replied, "You wicked, lazy servant! So you knew that I harvest where I have not sown and gather where I have not scattered seed? ²⁷ Well then, you should have put my money on deposit with the bankers, so that when I returned I would have received it back with interest.

'For everyone who has will be given more, and he will have an abundance.'

---

²⁸ ' "Take the talent from him and give it to the one who has the ten talents. ²⁹ For everyone who has will be given more, and he will have an abundance. Whoever does not have, even what he has will be taken from him. ³⁰ And throw that worthless servant outside, into the darkness, where there will be weeping and gnashing of teeth." '

DAY 281

MATT. 25. 31 — 46

The Sheep and the Goats

[31] 'When the Son of Man comes in his glory, and all the angels with him, he will sit on his throne in heavenly glory. [32] All the nations will be gathered before him, and he will separate the people one from another as a shepherd separates the sheep from the goats. [33] He will put the sheep on his right and the goats on his left.

[34] 'Then the King will say to those on his right, "Come, you who are blessed by my Father; take your inheritance, the kingdom prepared for you since the creation of the world. [35] For I was hungry and you gave me something to eat, I was thirsty and you gave me something to drink, I was a stranger and you invited me in, [36] I needed clothes and you clothed me, I was sick and you looked after me, I was in prison and you came to visit me.

[37] 'Then the righteous will answer him, "Lord, when did we see you hungry and feed you, or thirsty and give you something to drink? [38] When did we see you a stranger and invite you in, or needing clothes and clothe you? [39] When did we see you sick or in prison and go to visit you?"

[40] 'The King will reply, "I tell you the truth, whatever you did for one of the least of these brothers of mine, you did for me."

[41] 'Then he will say to those on his left, "Depart from me, you who are cursed, into the eternal fire prepared for the devil and his angels. [42] For I was hungry and you gave me nothing to eat, I was thirsty and you gave me nothing to drink, [43] I was a stranger and you did not invite me in, I needed clothes and you did not clothe me, I was sick and in prison and you did not look after me."

[44] 'They also will answer, "Lord, when did we see you hungry or thirsty or a

---

'I tell you the truth, whatever you did not do for one of the least of these, you did not do for me.'

---

stranger or needing clothes or sick or in prison, and did not help you?"

[45] 'He will reply, "I tell you the truth, whatever you did not do for one of the least of these, you did not do for me."

[46] 'Then they will go away to eternal punishment, but the righteous to eternal life.'

DAY 282

MATT. 26. 1 — 16

26 The Plot Against Jesus
When Jesus had finished saying all these things, he said to his disciples, [2] 'As you know, the Passover is two days away - and the Son of Man will be handed over to be crucified.'

[3] Then the chief priests and the elders of the people assembled in the palace of the high priest, whose name was Caiaphas, [4] and they plotted to arrest Jesus in some sly way and kill him. [5] 'But not during the Feast,' they said, 'or there may be a riot among the people.'

'I tell you the truth, whatever you did for one of the least of these brothers of mine, you did for me.'

Jesus Anointed at Bethany

While Jesus was in Bethany in the home of a man known as Simon the Leper, [7] a woman came to him with an alabaster jar of very expensive perfume, which she poured on his head as he was reclining at the table.

[8] When the disciples saw this, they were indignant. 'Why this waste?' they asked. [9] 'This perfume could have been sold at a high price and the money given to the poor.'

[10] Aware of this, Jesus said to them, 'Why are you bothering this woman? She has done a beautiful thing to me. [11] The poor you will always have with you, but you will not always have me. [12] When she poured this perfume on my body, she did to prepare me for burial. [13] I tell you the truth, wherever this gospel is preached throughout the world, what she has done will also be told, in memory of her.'

Judas Agrees to Betray Jesus

[14] Then one of the Twelve - the one called Judas Iscariot - went to the chief priests

> 'This perfume could have been sold at a high price and the money given to the poor.'

[15] and asked, 'What are you willing to give me if I hand him over to you?' So they counted out for him thirty silver coins. [16] From then on Judas watched for an opportunity to hand him over.

DAY 283

MATT. 26. 17 — 35

The Lord's Supper

¹⁷ On the first day of the Feast of Unleavened Bread, the disciples came to Jesus and asked, 'Where do you want us to make preparations for you to eat the Passover?'

¹⁸ He replied, 'Go into the city to a certain man and tell him, "The Teacher says: My appointed time is near. I am going to celebrate the Passover with my disciples at your house." ' ¹⁹ So the disciples did as Jesus had directed them and prepared the Passover.

²⁰ When evening came, Jesus was reclining at the table with the Twelve. ²¹ And while they were eating, he said, 'I tell you the truth, one of you will betray me.'

²² They were very sad and began to say to him one after the other, 'Surely not I, Lord?'

> **'But woe to that man who betrays the Son of Man! It would be better for him if he had not been born.'**

²³ Jesus replied, 'The one who has dipped his hand into the bowl with me will betray me. ²⁴ The Son of Man will go just as it is written about him. But woe to that man who betrays the Son of Man! It would be better for him if he had not been born.'

²⁵ Then Judas, the one who would betray him, said, 'Surely not I, Rabbi?'

Jesus answered, 'Yes, it is you.'

²⁶ While they were eating, Jesus took bread, gave thanks and broke it, and gave it to his disciples, saying, 'Take and eat; this is my body.'

²⁷ Then he took the cup, gave thanks and offered it to them, saying, 'Drink

> **'This is my blood of the covenant, which is poured out for many for the forgiveness of sins.'**

from it, all of you. ²⁸ This is my blood of the covenant, which is poured out for many for the forgiveness of sins. ²⁹ I tell you, I will not drink of this fruit of the vine from now on until that day when I drink it anew with you in my Father's kingdom.'

³⁰ When they had sung a hymn, they went out to the Mount of Olives.

Jesus Predicts Peter's Denial

³¹ Then Jesus told them, 'This very night you will all fall away on account of me, for it is written:

> "I will strike the shepherd,
>   and the sheep of the flock will be
>   scattered."

³² But after I have risen, I will go ahead of you into Galilee.'

³³ Peter replied, 'Even if all fall away on account of you, I never will.'

³⁴ 'I tell you the truth,' Jesus answered 'this very night, before the cock crows, you will disown me three times.'

³⁵ But Peter declared, 'Even if I have to die with you, I will never disown you.' And all the other disciples said the same.

DAY 284

MATT. 26. 36 — 56

Gethsemane

[36] Then Jesus went with his disciples to a place called Gethsemane, and he said to them, 'Sit here while I go over there and pray.' [37] He took Peter and the two sons of Zebedee along with him, and he began to be sorrowful and troubled. [38] Then he said to them, 'My soul is overwhelmed with sorrow to the point of death. Stay here and keep watch with me.'

[39] Going a little farther, he fell with his face to the ground and prayed, 'My Father, if it is possible, may this cup be taken from me. Yet not as I will, but as you will.'

[40] Then he returned to his disciples and found them sleeping. 'Could you men not keep watch with me for one hour?' he asked Peter. [41] 'Watch and pray so that you will not fall into temptation. The spirit is willing, but the body is weak.'

[42] He went away a second time and prayed, 'My Father, if it is not possible for this cup to be taken away unless I drink it, may your will be done.'

[43] When he came back, he again found them sleeping, because their eyes were heavy. [44] So he left them and went away once more and prayed the third time, saying the same thing.

[45] Then he returned to the disciples and said to them, 'Are you still sleeping and resting? Look, the hour is near, and the Son of Man is betrayed into the hands of sinners. [46] Rise, let us go! Here comes my betrayer!'

Jesus Arrested

[47] While he was still speaking, Judas, one of the Twelve, arrived. With him was a large crowd armed with swords and clubs, sent from the chief priests and the elders of the people. [48] Now the betrayer had arranged a signal with them: 'The one I kiss is the man; arrest him.' [49] Going at once to Jesus, Judas said, 'Greetings, Rabbi!' and kissed him.

[50] Jesus replied, 'Friend, do what you came for.'

Then the men stepped forward, seized Jesus and arrested him. [51] With that, one of Jesus' companions reached for his sword, drew it out and struck the servant of the high priest, cutting off his ear.

[52] 'Put your sword back in its place,' Jesus said to him, 'for all who draw the sword will die by the sword. [53] Do you think I cannot call on my Father, and he will at once put at my disposal more than twelve legions of angels? [54] But how then

---

'My Father, if it is not possible for this cup to be taken away unless I drink it, may your will be done.'

---

would the Scriptures be fulfilled that say it must happen in this way?'

[55] At that time Jesus said to the crowd, 'Am I leading a rebellion, that you have come out with swords and clubs to capture me? Every day I sat in the temple courts teaching, and you did not arrest me. [56] But this has all taken place that the writings of the prophets might be fulfilled.' Then all the disciples deserted him and fled.

DAY 285

MATT. 26. 57 — 75

Before the Sanhedrin

57 Those who had arrested Jesus took him to Caiaphas, the high priest, where the teachers of the law and the elders had assembled. 58 But Peter followed him at a distance, right up to the courtyard of the high priest. He entered and sat down with the guards to see the outcome.

59 The chief priests and the whole Sanhedrin were looking for false evidence against Jesus so that they could put him to death. 60 But they did not find any, though many false witnesses came forward.

Finally two came forward 61 and declared, 'This fellow said, "I am able to destroy the temple of God and rebuild it in three days." '

62 Then the high priest stood up and said to Jesus, 'Are you not going to answer? What is this testimony that these men are bringing against you?' 63 But Jesus

---

'Are you not going to answer?'

---

remained silent.

The high priest said to him, 'I charge you under oath by the living God: Tell us if you are the Christ, the Son of God.'

64 'Yes, it is as you say,' Jesus replied. 'But I say to all of you: In the future you will see the Son of Man sitting at the right hand of the Mighty One and coming on the clouds of heaven.'

65 Then the high priest tore his

clothes and said, 'He has spoken blasphemy! Why do we need any more witnesses? Look, now you have heard the blasphemy. 66 What do you think?'

'He is worthy of death,' they answered.

67 Then they spat in his face and struck him with their fists. Others slapped

---

'In the future you will see the Son of Man sitting at the right hand of the Mighty One...'

---

him 68 and said, 'Prophesy to us, Christ. Who hit you?'

Peter Disowns Jesus

69 Now Peter was sitting out in the courtyard, and a servant girl came to him. 'You also were with Jesus of Galilee,' she said.

70 But he denied it before them all. 'I don't know what you're talking about,' he said.

71 Then he went out to the gateway, where another girl saw him and said to the people there, 'This fellow was with Jesus of Nazareth.'

72 He denied it again, with an oath: 'I don't know the man!'

73 After a little while, those standing there went up to Peter and said, 'Surely you are one of them, for your accent gives you away.'

74 Then he began to call down curses on himself and he swore to them, 'I don't know the man!'

Immediately a cock crowed. 75 Then Peter remembered the word Jesus had spoken: 'Before the cock crows, you will disown me three times.' And he went outside and wept bitterly.

DAY 286
MATT. 27. 1 — 26

27

Judas Hangs Himself

Early in the morning, all the chief priests and the elders of the people came to the decision to put Jesus to death. ² They bound him, led him away and handed him over to Pilate, the governor.

³ When Judas, who had betrayed him, saw that Jesus was condemned, he was seized with remorse and returned the thirty silver coins to the chief priests and the elders. ⁴ 'I have sinned,' he said, 'for I have betrayed innocent blood.'

'What is that to us?' they replied. 'That's your responsibility.'

⁵ So Judas threw the money into the temple and left. Then he went away and hanged himself.

⁶ The chief priests picked up the coins and said, 'It is against the law to put this into the treasury, since it is blood money.' ⁷ So they decided to use the money to buy the potter's field as a burial place for foreigners. ⁸ That is why it has been called the Field of Blood to this day. ⁹ Then what was spoken by Jeremiah the prophet was fulfilled: 'They took the thirty silver coins, the price set on him by the people of Israel, ¹⁰ and they used them to buy the potter's field, as the Lord commanded me.'

Jesus Before Pilate

¹ Meanwhile Jesus stood before the governor, and the governor asked him, 'Are you the king of the Jews?'

'Yes, it is as you say,' Jesus replied.
¹² When he was accused by the chief priests and the elders, he gave no answer.

¹³ Then Pilate asked him, 'Don't you hear the testimony they are bringing against you?' ¹⁴ But Jesus made no reply, not even to a single charge - to the great amazement of the governor.

¹⁵ Now it was the governor's custom at the Feast to release a prisoner chosen by the crowd. ¹⁶ At that time they had a notorious prisoner, called Barabbas. ¹⁷ So when the crowd had gathered, Pilate asked them, 'Which one do you want me to release to you: Barabbas, or Jesus who is called Christ?' ¹⁸ For he knew it was out of envy that they had handed Jesus over to him.

¹⁹ While Pilate was sitting on the judge's seat, his wife sent him this message: 'Don't have anything to do with that innocent man, for I have suffered a great deal today in a dream because of him.'

²⁰ But the chief priests and the elders persuaded the crowd to ask for Barabbas and to have Jesus executed.

²¹ 'Which of the two do you want me to release to you?' asked the governor.

'Barabbas,' they answered.
²² 'What shall I do, then, with Jesus who is called Christ?' Pilate asked.

They all answered, 'Crucify him!'
²³ 'Why? What crime has he committed?' asked Pilate.

But they shouted all the louder, 'Crucify him!'

²⁴ When Pilate saw that he was getting nowhere, but that instead an uproar was starting, he took water and washed his hands in front of the crowd. 'I am innocent of this man's blood,' he said. 'It is your responsibility!'

²⁵ All the people answered, 'Let his blood be on us and on our children!'
²⁶ Then he released Barabbas to them. But he had Jesus flogged, and handed him over to be crucified.

DAY 287

MATT. 27. 27 — 44

The Soldiers Mock Jesus

27 Then the governor's soldiers took Jesus into the Praetorium and gathered the whole company of soldiers round him. 28 They stripped him and put a scarlet robe on him, 29 and then twisted together a crown of thorns and set it on his head. They put a staff in his right hand and knelt in front of him and mocked him. 'Hail, king of the Jews!' they said. 30 They spat on him, and took the staff and struck him on the head again and again. 31 After they had mocked him, they took off the robe and put his own clothes on him. Then they led him away to crucify him.

The Crucifixion

32 As they were going out, they met a man from Cyrene, named Simon, and they forced him to carry the cross. 33 They came to a place called Golgotha (which means The Place of the Skull). 34 There they offered Jesus wine to drink, mixed

---

'My God, my God, why have you forsaken me?'

---

with gall; but after tasting it, he refused to drink it. 35 When they had crucified him, they divided up his clothes by casting lots. 36 And sitting down, they kept watch over him there. 37 Above his head they placed the written charge against him: **THIS IS JESUS, THE KING OF THE JEWS**. 38 Two robbers were crucified with

him, one on his right and one on his left. 39 Those who passed by hurled insults at him, shaking their heads 40 and saying, 'You who are going to destroy the temple and build it in three days, save yourself! Come down from the cross, if you are the Son of God!'

41 In the same way the chief priests, the teachers of the law and the elders mocked him. 42 'He saved others,' they said, 'but he can't save himself! He's the King of Israel! Let him come down now from the cross, and we will believe in him. 43 He trusts in God. Let God rescue him now if he wants him, for he said, "I am the Son of God." ' 44 In the same way the robbers who were crucified with him also heaped insults on him.

DAY 288

MATT. 27. 45 — 66

The Death of Jesus

45 From the sixth hour until the ninth hour darkness came over all the land. 46 About the ninth hour Jesus cried out in a loud voice, 'Eloi, Eloi, lama sabachthani?' - which means, 'My God, my God, why have you forsaken me?'

47 When some of those standing there heard this, they said, 'He's calling Elijah.' 48 Immediately one of them ran and got a sponge. He filled it with wine vinegar, put it on a stick, and offered it to Jesus to drink. 49 The rest said, 'Now leave him alone. Let's see if Elijah comes to save him.'

50 And when Jesus had cried out again in a loud voice, he gave up his spirit. 51 At that moment the curtain of the temple was torn in two from top to

bottom. The earth shook and the rocks split. ⁵²The tombs broke open and the bodies of many holy people who had died were raised to life. ⁵³They came out of the tombs, and after Jesus' resurrection they went into the holy city and appeared to many people.

⁵⁴When the centurion and those with him who were guarding Jesus saw the earthquake and all that had happened, they were terrified, and exclaimed, 'Surely he was the Son of God!'

⁵⁵Many women were there, watching from a distance. They had followed Jesus from Galilee to care for his needs. ⁵⁶Among them were Mary Magdalene, Mary the mother of James and Joses, and the mother of Zebedee's sons.

The Burial of Jesus

⁵⁷As evening approached, there came a rich man from Arimathea, named Joseph, who had himself become a disciple of Jesus. ⁵⁸Going to Pilate, he asked for Jesus' body, and Pilate ordered that it be given to him. ⁵⁹Joseph took the body, wrapped it in a clean linen cloth, ⁶⁰and placed it in his own new tomb that he had cut out of the rock. He rolled a big stone in front of the entrance to the tomb and went away. ⁶¹Mary Magdalene and the other Mary were sitting there opposite the tomb.

The Guard at the Tomb

⁶²The next day, the one after Preparation Day, the chief priests and the Pharisees went to Pilate. ⁶³'Sir,' they said, 'we remember that while he was still alive that deceiver said, "After three days I will rise again." ⁶⁴So give the order for the tomb to be made secure until the third day. Otherwise, his disciples may come and steal the body and tell the people that he has been raised from the dead. This last deception will be worse than the first.'

⁶⁵'Take a guard,' Pilate answered. 'Go, make the tomb as secure as you know how.' ⁶⁶So they went and made the tomb secure by putting a seal on the stone and posting the guard.

'Surely he was the Son of God!'

DAY 289

MATT. 28. 1 — 20

28 The Resurrection

After the Sabbath, at dawn on the first day of the week, Mary Magdalene and the other Mary went to look at the tomb.

[2] There was a violent earthquake, for an angel of the Lord came down from heaven and, going to the tomb, rolled back the stone and sat on it. [3] His appearance was like lightning, and his clothes were white as snow. [4] The guards

> **'He has risen from the dead and is going ahead of you into Galilee. There you will see him.'**

were so afraid of him that they shook and became like dead men.

[5] The angel said to the women, 'Do not be afraid, for I know that you are looking for Jesus, who was crucified. [6] He is not here; he has risen, just as he said. Come and see the place where he lay. [7] Then go quickly and tell his disciples: "He has risen from the dead and is going ahead of you into Galilee. There you will see him." Now I have told you.'

[8] So the women hurried away from the tomb, afraid yet filled with joy, and ran to tell his disciples. [9] Suddenly Jesus met them. 'Greetings,' he said. They came to him, clasped his feet and worshipped him. [10] Then Jesus said to them, 'Do not be afraid. Go and tell my brothers to go to Galilee; there they will see me.'

The Guards' Report

[11] While the women were on their way, some of the guards went into the city and reported to the chief priests everything that had happened. [12] When the chief priests had met with the elders and devised a plan, they gave the soldiers a large sum of money, [13] telling them, 'You are to say, "His disciples came during the night and stole him away while we were asleep." [14] If this report gets to the governor, we will satisfy him and keep you out of trouble.' [15] So the soldiers took the money and did as they were instructed. And this story has been widely circulated among the Jews to this very day.

The Great Commission

[16] Then the eleven disciples went to Galilee, to the mountain where Jesus had told them to go. [17] When they saw him, they worshipped him; but some doubted. [18] Then Jesus came to them and said, 'All authority in heaven and on

> **'All authority in heaven and on earth has been given to me.'**

earth has been given to me. [19] Therefore go and make disciples of all nations, baptising them in the name of the Father and of the Son and of the Holy Spirit, [20] and teaching them to obey everything I have commanded you. And surely I am with you always, to the very end of the age.'

DAY 290

JAMES 1. 1 — 18

1 James, a servant of God and of the Lord Jesus Christ.

To the twelve tribes scattered among the nations:

Greetings.

Trials and Temptations

² Consider it pure joy, my brothers, whenever you face trials of many kinds, ³ because you know that the testing of your faith develops perseverance. ⁴ Perseverance must finish its work so that you may be mature and complete, not lacking anything. ⁵ If any of you lacks wisdom, he should ask God, who gives generously to all without finding fault, and it will be given to him. ⁶ But when he asks, he must believe and not doubt, because he who doubts is like a wave of the sea, blown and tossed by the wind. ⁷ That man should not think he will receive anything from the Lord; ⁸ he is a double-minded man, unstable in all he does.

⁹ The brother in humble circumstances ought to take pride in his high position. ¹⁰ But the one who is rich should take pride in his low position, because he will pass away like a wild flower. ¹¹ For the sun rises with scorching heat and withers the plant; its blossom falls and its beauty is destroyed. In the same way, the rich man will fade away even while he goes about his business.

¹² Blessed is the man who perseveres under trial, because when he has stood

Every good and perfect gift is from above.

the test, he will receive the crown of life that God has promised to those who love him.

¹³ When tempted, no-one should say, 'God is tempting me.' For God cannot be tempted by evil, nor does he tempt anyone; ¹⁴ but each one is tempted when, by his own evil desire, he is dragged away and enticed. ¹⁵ Then, after desire has conceived, it gives birth to sin; and sin, when it is full-grown, gives birth to death.

¹⁶ Don't be deceived, my dear brothers. ¹⁷ Every good and perfect gift is from above, coming down from the Father of the heavenly lights, who does not change like shifting shadows. ¹⁸ He chose to give us birth through the word of truth, that we might be a kind of firstfruits of all he created.

DAY 291
JAMES 1. 19 — 2.13

Listening and Doing

[19] My dear brothers, take note of this: Everyone should be quick to listen, slow to speak and slow to become angry, [20] for man's anger does not bring about the righteous life that God desires. [21] Therefore, get rid of all moral filth and the evil that is so prevalent, and humbly accept the word planted in you, which can save you.

[22] Do not merely listen to the word, and so deceive yourselves. Do what it says. [23] Anyone who listens to the word but does not do what it says is like a man who looks at his face in a mirror [24] and, after looking at himself, goes away and immediately forgets what he looks like. [25] But the man who looks intently into the perfect law that gives freedom, and continues to do this, not forgetting what he has heard, but doing it - he will be blessed in what he does.

[26] If anyone considers himself religious and yet does not keep a tight rein on his tongue, he deceives himself and his religion is worthless. [27] Religion that God our Father accepts as pure and faultless is this: to look after orphans and widows in their distress and to keep oneself from being polluted by the world.

2 Favouritism Forbidden

My brothers, as believers in our glorious Lord Jesus Christ, don't show favouritism. [2] Suppose a man comes into your meeting wearing a gold ring and fine clothes, and a poor man in shabby clothes also comes in. [3] If you show special attention to the man wearing fine clothes and say, 'Here's a good seat for you,' but say to the poor man, 'You stand there' or 'Sit on the floor by my feet,' [4] have you

Do not merely listen to the word.
Do what it says...

not discriminated among yourselves and become judges with evil thoughts?

⁵ Listen, my dear brothers: Has not God chosen those who are poor in the eyes of the world to be rich in faith and to inherit the kingdom he promised those who love him? ⁶ But you have insulted the poor. Is it not the rich who are exploiting you? Are they not the ones who are dragging you into court? ⁷ Are they not the ones who are slandering the noble name of him to whom you belong?

⁸ If you really keep the royal law found in Scripture, 'Love your neighbour as yourself,' you are doing right. ⁹ But if you show favouritism, you sin and are convicted by the law as law-breakers. ¹⁰ For whoever keeps the whole law and yet stumbles at just one point is guilty of breaking all of it. ¹¹ For he who said, 'Do not commit adultery,' also said, 'Do not murder.' If you do not commit adultery but do commit murder, you have become a law-breaker.

¹² Speak and act as those who are going to be judged by the law that gives freedom, ¹³ because judgment without mercy will be shown to anyone who has not been merciful. Mercy triumphs over judgment!

DAY 292

JAMES 2. 14 — 26

Faith and Deeds

¹⁴ What good is it, my brothers, if a man claims to have faith but has no deeds? Can such faith save him? ¹⁵ Suppose a brother or sister is without clothes and daily food. ¹⁶ If one of you says to him, 'Go, I wish you well; keep warm and well fed,' but does nothing about his physical needs, what good is it? ¹⁷ In the same way, faith by itself, if it is not accompanied by

...faith by itself, if it is not accompanied by action, is dead.

action, is dead.

¹⁸ But someone will say, 'You have faith; I have deeds.'

Show me your faith without deeds, and I will show you my faith by what I do. ¹⁹ You believe that there is one God. Good! Even the demons believe that - and shudder.

²⁰ You foolish man, do you want evidence that faith without deeds is useless? ²¹ Was not our ancestor Abraham considered righteous for what he did when he offered his son Isaac on the altar? ²² You see that his faith and his actions were working together, and his

As the body without the spirit is dead, so faith without deeds is dead.

faith was made complete by what he did. ²³ And the scripture was fulfilled that says, 'Abraham believed God, and it was credited to him as righteousness,' and he was called God's friend. ²⁴ You see that a person is justified by what he does and not by faith alone.

²⁵ In the same way, was not even Rahab the prostitute considered righteous for what she did when she gave lodging to the spies and sent them off in a different direction? ²⁶ As the body without the spirit is dead, so faith without deeds is dead.

DAY 293

JAMES 3. 1 — 18

3 **Taming the Tongue**
Not many of you should presume to be teachers, my brothers, because you know that we who teach will be judged more strictly. [2] We all stumble in many ways. If anyone is never at fault in what he says, he is a perfect man, able to keep his whole body in check.

> **Who is wise and understanding among you? Let him show it by his good life, by deeds done in the humility that comes from wisdom.**

[3] When we put bits into the mouths of horses to make them obey us, we can turn the whole animal. [4] Or take ships as an example. Although they are so large and are driven by strong winds, they are steered by a very small rudder wherever the pilot wants to go. [5] Likewise the tongue is a small part of the body, but it makes great boasts. Consider what a great forest is set on fire by a small spark. [6] The tongue also is a fire, a world of evil among the parts of the body. It corrupts the whole person, sets the whole course of his life on fire, and is itself set on fire by hell.

[7] All kinds of animals, birds, reptiles and creatures of the sea are being tamed and have been tamed by man, [8] but no man can tame the tongue. It is a restless evil, full of deadly poison.

[9] With the tongue we praise our Lord and Father, and with it we curse men, who have been made in God's likeness. [10] Out of the same mouth come praise and cursing. My brothers, this should not be. [11] Can both fresh water and salt water flow from the same spring? [12] My brothers, can a fig-tree bear olives, or a grapevine bear figs? Neither can a salt spring produce fresh water.

Two Kinds of Wisdom

[13] Who is wise and understanding among you? Let him show it by his good life, by deeds done in the humility that comes from wisdom. [14] But if you harbour bitter envy and selfish ambition in your hearts, do not boast about it or deny the truth. [15] Such 'wisdom' does not come down from heaven but is earthly, unspiritual, of the devil. [16] For where you have envy and selfish ambition, there you find disorder and every evil practice.

[17] But the wisdom that comes from heaven is first of all pure; then peace-loving, considerate, submissive, full of mercy and good fruit, impartial and sincere. [18] Peacemakers who sow in peace raise a harvest of righteousness.

DAY 294

JAMES 4. 1 — 17

4 **Submit Yourselves to God**
What causes fights and quarrels among you? Don't they come from your desires that battle within you? [2] You want something but don't get it. You kill and covet, but you cannot have what you want. You quarrel and fight. You do not have, because you do not ask God. [3] When you ask, you do not receive, because you ask with wrong motives, that you may spend what you get on

your pleasures.

⁴You adulterous people, don't you know that friendship with the world is hatred towards God? Anyone who chooses to be a friend of the world becomes an enemy of God. ⁵Or do you think Scripture says without reason that the spirit he caused to live in us envies intensely? ⁶But he gives us more grace. That is why Scripture says:

'God opposes the proud
    but gives grace to the humble.'

⁷Submit yourselves, then, to God. Resist the devil, and he will flee from you. ⁸Come near to God and he will come near to you. Wash your hands, you sinners, and purify your hearts, you double-minded. ⁹Grieve, mourn and wail. Change your laughter to mourning and your joy to gloom. ¹⁰Humble yourselves before the Lord, and he will lift you up.

¹¹Brothers, do not slander one another. Anyone who speaks against his brother or judges him speaks against the law and judges it. When you judge the law, you are not keeping it, but sitting in judgment on it. ¹²There is only one Lawgiver and Judge, the one who is able to save and destroy. But you - who are you to judge your neighbour?

Boasting About Tomorrow

¹³Now listen, you who say, 'Today or tomorrow we will go to this or that city, spend a year there, carry on business and make money.' ¹⁴Why, you do not even know what will happen tomorrow. What is your life? You are a mist that appears for a little while and then vanishes. ¹⁵Instead, you ought to say, 'If it is the Lord's will, we will live and do this or that.' ¹⁶As it is, you boast and brag. All such boasting is evil. ¹⁷Anyone, then, who knows the good he ought to do and doesn't do it, sins.

Come near to God and he will come near to you.

DAY 295

JAMES 5. 1 — 20

5 Warning to Rich Oppressors

Now listen, you rich people, weep and wail because of the misery that is coming upon you. [2] Your wealth has rotted, and moths have eaten your clothes. [3] Your gold and silver are corroded. Their corrosion will testify against you and eat your flesh like fire. You have hoarded wealth in the last days.

> **Therefore confess your sins to each other and pray for each other so that you may be healed.**

[4] Look! The wages you failed to pay the workmen who mowed your fields are crying out against you. The cries of the harvesters have reached the ears of the Lord Almighty. [5] You have lived on earth in luxury and self-indulgence. You have fattened yourselves in the day of slaughter. [6] You have condemned and murdered innocent men, who were not opposing you.

Patience in Suffering

[7] Be patient, then, brothers, until the Lord's coming. See how the farmer waits for the land to yield its valuable crop and how patient he is for the autumn and spring rains. [8] You too, be patient and stand firm, because the Lord's coming is near. [9] Don't grumble against each other, brothers, or you will be judged. The Judge is standing at the door!

[10] Brothers, as an example of patience in the face of suffering, take the prophets who spoke in the name of the Lord. [11] As you know, we consider blessed those who have persevered. You have heard of Job's perseverance and have seen what the Lord finally brought about. The Lord is full of compassion and mercy.

[12] Above all, my brothers, do not swear - not by heaven or by earth or by anything else. Let your 'Yes' be yes, and your 'No', no, or you will be condemned.

The Prayer of Faith

[13] Is any one of you in trouble? He should pray. Is anyone happy? Let him sing songs of praise. [14] Is any one of you sick? He should call the elders of the church to pray over him and anoint him with oil in the name of the Lord. [15] And the prayer offered in faith will make the sick person well; the Lord will raise him up. If he has sinned, he will be forgiven. [16] Therefore confess your sins to each other and pray for each other so that you may be healed. The prayer of a righteous man is powerful and effective.

[17] Elijah was a man just like us. He prayed earnestly that it would not rain, and it did not rain on the land for three and a half years. [18] Again he prayed, and the heavens gave rain, and the earth produced its crops.

[19] My brothers, if one of you should wander from the truth and someone should bring him back, [20] remember this: Whoever turns a sinner from the error of his way will save him from death and cover over a multitude of sins.

DAY 296

LUKE 1. 1 — 25

1 Introduction

Many have undertaken to draw up an account of the things that have been fulfilled among us, ² just as they were handed down to us by those who from the first were eye-witnesses and servants of the word. ³ Therefore, since I myself have carefully investigated everything from the beginning, it seemed good also to me to write an orderly account for you, most excellent Theophilus, ⁴ so that you may know the certainty of the things you have been taught.

The Birth of John the Baptist Foretold

⁵ In the time of Herod king of Judea there was a priest named Zechariah, who belonged to the priestly division of Abijah; his wife Elizabeth was also a descendant of Aaron. ⁶ Both of them were upright in the sight of God, observing all the Lord's commandments and regulations blamelessly. ⁷ But they had no children, because Elizabeth was barren; and they were both well on in years.

⁸ Once when Zechariah's division was on duty and he was serving as priest before God, ⁹ he was chosen by lot, according to the custom of the priesthood, to go into the temple of the Lord and burn incense. ¹⁰ And when the time for the burning of incense came, all the assembled worshippers were praying outside.

Then an angel of the Lord appeared to him, standing at the right side of the altar of incense. ¹² When Zechariah saw him, he was startled and was gripped with fear. ¹³ But the angel said to him: 'Do not be afraid, Zechariah; your prayer has been heard. Your wife Elizabeth will bear you a son, and you are to give him the name John. ¹⁴ He will be a joy and delight to you, and many will rejoice because of his birth, ¹⁵ for he will be great in the sight of the Lord. He is never to take wine or other fermented drink, and he will be filled with the Holy Spirit even from birth. ¹⁶ Many of the people of Israel will he bring back to the Lord their God. ¹⁷ And he will go on before the Lord, in the spirit and power of Elijah, to turn the hearts of the fathers to their children and the disobedient to the wisdom of the righteous - to make ready a people prepared for the Lord.'

¹⁸ Zechariah asked the angel, 'How can I be sure of this? I am an old man and my wife is well on in years.'

¹⁹ The angel answered, 'I am Gabriel. I stand in the presence of God, and I have been sent to speak to you and to tell you this good news. ²⁰ And now you will be silent and not able to speak until the day this happens, because you did not believe my words, which will come true at their proper time.'

²¹ Meanwhile, the people were waiting for Zechariah and wondering why he stayed so long in the temple. ²² When he came out, he could not speak to them. They realised he had seen a vision in the temple, for he kept making signs to them but remained unable to speak.

²³ When his time of service was completed, he returned home. ²⁴ After this his wife Elizabeth became pregnant and for five months remained in seclusion. ²⁵ 'The Lord has done this for me,' she said. 'In these days he has shown his favour and taken away my disgrace among the people.'

DAY 297

LUKE 1. 26 — 56

The Birth of Jesus Foretold

²⁶ In the sixth month, God sent the angel Gabriel to Nazareth, a town in Galilee, ²⁷ to a virgin pledged to be married to a man named Joseph, a descendant of David. The virgin's name was Mary. ²⁸ The angel went to her and said, 'Greetings, you who are highly favoured! The Lord is with you.'

²⁹ Mary was greatly troubled at his words and wondered what kind of greeting this might be. ³⁰ But the angel said to her, 'Do not be afraid, Mary, you

---

'For nothing is impossible with God.'

---

have found favour with God. ³¹ You will be with child and give birth to a son, and you are to give him the name Jesus. ³² He will be great and will be called the Son of the Most High. The Lord God will give him the throne of his father David, ³³ and he will reign over the house of Jacob for ever; his kingdom will never end.'

³⁴ 'How will this be,' Mary asked the angel, 'since I am a virgin?'

³⁵ The angel answered, 'The Holy Spirit will come upon you, and the power of the Most High will overshadow you. So the holy one to be born will be called the Son of God. ³⁶ Even Elizabeth your relative is going to have a child in her old age, and she who was said to be barren is in her sixth month. ³⁷ For nothing is

impossible with God.'

³⁸ 'I am the Lord's servant,' Mary answered. 'May it be to me as you have said.' Then the angel left her.

Mary Visits Elizabeth

³⁹ At that time Mary got ready and hurried to a town in the hill country of Judea, ⁴⁰ where she entered Zechariah's home and greeted Elizabeth. ⁴¹ When Elizabeth heard Mary's greeting, the baby leaped in her womb, and Elizabeth was filled with the Holy Spirit. ⁴² In a loud voice she exclaimed: 'Blessed are you among women, and blessed is the child you will bear! ⁴³ But why am I so favoured, that the mother of my Lord should come to me? ⁴⁴ As soon as the sound of your greeting reached my ears, the baby in my womb leaped for joy. ⁴⁵ Blessed is she who has believed that what the Lord has said to her will be accomplished!'

Mary's Song

⁴⁶ And Mary said:
    'My soul glorifies the Lord
⁴⁷   and my spirit rejoices in
            God my Saviour,
⁴⁸ for he has been mindful
        of the humble state of his
            servant.
    From now on all generations
            will call me blessed,
⁴⁹   for the Mighty One has
            done great things for me -
        holy is his name.
⁵⁰ His mercy extends to those
            who fear him,
        from generation to generation.
⁵¹ He has performed mighty
            deeds with his arm;
        he has scattered those who
            are proud in their inmost
            thoughts.
⁵² He has brought down rulers

from their thrones
but has lifted up the
humble.
[53] He has filled the hungry with
good things
but has sent the rich away empty.
[54] He has helped his servant
Israel
remembering to be
merciful
[55] to Abraham and his
descendants for ever,
even as he said to our
fathers.'

'He has filled the hungry with good things...'

[56] Mary stayed with Elizabeth for about three months and then returned home.

'Blessed is she who has believed that what the Lord has said to her will be accomplished!'

DAY 298
LUKE 1. 57 — 80

The Birth of John the Baptist

⁵⁷ When it was time for Elizabeth to have her baby, she gave birth to a son. ⁵⁸ Her neighbours and relatives heard that the Lord had shown her great mercy, and they shared her joy.

⁵⁹ On the eighth day they came to circumcise the child, and they were going to name him after his father Zechariah, ⁶⁰ but his mother spoke up and said, 'No! He is to be called John.'

⁶¹ They said to her, 'There is no-one among your relatives who has that name.'

⁶² Then they made signs to his father, to find out what he would like to name

---

> Her neighbours and relatives heard that the Lord had shown her great mercy, and they shared her joy.

---

the child. ⁶³ He asked for a writing tablet, and to everyone's astonishment he wrote, 'His name is John.' ⁶⁴ Immediately his mouth was opened and his tongue was loosed, and he began to speak, praising God. ⁶⁵ The neighbours were all filled with awe, and throughout the hill country of Judea people were talking about all these things. ⁶⁶ Everyone who heard this wondered about it, asking, 'What then is this child going to be?' For the Lord's hand was with him.

Zechariah's Song

⁶⁷ His father Zechariah was filled with the Holy Spirit and prophesied:

⁶⁸ 'Praise be to the Lord, the God of Israel,
 because he has come and
  has redeemed his people.
⁶⁹ He has raised up a horn of
  salvation for us
 in the house of his servant
  David
⁷⁰ (as he said through his holy
  prophets of long ago),
⁷¹ salvation from our enemies
 and from the hand of all
  who hate us -
⁷² to show mercy to our fathers
 and to remember his holy
  covenant,
⁷³ the oath he swore to our
  father Abraham:
⁷⁴ to rescue us from the hand of
  our enemies,
 and to enable us to serve
  him without fear
⁷⁵ in holiness and righteousness
  before him all our days.

⁷⁶ And you, my child, will be
  called a prophet of the
  Most High;
 for you will go on before
  the Lord to prepare the
  way for him,
⁷⁷ to give his people the
  knowledge of salvation
 through the forgiveness of
  their sins,
⁷⁸ because of the tender mercy
  of our God,
 by which the rising sun
  will come to us from heaven
⁷⁹ to shine on those living in

darkness
and in the shadow of death,
to guide our feet into the path
of peace.'

80 And the child grew and became strong in spirit; and he lived in the desert until he appeared publicly to Israel.

DAY 299

LUKE 2. 1 — 20

The Birth of Jesus

2 In those days Caesar Augustus issued a decree that a census should be taken of the entire Roman world. (2 This was the first census that took place while Quirinius was governor of Syria.) 3 And everyone went to his own town to register.

4 So Joseph also went up from the town of Nazareth in Galilee to Judea, to Bethlehem the town of David, because he belonged to the house and line of David. 5 He went there to register with Mary, who was pledged to be married to him and was expecting a child. 6 While they were there, the time came for the baby to be born, 7 and she gave birth to her firstborn, a son. She wrapped him in cloths and placed him in a manger, because there was no room for them in the inn.

The Shepherds and the Angels

And there were shepherds living out in the fields near by, keeping watch over their flocks at night. 9 An angel of the Lord appeared to them, and the glory of the Lord shone around them, and they were terrified. 10 But the angel said to them, 'Do not be afraid. I bring you good news of great joy that will be for all the people. 11 Today in the town of David a Saviour has been born to you; he is Christ the Lord. 12 This will be a sign to you: You will find a baby wrapped in cloths and lying in a manger.'

13 Suddenly a great company of the heavenly host appeared with the angel, praising God and saying,

14 'Glory to God in the highest,
and on earth peace to men
on whom his favour rests.'

15 When the angels had left them and gone into heaven, the shepherds said to one another, 'Let's go to Bethlehem and see this thing that has happened, which the Lord has told us about.'

16 So they hurried off and found Mary and Joseph, and the baby, who was lying in the manger. 17 When they had seen him, they spread the word concerning what had been told them about this child,

The shepherds returned, glorifying and praising God for all the things they had heard and seen, which were just as they had been told.

18 and all who heard it were amazed at what the shepherds said to them. 19 But Mary treasured up all these things and pondered them in her heart. 20 The shepherds returned, glorifying and praising God for all the things they had heard and seen, which were just as they had been told.

DAY 300

LUKE 2. 21 — 40

Jesus Presented in the Temple

²¹ On the eighth day, when it was time to circumcise him, he was named Jesus, the name the angel had given him before he had been conceived.

²² When the time of their purification according to the Law of Moses had been completed, Joseph and Mary took him to Jerusalem to present him to the Lord ²³ (as it is written in the Law of the Lord, 'Every firstborn male is to be consecrated to the Lord'), ²⁴ and to offer a sacrifice in keeping with what is said in the Law of the Lord: 'a pair of doves or two young pigeons'.

²⁵ Now there was a man in Jerusalem called Simeon, who was righteous and devout. He was waiting for the

---

'...Simeon took him in his arms and praised God...'

---

consolation of Israel, and the Holy Spirit was upon him. ²⁶ It had been revealed to him by the Holy Spirit that he would not die before he had seen the Lord's Christ. ²⁷ Moved by the Spirit, he went into the temple courts. When the parents brought in the child Jesus to do for him what the custom of the Law required, ²⁸ Simeon took him in his arms and praised God, saying:

²⁹ 'Sovereign Lord, as you have promised,
you now dismiss your servant in peace.

³⁰ For my eyes have seen your salvation,
³¹ which you have prepared in the sight of all people,
³² a light for revelation to the Gentiles
and for glory to your people Israel.'

³³ The child's father and mother marvelled at what was said about him. ³⁴ Then Simeon blessed them and said to

---

And the child grew and became strong; he was filled with wisdom.

Mary, his mother: 'This child is destined to cause the falling and rising of many in Israel, and to be a sign that will be spoken against, ³⁵ so that the thoughts of many hearts will be revealed. And a sword will pierce your own soul too.'

³⁶ There was also a prophetess, Anna, the daughter of Phanuel, of the tribe of Asher. She was very old; she had lived with her husband seven years after her marriage, ³⁷ and then was a widow until she was eighty-four. She never left the temple but worshipped night and day, fasting and praying. ³⁸ Coming up to them at that very moment, she gave thanks to God and spoke about the child to all who were looking forward to the redemption of Jerusalem.

³⁹ When Joseph and Mary had done everything required by the Law of the Lord, they returned to Galilee to their own town of Nazareth. ⁴⁰ And the child grew and became strong; he was filled with wisdom, and the grace of God was upon him.

DAY 301

LUKE 2. 41 — 52

The Boy Jesus at the Temple

Every year his parents went to Jerusalem for the Feast of the Passover. [42] When he was twelve years old, they went up to the Feast, according to the custom. [43] After the Feast was over, while his parents were returning home, the boy Jesus stayed behind in Jerusalem, but they were

'Didn't you know I had to be in my Father's house?'

unaware of it. [44] Thinking he was in their company, they travelled on for a day. Then they began looking for him among their relatives and friends. [45] When they did not find him, they went back to Jerusalem to look for him. [46] After three days they found him in the temple courts, sitting among the teachers, listening to them and asking them questions. [47] Everyone who heard him was amazed at his understanding and his answers. [48] When his parents saw him, they were astonished. His mother said to him, 'Son, why have you treated us like this? Your father and I have been anxiously searching for you.'

[49] 'Why were you searching for me?' he asked. 'Didn't you know I had to be in my Father's house?' [50] But they did not understand what he was saying to them.

[51] Then he went down to Nazareth with them and was obedient to them. But his mother treasured all these things in her heart. [52] And Jesus grew in wisdom and stature, and in favour with God and men.

DAY 302

LUKE 3. 1 — 38

3 John the Baptist Prepares the Way

In the fifteenth year of the reign of Tiberius Caesar - when Pontius Pilate was governor of Judea, Herod tetrarch of Galilee, his brother Philip tetrarch of Iturea and Traconitis, and Lysanias tetrarch of Abilene - [2] during the high priesthood of Annas and Caiaphas, the word of God came to John son of Zechariah in the desert. [3] He went into all the country around the Jordan, preaching a baptism of repentance for the forgiveness of sins. [4] As is written in the book of the words of Isaiah the prophet:

'A voice of one calling in the
    desert,
  "Prepare the way for the Lord,
    make straight paths for him.
[5] Every valley shall be filled in,
    every mountain and hill
      made low.
The crooked roads shall
    become straight,
  the rough ways smooth.
[6] And all mankind will see
    God's salvation." '

[7] John said to the crowds coming out to be baptised by him, 'You brood of vipers! Who warned you to flee from the

'The crooked roads shall become straight, the rough ways smooth. All mankind will see God's salvation'

coming wrath? ⁸ Produce fruit in keeping with repentance. And do not begin to say to yourselves, "We have Abraham as our father." For I tell you that out of these stones God can raise up children for Abraham. ⁹ The axe is already at the root of the trees, and every tree that does not produce good fruit will be cut down and thrown into the fire.'

'He will baptise you with the Holy Spirit and with fire.'

¹⁰ 'What should we do then?' the crowd asked.

¹¹ John answered, 'The man with two tunics should share with him who has none, and the one who has food should do the same.'

¹² Tax collectors also came to be baptised. 'Teacher,' they asked, 'what should we do?'

¹³ 'Don't collect any more than you are required to,' he told them.

¹⁴ Then some soldiers asked him, 'And what should we do?'

He replied, 'Don't extort money and don't accuse people falsely - be content with your pay.'

¹⁵ The people were waiting expectant and were all wondering in their hearts if John might possibly be the Christ. ¹⁶ John answered them all, 'I baptise you with water. But one more powerful than I will come, the thongs of whose sandals I am not worthy to untie. He will baptise you with the Holy Spirit and with fire. ¹⁷ His winnowing fork is in his hand to clear hi threshing-floor and to gather the wheat into his barn, but he will burn up the cha with unquenchable fire.' ¹⁸ And with mar other words John exhorted the people an preached the good news to them.

¹⁹ But when John rebuked Herod the tetrarch because of Herodias, his brothe wife, and all the other evil things he had done, ²⁰ Herod added this to them all: H locked John up in prison.

The Baptism and Genealogy of Jesus

When all the people were being baptised, Jesus was baptised too. And as he was praying, heaven was opened 22 and the Holy Spirit descended on him in bodily form like a dove. And a voice came from heaven: 'You are my Son, whom I love; with you I am well pleased.'

23 Now Jesus himself was about thirty years old when he began his ministry. He was the son, so it was thought, of Joseph,

the son of Heli, 24 the son of Matthat,
the son of Levi, the son of Melki,
the son of Jannai, the son of Joseph,
the son of Mattathias, the son of Amos,
the son of Nahum, the son of Esli,
the son of Naggai, 26 the son of Maath,
the son of Mattathias, the son of Semein,
the son of Josech, the son of Joda,
the son of Joanan, the son of Rhesa,
the son of Zerubbabel, the son of Shealtiel,
the son of Neri, 28 the son of Melki,
the son of Addi, the son of Cosam,
the son of Elmadam, the son of Er,
the son of Joshua, the son of Eliezer,
the son of Jorim, the son of Matthat,
the son of Levi, 30 the son of Simeon,

the son of Judah, the son of Joseph,
the son of Jonam, the son of Eliakim,
31 the son of Melea, the son of Menna,
the son of Mattatha, the son of Nathan,
the son of David, 32 the son of Jesse,
the son of Obed, the son of Boaz,
the son of Salmon, the son of Nahshon,
33 the son of Amminadab, the son of Ram,
the son of Hezron, the son of Perez,
the son of Judah, 34 the son of Jacob,
the son of Isaac, the son of Abraham,
the son of Terah, the son of Nahor,
35 the son of Serug, the son of Reu,
the son of Peleg, the son of Eber,
the son of Shelah, 36 the son of Cainan,
the son of Arphaxad, the son of Shem,
the son of Noah, the son of Lamech,
37 the son of Methuselah, the son of Enoch,
the son of Jared, the son of Mahalalel,
the son of Kenan, 38 the son of Enosh,
the son of Seth, the son of Adam,
the son of God.

DAY 303

LUKE 4. 1 — 15

4 **The Temptation of Jesus**
Jesus, full of the Holy Spirit,
returned from the Jordan and was
led by the Spirit in the desert, ² where for
forty days he was tempted by the devil.
He ate nothing during those days, and at
the end of them he was hungry.

³ The devil said to him, 'If you are the
Son of God, tell this stone to become
bread.'

⁴ Jesus answered, 'It is written: "Man
does not live on bread alone." '

⁵ The devil led him up to a high place
and showed him in an instant all the
kingdoms of the world. ⁶ And he said to
him, 'I will give you all their authority
and splendour, for it has been given to
me, and I can give it to anyone I want t
⁷ So if you worship me, it will all be you
⁸ Jesus answered, 'It is written:

> **'I will give you all their
> authority and splendour, for it
> has been given to me, and I
> can give it to anyone.'**

"Worship the Lord your God and serve
him only." '

⁹ The devil led him to Jerusalem an
had him stand on the highest point of t
temple. 'If you are the Son of God,' he
said, 'throw yourself down from here.
¹⁰ For it is written:

> "He will command his
> angels concerning you

The devil led him up to a high place and showed him in an instant all the kingdoms of the world.

to guard you carefully;
hey will lift you up in their
hands,
so that you will not strike
your foot against a
stone." '

¹² Jesus answered, 'It says: "Do not put
ᴇ Lord your God to the test." '
¹³ When the devil had finished all this
ᴍpting, he left him until an opportune
ᴍe.

ᴇsus Rejected at Nazareth

ᴊesus returned to Galilee in the power of
ᴇe Spirit, and news about him spread
ᴛrough the whole countryside. ¹⁵ He
ᴜght in their synagogues, and everyone
ᴀised him.

DAY 304

LUKE 4. 16 — 30

He went to Nazareth, where he had
ᴇen brought up, and on the Sabbath day
ᴇ went into the synagogue, as was his
ᴜstom. And he stood up to read. ¹⁷ The
ᴄroll of the prophet Isaiah was handed to
ᴍm. Unrolling it, he found the place
ᴡhere it is written:

¹⁸ 'The Spirit of the Lord is on me,
because he has anointed me
to preach good news to the poor.
He has sent me to proclaim
freedom for the prisoners
and recovery of sight for
the blind,
to release the oppressed,
¹⁹   to proclaim the year of the
Lord's favour.'

²⁰ Then he rolled up the scroll, gave it
back to the attendant and sat down. The
eyes of everyone in the synagogue were
fastened on him, ²¹ and he began by saying
to them, 'Today this scripture is fulfilled
in your hearing.'

²² All spoke well of him and were
amazed at the gracious words that came
from his lips. 'Isn't this Joseph's son?' they
asked.

²³ Jesus said to them, 'Surely you will
quote this proverb to me: "Physician, heal

> They were amazed at his
> teaching, because his message
> had authority.

yourself! Do here in your home town
what we have heard that you did in
Capernaum."

²⁴ 'I tell you the truth,' he continued,
'no prophet is accepted in his home
town. ²⁵ I assure you that there were
many widows in Israel in Elijah's time,
when the sky was shut for three and a
half years and there was a severe famine
throughout the land. ²⁶ Yet Elijah was not
sent to any of them, but to a widow in
Zarephath in the region of Sidon. ²⁷ And
there were many in Israel with leprosy in
the time of Elisha the prophet, yet not
one of them was cleansed - only Naaman
the Syrian.'

²⁸ All the people in the synagogue
were furious when they heard this.
²⁹ They got up, drove him out of the
town, and took him to the brow of the
hill on which the town was built, in
order to throw him down the cliff. ³⁰ But
he walked right through the crowd and
went on his way.

DAY 305

LUKE 4. 31 — 44

Jesus Drives Out an Evil Spirit

[31] Then he went down to Capernaum, a town in Galilee, and on the Sabbath began to teach the people. [32] They were amazed at his teaching, because his message had authority.

[33] In the synagogue there was a man possessed by a demon, an evil spirit. He

> **'I must preach the good news of the kingdom of God.'**

cried out at the top of his voice, [34] 'Ha! What do you want with us, Jesus of Nazareth? Have you come to destroy us? I know who you are - the Holy One of God!'

[35] 'Be quiet!' Jesus said sternly. 'Come out of him!' Then the demon threw the man down before them all and came out without injuring him.

[36] All the people were amazed and said to each other, 'What is this teaching? With authority and power he gives orders to evil spirits and they come out!' [37] And the news about him spread throughout the surrounding area.

Jesus Heals Many

[38] Jesus left the synagogue and went to the home of Simon. Now Simon's mother-in-law was suffering from a high fever, and they asked Jesus to help her. [39] So he bent over her and rebuked the fever, and it left her. She got up at once and began to wait on them.

[40] When the sun was setting, the people brought to Jesus all who had various kinds of sickness, and laying his hands on each one, he healed them. [41] Moreover, demons came out of many people, shouting, 'You are the Son of God!' But he rebuked them and would not allow them to speak, because they knew he was the Christ.

[42] At daybreak Jesus went out to a solitary place. The people were looking for him and when they came to where he was, they tried to keep him from leaving them. [43] But he said, 'I must preach the good news of the kingdom of God to the other towns also, because that is why I was sent.' [44] And he kept on preaching in the synagogues of Judea.

He went out to a solitary place.

DAY 306

LUKE 5. 1 — 26

The Calling of the First Disciples

One day as Jesus was standing by the lake of Gennesaret, with the people crowding round him and listening to the word of God, ² he saw at the water's edge two boats, left there by the fishermen, who were washing their nets. ³ He got into one of the boats, the one belonging to Simon, and asked him to put out a little from shore. Then he sat down and taught the people from the boat.

⁴ When he had finished speaking, he said to Simon, 'Put out into deep water, and let down the nets for a catch.'

⁵ Simon answered, 'Master, we've worked hard all night and haven't caught anything. But because you say so, I will let down the nets.'

⁶ When they had done so, they caught such a large number of fish that their nets began to break. ⁷ So they signalled to their partners in the other boat to come and help them, and they came and filled both boats so full that they began to sink.

⁸ When Simon Peter saw this, he fell at Jesus' knees and said, 'Go away from me, Lord; I am a sinful man!' ⁹ For he and all his companions were astonished at the catch of fish they had taken, ¹⁰ and so were James and John, the sons of Zebedee, Simon's partners.

Then Jesus said to Simon, 'Don't be afraid; from now on you will catch men.' ¹¹ So they pulled their boats up on shore, left everything and followed him.

The Man With Leprosy

¹² While Jesus was in one of the towns, a man came along who was covered with leprosy. When he saw Jesus, he fell with his face to the ground and begged him, 'Lord, if you are willing, you can make me clean.'

¹³ Jesus reached out his hand and touched the man. 'I am willing,' he said. 'Be clean!' And immediately the leprosy left him.

¹⁴ Then Jesus ordered him, 'Don't tell anyone, but go, show yourself to the priest and offer the sacrifices that Moses commanded for your cleansing, as a testimony to them.'

¹⁵ Yet the news about him spread all the more, so that crowds of people came to hear him and to be healed of their sicknesses. ¹⁶ But Jesus often withdrew to lonely places and prayed.

Jesus Heals a Paralytic

¹⁷ One day as he was teaching, Pharisees and teachers of the law, who had come from every village of Galilee and from Judea and Jerusalem, were sitting there. And the power of the Lord was present for him to heal the sick. ¹⁸ Some men came carrying a paralytic on a mat and tried to take him into the house to lay him before Jesus. ¹⁹ When they could not find a way to do this because of the crowd, they went up on the roof and lowered him on his mat through the tiles into the middle of the crowd, right in front of Jesus.

²⁰ When Jesus saw their faith, he said, 'Friend, your sins are forgiven.'

²¹ The Pharisees and the teachers of the law began thinking to themselves, 'Who is this fellow who speaks blasphemy? Who can forgive sins but God alone?'

²² Jesus knew what they were thinking and asked, 'Why are you thinking these

things in your hearts? ²³ Which is easier: to say, "Your sins are forgiven," or to say, "Get up and walk"? ²⁴ But that you may know that the Son of Man has authority on earth to forgive sins. . . .' He said to the paralysed man, 'I tell you, get up, take your mat and go home.' ²⁵ Immediately he stood up in front of them, took what he had been lying on and went home praising God. ²⁶ Everyone was amazed and gave praise to God. They were filled with awe and said, 'We have seen remarkable things today.'

DAY 307

LUKE 5. 27—6.11

The Calling of Levi

²⁷ After this, Jesus went out and saw a tax collector by the name of Levi sitting at his tax booth. 'Follow me,' Jesus said to him, ²⁸ and Levi got up, left everything and followed him.

²⁹ Then Levi held a great banquet for Jesus at his house, and a large crowd of tax collectors and others were eating with them. ³⁰ But the Pharisees and the teachers of the law who belonged to their sect complained to his disciples, 'Why do you eat and drink with tax collectors and "sinners"?'

Levi got up, left everything and followed him.

---

³¹ Jesus answered them, 'It is not the healthy who need a doctor, but the sick. ³² I have not come to call the righteous, but sinners to repentance.'

Jesus Questioned About Fasting

³³ They said to him, 'John's disciples often fast and pray, and so do the disciples of the Pharisees, but yours go on eating and drinking.'

³⁴ Jesus answered, 'Can you make the guests of the bridegroom fast while he is with them? ³⁵ But the time will come when the bridegroom will be taken from them; in those days they will fast.'

³⁶ He told them this parable: 'No-one tears a patch from a new garment and sews it on an old one. If he does, he will have torn the new garment, and the patch from the new will not match the old. ³⁷ And no-one pours new wine into old wineskins. If he does, the new wine will burst the skins, the wine will run out and the wineskins will be ruined. ³⁸ No, new wine must be poured into new wineskins. ³⁹ And no-one after drinking old wine wants the new, for he says, "The old is better." '

Lord of the Sabbath

6 One Sabbath Jesus was going through the cornfields, and his disciples began to pick some ears of corn, rub them in their hands and eat the grain. ² Some of the Pharisees asked, 'Why are you doing what is unlawful on the Sabbath?'

³ Jesus answered them, 'Have you never read what David did when he and his companions were hungry? ⁴ He entered the house of God, and taking the consecrated bread, he ate what is lawful only for priests to eat. And he also gave some to his companions.' ⁵ Then Jesus said to them, 'The Son of Man is Lord of the Sabbath.'

⁶ On another Sabbath he went into the synagogue and was teaching, and a man was there whose right hand was shrivelled. ⁷ The Pharisees and the

'I have not come to call the righteous, but sinners to repentance.'

eachers of the law were looking for a eason to accuse Jesus, so they watched im closely to see if he would heal on the abbath. [8] But Jesus knew what they were ninking and said to the man with the nrivelled hand, 'Get up and stand in ont of everyone.' So he got up and stood here.

[9] Then Jesus said to them, 'I ask you, which is lawful on the Sabbath: to do good or to do evil, to save life or to destroy it?'

[10] He looked round at them all, and then said to the man, 'Stretch out your hand.' He did so, and his hand was completely restored. [11] But they were furious and began to discuss with one another what they might do to Jesus.

DAY 308

LUKE 6. 12 — 36

The Twelve Apostles

[12] One of those days Jesus went out to a mountainside to pray, and spent the night praying to God. [13] When morning came, he called his disciples to him and chose twelve of them, whom he also designated apostles: [14] Simon (whom he named Peter), his brother Andrew, James, John, Philip, Bartholomew, [15] Matthew, Thomas, James son of Alphaeus, Simon who was called the Zealot, [16] Judas son of James, and Judas Iscariot, who became a traitor.

Blessings and Woes

[17] He went down with them and stood on a level place. A large crowd of his disciples was there and a great number of people from all over Judea, from Jerusalem, and from the coast of Tyre and Sidon, [18] who had come to hear him and to be healed of their diseases. Those troubled by evil spirits were cured, [19] and the people all tried to touch him, because power was coming from him and healing them all.

[20] Looking at his disciples, he said:

'Blessed are you who are
    poor,
    for yours is the kingdom of
        God.
[21] Blessed are you who hunger
    now,
    for you will be satisfied.
Blessed are you who weep
    now,
    for you will laugh.
[22] Blessed are you when men

hate you,
    when they exclude you
    and insult you
    and reject your name as
        evil,
    because of the Son of Man.

[23] 'Rejoice in that day and leap for joy, because great is your reward in heaven. For that is how their fathers treated the prophets.

[24] 'But woe to you who are rich,
    for you have already
        received your comfort.
[25] Woe to you who are well fed
    now,
    for you will go hungry.
Woe to you who laugh now,
    for you will mourn and
        weep.
[26] Woe to you when all men
    speak well of you,
    for that is how their fathers
        treated the false
        prophets.

Love for Enemies

[27] 'But I tell you who hear me: Love your enemies, do good to those who hate you, [28] bless those who curse you, pray for those who ill-treat you. [29] If someone strikes you on one cheek, turn to him the other also. If someone takes your cloak, do not stop him from taking your tunic. [30] Give to everyone who asks you, and if anyone takes what belongs to you, do not demand it back. [31] Do to others as you would have them do to you.

[32] 'If you love those who love you, what credit is that to you? Even "sinners" love those who love them. [33] And if you do good to those who are good to you, what credit is that to you? Even "sinners" do that. [34] And if you lend to those from

…om you expect repayment, what credit …that to you? Even "sinners" lend to …nners", expecting to be repaid in full. …But love your enemies, do good to them, …d lend to them without expecting to …t anything back. Then your reward will …great, and you will be sons of the Most …igh, because he is kind to the ungrateful …d wicked. ³⁶ Be merciful, just as your …ther is merciful.

DAY 309

LUKE 6. 37 — 49

…dging Others

…Do not judge, and you will not be …dged. Do not condemn, and you will …ot be condemned. Forgive, and you will …e forgiven. ³⁸ Give, and it will be given …you. A good measure, pressed down, …aken together and running over, will be …oured into your lap. For with the …easure you use, it will be measured to …ou.'

'No good tree bears bad fruit, nor does a bad tree bear good fruit.'

³⁹ He also told them this parable: 'Can a blind man lead a blind man? Will they not both fall into a pit? ⁴⁰ A student is not above his teacher, but everyone who is fully trained will be like his teacher.

⁴¹ 'Why do you look at the speck of sawdust in your brother's eye and pay no attention to the plank in your own eye? ⁴²How can you say to your brother, "Brother, let me take the speck out of your eye," when you yourself fail to see the plank in your own eye? You hypocrite, first take the plank out of your eye, and then you will see clearly to remove the speck from your brother's eye.

A Tree and Its Fruit

⁴³ 'No good tree bears bad fruit, nor does a bad tree bear good fruit. ⁴⁴ Each tree is recognised by its own fruit. People do not pick figs from thornbushes, or grapes from briers. ⁴⁵ The good man brings good things out of the good stored up in his heart, and the evil man brings evil things out of the evil stored up in his heart. For out of the overflow of his heart his mouth speaks.

The Wise and Foolish Builders

⁴⁶ 'Why do you call me, "…Lord, Lord," and do not do what I say? ⁴⁷ I will show you what he is like who comes to me and hears my words and puts them into practice. ⁴⁸ He is like a man building a house, who dug down deep and laid the foundation on rock. When the flood came, the torrent struck that house but could not shake it, because it was well built. ⁴⁹ But the one who hears my words and does not put them into practice is like a man who built a house on the ground without a foundation. The moment the torrent struck that house, it collapsed and its destruction was complete.'

DAY 310

LUKE 7. 1 — 28

7 **The Faith of the Centurion**
When Jesus had finished saying all this in the hearing of the people, he entered Capernaum. ²There a centurion's servant, whom his master valued highly, was sick and about to die. ³The centurion heard of Jesus and sent some elders of the Jews to him, asking him to come and heal his servant. ⁴When they came to Jesus, they pleaded earnestly with him, 'This man deserves to have you do this, ⁵because he loves our nation and has built our synagogue.' ⁶So Jesus went with them.

He was not far from the house when the centurion sent friends to say to him: 'Lord, don't trouble yourself, for I do not deserve to have you come under my roof. ⁷That is why I did not even consider myself worthy to come to you. But say the word, and my servant will be healed. ⁸For I myself am a man under authority, with soldiers under me. I tell this one, "Go", and he goes; and that one, "Come", and he comes. I say to my servant, "Do this", and he does it.'

⁹When Jesus heard this, he was amazed at him, and turning to the crowd following him, he said, 'I tell you, I have not found such great faith even in Israel.' ¹⁰Then the men who had been sent returned to the house and found the servant well.

Jesus Raises a Widow's Son

¹¹Soon afterwards, Jesus went to a town called Nain, and his disciples and a large crowd went along with him. ¹²As he approached the town gate, a dead person was being carried out - the only son of his mother, and she was a widow. And a large crowd from the town was with her. ¹³When the Lord saw her, his heart went out to her and he said, 'Don't cry.'

¹⁴Then he went up and touched the coffin, and those carrying it stood still. He said, 'Young man, I say to you, get up.' ¹⁵The dead man sat up and began to talk, and Jesus gave him back to his mother.

'God has come to help his people.'

---

¹⁶They were all filled with awe and praised God. 'A great prophet has appeared among us,' they said. 'God has come to help his people.' ¹⁷This news about Jesus spread throughout Judea and the surrounding country.

Jesus and John the Baptist

¹⁸John's disciples told him about all these things. Calling two of them, ¹⁹he sent them to the Lord to ask, 'Are you the one who was to come, or should we expect someone else?'

²⁰When the men came to Jesus they said, 'John the Baptist sent us to you to ask, "Are you the one who was to come, or should we expect someone else?" '

²¹At that very time Jesus cured many who had diseases, sicknesses and evil spirits, and gave sight to many who were blind. ²²So he replied to the messengers, 'Go back and report to John what you have seen and heard: The blind receive sight, the lame walk, those who have leprosy are cured, the deaf hear, the dead are raised, and the good news is preached to the poor. ²³Blessed is the man who does

ot fall away on account of me.'

²⁴ After John's messengers left, Jesus began to speak to the crowd about John: What did you go out into the desert to see? A reed swayed by the wind? ²⁵ If not, what did you go out to see? A man dressed in fine clothes? No, those who wear expensive clothes and indulge in luxury are in palaces. ²⁶ But what did you go out to see? A prophet? Yes, I tell you, and more than a prophet. ²⁷ This is the one about whom it is written:

> "I will send my messenger
> ahead of you,
> who will prepare your way
> before you."

²⁸ I tell you, among those born of women there is no-one greater than John; yet the one who is least in the kingdom of God is greater than he.'

DAY 311
LUKE 7. 29 — 50

²⁹ All the people, even the tax collectors, when they heard Jesus' words, acknowledged that God's way was right, because they had been baptised by John. ³⁰ But the Pharisees and experts in the law rejected God's purpose for themselves, because they had not been baptised by John.)

³¹ 'To what, then, can I compare the people of this generation? What are they like? ³² They are like children sitting in the market-place and calling out to each other:

> "We played the flute for you,

> and you did not dance;
> we sang a dirge,
> and you did not cry."

³³ For John the Baptist came neither eating bread nor drinking wine, and you say, "He has a demon." ³⁴ The Son of Man came eating and drinking, and you say, "Here is a glutton and a drunkard, a friend of tax collectors and 'sinners'." ³⁵ But wisdom is proved right by all her children.'

Jesus Anointed by a Sinful Woman

³⁶ Now one of the Pharisees invited Jesus to have dinner with him, so he went to the Pharisee's house and reclined at the table. ³⁷ When a woman who had lived a sinful life in that town learned that Jesus was eating at the Pharisee's house, she brought an alabaster jar of perfume, ³⁸ and as she stood behind him at his feet weeping, she began to wet his feet with her tears. Then she wiped them with her hair, kissed them and poured perfume on them.

³⁹ When the Pharisee who had invited him saw this, he said to himself, 'If this man were a prophet, he would know who is touching him and what

'Simon, I have something to tell you.'

kind of woman she is - that she is a sinner.'

⁴⁰ Jesus answered him, 'Simon, I have something to tell you.'

'Tell me, teacher,' he said.

⁴¹ 'Two men owed money to a certain money-lender. One owed him five

hundred denarii, and the other fifty. [42] Neither of them had the money to pay him back, so he cancelled the debts of

'Your faith has saved you; go in peace.'

both. Now which of them will love him more?'

[43] Simon replied, 'I suppose the one who had the bigger debt cancelled.'

'You have judged correctly,' Jesus said.

[44] Then he turned towards the woman and said to Simon, 'Do you see this woman? I came into your house. You did not give me any water for my feet, but she wet my feet with her tears and wiped them with her hair. [45] You did not give me a kiss, but this woman, from the time I entered has not stopped kissing my feet. [46] You did not put oil on my head, but she has poured perfume on my feet. [47] Therefore, I tell you, her many sins have been forgiven - for she loved much. But he who has been forgiven little loves little.'

[48] Then Jesus said to her, 'Your sins are forgiven.'

[49] The other guests began to say among themselves, 'Who is this who even forgives sins?'

[50] Jesus said to the woman, 'Your faith has saved you; go in peace.'

'Your faith has saved you; go in peace.'

DAY 312

LUKE 8. 1 — 21

8 ### The Parable of the Sower
After this, Jesus travelled about from one town and village to another, proclaiming the good news of the kingdom of God. The Twelve were with him, ² and also some women who had been cured of evil spirits and diseases: Mary (called Magdalene) from whom seven demons had come out; ³ Joanna the wife of Chuza, the manager of Herod's household; Susanna; and many others. These women were helping to support them out of their own means.

⁴ While a large crowd was gathering and people were coming to Jesus from town after town, he told this parable: ⁵ 'A farmer went out to sow his seed. As he was scattering the seed, some fell along the path; it was trampled on, and the birds of the air ate it up. ⁶ Some fell on rock, and when it came up, the plants withered because they had no moisture. ⁷ Other seed fell among thorns, which grew up with it and choked the plants. ⁸ Still other seed fell on good soil. It came up and yielded a crop, a hundred times more than was sown.'

When he said this, he called out, 'He who has ears to hear, let him hear.'

⁹ His disciples asked him what this parable meant. ¹⁰ He said, 'The knowledge of the secrets of the kingdom of God has been given to you, but to others I speak in parables, so that,

"though seeing, they may
   not see;

though hearing, they may
   not understand."

¹¹ 'This is the meaning of the parable: The seed is the word of God. ¹² Those along the path are the ones who hear, and then the devil comes and takes away the word from their hearts, so that they may not believe and be saved. ¹³ Those on the rock are the ones who receive the word with joy when they hear it, but they have no root. They believe for a while, but in the time of testing they fall away. ¹⁴ The seed that fell among thorns stands for those who hear, but as they go on their way they are choked by life's worries, riches and pleasures, and they do not mature. ¹⁵ But the seed on good soil stands for those with a noble and good heart, who hear the word, retain it, and by persevering produce a crop.

A Lamp on a Stand

¹⁶ 'No-one lights a lamp and hides it in a jar or puts it under a bed. Instead, he puts it on a stand, so that those who come in can see the light. ¹⁷ For there is nothing hidden that will not be disclosed, and nothing concealed that will not be known or brought out into the open. ¹⁸ Therefore consider carefully how you listen. Whoever has will be given more; whoever does not have, even what he thinks he has will be taken from him.'

Jesus' Mother and Brothers

¹⁹ Now Jesus' mother and brothers came to see him, but they were not able to get near him because of the crowd. ²⁰ Someone told him, 'Your mother and brothers are standing outside, wanting to see you.'

²¹ He replied, 'My mother and brothers are those who hear God's word and put it into practice.'

DAY 313

LUKE 8. 22 — 39

Jesus Calms the Storm

²² One day Jesus said to his disciples, 'Let's go over to the other side of the lake.' So they got into a boat and set out. ²³ As they sailed, he fell asleep. A squall came down on the lake, so that the boat was being swamped, and they were in great danger.

²⁴ The disciples went and woke him, saying, 'Master, Master, we're going to drown!'

He got up and rebuked the wind and the raging waters; the storm subsided, and all was calm. ²⁵ 'Where is your faith?' he asked his disciples.

In fear and amazement they asked one another, 'Who is this? He commands even the winds and the water, and they obey him.'

The Healing of a Demon-possessed Man

²⁶ They sailed to the region of the Gerasenes, which is across the lake from Galilee. ²⁷ When Jesus stepped ashore, he was met by a demon-possessed man from the town. For a long time this man had not worn clothes or lived in a house, but had lived in the tombs. ²⁸ When he saw Jesus, he cried out and fell at his feet, shouting at the top of his voice, 'What do you want with me, Jesus, Son of the Most High God? I beg you, don't torture me!' ²⁹ For Jesus had commanded the evil spirit to come out of the man. Many times it had seized him, and though he was chained hand and foot and kept under guard, he had broken his chains and had been driven by the demon into solitary places.

³⁰ Jesus asked him, 'What is your name?'

'Legion,' he replied, because many demons had gone into him. ³¹ And they begged him repeatedly not to order them to go into the Abyss.

³² A large herd of pigs was feeding there on the hillside. The demons begged Jesus to let them go into them, and he gave them permission. ³³ When the demons came out of the man, they went into the pigs, and the herd rushed down

> 'He commands even the winds and the water, and they obey him.'

the steep bank into the lake and was drowned.

³⁴ When those tending the pigs saw what had happened, they ran off and reported this in the town and countryside, ³⁵ and the people went out to see what had happened. When they came to Jesus, they found the man from whom the demons had gone out, sitting at Jesus' feet, dressed and in his right mind; and they were afraid. ³⁶ Those who had seen it told the people how the demon-possessed man had been cured. ³⁷ Then all the people of the region of the Gerasenes asked Jesus to leave them, because they were overcome with fear. So he got into the boat and left.

³⁸ The man from whom the demons had gone out begged to go with him, but Jesus sent him away, saying, ³⁹ 'Return home and tell how much God has done for you.' So the man went away and told all over the town how much Jesus had done for him.

DAY 314

LUKE 8. 40 — 56

A Dead Girl and a Sick Woman

⁴⁰ Now when Jesus returned, a crowd welcomed him, for they were all expecting him. ⁴¹ Then a man named Jairus, a ruler of the synagogue, came and fell at Jesus' feet, pleading with him to come to his house ⁴² because his only daughter, a girl of about twelve, was dying.

As Jesus was on his way, the crowds almost crushed him. ⁴³ And a woman was there who had been subject to bleeding for twelve years, but no-one could heal her. ⁴⁴ She came up behind him and touched the edge of his cloak, and immediately her bleeding stopped.

⁴⁵ 'Who touched me?' Jesus asked.

When they all denied it, Peter said, 'Master, the people are crowding and pressing against you.'

⁴⁶ But Jesus said, 'Someone touched me; I know that power has gone out from me.'

⁴⁷ Then the woman, seeing that she could not go unnoticed, came trembling and fell at his feet. In the presence of all the people, she told why she had touched him and how she had been instantly healed. ⁴⁸ Then he said to her, 'Daughter, your faith has healed you. Go in peace.'

⁴⁹ While Jesus was still speaking, someone came from the house of Jairus, the synagogue ruler. 'Your daughter is dead,' he said. 'Don't bother the teacher any more.'

⁵⁰ Hearing this, Jesus said to Jairus, 'Don't be afraid; just believe, and she will be healed.'

⁵¹ When he arrived at the house of Jairus, he did not let anyone go in with him except Peter, John and James, and the child's father and mother. ⁵²Meanwhile, all the people were wailing and mourning for her. 'Stop wailing,' Jesus said. 'She is not dead but asleep.'

⁵³ They laughed at him, knowing that she was dead. ⁵⁴ But he took her by the hand and said, 'My child, get up!' ⁵⁵ Her spirit returned, and at once she stood up. Then Jesus told them to give her something to eat. ⁵⁶ Her parents were astonished, but he ordered them not to tell anyone what had happened.

'Don't be afraid; just believe.'

DAY 315

LUKE 9. 1 — 27

9 **Jesus Sends Out the Twelve**
When Jesus had called the Twelve together, he gave them power and authority to drive out all demons and to cure diseases, ² and he sent them out to preach the kingdom of God and to heal the sick. ³ He told them: 'Take nothing for the journey - no staff, no bag, no bread, no money, no extra tunic. ⁴ Whatever house you enter, stay there until you leave that town. ⁵ If people do not welcome you, shake the dust off your feet when you leave their town, as a testimony against them.' ⁶ So they set out and went from village to village, preaching the gospel and healing people everywhere.

⁷ Now Herod the tetrarch heard about all that was going on. And he was perplexed, because some were saying that John had been raised from the dead, ⁸ others that Elijah had appeared, and still others that one of the prophets of long ago had come back to life. ⁹ But Herod

---

'...whoever loses his life for me will save it.'

---

said, 'I beheaded John. Who, then, is this I hear such things about?' And he tried to see him.

Jesus Feeds the Five Thousand
¹⁰ When the apostles returned, they reported to Jesus what they had done. Then he took them with him and they withdrew by themselves to a town called Bethsaida, ¹¹ but the crowds learned about it and followed him. He welcomed them and spoke to them about the kingdom of God, and healed those who needed healing.

¹² Late in the afternoon the Twelve came to him and said, 'Send the crowd away so they can go to the surrounding villages and countryside and find food and lodging, because we are in a remote place here.'

¹³ He replied, 'You give them something to eat.'

They answered, 'We have only five loaves of bread and two fish - unless we go and buy food for all this crowd.' ¹⁴ (About five thousand men were there.)

But he said to his disciples, 'Make them sit down in groups of about fifty each.' ¹⁵ The disciples did so, and everybody sat down. ¹⁶ Taking the five loaves and the two fish and looking up to heaven, he gave thanks and broke them. Then he gave them to the disciples to set before the people. ¹⁷ They all ate and were satisfied, and the disciples picked up twelve basketfuls of broken pieces that were left over.

Peter's Confession of Christ
¹⁸ Once when Jesus was praying in private and his disciples were with him, he asked them, 'Who do the crowds say I am?'

¹⁹ They replied, 'Some say John the Baptist; others say Elijah; and still others, that one of the prophets of long ago has come back to life.'

²⁰ 'But what about you?' he asked. 'Who do you say I am?'

Peter answered, 'The Christ of God.'

²¹ Jesus strictly warned them not to tell this to anyone. ²² And he said, 'The Son of Man must suffer many things and be rejected by the elders, chief priests and

teachers of the law, and he must be killed and on the third day be raised to life.'

²³ Then he said to them all: 'If anyone would come after me, he must deny himself and take up his cross daily and follow me. ²⁴ For whoever wants to save his life will lose it, but whoever loses his life for me will save it. ²⁵ What good is it for a man to gain the whole world, and yet lose or forfeit his very self? ²⁶ If anyone is ashamed of me and my words, the Son of Man will be ashamed of him when he comes in his glory and in the glory of the Father and of the holy angels. ²⁷ I tell you the truth, some who are standing here will not taste death before they see the kingdom of God.'

DAY 316
LUKE 9. 28 — 62

The Transfiguration

²⁸ About eight days after Jesus said this, he took Peter, John and James with him and went up onto a mountain to pray. ²⁹ As he was praying, the appearance of his face changed, and his clothes became as bright as a flash of lightning. ³⁰ Two men, Moses and Elijah, ³¹ appeared in glorious splendour, talking with Jesus. They spoke about his departure, which he was about to bring to fulfilment at Jerusalem. ³² Peter and his companions were very sleepy, but when they became fully awake, they saw his glory and the two men standing with him. ³³ As the men were leaving Jesus, Peter said to him, 'Master, it is good for us to be here. Let us put up three shelters - one for you, one for Moses and one for Elijah.' (He did not know what he was saying.)

³⁴ While he was speaking, a cloud appeared and enveloped them, and they were afraid as they entered the cloud. ³⁵ A voice came from the cloud, saying, 'This is my Son, whom I have chosen; listen to him.' ³⁶ When the voice had spoken, they found that Jesus was alone. The disciples kept this to themselves, and told no-one at that time what they had seen.

The Healing of a Boy With an Evil Spirit

³⁷ The next day, when they came down from the mountain, a large crowd met him. ³⁸ A man in the crowd called out, 'Teacher, I beg you to look at my son, for he is my only child. ³⁹ A spirit seizes him and he suddenly screams; it throws him into convulsions so that he foams at the mouth. It scarcely ever leaves him and is destroying him. ⁴⁰ I begged your disciples to drive it out, but they could not.'

⁴¹ 'O unbelieving and perverse generation,' Jesus replied, 'how long shall I stay with you and put up with you? Bring your son here.'

⁴² Even while the boy was coming, the demon threw him to the ground in a convulsion. But Jesus rebuked the evil

---

...they were all amazed at the greatness of God.

---

spirit, healed the boy and gave him back to his father. ⁴³ And they were all amazed at the greatness of God.

While everyone was marvelling at all that Jesus did, he said to his disciples, ⁴⁴"Listen carefully to what I am about to tell you: The Son of Man is going to be betrayed into the hands of men.' ⁴⁵ But they did not understand what this meant. It was hidden from them, so that they did

---

'For he who is least among you all - he is the greatest.'

---

not grasp it, and they were afraid to ask him about it.

Who will be the Greatest?

⁴⁶ An argument started among the disciples as to which of them would be the greatest. ⁴⁷ Jesus, knowing their thoughts, took a little child and made him stand beside him. ⁴⁸ Then he said to them, 'Whoever welcomes this little child in my name welcomes me; and whoever welcomes me welcomes the one who sent me. For he who is least among you all - he is the greatest.'

⁴⁹ 'Master,' said John, 'we saw a man driving out demons in your name and we tried to stop him, because he is not one of us.'

⁵⁰ 'Do not stop him,' Jesus said, 'for whoever is not against you is for you.'

Samaritan Opposition

⁵¹ As the time approached for him to be taken up to heaven, Jesus resolutely set out for Jerusalem. ⁵² And he sent messengers on ahead, who went into a Samaritan village to get things ready for him; ⁵³ but the people there did not welcome him, because he was heading for Jerusalem. ⁵⁴ When the disciples James and John saw this, they asked, 'Lord, do you want us to call fire down from heaven to destroy them?' ⁵⁵ But Jesus turned and rebuked them, ⁵⁶ and they went to another village.

The Cost of Following Jesus

⁵⁷ As they were walking along the road, a man said to him, 'I will follow you wherever you go.'

⁵⁸ Jesus replied, 'Foxes have holes and birds of the air have nests, but the Son of Man has nowhere to lay his head.'

⁵⁹ He said to another man, 'Follow me.'

But the man replied, 'Lord, first let me go and bury my father.'

⁶⁰ Jesus said to him, 'Let the dead bury

'I will follow you wherever you go.'

---

their own dead, but you go and proclaim the kingdom of God.'

⁶¹ Still another said, 'I will follow you, Lord; but first let me go back and say good-bye to my family.'

⁶² Jesus replied, 'No-one who puts his hand to the plough and looks back is fit for service in the kingdom of God.'

'For he who is least among you all - he is the greatest.'

DAY 317

LUKE 10. 1 — 24

10 ### Jesus Sends Out the Seventy-two

After this the Lord appointed seventy-two others and sent them two by two ahead of him to every town and place where he was about to go. [2] He told them, 'The harvest is plentiful, but the workers are few. Ask the Lord of the harvest, therefore, to send out workers into his harvest field. [3] Go! I am sending you out like lambs among wolves. [4] Do not take a purse or bag or sandals; and do not greet anyone on the road.

[5] 'When you enter a house, first say, "Peace to this house." [6] If a man of peace is there, your peace will rest on him; if not, it will return to you. [7] Stay in that house, eating and drinking whatever they give you, for the worker deserves his wages. Do not move around from house to house.

[8] 'When you enter a town and are welcomed, eat what is set before you. [9] Heal the sick who are there and tell them, "The kingdom of God is near you." [10] But when you enter a town and are not welcomed, go into its streets and say, [11] "Even the dust of your town that sticks to our feet we wipe off against you. Yet be sure of this: The kingdom of God is near." [12] I tell you, it will be more bearable on that day for Sodom than for that town.

[13] 'Woe to you, Korazin! Woe to you, Bethsaida! For if the miracles that were performed in you had been performed in Tyre and Sidon, they would have repented long ago, sitting in sackcloth and ashes. [14] But it will be more bearable for Tyre and Sidon at the judgment than for you. [15] And you, Capernaum, will you be lifted up to the skies? No, you will go down to the depths.

[16] 'He who listens to you listens to me; he who rejects you rejects me; but he who rejects me rejects him who sent me.'

[17] The seventy-two returned with joy

The seventy-two returned with joy...

---

and said, 'Lord, even the demons submit to us in your name.'

[18] He replied, 'I saw Satan fall like lightning from heaven. [19] I have given you authority to trample on snakes and scorpions and to overcome all the power of the enemy; nothing will harm you. [20] However, do not rejoice that the spirits submit to you, but rejoice that your names are written in heaven.'

[21] At that time Jesus, full of joy through the Holy Spirit, said, 'I praise you, Father, Lord of heaven and earth, because you have hidden these things from the wise and learned, and revealed them to little children. Yes, Father, for this was your good pleasure.

[22] 'All things have been committed to me by my Father. No-one knows who the Son is except the Father, and no-one knows who the Father is except the Son and those to whom the Son chooses to reveal him.'

[23] Then he turned to his disciples and said privately, 'Blessed are the eyes that see what you see. [24] For I tell you that many prophets and kings wanted to see what you see but did not see it, and to hear what you hear but did not hear it.'

DAY 318

LUKE 10. 25 — 42

The Parable of the Good Samaritan

²⁵ On one occasion an expert in the law stood up to test Jesus. 'Teacher,' he asked, 'what must I do to inherit eternal life?'

²⁶ 'What is written in the Law?' he replied. 'How do you read it?'

²⁷ He answered: ' "Love the Lord your God with all your heart and with all your soul and with all your strength and with all your mind"; and, "Love your neighbour as yourself." '

²⁸ 'You have answered correctly,' Jesus replied. 'Do this and you will live.'

²⁹ But he wanted to justify himself, so he asked Jesus, 'And who is my neighbour?'

'Love your neighbour as yourself.'

³⁰ In reply Jesus said: 'A man was going down from Jerusalem to Jericho, when he fell into the hands of robbers. They stripped him of his clothes, beat him and went away, leaving him half-dead. ³¹ A priest happened to be going down the same road, and when he saw the man, he passed by on the other side. ³² So too, a Levite, when he came to the place and saw him, passed by on the other side. ³³ But a Samaritan, as he travelled, came where the man was; and when he saw him, he took pity on him. ³⁴ He went to him and bandaged his wounds, pouring on oil and wine. Then he put the man on his own donkey, brought him to an inn and took care of him. ³⁵ The next day he took out two silver coins and gave them to the innkeeper. "Look after him," he said, "and when I return, I will reimburse you for any extra expense you may have."

³⁶ 'Which of these three do you think was a neighbour to the man who fell into the hands of robbers?'

³⁷ The expert in the law replied, 'The one who had mercy on him.'

Jesus told him, 'Go and do likewise.'

At the Home of Martha and Mary

³⁸ As Jesus and his disciples were on their way, he came to a village where a woman named Martha opened her home to him. ³⁹ She had a sister called Mary, who sat at the Lord's feet listening to what he said. ⁴⁰ But Martha was distracted by all the preparations that had to be made. She came to him and asked, 'Lord, don't you care that my sister has left me to do the work by myself? Tell her to help me!'

⁴¹ 'Martha, Martha,' the Lord answered, 'you are worried and upset about many things, ⁴² but only one thing is needed. Mary has chosen what is better, and it will not be taken away from her.'

DAY 319

LUKE 11. 1 — 23

11 ### Jesus' Teaching on Prayer

One day Jesus was praying in a certain place. When he finished, one of his disciples said to him, 'Lord, teach us to pray, just as John taught his disciples.'

² He said to them, 'When you pray, say:

> "Father,
> hallowed be your name,
> your kingdom come.
> ³ Give us each day our daily
> bread.
>
> ⁴ Forgive us our sins,
> for we also forgive
> everyone who sins
> against us.
> And lead us not into
> temptation." '

⁵ Then he said to them, 'Suppose one of you has a friend, and he goes to him at midnight and says, "Friend, lend me three loaves of bread, ⁶ because a friend of mine on a journey has come to me, and I have nothing to set before him."

⁷ Then the one inside answers, "Don't bother me. The door is already locked, and my children are with me in bed. I can't get up and give you anything." ⁸ I tell you, though he will not get up and give him the bread because he is his friend, yet because of the man's boldness he will get up and give him as much as he needs.

⁹ 'So I say to you: Ask and it will be given to you; seek and you will find; knock and the door will be opened to you. ¹⁰ For everyone who asks receives; he who seeks finds; and to him who knocks, the door will be opened.

¹¹ 'Which of you fathers, if your son asks for a fish, will give him a snake instead? ¹² Or if he asks for an egg, will give him a scorpion? ¹³ If you then, though you are evil, know how to give good gifts to your children, how much more will your Father in heaven give the Holy Spirit to those who ask him!'

Jesus and Beelzebub

¹⁴ Jesus was driving out a demon that was mute. When the demon left, the man who had been mute spoke, and the crowd was amazed. ¹⁵ But some of them said, 'By Beelzebub, the prince of demons, he is driving out demons.' ¹⁶ Others tested him by asking for a sign from heaven.

¹⁷ Jesus knew their thoughts and said to them: 'Any kingdom divided against itself will be ruined, and a house divided against itself will fall. ¹⁸ If Satan is divided against himself, how can his kingdom stand? I say this because you claim that I drive out demons by Beelzebub. ¹⁹ Now if I drive out demons by Beelzebub, by whom do your followers drive them out? So then, they will be your judges. ²⁰ But if I drive out demons by the finger of God, then the kingdom of God has come to you.

²¹ 'When a strong man, fully armed, guards his own house, his possessions are safe. ²² But when someone stronger attacks and overpowers him, he takes away the armour in which the man trusted and divides up the spoils.

²³ 'He who is not with me is against me, and he who does not gather with me, scatters.

DAY 320

LUKE 11. 24 — 36

²⁴ 'When an evil spirit comes out of a man, it goes through arid places seeking rest and does not find it. Then it says, "I will return to the house I left." ²⁵ When it arrives, it finds the house swept clean and put in order. ²⁶ Then it goes and takes seven other spirits more wicked than itself, and they go in and live there. And

---

'Blessed rather are those who hear the word of God and obey it.'

---

the final condition of that man is worse than the first.'

²⁷ As Jesus was saying these things, a woman in the crowd called out, 'Blessed is the mother who gave you birth and nursed you.'

²⁸ He replied, 'Blessed rather are those who hear the word of God and obey it.'

The Sign of Jonah

²⁹ As the crowds increased, Jesus said, 'This is a wicked generation. It asks for a miraculous sign, but none will be given it except the sign of Jonah. ³⁰ For as Jonah was a sign to the Ninevites, so also will the Son of Man be to this generation. ³¹ The Queen of the South will rise at the judgment with the men of this generation and condemn them; for she came from the ends of the earth to listen to Solomon's wisdom, and now one greater than Solomon is here. ³² The men of Nineveh will stand up at the judgment with this generation and condemn it; for

they repented at the preaching of Jonah, and now one greater than Jonah is here.

The Lamp of the Body

³³ 'No-one lights a lamp and puts it in a place where it will be hidden, or under a bowl. Instead he puts it on its stand, so that those who come in may see the light. ³⁴ Your eye is the lamp of your body. When your eyes are good, your whole body also is full of light. But when they are bad, your body also is full of darkness. ³⁵ See to it, then, that the light within you is not darkness. ³⁶ Therefore, if your whole body is full of light, and no part of it dark, it will be completely lighted, as when the light of a lamp shines on you.'

DAY 321

LUKE 11. 37 — 54

Six Woes

³⁷ When Jesus had finished speaking, a Pharisee invited him to eat with him; so he went in and reclined at the table. ³⁸ But the Pharisee, noticing that Jesus did not first wash before the meal, was surprised.

³⁹ Then the Lord said to him, 'Now then, you Pharisees clean the outside of the cup and dish, but inside you are full of greed and wickedness. ⁴⁰ You foolish people! Did not the one who made the outside make the inside also? ⁴¹ But give what is inside [the dish] to the poor, and everything will be clean for you.

⁴² 'Woe to you Pharisees, because you give God a tenth of your mint, rue and all other kinds of garden herbs, but you neglect justice and the love of God. You should have practised the latter without

'No-one lights a lamp and puts it in a place where it will be hidden.'

leaving the former undone.

[43] 'Woe to you Pharisees, because you love the most important seats in the synagogues and greetings in the market-places.

[44] 'Woe to you, because you are like unmarked graves, which men walk over without knowing it.'

[45] One of the experts in the law answered him, 'Teacher, when you say these things, you insult us also.'

[46] Jesus replied, 'And you experts in the law, woe to you, because you load people down with burdens they can hardly carry, and you yourselves will not lift one finger to help them.

[47] 'Woe to you, because you build tombs for the prophets, and it was your forefathers who killed them. [48] So you testify that you approve of what your forefathers did; they killed the prophets, and you build their tombs. [49] Because of this, God in his wisdom said, "I will send them prophets and apostles, some of whom they will kill and others they will persecute." [50] Therefore this generation will be held responsible for the blood of all the prophets that has been shed since the beginning of the world, [51] from the blood of Abel to the blood of Zechariah, who was killed between the altar and the sanctuary. Yes, I tell you, this generation will be held responsible for it all.

[52] 'Woe to you experts in the law, because you have taken away the key to knowledge. You yourselves have not entered, and you have hindered those who were entering.'

[53] When Jesus left there, the Pharisees and the teachers of the law began to oppose him fiercely and to besiege him with questions, [54] waiting to catch him in something he might say.

DAY 322

LUKE 12. 1 — 21

12

Warnings and Encouragements

Meanwhile, when a crowd of many thousands had gathered, so that they were trampling on one another, Jesus began to speak first to his disciples, saying: 'Be on your guard against the yeast of the Pharisees, which is hypocrisy. [2] There is nothing concealed that will not be disclosed, or hidden that will not be made known. [3] What you have said in the dark

---

> **'What you have said in the dark will be heard in the daylight...'**

---

will be heard in the daylight, and what you have whispered in the ear in the inner rooms will be proclaimed from the roofs.

[4] 'I tell you, my friends, do not be afraid of those who kill the body and after that can do no more. [5] But I will show you whom you should fear: Fear him who, after the killing of the body, has power to throw you into hell. Yes, I tell you, fear him. [6] Are not five sparrows sold for two pennies? Yet not one of them is forgotten by God. [7] Indeed, the very hairs of your head are all numbered. Don't be afraid; you are worth more than many sparrows.

[8] 'I tell you, whoever acknowledges me before men, the Son of Man will also acknowledge him before the angels of God. [9] But he who disowns me before men will be disowned before the angels of God. [10] And everyone who speaks a word

against the Son of Man will be forgiven, but anyone who blasphemes against the Holy Spirit will not be forgiven.

[11] 'When you are brought before synagogues, rulers and authorities, do not worry about how you will defend yourselves or what you will say, [12] for the Holy Spirit will teach you at that time what you should say.'

The Parable of the Rich Fool

[13] Someone in the crowd said to him, 'Teacher, tell my brother to divide the inheritance with me.'

[14] Jesus replied, 'Man, who appointed me a judge or an arbiter between you?' [15] Then he said to them, 'Watch out! Be on your guard against all kinds of greed; a man's life does not consist in the abundance of his possessions.'

[16] And he told them this parable: 'The ground of a certain rich man produced a good crop. [17] He thought to himself, "What shall I do? I have no place to store my crops."

[18] 'Then he said, "This is what I'll do. I will tear down my barns and build bigger ones, and there I will store all my grain and my goods. [19] And I'll say to myself,

---

> **'...a man's life does not consist in the abundance of his possessions.'**

'You have plenty of good things laid up for many years. Take life easy; eat, drink and be merry.' "

[20] 'But God said to him, "You fool! This very night your life will be demanded from you. Then who will get what you have prepared for yourself?"

[21] 'This is how it will be with anyone who stores up things for himself but is not rich towards God.'

DAY 323
LUKE 12. 22 — 40

Do Not Worry

[22] Then Jesus said to his disciples: 'Therefore I tell you, do not worry about your life, what you will eat; or about your body, what you will wear. [23] Life is more than food, and the body more than clothes. [24] Consider the ravens: They do not sow or reap, they have no storeroom or barn; yet God feeds them. And how much more valuable you are than birds! [25] Who of you by worrying can add a single hour to his life? [26] Since you cannot do this very little thing, why do you worry about the rest?

[27] 'Consider how the lilies grow. They do not labour or spin. Yet I tell you, not even Solomon in all his splendour was dressed like one of these. [28] If that is how God clothes the grass of the field, which is here today, and tomorrow is thrown into the fire, how much more will he clothe you, O you of little faith! [29] And do not set your heart on what you will eat or drink; do not worry about it. [30] For the pagan world runs after all such things, and your Father knows that you need them. [31] But seek his kingdom, and these things will be given to you as well.

[32] 'Do not be afraid, little flock, for your Father has been pleased to give you the kingdom. [33] Sell your possessions and give to the poor. Provide purses for yourselves that will not wear out, a treasure in heaven that will not be exhausted, where no thief comes near and no moth destroys. [34] For where your treasure is, there your heart will be also.

Watchfulness

[35] 'Be dressed ready for service and keep your lamps burning, [36] like men waiting for their master to return from a wedding banquet, so that when he comes and knocks they can immediately open the door for him. [37] It will be good for those servants whose master finds them watching when he comes. I tell you the truth, he will dress himself to serve, will have them recline at the table and will come and wait on them. [38] It will be good for those servants whose master finds them ready, even if he comes in the second or third watch of the night. [39] But understand this: If the owner of the house had known at what hour the thief was coming, he would not have let his house be broken into. [40] You also must be ready, because the Son of Man will come at an hour when you do not expect him.'

'Not even Solomon in all his splendour was dressed like one of these.'

DAY 324

LUKE 12. 41 — 59

⁴¹ Peter asked, 'Lord, are you telling this parable to us, or to everyone?'

⁴² The Lord answered, 'Who then is the faithful and wise manager, whom the master puts in charge of his servants to give them their food allowance at the proper time? ⁴³ It will be good for that servant whom the master finds doing so when he returns. ⁴⁴ I tell you the truth, he will put him in charge of all his possessions. ⁴⁵ But suppose the servant says to himself, "My master is taking a long time in coming," and he then begins to beat the menservants and maidservants and to eat and drink and get drunk. ⁴⁶ The master of that servant will come on a day when he does not expect him and at an hour he is not aware of. He will cut him to pieces and assign him a place with the unbelievers.

⁴⁷ 'That servant who knows his master's will and does not get ready or does not do what his master wants will be beaten with many blows. ⁴⁸ But the one who does not know and does things deserving punishment will be beaten with few blows. From everyone who has been given much, much will be demanded; and from the one who has been entrusted with much, much more will be asked.

Not Peace but Division

⁴⁹ 'I have come to bring fire on the earth, and how I wish it were already kindled! ⁵⁰ But I have a baptism to undergo, and how distressed I am until it is completed! ⁵¹ Do you think I came to bring peace on earth? No, I tell you, but division. ⁵² From now on there will be five in one family divided against each other, three against two and two against three. ⁵³ They will be divided, father against son and son against father, mother against daughter and daughter against mother,

'From everyone who has been given much, much will be demanded.'

mother-in-law against daughter-in-law and daughter-in-law against mother-in-law.'

Interpreting the Times

⁵⁴ He said to the crowd: 'When you see a cloud rising in the west, immediately you say, "It's going to rain," and it does. ⁵⁵ And when the south wind blows, you say, "It's going to be hot," and it is. ⁵⁶ Hypocrites! You know how to interpret the appearance of the earth and the sky. How is it that you don't know how to interpret this present time?

⁵⁷ 'Why don't you judge for yourselves what is right? ⁵⁸ As you are going with your adversary to the magistrate, try hard to be reconciled to him on the way, or he may drag you off to the judge, and the judge turn you over to the officer, and the officer throw you into prison. ⁵⁹ I tell you, you will not get out until you have paid the last penny.'

DAY 325

LUKE 13. 1 — 21

13

Repent or Perish

Now there were some present at that time who told Jesus about the Galileans whose blood Pilate had mixed with their sacrifices. ² Jesus answered, 'Do you think that these Galileans were worse sinners than all the other Galileans because they suffered this way? ³ I tell you, no! But unless you repent, you too will all perish. ⁴ Or those eighteen who died when the tower in Siloam fell on them - do you think they were more guilty than all the others living in Jerusalem? ⁵ I tell you, no! But unless you repent, you too will all perish.'

⁶ Then he told this parable: 'A man had a fig-tree, planted in his vineyard, and he went to look for fruit on it, but did not find any. ⁷ So he said to the man who took care of the vineyard, "For three years now I've been coming to look for fruit on this fig-tree and haven't found any. Cut it down! Why should it use up the soil?"

⁸ ' "Sir," the man replied, "leave it alone for one more year, and I'll dig round it and fertilise it. ⁹ If it bears fruit next year, fine! If not, then cut it down." '

A Crippled Woman Healed on the Sabbath

¹⁰ On a Sabbath Jesus was teaching in one of the synagogues, ¹¹ and a woman was there who had been crippled by a spirit for eighteen years. She was bent over and could not straighten up at all. ¹² When Jesus saw her, he called her forward and said to her, 'Woman, you are set free from your infirmity.' ¹³ Then he put his hands on her, and immediately she straightened up and praised God.

¹⁴ Indignant because Jesus had healed on the Sabbath, the synagogue ruler said to the people, 'There are six days for work. So come and be healed on those days, not on the Sabbath.'

¹⁵ The Lord answered him, 'You hypocrites! Doesn't each of you on the Sabbath untie his ox or donkey from the

---

> **Then he put his hands on her, and immediately she straightened up and praised God.**

---

stall and lead it out to give it water? ¹⁶ Then should not this woman, a daughter of Abraham, whom Satan has kept bound for eighteen long years, be set free on the Sabbath day from what bound her?'

¹⁷ When he said this, all his opponents were humiliated, but the people were delighted with all the wonderful things he was doing.

The Parables of the Mustard Seed and the Yeast

¹⁸ Then Jesus asked, 'What is the kingdom of God like? What shall I compare it to? ¹⁹ It is like a mustard seed, which a man took and planted in his garden. It grew and became a tree, and the birds of the air perched in its branches.'

²⁰ Again he asked, 'What shall I compare the kingdom of God to? ²¹ It is like yeast that a woman took and mixed into a large amount of flour until it worked all through the dough.'

DAY 326
LUKE 13. 22 — 35

The Narrow Door

²² The Jesus went through the towns and villages, teaching as he made his way to Jerusalem. ²³ Someone asked him, 'Lord, are only a few people going to be saved?'

He said to them, ²⁴ 'Make every effort to enter through the narrow door, because many, I tell you, will try to enter and will not be able to. ²⁵ Once the owner of the house gets up and closes the door, you will stand outside knocking and pleading, "Sir, open the door for us."

'But he will answer, "I don't know you or where you come from."

²⁶ 'Then you will say, "We ate and drank with you, and you taught in our streets."

²⁷ 'But he will reply, "I don't know you or where you come from. Away from me, all you evildoers!"

²⁸ 'There will be weeping there, and gnashing of teeth, when you see Abraham, Isaac and Jacob and all the prophets in the kingdom of God, but you yourselves thrown out. ²⁹ People will come from east and west and north and south, and will take their places at the feast in the kingdom of God. ³⁰ Indeed there are those who are last who will be first, and first who will be last.'

Jesus' Sorrow for Jerusalem

³¹ At that time some Pharisees came to Jesus and said to him, 'Leave this place and go somewhere else. Herod wants to kill you.'

³² He replied, 'Go tell that fox, "I will drive out demons and heal people today

and tomorrow, and on the third day I will reach my goal." ³³ In any case, I must keep going today and tomorrow and the next day - for surely no prophet can die outside Jerusalem!

³⁴ 'O Jerusalem, Jerusalem, you who kill the prophets and stone those sent to you, how often I have longed to gather your children together, as a hen gathers her chicks under her wings, but you were not willing! ³⁵ Look, your house is left to you desolate. I tell you, you will not see me again until you say, "Blessed is he who comes in the name of the Lord." '

'...enter through the narrow door.'

DAY 327

LUKE 14. 1 — 24

14

Jesus at a Pharisee's House

One Sabbath, when Jesus went to eat in the house of a prominent Pharisee, he was being carefully watched. There in front of him was a man suffering from dropsy. ³Jesus asked the Pharisees and experts in the law, 'Is it lawful to heal on the Sabbath or not?' ⁴ But they remained silent. So taking hold of the man, he healed him and sent him away.

⁵ Then he asked them, 'If one of you has a son or an ox that falls into a well on the Sabbath day, will you not immediately pull him out?' ⁶ And they had nothing to say.

⁷ When he noticed how the guests picked the places of honour at the table, he told them this parable: ⁸ 'When someone invites you to a wedding feast, do not take the place of honour, for a person more distinguished than you may have been invited. ⁹ If so, the host who invited both of you will come and say to you, "Give this man your seat." Then, humiliated, you will have to take the least important place. ¹⁰ But when you are invited, take the lowest place, so that when your host comes, he will say to you, "Friend, move up to a better place." Then you will be honoured in the presence of all your fellow guests. ¹¹ For everyone who exalts himself will be humbled, and he who humbles himself will be exalted.'

¹² Then Jesus said to his host, 'When you give a luncheon or dinner, do not invite your friends, your brothers or relatives, or your rich neighbours; if you do, they may invite you back and so you will be repaid. ¹³ But when you give a banquet, invite the poor, the crippled, the lame, the blind, ¹⁴ and you will be blessed. Although they cannot repay you, you will be repaid at the resurrection of the righteous.'

The Parable of the Great Banquet

¹⁵ When one of those at the table with him heard this, he said to Jesus, 'Blessed is the man who will eat at the feast in the kingdom of God.'

¹⁶ Jesus replied: 'A certain man was preparing a great banquet and invited many guests. ¹⁷ At the time of the banquet he sent his servant to tell those who had been invited, "Come, for everything is now ready."

¹⁸ 'But they all alike began to make excuses. The first said, "I have just bought a field, and I must go and see it. Please excuse me."

¹⁹ 'Another said, "I have just bought five yoke of oxen, and I'm on my way to try them out. Please excuse me."

²⁰ 'Still another said, "I have just got married, so I can't come."

²¹ 'The servant came back and reported this to his master. Then the owner of the house became angry and ordered his servant, "Go out quickly into the streets and alleys of the town and bring in the poor, the crippled, the blind and the lame."

²² ' "Sir," the servant said, "what you ordered has been done, but there is still room."

²³ 'Then the master told his servant, "Go out to the roads and country lanes and make them come in, so that my house will be full. ²⁴ I tell you, not one of those men who were invited will get a taste of my banquet." '

DAY 328

LUKE 14. 25 — 35

'Rejoice with me; I have found my lost sheep

The Cost of Being a Disciple

[25] Large crowds were travelling with Jesus, and turning to them he said: [26] 'If anyone comes to me and does not hate his father and mother, his wife and children, his brothers and sisters - yes, even his own life - he cannot be my disciple. [27] And anyone who does not carry his cross and follow me cannot be my disciple.

[28] 'Suppose one of you wants to build a tower. Will he not first sit down and estimate the cost to see if he has enough money to complete it? [29] For if he lays the foundation and is not able to finish it, everyone who sees it will ridicule him, [30] saying, "This fellow began to build and was not able to finish."

[31] 'Or suppose a king is about to go to war against another king. Will he not first sit down and consider whether he is able with ten thousand men to oppose the one coming against him with twenty thousand? [32] If he is not able, he will send a delegation while the other is still a long way off and will ask for terms of peace. [33] In the same way, any of you who does

---

> 'Salt is good, but if it loses its saltiness, how can it be made salty again?'

---

not give up everything he has cannot be my disciple.

[34] 'Salt is good, but if it loses its saltiness, how can it be made salty again? [35] It is fit neither for the soil nor for the manure heap; it is thrown out.

'He who has ears to hear, let him hear.'

DAY 329

LUKE 15. 1 — 32

15 The Parable of the Lost Sheep

Now the tax collectors and 'sinners' were all gathering round to hear him. [2] But the Pharisees and the teachers of the law muttered, 'This man welcomes sinners, and eats with them.'

[3] Then he told them this: [4] 'Suppose one of you has a hundred sheep and loses one of them. Does he not leave the ninety-nine in the open country and go after the lost sheep until he finds it? [5] And when he finds it, he joyfully puts it on his shoulders [6] and goes home. Then he calls his friends and neighbours together and says, "Rejoice with me; I have found my lost sheep." [7] I tell you that in the same way there will be more rejoicing in heaven over one sinner who repents than

ver ninety-nine righteous persons who
do not need to repent.

The Parable of the Lost Coin

Or suppose a woman has ten silver coins
and loses one. Does she not light a lamp,
sweep the house and search carefully until
she finds it? ⁹ And when she finds it, she
calls her friends and neighbours together
and says, "Rejoice with me; I have found
my lost coin." ¹⁰ In the same way, I tell
you, there is rejoicing in the presence of
the angels of God over one sinner who
repents.'

The Parable of the Lost Son

Jesus continued: 'There was a man who
had two sons. ¹² The younger one said to
his father, "Father, give me my share of
the estate." So he divided his property
between them.

¹³ 'Not long after that, the younger
son got together all he had, set off for a
distant country and there squandered his
wealth in wild living. ¹⁴ After he had
spent everything, there was a severe
famine in that whole country, and he
began to be in need. ¹⁵ So he went and
hired himself out to a citizen of that
country, who sent him to his fields to feed
pigs. ¹⁶ He longed to fill his stomach with
the pods that the pigs were eating, but
no-one gave him anything.

¹⁷ 'When he came to his senses, he
said, "How many of my father's hired men
have food to spare, and here I am starving
to death! ¹⁸ I will set out and go back to
my father and say to him: Father, I have
sinned against heaven and against you. ¹⁹ I
am no longer worthy to be called your
son; make me like one of your hired
men." ²⁰ So he got up and went to his
father.

'But while he was still a long way off
his father saw him and was filled with
compassion for him; he ran to his son,
threw his arms around him and kissed
him.

²¹ 'The son said to him, "Father, I
have sinned against heaven and against
you. I am no longer worthy to be called
your son."

²² 'But the father said to his servants,
"Quick! Bring the best robe and put it on
him. Put a ring on his finger and sandals
on his feet. ²³ Bring the fattened calf and
kill it. Let's have a feast and celebrate.

'...he was lost and is found.'

²⁴ For this son of mine was dead and is
alive again; he was lost and is found." So
they began to celebrate.

²⁵ 'Meanwhile, the older son was in
the field. When he came near the house,
he heard music and dancing. ²⁶ So he
called one of the servants and asked him
what was going on. ²⁷ "Your brother has
come," he replied, "and your father has
killed the fattened calf because he has
him back safe and sound."

²⁸ 'The older brother became angry
and refused to go in. So his father went
out and pleaded with him. ²⁹ But he
answered his father, "Look! All these
years I've been slaving for you and never
disobeyed your orders. Yet you never gave
me even a young goat so I could celebrate
with my friends. ³⁰ But when this son of
yours who has squandered your property
with prostitutes comes home, you kill the
fattened calf for him!"

³¹ ' "My son," the father said, "you are
always with me, and everything I have is
yours. ³² But we had to celebrate and be
glad, because this brother of yours was
dead and is alive again; he was lost and is
found." '

DAY 330

LUKE 16. 1 — 18

16 The Parable of the Shrewd Manager

Jesus told his disciples: 'There was a rich man whose manager was accused of wasting his possessions. ²So he called him in and asked him, "What is this I hear about you? Give an account of your management, because you cannot be manager any longer."

³'The manager said to himself, "What shall I do now? My master is taking away my job. I'm not strong enough to dig, and I'm ashamed to beg - ⁴I know what I'll do so that, when I lose my job here, people will welcome me into their houses."

⁵'So he called in each one of his master's debtors. He asked the first, "How much do you owe my master?"

⁶' "Eight hundred gallons of olive oil," he replied.

'The manager told him, "Take your bill, sit down quickly, and make it four hundred."

⁷'Then he asked the second, "And how much do you owe?"

' "A thousand bushels of wheat," he replied.

'He told him, "Take your bill and make it eight hundred."

⁸'The master commended the dishonest manager because he had acted shrewdly. For the people of this world are more shrewd in dealing with their own kind than are the people of the light. ⁹I tell you, use worldly wealth to gain friends for yourselves, so that when it is gone, you will be welcomed into eternal dwellings.

¹⁰'Whoever can be trusted with very little can also be trusted with much, and whoever is dishonest with very little will also be dishonest with much. ¹¹So if you

'You cannot serve both God and Money.'

have not been trustworthy in handling worldly wealth, who will trust you with true riches? ¹²And if you have not been trustworthy with someone else's property, who will give you property of your own?

¹³'No servant can serve two masters. Either he will hate the one and love the other, or he will be devoted to the one and despise the other. You cannot serve both God and Money.'

¹⁴The Pharisees, who loved money, heard all this and were sneering at Jesus. ¹⁵He said to them, 'You are the ones who justify yourselves in the eyes of men, but God knows your hearts. What is highly valued among men is detestable in God's sight.

Additional Teachings

¹⁶'The Law and the Prophets were proclaimed until John. Since that time, the good news of the kingdom of God is being preached, and everyone is forcing his way into it. ¹⁷It is easier for heaven and earth to disappear than for the least stroke of a pen to drop out of the Law.

¹⁸'Anyone who divorces his wife and marries another woman commits adultery, and the man who marries a divorced woman commits adultery.

DAY 331

LUKE 16. 19 — 17.10

he Rich Man and Lazarus

'There was a rich man who was dressed
purple and fine linen and lived in
xury every day. ²⁰ At his gate was laid a
:ggar named Lazarus, covered with sores
and longing to eat what fell from the
:h man's table. Even the dogs came and
:ked his sores.

²² 'The time came when the beggar

> ## The apostles said to the Lord,
> ## 'Increase our faith!'

ed and the angels carried him to
braham's side. The rich man also died
id was buried. ²³ In hell, where he was in
rment, he looked up and saw Abraham
r away, with Lazarus by his side. ²⁴ So he
illed to him, "Father Abraham, have
ty on me and send Lazarus to dip the tip
' his finger in water and cool my tongue,
:cause I am in agony in this fire."

²⁵ 'But Abraham replied, "Son,
member that in your lifetime you
ceived your good things, while Lazarus
ceived bad things, but now he is
imforted here and you are in agony. ²⁶ And
:sides all this, between us and you a great
1asm has been fixed, so that those who
ant to go from here to you cannot, nor
in anyone cross over from there to us."

²⁷ 'He answered, "Then I beg you,
ther, send Lazarus to my father's house,
for I have five brothers. Let him warn
1em, so that they will not also come to
iis place of torment."

²⁹ 'Abraham replied, "They have
Moses and the Prophets; let them listen
to them."

³⁰ ' "No, father Abraham," he said,
"but if someone from the dead goes to
them, they will repent."

³¹ 'He said to him, "If they do not
listen to Moses and the Prophets, they
will not be convinced even if someone
rises from the dead." '

17 Sin, Faith, Duty

Jesus said to his disciples:
'Things that cause people to
sin are bound to come, but woe to that
person through whom they come. ² It
would be better for him to be thrown into
the sea with a millstone tied round his
neck than for him to cause one of these
little ones to sin. ³ So watch yourselves.

'If your brother sins, rebuke him, and
if he repents, forgive him. ⁴ If he sins
against you seven times in a day, and
seven times comes back to you and says,
"I repent," forgive him.'

⁵ The apostles said to the Lord,
'Increase our faith!'

⁶ He replied, 'If you have faith as
small as a mustard seed, you can say to
this mulberry tree, "Be uprooted and
planted in the sea," and it will obey you.

⁷ 'Suppose one of you had a servant
ploughing or looking after the sheep.
Would he say to the servant when he
comes in from the field, "Come along
now and sit down to eat"? ⁸ Would he not
rather say, "Prepare my supper, get
yourself ready and wait on me while I eat
and drink; after that you may eat and
drink"? ⁹ Would he thank the servant
because he did what he was told to do?
¹⁰ So you also, when you have done
everything you were told to do, should
say, "We are unworthy servants; we have
only done our duty." '

DAY 332

LUKE 17. 11 — 37

Ten Healed of Leprosy

[11] Now on his way to Jerusalem, Jesus travelled along the border between Samaria and Galilee. [12] As he was going into a village, ten men who had leprosy met him. They stood at a distance [13] and called out in a loud voice, 'Jesus, Master, have pity on us!'

[14] When he saw them, he said, 'Go, show yourselves to the priests.' And as they went, they were cleansed.

[15] One of them, when he saw he was healed, came back, praising God in a loud voice. [16] He threw himself at Jesus' feet and thanked him - and he was a Samaritan.

[17] Jesus asked, 'Were not all ten cleansed? Where are the other nine? [18] Was no-one found to return and give praise to God except this foreigner?' [19] Then he said to him, 'Rise and go; your faith has made you well.'

The Coming of the Kingdom of God

[20] Once, having been asked by the Pharisees when the kingdom of God would come, Jesus replied, 'The kingdom of God does not come with your careful observation, [21] nor will people say, "Here it is," or "There it is," because the kingdom of God is within you.'

[22] Then he said to his disciples, 'The time is coming when you will long to see one of the days of the Son of Man, but you will not see it. [23] Men will tell you, "There he is!" or "Here he is!" Do not go running off after them. [24] For the Son of Man in his day will be like the lightning which flashes and lights up the sky from one end to the other. [25] But first he must suffer many things and be rejected by this generation.

[26] 'Just as it was in the days of Noah, so also will it be in the days of the Son of Man. [27] People were eating, drinking, marrying and being given in marriage up to the day Noah entered the ark. Then the flood came and destroyed them all.

> ...the Son of Man in his day will be like the lightning, which flashes and lights up the sky...

[28] 'It was the same in the days of Lot. People were eating and drinking, buying and selling, planting and building. [29] But the day Lot left Sodom, fire and sulphur rained down from heaven and destroyed them all.

[30] 'It will be just like this on the day the Son of Man is revealed. [31] On that day no-one who is on the roof of his house, with his goods inside, should go down to get them. Likewise, no-one in the field should go back for anything. [32] Remember Lot's wife! [33] Whoever tries to keep his life will lose it, and whoever loses his life will preserve it. [34] I tell you, on that night two people will be in one bed; one will be taken and the other left. [35] Two women will be grinding grain together; one will be taken and the other left.'

[37] 'Where, Lord?' they asked.

He replied, 'Where there is a dead body, there the vultures will gather.'

DAY 333

LUKE 18. 1 — 17

18

The Parable of the Persistent Widow

Then Jesus told his disciples a ̣rable to show them that they should ̣ways pray and not give up. ² He said: 'In ̣ertain town there was a judge who ̣ither feared God nor cared about men. ̣nd there was a widow in that town ̣o kept coming to him with the plea, ̣rant me justice against my adversary."

⁴ 'For some time he refused. But ̣ally he said to himself, "Even though I ̣n't fear God or care about men, ⁵ yet ̣cause this widow keeps bothering me, I ̣ll see that she gets justice, so that she ̣n't eventually wear me out with her ̣ming!" '

⁶ And the Lord said, 'Listen to what

> **'The kingdom of God does not come with your careful observation.'**

̣e unjust judge says. ⁷ And will not God ̣ing about justice for his chosen ones, ̣o cry out to him day and night? Will ̣ keep putting them off? ⁸ I tell you, he ̣ll see that they get justice, and quickly. ̣owever, when the Son of Man comes, ̣ll he find faith on the earth?'

̣he Parable of the Pharisee and ̣e Tax Collector

̣o some who were confident of their own righteousness and looked down on everybody else, Jesus told this parable: ¹⁰ 'Two men went up to the temple to pray, one a Pharisee and the other a tax collector. ¹¹ The Pharisee stood up and prayed about himself: "God, I thank you that I am not like other men - robbers, evildoers, adulterers - or even like this tax collector. ¹² I fast twice a week and give a tenth of all I get."

¹³ 'But the tax collector stood at a distance. He would not even look up to heaven, but beat his breast and said, "God, have mercy on me, a sinner."

¹⁴ 'I tell you that this man, rather than the other, went home justified before God. For everyone who exalts himself will be humbled, and he who humbles himself will be exalted.'

The Little Children and Jesus

¹⁵ People were also bringing babies to Jesus to have him touch them. When the disciples saw this, they rebuked them. ¹⁶ But Jesus called the children to him and said, 'Let the little children come to me, and do not hinder them, for the kingdom of God belongs to such as these. ¹⁷ I tell you the truth, anyone who will not receive the kingdom of God like a little child will never enter it.'

'Let the little children come to me.'

DAY 334

LUKE 18. 18 — 43

The Rich Ruler

¹⁸ A certain ruler asked him, 'Good teacher, what must I do to inherit eternal life?'

¹⁹ 'Why do you call me good?' Jesus answered. 'No-one is good - except God alone. ²⁰ You know the commandments: "Do not commit adultery, do not murder, do not steal, do not give false testimony, honour your father and mother." '

²¹ 'All these I have kept since I was a boy,' he said.

²² When Jesus heard this, he said to him, 'You still lack one thing. Sell everything you have and give to the poor, and you will have treasure in heaven. Then come, follow me.'

²³ When he heard this, he became very sad, because he was a man of great wealth. ²⁴ Jesus looked at him and said, 'How hard it is for the rich to enter the kingdom of God! ²⁵ Indeed, it is easier for a camel to go through the eye of a needle than for a rich man to enter the kingdom of God.'

²⁶ Those who heard this asked, 'Who then can be saved?'

²⁷ Jesus replied, 'What is impossible with men is possible with God.'

²⁸ Peter said to him, 'We have left all we had to follow you!'

²⁹ 'I tell you the truth,' Jesus said to them, 'no-one who has left home or wife or brothers or parents or children for the sake of the kingdom of God will fail to receive many times as much in this age and, in the age to come, eternal life.'

Jesus Again Predicts His Death

³¹ Jesus took the Twelve aside and told them, 'We are going up to Jerusalem, and everything that is written by the prophet about the Son of Man will be fulfilled. ³² He will be turned over to the Gentiles. They will mock him, insult him, spit on him, flog him and kill him. ³³ On the third

'Receive your sight; your faith has healed you.'

day he will rise again.'

³⁴ The disciples did not understand any of this. Its meaning was hidden from them, and they did not know what he was talking about.

A Blind Beggar Receives His Sight

³⁵ As Jesus approached Jericho, a blind man was sitting by the roadside begging. ³⁶ When he heard the crowd going by, he asked what was happening. ³⁷ They told him, 'Jesus of Nazareth is passing by.'

³⁸ He called out, 'Jesus, Son of David, have mercy on me!'

³⁹ Those who led the way rebuked him and told him to be quiet, but he shouted all the more, 'Son of David, have mercy on me!'

⁴⁰ Jesus stopped and ordered the man to be brought to him. When he came near, Jesus asked him, ⁴¹ 'What do you want me to do for you?'

'Lord, I want to see,' he replied.

⁴² Jesus said to him, 'Receive your sight; your faith has healed you.'

⁴³ Immediately he received his sight and followed Jesus, praising God. When all the people saw it, they also praised God.

DAY 335

LUKE 19. 1 — 27

19 Zacchaeus the Tax Collector

Jesus entered Jericho and was passing through. ² A man was there by the name of Zacchaeus; he was a chief tax collector and was wealthy. ³ He wanted to see who Jesus was, but being a short man he could not, because of the crowd. ⁴ So he ran ahead and climbed a sycamore-fig tree to see him, since Jesus was coming that way.

⁵ When Jesus reached the spot, he looked up and said to him, 'Zacchaeus, come down immediately. I must stay at your house today.' ⁶ So he came down at once and welcomed him gladly.

⁷ All the people saw this and began to mutter, 'He has gone to be the guest of a sinner".'

⁸ But Zacchaeus stood up and said to the Lord, 'Look, Lord! Here and now I give half of my possessions to the poor, and if I have cheated anybody out of anything, I will pay back four times the amount.'

⁹ Jesus said to him, 'Today salvation has come to this house, because this man, too, is a son of Abraham. ¹⁰ For the Son of Man came to seek and to save what was lost.'

The Parable of the Ten Minas

¹¹ While they were listening to this, he went on to tell them a parable, because he was near Jerusalem and the people thought that the kingdom of God was going to appear at once. ¹² He said: 'A man of noble birth went to a distant country to have himself appointed king and then to return. So he called ten of his servants and gave them ten minas. "Put this money to work," he said, "until I come back."

¹⁴ 'But his subjects hated him and sent a delegation after him to say, "We don't want this man to be our king."

¹⁵ 'He was made king, however, and returned home. Then he sent for the servants to whom he had given the money, in order to find out what they had gained with it.

¹⁶ 'The first one came and said, "Sir, your mina has earned ten more."

¹⁷ ' "Well done, my good servant!" his master replied. "Because you have been trustworthy in a very small matter, take charge of ten cities."

¹⁸ 'The second came and said, "Sir, your mina has earned five more."

¹⁹ 'His master answered, "You take charge of five cities."

²⁰ 'Then another servant came and said, "Sir, here is your mina; I have kept it laid away in a piece of cloth. ²¹ I was afraid of you, because you are a hard man. You take out what you did not put in and reap what you did not sow."

²² 'His master replied, "I will judge you by your own words, you wicked servant! You knew, did you, that I am a hard man, taking out what I did not put in, and reaping what I did not sow? ²³ Why then didn't you put my money on deposit, so that when I came back, I could have collected it with interest?"

²⁴ 'Then he said to those standing by, "Take his mina away from him and give it to the one who has ten minas."

²⁵ ' "Sir," they said, "he already has ten!"

²⁶ 'He replied, "I tell you that to everyone who has, more will be given, but as for the one who has nothing, even what he has will be taken away. ²⁷ But those enemies of mine who did not want me to be a king over them - bring them here and kill them in front of me." '

DAY 336

LUKE 19. 28 — 48

The Triumphal Entry

²⁸ After Jesus had said this, he went on ahead, going up to Jerusalem. ²⁹ As he approached Bethphage and Bethany at the hill called the Mount of Olives, he sent two of his disciples, saying to them, ³⁰ 'Go to the village ahead of you, and as you enter it, you will find a colt tied there, which no-one has ever ridden. Untie it and bring it here. ³¹ If anyone asks you, "Why are you untying it?" tell him, "The Lord needs it."

³² Those who were sent ahead went and found it just as he had told them. ³³ As they were untying the colt, its owners asked them, 'Why are you untying the colt?'

³⁴ They replied, 'The Lord needs it.'

³⁵ They brought it to Jesus, threw their cloaks on the colt and put Jesus on it. ³⁶ As he went along, people spread their cloaks on the road.

³⁷ When he came near the place where the road goes down the Mount of Olives, the whole crowd of disciples began joyfully to praise God in loud voices for all the miracles they had seen:

³⁸ 'Blessed is the king who comes in the name of the Lord!'

'Peace in heaven and glory in the highest!'

³⁹ Some of the Pharisees in the crowd said to Jesus, 'Teacher, rebuke your disciples!'

⁴⁰ 'I tell you,' he replied, 'if they keep quiet, the stones will cry out.'

⁴¹ As he approached Jerusalem and saw the city, he wept over it ⁴² and said, 'If you, even you, had only known on this day what would bring you peace - but now it is hidden from your eyes. ⁴³ The days will come upon you when your enemies will build an embankment against you and encircle you and hem you in on every side. ⁴⁴ They will dash you to the ground, you and the children within your walls. They will not leave one stone on another, because you did not recognise the time of God's coming to you.'

Jesus at the Temple

⁴⁵ Then he entered the temple area and began driving out those who were selling. ⁴⁶ 'It is written,' he said to them, "My house will be a house of prayer"; but you have made it "a den of robbers".'

⁴⁷ Every day he was teaching at the temple. But the chief priests, the teachers of the law and the leaders among the people were trying to kill him. ⁴⁸ Yet they could not find any way to do it, because all the people hung on his words.

DAY 337

LUKE 20. 1 — 26

20 The Authority of Jesus Questioned

One day as he was teaching the people in the temple courts and preaching the gospel, the chief priests and the teachers of the law, together with the elders, came up to him. ² 'Tell us by what authority you are doing these things,'

ey said. 'Who gave you this authority?'
³ He replied, 'I will also ask you a
question. Tell me, ⁴ John's baptism - was it
from heaven, or from men?'
⁵ They discussed it among themselves
and said, 'If we say, "From heaven", he
will ask, "Why didn't you believe him?"
But if we say, "From men", all the people
will stone us, because they are persuaded
that John was a prophet.'
⁷ So they answered, 'We don't know
where it was from.'
⁸ Jesus said, 'Neither will I tell you by
what authority I am doing these things.'

The Parable of the Tenants

He went on to tell the people this
parable: 'A man planted a vineyard,
rented it to some farmers and went away
for a long time. ¹⁰ At harvest time he sent
a servant to the tenants so they would
give him some of the fruit of the vineyard.
But the tenants beat him and sent him
away empty-handed. ¹¹ He sent another
servant, but that one also they beat and
treated shamefully and sent away empty-
handed. ¹² He sent still a third, and they
wounded him and threw him out.

> Jesus said, 'Neither will I tell
> you by what authority I am
> doing these things.'

¹³ 'Then the owner of the vineyard
said, "What shall I do? I will send my son,
whom I love; perhaps they will respect
him."
¹⁴ 'But when the tenants saw him,
they talked the matter over. "This is the
heir," they said. "Let's kill him, and the
inheritance will be ours." ¹⁵ So they threw

him out of the vineyard and killed him.
'What then will the owner of the
vineyard do to them? ¹⁶ He will come and
kill those tenants and give the vineyard
to others.'
When the people heard this, they
said, 'May this never be!'
¹⁷ Jesus looked directly at them and
asked, 'Then what is the meaning of that
which is written:

"The stone the builders rejected
has become the capstone"?

¹⁸ Everyone who falls on that stone will be
broken to pieces, but he on whom it falls
will be crushed.'
¹⁹ The teachers of the law and the
chief priests looked for a way to arrest
him immediately, because they knew he
had spoken this parable against them. But
they were afraid of the people.

Paying Taxes to Caesar

²⁰ Keeping a close watch on him, they sent
spies, who pretended to be honest. They
hoped to catch Jesus in something he said
so that they might hand him over to the
power and authority of the governor. ²¹ So
the spies questioned him: 'Teacher, we
know that you speak and teach what is
right, and that you do not show partiality
but teach the way of God in accordance
with the truth. ²² Is it right for us to pay
taxes to Caesar or not?'
²³ He saw through their duplicity and
said to them, ²⁴ 'Show me a denarius.
Whose portrait and inscription are on it?'
²⁵ 'Caesar's,' they replied.
He said to them, 'Then give to Caesar
what is Caesar's, and to God what is God's.'
²⁶ They were unable to trap him in what
he had said there in public. And astonished
by his answer, they became silent.

DAY 338

LUKE 20. 27 — 21.6

The Resurrection and Marriage

²⁷ Some of the Sadducees, who say there is no resurrection, came to Jesus with a question. ²⁸ 'Teacher,' they said, 'Moses wrote for us that if a man's brother dies and leaves a wife but no children, the man must marry the widow and have children for his brother. ²⁹ Now there were seven brothers. The first one married a woman and died childless. ³⁰ The second ³¹ and then the third married her, and in the same way the seven died, leaving no children. ³² Finally, the woman died too. ³³ Now then, at the resurrection whose wife will she be, since the seven were married to her?'

³⁴ Jesus replied, 'The people of this age marry and are given in marriage. ³⁵ But those who are considered worthy of taking part in that age and in the resurrection from the dead will neither marry nor be given in marriage, ³⁶ and they can no longer die; for they are like the angels. They are God's children, since they are children of the resurrection. ³⁷ But in the account of the bush, even Moses showed that the dead rise, for he calls the Lord "the God of Abraham, and the God of Isaac, and the God of Jacob". ³⁸ He is not the God of the dead, but of the living, for to him all are alive.'

³⁹ Some of the teachers of the law responded, 'Well said, teacher!' ⁴⁰ And no-one dared to ask him any more questions.

Whose Son is the Christ?

⁴¹ Then Jesus said to them, 'How is it that they say the Christ is the Son of David?

⁴² David himself declares in the Book of Psalms:

"The Lord said to my Lord:
'Sit at my right hand
⁴³ until I make your enemies
a footstool for your feet.' "

⁴⁴ David calls him "Lord". How then can he be his son?'

⁴⁵ While all the people were listening, Jesus said to his disciples, ⁴⁶ 'Beware of the teachers of the law. They like to walk around in flowing robes and love to be greeted in the market-places and have the most important seats in the synagogues and the places of honour at banquets. ⁴⁷ They devour widows' houses and for a show make lengthy prayers. Such men will be punished most severely.'

21 The Widow's Offering

As he looked up, Jesus saw the rich putting their gifts into the temple treasury. ² He also saw a poor widow put in two very small copper coins. ³ 'I tell you the truth,' he said, 'this poor widow has put in more than all the others. ⁴ All these people gave their gifts out of their wealth; but she out of her poverty put in all she had to live on.'

Signs of the End of the Age

⁵ Some of his disciples were remarking about how the temple was adorned with beautiful stones and with gifts dedicated to God. But Jesus said, ⁶ 'As for what you see here, the time will come when not one stone will be left on another; every one of them will be thrown down.'

DAY 339

LUKE 21. 7 — 38

'Teacher,' they asked, 'when will these things happen? And what will be the sign that they are about to take place?'

⁸ He replied: 'Watch out that you are not deceived. For many will come in my name, claiming, "I am he," and "The time is near." Do not follow them. ⁹ When you hear of wars and revolutions, do not be frightened. These things must happen

---

'Watch out that you are not deceived.'

---

first, but the end will not come right away.'

¹⁰ Then he said to them: 'Nation will rise against nation, and kingdom against kingdom. ¹¹ There will be great earthquakes, famines and pestilences in various places, and fearful events and great signs from heaven.

¹² 'But before all this, they will lay hands on you and persecute you. They will deliver you to synagogues and prisons, and you will be brought before kings and governors, and all on account of my name. ¹³ This will result in your being witnesses to them. ¹⁴ But make up your mind not to worry beforehand how you will defend yourselves. ¹⁵ For I will give you words and wisdom that none of your adversaries will be able to resist or contradict. ¹⁶ You will be betrayed even by parents, brothers, relatives and friends,

and they will put some of you to death. ¹⁷ All men will hate you because of me. ¹⁸ But not a hair of your head will perish. ¹⁹ By standing firm you will gain life.

²⁰ 'When you see Jerusalem being surrounded by armies, you will know that its desolation is near. ²¹ Then let those who are in Judea flee to the mountains, let those in the city get out, and let those in the country not enter the city. ²² For this is the time of punishment in fulfilment of all that has been written. ²³ How dreadful it will be in those days for pregnant women and nursing mothers! There will be great distress in the land and wrath against this people. ²⁴ They will fall by the sword and will be taken as prisoners to all the nations. Jerusalem will be trampled on by the Gentiles until the times of the Gentiles are fulfilled.

²⁵ 'There will be signs in the sun, moon and stars. On the earth, nations will be in anguish and perplexity at the roaring and tossing of the sea. ²⁶ Men will faint from terror, apprehensive of what is coming on the world, for the heavenly bodies will be shaken. ²⁷ At that time they will see the Son of Man coming in a cloud with power and great glory. ²⁸ When these things begin to take place, stand up and lift up your heads, because your

---

'At that time they will see the Son of Man coming in a cloud with power and great glory.'

---

redemption is drawing near.'

²⁹ He told them this parable: 'Look at the fig-tree and all the trees. ³⁰ When they sprout leaves, you can see for yourselves and know that summer is near. ³¹ Even so, when you see these things happening, you know that the kingdom of God is near.

never pass away.

[34] 'Be careful, or your hearts will be weighed down with dissipation, drunkenness and the anxieties of life, and that day will close on you unexpectedly like a trap. [35] For it will come upon all those who live on the face of the whole earth. [36] Be always on the watch, and pray that you may be able to escape all that is about to happen, and that you may be able to stand before the Son of Man.'

[37] Each day Jesus was teaching at the temple, and each evening he went out to spend the night on the hill called the Mount of Olives, [38] and all the people came early in the morning to hear him at the temple.

DAY 340

LUKE 22. 1 — 38

'Know that the kingdom of God is near.'

[32] 'I tell you the truth, this generation will certainly not pass away until all these

> **'They will fall by the sword and will be taken as prisoners...'**

things have happened. [33] Heaven and earth will pass away, but my words will

22 Judas Agrees to Betray Jesus

Now the Feast of Unleavened Bread, called the Passover, was approaching, [2] and the chief priests and the teachers of the law were looking for some way to get rid of Jesus, for they were afraid of the people. [3] Then Satan entered Judas, called Iscariot, one of the Twelve. [4] And Judas went to the chief priests and the officers of the temple guard and discussed with them how he might betray Jesus. [5] They were delighted and agreed to give him money. [6] He consented, and watched for an opportunity to hand Jesus over to them when no crowd was present.

The Last Supper

[7] Then came the day of Unleavened Bread on which the Passover lamb had to be sacrificed. [8] Jesus sent Peter and John, saying, 'Go and make preparations for us to eat the Passover.'

[9] 'Where do you want us to prepare for it?' they asked.

[10] He replied, 'As you enter the city, a man carrying a jar of water will meet you. Follow him to the house that he enters, [11] and say to the owner of the house, "The Teacher asks: Where is the guest room, where I may eat the Passover with my disciples?" [12] He will show you a large upper room, all furnished. Make preparations there.'

[13] They left and found things just as Jesus had told them. So they prepared the Passover.

[14] When the hour came, Jesus and his apostles reclined at the table. [15] And he said to them, 'I have eagerly desired to eat this Passover with you before I suffer. [16] For I tell you, I will not eat it again until it finds fulfilment in the kingdom of God.'

[17] After taking the cup, he gave thanks and said, 'Take this and divide it among you. [18] For I tell you I will not drink again of the fruit of the vine until the kingdom of God comes.'

[19] And he took bread, gave thanks and broke it, and gave it to them, saying, 'This is my body given for you; do this in remembrance of me.'

[20] In the same way, after the supper he took the cup, saying, 'This cup is the new covenant in my blood, which is poured out for you. [21] But the hand of him who is going to betray me is with mine on the table. [22] The Son of Man will go as it has been decreed, but woe to that man who betrays him.' [23] They began to question among themselves which of them it might be who would do this.

[24] Also a dispute arose among them as to which of them was considered to be greatest. [25] Jesus said to them, 'The kings of the Gentiles lord it over them; and those who exercise authority over them call themselves Benefactors. [26] But you are not to be like that. Instead, the greatest among you should be like the youngest, and the one who rules like the one who serves. [27] For who is greater, the one who is at the table or the one who serves? Is it not the one who is at the table? But I am among you as one who serves. [28] You are those who have stood by me in my trials. [29] And I confer on you a kingdom, just as my Father conferred one on me, [30] so that you may eat and drink at my table in my kingdom and sit on thrones, judging the twelve tribes of Israel.

[31] 'Simon, Simon, Satan has asked to sift you as wheat. [32] But I have prayed for you, Simon, that your faith may not fail. And when you have turned back, strengthen your brothers.'

[33] But he replied, 'Lord, I am ready to go with you to prison and to death.'

[34] Jesus answered, 'I tell you, Peter, before the cock crows today, you will deny three times that you know me.'

[35] Then Jesus asked them, 'When I sent you without purse, bag or sandals, did you lack anything?' 'Nothing,' they answered.

[36] He said to them, 'But now if you have a purse, take it, and also a bag; and if you don't have a sword, sell your cloak and buy one. [37] It is written: "And he was numbered with the transgressors"; and I tell you that this must be fulfilled in me. Yes, what is written about me is reaching its fulfilment.'

[38] The disciples said, 'See, Lord, here are two swords.'

'That is enough,' he replied.

DAY 341

LUKE 22. 39 — 71

Jesus Prays on the Mount of Olives

[39] Jesus went out as usual to the Mount of Olives, and his disciples followed him. [40] On reaching the place, he said to them, 'Pray that you will not fall into temptation.' [41] He withdrew about a stone's throw beyond them, knelt down and prayed, [42] 'Father, if you are willing, take this cup from me; yet not my will, but yours be done.' [43] An angel from heaven appeared to him and strengthened him. [44] And being in anguish, he prayed more earnestly, and his sweat was like drops of blood falling to the ground.

[45] When he rose from prayer and went back to the disciples, he found them asleep, exhausted from sorrow. [46] 'Why are you sleeping?' he asked them. 'Get up and pray so that you will not fall into temptation.'

Jesus Arrested

[47] While he was still speaking a crowd came up, and the man who was called Judas, one of the Twelve, was leading them. He approached Jesus to kiss him, [48] but Jesus asked him, 'Judas, are you betraying the Son of Man with a kiss?'

[49] When Jesus' followers saw what was going to happen, they said, 'Lord, should we strike with our swords?' [50] And one of them struck the servant of the high priest, cutting off his right ear.

[51] But Jesus answered, 'No more of this!' And he touched the man's ear and healed him.

[52] Then Jesus said to the chief priests, the officers of the temple guard, and the elders, who had come for him, 'Am I leading a rebellion, that you have come with swords and clubs? [53] Every day I was with you in the temple courts, and you did not lay a hand on me. But this is your hour - when darkness reigns.'

Peter Disowns Jesus

[54] Then seizing him, they led him away and took him into the house of the high priest. Peter followed at a distance. [55] But when they had kindled a fire in the middle of the courtyard and had sat down together, Peter sat down with them. [56] A servant girl saw him seated there in the firelight. She looked closely at him and said, 'This man was with him.'

[57] But he denied it. 'Woman, I don't know him,' he said.

[58] A little later someone else saw him and said, 'You also are one of them.'

'Man, I am not!' Peter replied.

[59] About an hour later another asserted, 'Certainly this fellow was with him, for he is a Galilean.'

[60] Peter replied, 'Man, I don't know what you're talking about!' Just as he was speaking, the cock crowed. [61] The Lord turned and looked straight at Peter. Then Peter remembered the word the Lord had spoken to him: 'Before the cock crows today, you will disown me three times.' [62] And he went outside and wept bitterly.

The Guards Mock Jesus

[63] The men who were guarding Jesus began mocking and beating him. [64] They blindfolded him and demanded, 'Prophesy! Who hit you?' [65] And they said many other insulting things to him.

Jesus Before Pilate and Herod

66 At daybreak the council of the elders of the people, both the chief priests and teachers of the law, met together, and Jesus was led before them. 67 'If you are the Christ,' they said, 'tell us.'

Jesus answered, 'If I tell you, you will not believe me, 68 and if I asked you, you would not answer. 69 But from now on, the Son of Man will be seated at the right hand of the mighty God.'

70 They all asked, 'Are you then the Son of God?'

He replied, 'You are right in saying I am.'

71 Then they said, 'Why do we need any more testimony? We have heard it from his own lips.'

DAY 342

LUKE 23. 1 — 25

23 Then the whole assembly rose and led him off to Pilate. 2 And they began to accuse him, saying, 'We have found this man subverting our nation. He opposes payment of taxes to Caesar and claims to be Christ, a king.'

3 So Pilate asked Jesus, 'Are you the king of the Jews?'

'Yes, it is as you say,' Jesus replied.

4 Then Pilate announced to the chief priests and the crowd, 'I find no basis for a charge against this man.'

5 But they insisted, 'He stirs up the people all over Judea by his teaching. He started in Galilee and has come all the way here.'

6 On hearing this, Pilate asked if the man was a Galilean. 7 When he learned that Jesus was under Herod's jurisdiction, he sent him to Herod, who was also in Jerusalem at that time.

8 When Herod saw Jesus, he was greatly pleased, because for a long time he had been wanting to see him. From what he had heard about him, he hoped to see him perform some miracle. 9 He plied him with many questions, but Jesus gave him no answer. 10 The chief priests and the teachers of the law were standing there, vehemently accusing him. 11 Then Herod and his soldiers ridiculed and mocked him. Dressing him in an elegant robe, they sent him back to Pilate. 12 That day Herod and Pilate became friends - before this they had been enemies.

13 Pilate called together the chief priests, the rulers and the people, 14 and said to them, 'You brought me this man as one who was inciting the people to rebellion. I have examined him in your presence and have found no basis for your charges against him. 15 Neither has Herod, for he sent him back to us; as you can see, he has done nothing to deserve death. 16 Therefore, I will punish him and then release him.'

18 With one voice they cried out, 'Away with this man! Release Barabbas to us!' (19 Barabbas had been thrown into prison for an insurrection in the city, and for murder.)

20 Wanting to release Jesus, Pilate appealed to them again. 21 But they kept shouting, 'Crucify him! Crucify him!'

22 For the third time he spoke to them: 'Why? What crime has this man committed? I have found in him no grounds for the death penalty. Therefore I will have him punished and then release him.'

23 But with loud shouts they insistently demanded that he be crucified, and their shouts prevailed. 24 So Pilate

decided to grant their demand. ²⁵ He released the man who had been thrown into prison for insurrection and murder, the one they asked for, and surrendered Jesus to their will.

Jesus said, 'Father forgive them, for they do not know what they are doing.'

DAY 343

LUKE 23. 26 — 56

The Crucifixion

26 As they led him away, they seized Simon from Cyrene, who was on his way in from the country, and put the cross on him and made him carry it behind Jesus. 27 A large number of people followed him, including women who mourned and wailed for him. 28 Jesus turned and said to them, 'Daughters of Jerusalem, do not weep for me; weep for yourselves and for your children. 29 For the time will come when you will say, "Blessed are the barren women, the wombs that never bore and the breasts that never nursed!" 30 Then they will say to the mountains, "Fall on us!" and to the hills "Cover us!"'

31 'For if men do these things when the tree is green, what will happen when it is dry?'

32 'Two other men, both criminals, were also led out with him to be executed. 33 When they came to the place called the Skull, there they crucified him, along with the criminals - one on his right, the other on his left. 34 Jesus said, 'Father, forgive them, for they do not know what they are doing.' And they divided up his clothes by casting lots.

35 The people stood watching, and the rulers even sneered at him. They said, 'He saved others; let him save himself if he is the Christ of God, the Chosen One.'

36 The soldiers also came up and mocked him. They offered him wine vinegar 37 and said, 'If you are the king of the Jews, save yourself.'

38 There was a written notice above him, which read: THIS IS THE KING OF THE JEWS.

39 One of the criminals who hung there hurled insults at him: 'Aren't you the Christ? Save yourself and us!'

40 But the other criminal rebuked him. 'Don't you fear God,' he said, 'since you are under the same sentence? 41 We are punished justly, for we are getting what our deeds deserve. But this man has done nothing wrong.'

42 Then he said, 'Jesus, remember me when you come into your kingdom.'

43 Jesus answered him, 'I tell you the truth, today you will be with me in paradise.'

Jesus' Death

44 It was now about the sixth hour, and darkness came over the whole land until the ninth hour, 45 for the sun stopped shining. And the curtain of the temple was torn in two. 46 Jesus called out with a loud voice, 'Father, into your hands I commit my spirit.' When he had said this, he breathed his last.

47 The centurion, seeing what had happened, praised God and said, 'Surely this was a righteous man.' 48 When all the people who had gathered to witness this sight saw what took place, they beat their breasts and went away. 49 But all those who knew him, including the women who had followed him from Galilee, stood at a distance, watching these things.

Jesus' Burial

50 Now there was a man named Joseph, a member of the Council, a good and upright man, 51 who had not consented to their decision and action. He came from the Judean town of Arimathea and he was waiting for the kingdom of God. 52 Going to Pilate, he asked for Jesus' body.

[53] Then he took it down, wrapped it in linen cloth and placed it in a tomb cut in the rock, one in which no-one had yet been laid. [54] It was Preparation Day, and the Sabbath was about to begin.

[55] The women who had come with Jesus from Galilee followed Joseph and saw the tomb and how his body was laid in it. [56] Then they went home and prepared spices and perfumes. But they rested on the Sabbath in obedience to the commandment.

DAY 344

LUKE 24. 1 — 35

24 The Resurrection

On the first day of the week, very early in the morning, the women took the spices they had prepared and went to the tomb. [2] They found the stone rolled away from the tomb, [3] but when they entered, they did not find the body of the Lord Jesus. [4] While they were wondering about this, suddenly two men in clothes that gleamed like lightning stood beside them. [5] In their fright the women bowed down with their faces to the ground, but the men said to them, 'Why do you look for the living among the dead? [6] He is not here; he has risen! Remember how he told you, while he was still with you in Galilee: [7] "The Son of Man must be delivered into the hands of sinful men, be crucified and on the third day be raised again." ' [8] Then they remembered his words.

[9] When they came back from the tomb, they told all these things to the Eleven and to all the others. [10] It was Mary Magdalene, Joanna, Mary the mother of James, and the others with them who told this to the apostles. [11] But they did not believe the women, because their words seemed to them like nonsense. [12] Peter, however, got up and ran to the tomb. Bending over, he saw the strips of linen lying by themselves, and he went away, wondering to himself what had happened.

On the Road to Emmaus

[13] Now that same day two of them were going to a village called Emmaus, about seven miles from Jerusalem. [14] They were talking with each other about everything that had happened. [15] As they talked and discussed these things with each other, Jesus himself came up and walked along with them; [16] but they were kept from recognising him.

[17] He asked them, 'What are you discussing together as you walk along?'

They stood still, their faces downcast. [18] One of them, named Cleopas, asked him, 'Are you only a visitor to Jerusalem and do not know the things that have happened there in these days?'

[19] 'What things?' he asked.

'About Jesus of Nazareth,' they replied. 'He was a prophet, powerful in word and deed before God and all the people. [20] The chief priests and our rulers handed him over to be sentenced to death, and they crucified him; [21] but we had hoped that he was the one who was going to redeem Israel. And what is more, it is the third day since all this took place. [22] In addition, some of our women amazed us. They went to the tomb early this morning [23] but didn't find his body. They came and told us that they had seen a vision of angels, who said he was alive. [24] Then some of our companions went to the tomb and found it just as the women had said, but him they did not see.'

²⁵ He said to them, 'How foolish you are, and how slow of heart to believe all that the prophets have spoken! ²⁶ Did not the Christ have to suffer these things and then enter his glory?' ²⁷ And beginning with Moses and all the Prophets, he explained to them what was said in all the Scriptures concerning himself.

²⁸ As they approached the village to which they were going, Jesus acted as if he were going further. ²⁹ But they urged him strongly, 'Stay with us, for it is nearly evening; the day is almost over.' So he went in to stay with them.

³⁰ When he was at the table with them, he took bread, gave thanks, broke it and began to give it to them. ³¹ Then their eyes were opened and they recognised him, and he disappeared from their sight. ³² They asked each other, 'Were not our hearts burning within us while he talked with us on the road and opened the Scriptures to us?'

³³ They got up and returned at once to Jerusalem. There they found the Eleven and those with them, assembled together ³⁴ and saying, 'It is true! The Lord has risen and has appeared to Simon.' ³⁵ Then the two told what had happened on the way, and how Jesus was recognised by them when he broke the bread.

DAY 345

LUKE 24. 36 — 53

Jesus Appears to the Disciples

³⁶ While they were still talking about this, Jesus himself stood among them and said to them, 'Peace be with you.'

³⁷ They were startled and frightened, thinking they saw a ghost. ³⁸ He said to them, 'Why are you troubled, and why do doubts rise in your minds? ³⁹ Look at my hands and my feet. It is I myself! Touch me and see; a ghost does not have flesh and bones, as you see I have.'

⁴⁰ When he had said this, he showed them his hands and feet. ⁴¹ And while they still did not believe it because of joy and amazement, he asked them, 'Do you have anything here to eat?' ⁴² They gave him a piece of broiled fish, ⁴³ and he took it and ate it in their presence.

⁴⁴ He said to them, 'This is what I told you while I was still with you: Everything must be fulfilled that is written about me in the Law of Moses, the Prophets and the Psalms.'

⁴⁵ Then he opened their minds so they could understand the Scriptures. ⁴⁶ He told them, 'This is what is written: The Christ will suffer and rise from the dead on the third day, ⁴⁷ and repentance and forgiveness of sins will be preached in his name to all nations, beginning at Jerusalem. ⁴⁸ You are witnesses of these things. ⁴⁹ I am going to send you what my Father has promised; but stay in the city until you have been clothed with power from on high.'

The Ascension

⁵⁰ When he had led them out to the vicinity of Bethany, he lifted up his hands and blessed them. ⁵¹ While he was blessing them, he left them and was taken up into heaven. ⁵² Then they worshipped him and returned to Jerusalem with great joy. ⁵³ And they stayed continually at the temple, praising God.

DAY 346
REV. 1. 1 — 20

Prologue

1 The revelation of Jesus Christ, which God gave him to show his servants what must soon take place. He made it known by sending his angel to his servant John, [2] who testifies to everything he saw - that is, the word of God and the testimony of Jesus Christ. [3] Blessed is the one who reads the words of this prophecy, and blessed are those who hear it and take to heart what is written in it, because the time is near.

Greetings and Doxology

[4] John,

To the seven churches in the province of Asia:

Grace and peace to you from him who is, and who was, and who is to come, and from the seven spirits before his throne, [5] and from Jesus Christ, who is the faithful witness, the firstborn from the dead, and the ruler of the kings of the earth.

To him who loves us and has freed us from our sins by his blood, [6] and has made us to be a kingdom and priests to serve his God and Father - to him be glory and power for ever and ever! Amen.

[7] Look, he is coming with the clouds,
and every eye will see him,
even those who pierced him;
and all the peoples of the earth will
mourn because of him.
So shall it be! Amen.

[8] 'I am the Alpha and the Omega,' says the Lord God, 'who is, and who was, and who is to come, the Almighty.'

One Like a Son of Man

[9] I, John, your brother and companion in the suffering and kingdom and patient endurance that are ours in Jesus, was on the island of Patmos because of the word of God and the testimony of Jesus. [10] On the Lord's Day I was in the Spirit, and I heard behind me a loud voice like a trumpet, [11] which said: 'Write on a scroll what you see and send it to the seven churches: to Ephesus, Smyrna, Pergamum, Thyatira, Sardis, Philadelphia and Laodicea.'

[12] I turned round to see the voice that was speaking to me. And when I turned I saw seven golden lampstands, [13] and among the lampstands was someone 'like a son of man', dressed in a robe reaching down to his feet and with a golden sash round his chest. [14] His head and hair were white like wool, as white as snow, and his eyes were like blazing fire. [15] His feet were like bronze glowing in a furnace, and his voice was like the sound of rushing waters. [16] In his right hand he held seven stars, and out of his mouth came a sharp double-edged sword. His face was like the sun shining in all its brilliance.

[17] When I saw him, I fell at his feet as though dead. Then he placed his right hand on me and said: 'Do not be afraid. I am the First and the Last. [18] I am the Living One; I was dead, and behold I am alive for ever and ever! And I hold the keys of death and Hades.

[19] 'Write, therefore, what you have seen, what is now and what will take place later. [20] The mystery of the seven stars that you saw in my right hand and of the seven golden lampstands is this: The seven stars are the angels of the seven churches, and the seven lampstands are the seven churches.'

DAY 347

REV. 2. 1 — 17

2 To the Church in Ephesus

'To the angel of the church in Ephesus write:

These are the words of him who holds the seven stars in his right hand and walks among the seven golden lampstands: ²I know your deeds, your hard work and your perseverance. I know that you cannot tolerate wicked men, that you have tested those who claim to be apostles but are not, and have found them false. ³You have persevered and have endured hardships for my name, and have not grown weary.

⁴Yet I hold this against you: You have forsaken your first love. ⁵Remember the height from which you have fallen! Repent and do the things you did at first. If you do not repent, I will come to you and remove your lampstand from its place. ⁶But you have this in your favour: You hate the practices of Nicolaitans, which I also hate.

⁷He who has an ear, let him hear what the Spirit says to the churches. To him who overcomes, I will give the right to eat from the tree of life, which is in the paradise of God.

To the Church in Smyrna

⁸'To the angel of the church in Smyrna write:

These are the words of him who is the First and the Last, who died and came to life again. ⁹I know your afflictions and your poverty - yet you are rich! I know the slander of those who say they are Jews and are not, but are a synagogue of Satan. ¹⁰Do not be afraid of what you are about to suffer. I tell you, the devil will put some of you in prison to test you, and you will suffer persecution for ten days. Be faithful, even to the point of death, and I will give you the crown of life.

¹¹He who has an ear, let him hear what the Spirit says to the churches. He who overcomes will not be hurt at all by the second death.

To the Church in Pergamum

¹²'To the angel of the church in Pergamum write:

These are the words of him who has the sharp, double-edged sword. ¹³I know where you live - where Satan has his throne. Yet you remain true to my name. You did not renounce your faith in me, even in the days of Antipas, my faithful witness, who was put to death in your city - where Satan lives.

¹⁴Nevertheless, I have a few things

'He who overcomes will not be hurt at all by the second death.'

---

against you: You have people there who hold to the teaching of Balaam, who taught Balak to entice the Israelites to sin by eating food sacrificed to idols and by committing sexual immorality. ¹⁵Likewise you also have those who hold to the teaching of the Nicolaitans. ¹⁶Repent therefore! Otherwise, I will soon come to you and will fight against them with the sword of my mouth.

¹⁷He who has an ear, let him hear what the Spirit says to the churches. To him who overcomes, I will give some of the hidden manna. I will also give him a white stone with a new name written on it, known only to him who receives it.

DAY 348

REV. 2. 18 — 3. 6

To the Church in Thyatira

[18] 'To the angel of the church in Thyatira write:

These are the words of the Son of God, whose eyes are like blazing fire and whose feet are like burnished bronze. [19] I know your deeds, your love and faith, your service and perseverance, and that you are now doing more than you did at first.

[20] Nevertheless, I have this against you: You tolerate that woman Jezebel, who calls herself a prophetess. By her teaching she misleads my servants into sexual immorality and the eating of food sacrificed to idols. [21] I have given her time to repent of her immorality, but she is unwilling. [22] So I will cast her on a bed of suffering, and I will make those who commit adultery with her suffer intensely, unless they repent of her ways. [23] I will strike her children dead. Then all the churches will know that I am he who searches hearts and minds, and I will

repay each of you according to your deeds. [24] Now I say to the rest of you in Thyatira, to you who do not hold to her teaching and have not learned Satan's so-called deep secrets (I will not impose any other burden on you): [25] Only hold on to what you have until I come.

[26] To him who overcomes and does my will to the end, I will give authority over the nations -

[27] "He will rule them with an iron sceptre;
he will dash them to pieces like pottery" -

just as I have received authority from my Father. [28] I will also give him the morning star. [29] He who has an ear, let him hear what the Spirit says to the churches.

3 To the Church in Sardis

'To the angel of the church in Sardis write:
These are the words of him who holds the seven spirits of God and the seven stars. I know your deeds; you have a reputation of being alive, but you are dead. [2] Wake up! Strengthen what remains and is about to die, for I have not found your deeds complete in the sight of my God. [3] Remember, therefore, what you have received and heard; obey it, and repent. But if you do not wake up, I will come like a thief, and you will not know at what time I will come to you.

[4] Yet you have a few people in Sardis who have not soiled their clothes. They will walk with me, dressed in white, for they are worthy. [5] He who overcomes will, like them, be dressed in white. I will never blot out his name from the book of life, but will acknowledge his name before my Father and his angels. [6] He who has an ear, let him hear what the Spirit says to the churches.

'He who has an ear, let him hear what the Spirit says to the churches.'

DAY 349

REV. 3. 7 — 22

To the Church in Philadelphia

[7] 'To the angel of the church in Philadelphia write:

These are the words of him who is holy and true, who holds the key of

---

'I am coming soon. Hold on to what you have, so that no-one will take your crown.'

David. What he opens no-one can shut, and what he shuts no-one can open. [8] I know your deeds. See, I have placed before you an open door that no-one can shut. I know that you have little strength, yet you have kept my word and have not denied my name. [9] I will make those who are of the synagogue of Satan, who claim to be Jews though they are not, but are liars - I will make them come and fall down at your feet and acknowledge that I have loved you. [10] Since you have kept my command to endure patiently, I will also keep you from the hour of trial that is going to come upon the whole world to test those who live on the earth.

[11] I am coming soon. Hold on to what you have, so that no-one will take your crown. [12] Him who overcomes I will make a pillar in the temple of my God. Never again will he leave it. I will write on him the name of my God and the name of the city of my God, the new Jerusalem, which is coming down out of heaven

from my God; and I will also write on him my new name. [13] He who has an ear, let him hear what the Spirit says to the churches.

To the Church in Laodicea

[14] 'To the angel of the church in Laodicea write:

These are the words of the Amen, the faithful and true witness, the ruler of God's creation. [15] I know your deeds, that you are neither cold nor hot. I wish you were either one or the other! [16] So, because you are lukewarm - neither hot nor cold - I am about to spit you out of my mouth. [17] You say, "I am rich; I have acquired wealth and do not need a thing." But you do not realise that you are wretched, pitiful, poor, blind and naked. [18] I counsel you to buy from me gold refined in the fire, so that you can become rich; and white clothes to wear, so that you can cover your shameful nakedness; and salve to put on your eyes, so that you can see.

[19] Those whom I love I rebuke and discipline. So be earnest, and repent. [20] Here I am! I stand at the door and knock. If anyone hears my voice and opens the door, I will come in and eat

---

'Here I am! I stand at the door and knock. If anyone hears my voice and opens the door, I will come in and eat with him, and he with me.'

---

with him, and he with me. [21] To him who overcomes, I will give the right to sit with me on my throne, just as I overcame and sat down with my Father on his throne. [22] He who has an ear, let him hear what the Spirit says to the churches.'

DAY 350
REV. 4. 1 — 11

4 **The Throne in Heaven**
After this I looked, and there before me was a door standing open in heaven. And the voice I had first heard speaking to me like a trumpet said, 'Come up here, and I will show you what must take place after this.' ² At once I was in the Spirit, and there before me was a throne in heaven with someone sitting on it. ³ And the one who sat there had the appearance of jasper and carnelian. A rainbow, resembling an emerald, encircled the throne. ⁴ Surrounding the throne were twenty-four other thrones, and seated on them were twenty-four elders. They were dressed in white and had crowns of gold on their heads. ⁵ From the throne came flashes of lightning, rumblings and peals of thunder. Before the throne, seven lamps were blazing. These are the seven spirits of God. ⁶ Also before the throne there was what looked like a sea of glass, clear as crystal.

In the centre, around the throne, were four living creatures, and they were covered with eyes, in front and behind. ⁷ The first living creature was like a lion, the second was like an ox, the third had a face like a man, the fourth was like a flying eagle. ⁸ Each of the four living creatures had six wings and was covered with eyes all around, even under his wings. Day and night they never stop saying:

'Holy, holy, holy
is the Lord God Almighty,
who was, and is, and is to come.'

⁹ Whenever the living creatures give glory, honour and thanks to him who sits on the throne and who lives for ever and ever, ¹⁰ the twenty-four elders fall down before him who sits on the throne, and worship him who lives for ever and ever. They lay their crowns before the throne and say:

¹¹ 'You are worthy, our Lord and God,
to receive glory and honour and power,
for you created all things,
and by your will they were created and have their being.'

'For you created all things...'

DAY 351

REV. 5. 1 — 14

5 The Scroll and the Lamb

Then I saw in the right hand of him who sat on the throne a scroll with writing on both sides and sealed with seven seals. [2] And I saw a mighty angel proclaiming in a loud voice, 'Who is worthy to break the seals and open the scroll?' [3] But no-one in heaven or on earth or under the earth could open the scroll or even look inside it. [4] I wept and wept because no-one was found who was worthy to open the scroll or look inside. [5] Then one of the elders said to me, 'Do not weep! See, the Lion of the tribe of Judah, the Root of David, has triumphed. He is able to open the scroll and its seven seals.'

[6] Then I saw a Lamb, looking as if it had been slain, standing in the centre of the throne, encircled by the four living creatures and the elders. He had seven horns and seven eyes, which are the seven spirits of God sent out into all the earth. [7] He came and took the scroll from the right hand of him who sat on the throne.

'Who is worthy to break the seals and open the scroll?'

[8] And when he had taken it, the four living creatures and the twenty-four elders fell down before the Lamb. Each one had a harp and they were holding golden bowls full of incense, which are the prayers of the saints. [9] And they sang a new song:

'You are worthy to take the scroll
 and to open its seals,
because you were slain,
 and with your blood you
  purchased men for God
from every tribe and language
 and people and nation.
[10] You have made them to be a
 kingdom and priests to serve our
 God,
and they will reign on the earth.'

'Worthy is the Lamb, who was slain, to receive power and wealth and wisdom...'

[11] Then I looked and heard the voice of many angels, numbering thousands upon thousands, and ten thousand times ten thousand. They encircled the throne and the living creatures and the elders. [12] In a loud voice they sang:

'Worthy is the Lamb, who was slain,
 to receive power and wealth
 and wisdom and strength
 and honour and glory and praise!'

[13] Then I heard every creature in heaven and on earth and under the earth and on the sea, and all that is in them, singing:

'To him who sits on the throne
 and to the Lamb
be praise and honour and glory
 and power,
 for ever and ever!'

[14] The four living creatures said, 'Amen', and the elders fell down and worshipped.

DAY 352

REV. 6. 1 — 17

6 **The Seals**
I watched as the Lamb opened the first of the seven seals. Then I heard one of the four living creatures say in a voice like thunder, 'Come!' ² I looked, and there before me was a white horse! Its rider held a bow, and he was given a crown, and he rode out as a conqueror bent on conquest.

³ When the Lamb opened the second seal, I heard the second living creature say, 'Come!' ⁴ Then another horse came out, a fiery red one. Its rider was given power to take peace from the earth and to make men slay each other. To him was given a large sword.

⁵ When the Lamb opened the third seal, I heard the third living creature say, 'Come!' I looked, and there before me was a black horse! Its rider was holding a pair of scales in his hand. ⁶ Then I heard what sounded like a voice among the four living creatures, saying, 'A quart of wheat for a day's wages, and three quarts of barley for a day's wages, and do not damage the oil and the wine!'

'Come!' I looked, and there before me was a black horse! Its rider was holding a pair of scales in his hand.

---

⁷ When the Lamb opened the fourth seal, I heard the voice of the fourth living creature say, 'Come!' ⁸ I looked, and there before me was a pale horse! Its rider was named Death, and Hades was following close behind him. They were given power over a fourth of the earth to kill by sword, famine and plague, and by the wild beasts of the earth.

⁹ When he opened the fifth seal, I saw under the altar the souls of those who had been slain because of the word of God and the testimony they had maintained. ¹⁰ They called out in a loud voice, 'How

---

'How long, Sovereign Lord, holy and true, until you judge the inhabitants of the earth and avenge our blood?'

---

long, Sovereign Lord, holy and true, until you judge the inhabitants of the earth and avenge our blood?' ¹¹ Then each of them was given a white robe, and they were told to wait a little longer, until the number of their fellow-servants and brothers who were to be killed as they had been was completed.

¹² I watched as he opened the sixth seal. There was a great earthquake. The sun turned black like sackcloth made of goat hair, the whole moon turned blood red, ¹³ and the stars in the sky fell to earth, as late figs drop from a fig-tree when shaken by a strong wind. ¹⁴ The sky receded like a scroll, rolling up, and every mountain and island was removed from its place.

¹⁵ Then the kings of the earth, the princes, the generals, the rich, the mighty, and every slave and every free man hid in caves and among the rocks of the mountains. ¹⁶ They called to the mountains and the rocks, 'Fall on us and hide us from the face of him who sits on the throne and from the wrath of the Lamb! ¹⁷ For the great day of their wrath has come, and who can stand?'

DAY 353

REV. 7. 1 — 8. 5

7 144,000 Sealed

After this I saw four angels standing at the four corners of the earth, holding back the four winds of the earth to prevent any wind from blowing on the land or on the sea or on any tree. ² Then I saw another angel coming up from the east, having the seal of the living God. He called out in a loud voice to the four angels who had been given power to harm the land and the sea: ³ 'Do not harm the land or the sea or the trees until we put a seal on the foreheads of the servants of our God.' ⁴ Then I heard the number of those who were sealed: 144,000 from all the tribes of Israel.

⁵ From the tribe of Judah
12,000 were sealed,
from the tribe of Reuben
12,000,
from the tribe of Gad
12,000,
⁶ from the tribe of Asher
12,000,
from the tribe of Naphtali
12,000,
from the tribe of Manasseh
12,000,
⁷ from the tribe of Simeon
12,000,
from the tribe of Levi
12,000,
from the tribe of Issachar
12,000,
⁸ from the tribe of Zebulun
12,000,

from the tribe of Joseph
12,000,
from the tribe of Benjamin
12,000.

The Great Multitude in White Robes

⁹ After this I looked and there before me was a great multitude that no-one could count, from every nation, tribe, people and language, standing before the throne and in front of the Lamb. They were wearing white robes and were holding palm branches in their hands. ¹⁰ And they cried out in a loud voice:

'Salvation belongs to our God,
who sits on the throne,
and to the Lamb.'

¹¹ All the angels were standing round the throne and around the elders and the four living creatures. They fell down on their faces before the throne and worshipped God, ¹² saying:

'Amen!
Praise and glory
and wisdom and thanks
and honour
and power and strength
be to our God for ever and ever.
Amen!'

¹³ Then one of the elders asked me, 'These in white robes - who are they, and where did they come from?'

¹⁴ I answered, 'Sir, you know.'

And he said, 'These are they who have come out of the great tribulation; they have washed their robes and made them white in the blood of the Lamb. ¹⁵ Therefore,

A great star, blazing like a torch, fell from the sky.

there was silence in heaven for about half an hour.

[2] And I saw the seven angels who stand before God, and to them were given seven trumpets.

[3] Another angel, who had a golden censer, came and stood at the altar. He was given much incense to offer, with the prayers of all the saints, on the golden altar before the throne. [4] The smoke of the incense, together with the prayers of the saints, went up before God from the angel's hand. [5] Then the angel took the censer, filled it with fire from the altar, and hurled it on the earth; and there came peals of thunder, rumblings, flashes of lightning and an earthquake.

DAY 354
REV. 8. 6 — 9. 21

they are before the throne of God
and serve him day and night
in his temple;
and he who sits on the throne will
spread his tent over them.
[16] Never again will they hunger;
never again will they thirst.
The sun will not beat upon them,
nor any scorching heat.
[17] For the Lamb at the centre of the
throne will be their shepherd;
he will lead them to springs of
living water.
And God will wipe away every tear
from their eyes.'

The Trumpets
[6] Then the seven angels who had the seven trumpets prepared to sound them.

[7] The first angel sounded his trumpet, and there came hail and fire mixed with blood, and it was hurled down upon the earth. A third of the earth was burned up, a third of the trees were burned up, and all the green grass was burned up.

[8] The second angel sounded his trumpet, and something like a huge mountain, all ablaze, was thrown into the sea. A third of the sea turned into blood, [9] a third of the living creatures in the sea died, and a third of the ships were destroyed.

[10] The third angel sounded his trumpet, and a great star, blazing like a torch, fell from the sky on a third of the rivers and on the springs of water - [11] the name of the star is Wormwood. A third of the waters turned bitter, and many people

8 The Seventh Seal and the Golden Censer
When he opened the seventh seal,

died from the waters that had become bitter.

[12] The fourth angel sounded his trumpet, and a third of the sun was struck, a third of the moon, and a third of the stars, so that a third of them turned dark. A third of the day was without light, and also a third of the night.

[13] As I watched, I heard an eagle that was flying in mid-air call out in a loud voice: 'Woe! Woe! Woe to the inhabitants of the earth, because of the trumpet blasts about to be sounded by the other three angels!'

9

The fifth angel sounded his trumpet, and I saw a star that had fallen from the sky to the earth. The star was given the key to the shaft of the Abyss. [2] When he opened the Abyss, smoke rose from it like the smoke from a gigantic furnace. The sun and sky were darkened by the smoke from the Abyss. [3] And out of the smoke locusts came down upon the earth and were given power like that of scorpions of the earth. [4] They were told not to harm the grass of the earth or any plant or tree, but only those people who did not have the seal of God on their foreheads. [5] They were not given power to kill them, but only to torture them for five months. And the agony they suffered was like that of the sting of a scorpion when it strikes a man. [6] During those days men will seek death, but will not find it; they will long to die, but death will elude them.

[7] The locusts looked like horses prepared for battle. On their heads they wore something like crowns of gold, and their faces resembled human faces. [8] Their hair was like women's hair, and their teeth were like lions' teeth. [9] They had breastplates like breastplates of iron, and the sound of their wings was like the thundering of many horses and chariots rushing into battle. [10] They had tails and stings like scorpions, and in their tails they had power to torment people for five months. [11] They had as king over them the angel of the Abyss, whose name in Hebrew is Abaddon, and in Greek, Apollyon.

[12] The first woe is past; two other woes are yet to come.

[13] The sixth angel sounded his trumpet, and I heard a voice coming from the horns of the golden altar that is before God. [14] It said to the sixth angel who had the trumpet, 'Release the four angels who are bound at the great river Euphrates.' [15] And the four angels who had been kept ready for this very hour and day and month and year were released to kill a third of mankind. [16] The number of the mounted troops was two hundred million. I heard their number.

[17] The horses and riders I saw in my vision looked like this: Their breastplates were fiery red, dark blue, and yellow as sulphur. The heads of the horses resembled the heads of lions, and out of their mouths came fire, smoke and sulphur. [18] A third of mankind was killed by the three plagues of fire, smoke and sulphur that came out of their mouths. [19] The power of the horses was in their mouths and in their tails; for their tails were like snakes, having heads with which they inflict injury.

[20] The rest of mankind that were not killed by these plagues still did not repent of the work of their hands; they did not stop worshipping demons, and idols of gold, silver, bronze, stone and wood - idols that cannot see or hear or walk. [21] Nor did they repent of their murders, their magic arts, their sexual immorality or their thefts.

DAY 355
REV. 10. 1 — 11

10 **The Angel and the Little Scroll**
Then I saw another mighty angel coming down from heaven. He was robed in a cloud, with a rainbow above his head; his face was like the sun, and his legs were like fiery pillars. ²He was holding a little scroll, which lay open in his hand. He planted his right foot on the sea and his left foot on the land, ³and he gave a loud shout like the roar of a lion. When he shouted, the voices of the seven thunders spoke. ⁴And when the seven thunders spoke, I was about to write; but I heard a voice from heaven say, 'Seal up what the seven thunders have said and do not write it down.'

⁵Then the angel I had seen standing on the sea and on the land raised his right hand to heaven. ⁶And he swore by him who lives for ever and ever, who created the heavens and all that is in them, the earth and all that is in it, and the sea and all that is in it, and said, 'There will be no more delay! ⁷But in the days when the seventh angel is about to sound his trumpet, the mystery of God will be

> **'You must prophesy again about many peoples, nations, languages and kings.'**

accomplished, just as he announced to his servants the prophets.'

⁸Then the voice that I had heard from heaven spoke to me once more: 'Go, take the scroll that lies open in the hand of the angel who is standing on the sea and on the land.'

⁹So I went to the angel and asked him to give me the little scroll. He said to me, 'Take it and eat it. It will turn your stomach sour, but in your mouth it will be as sweet as honey.' ¹⁰I took the little scroll from the angel's hand and ate it. It tasted as sweet as honey in my mouth, but when I had eaten it, my stomach turned sour. ¹¹Then I was told, 'You must prophesy again about many peoples, nations, languages and kings.'

DAY 356
REV. 11. 1 — 19

11 **The Two Witnesses**
I was given a reed like a measuring rod and was told, 'Go and measure the temple of God and the altar, and count the worshippers there. ²But exclude the outer court; do not measure it, because it has been given to the Gentiles. They will trample on the holy city for 42 months. ³And I will give power to my two witnesses, and they will prophesy for 1,260 days, clothed in sackcloth.' ⁴These are the two olive trees and the two lampstands that stand before the Lord of the earth. ⁵If anyone tries to harm them, fire comes from their mouths and devours their enemies. This is how anyone who wants to harm them must die. ⁶These men have power to shut up the sky so that it will not rain during the time they are prophesying; and they have power to turn the waters into blood and to strike the earth with every kind of plague as often as they want.

[7] Now when they have finished their testimony, the beast that comes up from the Abyss will attack them, and overpower and kill them. [8] Their bodies will lie in the street of the great city, which is figuratively called Sodom and Egypt, where also their Lord was crucified. [9] For three and a half days men

'The kingdom of the world has become the kingdom of our Lord and of his Christ, and he will reign for ever and ever.'

from every people, tribe, language and nation will gaze on their bodies and refuse them burial. [10] The inhabitants of the earth will gloat over them and will celebrate by sending each other gifts, because these two prophets had tormented those who live on earth.

[11] But after the three and a half days a breath of life from God entered them, and they stood on their feet, and terror struck those who saw them. [12] Then they heard a loud voice from heaven saying to them, 'Come up here.' And they went up to heaven in a cloud, while their enemies looked on.

[13] At that very hour there was a severe earthquake and a tenth of the city collapsed. Seven thousand people were killed in the earthquake, and the survivors were terrified and gave glory to the God of heaven.

[14] The second woe has passed; the third woe is coming soon.

The Seventh Trumpet

[15] The seventh angel sounded his trumpet, and there were loud voices in heaven, which said:

'The kingdom of the world has
    become the kingdom of our Lord
    and of his Christ,
and he will reign for ever and ever.'

[16] And the twenty-four elders, who were seated on their thrones before God, fell on their faces and worshipped God, [17] saying:

'We give thanks to you, Lord God
    Almighty,
    the One who is and who was,
because you have taken your great
    power
    and have begun to reign.
[18] The nations were angry;
    and your wrath has come.

And there came flashes of lightning, rumblings, peals of thunder, an earthquake and a great hailstorm.

The time has come for judging the
    dead,
    and for rewarding your servants the
    prophets
and your saints and those who
    reverence your name,
    both small and great -
and for destroying those who
    destroy the earth.'

[19] Then God's temple in heaven was opened, and within his temple was seen the ark of his covenant. And there came flashes of lightning, rumblings, peals of thunder, an earthquake and a great hailstorm.

DAY 357

REV. 12. 1 — 18

12 The Woman and the Dragon

A great and wondrous sign appeared in heaven: a woman clothed with the sun, with the moon under her feet and a crown of twelve stars on her head. [2] She was pregnant and cried out in pain as she was about to give birth. [3] Then another sign appeared in heaven: an enormous red dragon with seven heads and ten horns and seven crowns on his heads. [4] His tail swept a third of the stars out of the sky and flung them to the earth. The dragon stood in front of the woman who was about to give birth, so that he might devour her child the moment it was born. [5] She gave birth to a son, a male child, who will rule all the nations with an iron sceptre. And her child was snatched up to God and to his throne. [6] The woman fled into the desert to a place prepared for her by God, where she might be taken care of for 1,260 days.

[7] And there was war in heaven. Michael and his angels fought against the dragon, and the dragon and his angels fought back. [8] But he was not strong enough, and they lost their place in heaven. [9] The great dragon was hurled down - that ancient serpent called the devil, or Satan, who leads the whole world astray. He was hurled to the earth, and his angels with him.

[10] Then I heard a loud voice in heaven say:

'Now have come the salvation
and the power and the kingdom
of our God,
and the authority of his Christ.
For the accuser of our brothers,
who accuses them before our God
day and night,
has been hurled down.
[11] They overcame him
by the blood of the Lamb
and by the word of their testimony;
they did not love their lives so much
as to shrink from death.
[12] Therefore rejoice, you heavens
and you who dwell in them!
But woe to the earth and the sea,
because the devil has gone down
to you!
He is filled with fury,
because he knows that his time
is short.'

[13] When the dragon saw that he had been hurled to the earth, he pursued the woman who had given birth to the male child. [14] The woman was given the two wings of a great eagle, so that she might fly to the place prepared for her in the desert, where she would be taken care of for a time, times and half a time, out of the serpent's reach. [15] Then from his mouth the serpent spewed water like a river, to overtake the woman and sweep her away with the torrent. [16] But the earth helped the woman by opening its mouth and swallowing the river that the dragon had spewed out of his mouth. [17] Then the dragon was enraged at the woman and went off to make war against the rest of her offspring - those who obey God's commandments and hold to the testimony of Jesus. [18] And the dragon stood on the shore of the sea.

DAY 358

REV. 13. 1 — 18

13

The Beast out of the Sea

And I saw a beast coming out of the sea. He had ten horns and seven heads, with ten crowns on his horns, and on each head a blasphemous name. ² The beast I saw resembled a leopard, but had feet like those of a bear and a mouth like that of a lion. The dragon gave the beast his power and his throne and great authority. ³ One of the heads of the beast seemed to have had a fatal wound, but the fatal wound had been healed. The whole world was astonished and followed the beast. ⁴ Men worshipped the dragon because he had given authority to the beast, and they also worshipped the beast and asked, 'Who is like the beast? Who can make war against him?'

⁵ The beast was given a mouth to utter proud words and blasphemies and to exercise his authority for forty-two months. ⁶ He opened his mouth to blaspheme God, and to slander his name

> He was given power to make war against the saints and to conquer them.

and his dwelling-place and those who live in heaven. ⁷ He was given power to make war against the saints and to conquer them. And he was given authority over every tribe, people, language and nation. ⁸ All inhabitants of the earth will worship the beast - all whose names have not

been written in the book of life belonging to the Lamb that was slain from the creation of the world.

⁹ He who has an ear, let him hear.

¹⁰ If anyone is to go into captivity,
  into captivity he will go.
If anyone is to be killed with the
    sword,
  with the sword he will be killed.

This calls for patient endurance and faithfulness on the part of the saints.

The Beast out of the Earth

¹¹ Then I saw another beast, coming out of the earth. He had two horns like a lamb, but he spoke like a dragon. ¹² He exercised all the authority of the first beast on his behalf, and made the earth and its inhabitants worship the first beast, whose fatal wound had been healed. ¹³ And he performed great and miraculous signs, even causing fire to come down from heaven to earth in full view of men. ¹⁴ Because of the signs he was given power to do on behalf of the first beast, he deceived the inhabitants of the earth. He ordered them to set up an image in honour of the beast who was wounded by the sword and yet lived. ¹⁵ He was given power to give breath to the image of the first beast, so that it could speak and cause all who refused to worship the image to be killed. ¹⁶ He also forced everyone, small and great, rich and poor, free and slave, to receive a mark on his right hand or on his forehead, ¹⁷ so that no-one could buy or sell unless he had the mark, which is the name of the beast or the number of his name.

¹⁸ This calls for wisdom. If anyone has insight, let him calculate the number of the beast, for it is man's number. His number is 666.

DAY 359

REV. 14. 1 — 20

14

The Lamb and the 144,000

Then I looked, and there before me was the Lamb, standing on Mount Zion, and with him 144,000 who had his name and his Father's name written on their foreheads. ² And I heard a sound from heaven like the roar of rushing waters and like a loud peal of thunder. The sound I heard was like that of harpists playing their harps. ³ And they sang a new song before the throne and before the four living creatures and the elders. No-one could learn the song except the 144,000 who had been redeemed from the earth. ⁴ These are those who did not defile themselves with women, for they kept themselves pure. They follow the Lamb wherever he goes. They were purchased from among men and offered as firstfruits to God and the Lamb. ⁵ No lie was found in their mouths; they are blameless.

The Three Angels

⁶ Then I saw another angel flying in mid-air, and he had the eternal gospel to proclaim to those who live on the earth - to every nation, tribe, language and people. ⁷ He said in a loud voice, 'Fear God and give him glory, because the hour of his judgment has come. Worship him who made the heavens, the earth, the sea and the springs of water.'

⁸ A second angel followed and said, 'Fallen! Fallen is Babylon the Great, which made all the nations drink the maddening wine of her adulteries.'

⁹ A third angel followed them and said in a loud voice: 'If anyone worships the beast and his image and receives his mark on the forehead or on the hand, ¹⁰ he, too, will drink of the wine of God's fury, which has been poured full strength into the cup of his wrath. He will be tormented with burning sulphur in the presence of the holy angels and of the Lamb. ¹¹ And the smoke of their torment rises for ever and ever. There is no rest day or night for those who worship the beast and his image, or for anyone who receives the mark of his name.' ¹² This calls for patient endurance on the part of the saints who obey God's commandments and remain faithful to Jesus.

¹³ Then I heard a voice from heaven say, 'Write: Blessed are the dead who die in the Lord from now on.'

'Yes,' says the Spirit, 'they will rest from their labour, for their deeds will follow them.'

The Harvest of the Earth

¹⁴ I looked, and there before me was a white cloud, and seated on the cloud was one 'like a son of man' with a crown of gold on his head and a sharp sickle in his hand. ¹⁵ Then another angel came out of the temple and called in a loud voice to him who was sitting on the cloud, 'Take your sickle and reap, because the time to reap has come, for the harvest of the earth is ripe.' ¹⁶ So he who was seated on the cloud swung his sickle over the earth and the earth was harvested.

¹⁷ Another angel came out of the temple in heaven, and he too had a sharp sickle. ¹⁸ Still another angel, who had charge of the fire, came from the altar and called in a loud voice to him who had the sharp sickle, 'Take your sharp sickle and gather the clusters of grapes

om the earth's vine, because its grapes re ripe.' [19] The angel swung his sickle on ne earth, gathered its grapes and threw nem into the great winepress of God's rath. [20] They were trampled in the inepress outside the city, and blood owed out of the press, rising as high as ne horses' bridles for a distance of 1,600 adia.

DAY 360
REV. 15. 1 — 8

15
Seven Angels With Seven Plagues

I saw in heaven another reat and marvellous sign: seven angels ith the seven last plagues - last, because ith them God's wrath is completed. And I saw what looked like a sea of glass ixed with fire and, standing beside the ea, those who had been victorious over ne beast and his image and over the umber of his name. They held harps ven them by God [3] and sang the song of oses the servant of God and the song of the Lamb:

'Great and marvellous are your deeds,
Lord God Almighty.
Just and true are your ways,
King of the ages.
[4] Who will not fear you,
O Lord,
and bring glory to your name?
For you alone are holy.
All nations will come
and worship before you,
for your righteous acts have been
revealed.'

[5] After this I looked and in heaven the temple, that is, the tabernacle of the Testimony, was opened. [6] Out of the temple came the seven angels with the seven plagues. They were dressed in clean, shining linen and wore golden sashes round their chests. [7] Then one of the four living creatures gave to the seven angels seven golden bowls filled with the wrath of God, who lives for ever and ever. [8] And the temple was filled with smoke from the glory of God and from his power, and no-one could enter the temple until the seven plagues of the seven angels were completed.

'Great and marvellous are your deeds, Lord God Almighty.'

DAY 361

REV. 16. 1 — 21

16

The Seven Bowls of God's Wrath

Then I heard a loud voice from the temple saying to the seven angels, 'Go, pour out the seven bowls of God's wrath on the earth.'

² The first angel went and poured out his bowl on the land, and ugly and painful sores broke out on the people who had the mark of the beast and worshipped his image.

³ The second angel poured out his bowl on the sea, and it turned into blood like that of a dead man, and every living thing in the sea died.

⁴ The third angel poured out his bowl on the rivers and springs of water, and they became blood. ⁵ Then I heard the angel in charge of the waters say:

'You are just in these judgments,
    you who are and who were,
        the Holy One,
    because you have so judged;
⁶ for they have shed the blood of
        your saints and prophets,
    and you have given them blood
        to drink as they deserve.'
⁷ And I heard the altar respond:
    'Yes, Lord God Almighty,
        true and just are your judgments.'

⁸ The fourth angel poured out his bowl on the sun, and the sun was given power to scorch people with fire. ⁹ They were seared by the intense heat and they cursed the name of God, who had control over these plagues, but they refused to repent and glorify him.

¹⁰ The fifth angel poured out his bowl on the throne of the beast, and his kingdom was plunged into darkness. Men gnawed their tongues in agony ¹¹ and cursed the God of heaven because of their pains and their sores, but they refused to repent of what they had done.

¹² The sixth angel poured out his bowl on the great river Euphrates, and its water was dried up to prepare the way for the kings from the East. ¹³ Then I saw three evil spirits that looked like frogs; they came out of the mouth of the dragon, out of the mouth of the beast and out of the mouth of the false prophet. ¹⁴ They are spirits of demons performing miraculous signs, and they go out to the kings of the whole world, to gather them for the battle on the great day of God Almighty.

¹⁵ 'Behold, I come like a thief! Blessed is he who stays awake and keeps his clothes with him, so that he may not go naked and be shamefully exposed.'

¹⁶ Then they gathered the kings together to the place that in Hebrew is

'Yes, Lord God Almighty, true and just are your judgments.'

called Armageddon.

¹⁷ The seventh angel poured out his bowl into the air, and out of the temple came a loud voice from the throne, saying 'It is done!' ¹⁸ Then there came flashes of lightning, rumblings, peals of thunder and a severe earthquake. No earthquake like it has ever occurred since man has been on earth, so tremendous was the quake. ¹⁹ The great city split into three parts, and the cities of the nations collapsed. God remembered Babylon the Great and gave her the cup filled with the wine of the fury

f his wrath. ²⁰ Every island fled away and he mountains could not be found. ²¹ From he sky huge hailstones of about a hundred ounds each fell upon men. And they ursed God on account of the plague of ail, because the plague was so terrible.

DAY 362
REV. 17. 1 — 18

17 The Woman on the Beast

One of the seven angels vho had the seven bowls came and said o me, 'Come, I will show you the unishment of the great prostitute, who its on many waters. ² With her the kings of the earth committed adultery and the nhabitants of the earth were intoxicated vith the wine of her adulteries.'

³ Then the angel carried me away in he Spirit into a desert. There I saw a voman sitting on a scarlet beast that was overed with blasphemous names and had even heads and ten horns. ⁴ The woman vas dressed in purple and scarlet, and was littering with gold, precious stones and earls. She held a golden cup in her hand, illed with abominable things and the ilth of her adulteries. ⁵ This title was vritten on her forehead:

MYSTERY
BABYLON THE GREAT
THE MOTHER OF PROSTITUTES AND
OF THE ABOMINATIONS OF THE
EARTH.

I saw that the woman was drunk with he blood of the saints, the blood of those vho bore testimony to Jesus.

When I saw her, I was greatly astonished. ⁷ Then the angel said to me: 'Why are you astonished? I will explain to you the mystery of the woman and of the beast she rides, which has the seven heads and ten horns. ⁸ The beast, which you saw, once was, now is not, and will come up out of the Abyss and go to his destruction. The inhabitants of the earth whose names have not been written in the book of life from the creation of the world will be astonished when they see the beast, because he once was, now is not, and yet will come.

⁹ 'This calls for a mind with wisdom. The seven heads are seven hills on which the woman sits. ¹⁰ They are also seven kings. Five have fallen, one is, the other has not yet come; but when he does come, he must remain for a little while. ¹¹ The beast who once was, and now is not, is an eighth king. He belongs to the seven and is going to his destruction.

¹² 'The ten horns you saw are ten kings who have not yet received a kingdom, but who for one hour will receive authority as kings along with the beast. ¹³ They have one purpose and will give their power and authority to the beast. ¹⁴ They will make war against the Lamb, but the Lamb will overcome them because he is Lord of lords and King of kings - and with him will be his called, chosen and faithful followers.'

¹⁵ Then the angel said to me, 'The waters you saw, where the prostitute sits, are peoples, multitudes, nations and languages. ¹⁶ The beast and the ten horns you saw will hate the prostitute. They will bring her to ruin and leave her naked; they will eat her flesh and burn her with fire. ¹⁷ For God has put it into their hearts to accomplish his purpose by agreeing to give the beast their power to rule, until God's words are fulfilled. ¹⁸ The woman you saw is the great city that rules over the kings of the earth.'

DAY 363

REV. 18. 1 — 19. 4

18 **The Fall of Babylon**
After this I saw another angel coming down from heaven. He had great authority, and the earth was illuminated by his splendour. ² With a mighty voice he shouted:

'Fallen! Fallen is Babylon the Great!
    She has become a home for
        demons
and a haunt for every evil spirit,
    a haunt for every unclean
        and detestable bird.
³ For all the nations have drunk
    the maddening wine of
        her adulteries.
The kings of the earth committed
        adultery with her,
    and the merchants of the earth grew
        rich from her excessive
        luxuries.'

⁴ Then I heard another voice from heaven say:

'Come out of her, my people,
    so that you will not share in her
    sins, so that you will not receive
        any of her plagues;
⁵ for her sins are piled up to heaven,
    and God has remembered
        her crimes.
⁶ Give back to her as she has given;
    pay her back double for
        what she has done.
    Mix her a double portion from
        her own cup.
⁷ Give her as much torture

and grief as the glory and luxury sh▸
    gave herself.
In her heart she boasts,
    "I sit as queen; I am not a widow,
    and I will never mourn."
⁸ Therefore in one day her plagues
        will overtake her:
    death, mourning and famine.
She will be consumed by fire,
    for mighty is the Lord God who
        judges her.

⁹ 'When the kings of the earth who committed adultery with her and shared her luxury see the smoke of her burning, they will weep and mourn over her. ¹⁰ Terrified at her torment, they will stand far off and cry:

"Woe! Woe, O great city,
    O Babylon, city of power!
In one hour your doom has come!"

¹¹ 'The merchants of the earth will weep and mourn over her because no-one buys their cargoes any more - ¹² cargoes o▸ gold, silver, precious stones and pearls; fine linen, purple, silk and scarlet cloth; every sort of citron wood, and articles of every kind made of ivory, costly wood, bronze, iron and marble; ¹³ cargoes of cinnamon and spice, of incense, myrrh and frankincense, of wine and olive oil, fine flour and wheat; cattle and sheep; horses and carriages; and bodies and soul▸ of men.

¹⁴ 'They will say, "The fruit you long▸ for is gone from you. All your riches and splendour have vanished, never to be recovered." ¹⁵ The merchants who sold these things and gained their wealth from her will stand far off, terrified at her torment. They will weep and mourn ¹⁶ an▸ cry out:

"Woe! Woe, O great city,
 dressed in fine linen,
  purple and scarlet,
 and glittering with gold, precious
  stones and pearls!
[17] In one hour such great wealth has
  been brought to ruin!"

'Every sea captain, and all who travel
by ship, the sailors, and all who earn their
living from the sea, will stand far off.
[18] When they see the smoke of her
burning, they will exclaim, "Was there
ever a city like this great city?" [19] They
will throw dust on their heads, and with
weeping and mourning cry out:

"Woe! Woe, O great city,
 where all who had ships on
  the sea
 became rich through her wealth!
In one hour she has been brought to
  ruin!
[20] Rejoice over her, O heaven!
 Rejoice, saints and apostles
  and prophets!
God has judged her for the way she
  treated you." '

[21] Then a mighty angel picked up a
boulder the size of a large millstone and
threw it into the sea, and said:

'With such violence
 the great city of Babylon will be
  thrown down,
 never to be found again.
[22] The music of harpists and musicians,
 flute players and trumpeters,
 will never be heard in you again.
No workman of any trade
 will ever be found in you again.
The sound of a millstone
 will never be heard in you again.
[23] The light of a lamp

will never shine in you again.
The voice of bridegroom and bride
 will never be heard in you again.
Your merchants were the world's
 great men.
By your magic spell all the nations
 were led astray.
[24] In her was found the blood of
 prophets and of the saints,
 and of all who have been killed on
  the earth.'

19 Hallelujah!

After this I heard what
sounded like the roar of a
great multitude in heaven shouting:

'Hallelujah!
Salvation and glory and power
 belong to our God,
[2] for true and just are his judgments.
He has condemned the great
 prostitute
 who corrupted the earth by her
  adulteries.
He has avenged on her the blood of
 his servants.'

[3] And again they shouted:

'Hallelujah!
The smoke from her goes up
 for ever and ever.'

[4] The twenty-four elders and the four
living creatures fell down and worshipped
God, who was seated on the throne. And
they cried:

 'Amen, Hallelujah!'

DAY 364

REV. 19. 5 — 21

[5] Then a voice came from the throne, saying:

> 'Praise our God,
>   all you his servants,
> you who fear him,
>   both small and great!'

[6] Then I heard what sounded like a great multitude, like the roar of rushing waters and like loud peals of thunder, shouting:

> 'Hallelujah!
>   For our Lord God Almighty reigns.
> [7] Let us rejoice and be glad
>   and give him glory!
> For the wedding of the Lamb has
>   come,
>   and his bride has made herself ready.
> [8] Fine linen, bright and clean,
>   was given her to wear.'

(Fine linen stands for the righteous acts of the saints.)

[9] Then the angel said to me, 'Write: "Blessed are those who are invited to the wedding supper of the Lamb!"' And he added, 'These are the true words of God.' [10] At this I fell at his feet to worship him. But he said to me, 'Do not do it! I am a fellow-servant with you and with your brothers who hold to the testimony of Jesus. Worship God! For the testimony of Jesus is the spirit of prophecy.'

The Rider on the White Horse

[11] I saw heaven standing open and there before me was a white horse, whose rider is called Faithful and True. With justice he judges and makes war. [12] His eyes are like blazing fire, and on his head are many crowns. He has a name written on him that no-one knows but he himself. [13] He is dressed in a robe dipped in blood, and his name is the Word of God. [14] The armies of heaven were following him, riding on white horses and dressed in fine linen, white and clean. [15] Out of his mouth comes a sharp sword with which to strike down the nations. 'He will rule them with an iron sceptre.' He treads the winepress of the fury of the wrath of God Almighty. [16] On his robe and on his thigh he has this name written:

KING OF KINGS AND LORD OF LORDS

[17] And I saw an angel standing in the sun, who cried in a loud voice to all the birds flying in mid-air, 'Come, gather together for the great supper of God, [18] so that you may eat the flesh of kings, generals, and mighty men, of horses and their riders, and the flesh of all people, free and slave, small and great.'

[19] Then I saw the beast and the kings of the earth and their armies gathered together to make war against the rider on the horse and his army. [20] But the beast was captured, and with him the false prophet who had performed the miraculous signs on his behalf. With these signs he had deluded those who had received the mark of the beast and worshipped his image. The two of them were thrown alive into the fiery lake of burning sulphur. [21] The rest of them were killed with the sword that came out of the mouth of the rider on the horse, and all the birds gorged themselves on their flesh.

DAY 365

REV. 20 — 22

20
The Thousand Years

And I saw an angel coming down out of heaven, having the key to the Abyss and holding in his hand a great chain. ² He seized the dragon, that ancient serpent, who is the devil, or Satan, and bound him for a thousand years. ³ He threw him into the Abyss, and locked and sealed it over him, to keep him from deceiving the nations any more until the thousand years were ended. After that, he must be set free for a short time.

⁴ I saw thrones on which were seated those who had been given authority to judge. And I saw the souls of those who had been beheaded because of their testimony for Jesus and because of the word of God. They had not worshipped the beast or his image and had not received his mark on their foreheads or their hands. They came to life and reigned with Christ for a thousand years. ⁵ (The rest of the dead did not come to life until the thousand years were ended.) This is the first resurrection. ⁶ Blessed and holy are those who have part in the first resurrection. The second death has no power over them, but they will be priests of God and of Christ and will reign with him for a thousand years.

Satan's Doom

⁷ When the thousand years are over, Satan will be released from his prison ⁸ and will go out to deceive the nations in the four corners of the earth - Gog and Magog - to gather them for battle. In number they are like the sand on the seashore. ⁹ They marched across the breadth of the earth and surrounded the camp of God's people, the city he loves. But fire came down from heaven and devoured them. ¹⁰ And the devil, who deceived them, was thrown into the lake of burning sulphur, where the beast and the false prophet had been thrown. They will be tormented day and night for ever and ever.

The Dead Are Judged

¹¹ Then I saw a great white throne and him who was seated on it. Earth and sky fled from his presence, and there was no place for them. ¹² And I saw the dead, great and small, standing before the throne, and books were opened. Another book was opened, which is the book of life. The dead were judged according to what they had done as recorded in the books. ¹³ The sea gave up the dead that were in it, and death and Hades gave up the dead that were in them, and each person was judged according to what he had done. ¹⁴ Then death and Hades were thrown into the lake of fire. The lake of fire is the second death. ¹⁵ If anyone's name was not found written in the book of life, he was thrown into the lake of fire.

21
The New Jerusalem

Then I saw a new heaven and a new earth, for the first heaven and the first earth had passed away, and there was no longer and sea. ² I saw the Holy City, the new Jerusalem, coming down out of heaven from God, prepared as a bride beautifully dressed for her husband. ³ And I heard a loud voice from the throne saying, 'Now the dwelling of God is with men, and he will live with them. They will be his people, and God himself will be with them and be their God. [4] He will wipe every tear from their eyes. There will be no more death or mourning or crying or pain, for the old order of things has passed away.'

[5] He who was seated on the throne said, 'I am making everything new!' Then he said, 'Write this down, for these words are trustworthy and true.'

[6] He said to me: 'It is done. I am the Alpha and the Omega, the Beginning and the End. To him who is thirsty I will give to drink without costs from the spring of the water of life. [7] He who overcomes will inherit all this, and I will be his God and he will be my son. [8] But the cowardly, the unbelieving, the vile, the murderers, the sexually immoral, those who practise magic arts, the idolaters and all liars — their place will be in the fiery lake of burning sulphur. This is the second death.'

[9] One of the seven angels who had the seven bowls full of the seven last plagues came and said to me, 'Come, I will show you the bride, the wife of the Lamb.' [10] And he carried me away in the Spirit to a mountain great and high, and showed me the Holy City, Jerusalem, coming down out of heaven from God. [11] It shone with the glory of God, and its brilliance was like that of a very precious jewel, like a jasper, clear as crystal. [12] It had a great, high wall with twelve gates, and with twelve angels at the gates. On the gates were written the names of the twelve tribes of Israel. [13] There were three gates on the east, three on the north, three on the south and three on the west. [14] The wall of the city had twelve foundations, and on them were the names of the twelve apostles of the Lamb.

[15] The angel who talked with me had a measuring rod of gold to measure the city, its gates and its walls. [16] The city was laid out like a square, as long as it was wide. He measured the city with the rod and found it to be 12,000 stadia in length, and as wide and high as it is long. [17] He measured its walls and it was 144 cubits thick, by man's measurement, which the angel was using. [18] The wall was made out of jasper, and the city of pure gold, as pure as glass. [19] The foundations of the city walls were decorated with every kind of precious stone. The first foundation was jasper, the second sapphire, the third chalcedony, the fourth emerald, [20] the fifth sardonyx, the sixth carnelian, the seventh chrysolite, the eighth beryl, the ninth topaz, the tenth chrysoprase, the eleventh jacinth, and the twelfth amethyst. [21] The twelve gates were twelve pearls, each gate made of a single pearl. The great street of the city was of pure gold, like transparent glass.

[22] I did not see a temple in the city, because the Lord God Almighty and the Lamb are its temple. [23] The city does not need the sun or the moon to shine on it, for the glory of God gives it light, and the Lamb is its lamp. [24] The nations will walk by its light, and the kings of the earth will bring their splendour into it. [25] On no day will its gates ever be shut, for there will be no night there. [26] The glory and honour of the nations will be brought into it. [27] Nothing impure will ever enter it, nor will anyone who does what is shameful or deceitful, but only those whose names are written in the Lamb's book of life.

22 The River of Life

Then the angel showed me the river of the water of life, as clear as crystal, flowing from the throne of God and of the Lamb [2] down the mddle of the great street of the city. On each side of the river stood the tree of life, bearing twelve crops of fruit, yielding its fruit every month. And the leaves of the tree are for the healing of the nations. No longer will there be any curse. The throne of God and of the Lamb will be in the city and his servants will serve him. They will see his face, and his name will be on their foreheads. ⁵There will be no more night. They will not need the light of a lamp or the light of the sun, for the Lord God will give them light. And they will reign for ever and ever.

⁶The angel said to me, 'These words are trustworthy and true. The Lord, the God of the spirits and the prophets, sent his angel to show his servants the things that must soon take place.'

Jesus is coming

'Behold, I am coming soon! Blessed is he who keeps the words of the prophecy in this book'

⁸I, John, am the one who heard and saw these things. And when I had heard and seen them, I fell down to worship at the feet of the angel who had been showing them to me. ⁹But he said to me, Do not do it! I am a fellow servant with you and with your brothers the prophets and of all who keep the words of this book. Worship God!'

¹⁰Then he told me, 'Do not seal up the words of the prophecy of this book, because the time is near. ¹¹Let him who does wrong continue to do wrong; let him who is vile continue to be vile; let him who does right continue to do right; and let him who is holy continue to be holy.'

¹²'Behold, I am coming soon! My reward is with me, and I will give to everyone according to what he has done.

¹³I am the Alpha and Omega, the First and the Last, the Beginning and the End.

¹⁴'Blessed are those who wash their robes, that they may have the right to the

---

'Behold, I am coming soon! Blessed is he who keeps the words of the prophecy in this book.'

---

tree of life and may go through the gates into the city. ¹⁵Outside are the dogs, those who practise magic arts, the sexually immoral, the murderers, the idolaters and everyone who loves and practises falsehood.

¹⁶'I, Jesus, have sent my angel to give you this testimony for the churches. I am the Root and the Offspring of David, and the bright Morning Star.'

¹⁷The Spirit and the bride say, 'Come!' And let him who hears say, 'Come!' Whoever is thirsty, let him come; and whoever wishes, let him take the free gift of the water of life.

¹⁸I warn everyone who hears the words of the prophecy of this book: If anyone adds anything to them, God will add to him the plagues described in this book. ¹⁹And if anyone takes words away from this book of prophecy, God will take away from him his share in the tree of life and in the holy city, which are described in this book.

²⁰He who testifies to those things says, 'Yes, I am coming soon.'

Amen. Come, Lord Jesus.

²¹The grace of the Lord Jesus be with God's people. Amen.